Louis D. Brandeis

By the Same Author:

Presidential Power
and American Democracy

The Supreme Court
and Political Questions

Louis D. Brandeis

Justice
for
the People

Philippa Strum

SCHOCKEN BOOKS
NEW YORK

In Memoriam

Laura Segelstein (1968–1981)
Eric Louis Segelstein (1971–1981)

Strum, Philippa.
    Louis D. Brandeis: justice for the people.

    Reprint. Originally published: Cambridge, Mass.:
Harvard University Press, 1984.
    Bibliography: p.
    Includes index.
    I. Brandeis, Louis Dembitz, 1856–1941.
    2. Judges—United States—Biography.   I. Title.
[KF8745.B67S78   1989].   347.73'2634   88-43284
    ISBN 0-8052-0884-4   347.3073534

Contents

Illustrations

Preface

Louis Dembitz Brandeis was born on November 13, 1856, in Louisville, Kentucky—his first memory was of the Union Army camped outside his family's home—and he died on October 5, 1941, on the eve of another war. He was part of almost every important American social and economic movement during his long adult life: trade unionism; trust-busting; Progressivism; women's suffrage; scientific management; expansion of civil liberties; hours, wages, and unemployment legislation; Woodrow Wilson's New Freedom; Franklin Roosevelt's New Deal. He invented savings bank life insurance and the preferential union shop, and he earned over two million dollars practicing law between 1878 and 1916, while serving so actively in public causes that he became known throughout the country as the "people's attorney."

Creating a new method of arguing cases in 1908, he used it until 1916 and encouraged its adoption while he sat on the Supreme Court of the United States from 1916 to 1939; the effect was the alteration of American jurisprudence. He led American Zionism from 1914 through 1921 and again from 1930 until his death. Among those he advised were Robert La Follette, Woodrow Wilson, Herbert Hoover, Josephus Daniels, William McAdoo, Franklin D. Roosevelt, Frances Perkins, Harold Ickes, David Lilienthal, Samuel Gompers, Herbert Croly, and Harry Truman.

Brandeis's ideas about people, society, and government developed along with American industrialization. First, as befit the son of a successful small-scale merchant, he favored a nation of many such businesses. Then, as his public service activities uncovered the massive power inherent in big business, he began to believe that industrial unions were needed to balance the power of employers. Later he came to believe that concentration of money leads to power beyond that which human beings can manage intelligently and that trusts and monopolies were unethical and inefficient. His goals of justice and efficiency led him to argue that corporate profits should be shared with employees. But he was concerned that although technological expansion and assembly lines could produce wealth for employers and employees, they could also produce workers who were mindless automatons instead of the thinking human beings necessary to a democratic society. If it was possible to share profits with employees, he reasoned, decision making could also be a joint endeavor. By logical progression, he concluded that businesses should be run as cooperatives, with workers also serving as managers.

Brandeis countered arguments of the experts that economic bigness was inevitable by charging that bigness existed only because of government encouragement and that without it, outsize corporations, and even oligopolies, which were unnatural, would collapse. Large-scale industrial development was a product, in part, of the political decision making process.

Because individual liberty was the value he held highest, Brandeis wanted workers' jobs to be as fulfilling as possible. Technology was not to be abused to create bigness, for although it could make businesses large, it could not make them efficient; only human beings could do that. When Brandeis postulated reasonable-sized businesses, however, he was faced with the consequences of businesses controlling technology. They would decide on the products to be produced and their prices. Brandeis saw a need for a balancing power and found it in consumers' cooperatives.

One outcome of Brandeis's intellectual odyssey was that he brought Jeffersonianism up to date by making it relevant to an industrial society. His mechanism of worker-management was new, yet Brandeis and Jefferson held startlingly similar ideas about men and the body politic: the goodness but fallibility of human beings; democracy as the best possible political system; the central role of education in a democracy; the inability of economically dependent citizens to be politically independent; the desirability of small, controllable governmental units as close as possible to the people being governed. Brandeis's central vision that citizens must be economically independent in order to be politically free brought him to support first unionism and then worker-participation.

Brandeis was much influenced by the Greek polis of the fifth century B.C., which he considered the acme of civilized existence. There, he thought, in the years leading to Pericle's great funeral oration (which Brandeis quoted in his most important civil liberties opinion), citizen participation in public life flourished, the properly small state was therefore well run, and human beings were able to attain heights of culture and self-fulfillment. The highest compliment Brandeis could give, and one he saved for the uncle whose last name he took as his own middle name, was to say that someone "reminded one of the Athenians." He continued to read Greek history and poetry throughout his life.

In his late fifties, Brandeis turned to Zionism suddenly and intensely, and it became a dominating theme of his life. Zionism was a seemingly surprising departure for a thoroughly assimilated Jew who had deplored the phenomenon of "hyphenated Americans," but Brandeis's vision of Zion and his dream of American worker-participation both reflect his emphasis on smallness, his fear that modern technology was turning workers into wage-slaves, his belief that democracy could not function without active citizen participation, his recognition of economic independence as a necessary precondition of political independence, and his fear of concentrated and irresponsible power. Fired by the work of Alfred Zimmern, author of *The Greek Commonwealth*, who compared Periclean Athens to ancient Palestine, Brandeis envisaged a small, democratic, agrarian Jewish state in Palestine that would revive the virtues of the Athenian polis.

There are other puzzles in Brandeis's life that need examination. How did a German son of immigrants manage to get himself accepted by the late nineteenth century world of Harvard, and then of Brahmin Boston? How did a man who became one of the richest lawyers of his time earn the sobriquet the "people's attorney," the respect of Americans who saw him as a fighter for the public good, and the almost violent hatred of the rich and powerful? In light of the work of Roscoe Pound and Oliver Wendell Holmes, how important was Brandeis to the development of sociological jurisprudence? Why did he emphasize facts rather than legal axioms as the foundation for judicial decision? How did his battles on behalf of the public tinge his political beliefs? Did those beliefs in turn affect his work as a judge? How involved was he in the workings of the Wilson and Roosevelt administrations? How did he reconcile his political activities with his strong ethical code? Finally, what was the extent of Brandeis's impact on American law and politics?

A close examination reveals some elements of personal ideological change. For example, the carefree young attorney whose Kentucky brother kept him supplied with bourbon and who served sherry during the early years of his marriage became an advocate of Prohibition. The lecturer against women's suffrage became an eager champion of the cause and an admiring advocate of women who sought careers. But because information on Brandeis the man is sparse, his personal life will remain something of a mystery. Brandeis was portrayed in his lifetime as a jealous guardian of his privacy. One observer said there was "no niggardly husbanding of resources, but rather, I think, a sense of personal dignity which would not be consistent with an easy opening of doors to everyone who knocked." Those who got through those portals, however, were rewarded by a relationship with a man who was warm, thoughtful, humorous, and unaffected. Only rarely was he the cold and ascetic intellectual. Yet the conflicted impression that remains is very much Brandeis's own doing. He "divorced his public from his private life because he so jealously valued both." The destruction of many of his personal papers, along with the sense of privacy that became part of his legacy to his family, makes it difficult to discover Brandeis even decades after his death. The few bits of information that can be culled from his household bills, his remaining letters, and the recollections of friends and family barely hint at the charisma of a man who was a figure of both love and awe to almost everyone who knew him. His brilliance and his vision led those around him to call Brandeis "Isaiah." His message, like that of the prophets of old, holds much that is relevant today.

Acknowledgments

Louis Dembitz Brandeis had a profound understanding of the limited capabilities of all human beings. That insight explains in part his insistence on the need for small institutions, for leisure, for constant experimentation, for human beings to confine themselves to undertakings that do not exceed their capacities. I hope I have not violated the last injunction by writing this volume, and I am quite certain I could not have completed it without the help of a large number of extraordinary people.

Beryl Trapp has loved and taken a large measure of responsibility for my children throughout the writing of this book. Every working parent will understand my gratitude for her presence, her sense of responsibility, and her patience. Doris Glassman deciphered and produced readable copies of drafts of this biography. It was my very good fortune to be the child of Ida and Joseph Strum, who raised both their daughters with the once-unfashionable idea that they could achieve anything they really chose to work at, and who have remained an inexhaustible source of moral support and intelligent advice.

Professor James MacGregor Burns deserves special thanks for the tireless encouragement and shared wisdom he provided during the decade it took to complete this volume. The colleagues who generously read various parts of this volume and offered their comments and suggestions include professors Judith Baer, Bernard Bellush, Gayle Binion, Samuel Hendel, Samuel Krislov, Jeffrey Morris, Mary Cornelia Porter, Robert Scigliano, and Melvin I. Urofsky. I owe an immense debt to four Israeli colleagues for their knowledge of Zionism: professors Asher Arian, Yigal Elam, Allon Gal, and Yonathan Shapiro.

Professors James David Barber, Walter Berns, Alexander George, Betty Glad, Charles Hardin, C. Herman Pritchett, David Riesman, and John P. Roche graciously supported my requests for grants from the Penrose Fund of the American Philosophical Society, the American Council for Learned Societies (a fellowship made possible by a grant to ACLS from the National Endowment for the Humanities), and the City University of New York–Professional Staff Congress Faculty Research Award Program.

My gratitude toward archivists is unbounded. They include Erika Chadbourn, Curator of Manuscripts and Archives, Harvard Law School Library; Janet B. Hodgson, Brandeis Project Archivist, University of Louisville Archives; Professor Gene Teitelbaum, Law Librarian, University of Louisville; and Morrison C. Haviland, University Archivist and Campus Records Officer, State University of New York-Albany. Grateful acknowledgment is made to the University of Louisville Law Library and the University of Louisville Archives for permission to quote from the Brandeis Papers and to the State University of New York Press for permission to quote from Melvin I. Urofsky and David W. Levy, *Letters of Louis D. Brandeis* (5 vols.)

Three first-rate scholars who generously shared then-unpublished information with me are Nelson L. Dawson, Leonard Baker, and Melvin I. Urofsky. Professor Urofsky and Professor David Levy are the editors of the five-volume *Letters of Louis D. Brandeis,* which have been of great assistance to me and which will be a tool of the greatest importance to all future Brandeis scholars.

A number of Brandeis's former law clerks and members of the Brandeis family sat patiently through what must have seemed endless questioning. Their forbearance and insightful suggestions were no doubt in the Brandeis tradition, but that does not diminish my debt to H. Thomas Austern; Professors Paul A. Freund, Willard Hurst, and David Riesman; Professor Mary K. Tachau; and, particularly, Mrs. Elizabeth Brandeis Raushenbush, who at age eighty-four put up with two days of interviews and a stream of correspondence. Laurence Arato and Andrew Kolin of the City University of New York Graduate Center Program in Political Science provided tireless and painstaking assistance in research and organization. Larry Raymond's expertise made possible the reproduction of old photographs in the Louisville Archives. I owe thanks to Harvard University Press, and especially to my editors, Aida D. Donald and Denise Thompson-Smith, for raising penetrating questions about substance and style with grace and wit.

Thanks are also due to my son, David Strum Weiss, who considers his mother's chosen form of recreation rather odd but who nonetheless contributed in his own way by playing elsewhere whenever he heard the sound of the typewriter and by agreeing not to jump all over the manuscript.

My joyous, loving children, Laura Segelstein and Eric Louis Segelstein, were old enough to be patient with a mother whose thoughts were often back in the "olden days" and to be sympathetic and encouraging whenever the pangs of authorship became overwhelming. Intelligent and sensitive, they had already demonstrated the kind of respect for human dignity and interest in serving the community that were among Brandeis's most notable characteristics. They lived through most of the work on the book but not through its completion; they and their father were killed in an airplane accident on September 5, 1981. This volume is therefore dedicated to them, as an expression of my endless gratitude for the wonderful years we shared.

New York City
September 5, 1983

Chronology

November 13, 1856	Born in Louisville, Kentucky
1873–1875	Student at Annen-Realschule, Dresden, Germany
1875–1878	Student and graduate student, Harvard Law School
1878–1879	Practiced law in St. Louis, Missouri
1879–1897	Partner in Warren & Brandeis, Boston, Massachusetts
1882–1883	Taught "Evidence" at Harvard Law School
March 23, 1891	Married Alice Goldmark
1892–1894	Taught "Business Law" at Massachusetts Institute of Technology
February 27, 1893	Daughter Susan born
April 25, 1896	Daughter Elizabeth born
1897–1916	Senior partner in Brandeis, Dunbar & Nutter, Boston, Massachusetts
1900–1902	Leader in fight to preserve Boston subway system
1905–1907	Created savings bank life insurance
1905–1913	Involved in New Haven Railroad fight
1908	Created "Brandeis brief" in case of *Muller* v. *Oregon*
1910	Counsel for *Collier's Weekly* in Pinchot-Ballinger hearings
1910	Arbitrator in New York City garment workers' strike
August 1914	Became leader of American Zionist movement
1916–1939	Associate Justice of the Supreme Court of the United States
Summer 1919	Trip to Palestine
February 13, 1939	Resigned from U.S. Supreme Court
October 5, 1941	Died in Washington, D.C.

1 | Beginnings

Cincinnati, Ohio—a thriving metropolis in the mid-nineteenth century—in 1849 became the temporary home of yet another group of immigrants fleeing the political repression and economic chaos that had accompanied the German revolutionary movement of 1848. Twenty-seven-year-old Adolph Brandeis had rented a four-story house for one month for himself and the twenty-six other members of his extended family group while they decided where their American future lay. The newcomers were members of the Brandeis, Wehle, and Dembitz families. Distantly related and neighbors in Prague, the families were to be related even more closely in the near future, for Adolph Brandeis was engaged to Frederika Dembitz, and his brother Samuel Brandeis was engaged to Lotti Wehle. They were all members of the Jewish merchant class with high hopes of beginning a new life in America.

Their ideas and their history strongly influenced Louis David Brandeis, youngest child of Adolph and Frederika, who would be born six years later. In order to understand how the major strands of Brandeis's thought—the importance of liberty, the duty to participate in public life, the need to develop oneself intellectually and culturally, the paramount place of education in the life of any citizen who would be both free and cultured, an emphasis on the small businessman as the backbone of a free society—came together, one must first know something of the family that produced him.

His maternal grandfather, one of the Pilgrims of '48 (as they would be called by Josephine Goldmark, Brandeis's sister-in-law, in her book with that title), was Sigmund Dembitz, a surgeon. Sigmund had wanted to practice medicine in Prague but, characteristically, ignored the Austrian law permitting only graduates of Austrian medical schools to practice in Austria and chose to study medicine at the University of Konigsberg in Prussia. When he had taken his degree, therefore, he and his wife Fanny Wehle Dembitz became wanderers through Poland, moving from one small town to another in ceaseless search of a profitable practice. In spite of the family's lack of money, however, Dr. Dembitz was sufficiently well thought of to be received by Polish nobility and to treat the Duke of Brunikowsky.

Fanny Dembitz gave birth to a daughter, Frederika, in 1829; later two sons were born. Frederika remembered her migratory childhood as a warm and happy one. Although the family was Jewish, Frederika's clearest memories indicate that it was nonreligious and assimilated. In Zirke, Poland, where her father was physician to the count, Frederika had her first Christmas tree. The only "religion" the young Dembitzes seem to have been taught was the longing for Prague, which their parents spoke about with the "kind of love and longing" that Frederika associated with the feelings of the more pious for Jerusalem or Mecca. Fanny took her children on a pilgrimage to Prague almost yearly, to visit the house which had been her family's for generations.[1]

During the Polish Revolution of 1831, although he professed sympathy with the Poles, the doctor's Austrian origins made him such a target of anti-German feeling that the family moved to Prussia. Then when Frederika was eleven, disaster struck: her youngest brother Theodore died. Within months, his death was followed by the death of her mother. Frederika was so devastated that she wrote in her *Reminiscences* only: "Let me be silent about those days and weeks. Did ever a twelve-year-old child feel more forsaken?"[2]

The doctor was equally shaken. He moved Frederika and her remaining brother, Lewis, from place to place throughout what would become the Austro-Hungarian Empire, mourning and restlessly seeking his always elusive fortune. And as they wandered, Dr. Dembitz tutored his daughter. Her formal education consisted only of six months at a Muncheberg public school and a year of high school in Frankfurt. Although she had occasional tutors, it was her father who taught her writing, arithmetic, French, and liberal politics. Frederika would later describe him as "full of eloquence and enthusiasm . . . more brilliant than most men . . . the older I grow the more I admire his enlightenment, his conception of the world."[3]

Frederika was sent to Prague for frequent visits with her aunt and uncle Wehle, owners of a linen store. There, her education came as much from the milieu as from the dancing and drawing lessons she took. The Wehle social circle, for example, included the German poets and writers Moritz Hartmann and Alfred Meissner. Her younger uncle, Siegmund, gave her free access to his library. There she immersed herself in eighteenth-century French writers, Goethe, Homer, Bulver, the poems of Karl Beck, and the letters of Bettina von Arnim; as a young teenager, she wrote plays and poems. Josephine Goldmark commented that "it is significant of her always keen intellectual interests that the record of her [girlhood] friendships is always a record of books and reading shared with a friend." The German-Jewish middle class took the world's literature and history as part of its legacy; Frederika would make this part of her children's legacy as well.[4]

Across the street from the Wehle house stood the cotton-printing mill of the Brandeis family, whose history dated back to the early fifteenth century. However old the family might have been and however famous at least one of its offspring might later become, in the 1840s the Brandeis family was not doing well. The textile industry was in trouble, as were all Austrian industries; in addition, Jews suffered from special taxes and restrictions. When the outbreaks of 1848 added political persecution to the already discouraging economic conditions, it became sadly clear that Prague was no longer a good home. Young Adolph Brandeis was designated to go abroad and seek a new life for the families.

Born in 1822, Adolph had studied in Prague and decided to become a chemist, but financial exigencies forced him to give up his ambitions and turn instead to managing the cotton mill. His family, however, realized that its handblock method of printing textiles would not be able to compete with machine technology and so sent Adolph off to technical school, the Prague Technischen Lehranstalt im Schuljabre, from which he received a certificate for studies in the management of agricultural estates and marketing. Despite his training, he did not get a job in Prague, and he spent two years traveling to Hamburg, England, and Holland, seeking his fortune. Finding no greater success there, he began to consider leaving Europe. Economic vicissitudes did not curb his natural ebullience or impair his attractiveness, for when he returned to Prague, Frederika found him charming and graceful, with "unusually attractive manners." Josephine Goldmark considered "his courageous optimism, his good judgment, and his charm of manner" qualities that he displayed throughout his life.[5]

Frederika and Adolph became engaged during the Revolution of 1848. Adolph had rushed home as soon as he heard about the uprising, and only an attack of typhoid prevented him from participating in it. The families were entirely sympathetic to the aims of the revolutionaries, and

Adolph spoke of 1848 as the "wonderful year" when "the spirit of the Lord informed the peoples of Europe and His mighty voice overthrew the tyrants." But Adolph could not remain in Austria; he was the logical person to send across the Atlantic to explore the territory for the Brandeis, Dembitz, and Wehle families.

Descriptions of the United States had made it sound like a veritable Utopia to the families: "there came tidings of the new, the incredible fertility of nature in the new world; of farmlands and ranches to be had almost for the asking; and above all, of the political, civil, and religious liberty." The contrast with Prague could not have been greater, particularly to a group of intellectuals thoroughly imbued with the pastoral doctrines of Rousseau. Romantic liberals all, they responded as did many other educated Europeans to Rousseau's invitation to return to nature. Thus, full of naive enthusiasm for the agrarian Eden he would find, Adolph sailed for New York.[6]

There, as in his travels through the Midwest, Adolph was forced to realize that the sophisticated urbanites whose emissary he was would not adapt easily to farm life. A stint as a farmworker in Ohio showed him that the agrarian existence was not necessarily Rousseauian; instead, it meant a kind of "tedium" that "can become the most deadly poison in family life" and the possibility that a man could "sink to being a mere common beast of burden." The toil was ceaseless, back-breaking, monotonous; city people he met attempting to farm soon gave up "because they could not make a living" and found the rural life "unbearable." He was undiscouraged, nonetheless, and told Frederika, "Our future doesn't cause me the least worry . . . The resources of this country are so great that after a short time of privation anyone can acquire a peaceful, satisfactory livelihood." He took a job in a Cincinnati grocery store and decided that the families should set up their own business, urging them to learn all they could at home about the manufacture of fine starch made from corn. Starch in the United States was manufactured from wheat; Adolph was certain that the Bohemian corn-based method produced a finer product and would prove lucrative. On April 8, 1849, the party of twenty-six, including Frederika's father and brother, Adolph's brother Samuel, Frederika's aunt and uncle Wehle and their twelve children and governess, Frederika herself, and assorted other Wehles, sailed for New York.[7]

The three families were coming to America not only for economic opportunity, but for freedom as well. Adolph's letters made it clear that he was enchanted by the atmosphere of liberty he found. Patriotism flourished in the fresh air of the United States; indeed, he told Frederika, "I have often thought that even the hard work of these people is a kind of patriotism. They wear themselves out to make their country bloom, as though each one of them were commissioned to show the despots of the old world what a free people can do." He got a book with the "messages of all the presidents,"and read it eagerly. One week he read about "the progress made in Washington's day, and I felt as proud and happy about it as though it had all been my own doing." The history of the United States was the history of "the triumph of the rights of man . . . in which we rejoice." And the more he learned about the "splendid" American institutions, the more he felt his patriotism growing. He took out first citizenship papers within two months of his arrival, and his certificate of citizenship was one of the first documents later placed in Louis Brandeis's scrapbooks.[8]

The Forty-eighters came not only with a love of liberty but with a sense of culture. They considered themselves the inheritors of a classical tradition based on the love of learning, music, and the arts. Back in Prague, Frederika's aunt Eleanore Wehle had not only supervised the raising of her twelve children (with the aid of five servants, a governess, a seamstress, and a music teacher) and worked daily in the family linen store, but also found time to give dinner parties at which all the children were expected to recite in German and French and to display their musical proficiency. During Adolph's scouting trip to America, he quoted Heine's poetry in his letters to Frederika. And the two family pianos and pieces of music, as well as cases of books, were included in the family's baggage as a matter of course.[9]

Shipment of the pianos did not mean that the families were frivolous or unrealistic. It was unthinkable that they would not have pianos wherever they lived, and Adolph had warned them that prices in the United States were high. Frederika had asked Adolph "to look at the ladies— to look at their dresses and lace collars." This brought the practical advice in turn that "you ought to make yourself some dresses and even some silk ones . . . things are certainly much cheaper over there [in Prague] than here . . . So provide yourself with as much as is necessary to look well, and in order not to get out of fashion you had better choose dark colors." Adolph's admonition reflected a tacit assumption that of course his wife would want to look fashionable.[10]

These, then, were the people who would be closest to the young Louis Brandeis: educated, cultured, intelligent, idealistic, patriotic, moral, ambitious, family-oriented, politically aware. Their heritage would leave clear imprints on his mind.

In the summer of 1849 all the members of the families except Dr. Dembitz and his son Lewis, who stayed in Cincinnati, moved to Madison, Indiana.

Adolph had traveled extensively looking for the best location for the now-agreed-upon starch factory and store, and he was certain that a prosperous future lay in Madison. Although the city had only ten thousand inhabitants, it was on the heavily trafficked Ohio River and boasted the terminal of the Indianapolis and Madison Railroad, the first railway to be built in Indiana. The railroad was a vital link in the chain that ran from the interior of Indiana all the way to the port of New Orleans. The families were attracted not only by Madison's economic potential but also by the fact that during a recent nearby cholera epidemic that had killed hundreds, Madison had had no cases of cholera at all. Leaving Dr. Dembitz in Cincinnati to practice medicine and Lewis to study law there, the rest of the group moved to a big house in which everyone but the unmarried men lived. This arrangement lasted only a few months, until September 5, 1849. On that day, Adolph Brandeis married Frederika Dembitz and Samuel Brandeis married Lotti Wehle in a double ceremony. The two couples moved to a small two-story house, near the house that the two young women had just left.[11]

Adolph and the Wehles set up the starch factory, as well as the grocery and general produce store of G. & M. Wehle, Brandeis & Company. The starch factory, undercapitalized and poorly managed by the neophyte partners, had to be sold at a loss after two years, but the grocery and produce business prospered. Samuel Brandeis, trained as a physician, decided he wanted to practice medicine, and Adolph felt capable of building on his commercial experience in a bigger metropolis. The two brothers, therefore, moved their families to Louisville, Kentucky, in 1851. Adolph immediately set about developing a wholesale grain and produce business; in 1855 he joined with Charles W. Crawford in establishing the firm of Brandeis & Crawford, which a local newspaper called "the pioneer of the grain trade in the Ohio Valley, as conducted on modern lines." When the wheat crop of New York's Genesee Valley failed that year, the firm sent to New York the first wheat shipment ever to go from Kentucky to the eastern states. Although small, the shipment soon led to an extensive trade with millers in the Genesee Valley. The firm further added to its business during the Civil War, when it became a major supplier of grain and other produce to the Union forces. The Brandeis family grew prosperous.[12]

Louis David Brandeis was born in Louisville on November 13, 1856. "My earliest memories," he recalled, "were of the war . . . I remember helping my mother carry out food and coffee to the men from the North. The streets seemed full of them always. But there were times when the rebels came so near that we could hear the firing. At one time my father moved us over the river" to the comparative safety of Indiana.[13]

The Brandeises were convinced abolitionists. They were wealthy enough to build a substantial house in an exclusive area of Louisville and employ black servants, at least some of whom became family retainers. Servants, however, whatever their color, were not slaves, and numerous family anecdotes indicate that they were not so treated. The antislavery stance of the Brandeises and their extended family made them unpopular in Louisville, which seems to have concerned them not at all. They were pleased when Lewis Dembitz, Brandeis's favorite uncle, became involved in Lincolnian politics through his friend James Speed, brother of Joshua Speed, Lincoln's former roommate. Dembitz delighted the Brandeis clan further in 1860 by being named a delegate to the convention that nominated Lincoln for president.[14]

The Brandeises' involvement in the slavery issue was inevitable, given their continuing interest in public affairs. Adolph had "talked politics" in his commercial travels throughout the Midwest. He considered one of the distinguishing traits of Americans to be a sense of personal identification with the success or failure of democratic institutions, and he shared it. Public affairs were a staple of the dinner table; indeed, Frederika banned all discussion of money and other vulgar matters from dinner conversation.[15]

Louis grew up in a house of books, music, sociability, and warmth. Frederika encouraged the literary interests of her four children: Fannie, born in 1851; Amy, in 1852; Alfred, in 1854; and Louis, two-and-a-half years later. There were no financial worries. Brandeis & Crawford not only sold grain and produce; it also owned a flour mill, a tobacco factory, an eleven-hundred-acre farm, and a river freighter. When Brandeis was four, his parents moved from their little house on Center Street, between Chestnut and Walnut, to a larger one on First Street, which they had remodeled. A few years later they moved again, this time to an impressive limestone-fronted house they had built on fashionable Broadway. A flourishing business, a large home filled with happy children and a retinue of servants, an extended family that remained close as it prospered: Adolph and Frederika had no reason to question the reality of the American dream. Neither did their children, then or later.[16]

Louis and Alfred developed a particularly close friendship that delighted Frederika and lasted throughout their lives. Together, they rode horseback, teased little girls, thought up pranks to frighten maids, fought with other boys, and generally enjoyed their lives as sons of a wealthy family in a border state of the mid-nineteenth century. They also got into trouble together. Louis was nine and Alfred almost twelve on July 4, 1865, when they experimented with homemade firecrackers. Suddenly, their supply of powder exploded; and the two boys, thrown backwards, found themselves with burned and blackened faces. They were too terrified to tell what they had done until the pain forced them to call for help. But they were forgiven, and the story became a family favorite.[17]

Pictures from the period show Frederika as self-assured, looking at the camera with eyes that were both calm and full of curiosity. Her wavy hair was parted in an absolutely straight line down the middle of her head, pulled over her ears, and then piled in a braid on the top. Not a hair was out of place. Straight thick eyebrows sat above large eyes. Her dress was fashionable, with ruffled collars, cameos, gowns tight at the waist and flaring into full skirts. She gave the impression of an upright, proper lady, but one with a sense of humor. Her husband, dressed in the long-jacketed suit of the day and with his hair modishly placed over the tops of his ears, somehow seems less of a presence than his wife, although he was a self-confident, smiling man, with a Theodore Roosevelt mustache, a high forehead gradually being made higher by a receding hairline, and eyes and mouth that looked out on the world with confidence and amusement.

A picture of Louis at two shows what can only be described as a very funny-looking child. His head was enormous; his ears stuck out; huge solemn eyes peered at the camera in bewilderment; and he sat slouched in what appears to be a checked dress pulled over short pants. By the time he was fifteen, however, he had become a prepossessing boy. Straight dark hair was parted at one side and allowed to flop over his ears; the huge eyes had eyebrows like his father's arched over them; a slightly curved nose complemented a mouth that was generous, even sensuous; his starched white shirt, dark tie, and jacket became him well.[18]

Childhood was fun for Louis, but it was not all play. In his first letter extant, written to his mother when he was fourteen and she was visiting relatives in St. Louis, he presents a picture of a warm but disciplined life in Louisville:

September 7, 1870

My dear darling Ma:

As I can't write to you tomorrow morning, I use my time tonight to write a few lines and congratulate my dear Ma on her wedding day, the first one I have not been with you . . .

Today the regular lessons began and there was yawning down in our room which would have done justice to Pa. I study only French, Latin, Chemistry, German, Algebra, Composition, Trigonometry: Mathematics and Languages being the principal studies.

We went out riding with Aunt Rosa on the river road yesterday . . . Pa is at the Opera House meeting tonight. Fanny is going to the Prussian meeting tomorrow afternoon. Mr. Hirschbull is going to raffle off the picture HEIDELBERG he used to have hanging in his store, for the wounded. Has Pa written you of his proposed punishment for Napoleon? It is this: He should be put in prison with no book but Kinglake's Crimea . . . Hoping you will soon be back to your

Loving son
Louis[19]

The letter, with its casual listing of a range of subjects that would be considered overwhelming today, is indicative of the kind of intellectual background that illuminated Brandeis's thinking. His formal education began at Miss Wood's school in Louisville when he was seven, and he kept Goodrich's *First School Reader* as a memento of that year. He went on to the German and English Academy, where the principal wrote on his almost perfect report card, "Louis deserves special commendation for conduct and industry." The course of study he described in his letter was undertaken during his first year in the Louisville Male High School. During the following year, he studied belles lettres, Latin, Greek, pure mathematics, chemistry and technology, French, and German. Among the schoolbooks he preserved were Xenophon's *Expeditio Cyri* in Latin and *Herodotos* by Heinrich Stein (the latter in Greek with German footnotes). In seven marking periods his general class standing varied between 5.94 and 5.98, out of a possible 6; his deportment grade was always 6, and his report card showed no demerits or absences. One year later, when he was sixteen, the University of the Public Schools in Louisville awarded him a gold medal "for pre-eminence in all his studies." The gold medal winner each year was expected to make a speech at graduation, but Louis, "overcome with terror at the thought of making a speech," was spared that ordeal by the discovery on graduation morning that he had laryngitis. All he remembered about the graduation ceremonies was that one of the trouser legs of the distinguished Louisville gentleman who made the major address became caught in the top of his fashionably high boot. The speaker was unaware of this, and the adolescent Louis and his fellow students found that fact hilarious.[20]

The home in which Louis grew up was not one that adhered to formal religion or engaged in religious activities. His family practiced what might be called the secular Christianity of the United States, sending each other Christmas greetings and gifts. Frederika wrote "I do not believe that sins can be expiated by going to divine service and observing this or that formula; I believe that only goodness and truth and conduct that is humane and self-sacrificing towards those who need us can bring God nearer to us, and that our errors can only be atoned for by acting in a more kindly spirit." She reared her children without a formal religion because she "wanted to give them something that neither could be argued away nor would have to be given up as untenable, namely, a pure spirit and the highest ideals as to morals and love." She was very much aware of being a Jew, however. She did not know what particular doctrines her parents had believed in, but she knew "that they believed in goodness for its own sake and they had a lofty conception of morality with which they imbued us and which I developed further for myself . . . I saw that my parents were good Jews, and yet did not associate with Jews and were different from them and so there developed in me more affection for our race as a whole than for individuals." Thus spoke the thoroughly assimilated German Jew. To Frederika, Judaism meant no more than belonging to a group of people with an especially lofty sense of morality, and she successfully inculcated this attitude in her children. Years later, Alfred married a non-Jew, the daughter of an old friend of Adolph's, and the elder Brandeises were delighted at the match. Later still, one of Louis's two daughters would marry a Christian, the son of a minister and theologian; Brandeis described him as "a rare find" and was clearly pleased at his daughter's choice.[21]

Frederika's secular ethic, with its emphasis on moral duty to others, did have a religious counterpart within the family. Her beloved brother Lewis, after whom she named her younger son, was an ardent Jew. And he was ultimately second only to Frederika in his impact on Brandeis.

Lewis Naphtali Dembitz was born four years after his sister Frederika and studied law in Austria for one semester before the family moved to the United States. After reading law in Cincinnati, he moved to Louisville to practice, write, participate in public life, and become the intellectual leader of the combined Dembitz and Brandeis families. He was a constant caller at the Brandeis home and the dominant figure in the extended family circle. Five feet tall and a frail one hundred pounds, he was a balding man who peered intensely at the world through rimless glasses that perched on his nose and barely corrected his poor vision. His range of achievements was almost incredible: lawyer, legal writer, civil servant, political activist, astronomer, linguist, mathematician. He was a follower of Henry Clay, after whom he named his oldest son, as well as of Lincoln, after whom he named his second son. He read a dozen languages; he forecast the 1869 eclipse of the sun to the minute, using his own calculations; he contributed to encyclopedias and wrote authoritative works on Kentucky law and jurisprudence. He was absentminded, good-humored, a natural teacher, and particularly fond of children.

Louis adored his uncle. Although he already bore his uncle's first name, the teenaged Louis changed his middle name of David to Dembitz in his honor. And he paid tribute to his uncle's influence all his life. His uncle, Brandeis said, had been "a living university. With him, life was unending intellectual ferment . . . In the diversity of his intellectual interests, in his longing to discover truths, in his pleasure in argumentation and the process of thinking, he reminded one of the Athenians."[22]

Lewis Dembitz was sufficiently knowledgeable about the culture, history, ritual, and theology of Judaism to write about it, but it was not merely an intellectual concern to him; he was an orthodox Jew and observed all the prescribed laws. Brandeis had no experience of the Jewish Sabbath in his parents' home, nor did he observe it in his own. But he remembered, "vividly," the details of his uncle's Sabbath: "the joy and awe with which my uncle, Lewis Dembitz, welcomed the arrival of the day and the piety with which he observed it. I remember the extra delicacies, lighting of the candles, prayers over a cup of wine, quaint chants, and Uncle Lewis poring over books most of the day. I remember more particularly an elusive something about him which was spoken of as the 'Sabbath peace' and which years later brought to my mind a passage from Addison in which he speaks of stealing a day out of life to live . . . Uncle Lewis used to say that he was enjoying a foretaste of heaven."[23]

In 1872 Adolph Brandeis realized that the country was about to face a major recession. He decided to cut his losses, dissolve his firm, and take his family on a fifteen-month trip to Europe, after which he expected busness conditions to improve and the family to return and reestablish itself. As it turned out, the European trip lasted three years, and the family did not return until 1875. They were in good health and excited when they left for Europe on August 10, 1872. They saw a bit of England and much of Germany, Austria, Italy, and Switzerland. It had been planned that Brandeis would enter the Vienna Gymnasium to continue his formal education, but his Louisville education proved insufficient; he failed the entrance exam. He therefore spent the winter of 1872 in Vienna being tutored, listening to lectures at the university, and attending concerts and plays; then he journeyed slowly through Italy and Switzerland with his family. They visited Venice, Bologna, Naples, Genoa, Pisa, Milan, Lake Como, and various places in Switzerland, with Frederika making certain that they appreciated the art and architecture at each stop and Adolph and Alfred encouraging Louis to join them in testing themselves against the Alps. Louis occasionally became exasperated with Alfred's greater zest for athletics—on one Alpine climbing expedition, as Louis lay exhausted under some trees, his brother suggested that they seek the source of the river running nearby, and Louis snapped, "I don't see why I should have to find the source of every damned river in Europe!"—but he found the trip exhilarating. Memories of it reappeared in his letters to his brother for the next fifty years. His reading, already wide in scope, was stimulated further, as he sought to learn more about the places he visited.[24]

When the summer of 1873 ended and the weather began to turn chilly, Alfred sailed back to Louisville to work for Reed & Ferguson, Grocer's Sundries. The family had decided to take Louis to Dresden, in hopes of enrolling him in the Annen-Realschule. But Amy had been stricken with typhoid fever in Milan in May, and she was still too sick either to journey to Dresden or to be left alone. Sixteen-year-old Louis therefore had to get himself to Dresden and into the school. It was his first attempt to meet the world on his own, and he did not do badly. Having arrived in Dresden, he discovered that the friend who was to introduce him to the rector of the school was temporarily unavailable, so he determined to make the initial approach himself. After circling the building long enough to work up his courage, he marched into the rector's office and presented himself. That worthy was not impressed; admission was impossible, he said, without proof of birth, a vaccination certificate, and an examination. Louis stoutly replied, "The fact that I am here is proof of my birth; and you may look at my arm for evidence that I was vaccinated." The rector, softening, advised Louis to take private lessons from the faculty during the three weeks remaining until the midyear examinations. The youth took the advice and threw himself into a self-imposed schedule of studying for thirteen hours a day. When the new term began, he simply started classes; nothing further was said about taking the examination.[25]

Brandeis remained at the Annen-Realschule for three terms and justified his unorthodox admission by becoming an outstanding student. He took courses in French, Latin, German, literature, mineralogy, geography, physics, chemistry, and mathematics, and did so well that in March 1875, the faculty awarded him a prize "for diligence and good conduct." He was permitted to pick his prize and chose A. W. Becker's *Charackterbilder aus der Kunstgeschicte*, a book about Greek art. Although he found the authoritarianism of the school stifling, he later told his law clerk and friend Paul Freund that his German education had been memorable. According to Freund, Brandeis credited his Dresden experience with teaching him how to think. While preparing an essay on a subject about which he had known nothing, he made the exciting discovery that "ideas could be evolved by reflecting on your material." The lesson was a significant one. Nonetheless he was homesick: "I wanted to go back to America and I wanted to study law. My uncle, the abolitionist, was a lawyer; and to me nothing else seemed really worth while."[26]

The family returned to the United States in May 1875 and stayed in Massachusetts long enough for Brandeis to organize his admission to law school. In his eighties, he remarked "sometimes [I] think I might have had more education—eighteen and nineteen when I was in Law School." But he was filled with "the enthusiasm and fire of youth," and he was eager to begin his study of the law. So he arranged to enter Harvard Law School in the fall. Then the Brandeises went home to Louisville.[27]

Adolph Brandeis was unable to offer his son Louis any financial help at Harvard Law School. When the family returned from Europe, Adolph established a cotton business, but he gave it up in 1877 and spent his time attempting to collect bad debts. He lost the optimism of his early days and wrote to Louis, "This up to now, is my sole occupation, for nothing new has turned up . . . My people say I am looking very well, so at least one doesn't notice what it looks like inside me." He admonished Louis, now a student at Harvard Law School, "Enjoy this beautiful time with all your might and be conscious of it, because it won't always remain as beautiful as it is now even if luck, with God's help, will favor you." A few months later he added, seemingly philosophically, "I have more or less accepted my situation and live for the day like a real proletarian. Misery likes Company, and I have plenty of that now, and the circle of miserable merchants is becoming larger and more respectable every day." But he was not really resigned: "I hope," he noted, "that once things change . . . I can become active again." In 1878 the retail store of A. Brandeis & Son (the son being Alfred) was formed. The firm's early years were not easy, and Alfred wrote constantly to his brother of the hard work he and his father were doing for relatively little reward. As late as 1890 Adolph wrote, "Business is a perfect blank and prospects not very good ahead."[28]

The firm ultimately succeeded, but the bad days appeared to have left their mark on Adolph. Later, when Louis gave up a "safe" teaching job for the more tenuous life of a legal practitioner, Adolph wrote to him,

It may have been unwise on my part to have told you my opinion so very frankly. In no way do I intend to divert you from the path you have planned for yourself, and from seeking your fortune where you think you can find it most quickly. Maybe it is cowardice that I have such little inclination for and joy in fighting, and I should congratulate myself that my sons are made of better metal. I believe though, that all my life I have tried to do my duty, and this sense of duty my sons have inherited from me. Luckily, they have received as a heritage from their mother the will to fight and some ambition, and that is why they are such fine fellows whom God may protect.[29]

Alfred kept the business going until his death in 1928, and the brothers' letters in the first three decades of the twentieth century are full of information about the effects on small business of tariffs, monopolies, "free silver," and so on. Brandeis's roots were in the world of small business, and his interest in it remained constant throughout his life. It seems legitimate to postulate that the impact on Adolph of his business's temporary failure, caused by forces beyond his control, affected Brandeis's attitude toward both small business and the forces he perceived as responsible for economic conditions.

Before following Brandeis to Harvard and Boston, where he would remain until his elevation to the Supreme Court in 1916 and where he would change from a German-American Puritan into a Bostonian Progressive, it seems appropriate to look back for one last moment at the influence of Germany, Kentucky, and the Brandeises. It is clear that Brandeis first encountered many of the ideas he would work into his political philosophy within his family circle. And it can be hypothesized that his willingness to learn from his family and his continued devotion to it reinforced those ideas as he experimented with them in the larger world. A Jewish agnostic, cultured, intelligent, devoted to family and nation, imbued with respect for the dignity of every individual, reared to believe that the best of both the Old and the New Worlds was his for the asking—young Louis Dembitz Brandeis was ready to reverse Horace Greeley's advice and go east.

2 | The World of the Boston Brahmin

Brandeis began his studies at Harvard Law School on September 27, 1875. He arrived during a halycon moment in the intellectual history of Boston and Cambridge. The Puritans who had settled the Massachusetts Bay Colony had stamped their beliefs on all the towns and villages that grew up in what became the Commonwealth of Massachusetts. Since the Puritans believed in predestination, knowing whether they were going to Heaven or Hell became an obsession with most of them. Part of their doctrine, which emphasized the individual's direct relationship with God, minimized the unbearable uncertainty: if God had blessed one with His grace, He surely would not permit one to suffer unduly on earth. There-fore, it was postulated, those who did well economically could take their success as an indication that they were among God's chosen. This equa-tion of economic success with moral value gradually became secularized as the colonies expanded and united. Benjamin Franklin's writings are a good example, Andrew Carnegie's another, although both men also drew on additional sources for their thinking.

The Puritans believed that as God's chosen people, they were different from all others and had special responsibilities. They rejoiced in their uniqueness, suffered from grave doubts about their salvation, manifested the gravest pessimism, and yet created institutions that helped make life on earth meaningful. Possessing what Arthur Schlesinger has called an "intense moral zeal both for [their] own salvation and for that of the community," they also had a notion of stewardship; a great trust in the human capacity for brotherhood; high intellectual standards; a passion for work; unbounded resolution and fortitude; an unusual talent for the concerted effort that led to the development of congregations, town meetings, public schools, and Harvard College; and a fear of the arts and graces as corrupting, combined with a respect for learning and the books and organizations that embodied art and grace.[1]

By the 1870s the Puritan ethic in Boston had been transformed into Brahminism, and although many descendants of the old Boston families had converted from Puritanism to Unitarianism and would become Episcopalians in the 1880s, the new ethic retained many elements of the Puritan creed. The Brahmins were very aware of their colonial descent, which, they believed, imbued them with both superiority and responsibility. The Puritan sense of God-imposed duty had become a secularized tradition of disinterested public service. Their interest in the "higher things" of life was expressed in an ostensible disdain for the overt pursuit of wealth and in an obsession with culture and education. Duane Lockard describes them as tending "to distrust basic human instincts . . . to regard the state as a [necessary] . . . instrument for the ordering of society, and to favor government of the majority by a specialized, responsible minority." The Boston Brahmins retained the Puritans' emphasis on the individual, on self-reliance, and on making the most of one's abilities— all elements of Frederika Brandeis's code, and all enshrined in the works of Brandeis's favorite Boston author, Ralph Waldo Emerson, the great advocate of Self-Reliance.[2]

The Brahmins whom Brandeis began to meet in the mid-1870s were origin conscious but not exclusive. Although well over half of Boston's population was either foreign-born or the children of the foreign-born by then, living in ghettoes in the West End or South End, the new residents, as individuals, could find a place in the Brahmin world. Such Brahmin thinkers as Emerson, Julia Ward Howe, Wendell Phillips, Edward Everett Hale, and Thomas Wentworth Higginson emphasized what one did rather than who one was and upheld the right of the newcomers to join the American democracy by accepting the values of intellectual Brahminism. Mark Twain summarized this attitude by commenting that "In Boston they ask, How much does he know? in New York, How much is he worth? in Philadelphia, Who were his parents?"[3]

Individualism was but one tenet of intellectual Brahminism. Individuals had to be active in public life, separately and in groups, not only to restrain a potentially interfering government, but to demonstrate their sense of humanity by helping those less fortunate than themselves. This meant honest business practices as well as private charity. Brandeis copied into his notebook Emerson's remark, "Every man takes care that his neighbor shall not cheat him. But a day comes when he begins to care that he does not cheat his neighbor. Then all goes well. He has changed his market cart into a chariot of the sun." A sense of responsibility for one's fellow citizens, which in turn proved one's own worth, permeated the Brahmin tradition. It had also permeated the Brandeis home.[4]

The sense of social responsibility found in Boston was unusual. Massachusetts was well ahead of almost all the other states in the antislavery movement, the drive against child labor, and movements for women's suffrage, prison and asylum reform, and public education. By the time Brandeis reached Boston, the obligation of the state to engage in such activities as the regulation of working hours for women and children and the inspection of factory working conditions was taken for granted; in most other states, such activities were still considered radical and would take many years to be enacted.[5]

Familiar with these ideas from home, Brandeis seems to have felt no strangeness in adopting their Protestant Brahmin manifestations. Being a Jew was not a bar to intellectual Brahminism; on the contrary, being a Jew in the Boston of the late 1870s and early 1880s was an advantage (as long as one was a Harvard-connected, intellectually gifted Jew). Puritans habitually linked themselves with Jews in being "chosen people". Educated Puritans read Hebrew, which was taught at Harvard almost from the time that institution was established. Thus, discrimination against the Jews was not acceptable to Brahmins. When a New England hotel he had frequented sent William James a circular stating that "applications from Hebrews cannot be considered," that philosopher and epitome of Boston society wrote back, "I propose to return the boycott." Elizabeth Glendower Evans, the socially impeccable Bostonian who became a close friend of Brandeis and his wife, did not know for a while that he was Jewish. The discovery that he was, she later reported, "gave an aroma to his personality." She excitedly recalled, "A Jew! He belonged then to Isaiah and the Prophets." Indeed, one of the most respected men in Boston was Rabbi Solomon Schindler of Temple Adath Israel, an assimilated Reform Jew who moved easily through the world of literary and intellectual Boston. Leading journals published his opinions; newspapers reported on his sermons; by the 1880s, as many non-Jews as Jews went to hear his Sunday sermons; and he became the first person in Boston to be nominated for the School Committee by both political parties.[6]

Although demographics made inevitable the loss of the Brahmins' political hegemony over Boston, they retained control of its intellectual life. And even though some Brahmins clung to birth as a criterion for inclusion in the clan, Brahminism became almost entirely an intellectual creed. The path to that world of Emerson, William James, Henry Wadsworth Longfellow, and Oliver Wendell Holmes lay through Harvard.

There Brandeis achieved one of the great triumphs of his life. When he arrived at Harvard Law School in the fall of 1875, he was eighteen-going-on-nineteen, without a college degree, a Jew who spoke with a Kentucky accent, an almost penniless young man in one of the citadels of the American aristocracy. He left Harvard three years later, having achieved the highest scholastic record of any Harvard Law School student (and this record remains unsurpassed) a special exemption from the Board of Trustees so that he could receive his degree at a younger age than the school's rules allowed, and acceptance by the Brahmin intelligentsia and Boston society. He had even managed to save the first few dollars of what would become a multimillion-dollar fortune.

One of his classmates described Brandeis as having "the pleasant voice of the youthful student," a "keen intellectual face," a "lithe figure," a "dark yet handsome aspect, and finally the unaffected suavity of his manner, that had in it something of the Old World. Intellect, refinement, an alert and receptive spirit, were written all over his attractive personality." Another observer noted the "detectable Southern softness in his voice" and pictured him as a "black-haired, blue-eyed fellow, with high color suffusing his olive skin" and "the polish and poise of a gifted actor." A picture taken when Brandeis was twenty shows the same high-browed face of his younger days, with the features now more sculpted and less boyish, the hair short and smooth, the eyes more sophisticated.[7]

The 1875 Law School student body was made up of about two hundred men, most of whom had graduated with high grades from prestigious New England colleges. The social pecking order was dominated by the scions of wealthy New England families and by those who had graduated from Harvard College. They lived in "Harvard style" brick buildings and attended classes in two-storied Dane Hall, its front doors bordered by the columns that characterize the early Harvard buildings. The only innovation at the Law School lay in its curriculum.[8]

Most American lawyers had become such by "reading law" in a lawyer's office. Law schools were unlike lawyers' offices in that one did not concentrate on specific cases but instead read textbooks and heard lectures. The Law School method was changed by Christopher Columbus Langdell, Dane Professor of Law at Harvard since 1870, and it was Langdell's approach to the law that Brandeis learned and adopted.

In an article that he wrote in 1889 for Harvard's magazine, *The Green Bag*, Brandeis explained the difference Langdell had made to Harvard. He instituted stringent admission requirements, including examinations in Latin or French and in Blackstone's *Commentaries*. Degrees were given only to students who had attended lectures regularly and taken examinations in their courses. More important, Langdell and his fellow faculty members "believed that the law was a science, and should be studied as such." They therefore established a rigorous set of courses to be taken in sequence, including such subjects as contracts, property, torts, civil procedure, criminal law, evidence, equity, trusts, and constitutional law. And most important of all, Langdell introduced what has come to be known as the case method of instruction.[9]

Brandeis quoted Langdell's own explanation of the method, which appeared in the preface to his *Selected Cases on Contracts* (the first casebook ever published in the United States): "Law . . . consists of certain principles or doctrines . . . Each of these doctrines has arrived at its present state by slow degrees . . . This growth is to be traced in the main through a series of cases; and much the shortest and best, if not the only way of mastering the doctrine effectually is by studying the cases in which it is embodied . . . To have such a mastery of these as to be able to apply them with constant facility and certainty to the ever-tangled skein of human affairs, is what constitutes a true lawyer; and hence to acquire that mastery should be the business of every earnest student of the law."[10]

As Brandeis explained the application of Langdell's approach, students studied between two and six cases for each class. "In the classroom some student is called upon by the professor to state the case, and then follows an examination of the opinion of the court, an analysis of the arguments of counsel, a criticism of the reasoning on which the decision is based, a careful discrimination between what was decided and what is a *dictum* merely. To use the expression of one of the professors, the case is 'eviscerated.' Other students are either called upon for their opinions or volunteer them,—the professor throughout acting largely as moderator." Brandeis excelled at the "evisceration." A classmate reminisced, "Mr. Brandeis had hardly taken his seat in our class room before his remarkable talents were discovered and his claim to immediate distinction allowed," and added of the class of 1877, "I think it would be admitted by every surviving member of that class, however distinguished, that Mr. Brandeis, although one of the youngest men present, had the keenest and most subtle mind of all." Brandeis described the "animated discussions in the class-room" as encouraging each student "to resort to every means of fortifying himself, either for his own instruction or in order to overthrow his adversary in discussion, be it professor or fellow-student." He believed that he was depicting his classmates as well as himself when he wrote, "Their interest is at fever heat." The case method, for Brandeis, engendered "intellectual self-reliance and the spirit of investigation."[11]

Clearly, Brandeis had fallen in love with the law. His letters to his family were full of enthusiasm, and he would always refer to his Harvard experience as "the wonderful years" and the "happiest of my life." Writing to Lewis Dembitz's former partner, the man who would soon become one of his brothers-in-law, Brandeis said, "Law schools are splendid institutions. Aside from the instruction there received, being able continually to associate with young men who have the same interest and ambition, who are determined to make as great progress as possible in their studies and devote all their time to the same—must alone be of inestimable advantages. Add to this the instruction of consummate lawyers, who devote their whole time to *you*, and a complete law-library of over fifteen thousand volumes." In addition, there were the law clubs, similar to today's moot courts, in which students argued cases for practice. Brandeis called them "grand institutions," and he participated enthusiastically in his own (dubbed the Pow-Wow Club). "Law seems so interesting to me in all its aspects," he rejoiced to his sister; "it is difficult for me to understand that any of the initiated should not burn with enthusiasm." He kept his casebooks long after he left Harvard, and in 1917, when his daughter Susan was studying law at the University of Chicago, he would send her his own copies of casebooks and treatises by Langdell, Ames, Kent, and Thayer as well as the notebooks from his courses.[12]

The "consummate lawyers" of whom Brandeis wrote included such outstanding professors as Charles Saunders Bradley and James Bradley Thayer. Brandeis occasionally dined at Bradley's home and met other professors. When Brandeis was awarded a scholarship at the end of his first year, Bradley advised him against accepting it and instead offered him a job tutoring his son. Years later Brandeis wrote to his fiancée that Thayer "was my best friend among the instructors at the Law School." It was at Bradley's house that Brandeis met Nathanial Southgate Shaler, also a Kentuckian and an outstanding professor of geology. They became sufficiently intimate for Brandeis to consult Shaler about his post–law school plans. He was impressed also by Professor James B. Ames, whom he described as "a man of the most eminent abilities." Ames, a graduate of Harvard College and the Law School, would become dean of the Law School in 1895, and Brandeis would then work closely with him in his activities as an alumnus.[13]

Brandeis's professors began to introduce him to some of the leading citizens of Boston and their offspring. Denman Ross, who occasionally lectured on architecture and design at Harvard, invited Brandeis to attend a discussion group and to meet eligible young ladies at his home; Ephraim Emerton, professor of German and ecclesiastical history at Harvard, whom Brandeis had met in Europe, frequently asked him and other students to dine. As a result of these invitations, Brandeis was present when Ralph Waldo Emerson delivered his lecture "Education" to a small group; he heard lectures by Henry Adams and Charles Eliot Norton; and at one reception he "saw (literally) Longfellow & Holmes & just missed [George Ticknor] Curtis and [John Greenleaf] Whittier." Indeed, Boston and Cambridge were so full of the famous that Brandeis wrote to his brother, "Celebrities are so numerous here one cannot take the trouble to look at all of them." His mother, responding to the copious details in his letters, concluded, "How pleasant your life in Cambridge is! How refreshing and wholesome this gay, intellectual atmosphere!" To his sister, Brandeis wrote, perhaps a bit proud of himself, "I have been quite a society man for the past week—out for breakfast, out for lunch, out for dinner, out out [*sic*] for teas—almost less 'ins' than 'outs.' " Much as he enjoyed these occasions, however, he could still discriminate; after another "very enjoyable evening," he commented, "it must be confessed that all Cambridge people are not intellectual giants."[14]

His outings, though, were not entirely intellectual. One evening at the Rosses', where he went to dine and stayed "till near midnight," there were "three or four young ladies & same number of gents." The assembled throng played " 'chumps', an improvement on 'Yes & No' which you ought to introduce in the West if not already known there. The company divides itself into two 'camps', each occupying a separate room. One emissary from each camp goes out of the room, the two choose a question and the emissary from Camp A. goes into Camp B. and vice versa. The company i.e. the soldiers of each camp, asks the enemy's emissary as many questions as possible . . . The camp which guesses the problem first retains the emissary as captive and receives back its own emissary in triumph." Judging from Brandeis's next words, the young ladies playing were from Boston society, but not entirely impressive: "The game taught me, at least, that Cambridge young ladies, who have had the advantages of a European Education are not necessarily omniscient; the problem to be solved by the camps was the 'Shadow of the Pyramids of Egypt' and the two young ladies who proposed it, concurred in the opinion that Egypt is in Asia."[15]

Brandeis soon became fast friends with Samuel Dennis Warren, whose socially prominent New England family owned paper mills and who graduated second in their class, behind Brandeis. Another classmate with whom he roomed for a while and with whom he corresponded at least until 1890 was Walter Bond Douglas. Douglas practiced in St. Louis after graduating from Harvard and then became a law professor and state circuit court judge in Missouri. Brandeis also received letters from William Reuben Richards, who came from an old Massachusetts family and was later of great importance in organizing the construction of Boston's first subway. Richards was one of the friends who read to Brandeis and remained on sufficiently good terms that Brandeis in the summer of

1879 considered a fall walking tour with him. No other Harvard friends are mentioned in Brandeis's letters home. Since many of these letters have been lost, references to other friends may have vanished with them; although a close student of Brandeis has argued that his Jewishness precluded Brandeis's acceptance by Brahmin society. However, no record of social exclusion exists, and to Brandeis, the Harvard years were the "wonderful" ones.[16]

A more reasonable explanation for the few references to friends lies in Brandeis's insistence, demonstrated rather early, that he would choose his own society. In the letter in which he talked of having "been quite a society man for the past week," he added, "This, however, was an unusual rush and seeing only comparitively little 'Society' I generally enjoy myself in it. Very much of society would surely bore me . . . How many times one does make the same remark." Brandeis may have been awed, initially, at the great men he met, but he was soon convinced that greatness was evidenced by intelligence rather than social standing. He kept a notebook in which he jotted down not only passages that he had read but remarks that had been made by the men he admired. He made notes of passages from Emerson, Shakespeare, Swift, Walpole, De Quincey, Lowell, Matthew Arnold, Milton, Tennyson, Swinburne, Longfellow, and Stevenson, as well as remarks by Shaler. The excitement of Harvard and Boston, for Brandeis, was the excitement of ideas—particularly those of Boston Brahminism. Nothing in Brandeis's childhood and nothing in his own jottings or memories of Harvard and Boston indicates that he was at all interested in idle chatter, no matter how socially prominent the chatterers.[17]

Brandeis may have narrowed his social circle deliberately in order to protect his time for other things. The Brandeis children had all been expected to play musical instruments, but Brandeis, who had never thought much of his attempts to scratch away on the violin, deliberately gave it up at Harvard, because he could make better use of his limited time. Taught from childhood that one had to be both self-disciplined and a participant in the public life of one's country, he went through life making conscious choices about how to fulfill these expectations. He copied down Emerson's "They can conquer who believe they can" as well as his "The Golden Age is not behind but before you"; from Tennyson, he took "Drink deep until the habits of the slave / The sins of emptiness, gossip and spite, / and slander die . . . Besides the brain was like the hand and grew with using."

At Harvard, he plunged into the demanding world of law and of the intellect; later in Boston, as an attorney, he would balance the demands of clients, a growing family, and a variety of public service activities. As for society, one biographer claims that "ever since law-school days Brandeis had been in good standing with the 'best' people of Cambridge and Boston" and another maintains that in later years "none of this circle served to buttress Brandeis' place in society . . . the real reason for his unpopularity was, as an established local lawyer knowledgeably assessing Brandeis' place in the city concluded, that he was 'an outsider, successful, and a Jew.' " The point may be moot. Brandeis may well have cared very little for Brahmin society; it was the Puritan-Brahmin ethic which he felt to be congenial—and as the Brahmins began to lose touch with that ethic, he lost interest in them.[18]

One other Harvard-related phenomenon had an impact far beyond the Harvard years. Brandeis's eyes began to fail. He read constantly and suffered the eyestrain common to law students who read by gaslight. His eyes gave out completely, however, during the summer after his first year at Harvard, while he was "reading law" in Louisville with his brother-in-law. The Cincinnati oculist he consulted told him he would have to give up all reading, including the law. He returned to Harvard nonetheless to consult a Boston doctor; the advice was the same. Refusing to heed it, he went to a Dr. Knapp, who was an oculist well known in New York. Finding nothing organically wrong with Brandeis's eyes, Dr. Knapp counseled him to think more and read less. Brandeis decided that he could do so if his friends read to him, and it was in this fashion that he completed law school.

On January 31, 1878, he wrote about his eyes to a friend, "I am able to use them hardly three or four hours with most careful use but my oculists promise me a brilliant future. Hence am not doing very much nor very satisfactory work this year. Take 'Sales,' the different courses on R.P. [Real Property] & Wills but am relying greatly on the absorbing process. Also attend lectures on B & N [Bills and Notes] & Evidence. Am doing considerable work with kind friends who read to me." A few months later he reported to his brother, "To-day I reached one hour in my reading & shall hence forth be allowed to write one half hour each day instead of so much reading . . . I hope by September to have my eyes strong again." Brandeis was already gifted with an unusually good memory, and the need to rely on the "absorbing process" made it even more acute. Within his family circle, he was credited with a photographic memory.[19]

In the spring of 1877, after what was then the normal two years of law school, Brandeis was ready to graduate. He had the highest grades earned by anyone in his class and was one of six men chosen by the class to write the oration that would be presented at graduation. Once the six had written the oration, the faculty chose the man who would actually deliver it. But when the faculty voted for Brandeis, they suddenly found themselves in an embarrassing position, for the rules of Harvard provided that no one under the age of twenty-one could graduate. This troubled Professor Langdell particularly; Brandeis was one of his favorites, and he wanted him to have the honor of delivering the oration. Langdell sent Brandeis to President Charles Eliot for a ruling. Eliot, whom Brandeis had never met before, was firm: "The rule is that the orator is to be one of those who receive a degree. The law says that you can't have a degree before you are twenty-one. You will not be twenty-one until November. Commencement is in June. I don't see, Mr. Brandeis, how you can be the orator." That settled that, in less than three minutes. Brandeis later told his secretary and assistant that his mental reaction was, "There is an example of the efficient executive." Eliot, however, must not have been entirely happy with his ruling, for at a hurried meeting before commencement the following morning the trustees met to suspend the age rule and allow Brandeis to graduate with his cum laude degree. The orator having already been chosen, Brandeis again sat through a commencement without speaking.[20]

Brandeis was clearly not in a hurry to leave Harvard. He had originally borrowed a few hundred dollars from Alfred, and that sum constituted all the money Brandeis was to receive from home during his Harvard years, since his father was still in financial difficulties. Professor Bradley's offer of a tutorship had been followed by others, and in addition Brandeis had been relieved of the necessity to pay rent by his appointment as a proctor in the spring of 1877, replacing Ephraim Emerton, who had married. Knowing that he could count on his tutoring jobs and proctorship, Brandeis decided to do a year's graduate work at Harvard, and once again took up residence at 29 Thayer Hall. He continued to take courses in what must have been very small classes. He wrote to Douglas that "Law School has increased—2—this year, number being 189. Third year 13. Second year 78. First year 72. Special students 26." Nevertheless, Brandeis did not view the Law School as small; he had lamented that "the Law School, is unfortunately, very popular—we have an increase of nearly thirty students over last year's number and the library is consequently overcrowded."[21]

During this time, Brandeis added to his income by proctoring examinations, receiving payment of $1.00 an hour. The sum was not negligible, as is perhaps indicated by the Harvard Bursar's Record of Payment Received from Brandeis for the spring semester of 1877. The fee for "Instruction and Library" was $50.00; that for "Board at Harvard Dining Association," $38.25. Another indication of comparative costs came from Alfred during Brandeis's third year at Harvard: "we are going to have the parlor furniture covered for Ma's birthday. You will owe me $4.00 on it and I want you to take the money and use it for room decoration or something else as a birthday present from me."[22]

Brandeis accumulated money by working hard and living frugally, as he would throughout the rest of his life. He had already discovered that to the extent that he scaled down his expenses, he would be sufficiently freed of financial exigencies to spend his time as he chose. Perhaps he kept in mind the fate of his father, who had spent freely when times were good and had then been devastated when the economy destroyed his fortune. At any rate, by 1878 Brandeis not only had managed to repay his brother but had saved between $1,200 and $1,500. He used $600 to buy a bond of the Atchison Railroad, which he kept in his portfolio long after he had become a multimillionaire. By the end of his third year at Harvard, he was able to send Al "two drafts; one for four hundred & thirty five Dols ($435) on Merchants Nt Bk of Boston, the other on Boylston Nt Bk of Boston for sixty five Dols (together $500) . . . Please invest proceeds in U.S. four (4)% Bonds deposit them in my name in the safest place at Louisville." A few weeks later he sent another "draft on Boston for Two Hundred & Fifty (250) Dols. which you will also please invest in U.S. 4% Bonds."[23]

His financial problems were at last over, but now he was in a quandary: what to do when the third year was up. His family sent a stream of letters urging him to return to the Midwest. His parents urged him to practice in Louisville, where he could be assured of his father's firm's legal business; his oldest sister, Fannie, begged him to join her husband Charles Nagel in his law practice in St. Louis; Sam Warren wanted Brandeis to become *his* partner in Boston. Brandeis put off a decision as long as possible. Late in June of 1878, when the school year was over, he wrote to his brother, "My plans for the summer are still unsettled. Dr. Derby [the oculist] thinks it inadvisable for me to go to Louisville at present fearing that the heat may debilitate me & thus injuriously affect the eyes. It is probable that I shall remain in New England . . . Cambridge is beautiful now & I am becoming more & more attached to the place." Lest he be thought indecisive or unwilling to return to the bosom of the family, he quickly added, "It is possible that I may go out to Judge Bradley's farm and tutor his son for four or six weeks. Shall do it if I can." But the decision had to be made, and Brandeis, apparently unwilling to tie himself too closely to his family, opted to go to work for a St. Louis firm other than his brother-in-law's. Even so, he could not escape family ties: the firm he chose was headed by James Taussig, who belonged to a family long associated with the Brandeises and who was the uncle of Alfred's wife. But at least St. Louis was not Louisville and Taussig was not his brother-in-law. Why Brandeis did not accept Sam Warren's offer is unclear. Perhaps Brandeis felt that any partnership would depend too heavily on Warren's extensive connections among socially prominent Bostonians and therefore place Brandeis in a de facto junior position.[24]

Having decided to leave Cambridge, Brandeis was not at all certain that he had done well to choose St. Louis over Louisville. He wrote to "Dearest Mama" on August 2, 1878, "I have doubted somewhat whether I was right in the course I pursued in this matter. If after reading the letter you think I was *wrong*, I most humbly beg your pardon." His mother replied that he "had the right to follow your *inclination*, for you are so young that you can afford a risk, and I am convinced that whatever you will undertake is going to be of advantage to you as a step in your development. So I am leaving everything to you in happy confidence, and give you my blessings. A temporary separation from any of you is probably unavoidable, and I only hope that it will be given to us, your parents, to have you with us alternately . . . I had given up hope that you would settle here, and therefore the news that you had decided for St. Louis was not a great disappointment for me." The letter goes on to indicate Frederika's understanding that Brandeis might well want to practice "before deciding to retire to a purely scientific career." Frederika's mention of a "purely scientific career" is somewhat puzzling. This may have referred to a hope that Brandeis would ultimately choose the life of a scholar. He had written to his younger sister about legal writing: "What a delightful occupation for leisure moments . . . Giving has always seemed better to me than receiving—Why always absorb—why be forever reading, reading, reading—& never produce, never give anything in return. I wish my eyes would let me do some independent work, I should revel in it . . . I am anxiously looking forward to the time when I shall again be able to satisfy my desperate longing for more law."[25]

Brandeis put off his return to the Midwest as long as he could. He did secure the job tutoring Judge Bradley's son at the family home in Providence, Rhode Island, and stayed there through August. Then he returned to Massachusetts and became ill; on September 22, 1878, Taussig wrote, "I shall endeavor to keep the position open for you, and would venture to suggest that you take all the time necessary for a radical cure." Brandeis finally got to St. Louis sometime between then and November and was admitted to the Missouri bar. His distaste for St. Louis—or, perhaps, for anything that was not Cambridge—showed itself early. He lamented to one of his sisters that social life required him to participate in "tableaux" and hoped that he would "be called off to Washington to argue a case before the Supreme Court—merely for the purpose of escaping this trial."[26]

It was not merely that tableaux were not as exciting as "chumps." He complained about his salary, and although he admitted that he had been doing some "interesting & instructive work," he also noted that he was about to try what was apparently his first case, "which we . . . fully expect to lose; in fact, our only chance of winning rests in the possibility of total mental aberration of the judge." He thought that was probably the reason the case had been given to him. Shortly thereafter, he lamented, "I suppose the Cambridge letters may have greatly conduced to my impatience with ballroom superficiality and vapidity." And there was not much promise professionally: "The quantity of young & old lawyers here without practice is appalling." "Litigation & legal business is very much depressed here. Everybody complains & most with reason. Even in our office business is poor." To make matters worse, Brandeis suffered repeated attacks of malaria. All in all, St. Louis seemed a good place to leave.[27]

And Brandeis was planning to do exactly that. He had kept up a correspondence with Sam Warren, who had never ceased urging Brandeis to return to Boston and a partnership. In May Warren found out that the *Law Reporter* and the *Law Review* might both have editorial vacancies. He quickly wrote to Brandeis that if they managed to get the positions, they would be assured of enough income to begin their own practice. Brandeis's reply sounded cautious. "If," he wrote, the editorship of one or the other periodicals "would give me a living salary—that would enable me to disregard what otherwise would be a great obstacle to my going into partnership with you." Warren, of course, had great financial resources, which Brandeis's bit of capital tucked away in 4 percent bonds could not match. But it was not the editorship as such he really wanted; it was "essential that the position should not monopolize our time . . . For, although I am very desirous of devoting some of my time to the literary part of the law, I wish to become known as a practicing lawyer . . . Furthermore, my eyes, though quite strong again, allowing me to work practically the whole day and as much as [is] ordinarily required in a lawyer's practice, must be still carefully used and would not, I fear, be able to stand much or regular nightwork." If the editorships did not materialize, Brandeis was not ready to commit himself; he wrote, "I wish particularly for your letter giving the results of our examination of the prospects of a young law firm and more particularly your own prospects of securing business through your social and financial position."[28]

It is interesting that Brandeis wrote that he wished "to become known" as a practicing lawyer, not merely that he wished to become a practicing lawyer; clearly, he was thinking of the kind of reputation he would wish to have in his beloved Boston. It no longer seemed to bother him that the business would depend, at least initially, on Warren's contacts. Perhaps his intense distaste for St. Louis and his disinclination to return to the family fold in Louisville had become more important than his pride.

But Brandeis did not have to wait for more news about the editorship; he was offered a position by Chief Justice Horace Gray of the Massachusetts Supreme Judicial Court "as his Secty & Assistant which gives me a salary about $500." Professors Bradley, Thayer, and Langdell were apparently involved in securing the position for him and advised that it would be "very valuable as a stepping stone. Most of the work . . . falls in summer so that it will not greatly interfere" with time for private clients. Barely a month after telling Warren that he was unsure about the move, Brandeis was to be found in Cambridge, writing to a friend that "my last year was not a contented one . . . I longed for something I had had before—& I hope & pray I may find it here." He suggested that mail be sent to him care of Warren, although they had not as yet finished arranging the details of their partnership. One detail that might have caused problems was Brandeis's admission to the Massachusetts bar. Warren was of course a member of it, but no bar examination was planned until the following fall. Justice Gray arranged to have Brandeis admitted in July, "without an examination and contrary to all principles and precedent," as Brandeis jubilantly reported to his brother. Since Warren was senior in bar membership, it was appropriate to have his name come first, and the firm of Warren & Brandeis thus came into existence.[29]

Brandeis got to Boston just before the large-scale migration of Eastern European Jews and the threat of the combined political power of Jews, Irish, and Italians led to a xenophobia new to Boston. Anti-Semitism was frowned upon by Harvard during Brandeis's student days. President Eliot summed up his feelings by calling the Jewish race "the source of all the highest conceptions of God, man, and nature." Even during the later heyday of the Immigration Restriction League, Eliot stood firm for free immigration and favored the preservation of the unique characteristics and individuality of Judaism. The Brahminism of Harvard, of Brandeis's hero Emerson, and of men like William Ellery Channing, the father of Unitarianism, has been summarized by a historian of the period as being founded on "respect for the individuality of each man plus faith in the universality of all men," and an understanding and tradition of "civil and religous liberties." These sentiments were antithetical to anti-Semitism.[30]

Nonetheless, a fear of "outsiders" developed among the younger generation of Brahmins in the 1880s and 1890s, particularly with the rise of Irish Catholic political power. Hugh O'Brien, Boston's first Irish mayor, was elected in 1884. By then, even Professor Shaler was advocating limitations on immigration. The Immigration Restriction League of the 1890s fought against admission of southern and eastern European immigrants (but approved of those from Britain, Germany, and Scandinavia.) The league and its friends campaigned vigorously for a bill that would exclude the illiterate undesirables; in 1917 the United States Congress passed such a bill and repassed it over President Woodrow Wilson's veto.[31]

Throughout the xenophobic period, however, a curiously schizoid approach to Jews could be found. The old Puritan admiration for German Jews persisted and was enhanced by a new emphasis on the Teutonic origins of Anglo-Saxon institutions. It was the Russian and Polish Jews who were feared, along with the Irish and Italian Catholics.[32]

Thus, Brandeis would not have had any qualms about returning to Boston because of his Jewishness. In the 1870s, restrictionism was not respectable. His experience of the Brahminism of Harvard and of the Boston intellectuals he met had taught him that Jews were welcome. As Sam Warren's partner he would gain membership in the exclusive social clubs of Boston and its environs: the Union, Exchange, Union Boat, and the Dedham Polo Club. It has been suggested that he was tolerated solely because of his Harvard connection and his relationship with Warren. For whatever reasons, Brandeis was indeed accepted. At one point in 1891, he and the Secretary of the Union Boat Club exchanged letters after the Club's Executive Commmttee decided to ask Brandeis to undertake an investigation into a minor complaint made by some members. The tone of the letters is mock-serious, as befits two men of affairs called upon to deal with one of life's petty annoyances. If there was any hostility shown to Brandeis by the Union Club or any other of his fellow Brahmins, no record of it remains.[33]

"Fellow Brahmins" they were. He had no difficulty shifting from his family's world to that of Harvard and the Boston Brahmins; essentially, the two credos were the same. By the end of the 1870s Brandeis had adopted both Boston and intellectual Brahminism as his own, and he would remain true to the Brahminism of Emerson and Eliot for the rest of his life.[34]

3 | Practicing Law

In the summer of 1879, Brandeis moved to Boston and found room and board at a Mrs. Smith's, 21 Joy Street, where three of his former Harvard classmates also resided. It was near both Warren and the State House. In the fall, however, he moved into the Warren house, on Mt. Vernon Street. His sister Amy sent him an easel and pictures, which "are nicely placed in my room," and his father contributed a print, which Brandeis called "one of the prettiest I have seen." His approach to furnishings was summarized in a letter home:

> To Al.
> Can give only two bits of advice about furnishing rooms
> I. Buy nothing that is not irresistably handsome.
> II. Buy nothing which your grandchildren cannot use.

He also sent a message to his mother: "Have the shirts washed in Louisville." But frugality did not mean that Brandeis was unconscious of appearance. Not only did he buy furnishings for his room, he also bought himself "a new square top-hat" which he described as "quite swell." Now he was ready to conquer Boston.[1]

Warren & Brandeis opened for business in a room at 60 Devonshire Street, which Brandeis called a "desirable location . . . in the 3rd story (2 flights) . . . The room (no. 5) is only $200 a year—very cheap everybody says." For three dollars a week, the partners hired a messenger boy. Brandeis pronounced himself pleased with the partnership: "What I have seen of him [Warren] since I am here has raised my opinion in every respect . . . I think we will work well together and that he is a good supplement to me. I like his push and obstinacy and his ambition. He is a person with a fine sense of profession and commercial honor and is smart enough to lay aside his seeming hautiness which made him enemies at Cambridge. His first appearance in Court Wednesday a week ago and Monday last earned for him many compliments." He added, "He is bent now on making clients and getting business and I think he will do it. Already he has quite a number of small claims with a prospect of some larger ones. If matters continue to come in as now, we are safe." They were all the safer for having the business of S. C. Warren & Company, the paper manufacturing concern owned by Warren's father.[2]

Still, Brandeis had doubts about having moved so far from his family. He wrote to his mother, "When I received your letter and those of the others, it seems to me as if I were a fool to have settled here so far away, instead of staying with you and enjoying you and your love." But he recognized that stronger emotions were pulling at him: "Of course one can live anywhere, but there is also ambition to be satisfied . . . man is strange, at least this one is; he does not enjoy what he has—and he always wants what he does not yet have. That probably is called ambition . . . And so I think that I shall be happier here, in spite of being alone, and if I can write you of successes, I shall be compensated for all I am missing. I think you will be too."[3]

He was not entirely certain that he wanted to remain alone; to his brother-in-law, whom he called his sister Fannie's partner, he wrote, "Living away from you all I think I shall be looking around for some such partner when my income justifies such a step." But then he drew back, writing "—Later—The brilliant ideas expressed in the last few lines were conceived in a moment of loneliness. That condition having passed away, I take this all back." Indeed, he would not marry for more than a decade. Nevertheless, he had flirtations. He sent his sister a long description of a lady of twenty-eight, who had a "finely chiseled" face, "sparkling jet eyes," a "delicate look," and "conversation . . . of unusual character and quality." But after praising her at length, he added, "You, of course, are very much interested in this young lady because you think I am smitten with her. But Alas! it is not so. One mistress only claims me. The 'Law' has her grip on me."[4]

Although the firm's start struck Brandeis as slow at first, the partnership actually picked up business rather quickly. After only a few months, Brandeis wrote to his brother, "We are pretty scared about some cases we are to try next week. Can't you send us some clients." In December 1879 he reported, "Nothing new this week in business—awfully dull," but by January he was writing, "Things look pretty bright in our practice.

My individual clientage is almost nothing, but then I shall watch and wait and exist. Meanwhile I get practice (in another sense) and am learning considerable about affairs." Brandeis's former professor, Bradley, had recommended him as counsel in a case being brought before the Rhode Island Supreme Court. He argued it successfully in March 1880 and returned to Boston with a large fee and the friendship of a number of Rhode Island lawyers and businessmen. Brandeis called the experience "delightful throughout and people have said so many kind things about my briefs and arguments that I hope something more substantial than glory may come out of it." In fact, although the decision on the point Brandeis argued was a victory, the entire case was later reargued and Brandeis's clients lost. This, however, was generally seen as the result of a weak case rather than a poor lawyer.[5]

While Brandeis was in Providence, Warren wrote that he had gotten several new cases, including one of an estate of "over half a million," and exulted, "The success of W. & B. is assured." A few months later, Brandeis could report that "the cases begun before the vacation are coming to a head now and we look forward to a busy half year . . . On the whole the second year opens well enough and we should be satisfied if the improvement in practice continues as it has since Jan. 1880." A paper manufacturer had turned four cases in New Hampshire over to the firm, and a steamship company became a major client. With the additional work the partners had taken on a senior at Harvard Law School part-time as an aide, a practice they would continue both for its convenience to themselves (Brandeis called the student aides "convenient articles") and as a gesture of support to the Law School.[6]

In fact, the Harvard connection produced more than "convenient articles." Brandeis remained close to the professors and alumni of the Harvard Law School and eventually drew all his full-time associates and future partners from the school. He was a major force in the creation of the Harvard Law School Alumni Association and became its first secretary on September 23, 1886. Law School alumni, who knew of his legendary scholarship and his burgeoning reputation as a practitioner, spread his reputation throughout the United States. In 1910 a young man named Jacob J. Kaplan was about to graduate from the Law School and received an offer from Brandeis's firm. He sought advice from two of his teachers, both among the most influential law professors in the country: James Barr Ames and Samuel Williston, both of whom urged him to accept the invitation. Williston added that he himself went to Brandeis's firm when he needed a lawyer.[7]

Meanwhile, Brandeis was also clerking for Chief Justice Gray. He found his work even more pleasant than he had anticipated and praised

Justice Gray for "patiently listening to suggestions and objections and even contradiction . . . Our mode of working is this. He takes out the record and briefs in any case, we read them over, talk about the points raised, examine the authorities' arguments—then he makes up his mind if he can, marks out the line of argument for his opinion, writes it, and then dictates it to me . . . I am treated in every respect as a person of co-ordinate position. He asks me what I think of his line of argument and I answer candidly. If I think other reasons better, I give them; if I think his language is obscure, I tell him so; if I have any doubts I express them and he is very fair in acknowledging a correct suggestion or disabusing one of an erroneous idea." Perhaps Justice Gray showed Brandeis none of "the unpleasant peculiarities" for which he was noted because he regarded Brandeis so highly. In November 1880, Brandeis's father heard in a roundabout way that Gray had said, "I consider Brandeis the most ingenious and most original lawyer I ever met, and he and his partner are among the most promising law firms we have got."[8]

Brandeis also began bringing business into the firm. Professor Bradley apparently sent other clients to him. Now the German-Jewish community, inclined to give its business to its own, turned to Brandeis. Previously, only one lawyer, Godfrey Morse, had handled accounts for German-American Jews, but one lawyer could not manage to do all the work generated by the community. Jacob H. Hecht, a merchant and leader of the Boston Jewish community, brought Brandeis the first case he would argue before the Massachusetts Supreme Judicial Court. Brandeis recognized the usefulness of the German-American connection and wrote to his sister, "I must go soon to the Turnverein and try and be captivating . . . and get some clients." The Turnverein was a German-American athletic and social club. Brandeis later helped found a Germanic museum, joined the German Club, and contributed to the Deutscher Hilfsverein (a German philanthropic organization). If Warren could "work" Brahmin Boston, Brandeis could do his bit with Boston's German-Americans. The majority of Warren & Brandeis's clients, and of its successor, Brandeis, Dunbar and Nutter (renamed after Sam Warren left to take over the family business) were not Jewish; but merchants like the Eisemanns and Liebmanns (wool merchants), the Filenes (Filene's Department Store), the Franks, the Vorenbergs, Lehman Pickert and Company, Charles Weil and Company, Jacob Dreyfus and Sons, and, of course, the Hechts, accounted for a substantial part of the firm's business. Eventually, Brandeis developed the habit of having a Jewish junior associate to handle many of the Jewish clients. Thus, in 1896, David A. Ellis, who had received his degree from the Harvard Law School, was hired. In 1903 after Ellis left to begin practice on his own, Walter S. Heilborn, whose father was a leading member of the Jewish community and a client of Brandeis's, was brought in; when he left in 1910, Jacob J. Kaplan was hired.[9]

Much of that, however, was in the future. But even in its early days, the firm prospered; at the end of their first year, each of the partners had a net profit of $1,200. In July 1881 Brandeis wrote to Al, "Our fiscal year ends today. It shows up about $3600 gross earnings which makes $3000 (little less) net profits for the year. Last year's gross earnings were something over $3400 but $435 of that came from the Chief Justice, so that legitimate fees are considerably in excess of last year." In a mixture of pessimism and high spirits, he continued, "The outlook for next year is not good. If I were a Sec'ty of Treasury making our estimates I should prepare the country for a strong deficit in the budget. . . don't expect my practice to amount to much for the next fifteen years but I do expect to have a high old time for the twenty five following." But Brandeis was wrong. By 1889 the firm had grown so successful that it moved to larger quarters at 220 Devonshire Street. Warren & Brandeis was among the first Boston law firms to install a telephone, putting efficiency before preference. (Brandeis himself loathed the instrument and used it as little as possible throughout his life.)

Brandeis argued his first case before the United States Supreme Court in 1889. Brought in by Judge Jeremiah Smith, who had been hired to represent the Wisconsin Central Railroad, he helped to prepare the brief and traveled to Washington to hear Smith argue the case. But when Smith was late, Brandeis hurriedly borrowed a frock coat and stepped in for him. The experience added to his fame; by 1890 he was earning more than $50,000 a year, at a time when 75 percent of the country's lawyers made less than $5,000. His earnings continued to rise, averaging $73,000 a year from 1901 to 1915, with $105,758 in 1912. His income, combined with frugal living and conservative investments, enabled him to accumulate $1 million by 1907. By the time he was elevated to the Court in 1916, he was a millionaire twice over, and when he died in 1941, his estate was worth over $3 million.[10]

Brandeis's intellectual life also flourished, and his notebooks reveal the people he met, such as Francis Lowell, Robert Gardiner, Morris Grey, and F. J. Stimson—good Brahmins all. Referring to an afternoon at the home of Mrs. Anne Fields, a well-known New England hostess, he said "I had actually been invited to the Fields to enjoy Longfellow who had promised to spend Sunday with them, but who did not appear on account of the rain." Two days later "Holmes, Warren and I spent [the evening] at Warren's room over a glass of _____ [mixture of champagne and beer] telling jokes and talking Summum bonum. i.e. Warren and Holmes talked and I lay outstretched on a ships chair." Warren had introduced Brandeis to Oliver Wendell Holmes, his former employer, when Warren and Brandeis became partners. Brandeis spent a weekend with the Holmeses in the country during the summer of 1879, and their friendship continued with dinners together at the Parker House and meetings with Warren in a nearby tavern. Holmes thought highly of Brandeis. He had been impressed by Brandeis's article on the liability of trust-estates, and he asked Brandeis to listen to a draft of his own article "Trespass and Negligence." Clearly, Brandeis was back in the Boston intellectual and cultural life he loved. A side benefit was that some of the intelligentsia were in business and turned their legal affairs over to him.[11]

He had only two major problems, one pleasant, the second less so. The first was the dilemma of whether to concentrate on litigation or to join the academic community. Even as he moved back to Boston and the partnership with Warren, Brandeis had admitted that one of his reasons for doing so was the possibility of obtaining a position at Harvard. The partnership would enable him to maintain the security of a private practice while getting a taste of teaching. He could not be certain what he would do if a position were offered, but, if his eyes allowed, he thought he would take it. He loved the law as an intellectual working-out of ideas and recognized that practitioners do not have the leisure for such cerebral games: "The law as a logical science has very great attractions for me. I see it now again by the almost ridiculous pleasure which the discovery or invention of a legal theory gives me; and I know that such a study of the law cannot be pursued by a successful practitioner nor by a Judge (I speak now from experience). Teaching would mean for me writing as well. However, this is all talk. I may feel differently in three months and the wrangling of the Bar may have the greatest attraction for me. It surely is not distasteful to me now. It is merely a question of selecting between two good things—They are both good enough for me. I question only which I am good for."[12]

He was soon to have the opportunity to find out. When Professor James Bradley Thayer planned to go on leave from the Law School in 1881, he suggested that Brandeis be invited to teach his course on evidence. Thayer's leave was postponed, however. In 1882 a leave was planned once again, and this time President Eliot himself wrote Brandeis asking him to take on the course, lecturing twice weekly at a salary of $1,000. Brandeis accepted, and his family was elated. His uncle Dembitz wrote that when he saw President Eliot's letter of appointment made out to Louis Dembitz Brandeis, it was "the first time that I felt glad at your changing your middle name from 'David' to 'Dembitz.'" His mother exulted, "My dearest child, how happy you make me feel! My heart is a prayer of thanksgiving." His father pronounced the appointment "the greatest honor that can be given to a young man of your age." Apparently Adolph Brandeis had been urging a teaching career, for he was afraid that his son had accepted the position to satisfy him: "I simply cannot help being aware that the profession of an academic teacher and possibly a writer is the most satisfying and desirable, and it may have been imprudent on my part to have expressed my opinion so unreservedly . . . if your new duties should induce you to overexert yourself even a very little, I would reproach myself terribly for ever having expressed my feeling about it."[13]

The course was a great success. Oliver Wendell Holmes even asked one student for his notes. The faculty, equally impressed, offered Brandeis the job of assistant professor. He was only twenty-five years old, Harvard had the country's most prestigious law school, and it was one that he loved.[14]

Here Brandeis ran up against his other problem—his uncertain health. The fear of illness and possible death permeates Adolph's and Frederika's letters to Brandeis and his own letters to the people for whom he cared. He grew up hearing about the fatal illnesses of Frederika's mother and brother and remembering his sister Amy's typhoid fever attack in Euripe; the death of his nephew Alfred in 1889, from typhoid fever; the death of his sister Fannie in 1890; and the entire family's bouts with malaria. In Louisville malaria had been such a constant companion that Brandeis always remembered the bowl of antimalaria pills that stood on the dining-room table throughout his childhood. And he had had at least one "bad case" of malaria during his year in St. Louis. Although he had enjoyed horseback riding as a boy, by the time Brandeis got to Harvard the director of the Hemenway Gymnasium had told him that muscularly he was one of the weakest students he had ever seen. He prescribed a program of regular physical exercise to which Brandeis adhered and which helps explain the time he continued to devote to riding and boating no matter how busy he became. During Brandeis's second year back in Boston, he wrote to his brother, "I am a little provoked about my health; for in spite of my vacations I do not feel in real working condition as I should. Suppose however I must reconcile myself to the idea of not accomplishing at present what I should like to and that this state of things must last a year or two." He was doing his best to remedy the situation, however, walking regularly in the morning and rowing before dinner. Once the weather ended the rowing season, he exercised in the gymnasium. His membership in the Turnverein was partly for business purposes, but partly for the sake of its athletic facilities.[15]

When faced with the decision about teaching, Brandeis wrote to his father, "I am rather disgusted with myself physically. I have taken very good care of myself—worked moderately, and still find myself much below par; that is, I am easily exhausted and worn out, without adequate reason." That became a consideration in making his decision, for it was assumed that even as a professor he would continue his private practice. This raised health problems: "You and mother seem to think that Warren could relieve me of much work if he wanted to. That is not true to any extent." He thought, therefore, that he might turn down the Harvard offer "with a view to working less next year."[16]

It was not only reasons of health that made him reluctant to accept the offer. He wanted more experience of litigation before choosing—as his health would force him to do—between practice and teaching: "I feel I am weak in this experience and think that with practice I could do well at it." Professor Shaler, his hero of student days, advised him to leave the partnership: "You're too sensitive. A lawyer should be made of sterner stuff. You won't be able to stand the gaff of opposition." But the joys of practice won, and he declined the Harvard position. According to one biographer, he had the following conversation with Langdell, by then dean of the Law School:

Brandeis: "I'm not ready for it. I want other experiences first."
Langdell: "Perhaps we won't be ready when you are."
Brandeis: "That's a chance I'll have to take."[17]

Shaler did not perceive the extent of Brandeis's psychological strength. Certainly making a decision that ran counter to the expressed wishes of his parents, his uncle, and his former and much revered teachers took a good amount of "stern stuff." And Brandeis was content with his decision. A few years later he wrote to Alfred, "Except a few cases before the Supreme Court this month I have tried few causes within the last weeks, and I really long for the excitement of the contest—that is a good prolonged one covering days or weeks. There is a certain joy in the draining exhaustion and backache of a long trial, which shorter skirmishes cannot afford." In 1892–93 Brandeis did give a course at the Massachusetts Institute of Technology on business law, which he repeated two years later, but then he dropped the course on his own initiative. He discovered, however, that he would be able to combine litigation with more abstract intellectual endeavors. Brandeis and Sam Warren published two law review articles, "The Watuppa Pond Cases" and "The Law of Ponds," in 1888 and 1889. Then, distressed by the lurid newspaper coverage given to Warren's engagement and marriage to the daughter of Senator Thomas Bayard, they wrote "The Right to Privacy," arguing that such a right was inherent in American law. Roscoe Pound later declared that the path-breaking article, published in the *Harvard Law Review*, "did nothing less than add a chapter to our law."[18]

Brandeis practiced commercial law, representing businessmen in their dealings. Initially, he was content to plead their causes, particularly if doing so involved litigation. He wrote of "the excitement of trying a number of cases," and it was clear that his ability to master the facts of any case (based in part on his phenomenal memory) and his brilliance as a legal technician made him an outstanding trial lawyer. Had Brandeis wished, he could have been an extremely successful business lawyer in the traditional sense, taking whatever cases wealthy customers brought to him and fighting their battles in court. But this was not what he opted to do. Brandeis wanted to pick and choose his clients. "I would rather have clients," he said, "than be somebody's lawyer." He did not see clients as his employers but almost as supplicants, coming to ask if he would consider helping them. He refused to pamper them. His office was furnished as austerely as possible, without rug or easy chair, and the temperature was deliberately kept so low that clients had to keep on their overcoats in winter. He wasted no time on niceties; one client "remarked that he could not stay in Brandeis' office except by clinging to some substantial object." His time sheets show that clients were permitted anywhere between fifteen minutes and an hour and a half, with the greatest number of appointments lasting no more than half an hour. He insisted on punctuality, which a reporter called his sine qua non: "One of his secretaries had made the appointment for 3:15 P.M., and precisely on the dot she said: 'Mr. Brandeis will see you now.' " He knew his health limited his work hours; so he organized his time to accomplish all that he wished to do.[19]

Nor were his punctuality and brevity signs of coldness or disinterest. Rather, he was abrupt in part because he quickly understood all that was necessary—and all that was necessary included not only the wishes of his client but the entire situation that had brought the client to him. Here his interest and his understanding frequently went beyond what his client expected. He expressed this need for a deeper understanding in an oft-quoted letter to a young man in his firm who was not doing as well as Brandeis thought he should. The letter sums up the philosophy of Brandeis the lawyer:

> Cultivate the society of men—particularly men of affairs . . . Lose no opportunity of becoming acquainted with men, of learning to feel instinctively their motivation, of familiarizing yourself with their personal and business habits; use your ability in making opportunities to do this . . .
> The knowledge of men, the ability to handle, to impress them, is

needed by you—not only in order that clients may appreciate your advice and that you may be able to apply the law to human affairs— but also that you may more accurately and surely determine what the rules of law are, that is, what the courts will adopt. You are prone in legal investigations to be controlled by logic and to underestimate the logic of facts. Knowledge of the decided cases and of the rules of logic cannot alone make a great lawyer. He must know, must feel "in his bones," the facts to which they apply—must know, too, that if they do not stand the test of such application, the logical result will somehow or other be avoided. You are sometimes inclined to the attitude of "then so much the worse for facts" . . .

Knowledge of decisions and powers of logic are mere hand maidens—they are servants, not masters. The controlling force is the deep knowledge of human necessities . . . The man who does not know intimately human affairs is apt to make of the law a bed of Procrustes. No hermit can be a great lawyer, least of all a commercial lawyer. When from a knowledge of the law, you pass to its application, the need of a full knowledge of men and of their affairs becomes even more apparent. The duty of a lawyer today is not that of a solver of legal conundrums: he is indeed a counsellor at law. Knowledge of the law is of course essential to his efficiency, but the law bears to his profession a relation very similar to that which medicine does to that of the physicians. The apothecary can prepare the dose, the more intelligent one even knows the specific for most common diseases. It requires but a mediocre physician to administer the proper drug for the patient who correctly and fully describes his ailment. The great physicians are those who in addition to that knowledge of therapeutics which is open to all, know not merely the human body but the human mind and emotions, so as to make themselves the proper diagnosis—to know the truth which their patients fail to disclose and who add to this an influence over the patient which is apt to spring from a real understanding of him.

Your law may be perfect, your ability to apply it great, and yet you cannot be a successful adviser unless your advice is followed; it will not be followed unless you can satisfy your clients, unless you impress them with your superior knowledge, and that you cannot do unless you know their affairs better than they do because you see them from a fullness of knowledge. The ability to impress them grows with your success in advising others, with the confidence which you yourself feel in your powers. That confidence can never come from books: it is gained by human intercourse.[20]

The notion that the lawyer's role was not merely to achieve whatever goal the client thought he wanted but to tell the client what to do about his problem—and to convince the client that the proposed course of action was correct—was extraordinary at a time when lawyers were increasingly becoming no more than lackeys for growing corporations, taking upon themselves whatever battles their employers were fighting and seeking to get business-oriented courts to help them win. Brandeis was not merely interested in winning cases, much as he loved litigation; he was concerned with whether or not the battle was just.

The underlying tenet of the adversary system is that all litigants must be treated by their lawyers as if they are right and that it is up to a judge or jury to decide the issue. But Brandeis would have none of the idea that lawyers are legal guns for hire, using their skills for whichever side seeks them out. His frugality was destined in part to permit him to make value judgments about the cases for which his services were sought. If he did not believe a prospective client's claim to be legitimate, he would not take his case. And if, through his knowledge of his clients' affairs, he could help them to organize their businesses and dealings so as to minimize the need for litigation, he was delighted to do so. Among his papers is a memorandum in his handwriting entitled "The Practice of the Law." It says, in part, "Know not only specific cases. but whole subject. can't know the facts. know thoroughly Each fact. Don't believe client witness—Examine Documents. Reason. Use imagination. Know the whole Subject. Know bookkeeping the universal language of business . . . Know not only those facts which bear on direct controversy, but know all facts that Surround. Advise client what he should have—not what he wants."[21]

He commented later in life that his own investigations of all the facts involved in clients' problems led him to believe that "many things sanctioned by expert opinion . . . were wrong." As Brandeis was to reflect later, "When I began to practice law . . . I trusted only expert opinion." But "experience of life" made him "democratic" in the sense of realizing that wisdom was not the possession of experts only. Insistence on knowing the facts, organizing and analyzing them, fashioning creative solutions to seemingly intractable problems—that to Brandeis was the job of the lawyer.[22]

Brandeis explained his approach to the law in the address "The Opportunity in the Law," delivered to the Harvard Ethical Society at Phillips Brooks House on May 4, 1905. He praised the "whole training" of lawyers in law school and in everyday practice—as leading to the "development of judgement [and] . . . the memory of the reasoning faculties" as well as the art of research and the practice of logic, resulting in the lawyer's eventual fitness for his "position of the adviser of men." Brandeis noted that in the early United States "nearly every great lawyer was then a statesman; and nearly every statesman, great or small, was a lawyer." Brandeis felt that, in an industrialized society, "the particular mental attributes and attainments which the legal profession develops are demanded in the proper handling of these large financial or industrial affairs . . . The magnitude, difficulty and importance of the problems involved are often as great as in the matters of state with which lawyers were formerly frequently associated."[23]

However, the citizenry now accorded the lawyer far less respect than it had seventy-five years earlier. The reason, Brandeis found, was that lawyers had abused their trust: "Instead of holding a position of independence, between the wealthy and the people, prepared to curb the excesses of either, able lawyers [had], to a large extent, allowed themselves to become adjuncts of great corporations and [had] neglected the obligation to use thei powers for the protection of the people." Brandeis lamented that it was all too infrequent for anyone to be called the "people's lawyer" (the name by which he would later be known).

He inveighed against the unthinking involvement of attorneys in corporate attempts to affect legislative policymaking. Corporations were able to hire the most talented lawyers for such tasks, "while the public [was] often inadequately represented or wholly unrepresented." The result was the passage of unfair laws and the defeat of good ones. Lawyers had even been known to fight before legislatures for bills that they as citizens deplored. Worse still, lawyers went on acting for corporations before legislatures even if they knew that their clients had bribed members of those bodies or "corrupted public opinion" through manipulation of the media. And the public, vaguely aware of this, no longer gave the bar the respect that could be its due. The remedy could be found in a twofold vision of the lawyer: as an adviser in his private practice to those who in effect controlled the economy and as a public servant, morally obligated to act in the public sector for the solutions to the problems that beset an industrial society.[24]

How did a young lawyer, initially anxious about securing clients, representing merchants whose major interest was profit making, come to develop this two-pronged idea of the lawyer as the servant of the community? Part of the answer, of course, lies in the ethic of public service that had been taught by Brandeis's parents and by the Brahmins at Harvard. But Brandeis was an empiricist. His principles, he said, were derived from "run[ning] up against a problem" and then "painfully . . . think[ing] it out." To understand the transformation of Brandeis, the private practitioner and former law professor, into Brandeis, the "people's lawyer," one must turn to his early professional experiences in the world of politics (discussed in Chapter 5).[25]

4 | Family Life

One of the most astonishing things about Brandeis was the number of his interests and the amount of work he completed, while insisting on maintaining a regulated life with reasonably short work days and regular vacations. This was the result of a deliberate decision, taken for reasons both of health and of efficiency. To Harold Laski, he wrote, "each [man] is a weak thing, despite the aids and habiliments with which science, invention and organization have surrounded him." Of himself he said, "I soon learned that I could do twelve months' work in eleven months, but not in twelve." When the twelfth month arrived, Brandeis went on vacation, almost always in August.[1]

He also believed that lawyers had a particular need for leisure and wrote to a young employee, "A bookkeeper can work 8 or 10 hours a day and perhaps 12, year in—year out, and possibly his work may be always good (tho' I doubt it). But a man who practices law, who aspires to the higher places of his profession must keep his mind fresh. It must be alert and be capable of meeting emergencies, must be capable of the *tour de force*. This is not possible for him who works alone, not only during the day but much of the night, without change, without turning the mind into new channels, with the mind always at some tension. The bow must be strung and unstrung; work must be measured not merely by time but also by its intensity. There must be time for that unconscious thinking which comes to the busy man in his play." Brandeis thus left work regularly in the late afternoon and spent his evenings in good conversation, reading, or at the theater or concerts.[2]

During the year, he was "quite active . . . socially" and wrote home about meetings with such people as "an extraordinary man—Berenson, I think, is his name. A student at Harvard of great talents—particularly literary talent. A Russian Jew I surmise, a character about whom I must know more. He seemed as much of an exotic lure as the palm or the cinnamon tree." This, of course, was Bernard Berenson, who became the famous art collector and connoisseur. Brandeis went to the Art Club and served as its secretary. He read books such as Margaret Wade Campbell Deland's *John Ward, Preacher*. Indeed, he became close friends with Mrs. Deland and her wealthy husband, a dabbler in the theater and in an advertising agency.[3]

Brandeis also became fast friends with Mr. & Mrs. Glendower Evans, two wealthy Brahmins, and took Elizabeth Glendower Evans (later described by Felix Frankfurter as "a very beautiful young thing" with an "awfully good brain") under his wing when her husband died unexpectedly in 1886 at the age of thirty. Mrs. Evans remained a close friend of Brandeis and later of his wife and daughters, spending her summers with the Brandeises, being treated as a member of the household, and joining in their public affairs battles. Brandeis visited the Evanses frequently, dropping in to talk or for dinner, and boating or walking with them on Sunday mornings.[4]

He owned a horse, and, depending on the weather, went riding and canoeing. Brandeis loved the excitement of pitting himself against nature, particularly in a canvas canoe. Those who saw him doing so a few years later, when he vacationed regularly in South Yarmouth, Massachusetts, said of anyone taking chances in a canoe, "That must be Mr. Brandeis." In August 1885 he took a hiking and canoeing trip in Canada with friends, snapping photographs all the way; these he pasted into a scrapbook and sent to his mother. Other summers were spent in Dedham, where Brandeis stabled his horses at the Polo Club (but where he never played polo, disdaining athletic competition against men rather than nature). Brandeis recognized that exercise was necessary for his health, about which he still worried constantly: "The cold wave has rendered the question of visiting in the rain an immaterial issue. Were it not so I should really be in a position of difficulty. Face to face with the danger of the devil of rheumatism, on the one hand, if I ride—and the certainty of a deep sea of stuffed head and sleeplessness if I don't. However the brisk cold weather which has come settles the question." He would ride even in the rain, speculating at one point that "I really think there is something in the theory that if rain fairly sets in, there is no reason why it should ever stop. I ride now generally in rubbers and come home drenched nevertheless." He wrote in one letter to his brother of "a paltry twenty miles which I traversed in the saddle today."[5]

Brandeis's sister, Fannie Nagel, died on March 5, 1890, and Brandeis of course went home for the funeral. While he was in Louisville, he visited his uncle Samuel Brandeis and found that his second cousin Alice Goldmark was also visiting. Brandeis and Alice had met in New York at her home but had shown no great interest in each other; after the meeting in Louisville, however, this changed. The following summer the Goldmark and Brandeis families vacationed together in the Adirondacks. Brandeis joined his family late in August, and by September 4 Alice could write in her diary, "His eyes are always upon me. We go down to the river and he tells me his story—we have found each other." They became engaged and were married on March 23, 1891. The letters he wrote to her in the interim are among the most revealing of those still extant.[6]

Brandeis reported to Alice a conversation he and his father had had the previous summer. "He referred to some petty success of mine and remarked, 'You must be proud of that honor.' I told him that I could not recall ever having been proud of anything accomplished or to have deemed any recognition an honor. Indeed, I believe that the little successes I may have had, were due wholly to the pressure from within—proceeding from a deep sense of obligation and in no respect to the allurement of a possible distinction." Brandeis also wrote of his sense of purpose: "You speak my thoughts in what you say about right living. The value of that is surely underestimated by even the good people of the world. I mean the value of example . . . To use the potency of example seems very great." He thought about writing an article called "The Duty of Publicity," which would discuss "the wickedness of people shielding wrongdoers and passing them off . . . as honest men." His faith in the populace and in education was reflected in his comment, "If the broad light of day could be let in upon men's actions, it would purify them as the sun disinfects."[7]

When Fannie was ill, Brandeis had written to his father about believing in a Providence. He told Alice that character was to be admired even if character did not produce results; "It is the effort—the attempt—that tells. Man's work is, at best, so insignificant compared to that of the Creator—it is all so Lilliputian, one cannot bow before it." However, the Creator that Brandeis envisioned was tied to no specific religion. Brandeis and Alice were to be married by her brother-in-law, Felix Adler, the founder of the New York Society for Ethical Culture, in a civil service. It is questionable whether Brandeis's Jewishness was of any importance to him during this period except as it was useful in establishing a relationship with some of his Boston clients.[8]

As he and Alice shared their various opinions, Brandeis found that they were of one mind on most things. It gave him great happiness "to find on the fly-leaf of [Alice's] diary those lines of Matthew Arnold's . . . 'Life is not a having and a getting; but a being and a becoming.' " The view of life as an unfolding process was one Brandeis would always retain. But while that process was going on, Brandeis wanted Alice at his side: "I long for the time when you will be with me always. You have become so large a part of my life that I rattle about sorely when you are absent. Is it not strange? For seventeen years I have stood alone—rarely asking—still less frequently caring, for the advice of others. I have walked my way all these years but little influenced by any other individual. And now, Alice, all is changed. I find myself mentally turning to you for advice and approval—indeed, also for support, and I feel my incompleteness more each day. I feel myself each day growing more into your soul, and I am very happy."[9]

The "seventeen years" to which Brandeis referred were presumably those since he had left his family to study in Germany. It is interesting that he considered himself to have been "but little influenced by any other individual," considering that his approach to the law had come entirely from Langdell, that his notebooks were replete with quotations from Emerson and William James, and that he would continue to cite Professor Shaler throughout his life. In this case, however, Brandeis's words may indicate nothing more than that he was finally in love.[10]

Love was one thing, but there were practical matters to be arranged, and it was Brandeis who arranged them. Alice was not blessed with great physical stamina and was to be attended by various doctors throughout their marriage. Precisely what was wrong with her is impossible to determine. The family described her as "having 'the vapors,' " which was the general nineteenth and early twentieth century description for any mild and debilitating illness of unknown cause that affected women. It may well be that, along with other women of her generation, she was a victim of a lack of exercise and a lack of medical knowledge about the illnesses and infections specific to women. At any rate, almost from the time of their engagement, Brandeis took upon himself the management of their lives and households. It was he who paid bills, arranged for house repairs, sought out and rented summer cottages, dealt with utility companies, and generally undertook to relieve his wife of life's little nuisances.[11]

This is not to imply that Alice was helpless. The daughter of an extremely cultured family that was involved in public affairs, she not only worked with reformist groups in Boston but actively assisted Sacco and Vanzetti and their families during the 1920s, involved herself in moves to reform juvenile courts, and threw her support behind the presidential campaigns of Robert M. La Follette and Alfred E. Smith. In addition, particularly in later years, she arranged the dinners and teas for which Brandeis became well known in Washington and organized his leisure hours to minimize the strains upon his energy and health. But the limits on her physical strength were severe, and she was never able to join her husband in his athletic activities. Because Alice could not be expected to ride horseback, Brandeis trained one of his horses to pull a buggy. Alice equipped herself with a red Shaker cloak in which, one friend said, she looked "like a joyous school girl," and the two would go riding through Boston. It is probably because of Alice's health that the Brandeises did not travel abroad, though Brandeis wrote ecstatic letters home during the few times that public matters sent him out of the country. Eventually Brandeis would make his daughters his companions at sports and travel. When Susan was in her twenties, she and her father would take canoeing trips to Canada and on the Potomac. Elizabeth accompanied her father canoeing and sailboating from the time she was in her teens. Yet there is no indication that Brandeis resented the restrictions Alice's health placed on their activities, and he took on his additional duties with his usual organization and efficiency.[12]

The first matter to be taken care of was a place to live. Brandeis bought a narrow brick house at 114 Mt. Vernon Street in a good section of Boston and next to the home of his friends the Delands. He and Deland decided what needed to be done and sent estimates to Alice: $25.25 for 25 shades; $72.43 for wallpapering the hall, reception room, dining room, library, spare room, and two rooms on the third floor. He organized a crew of carpenters, plasterers, and paperhangers and had a fourth story added to the house.[13]

Alice was expected to do her part with furnishings too. "Poor child," Brandeis commiserated with her, "there will be more shopping for you soon. I wish sometimes that the idea of a house had never entered my mind, & that we had contented ourselves with a couple of attic rooms and bare walls." She also had to shop for a trousseau, and she hated all of it. Brandeis chided her gently: "When a woman happens to be both handsome and artistic a certain obligation rests upon her; there is a call upon her thought and taste. With a woman of mind and of taste, there is the same reason why her dress should be more effective as there is that her house should be more attractive and her table better." Later he added, "I don't know whether to be sorry or glad that clothes and the like seem such a nuisance to you. I believe in good clothes; it is only the unreasonable accumulation of them which is objectionable . . . you know I shall be very exacting about your *dress*." He encouraged her by comparing her favorably to the women he had met at an "official dinner." And he added, "Pray devote some deep thought to the house and its furnishings—in order that your individuality may be stamped upon it . . . it should bear [your expression]: pure, noble, tender, simple."[14]

The couple of course received wedding presents, many of which they kept for years. The estate inventory of Brandeis's Washington apartment included "1 Painting (Jules Dupre), 2 Oriental rugs, 1 Afghan rug, 1 Cashmere rug, and Silver" in the "dining Room and Closet," all of which were wedding presents. It also listed "1 Tall grandfather clock" in the dining room of which Brandeis had written, "Alice we shall not be able to escape one of those tall clocks. That client of mine, Mr. Ellis, insists upon presenting us one—of fabulous cost and wants me to select the kind of wood."[15]

The Brandeises' use, throughout life, of wedding presents is notable primarily because, as multimillionaires, they could easily have replaced their early acquisitions. But they had decided early in their marriage to live unostentatiously. Brandeis understood the importance of financial independence; he was quoted as saying that "in this age of millions, the man without some capital can only continue to slave and toil for others to the end of his days." He had no aversion to the acquisition of money. Much of the money, however, was given away: Brandeis donated $1,496,094.52 to various causes, according to one biographer.

Brandeis's money also was shared with needy members of the family, and, later, with friends. He and his brother made regular monthly payments to cousins, aunts, and uncles. Brandeis deposited small amounts in the bank account of Edward G. Gardiner, Mrs. Evans's brother, throughout the years at the turn of the century, and later he would send monthly or quarterly checks to such friends as Felix Frankfurter, Henrietta Szold, and Jacob de Haas, his lieutenant in the Zionist movement.[16]

The money that the Brandeises did spend went for "good" things. After their marriage, Alice shopped at such "quality" retailers as S. S. Pierce, W. & J. Sloan, and Jordan Marsh. Brandeis spent freely on canoes and equipment for horses. He bought few clothes, but what he did buy was expensive; for example, in 1913 he spent $100.00 for a dress suit. Alice bought herself suits for $75.00 and $90.00, one gown for $45.00, and another, in black velvet, for $125.00. They shipped their piano to whatever house they rented for the summer, until they bought their own summer home. Nonetheless, although they bought well, they did not buy much of anything, and there are far more bills for books than there are for such things as furniture or silverware.[17]

Good clothing did not mean ostentation. Although one reporter, writing many years later, said that in his early Boston days Brandeis was "a fastidious dresser ... fond of good company and rather interested in horses," he was better known as a man who took little interest in his appearance. In the country, he dressed in "a few old woolen suits and sweaters"; the inventory of his Chatham summer home lists "old clothes (bathrobe, shirts and shoes) no value" as all the clothing in his room. A reporter who had traveled to Boston to interview Brandeis was surprised to find him walking to work. "I found out later why he didn't [drive his car to work]. He had no car ... Cars, I gather, are things he just doesn't feel he needs." The interviewer also noted, rather apologetically, that when Brandeis went to Washington on business he stayed at a hotel that was "certainly not at all like the Shoreham or the New Willard." Brandeis saw no need for a car or an expensive hotel; therefore he did not buy the former or stay in the latter. He was guided by necessity rather than conspicuous consumption. This led to his being described as leading a life "of a simplicity almost ascetic." It was not; certainly ascetics do not indulge in horses, canoes, summer homes, servants (the Brandeises hired a cook when they were married, as well as a "second girl" who was paid four dollars a week, and after they became parents they added a nurse to their household), and private schools for their daughters. Brandeis bought the things he considered necessary and ignored the rest.[18]

In 1893 the Brandeises' first child, Susan, was born; in 1896, their second and last, Elizabeth, named for Elizabeth Glendower Evans. Brandeis described Alice in her first pregnancy as "even lovelier than before. There has been much of the time a calm madonna-like serenity and strength which seemed to lift her above things worldly." He was similarly delighted with his role as a father, writing to his sister some months later that when he and Alice returned from a buggy drive "Susan had much to tell us ... She has actually accomplished 'Papa'—but occasionally confuses it with 'Baby-ba.' " Once the two girls were old enough to sit at table, they joined their father for breakfast every morning at seven. When they were a little older, he would hold serious discussions with them at table, talking about history or mathematics or specific books. Frequently they read, having agreed the evening before upon the morning's reading. The books reportedly ranged from Robert Louis Stevenson's *Kidnapped* to Bury's *Later Roman Empire*.[19]

After breakfast, Brandeis would leave for the office, occasionally accompanied by one of his daughters on the way to school. He would arrive promptly at 8:20, stay until 1:10, lunch at one of his clubs, and return to work until 5:00. Then, with or without his children, he would go canoeing or walking or riding until it was time to bathe for dinner at 7:00. At dinner there might be a "judicious selection" of dinner guests.

A reporter noted that wealth did not gain one entry to dinner at the Brandeises'; their standards had more to do with intellect and knowledge. He went on to marvel that "when one considers his [Brandeis's] high social standing, their dinner really is a wonderful affair . . . Their meals do not cost any more than those of the average mechanic and they never go into what commonly is referred to as society." One of the reasons for Brandeis's eventual undeserved reputation for coldness, in fact, came from the exclusion of most Boston lawyers from the "judicious selection," and from his insistence on intellectual conversation and habits. He played neither poker nor golf; refused to join lodges, smokers, or men's clubs; and declined to listen to dirty stories. Once again, there is no indication whatsoever that the Brandeises were excluded from "society" because of their Jewishness, but, rather, that they were quite choosy about the people with whom they socialized, as any members of society might be.[20]

Brandeis and his brother, Alfred, exchanged letters almost daily from the time Louis began Harvard Law School in 1877 until Alfred's death in 1928. The early letters, in which, for some unexplained reason, Alfred frequently addresses Louis as "Sam," "Sammy" or, occasionally, "Sammie" (Alfred's spelling was spasmodic), are full of breezy exchanges on social life and young ladies; later, the two men shared their thoughts about political events. Even as young men, the Brandeises' interests were sophisticated; they quoted Longfellow and Artemus Ward, talked about the operas they had seen, and mentioned the books they had sent each other—although Alfred also occasionally sent "a case of Budweiser" or some Kentucky bourbon. Louis told him, "It is a great comfort to know that so good a supply is near." Later, as Brandeis and his wife gradually eliminated from their lives anything they considered excessive, including alcoholic beverages, the shipments of whiskey were replaced by whole hams. Louis meticulously wrote and told Alfred to whom they had been served. The flow of presents went in both directions. In 1906, when Alfred decided to buy a farm outside Louisville, Brandeis wrote, "I want to have some part in the creation of your farm which you love so much and I want therefore to make you a birthday present, either of such part of Walter's land as you think you need to give you a scientific frontier, if you can buy it at any price you think reasonable—or to put your house into condition for winter use—or anything else for the place you want."[21]

Letter-writing was demanded by each successive group of Brandeis elders, both as a means of communication and as a symbol of the younger generation's respect. In 1891, when he was a married man of over thirty-four, Brandeis wrote to his sister, "The convenience of a correspondent in my own family has relieved me for months of the *necessity* of writing even to Mother—I find that the temptation of silence, unresisted, was altogether too great." Alice had taken over the chore of writing to her mother-in-law. Apparently, this did not satisfy Frederika, for on March 27, 1893, Brandeis's father wrote, "I hope Mama has released you from writing daily." Three days later he wrote again, "I had this morning your letter of the 27th and agree with everything you say. I had already said to Mama a few days ago that I wrote you that three letters weekly would now be sufficient, and she seemed to accept this without difficulty. In view of what you say I really believe that two letters a week should be enough and I will try to get Mama's consent to this." In 1888 Brandeis sent his mother a birthday letter: "I must send you another birthday greeting and tell you how much I love you; that with each day I learn to extol your love and your worth more—and that when I look back over my life, I can find nothing in your treatment of me that I would alter. You often said, dearest mother, that I find fault—but I always told you candidly that I felt and sought to change only that little which appeared to me to be possible of improvement. I believe, most beloved mother, that the improvement of the world, reform, can only arise when mothers like you are increased thousands of times and have more children." Brandeis passed the discipline on to his children; according to one of his closest friends, Susan and her father exchanged letters every day long after Susan's own marriage.[22]

Brandeis read incessantly: books, newspapers, magazines, reports of all kinds. Frequently he and Alice read together, sometimes to save his eyes from strain, sometimes because their interests overlapped. Among the books they read during their first summer of married life were Sir Walter Scott's *Journal,* Overbeck's *Pompeji in Seinen Gebauden,* Froude's *Caesar,* Goethe's *Aus meinem leben,* Matthew Arnold's *Essays in Criticism,* Kingsley's *Westward Ho!,* and some of Kipling. A few years later Brandeis wrote that he and Alice were braving the Massachusetts winter by "feeding our imagination with Whympers' Ecuador and I have been taking a 'vacation trip to Cuba' with Richard Henry Dana" (referring to the title of Dana's book, *To Cuba and Back: A Vacation Voyage).*[23]

At a dinner party in 1916, shortly after he had been nominated to the Supreme Court, Brandeis cited a statistic from a consular report. Such reports, he told the company, were highly interesting and should be read daily. The company, none of which read them even annually, found itself listening to a resumé of consular reports on German and English industry. He also quoted poetry, knowing a great deal of it by heart, favoring Heine and Euripides particularly. After listening to Brandeis through a number of interviews, a journalist commented drily that Euripides apparently had the last word on virtually every subject. And, rather surprisingly, Brandeis read detective stories. He told a Boston reporter that he liked Sherlock Holmes "best of all," and compared his own method of investigating public matters to that of Holmes: "I use practically the same method . . . It's a matter of having special knowledge and being able to draw the only possible conclusion. Sometimes," he added, "I have been able to figure out the solutions to detective stories before I read to the end. But usually the author conceals some of the important facts in order to surprise the reader. In the case of Sherlock Holmes he possessed much special knowledge, knowing various cigar ashes, etc. Without that knowledge revealed by the author, no one could solve the mystery in advance." Asked whether he had ever attempted to solve real crimes, he replied that he had not, but that "I think I should like to try to catch a murderer sometime." It was this delight in facts and special knowledge that made Brandeis so effective in the courtroom; during cross-examination, he would frequently know more facts than the witnesses and would use this knowledge to discredit them.[24]

Weekends were spent in the country, where Brandeis sometimes worked on a Sunday morning but otherwise devoted himself to the family. With the children, he would ride, skate, ski, canoe, and play tennis. The two girls were sent to the fashionable Winsor School, described by Elizabeth as the best school in Boston, where they received an enlightened education that included carpentry, then called *sloyd*. The sloyd lessons led to Susan's successful request for a workbench in the country, at which she and her father built a big playhouse.[25]

Summers were initially spent in rented houses in various parts of Massachusetts. The rent for their summer house in Dedham in 1897 was $90 per month, plus gas and water charges. By 1909 they were paying $200 for the month of August in South Yarmouth, in a cottage that its owner described as having a living room, dining room, kitchen, pantry, three bedrooms on the first floor, three on the second, an "open fire" in the living room and two "piazzas." Brandeis wrote back to ask "whether there is a carving knife and fork and ice cream freezer in the house." Although they traveled to their summer residence with their three servants, they were clearly not renting palaces. Eventually they bought a summer home in Chatham, Massachusetts, on Cape Cod. That, and the little house on Mt. Vernon Street, were the only homes they ever owned. The house in Chatham was modest and was furnished modestly. The inventory made after Brandeis's death noted that there was "no complete set of dishes" in the china closet; there were all of 11 dinner plates and 4 teacups and saucers. The entire contents of what had by then become Alice's room were a bed, a table, two chairs, a bureau, two cotton rugs, and "1 very old boat shaped couch with old plush cover." Brandeis's room was more elaborate; it had a wooden armchair, a wicker armchair, a bedroom chair, a braided rug, and a small electric radiator.[26]

There are various descriptions of Brandeis during the three and a half decades he spent practicing law in Boston, but most date from 1910 or after, when he had become a figure on the national scene. One photograph taken in the 1890s, when he was in his late thirties or early forties, shows what seems to be a youth of twenty: tall, high-browed, square-faced, with inward-looking eyes set under dark eyebrows. Although his eye problems required him to wear glasses, he was sufficiently vain not to wear them in photographs of this time; in later years, a photographer occasionally caught him with his round spectacles perched on his nose.

Brandeis looked younger than his years until shortly before he died. In 1910, a Louisville newspaper depicted him as being "in his fifties, but doesn't look it . . . his smooth face is square and strong, but irregular, and expresses a lively sense of humor. His eyes twinkle behind his nose glasses . . . Brandeis has a large frame, but sparingly filled out. His voice is soft and drawling, but it can snap like a whip lash on occasion. One finds a deal of charm and attraction in him on personal contact." Another account said that when he began to talk, "his face [lit] up with . . . intense interest." Over and over again, interviewers found him to be warm and to resemble Lincoln. Ray Stannard Baker, who met Brandeis around 1910, said that "especially in repose" Brandeis "recall[ed] almost star-tlingly one of the portraits of Abraham Lincoln," although "more like Lincoln above . . . less broadly and commonly Lincoln below, in the mouth and chin." He had "a large head . . . stubborn black hair streaked with iron gray . . . [a] striking, dark face . . . sensitive hands—he has the hand of a musician." All in all, Baker thought, Brandeis "gave one singularly an impression of originality and power."[27]

His attractiveness and his ability to convince people that his way should be theirs was felt by his children as well as by his clients. The results of the educational routine he had worked out for his daughters delighted Brandeis. When he was engaged in a drawn-out battle to prevent the New York, New Haven & Hartford railroad from acquiring local trolley lines, Susan, then 14, of course heard all about her father's endeavors. Of the railroad's takeover bid she immediately commented, "Where would there then be any competition?" Brandeis recounted the incident with great pride. Susan went on to law school, a legal practice in New York, and involvement in Zionism; Elizabeth became an economist at the University of Wisconsin and, with her husband, helped create the Wisconsin unemployment act that was the precursor of the Wagner Act. The children made up a good deal of his life, and he theirs. They worked at causes to which he had introduced them, and they routinely brought their husbands and children to spend the summers with their parents at Chatham. Brandeis acted with his children as he was later to act with his law clerks and the young men and women who flocked to his teas in Washington. Nothing was more important to Brandeis than the process of education, and as an educator, in his private life as well as in his speeches and judicial opinions, he excelled.[28]

5 | A Public Career

Brandeis's parents had taught him that involvement in public life was a matter of duty; Harvard had added to his sense of noblesse oblige; and the Boston Brahmins he knew participated in the running of Boston as a matter of course. Furthermore, it was assumed in the United States that public activity was the natural extension of a career in the law. Thus, it was almost inevitable that Brandeis would become an actor on the public scene.

In fact his thriving law practice, his social circle, and his interests led to his being called on to undertake various public activities. Brandeis wrote proudly to Al in 1884, "Have had a public career of late. Lecture on Taxation Sunday [,] Spoke against 'Woman Suffrage' before the Legislative Com[mit]tee yesterday & appeared before the Insurance Com[mit]tee yesterday & today." The lecture on taxation had taken place at South Congregational Church (Unitarian), where the minister was the well-known Edward Everett Hale. Brandeis told a Sunday school class that taxation was a necessary evil and that it was a duty for citizens both to pay taxes and to try to minimize the need for them. The state Insurance Committee before which he spoke was holding hearings on a bill designed to value policies uniformly for purposes of taxation. The speech against women's suffrage held that the franchise was not a right but a privilege and that the duties involved in exercise of the privilege should be imposed only upon men. These topics recurred throughout Brandeis's career. He never changed his belief that government should be minimal, and his interest in insurance matters grew in the years to come, but his views about women's suffrage changed drastically.[1]

Frequently, Brandeis's private practice led him to broader public issues. For example, the interests of several clients induced him to learn about and then fulminate against a monopoly held by the Boston Disinfecting Company. A number of paper manufacturers hired Warren & Brandeis to petition the Common Council to repeal a city ordinance that required all imported rags to be disinfected in Boston as a health measure. Boston Disinfecting charged five dollars a ton for disinfecting rags that the importers had already been forced to pay to have disinfected abroad. "The fight now is against the Boston Board of Health," Brandeis wrote to his brother in 1886, "which is sustaining the grinding monopoly & fraud entitled—the Boston Disinfection Co . . . We have evidence—both practical & scientific on our side—and the chances are quite good that political influence will not be potent enough to overcome that. Popular prejudice and ignorance may make us some trouble but we are in the right and must, in the end, come out successful. The more the matter is canvassed & discussed (and the papers have taken up the question now), the better for us. It is only ignorance and dark dealing that we must fear." Brandeis was too sanguine; the statute was not repealed. His firm handled the case subsequently brought against the law by one of the paper manufacturers but lost it. The letter, however, indicates that Brandeis's attitude toward public causes was set quite early. According to one of his daughters, it was the rag fight that awakened him to the dangers of monopoly.[2]

Brandeis learned more about issues and politics in Massachusetts by becoming involved briefly in temperance legislation (he disapproved of excessive drinking, but opposed as unenforceable a law that prohibited the sale of liquor except with a meal), moves to limit the impact of lobbies on the state legislature, and Boston's treatment of its poor. Then, in 1897, he made his debut on the national political scene, when the interests of his clients and his own predilection for free trade led him to Washington. The New England Free Trade League, of which Brandeis and many of his associates were members, was composed largely of manufacturers of wool, paper, metal goods, and carpets. Opposed to tariffs in general, both as reformers and as owners of businesses dependent on imported raw materials, they were particularly concerned at the introduction in the House of Representatives of the Dingley bill, designed to raise tariffs as a protective measure. The Free Trade League asked Brandeis to state its case at the hearings in the House.[3]

The House Ways and Means Committee, chaired by Representative Dingley, had heard a succession of lobbyists pleading for their industries' inclusion in the protective legislation. When Brandeis was asked which articles of trade he wished to speak about and replied that he represented the Free Trade League, there was laughter from the committee, whose immediate purpose seems to have been to get as much "protection" for American manufacturers as possible into the bill. Brandeis nonetheless continued solemnly, "I desire to speak in behalf of those who form, I believe, a far larger part of the people of the United States than any who have found representation here. I appear for those who want to be left alone, those who do not come to Congress and seek the aid of the sovereign powers of the government to bring them prosperity . . . What I have undertaken to do is to appear on behalf of the consumer and a large number of workingmen in New England. I have undertaken to object to a change of conditions which is very far removed from free trade. Where duties are largely over 40 per cent, I think it can hardly be called free trade. What I make an argument for is that we be left undisturbed in business . . . The business man, and the laboring man, as a whole, want to be left alone in their business, without sudden changes in the tariff."[4]

The Committee was alternately dumbfounded and exasperated at this attempt to represent interests irrelevant to big manufacturers and finally contemptuously cut Brandeis off with the announcement that his time had expired. Massachusetts newspapers expressed outrage at Brandeis's treatment; so did William Lloyd Garrison, who castigated the hearings, charging that "With one exception, not one word of public spirit, not one sentiment implying a thought of equal rights and privileges, has relieved the monotonous record of corporate and private greed which casts its shame upon popular government." The exception, "for which let us be thankful," was Brandeis, "one of Boston's most respected lawyers . . . He carried a brief for no mendicant industry, but modestly essayed to speak for the consumer, 'the forgotten man' in every tariff scheme." Garrison explained the committee's attitude toward Brandeis: "The revelation that the speaker had no plunder in view was a signal for impatience and contemptuous treatment."[5]

Unnoticed by the committee and by Garrison was that Brandeis spoke not only for the consumer but for a limited government. "This asking for help from the government for everything should be deprecated. It destroys the old and worthy sturdy principle of American life which existed in the beginning when men succeeded by their own efforts. That is what has led to the evil of protective tariff and other laws to that end, by which men seek to protect themselves from competition." The committee, as noted, was not impressed by Brandeis's first articulation of his still half-formed political views in the halls of Congress. Brandeis returned to Boston, there to refine his opinions with further work in the service of the public.[6]

Back in 1893, Brandeis had become involved in his first long-term fight on behalf of the public. At that time Boston had a population of over half a million, which had increased by more than 25 percent in ten years. It needed a public transportation system, and private companies had met the need by setting up a series of trolley lines. One of them, the West End Railway, decided that it would make sense to run a track across Boston Common. Brandeis disagreed and took his argument against the signing away of public park land to the legislative hearings. There he spoke forcefully of his belief that franchises over public lands had to be given with great care. One spectator wrote to him, "Never before this morning had it been my good fortune to hear so logical, clear and convincing an argument on the very important question of street franchises as that made by you at the State House." The legislature agreed with Brandeis and other opponents and denied the West End the franchise.[7]

The congestion in downtown Boston, however, had become intolerable. Eventually, the city built a subway under Tremont and Boylston Streets and leased it to the West End for a term of twenty years. The term of the lease had been hotly debated, with the West End, supported by the legislature, insisting on a long-term lease. Traditionally, however, Boston granted traction rights for just a few years, reserving its option to revoke the lease thereafter, in order to keep fares low and to insure that the public would be compensated properly. In this case public outcry supported the city's position.[8]

In 1897, however, a new company, the Boston Elevated Railway, quietly got the legislature to give it long-term franchise rights to operate on many of the city's most important thoroughfares at fares not below five cents for the next thirty years. The back room agreement was kept secret almost until it was due to go into effect. When Brandeis found out about it, he immediately called for public protest against the charter, which was "at odds with the established policy of the Commonwealth" and which would "sacrifice the interests of the public to that of a single corporation." Other cities had managed to reduce fares to below five cents, Brandeis wrote angrily in a letter to the *Boston Evening Transcript*, and the long-term lease would deny the next generation the money-saving benefits of new inventions. In addition, the guaranteed five-cent fare applied to passengers of all ages and to rides of any length. Brandeis had the facts and publicized the exact amount that the company would pay Boston, as opposed to the much greater amount paid to New York by a similar company operating in that city. He urged that action wait for the report from a recently appointed commission on proper compensation for street franchises. Members of the Boston business community, opposed to the legislation, had organized a Municipal Transportation League, and Brandeis had become chairman of its Transportation Committee; however, he wrote his letter to the *Transcript* as a private citizen.[9]

Boston Elevated Railway retaliated for the letter and for Brandeis's susequent appearance before the legislature's Joint Committee on Metropolitan Affairs and Street Railways (at which Brandeis did represent the Municipal Transportation League) by spreading rumors that Brandeis was receiving a fat fee from the league for opposing the legislation and that he was being paid by Lee Higginson & Company. Lee Higginson, a brokerage and banking firm, was considered a financial rival of J. P. Morgan & Company, which held an interest in the Boston Elevated Railway. Brandeis wrote to William Bancroft, the chairman of the board of the Elevated, about the first rumor: "I have been retained by no person, association or corporation, directly or indirectly in this matter, and I have opposed it solely because I believe that the bill, if passed, would result in great injustice to the people of Massachusetts, and eventually great injustice to the capitalist classes whom you are now representing, and with whom I, as well as you, are in close connection." He wrote a similar letter about the second rumor to Albert Pillsbury, the Elevated's lawyer. The rumors were creditable (although not true) in part because Brandeis was indeed a lawyer for "the capitalist classes," whose business was quickly turning him into a millionaire. His letters were addressed to "My Dear Colonel Bancroft" and "My Dear Pillsbury," indicating that he had more than a passing acquaintance with his two adversaries. What none of the men quite realized as yet was that Brandeis would remain a friend of capitalism and capitalists, but that he was rapidly coming to exclude from these categories trusts and tycoons. In early 1897 Brandeis was still perceived as a friend of capitalism and capitalists; by the end of the fight over traction, which would last until 1911, Brandeis would be seen by many of the Brahmins as a traitor to his class.[10]

Despite the efforts of Brandeis and the league, the Elevated got its lease. But another round in the fight was just beginning. The subway proved to be such a success that in 1910 a group of citizens petitioned for the building of an additional line under Washington Street. The Elevated asked for the right to build the subway (which it would then own), to build and own a connecting subway to Cambridge, and to extend its lease of the existing subway for twenty years past its scheduled expiration date (that is, until 1937). Clearly, the Elevated was seeking control over Boston's transportation system.[11]

Opposition to the plan was organized by the Public Franchise League, formed in 1897 to prevent private control of street transportation, and the Associated Board of Trade. The Public Franchise League's members included Brandeis's friend and client Edward A. Filene of Filene's Department Store; Robert Treat Paine, Jr., a former gubernatorial candidate; Dr. Morton Prince, the son of a former mayor; and other Brahmins with progressive leanings. Filene's participation was crucial, since he had money, organizing talents, and ties to the local newspapers. The Board of Trade was made up of local merchants and manufacturers, all of whom had an interest in cheap transportation for consumers and some of whom were also Brandeis's clients.

It was the Board of Trade that Brandeis formally represented when he appeared before the Committee on Metropolitan Affairs. Its hearings and the general legislative debate extended through 1900 and into June of 1901. Then the Elevated offered to build the subway, turn it over to the city, and receive a fifty-year lease. Delighted that someone else would pay for construction costs, the legislature enacted the proposal. Brandeis, however, anticipating this, had written to Governor Winthrop M. Crane, whom he had met some months before. He also had the Board of Trade and the Public Franchise League write and ask to speak with the governor. Their arguments convinced Crane, who vetoed the bill, and the legislature proved unable to override the veto.[12]

The fight against the Elevated was notable as an early example of techniques Brandeis would perfect and use in subsequent battles. He poured out letters to supporters, giving them facts with which to argue, suggestions for tactics, and encouragement. He solicited support from prominent citizens, legislators, and friendly journalists. To Edward Filene, who had become head of the Public Franchise League's Publicity Bureau, he wrote, "Have editorials and similar notices in various papers, particularly the Springfield Republican, the Worcester Spy, and the Pittsfield papers . . . Have the labor organizations repeat their protest against the modified Elevated bill . . . Have personal letters written to members from the Metropolitan District, particularly from Boston, by their constituents, and have these persons ask for seats in the House during the debate . . . Get as many letters into the Boston papers as you can." Telling Filene "our success will depend largely upon the thoroughness" with which these instructions were carried out, Brandeis added as a postscript, "We rely upon you for hard work." Getting the facts out to the people, and then getting the people after their legislators would characterize Brandeis's public service career. In believing that education and democracy went hand in hand, Brandeis was a true Jeffersonian.[13]

He was also a fighter who looked ahead. The Elevated bill had been beaten, but there was nothing to stop the company from repeating its campaign during successive legislative sessions, and Crane would not always be governor. The Public Franchise League and the Associated Board of Trade therefore devised a bill providing for city construction of the Washington Street subway, with a lease to the Elevated for no more than twenty-five years, and a rental of 4.5 percent of the construction cost. The Elevated countered with its own bill, giving the city ownership of the subways but leaving ownership of subway tunnels in the hands of the company. The distinction between "subways" and "tunnels" was obviously a piece of sophistry aimed at achieving the Elevated's original goal of long-term monopoly. Once again Brandeis threw himself into the fray, chiding allies for being out of Boston at any time during the fight, lecturing them if they missed any strategy sessions, and stressing the role of the newspapers. Brandeis was always urging on his troops: "I realize fully how busy you are, but everybody else who is working in this cause is equally busy, and unless all the work that has been done is to be thrown away, you must put your hand to the wheel now"; "I wish you would write at once a letter"; "I think it absolutely necessary that you take up this matter yourself now"; "You must get to work with your accustomed energy"; "Please write another letter." He believed that those engaged in the peoples' work had to give it as much energy and attention as he was prepared to contribute—and that was a formidable amount.[14]

Brandeis's penchant for facts served him well in the struggle with the Elevated. During the last moments of the final committee hearings on April 14, 1902, the Elevated's counsel suddenly poured out a stream of statistics designed to show that the company was losing money and that it could not possibly function under the Board of Trade's proposed bill. He asked that all action be postponed, believing that postponement would dissipate Brandeis's support and that the Elevated would do better to wait for a more sympathetic governor. The claim of potential insolvency was completely new and was kept for the last moments to prevent Brandeis and the board from mustering an adequate reply. But Brandeis remembered the figures and promptly responded with his own statistics. The Elevated had raised its dividend from 4 to 6 percent, Brandeis told the committee, paying $600,000 in dividends; its stock had gone up from $105 to $170 during the last four years. When the Committee on Metropolitan Affairs decided to reopen hearings, Brandeis appeared with a fifteen-page statement, filled with statistics about the Elevated. "This statement is incorrect," he told the committee about one of the company's claims; "This statement is grossly misleading," he said about another; and on and on, until the company's figures were demolished. Then the Elevated, without replying directly to Brandeis's facts, attacked his plan as impractical. However, the legislature was impressed by his analysis of the Elevated and passed a bill including the league's provisions. The company capitulated and accepted the terms, which were ratified in a popular referendum on December 9, 1902. "Boston has thus," Brandeis wrote, "established conclusively the policy of retaining control of its transportation system." The battle had been won.[15]

Brandeis called the Boston franchise fight "my first important public work." Edwin Hale Abbot, president of the Wisconsin Central Railroad and Boston philanthropist, congratulated him "on your good and skillful work . . . You are on your way into public life I see clearly, and you ought to be in it. You are needed." The Board of Trade voted unanimously to convey its thanks to Brandeis, particularly for representing it without fee. According to Edward Filene, who had pressed him to present a bill, Brandeis explained that "he never made a charge for public service of this kind; that it was his duty as it was mine to help protect the public rights; and . . . that he resolved early in life to give at least one hour a day to public service, and later on he hoped to give fully half his time." Initially, Brandeis had given fees for public service undertakings to charity, but he eventually decided that taking fees at all was wrong. He then went further and reimbursed his firm for the working hours he spent in public service. Although his partners had not approached him about the matter, Brandeis felt that they and the nonlawyers working for the firm (all of whom participated in a profit-sharing plan) should not be "affected by [his] own feeling" about the causes he took on. He therefore substituted himself "as the client of the firm" and paid his firm as much as $25,000 on one public service matter alone. In at least one instance, he represented a consumer group without fee, reimbursed his firm for his services, and paid court costs. By this time Brandeis had become one of the most successful lawyers in the United States, and neither he nor his family was deprived of anything because of his decision. Brandeis delighted in being a "free man" who could donate his labor to public service. "Some men buy diamonds and rare works of art," he told an interviewer; "others delight in automobiles and yachts. My luxury is to invest my surplus effort, beyond that required for the proper support of my family, to the pleasure of taking up a problem and solving, or helping to solve it, for the people without receiving any compensation. Your yachtsman or automobilist would lose much of his enjoyment if he were obliged to do for pay what he is doing for the love of the thing itself. So I should lose much of my satisfaction if I were paid in connection with public services of this kind."[16]

By 1902 Brandeis had developed certain beliefs about the democratic process, which seemed to be borne out by the traction case. He viewed democracy as free citizens making intelligent choices about matters affecting their joint lives. "Free" citizens were those who were economically independent and who had a voice and vote in matters involving their political and economic well-being. Brandeis had always put democracy into a capitalistic context; American democracy, in his eyes, had as its backbone small tradespeople, merchants, and manufacturers, with a sprinkling of professionals—very much, in fact, like the extended Brandeis-Dembitz-Wehle family. Gradually, he had recognized that the last decades of the nineteenth century had brought about concentrations of wealth that did not fit into this scheme. Groups like the Morgan-backed syndicate that controlled the Elevated had access to huge amounts of capital, with which they could buy out or force out competition and bribe state legislators. If the good of individuals, organized through government, could be negated by concentrations of capital, then such concentrations and their consequence had to be opposed. The mechanism for doing so was Jeffersonian: the vote, exercised by an educated and well-informed public. And education was not a process confined to the schoolroom; a major educative function was performed by the press. It exposed the citizenry to ideas, it enabled them to know what was going on in the halls of their legislature, it could mobilize them to protect their rights when vested interests attacked them. And central to an alert electorate was the work of public-spirited citizens who would monitor the governmental process. Indeed, there was a strong element of noblesse oblige in Brandeis's ideology. Those who were well-educated, whose careers (or inheritances) gave them the leisure for public affairs had an obligtion to keep the society free and just for their fellow citizens. It was, as Brandeis's opponents would charge, a romantic and idealistic vision. It was also a highly democratic one and, as Brandeis would prove, an eminently practical one. Brandeis believed, quite simply, that with good will and a great deal of effort, democracy could be made to work.

In 1890 his partner, Samuel Warren, had sent Brandeis the lines from Euripides' *The Bacchae* that became the keynote of Brandeis's public life:

> Thou has heard men scorn the city, call her wild
> Of counsel, mad; thou has seen the fire of morn
> Flash from her eyes in answer to their scorn!
> Come toil on toil, 'tis this that makes her grand.
> Peril on peril! And common states that stand
> In caution, twilight cities, dimly wise—
> Ye know them; for no light is in their eyes!
> Go forth, my son, and help.

A year later, Warren had written to Brandeis, "Your life is very largely before you—with a great lead over all contemporaries . . . Consider whether or not you will direct your course toward public life. I think you are fitted for it. This would not mean to seek office or place, but to command the leisure for public service as opportunity presents." Brandeis had taken the advice and was already learning that public life could bring both praise and opprobrium. His appearance on behalf of the public had led to his being called the "People's Attorney," particularly by those newspapers that approved of his efforts. Some of Boston's elite, however, found his opposition to established interests inexplicable and concluded that he had become a radical. This meant that he and his wife were no longer socially acceptable, and a number of their Brahmin friends began to cut them. Alice was bothered at first by their sudden ostracism, but there is no evidence that Brandeis took much notice of it.[17]

The traction fight had brought a larger problem to Brandeis's attention: the corruption of legislators. During the traction battle, he had drafted two bills making it illegal for legislators to seek favors from quasi-public corporations such as the Elevated. As he wrote a few months later, "In our subway fight, we found the great evil that we had to deal with was the influence of the corporation, due largely to the patronage which it exerts . . . The legislators, councilmen and others in position rely upon the public service corporations who are getting favors from them to furnish places to the men who work for the nomination and election of the respective candidates, some aldermen and senators having from one to two hundred men in this way on the pay-roll of the companies." The civil service law in Massachusetts had not been broad enough to end this "most serious and widespread form of corruption." The Public Franchise League had decided, however, that "it was best not to complicate the specific fight we were making on the subway with the general fight against these practices." Now that the subway fight was over, the time had come to act on patronage. "We are proposing this year to endeavor to educate the public and to ultimately pass a bill" drawn up by the league.[18]

Brandeis began agitating in favor of the bill by collecting additional facts, firing off memoranda to supporters, getting the *Boston Evening Transcript* to publish a favorable editorial, successfully urging the new governor to include mention of the issue in his inaugural address, arranging for the bill to be introduced in the legislature, and lecturing in public about the matter (making certain that his remarks received press coverage). His lectures were in fact given wide coverage. The *Boston Herald* of March 19, 1903, trumpeted "Corruption At City Hall, Says Brandeis." A few weeks later the same newspaper announced in even bigger type, "Use Searchlight on the City Hall," and in slightly smaller letters, "Brandeis Says It Is High Time to Delve Into Corruption in City Affairs." The *Boston Journal* covered the same speech, in which Brandeis said that good citizens are indifferent to the problem of corruption "because they are ignorant of the facts."[19]

He expanded upon this sentiment in a speech in Brighton on December 2, 1904. "Few things in the world are worth while having that are not attained by struggle," he told his audience. "But whether or not we deserve to have good government without struggle, it is obvious that in a democratic community we cannot have it. Democracy means that the people shall govern, and they can govern only by taking the trouble to inform themselves as to the facts necessary for a correct decision, and then by recording that decision through a public vote." He went on, "It is customary for people to berate politicians, to speak with horror of those who take an active interest in elections. But after all, the politicians, even if their motives are not of the purest, come much nearer performing their duties as citizens than the so-called 'good' citizens who stay at home." A few days earlier, at a meeting at Tremont Temple in Boston, Brandeis had noted that Jefferson, "the father of democracy," had asked whether a candidate was honest, capable, and faithful to the Constitution. In 1904, however, it was necessary to ask as well, "Will he devote himself to the honor and the best interest of the community?"[20]

Having learned from the franchise fight how important it was to have allies well organized and at hand, Brandeis joined the Election Laws League, becoming a member of its Executive Committee, and helped organize the Good Government Association and the Aldermanic Association (of which he became chairman), quietly merging the Public Franchise League into the last. He became active in the Public School Association, the People's Lobby, and the Citizens' Committee of One Hundred. Indeed, he urged organization to anyone who wanted to make a difference in public life. Speaking at a convention of the Massachusetts Medical Society, he pointed out that a legislative appropriation for a hospital for consumptives, favored by the doctors, had not in fact been spent on a hospital. "You physicians are of no political significance" he announced. "Your citizenship can be an intelligent, a working citizenship only through organization." Fortunately, he added, a mechanism was at hand; "the existence of the Good Government Association affords you an easy means toward the organization of your forces." Presumably the presence of the doctors would be welcomed in the Good Government Association not merely to get their hospital but to join in the effort against corruption. His first major speech in the anticorruption fight had been to the businessmen of the Boston Boot & Shoe Club, to whom he said that if "the businessman" (used interchangeably with "good citizens") involved himself in "follow[ing] the various departments of our government from day to day," the result would be that ward heelers, those "miserable fellows who cannot or will not earn a living for themselves," would "have to seek elsewhere." In a sentence that stunned the city, Brandeis declared, "We should not allow ourselves to be represented by thieves and convicts."[21]

Some years before a member of the legislature had told him he was attacking the wrong people. "The men to blame," the member had said, "are not the poor fellows up here . . . If you want to go to the bottom, get after the men in the fur coats. It is the fur coat section which deserves the censure." This view was echoed during the 1903 debate by George Tinkham, a former alderman of Boston and ally of Brandeis. A Pittsfield newspaper reported a conversation with Tinkham. "When the resolution favoring public ownership of the Washington street subway was before the board of aldermen, the members voted against it, although it was favored by the majority of their constituents. They told Mr. Tinkham that they voted against it because the Boston Elevated would punish them if they did not, by refusing to give positions to their constituents." Tinkham brought to the hearings with him a former Elevated employee who had lost his job when he adopted a political stance unacceptable to the Elevated. Going after "the men in the fur coats" as well as the ward heelers, the Public Franchise League designed its bill to make a public official's soliciting a job from a quasi-public corporation and the favorable response by any such corporation a crime.[22]

Brandeis's personality was a major factor in the fight, not only because of his tactics but also because of the impact his presence made at hearings. "Mr. Brandeis is an interesting man," one newspaper told its readers, "and has an attractive personality. He is not handsome, as that term is generally applied, but after one has taken a first look at this attorney he grows in attractiveness until one gets to watching his conduct of a case with an absorbing interest." Brandeis's passionate belief in his causes, usually communicated in calm tones, quite frequently led his listeners to be taken not only with his manner but also with his arguments. When speaking before those whom he expected to join him in a cause rather than before legislators, he permitted himself a more picturesque style and hortatory manner. For example, he urged support of the anticorruption bill upon a group of businessmen at a Good Government Association meeting. "As men of honor," he lectured them, "you cannot submit meekly to be represented and to be governed by men criminal or inefficient. As men of honor, you cannot without a struggle permit the City of Boston, around which cluster the noblest and most sacred memories of American history,—the City of Boston which you love, and whose fair name and welfare are now entrusted to your care, to be disgraced by the election to high office of men whose criminal practices are . . . known . . . Every criminal in the public service is a plague spot spreading contagion on every hand. Think what a heritage we shall leave to our children if corruption is allowed to stalk about unstayed. The ships (Brandeis's original notes had this sentence beginning with "Your ships") which carry the products of our rich country to other lands come back freighted with thousands of men and women and children who, fleeing from the oppression or the hopelessness of their old homes, seek this as the land of liberty and opportunity. Shall we permit these, our fellow-citizens—perhaps our future rulers—to be taught that in Boston liberty means license to loot the public treasury—that in Boston opportunity means the chance for graft?" Having urged the group to prove its patriotism and devotion to liberty by working for passage of the anti-corruption bill, Brandeis closed by exhorting his listeners: "You must have good government because it is a disgrace in a free country to submit to the government of the bad; and if you do strive,—strive earnestly, persistently—you will not fail." Brandeis and his colleagues, many of them comrades in the franchise battles, hammered away at the public and the legislature until the latter enacted the Public Franchise League's bill of 1906.[23]

Brandeis interested himself in many other civic causes: the relative powers of the Boston School Board and School Committee over the construction of new schools; the Public School Association, which ran its own candidates for the School Committee; an investigation into the possibility of state support for widows with dependent minor children; and maintaining clear separation of church and state. The result of all his exposure to the public eye was the suggestion by well-wishers that Brandeis run for public office. Indeed, his suspicious opponents found it impossible to understand that a corporation lawyer could engage in publicity-generating activities without hoping they would lead to public office. For example, the *Boston Traveler* "discovered," during the anticorruption campaign, that Brandeis meant to be the reform candidate for mayor. Asked about his candidacy by the *Boston Herald*, Brandeis retorted, "Nothing could be further from my thought than to be candidate for mayor, or for any other public office. What I have desired to do is to make the people of Boston realize that the most important office, and the one which all of us can and should fill, is that of private citizen. The duties of the office of private citizen cannot under a republican form of government be neglected without serious injury to the public." He could not understand, he wrote to a leading Boston reformer and educator, "anyone being really sensible who was not a reformer, as well as earnest and progressive."[24]

Brandeis had decided early on that he would not be a candidate for office, because politics should be entered into wholeheartedly or not at all, and he was not about to give up either his law practice or the various reform movements which came to interest him. Coming from a family that supported Lincoln, he had originally considered himself a Republican. But in 1884 when the party nominee for president was James G. Blaine, who had been implicated in the railroad scandals, Brandeis shifted to the Democrats along with other "mugwumps." He wrote to his then-fiancée in 1890, "A very urgent invitation came today from the Democratic State Central Committee to accept the nomination for Representative to the Legislature from Ward IX. It could be very interesting, but of course I cannot do it. It is one of the many things one must postpone or leave wholly undone." He may also have declined because the Republicans had taken the unusual step of naming a black man as their candidate. In fact, Brandeis may not have realized how fortunate he was that his personality, his beliefs, his talents, and his historical moment dovetailed to give him enormous self-fulfillment without the compromises and invasions of privacy that inevitably would have accompanied partisan politics.[25]

Because Brandeis had a talent for economics and detail, he could turn with gusto to the seemingly dull and arcane matter of gas rates. The Massachusetts legislature had passed a bill at the request of the eight gas companies serving Boston and nearby Brookline, permitting them to combine as the Boston Consolidated Gas Company in 1903 to end costly duplication of facilities. The law provided that the new company could issue stock up to an amount equal to the "fair value" of the company's assets. Fearing both monopoly and potential stock watering, the Public Franchise League opposed the bill, but to no avail. (Brandeis, busy elsewhere, was not involved in the dispute.) The league's fears seemed about to be realized in 1904, when Edward Warren, brother of Brandeis's former law partner and an ally in the franchise fight, wrote Brandeis an angry letter warning that the Boston Board of Gas and Electric Light Commissioners was about to assess the company's assets at a ridiculously high figure and permit it to issue concomitantly worthless stock. Brandeis agreed that the league should involve itself in the decision about the capitalization rate that would be set for Consolidated Gas, because stock watering was one of the issues that had arisen during the franchise fight, and the league was, of course, against it.[26]

When Brandeis studied the matter he found that although the companies claimed that the cost of their properties was $24,000,000.00 and that the "fair value" of the new company should therefore be set at no less than $20,609,989.99, the Public Franchise League believed that stockholders had actually spent only $15,124,121.00. Any money beyond that, the league argued, had been accumulated through excessively high rates, and the company should not reap the rewards of its wrongdoing by including the additional sum in its assets for stock-issuing purposes. In addition, the Public Franchise League wanted the commissioners to set a gas rate that would permit no more than a fair return on the company's investment. The company insisted it could not operate unless it charged its current price of $1.00 per thousand cubic feet of gas; one of the league's allies, the *Boston American*, suggested that $.80 would be fairer. Thus, at issue were both the capitalization figure and the rate to be charged.[27]

Brandeis himself took a position midway between that of the company and that of the league. He agreed that capitalization should be honest to prevent stock watering, but he felt that since the public had in effect permitted the company to accumulate surplus capital it would be confiscatory to exclude that capital from the company's assets. However, the company and its stockholders should not be permitted as great a return on surplus as should be allowed on capital actually invested by shareholders. He suggested that the dividends paid on surplus should be no greater than the rate at which money could be borrowed, but the dividends on capital invested should be commensurate with the risk assumed.[28]

This position pleased neither Consolidated Gas, which wanted to issue a high dividend on all its earnings, nor those members of the Public Franchise League who agreed with Edward Warren that Brandeis was not standing firm against stock watering. It seemed reasonable to the Massachusetts State Board of Trade, however, and its Committee on Transportation and Legislation accepted Brandeis's offer to represent it before the legislature and the governor. The issue was a difficult one, and before the fight was over both the league and the State Board of Trade had dissolved into factions. The league hired George W. Anderson as its counsel (Brandeis, of course, served the State Board of Trade without fee).[29]

In the midst of the controversy, all the reformers were dramatically reminded of the powerful interests with which they had to contend. J. Harvey White, an official of the Elevated, sent an advertisement stating that the public agreed with the Consolidated Gas position to a number of Massachusetts newspapers outside Boston. White directed the newspapers to print the advertisement "without advertising marks of any sort . . . set as news matter in news type, with a news head at the top of the column." Samuel Bowles, publisher and editor-in-chief of the *Springfield Republican,* printed White's letter as well as his "advertisement." The *Boston American* then published a story entitled "Gas Trust Exposed by Endeavor to Buy Press," making the ruse public, and Brandeis praised Bowles for having called attention to "what is probably one of our greatest dangers—corruption of the sources of public opinion by the suppression of a free press" and the use of corporate money to buy news space for the purpose of suppressing the "public's side of the question."[30]

At approximately the same time, Brandeis's reading had led him to the London system of "sliding-scale" utility rates: if utility companies were able to lower rates to their customers, they were permitted to increase dividends to their shareholders. This incentive to efficiency, which also constituted a kind of profit sharing between consumer and shareholder, immediately fired Brandeis's imagination. He explained the system to Edward Warren: "in fixing the price of gas, the Board would determine from time to time, according to circumstances then existing, what it was proper that the company should have, and that the amount the company should have should depend, in my opinion, upon what was given to the community. If they gave, for instance, 75 cent gas, they ought to be allowed to receive more in dividend than if they gave $1.00 gas." Brandeis also presented this idea to the legislature's Joint Committee on Public Lighting, as a bill proposed by the State Board of Trade. The sliding-scale idea went beyond the one-time capitalization issue to take care of the future, when Consolidated Gas could be counted upon to ask for rate increases unrelated to capitalization. The Public Franchise League rallied behind the idea, but Warren and a few others remained bitterly convinced that Brandeis had betrayed their ideals.[31]

More remarkable than the league's conversion was that of James L. Richards, chairman of the board of Consolidated Gas and the wealthy representative in gas matters for the brokerage house of Kidder, Peabody & Company (which was allied with J. P. Morgan & Company). Richards was introduced to Brandeis by a mutual friend, Brandeis's client Charles P. Hall. Richards came to Brandeis's office on the morning of April 24 and stayed for two hours (Brandeis swept most of his clients out within half an hour). The two men met again that afternoon. Brandeis was inclined to treat Richards as one who needed to be educated, rather than as an adversary, and the approach worked. He convinced Richards of the immorality of stock watering and the need for a compromise that would protect both public and investors. Brandeis suggested that the company agree to be consolidated on the basis of the Public Franchise League's capitalization figure of $15,124,121; accept a dividend rate of

7 percent; and work with the league to have the legislature pass the sliding-scale bill. Brandeis used both the carrot and the stick. He told Richards that the sliding-scale system would enable the company to raise its dividends. At the same time, he warned him that legislation that struck the public as overly favorable to Consolidated Gas would be viewed as the result of bribery and would be "merely the beginning of new trouble." Brandeis was, as he reported, "perfectly frank," and he thought that Richards was "at least somewhat shaken in his views after our interview." Brandeis was clearly correct; within ten days, Consolidated Gas had agreed to Brandeis's proposal, and Brandeis presented to the league and the State Board of Trade the draft of a bill drawn up by Consolidated Gas in consultation with Brandeis.[32]

From that time on, Brandeis and Richards worked together behind the scenes to achieve the result that they now both wanted. Richards exhibited a strong political sense, and wrote to Brandeis about the sliding-scale bill, "It seems wiser that a bill upon these lines should be introduced by the Public Franchise League rather than by us and that it will be better also to introduce the bill without saying specifically that we agree to its terms." Then, rather remarkably, he put his concurrence into writing: "I write this to say that if a bill is passed on these lines, substantially in the form which you and we agree upon, our company will accept the bill within the time provided by the act." But, he added quickly, "if this bill should for any reason not pass we are not to be quoted in any way as having assented to 7 per cent as being a proper dividend." Clearly, Richards had come to trust Brandeis not to betray him. Brandeis reciprocated Richards's trust, telling the Boston newspapers that Richards's support of the bill "is strong evidence that he recognizes [that] the paramount function of a public service corporation is to serve the public." It was a remarkable collaboration between the mogul and the reformer. To Brandeis, however, it was not at all unlikely. He was confident that people of good will could work together to deal with virtually any situation. Brandeis's view of his work was that of a good capitalist striving to make capitalism socially responsible, and he believed firmly that if capitalism did not clean its own house the people would eventually be driven to undo the capitalists. The role of the lawyer was to help businesses flourish in the new industrialized world, and Brandeis proposed to do this in his public as well as in his private work.[33]

After a substantial fight the compromise worked out by Brandeis and Richards was adopted by the legislature, and Brandeis was delighted. Consolidated Gas had been prevented from watering its stock, an incentive for cheap gas had been written into law, and the specter of government ownership of a utility had been avoided. Brandeis rejoiced to Al,

"I consider this a most important step in public economics and govern-ment—an alternative for municipal ownership—which will keep the Gas Co. out of politics. If, as I anticipate, this succeeds well in Boston, there will be many followers, also in other lines of public service." He explained to a member of the Massachusetts legislature that prevention of monopoly and the high rates that a monopoly would inevitably charge was not the only reason for the regulation of public service corporations. In addition, there was "the fact that they use public property, namely, the streets;" second, they were "performing a function recognized as a governmental function," and any such function should be susceptible to the will of the people.[34]

There was some anger when the consolidated gas bill was passed, because it provided for gas at the relatively high rate of $.90 per thou-sand cubic feet. Brandeis replied that his bill would not only make cheaper gas a certainty within the near future but that it would also permit the company a satisfactory return on its investment. He was right. When the sliding-scale system went into effect in 1906, Consolidated Gas reduced the rate to $.85 in order to raise its dividends. Within a year the price went down to $.80 and the dividend went up to 9 percent. This was good for the consumers, who were saving $800,000 a year over the rates that had been charged before consolidation, and for the shareholders, who were benefited both by high dividends and by the rise of the company's stock from $44.50 in 1904 to $57.50 in 1907. It was good for the public, because "the officers and em-ployees of the gas company now devote themselves strictly to the busi-ness of making and distributing gas, instead of dissipating their abilities, as heretofore, in lobbying and political intrigue." It was also good for Brandeis's growing reputation as an exceptional public advocate. The chairman of the Committee on Public Lighting had sent him a letter of appreciation when the sliding-scale bill passed, saying that Brandeis had been "the largest factor in obtaining so satisfactory a piece of legis-lation." Brandeis himself gave much of the credit for the actual work-ing of the system to Richards's "enlightened leadership," which he saw as the result of Richards's "conversion" that fateful day in his office.[35]

What excited Brandeis about the sliding-scale system, in addition to its being an equitable solution, was that it encouraged efficiency in busi-ness. The article that he wrote about Boston's gas problem made it clear that the sliding-scale system depended on Consolidated Gas's adoption of efficient methods for the sake of increasing its profits. What Consol-idated Gas needed was "the kind of management most likely to produce and distribute gas at the lowest possible cost . . . no self-sustaining system of supplying gas can give to the people cheap gas unless it rests upon high efficiency in management."[36]

Once the sliding-scale bill was adopted, Richards introduced what Brandeis called an "extension" of the sliding-scale principles to those employees who elected to participate. Six hundred eighty-one employees received not only wages but also a dividend on their wages equal to the dividend paid stockholders. They took their dividend in stock, thereby becoming owners as well as workers. The workers thus shared management's incentive to raise profits, which meant that they were all interested in efficiency. Efficiency brought lower rates; lower rates meant greater sales, which permitted even lower rates; and under the sliding-scale system, every reduction in rates by five cents enabled the company to increase its dividend by one percent.[37]

Others might label Brandeis a radical for his attacks on large corporations, but he considered himself a conservative capitalist. A good Brahmin and champion of small business, he had an almost instinctive fear of socialism; later, this attitude would be strengthened as he articulated the belief that concentration of power in any bureaucracy, state or private, was to be avoided. In 1905 he spoke of reform as an answer to the vague threats of socialism. The *Boston Transcript* reported his statement to the House Committee on Public Lighting during the gas hearings that "the conservative classes in the community are not to be considered those who wish to leave unrestricted the power of wealth, but those who in economic relations are working for justice to capitalist and the public alike." If the public perceived overconcentrations of wealth as unfair, the forces of revolution would triumph: "Those who have sought in the past and now are seeking to keep capital down are doing all they can to keep the communistic element down also, and in this country unless corporate wealth is held within bounds, individual wealth will be swept away . . . It is of the greatest importance to capitalistic interests" that measures as equitable as the sliding-scale law be enforced.[38]

By 1905 Brandeis was deeply immersed in public activities. In May, for example, he was seeking a solution for a labor conflict that had arisen between the musicians' union of the Boston Symphony Orchestra and Henry Lee Higginson, who paid its expenses and wanted to control it totally; he was lobbying vigorously for the sliding-scale gas bill; he delivered an address entitled "The Opportunity in the Law" to the Harvard Ethical Society; he participated in the Industrial League, a society that attempted to work out solutions to general industrial problems; he accepted membership on the Advisory Committee of the National Municipal League's Municipal Taxation Committee; and he was of course busy with both his private law work and his family. Two months later he was sending letters and clippings to his father about London's improvement of streets in working-class areas, a meeting of Chinese-Americans about American policy in China, domestic unrest in Russia, temperance in England, the proposed Panama Canal, immigration, the cranberry industry in Massachusetts, and the conclusion of the Russo-Japanese War. He asked the American Bar Association to discuss the issues he had raised in "The Opportunity in the Law"; he continued his correspondence about street railways; he wrote to various state officials, including the commissioners of the State Board of Charities, the State Board of Prison Commissioners, the Board of Insanity, and the Bureau of Statistics of Labor, criticizing their public reports and suggesting alterations in methods of data collection and circulation; he followed the progress of the Consolidated Gas Company; he advised local civic reformers about organizing a particular ward of the city; he made suggestions to the Metropolitan Park Commission on the lands it should acquire; he worked at his practice, getting ready for his August vacation; and he found time to go on typical summer outings—canoe rides, picnics—with his family. He was also well into his study of the insurance industry—an endeavor that would result in what he considered for many years to be his life's greatest achievement.[39]

6 | Reforming Life Insurance

On any given workday in 1905, over 20,000 life insurance salesmen could be found knocking on the doors of industrial workers, selling new policies or collecting the weekly premiums on policies they had previously sold. They would frequently be told that a family could not afford to keep up its payments of $.50 a week. In fact, two-thirds of the industrial life insurance policies they sold could be counted on to lapse in this manner within 3 years. The worker, of course, lost all payments already made.

Three companies—the Metropolitan of New York, the Prudential of New Jersey, and the John Hancock of Massachusetts—were responsible for 94 percent of all industrial insurance sold in the United States. Of the industrial policies they held in 1904, 2,761,449 (out of over 14,000,000) were ended by death, surrender, or lapse. Payment to the holder or heirs was made in only one-eighth of the cases; in all the others—2,414,377— no money at all was paid out by the insurance companies. The payment made to the lucky one-eighth averaged about $140.00, and served primarily to pay funeral expenses and perhaps some of the bills resulting from long illness.

If a male industrial worker had faithfully made payments every week from age 21 until he reached the average male life expectancy of 61.25 years, his family would collect $820.00. If, instead, he had put his $.50 a week into a savings bank, then paying an average interest of 3.5 percent a year, his family would inherit $2,265.90. Had he taken out an industrial life insurance policy and found after 20 years that he could no longer afford to maintain it, he could surrender it and the company would give him $165. After 20 years in a savings bank, the same $.50 a week would yield him $746.20. Nonetheless, eager to protect their families, uncomfortable with banks, and responsive to the extensive soliciting of the insurance companies, 15,678,310 American workers had put their money into industrial policies in 1905 alone.

Industrial life insurance differed from regular life insurance in a number of ways. The premiums were fixed according to age and rose in multiples of $.05. A one-year-old child, for example, was insurable at a rate of $.10 a week. The premium percentage remained the same no matter what amount of insurance was bought, whereas in ordinary life insurance the percent paid in premiums decreased as the amount purchased rose. Ordinary life insurance premiums were paid anywhere from one to four times a year, and policyholders took or sent their premiums to the company's offices. Industrial insurance premiums were collected weekly, and policyholders had the "luxury" of a weekly reminder in the form of a visit from an agent.

The price of the luxury came high. A 40-year-old with an industrial policy bought from the Prudential would pay a total of $26.00 a year for a policy worth $500.00. A regular life insurance policy bought from the same company by a 40-year-old would cost $27.03 for $1,000.00 worth of coverage, approximately half the cost. In addition, two-thirds of all industrial policies ended in total forfeit of all premiums because payments lapsed before the minimum 3 years were up. For what some saw as a shocking fraud perpetrated on the working class the insurance companies offered a number of reasons: The high attrition rate, coupled with the time spent by the solicitor and the agent, and added to the amount of "reserve" capital that states required the companies to hold, meant the industrial insurance did not pay for itself unless policies were held for 3 years. Twenty percent of the premium went to the agent and another 20 percent was spent on supervision and accounting. The agent system was at the heart of industrial life insurance, which provided protection to people who could not afford to insure themselves for the amount of coverage available in regular life insurance; the ignorance and habits of the working class were such that without agents they would not know how, or would forget, to make regular payments; without small weekly payments, they would not accumulate the money for premiums. The insurance companies were thus offering a great service to the working class. Or so, at any rate, said the insurance companies.[1]

Brandeis did not agree that industrial insurance was a great service, nor did he think that insurance companies in general were well run. He was introduced to the life insurance system in 1905, when a dispute erupted between the president and vice-president of the New York-based Equitable Assurance Company. Tales of mismanagement—the vice-president's charging the Equitable for the salary of his gardener, dinners for the French nobility, entertainments in his French château—began to leak to the public. Almost a million dollars per year in premiums was going to the Equitable from Bostonians, some of whom organized the New England Policy-Holders' Protective Committee and sought out Brandeis to act as their counsel. He agreed to act as counsel but would take no fee, so that he might do whatever he felt needed doing in the public interest as well as for the committee.

Even before the committee approached him, Brandeis had written to one of the New York investigators, "I am well aware that it is not fashionable at the present time to suggest that anything can be too large, and I am disposed to think that in regard to most businesses, it would not be wise to place any limit upon size, but I am inclined to think that the evils which inhere in and surround the life insurance business cannot be fully met without placing some limitation upon the size of an insurance company." Within a few years he would change his mind about not setting limits on most businesses.[2]

To begin functioning as the committee's counsel, he immediately immersed himself in the reports of various life insurance companies, seeking information not only about the Equitable but about the subject in general. The New England Committee's first report on May 19 was presented as no more than the beginning of the inquiry. Clearly, the Equitable had mismanaged the money entrusted to it and its officers were culpable, but the matter could not rest with an alteration of management. There were no legal safeguards protecting purchasers of insurance policies as there were for savings banks depositors, nor was there any requirement that insurance companies use proper accounting methods.

Two other inquiries were taking place simultaneously. Members of the Equitable's Board of Directors had set up their own investigative committee, headed by Henry Clay Frick, and public outcry in New York had led to an official investigation by New York Superintendent of Insurance Francis Hendricks. This did not reassure the Bostonians; after all, Hendricks had had jurisdiction over the Equitable when mismanagement had been rife. Nonetheless, the report of the Frick Committee, issued May 31, and that of Hendricks, published June 21, went even further than that of the New England Committee in detailing the "excessive salaries, excessive commissions, excessive expenses, superfluous offices, and a general lack in the organization of that strong moral fibre so essential for the accomplishment of satisfactory results."[3]

Meanwhile, the high-living vice-president responsible for the scandal had sold his stock to Thomas Fortune Ryan—a major force on Wall Street—who put the stock into a trust controlled by three citizens of impeccable virtue: Grover Cleveland, former president of the United States; Morgan J. O'Brien, a judge of the New York Supreme Court; and George Westinghouse, an inventor and industrialist. The trustees named the chairman of the New England Committee as a director of the Equitable and invited Brandeis and the committee to submit recommendations about the future management of the company. Brandeis's recommendations, sent on July 12, constituted the first indication of his approach to this new field of endeavor.[4]

Some years earlier, Governor Murray Crane of Massachusetts had asked Brandeis to serve as unpaid counsel for a group about to propose legislation governing savings banks. When the Equitable scandal broke and Brandeis began his studies of the insurance industry, he was struck by the differences between the way the insurance industry operated and the efficiency and good management of savings banks. His, and the committee's, recommendations therefore focused on means by which the former could emulate the latter: by demobilizing the army of sales agents, by stopping advertising, by ending the practice of selling policies to people who could not afford them, by enforcing rigorous accounting and disclosure methods, and by preventing officers from holding positions in other corporations. Most radically, the committee urged the "complete mutualization of the Society"; that is, it was to be "brought under the absolute control of the policy holders." No one doubted the integrity of the trustees, but the fact of the matter was that a controlling share of the Equitable's stock still belonged to Thomas Fortune Ryan.[5]

One newspaper, the *New York World,* began a campaign to separate Ryan and the Equitable. It stimulated what became a public demand for a legislative investigation. Senator William Armstrong became chairman of the joint investigative committee, and Charles Evans Hughes, a lawyer with a reputation for investigative work (and a future Chief Justice of the Supreme Court) was named chief counsel. The *World* kept close watch on the Armstrong Committee's hearings and trumpeted each new revelation of malfeasance, adding to the excitement with a total of 202 editorials telling readers what should be done next. Brandeis was much impressed by this demonstration of the power of the press and wrote, "The debt which the American people owes to *The New York World* in handling this subject of insurance cannot be overestimated. Its editorials . . . were invaluable."[6]

One of the villains who emerged during the Armstrong investigation was George W. Perkins, a partner in J. P. Morgan and Company. He chaired the finance committee of the New York Life Insurance Company, which in 1904 had contributed $48,702.50 to the presidential campaign of Theodore Roosevelt. Along with the Equitable and the Mutual Life Insurance Company, New York Life had maintained a fund from which legislators had been paid to kill state proposals designed to regulate the insurance industry. The books of all three companies were juggled to hide the existence of the fund, and one of Perkins's jobs had been to manipulate the books and the stocks of New York Life. The deliberate fraud thus perpetrated on the public infuriated Brandeis. He stormed, "Talleyrand said, 'Language was made to conceal thought.' George W. Perkins would teach us that 'Bookkeeping was made to conceal facts.' " There was almost nothing worse, to Brandeis, than manipulating facts. Just as Brandeis remembered the role of the press in the insurance controversy, so he would remember the revelations about Perkins.[7]

As Brandeis collected facts, taking home suitcases filled with reports from insurance and banking companies, he became convinced that Theodore Roosevelt, who had received campaign contributions from insurance companies, was mistaken in advocating federal supervision of the companies. If government power had to be extended into yet another area of life, Brandeis thought, concentration of that power could be avoided by distributing it to the states. He was also suspicious of the companies' support for federal supervision, recognizing that the companies preferred concentrated power because it meant that only one legislature had to be bought off.[8]

On October 26, 1905, Brandeis delivered a lecture to the Boston Commercial Club entitled "Life Insurance: The Abuses and the Remedies." As he had done in the first report of the New England Committee, he compared the life insurance companies to the savings banks and found the former sadly lacking in rationality and good management. He pointed to the "188 modest Massachusetts savings banks," run by "faithful treasurers" and supervised only by "obscure but conscientious citizens." In 1904 the banks had earned an average of 4.4 percent, which was 5 percent more than the insurance companies' earnings, while spending seventeen times less, proportionately, than the biggest three insurance companies. The banks had no agents, no solicitors, no lavish advertising. Insurance companies, too, should be able to do without such extravagances. And the companies not only wasted money; they put much of the money they collected from policyholders to pernicious use. They deposited huge amounts in banks, thus gaining effective control over them; similarly, they invested in various manufacturing and transportation industries, which became dependent upon the capital and whims of the insurance magnates. In one way or another, the money of the "big three" (Hancock, Metropolitan, and Prudential) affected half the population of the United States.[9]

The speech, which was widely reported throughout the United States, merely hinted at the way Brandeis's thoughts were running. At about the same time, he wrote triumphantly to Alice Grady, his executive secretary, "We've found the answer. The savings banks *can* be adapted to the writing of life insurance." But he was not yet ready to share this idea with the public. He asked the Insurance Commissioners and the Board of Savings Bank Commissions of New York, New Hampshire, Vermont, Maine, Connecticut, and Pennsylvania for their 1905 reports.[10]

At the end of December the Armstrong Committee closed its hearings; in February 1906 it presented to the legislature its report of almost five hundred pages, which drew extensively on Brandeis's suggestions. Many of its ideas about regular life insurance were subsequently adopted by the New York legislature. Massachusetts, along with other states such as Wisconsin, Indiana, and Ohio, created commissions on insurance to consider the insurance problem and propose courses of action. Unfortunately, however, none of the states did anything about industrial life insurance. The Armstrong Committee had accepted the conclusions of the insurance industry, repeated endlessly during the hearings, that there was no way to lower the costs of industrial insurance. Perhaps, the report suggested meekly, establishment of branch offices might eliminate the expenses of solicitors and agents, but the companies had assured the committee that the number of "thrifty poor" who would seek out such offices would not make their establishment economical. "Miss Grady," Brandeis said to his secretary, "Let's take them at their word. They can't give cheaper insurance. Very well, we'll devise a means of getting it." While doing research, Brandeis had discovered the work of Elizur Wright, Massachusetts's first insurance commissioner, who had urged the Boston Board of Trade in 1874 to combine the functions of banks and insurance companies. When nothing was done, he applied for a charter for a Massachusetts Family Bank that would be owned by a stock company and sell insurance over the counter. But he was too elderly to pursue the matter, and it came to nothing. A quarter of a century later, however, Brandeis seized upon Wright's idea. Wright's son, Walter, had written to Brandeis while the latter was still counsel to the New England Committee and had offered his services. Brandeis replied enthusiastically, with an invitation saying "I shall want to talk with you soon about a matter which in the first instance is of a public nature, but which I think may ripen into a matter in which your services will be required professionally." (The professional services Wright could offer were his skills as a consulting actuary.)[11]

The two men soon met, and Brandeis followed up with a lengthy letter reiterating his ideas and asking Wright to do the statistical work necessary to prove that the ideas were feasible. Savings banks should open insurance departments, Brandeis wrote. They would have to do no more in the way of advertising than to put slips announcing the service into the bankbooks of depositors, who would find it an "easy and natural step" to buy insurance from the banks in whose financial stability they already trusted. Few additional employees would be needed, which meant that the project should not be expensive for banks. The policyholder would not be faced with the prospect of forfeiture, for the money already paid in premiums could remain in his or her name; within a maximum limit, insurance could be bought for as little or as much as the policyholder wished; if circumstances prevented the payment of a large premium at any given time, the policy could simply be converted to one for a lesser benefit; and, as in the savings department of the bank, if the insured wished to drop the policy, his or her money would be returned and all that would be lost was the fee paid for a medical examination before the issuance of the policy. "In other words," wrote Brandeis, "make the investment of insurance practically convertible into a savings bank investment."[12]

Brandeis recognized that he was suggesting something quite new: "the experiment could be tried in connection with existing savings banks without involving the large financial and moral risk of failure attendant upon making the experiment of an entirely new institution." If, as he had understood Wright to say, a bank would have to hold no more than 200 or 300 such policies to cover its expenses, "it would be possible for practically any savings bank in the Commonwealth to put the plan in operation," and Brandeis would propose a law "under which the business might be entered upon by any savings bank willing to make the experiment." Brandeis was convinced that using a relatively small institution to experiment was the only rational way to approach social engineering; hence his fervent support for the American federal system, with the concomitant ability of the states to experiment and to learn from each other's successes and failures. Some of the details to be worked out in the experiment of savings bank life insurance were what the maximum policy might be—whether it should be the existing average of $150 or $200 for industrial policies, or, as he thought might be preferable, the $1000 limit on savings bank deposits; and whether the kinds of policies, for the sake of economy, might be limited to two or three, utilizing standard forms.[13]

Leaving Wright to work out the actuarial details, Brandeis swung into action. Even before he was ready to make his plan public, Brandeis had, as usual, encouraged public discussion of the matter. Invited to speak to the Providence Economic Club, he had suggested that the topic be insurance and that a representative of one of the insurance companies be invited to speak as well. He got the Boston Industrial League to put industrial insurance on the agenda for its November meeting and urged the subject as one for discussion upon the National Civic Federation. When the illness of his father made it unlikely that he would be able to speak before the Providence Economic Club, which had secured the president of the Phoenix Mutual Life Insurance Company as a cospeaker, he proposed that they invite instead the editor of the *New York World* responsible for the reports on corruption in the insurance companies.[14]

Brandeis himself lectured tirelessly. In a letter reporting to his brother that he was going to speak in the next few days to the Central Labor Union, the Unitarian Club, the Amalgamated Sheet Metal Workers, and the Industrial League, all of Boston, as well as to the Unitarian Church in Needham, he wrote, "I am having nearly every day requests to address some audience on the subject." A few weeks later the pace was still hectic. He wrote to Al, "This is a pretty busy Insurance week. Shall speak six times—having had two meetings last evening. We are having quite a resistance from the ultra-conservatives . . . but the movement has acquired such a momentum that it will be very hard for them to stop us now. They began too late." He was certain he would win but, recognizing that victory would come only after a good deal of hard work, he spent six months speaking about insurance from two to six nights every week. Each occasion was carefully orchestrated. He asked the sponsors to invite specific members of the community, including trustees of savings banks, philanthropists, the press, and state representatives. His audiences included trade unions, boards of trade, and church groups. Social engagements were cancelled; all his time had to be spent educating the public. He kept a set of dinner clothes in his office in case he was suddenly called to a dinner meeting. He urged others to speak whenever and wherever they could, but, although he did not say so, it is clear that most audiences wanted the most authoritative voice, his. He used his lectures to generate publicity, and then used the publicity to secure more lectures. Brandeis understood that public attention could be maintained only through drama. Sending his father "some more twaddle on Equitable," he mused, "It is extremely fortunate that the Equitable disclosures came out so gradually. If all the 'exposures' had come at one time the country would have been shocked & then have quickly forgotten the matter as it is apt to with abuses. But the deferred New York legislative investigation will carry the matter along for nine months more and other legislatures will doubtless be ready to take a hand. So we shall have life insurance activity on all hands for a year to come, and the business has a fair chance of being put upon a proper basis at the end of that time."[15]

Brandeis wrote to the incoming governor of Massachusetts, Curtis Guild, Jr., whom he had known when Guild was lieutenant governor, asking him to mention life insurance in his inaugural address to pave the way for legislation. Brandeis had prepared the ground with publicity; now it was time for more direct political action. And it is clear that Brandeis's manipulations were conscious. He told his brother, "I think I can work my Savings Bk Industrial Scheme" through people he knew in the savings banks "& through Whitman whom I had put on the Special Insurance Com^{te} . . . A Mutual Life Com^{te} is also forming as to which I am advising." William Whitman was the head of the New England Committee, whom Brandeis had earlier put on the reorganized board of the New York Equitable. Governor Guild had indeed mentioned insurance in his inauguration message, and the legislature eventually established an Insurance Committee to organize existing state laws on insurance and recommend any others it considered necessary. Brandeis immediately met with the Speaker of the House about the people to be appointed to the committee, and got him to name three supporters of the Brandeis plan. Another supporter was named by the president of the senate. The Speaker, the senate president, and the eight members of the governor's insurance commission constiuted the remainder of the new committee, designed to act in a way Brandeis found proper.[16]

However, the insurance interests were powerful, and Brandeis knew he could not merely rely upon the state committee. He therefore organized a series of speakers, himself included, to appear before it. Then, learning that the committee might nonetheless vote against his plan, he mustered outside pressure. The press, thoroughly sympathetic to Brandeis, "leaked" rumors that he and the governor were meeting regularly, and that the governor was preparing a strong endorsement for his January message. The more fervent Brandeis supporters on the committee threatened to issue a minority report if the outcome was not favorable. The Mutual Life Committee was reorganized and enlarged as the Massachusetts Savings Bank Insurance League. Its members included former Democratic Governor William L. Douglas (president); former Republican Governor John L. Bates (vice-president); Bishop William Lawrence; President Eliot of Harvard; Bishop William O'Connell; the Reverend A. A. Berle, Sr.; J. J. Storrow of Lee Higginson & Company; the president of the First National Bank of Boston; George Wigglesworth, a lawyer, textile manufacturer, and bank trustee; Louis Frothingham, former Speaker of the House; and so many other distinguished business and professional leaders that, in order to give all of them the status in the league their positions demanded, it was necessary to create more than twenty vice-presidencies, an Executive Committee, and a Committee of One Hundred. But these

Brahmins were not the only members of the league; by March 1907 it had over seventy thousand members.[17]

In the course of the fight to muster public opinion, Brandeis made a new ally who would prove to be of major importance for years to come. He was Norman Hapgood, editor of *Collier's Magazine*. Hapgood had written favorably about Brandeis's insurance speech to the Commercial Club. Brandeis's letter thanking him became the first of hundreds of letters they exchanged. It was always Brandeis's assumption that someone who acted in one good cause could be induced to act for another. Therefore, he enclosed in his letter a copy of his public franchise speech, given before the Cooper Union some months earlier. New York and *Collier's* were in the midst of a fight on that issue, and Brandeis had made reference to the New York system in his speech. Four months later Brandeis sent Hapgood a lengthy letter announcing the signing of Massachusetts's sliding-scale gas bill and enclosing a copy of a Public Franchise League pamphlet explaining it. Within a month he had also forwarded a copy of his paper "Wage Earners' Life Insurance: A Great Wrong and a Remedy." Now, it appeared, Brandeis was ready to use *Collier's*. "In considering the best method of undertaking to secure to our working people life insurance under proper conditions," he suggested to Hapgood, "it seemed to me that you might deem it wise to have Collier's lead in the movement . . . If you deem it wise for Collier's to take up the work, I should like to have your suggestion as to when the best time would be to open the campaign." He confided to Hapgood that he was planning to introduce his plan to the Massachusetts legislature in January, and Hapgood agreed to publish the article. Brandeis wrote to him, "I feel confident now that we shall succeed." When it appeared that the movement had indeed succeeded, and that only the formality of senate passage and the governor's signing the bill remained, Brandeis sent *Collier's* his thanks. He told Mark Sullivan, the magazine's chief correspondent, "The work that Collier's did in giving publicity to the plan . . . has been of immense service to us, and you and Mr. Hapgood may well feel that if as we hope the plan becomes a success in its working, you and he have largely contributed to that result." On the same day, another letter to Sullivan accompanied a copy of a newspaper article on the success of the sliding-scale gas system with a suggestion that *Collier's* "will be interested in noting" it "in some subsequent number."[18]

Hapgood was a fellow graduate of the Harvard Law School, as well as of Harvard College. He had been, in turn, a practicing attorney, a drama critic, and a biographer (of Webster, Washington, and Lincoln). He went to *Collier's* in 1903 and rapidly turned it into a key force for progressivism, and, ultimately, a vehicle for Brandeis's public crusades. The relationship between the two men quickly ripened into a close friendship, and Hapgood became one of the few people with whom Brandeis was on a first-name basis. His picture was given a place of honor in Brandeis's study. They would battle together for various Progressive causes, including public control of land, abolition of the money trust and other oligopolies, and the presidential campaign of Robert La Follette. Eventually, Hapgood became one of Brandeis's conduits to Franklin Roosevelt and the New Deal administration.[19]

Brandeis's insurance article, published by *Collier's,* was one over which he had labored at great length. Uncharacteristically, he had gotten comments on the draft from Walter Wright, Charles Evans Hughes, George Wigglesworth, William Whitman, Edward Filene, and at least a dozen more friends, colleagues, and experts on insurance. This not only assured him of competent criticism; it also encouraged support for his plan. Then Brandeis arranged for the article to be seen by thousands of people who did not read *Collier's.* He informed the editors of the three most influential Massachusetts newspapers (the *Boston Post,* the *Springfield Republican,* and the *Boston Evening Transcript*) that the article was forthcoming and that *Collier's* had agreed to permit simultaneous publication in local newspapers. The *Boston Evening Transcript* published the article in full; the *Boston Post* issued a series of its own articles, supporting the plan; and virtually every newspaper in Massachusetts reported on the plan and ran editorials about it. The Massachusetts Savings Bank Insurance League had the *Collier's* article reprinted and sent hundreds of copies to people throughout the state. Not con..nt with in-state coverage, Brandeis had written to the financial editor of the *New York Evening Post,* which along with other papers around the country carried stories discussing the plan.[20]

The importance of the article and of Brandeis's testimony before the legislature went beyond publicity and education. The major criticism made by the insurance companies of the plan was that it constituted no more than the well-intentioned but totally impractical ravings of someone who knew nothing about the insurance business. The *Collier's* article, the much publicized Commercial Club speech, and Brandeis's cool legislative performances gave the lie to that claim. His method of collecting facts, organizing them, and citing them—facts about the number of policies, the attrition rate, the costs to the policyholders, the profits of the companies, the functioning of savings banks, the exact amounts that banks would have to spend on insurance departments, the savings that would accrue to policyholders—proved to be as important as his political skills. Statistics and a flair for publicity came together, with the publicity making the public aware of the statistics and the statistics in turn generating additional publicity.

Recognizing the enormous influence of the insurance interests, Brandeis left nothing to chance. By the time the legislative Insurance Committee was ready to report, Brandeis had involved much of the Boston and Massachusetts elite in his plan, had begun putting together his prestigious Savings Bank Insurance League, had published his overview of the insurance industry and his arguments for savings bank life insurance in *Collier's*, had turned the press into an ally and a public relations outlet, and had made the possibility of savings bank life insurance part of the political agenda of the day. He also made certain that, before the committee voted, Governor Guild gave the plan a ringing public endorsement. Five days later the committee issued its unanimous report, incorporating many of the points made in Brandeis's *Collier's* article.[21]

Although Brandeis wanted Massachusetts to iron out all of the problems of savings bank life insurance before the experiment was adopted by other states, he was intrigued by the interest of President Theodore Roosevelt in the subject and by the possibility of his public support. Brandeis, therefore, wrote to Henry Beach Needham of the People's Lobby, "Will you undertake to bring this matter to the attention of President Roosevelt? It is a subject on which I should think he would be willing to express himself." He enclosed a copy of his *Collier's* article as well as the earlier pamphlet. Roosevelt read the two articles "with great interest (altho not with as much knowledge of the subject as I should like to have)" and sent Brandeis, for his comments, a report by the District of Columbia insurance commissioner. Brandeis replied with detailed comments about the commissioner's proposal for a model insurance bill, and Roosevelt submitted Brandeis's letter to Congress when he sent it the commissioner's report. The public now knew that the president of the United States considered Brandeis an expert on insurance matters.[22]

The matter then went to the two houses of the Massachusetts legislature, where a bitter fight ensued. Some of Boston's most renowned business leaders, led by Henry Higginson of Lee Higginson & Company, had suggested a plan for a private company that would sell over-the-counter industrial insurance, and the insurance companies now began to endorse the plan. Brandeis recognized that the companies hoped "to accomplish two things: to make an apparent concession to the demand of the community for eliminating the expense of solicitation and collection of the business, and then by the failure of this company to accomplish this end—to show that the old method of doing the business must be adhered to." In other words, Brandeis explained, the company Higginson wanted set up would make little attempt to secure policies but would destroy savings bank life insurance by gaining legislative acceptance as a substitute for it. Brandeis did not ask the legislature to ignore the Higginson plan; on the contrary, it seemed to him "eminently proper that the Higginson Company should have a charter; indeed that under the general law any persons under proper safeguards should be permitted to engage in the life insurance business." He simply did not want the Higginson plan endorsed at the expense of his own. In fact, Brandeis's display of fairness was tactical; he doubted anything would ever come of the Higginson plan if both it and savings bank life insurance were approved. He was right: the Higginson plan received legislative endorsement, and the Higginson group was given until 1910 to file a certificate of incorporation with the state insurance commissioner. It never did, and subsequent events proved that Higginson did not forgive Brandeis.[23]

On March 21, 1907, the Joint Legislative Committee convened to hold hearings on the Brandeis plan, which drew the largest audience that had ever attended such an event at the State House. The Higginson forces mounted an impressive campaign, pointing out to the committee the number of bank officials in the state who were opposed. They, of course, neglected to mention that the officials named also had connections with the insurance companies, on whose boards many of them sat as trustees. On March 23 Brandeis, therefore, sought political advice from Municipal Court Judge Warren Reed, a friend from Harvard. Reed counseled him that "laws are passed in answer to a public demand, rather than because they are good" and advised him to get the labor unions behind the bill. "The moment they show interest, the two political parties will vie with each other, but until the wage-earners ask for our bill themselves, the Legislature will ignore it." Brandeis agreed and always remembered Reed's dictum about the reason laws are passed. He also accepted Reed's suggestion that savings bank leaders who supported the plan ought to appear before the committee. He began to work out the details of his strategy. Reed would appear before the committee, with a telegram from former Governor William Douglas; Brandeis would then call upon savings bank trustees. He sent a list of ten to an associate, asking that he think of more. He also orchestrated the issuance by the league of pamphlets containing letters from noteworthy Massachusetts citizens endorsing the plan. Meanwhile, 140 labor organizations in the state had come out for the plan; Brandeis asked Henry Abrahams, secretary of the Boston Central Labor Union and assistant secretary of the league, to present a list of them to the committee. He made sure that the editor of the supportive *Boston Post* knew in advance of the witnesses' appearance. He asked influential individuals to speak to legislators. The labor unions were also asked to send representatives to see their legislators, and the league sent

its members postcards telling them who their legislators were and urging
that they write. It also issued pamphlets containing letters from noteworthy Massachusetts citizens endorsing the plan.[24]

The response was impressive. Leaders of labor, industry, both political
parties, and religious groups appeared before the committee; Edwin Grozier, editor of the *Post,* kept up a drumfire of editorials, both during and
after the committee's deliberations; and it became clear that the massive
effort would result in committee approval. The vote for the bill was 10
to 4. The next step was the House Ways and Means Committee, to which
the bill was sent, and Brandeis immediately mobilized the same forces,
with the same result. Then came debate and a vote by the entire House.
Brandeis supplied his legislative supporters with material for the debate,
again successfully: the bill passed and was sent to the Senate Ways and
Means Committee. Brandeis pulled out all the stops, mustering an array
of star speakers for the hearing on June 12; lobbying the legislators
himself and urging others to do so; utilizing all the influence at the
command of various labor and business leaders. His success was reported
in a series of letters to his brother. June 13: "The Senate Ways & Means
Com[tee] has reported the Savings Ins bill." June 18: "the Senate voted
yesterday 23 to 3 to order the Savings Insurance Bill to a third reading."
June 19: "The enemy is still worrying us. At yesterday's Senate meeting
a lot of amendments were introduced to the Savings Insurance Bill. Hope
we shall brush them away without injury today." June 19: "4 P.M. Senate
voted down all amendments and passed the Insurance bill to be engrossed
by vote 28 to 4." On June 26, the governor signed the bill. Brandeis had
written to Al that if the bill was signed, "a respite in work would follow
this much desired consummation, but a respite only, as it will take much
more work to make the bill a practical success than it has to march it
along so far."[25]

Considering the amount of work Brandeis had done to "march it along
so far," the prospect of "much more work" might seem overwhelming.
But Brandeis had learned that laws once passed do not administer themselves. The bill contained provision for the establishment of a supervising
General Insurance Guaranty Fund made up of seven gubernatorial ap-
pointees. The day before the bill was signed, Brandeis sent "My dear
Curtis" (Governor Guild) a list of seven proposed trustees. Guild appointed all but one, arguing that the one would spoil the geographic
balance of the board; Brandeis suggested a substitute, and Guild appointed him. The board chose an actuary, Robertson Hunter, to prepare
rates and policy forms; Brandeis sent him detailed suggestions, most of
which were accepted. Various formalities and details—including the
working out of medical criteria for the acceptance of future policyholders,

the establishment of guaranty funds by participating banks, and bureau-cratic procedures—delayed the implementation of the bill for a year. Finally, on June 22, 1908, after a great deal of pulling and tugging by Brandeis, the Whitman Savings Bank opened its insurance department. The first policy was purchased by Charles Henry Jones, a Boston shoe manufacturer who was one of Brandeis's clients and friends. On Novem-ber 2, the People's Savings Bank of Brockton followed suit. Savings bank life insurance was in business.[26]

But it was not much of a business. Very few people took out policies. Brandeis had foreseen this, warning as soon as the bill was passed that the "promoters of this legislation do not underrate the difficulty of mak-ing this movement a practical success by educating the people to avail themselves of the opportunity which the legislation affords." Judge Reed was perplexed, a month after the Brockton bank opened its department, to find so little interest. "I had expected that after it had been fully explained to the working people here, there would be a movement by them toward the acceptance of the advantages obtained for them. For some reason the people do not come forward." Alice Grady replied that she was not surprised: "The whole thing is a campaign of ed-ucation, and I don't know why the slight talk or explanation that you have given the people should be deemed equivalent to an education." Brandeis and Edward Filene induced the Boston Chamber of Com-merce to set up a Wage Earners' Committee on Insurance, with the aim of getting more banks to open departments and manufacturers to open "agencies," which were in effect tiny bank branch offices to handle insurance (this was permitted 'by the statute). The new committee, working with the Massachusetts Savings Bank Life Insurance League, also prepared circulars to be placed in pay envelopes and noon-hour educational meetings for employees as ways of increasing employee participation. The tactic worked: where this kind of drive was under-taken, between one-third and one-half of a manufacturer's employees took out insurance.[27]

The system began to show that it was economically sound. The second policy anniversary on June 12, 1910, found it paying a dividend of $12\frac{1}{2}$ percent—$8\frac{1}{3}$ percent to be paid at once and the remainder in 1911. On August 1, 1911, the Berkshire County Savings Bank became the third to open an insurance department; on July 15, 1912, the City Savings Bank of Pittsfield became the fourth. Governor David I. Walsh was sufficiently impressed to urge, in his inaugural address on January 7, 1915, that the state appropriate money to publicize the system. The insurance companies were also impressed. Savings bank life insurance was not big, but it was threatening, and the companies responded accordingly. They cut their charges by 10 percent in 1907 and by another 10 percent in 1909. This meant that policyholders in Massachusetts alone were able to save over one million dollars a year.[28]

Brandeis spent much time over the next years on what he called his "propaganda" effort to further savings bank life insurance. "We have before us the work of putting the law into successful practice," he wrote shortly after its passage, "and that means a good deal of educating the public." He poured money as well as time into the effort, contributing half the budget of the league. Over the course of his lifetime he spent more than $200,000 on the cause. He could normally devote half his working hours to public matters, but, especially in the early days of the insurance plan, he found this insufficient. "My office is pretty busy now," he complained to his brother, "and even 'Father' must work. This interrupts considerably my Savings Bank Insurance Campaign, which badly needs my prodding. I manage to get in a little lick most days, but it needs a lot of boosting to keep people in motion." One form of "boosting" was to send endless letters to Massachusetts businessmen, urging them to set up insurance agencies. Each letter included a list of the businesses that had already done so: the Regal Shoe Company, Commonwealth Shoe & Leather Company, W. H. McElwain Company, the Phelps Publishing Company of Springfield, Filene's, the Boston Bookbinding Company, the Laboratory Kitchen, Henry Siegal Company, the United Shoe Machinery Company, American Hide & Leather Co., Women's Educational and Industrial Union, Talbot Mills, Dennison Manufacturing Co.. All told, by 1912 more than 160 manufacturers had set up agencies, and 13 savings banks that had not themselves created insurance departments had become agencies for those that had. Notable among the businesses on the list were Brandeis's clients and others engaged in similar kinds of manufacturing: shoes, textiles, books.[29]

Brandeis also spewed out ideas constantly to his associates. Savings books should have information about insurance pasted on their covers and inserted between the pages, and new insertions should be made each time the book was used; men's Bible classes should be explored as a place to recruit depositors; children could be told about the system in school; all circulars should be "very carefully and attractively prepared"; "voluntary associations like the Young Men's Christian Association" might become participants; agencies should be provided with a "small, simple, but attractive cabinet" for papers connected with insurance, and the cabinet should be sufficiently attractive "that it can be put in a prominent place in the store or institution." Of course it was expected that arrangements would be made for the cabinets to be manufactured "at a very small cost in wholesale quantities."[30]

Brandeis demanded streams of information. He asked that instructors, hired by employers to explain the system to their employees, keep daily files on the basis of which they would turn in regular reports. He hired a clipping service to send him all newspaper articles that appeared on the subject. The purpose was to know where and how best to continue the work of education. "I am convinced that the success of the system is wholly dependent upon our ability to educate the public," he wrote; "it is merely a matter of education," but "publicity is of the utmost importance to our cause."[31]

Fortunately, he was aided in the cause by Alice Grady, his executive secretary and chief assistant in his insurance activities. Her steady work for insurance was so important that a major enemy of the system declared, "Frankly, I think that without Miss Grady savings bank insurance would atrophy." She became financial secretary and then executive secretary of the league, and a movie impresario as well. Recognizing the importance of that medium while it was still in its infancy, she wrote and directed a movie about the system that was shown throughout Massachusetts. Absolutely undaunted by rank, wealth, or personality when it came to what she had made her personal crusade, Grady insisted that former Governor David Walsh, a number of New England financiers, and Brandeis himself serve as her cast. No one else, Brandeis said, could ever have gotten him to do such a thing. Grady, however, was a force to be reckoned with. She was hired as a secretary by Warren & Brandeis while still a girl and, quickly becoming Brandeis's private secretary, assumed responsibility for the entire secretarial staff. She managed his clients, his work, his bills, and his family, earning Brandeis's total confidence and the affection of his family. It would be hard to say whether her first love was Brandeis or the insurance system. She was always on call for Brandeis, but her nights, her Sundays, and her holidays were devoted to insurance. Her loyalty was rewarded when in 1919 she was named Deputy Commissioner of Savings Bank Life Insurance for Massachusetts. She remained in that position until her death in 1934 at the age of sixty-one. An appreciation of her numerous talents was a factor in Brandeis's conversion to the cause of women's suffrage.[32]

At least until he began his work in Zionism, Brandeis considered savings bank life insurance his greatest achievement. "Far more has been accomplished by the savings bank insurance movement," he wrote to Lincoln Steffens, "than even its most ardent supporters had dared hope for." The policies themselves were "but a very small part of the achievement . . . Its greatest success by far has been in its effect upon the industrial insurance companies." Not only had the companies reduced their premium rates; they now paid the full amount if death occurred after six months (rather than three years), or if the policy was surrendered after ten years (instead of twenty). Within a few years, Brandeis predicted, the reforms would save American workers between $10 and $15 million annually.[33]

Brandeis's concern with life insurance was not based solely, or even primarily, on a desire to give workers' families either a fund from which to cover funeral expenses or a small inheritance. The more important goal was to give workers the assurance that they would not be penniless in their old age. Brandeis explained his thinking to a journalist: the "American standard of living" had to include provision for the future. If a "living wage" provided only for food, shelter, clothing, education and recreation, it was insufficient. (In an age when most reformers were struggling simply to secure workers' wages adequate for the necessities of life, Brandeis was insistent that education and recreation had to be included among such necessities. As he frequently said, he was not interested in producing machine-slaves but citizens, and citizens needed the skills and leisure to think.) "Provision for the future"—unemployment, illness, accident, death, and "superannuation"—had to come from the living wage. This meant that workers had to make a "daily pro rata contribution" to a fund for the future. "The cost of such a provision is a fixed charge on the workingman's living, just as much as the cost of repairs or depreciation of machinery are a fixed charge in the cost of manufacturing." Brandeis rejected the paternalistic model of Germany where both employee and employer were compelled to contribute to a fund that covered injuries, illness, and old-age: "Such compulsory thrift on the part of the wage earner, and other contribution, are not in harmony with the American ideas of individual liberty. The American spirit demands that provision for the workingman's future be made through his own efforts to secure a wage sufficiently large to leave a surplus applicable to such purpose and to the development on his part of strength of character and self-control which shall induce him voluntarily so to apply it." He had told Judge Reed, "What we want is to have the workingman free, not to have him the beneficiary of a benevolent employer, and freedom demands a development in the employees of that self-control which results in thrift and in adequate provision for the future."[34]

At all times, Brandeis saw the state's role in insurance as "supplying institutions which, combining the best possible conditions of management by private citizens with adequate State supervision, will care for the funds which the workingman does set apart as a provision for the future." This was the purpose of his legislation. In addition, as he pointed out, while most states had savings bank systems, and private companies had supplied life insurance (at an exorbitant price), there was virtually no such thing as old-age annuities for workers. His plan was to combine all three functions, which were "inherently the same," and which therefore could be united through use of "our admirable system of savings banks." The law provided that all money paid in was returnable after premiums had been paid for six months (the entire amount was payable in case of death from the time the policy was signed). Most legislators probably thought of the provision as a guarantee that a worker unable to meet payments would not lose the money already paid in. To Brandeis, however, the clause meant that insurance policies could also function as a nest egg for old age.[35]

When the law went into effect, he was ready to make public what had come to seem to him its element of greatest potential. He wrote to Lawrence F. Abbott, editor of the *Outlook,* thanking him for writing about the legislation during the campaign, "I think that it will prove in the end," he wrote, "that an even greater merit of the plan rests in its affording workingmen an opportunity of providing themselves with old age annuities." He enclosed an article by Robertson Hunter entitled "Who will Pay Your Wages When You Are Old and Grey," and added, "We have great faith in the possibilities of educating our people." Abbott took the hint and published an editorial on the early success of the Massachusetts system. Brandeis sent Samuel Gompers, the president of the American Federation of Labor, his manuscript entitled "Massachusetts Old Age Annuities," which he hoped Gompers would "deem worthy of a place in an early number of the Federationist." Gompers, too, complied. Another article appeared as "Massachusetts's Substitute for Old Age Pensions," and yet another version appeared as "Massachusetts Savings Insurance and Annuity Banks" in *The Banker's Magazine.*[36]

Brandeis was particularly pleased that "enlightened representatives of labor and capital" had cooperated to make the movement a success. The unions were helping to educate workers about the program and so were manufacturers. Brandeis believed that enlightened capitalism could work for both groups, particularly if they joined with him in combatting their mutual enemy, the trusts. Measures such as industrial insurance proved that the business world, properly educated, could be induced to care about its workers, for it was through manufacturers' efforts in their factories that many of the policies were being sold. (It had not yet occurred to Brandeis that businesses might have an obligation to contribute to the insurance and pension funds of their employees.) Labor, an active participant in the legislative struggle, had been shown to be able to fight for itself, thereby obviating the need for paternalism. Together, labor and capital had made state insurance unnecessary, which was a great victory for democracy and decentralization of power. This kind of cooperation had to be pushed further in the future, particularly in the direction of unemployment insurance. "The wide distribution of insurance would go very far towards remedying existing industrial evils and social discontent," Brandeis predicted.[37]

7 | Trade Unionism

Brandeis's private clients were, for the most part, either small manufacturers of such goods as shoes and paper or retail merchants. Given the growing labor movement, Brandeis's view of the lawyer as a consultant as well as an advocate, and his catholic interests, it was inevitable that his clients' labor problems would come to his attention. One of the most important legacies Brandeis had from his parents, and the one that would figure prominently in his approach to industrial democracy, was respect for the dignity of the individual, whether Brahmin or servant. Brandeis agreed with Jefferson that all human beings were equal in their possession of reason and the capacity to use it, however different the level of one human being's intelligence might be from that of another's. All needed education, not only to be good citizens, but to live the well-rounded lives that presumably differentiated people from other animals. People had to have time for study, for thinking, and for leisure, as well as for work. The view that Brandeis would bring to his clients about their employees was expressed in Matthew Arnold's lines, "Life is not a having and a getting; but a being and a becoming."[1] All human beings had to be given a chance to "be" and to "become." In 1892 he discovered with shock that his view of human beings was not shared by everyone.

Through Elizabeth Glendower Evans, Brandeis had become friendly with Mary Kenney, a labor organizer, and her future husband, John F. O'Sullivan, president of the Boston Central Labor Union and a reporter on labor matters for the *Boston Globe*. In 1892 Brandeis was completing his notes for his course on business law at the Massachusetts Institute of Technology. He had put together a series of lectures showing how the common law had evolved along with industry and commerce, when one morning he picked up his newspaper and read of the violence that had erupted at the Carnegie steel works in Homestead, Pennsylvania, after Carnegie decided not to renew its contract with the steel workers and refused to deal with a union. Mary Kenney had traveled to Homestead while the contract was still in effect and later described to Brandeis the walls with apertures for guns that the company had erected around the steel mill grounds. The company was clearly expecting a small war when the contract ran out. The contract expired; wages were slashed; and the steel workers went on strike. Henry Clay Frick, Carnegie's manager, hired Pinkerton guards and sailed them up the Ohio River to protect strikebreakers. The strikers dug in on the bank of the river. As the Pinkertons arrived, and realized that the strikers would not permit them to land, they began to fire their Winchesters. The steel workers suffered most of the casualties in the ensuing battle. Brandeis later remembered his reaction to the "pitched battle between the Pinkertons on the barge and barricaded steel workers on the bank" reported in the newspaper: "I saw at once that the common law, built up under simpler conditions of living, gave an inadequate basis for the adjustment of the complex relations of the modern factory system. I threw away my notes and approached my theme from new angles. Those talks at Tech marked an epoch in my own career."[2]

His introductory lecture had originally asserted that the study of law was valuable "as part of a liberal education, because the conduct of life is to so large an extent determined by the existing legal institutions, that an understanding of the legal system must give you a clearer view of human affairs in their manifold relations." Nothing in the formal legal institutions, Brandeis suddenly realized, explained "human affairs in their manifold relations" as they existed in Homestead. It was Homestead, he said, that made him think seriously for the first time "about the labor problem . . . it took the shock of that battle, where organized capital hired a private army to shoot at organized labor for resisting an arbitrary cut in wages, to turn my mind definitely toward a searching study of the relations of labor to industry." The course as originally conceived had begun with somewhat abstract lectures on the nature of law; as revised after the Homestead strike, the casebook started with a chapter entitled "Legal Relation of Labor and Capital." His training at Harvard under Langdell was given new meaning by current events: law was a dynamic entity, reflecting changing social conditions, and the law of the twentieth century had to keep pace with the new phenomenon of highly concentrated capital—at least if it was to be truly moral. As Horace Kallen commented, the Homestead strike forced Brandeis to choose between legalism and morality.[3]

Homestead taught Brandeis the fallacy of his assumption that all Americans were equal under the law, for the law upheld Carnegie's right to guard his property from striking workers and to use his far greater funds to hire scabs and the forces to protect them, while denying the workers a balancing right to unionize or a means by which they could use their limited resources to press their economic demands. Clearly, labor was not the legal equal of capital, nor was labor capital's equal in political power; the law gave capital excessive unbalanced power. Suddenly made aware of the economic injustices inherent in American society and the role of law in perpetuating the inequalities, Brandeis began to think less about what the courts accepted as legitimate and more about what public policies would be morally right.

In 1902 he had the opportunity to see at first hand the difficulties of the capital-labor relationship. One of his clients was William H. McElwain of Bridgewater, Massachusetts, whom Brandeis later described as "one of the largest shoe manufacturers in the world." In fact, when McElwain died in 1908, his company was making $8,691,274 a year. But in 1902, he was confronted with bad times, and asked his employees to accept a wage cut. They refused, and he called in Brandeis. Not only was business in a slump, McElwain told Brandeis, but his laborers had also been earning unusually high wages and enjoyed good working conditions.[4]

Brandeis decided to visit the plant. Discovering that the employees were indeed paid well when they worked but that their work was seasonal and that there were many days when no work was to be had, he asked McElwain, "Are you giving me the average pay they receive for fifty-two weeks of the year, or are you giving me the pay they earn while they are working?" He was shocked to find that McElwain did not know his workers' yearly income. "You say your factory can not pay the wages the men have been earning," he thundered at McElwain. "How much money do they lose through irregularities in their work? You don't know? Do you undertake to manage this business and to say what wages it can afford to pay while you are ignorant of facts such as these? Are not these things that you should have understood and which you should have seen that your men too understood, before you went into this fight?" He called in John Tobin, the head of the International Boot and Shoe Workers' Union, who was acting as the striking workers' representative. Tobin's version of the situation—relatively high but seasonal wages—was the same as McElwain's. When Tobin finished his recital, Brandeis, the employer's lawyer, startled the labor leader by commenting, "You're perfectly right."[5]

Now Brandeis asked for a record of each worker's employment, indicating how many days each man worked per year, his wage, and what this amounted to annually. The more he studied the situation, he recalled later, "the more it seemed to me absurd that men willing to work should have to be idle during ten or fifteen weeks of each year. I said: 'This is unnecessary. It is an outrage that in an intelligent society a great industry should be so managed.' " McElwain talked to Brandeis about the average wage earned. Brandeis's reaction was, "I abhor averages. I like the individual case. A man may have six meals one day and none the next, making an average of three per day, but that is not a good way to live." He was particularly annoyed at unemployment in the shoe industry, because, as he pointed out to McElwain, neither raw material nor finished product was perishable.[6]

McElwain's proposed solution was to pay the workers on a piece-work basis; Tobin wanted wages calculated on the basis of time worked. Brandeis, however, proposed that the work be spread out during the year to prevent irregularity of employment. He counseled McElwain to show samples and get orders far enough in advance to provide work throughout the year. Brandeis told McElwain to make certain that his goods were delivered when promised, and this, taken with the securing of orders in advance, would permit him to regularize employment in his factory. McElwain took the advice, insisting that he would take no "rush" orders but pledging that orders placed in advance would be delivered on the exact date agreed. The net result was that the factory was kept operating 305 days every year, wages were both substantial and regular, the business prospered, and McElwain, Tobin, and the workers were satisfied.[7]

Tobin and Brandeis remained in contact. When three years later Tobin wrote an article for the *Shoe Workers' Journal,* arguing that employers should have the right to fire employees for valid reasons, Brandeis wrote to him, commending his position and noting that it "eliminates one of the greatest objections which has been urged in many cases against unions." McElwain, in turn, earned Brandeis's respect as the model employer, and whenever Brandeis described the regularization of employment at the McElwain plant he gave entire credit to its owner, saying that he "worked for nobler ends than mere accumulation or lust of power." In the course of his short career (he died in 1908 at age forty-one) McElwain "revolutionized shoe manufacturing. He found it a trade; he left it an applied science." The science lay in guaranteeing regularity of employment.

McElwain, of course, remained Brandeis's client; he also became his comrade-in-arms in the fights against municipal corruption and for savings bank life insurance. After McElwain's death, Brandeis wrote to Alfred that he was "greatly distressed" in part because "[McElwain] was in my opinion really the greatest man of my acquaintance."[8]

There were at least two lessons to be learned from the McElwain experience. Of utmost importance was that irregularity of employment demoralized the workers, reduced their annual earnings to an amount far below that which a casual survey of their daily wage would seem to indicate, and made it impossible for them and their families to plan their budgets or to live without economic fear. Brandeis became convinced that this was *the* major labor problem, and he began a crusade to teach this lesson to unions and employers alike. Regularization of employment would help employers reduce costs by running machinery all year and recouping their initial investment on machinery; they would be able to increase production and, perhaps, lower prices as a result of added volume, thus adding to their profits; and they might also find that employees who were guaranteed regular employment would be willing to accept a lower wage per piece or per day. He therefore told Clarence Darrow, lawyer for the miners in the 1902 strike against the Pennsylvania Coal Company, "I feel very strongly that one of the great evils from which the employees suffer is the lack of continuous occupation, and that it would be possible for the railroads, by some change in their method of doing business, as well as by a somewhat lessened market price, to run their mines continuously, and with a practically average output each day."[9]

The most satisfying lesson learned from McElwain was that labor and capital could both behave reasonably. To bring this about, facts were an absolute necessity; without facts, no reasonable solution could possibly be fashioned, and neither business nor capital always had all the facts. It therefore became the function of the lawyer to gather facts, bring them to the attention of both sides and, acting as a mediator, use them as the basis for a solution. Answers could be found that brought justice to the employees without sacrificing profit to the employers; indeed, a truly creative solution would frequently add to both profits and wages.

A few years later Brandeis said, "I am convinced that little of real value can be accomplished without . . . specific detail. A study of the facts in individual cases is essential to working out not only individual reform but to devising broader reform measures." But more than expediency lay behind Brandeis's preference for individual cases. He realized that behind the statistics were people with specific wants, needs, desires, problems, and aspirations. The gradual working-out of an answer to such problems as irregularity of employment was in part an exciting intellectual exercise, but it was also a response to the fact that human beings were hurt by irregular employment. Brandeis was offended by the continued existence of preventable human suffering. His sensitivity to the human condition was the logical outcome of his parents' humanism; and, perhaps, it was in part the result of the tales of the "Pilgrims of '48" as well as his reaction to his mother's suffering from family deaths when she was a child, the illnesses and deaths in his family, and his own tenuous health. The self-confidence that had been instilled in the adored younger son of a loving family and enhanced by his proven ability to meet the world on its own terms brought with it a psychological openness. He was able to speak to labor leaders with the same naturalness with which he spoke to manufacturers and to listen to both with equal interest. Indeed, his interest in the human condition and his thirst for knowledge made him extremely difficult to interview, as journalists found to their exasperation; he was more interested in interviewing them. And he learned from experience. In an interview in which he discussed the McElwain strike, he was asked, "How came you by your democracy? You were not bred to it?" His answer was illuminating: "No; my early associations were such as to give me greater reverence than I now have for the things that are because they are. I recall that when I began to practice law I thought it awkward, stupid, and vulgar that a jury of twelve inexpert men should have the power to decide. I had the greatest respect for the Judge. I trusted only expert opinion. Experience of life has made me democratic. I began to see that many things sanctioned by expert opinion and denounced by popular opinion were wrong." Asked to give an example, he turned to the McElwain strike as his first experience with irregularity of employment and the beginnings of his belief that it was an unnecessary evil.[10]

Edward A. Filene gave Brandeis the unique experience of observing and shaping one of the country's first experiments with employee participation in management. Filene was the son of William Filene, who in 1881 had opened a women's clothing store at 10 Winter Street in Boston. The store quickly grew into what was described as a "department specialty shop," selling men's and women's clothing and accessories and boasting the bargain basement for which it is still well known. William Filene turned the store over to his sons, Edward Albert and Abraham Lincoln Filene in 1901. The two young men were most unusual in believing that employer-employee relations were a matter not only of money-making but of social justice. Convinced that commercial success depended in large part on the workers, the Filenes organized the corporation that owned the store and the store itself so as to involve employees in decision making.[11]

An appeal to Edward Filene after a cashier had been charged for a shortage in her cash account had resulted in the establishment in 1901 of an Arbitration Board, with members elected by employees, to hear cases relating to fines. This was quickly extended to cases of dismissal as well. Then in 1903 the board acquired jurisdiction over all controversies between the company and an employee as well as those between employees. The most amazing feature of the board was that management was given no voice on it whatsoever and yet accepted its decisions. The Filenes were firm in their belief that a group of employees, given full facts about a controversy such as a dismissal, would learn to exercise their responsibility and judgment well, and that as a result friction between management and labor would be minimized. Management would benefit from the reduction in friction and from the more amiable atmosphere; labor would benefit from training in responsibility and from the knowledge that it would be treated fairly. This was Brandeis's first experience of an arbitration board, and he undoubtedly drew upon it when he created one for the New York garment industry in 1910.[12]

William Filene had instituted informal meetings with employees, during which workers were encouraged to discuss whatever store-related issues they chose. The Filene brothers, however, decided that informal discussions and a beneficent management did not result in the kind of democratic system they wanted to achieve. Somewhere around 1898 the firm had turned over to the employees responsibility for management of the lunchroom and of the relief and entertainment funds. The employees' success with these endeavors quickly convinced the Filenes that their workers were capable of helping to run the store itself. The practices that gradually developed as a result of this realization were organized, articulated, and codified in the 1903 constitution of the Filene Co-operative Association, which Brandeis helped write. The constitution was considered by both management and labor to be a binding document, although in fact it carried no legal weight. Edward Filene summarized their experience when he spoke at a dinner of the Filene Co-operative Association in 1904:

> After many experiments arising from a desire on our part to do the right thing for our employes, after many experiments with lunchrooms and other types of what is called welfare work, we finally came to the point where we had to acknowledge our work had been a failure [and] . . . to acknowledge we had not done our work in a way suitable to the environment in which we were trying to do it . . . in the beginning we had tried to do the work for our people

under well-meant but still despotically benevolent principles. But grown wise and more democratic by our failures, we agreed to do nothing for our people, but to help them with all our minds and strength to do everything for themselves.[13]

Every Filene's employee was automatically a member of the association, whose purpose was "to give its members a voice in their government, to increase their efficiency and add to their social opportunities, to create and sustain a just and equitable relation between employer and employe." The association was given the right to make rules concerning every aspect of employment but not store policy (that is, merchandising decisions). A profit-sharing plan for executives and other high-level personnel was put into effect immediately and lasted until 1912. The plan was supposed to be extended to all employees in 1913; for various reasons this did not occur, and instead an annual bonus plan was instituted. The 1912 By-Laws provided for the acquisition by the association of the Filene brothers' voting common stock upon their retirement, leaving 52 percent of the voting stock in the hands of what had by then become the remaining two owners. Again the shareholding plan fell through, in part because Lincoln Filene and the two nonfamily owners turned against it; in part because Edward was as discouraged as the others by the failure of the employees to participate more actively in management. A Russell Sage Foundation study in 1930 found that much of the failure in both instances could be attributed to the fact that the idea of worker-management was instituted from above, and said that the employees' "lack of initiative in using their powers for participation in management has been conspicuous." The report suggested that "where the workers are not affiliated with others outside," active worker involvement might be "dependent on the continuous supervision and leadership of the management." Since management had gradually lost its enthusiasm for the all-important profit-sharing and stock-sharing aspects of the program, the report's critique implied that industrial democracy could best be achieved through unionization. That, at any rate, was the conclusion Brandeis reached many years before the foundation's investigation. Nevertheless, he urged Edward Filene to bring the experiment "to the attention of the country," perhaps through an article in a magazine like *McClure's* or the *World's Work* or the *Review of Reviews*. "A great deal has been accomplished in your store," he told Filene, "but the best results of any form of industrial co-operation cannot be attained by working out the problem in a single establishment. What you are trying to accomplish can be best reached by having your work and ideas supplemented by the independent work and ideas of others that may be started under different conditions and in different places on the same general lines."[14]

Brandeis viewed the Filene Co-operative Association as a great experiment in industrial democracy. Indeed, he told the association members in 1905, "If this experiment fails, a great deal of the hope which there is for the improvement of the condition of the employee goes out of the world for some time . . . The civilized world today believes that we must adhere to the system which we have known as the monarchical system, the system of master and servant, or, as now more politely called, employer and employee. It rests with this century and perhaps with America to prove that as we have in the political world shown what self-government can do, we are to pursue the same lines in the industrial world." In 1905 Brandeis was still viewed as a good Brahmin—a bit eccentric and perhaps too inclined to enthusiasm for his own well-being, but a Brahmin nonetheless. At worst, he could be seen as a "misguided" Progressive in what would become the Wilsonian sense; that is, essentially a conservative who wanted to return to a small-scale market economy in order to preserve capitalism. But it was scarcely using the voice of conservatism to equate employers with monarchs and employees with servants.[15]

At the same time, Brandeis proclaimed that "Democracy is only possible, industrial democracy, among people who think; among people who are above the average intelligence." While he added that "thinking is not a heaven-born thing . . . It is a gift men and women make for themselves . . . it is earned by effort . . . The brain is like the hand. It grows with using," this encouragement of a mental work effort does not negate the statement about democracy and above-average intelligence. Brandeis was all for industrial democracy, but he was not yet certain how far down into the economic and intellectual strata one could take it. And yet he was pushing himself, and the Filene workers, toward taking the risk. "The constitution of this business is today far from the perfection of industrial democracy," he told them; "I view it as only in its early stages." The workers' acts would determine "how far this experiment shall go."[16]

His short speech, containing as it does both a proclamation of faith in industrial democracy and the remains of aristocratic doubt, indicates how long a road Brandeis had to travel from the successful Boston corporation lawyer to the advocate of worker-participation. He had to reconcile his belief in individual dignity and possibilities with the spectacle of human degradation that smacked one in the face when one left Beacon Street for the interior of the average factory. The very essence of Brahminism was a sense of noblesse oblige, but noblesse oblige implies the existence of noblesse—of those who, by being particularly favored, bear testimony that there are others who are not. And Brandeis's Brahminism was still much with him. Could one really willingly turn power over to the less favored, the less educated, the less intelligent? The question had also been posed by Jefferson as it must be by any thinking person. The difference between the elitist and the democrat lies in the answer.

Brandeis and the Filenes also set up the Industrial League, whose purpose was "to promote the investigation and study of economic and industrial questions and aid in improving relations between employers and employees." Edward Filene was so enthusiastic about the organization that he made it his residual legatee in his will. Brandeis was president, Edward Filene chaired the executive committee, and Lincoln Filene was the treasurer. Brandeis described the organization to a fellow attorney as "composed largely of representatives of great manufacturing enterprises, some labor men, and some men, who like us, are supposed not to labor." Fifteen or twenty of them met monthly at 6:45 at the Technology Club in Boston for a discussion of industrial questions over dinner, and from time to time Brandeis would invite as his guest someone who he thought might be particularly interested in the subject of the evening.[17]

Brandeis also became a vice-president of the Civic Federation of New England, which offered its services to both labor and management during a strike, hoping that an informal meeting of representatives of the two sides with a disinterested outsider might help them reach some agreement. "Personally," Brandeis told one such employer, "I have a strong belief in the value of such conferences, when conducted between the right parties and in the right spirit, having had rather intimate connection with the practical working of these matters on a number of occasions." The federation's reputation for disinterestedness grew, and it was sometimes asked for its services by employer and employees. At other times, one side—usually the employer—would reject the idea of "interference" by outsiders. And occasionally, as in the strike by the members of the American Federation of Musicians in the Boston Symphony Orchestra against Henry Lee Higginson, the federation's mediation efforts were successful.[18]

Brandeis was also asked to serve on the National Committee being put together by the Economic Clubs of various cities. In accepting he noted, "It is essential to the accomplishment of any satisfactory results that there should be upon the Committee and in the local clubs a large and strong representation of the labor interests. The labor question is and for a long time must be the paramount economic question in this country." Furthermore, club discussions should be held "under the auspices of an organization in which the employers, the employed, and the community are all fairly represented." He felt that the committees of the National Civic Federation could serve as a model. The president of the

New England branch was Lucius Tuttle, president of the Boston & Maine Railway. Among its activists were Amory Appleton Lawrence, head of several textile mills and president of the Boston Merchants Association; Arthur T. Lyman, owner of textile and carpet factories and the president of the Boston Athenaeum; Charles H. Taylor, president of the American Newspaper Publishers Association and manager and treasurer of the *Boston Globe;* Dennis D. Driscoll, secretary of the Massachusetts branch of the American Federation of Labor; and Frank McCarthy, another Boston labor leader. The extraordinary mixture of social and economic strata the group represented is illustrated by an afterthought in a letter from Brandeis to Lawrence, mentioning a dinner meeting of one of the committees at Brandeis's home. Brandeis wrote to the aristocratic business leaders, "In view of the Labor element we think it best to dine without evening dress."[19]

Brandeis's behavior frequently confused both management and labor because they misunderstood his basic premises: human beings had the right to govern themselves, whether in the political or economic sphere, but they did not have the right to behave stupidly, immorally, or illegally. When they did behave improperly, they had to take responsibility for their acts. Thus, Brandeis differed with Samuel Gompers, leader of the American Federation of Labor, on whether unions should be incorporated. The two men were brought together by the Economic League to debate, in Tremont Temple on December 4, 1902, the desirability of such incorporation. Brandeis and Gompers each spoke for thirty minutes and each had forty-five minutes in reply. Brandeis praised labor in glowing terms for its "enlightened self-sacrifice," saying, "If you search for the heroes of peace, you will find many among humble workmen who have braved idleness and poverty for principle." But even "the best friends of labor unions" had to admit that action taken by unions "is frequently hasty and ill-considered, the result of emotion rather than of reason; that their action is frequently arbitrary, the natural result of the possession of great power by persons not accustomed to its use; that the unions frequently ignore laws which seem to hamper them in their efforts and which they therefore regard as unjust." Incorporation of unions would make them legally liable and their funds subject to court-imposed fines. This would protect unions "from their own arbitrariness." Brandeis fully understood that the courts had been unfair to unions, and in his speeches to lawyers he lectured them about it, but he could not believe that civilization would be advanced through lawbreaking.[20]

Gompers, however, was infuriated. "The well organized body of working men and women know something of restraint," he replied. "They have respect for law and order, and it is an outrage to claim or to even insinuate that they are violators of the law." It was true, he noted, that frustrated nonunion laborers occasionally resorted to violence, but the law already enabled them—or violent union members—to be prosecuted. Incorporation would destroy unions by letting corrupt antilabor judges seize their funds. Gompers declared, "I am second to no man in my respect for the law and for the judges of our courts, but I will say this— that the judiciary looks upon the workingman as a piece of property and not as a human being. We do not question the integrity of the judges but we know that in order that they may get their appointment or election they must have certain convictions upon particular subjects."21

The *Boston Herald,* which was clearly on Brandeis's side, reported the demeanor of each debator. "The attitude of Mr. Brandeis was that of a man who has not an interest in the matter beyond that of every public-spirited man properly affected by movements which concern his country. He spoke in a calm, dispassionate manner . . . He made no effort at oratorical effect and assumed a conversational tone and manner, leaning for the most part of the time with his left arm on the desk and with his right hand in his trousers pocket, from which it was seldom removed. He spoke slowly and deliberately, and paused from time to time, apparently to let his words sink in, and seemed content to let his argument rest on its logic." Gompers, however, "soon made it felt that the subject was one that commands his deepest interest. His was not the argument of one who looks from above, but of one whose life work is at stake, and he rallied to its support with a vehemence of gesture and expression that left no doubt as to his sincerity . . . His statements were forcibly delivered and were accompanied by gestures that may be described as violent. As he told how trade unions had suffered at the hands of law courts his manner became contemptuous." Gompers lashed out at Brandeis's defense of the judicial system. "We want only fair play," he exclaimed. "What chance have labor and the laborers for fair play when the whole history of jurisprudence has been against the laborer? There never was a tyrant in the history of the world but who found some judge to clothe in judicial form the tyranny exercised and the cruelty imposed on the people." He drew blood, for Brandeis was not prepared to agree in public that the legal system should be flouted. Brandeis's initial attitude "gave way to one more combative . . . He spoke earnestly and indulged at times in a fine sarcasm, which was phrased with a dignity that rendered it all the more biting." Brandeis called Gompers emotional; Gompers replied that "it is true that I am emotional but I am also emphatic."22

The audience "of the most cosmopolitan character" that heard the two men overflowed Tremont Temple's Chipman Hall and was constituted of an extraordinary melange of lawyers, businessmen, and academicians. If there were union members present, the newspapers did not report that fact. The listeners were not prepared to condemn labor, but their attitudes nonetheless varied widely. For example, Professor E. Dana Durand of Harvard, who supported incorporation, "caused a sensation" when he suggested that picketing during a strike be made legal.[23]

Brandeis, like many in the audience, was a reformer. His economic ideas, and his willingness to fight for them, would eventually make him anathema to the Brahmins, but did not keep him from becoming one of the country's richest attorneys. Gompers, who spoke passionately about becoming involved with labor when he was fourteen (at which age Brandeis was riding his still-wealthy family's horses and studying in Louisville), did indeed feel that "his life work [was] at stake." He had no opportunity to look coolly at the fray from above. It was the classic chasm between those on the front lines of battle and their supporters. Unionites, caught up in the horrors of underpaid and overworked laborers toiling in inhumane conditions, fought furiously for and were satisfied when they managed to achieve better wages, shorter hours, and decent working conditions. Brandeis never knew want, but he could see that satisfactory conditions of labor were a far cry from industrial democracy and that only a reconciliation of the interests of labor and capital could focus attention on the kinds of human beings who were being produced by the new economic system.[24]

However, his disagreement with Gompers did not keep the two men from working together or from appearing together on other platforms. For example, Gompers turned to Brandeis for an opinion when a bill was introduced in Congress in 1905 that would have prohibited a court's granting an injunction against a union in a labor dispute before the union had been notified. This would have prevented the existing practice of corporations seeking and getting such *ex parte* injunctions. Gompers, writing an editorial supporting the bill for the *American Federationist,* asked Brandeis for his views. Brandeis objected to the bill as an abridgement of traditional judicial power and told Gompers, "You can doubtless cite some cases of unusual hardship resulting from the improvident issue of ex parte injunctions; cases too where the judges' action appears to have been due to prejudice against labor." In April 1905 the two men discussed the question "How far does associated effort in industries interfere with individual liberty?" before the first meeting of the National Civic Federation's Industrial Economics Department. And the Massachusetts branch of the American Federation of Labor invited Brandeis to speak to the Boston Central Labor Union about trade unionism and employers. Over a thousand people heard him urge unions to end the evil of irregular employment and to work with employers to increase profits so that workers' earnings could be increased. The speech was so successful that he was urged to publish it and did so in the *National Civic Federation Monthly Review*. Later Brandeis was supported by the Massachusetts branch of the American Federation of Labor during the savings bank life insurance fight. Brandeis discussed the insurance proposal with Gompers, and when the bill was passed, Brandeis wrote to him, calling the bill's passage "one of the victories of organized labor" and reminding him that the "practical success of this measure depends wholly upon our ability to educate the workingmen to avail themselves of the opportunities afforded." Their mutual respect was sufficiently great for Lincoln Filene, who wanted to get Brandeis involved in a labor dispute, to tell his brother that "it is my intention to get Gompers to secure Brandeis." They had clearly agreed to disagree, at least about incorporation, because in 1912 Brandeis was still referring union leaders to his remarks in the 1902 debate.[25]

Just as Brandeis saw no reason not to differ in public with Gompers, he perceived no paradox in his lecturing about the virtues of unions to employers whom he had just represented in a battle against workers. For example, in 1904 when Boston Typographical Union No. 13 went out on strike for higher wages, Brandeis considered the action "shockingly bad business," for the workers had asked that the minimum wage be raised from $16.50 a week to $18.00. The Boston Typothetae, which was the employers' organization, offered $17.00 the first year and $18.00 thereafter. As Brandeis pointed out, the $52.00 extra a year that would have been earned had wages been raised to $18.00 was lost by each worker who remained on strike for three weeks. But what brought Brandeis into the struggle was the sympathetic strike by pressmen and feeders, in violation of a contract that provided for arbitration of grievances and prohibited sympathetic strikes. Indeed, the strike began in spite of the pleas of Martin Higgins, president of the International Printing Pressmen and Assistants' Union to which the pressmen and feeders in question belonged. Brandeis was employed by the Typothetae to obtain an injunction against the pressmen and feeders. After he had done so, the president and members of the Executive Committee of the International Typographical Union came to Boston to investigate and sent their union members back to work. The strike thus ended with no gains for the union, loss of jobs for many of those who had struck in sympathy, and the collapse of the power of the local union leader. To Brandeis, it was an example of bad unionism.[26]

But when he was asked to speak at the annual banquet of the Boston

Typothetae whose representative he had been, he told its members that labor unrest was largely their fault and laid down six principles to be followed if there was to be industrial peace and prosperity. The first contained the seeds of a radical philosophy: "Industrial liberty must attend [that is, go along with] political liberty . . . Some way must be worked out by which employer and employee, each recognizing the proper sphere of the other, will each be free to work for his own and for the common good, and that the powers of the individual employee may be developed to the utmost." It was as wrong for employers to be masters of their employees as it would be for the employees to be masters of their employers, for the "sense of unrestricted power is just as demoralizing for the employer as it is for the employee. Neither our intelligence nor our characters can long stand the strain of unrestricted power." This first principle of equality of power between employer and employee is worth examining as an indication of how Brandeis's thinking differed from that of many union leaders, who wished to gain dominance over employers. His primary concern was the limitations and possibilities of the human being. In a sense, he was updating Acton's dictum about the corrupting effects of power and bringing it from the political into the economic sphere. But at the same time that Brandeis feared unlimited power, he emphasized a system under which "the powers of the individual employee may be developed to the utmost." These were the powers of intellect and character, which would thrive from the assumption of responsibility but which would wither under a system of industrial despotism. There were almost no limits to the possible development of human beings as long as they were not the victims of power, either by virtue of having too little or by virtue of having too much. The problem, however, was to maintain the Jeffersonian ideal of economic independence in the industrial era.[27]

Brandeis addressed that problem with his second principle: employers had to understand the benefits that would flow from unionization. "The employer needs the union 'to stay him from the fall of vanity,' " and union leaders "will adequately feel the terrible responsibility resting upon them" and will become "reasonable and conservative" only if they represent strong unions. Brandeis acknowledged that unions had committed excesses but pointed out, "We believe in democracy despite the excesses of the French Revolution." Unions were the key to industrial democracy.[28]

His third principle was that employees were entitled to representation by their union officers; his fourth, the seemingly naive dictum "Employers and employees should try to agree." Underneath the dictum lay the core of Brandeis's approach to problems: "Nine-tenths of the serious controversies which arise in life result from misunderstanding, result from one man not knowing the facts which to the other man seem important, or otherwise failing to appreciate his point of view. A properly conducted conference involves a frank disclosure of such facts—patient, careful argument, willingness to listen and to consider." On the basis of his experience, he could not accept the premise that the objectives of labor and management differed. Both would benefit from the success of the business, and both therefore had to be interested in making the business a success. To workers who had been shot at by employers' armies and to employers whose buildings had been blown up by frustrated workers he said, "Come, let us reason together"; their interests were the same.[29]

The emphasis he put on the reasoning process led to his fifth principle, which was that conferences had to be attended by those who actually owned or managed the business. Management had to be exposed to the views of labor, just as labor had to hear the thinking of those in the best position to understand the finances and working of the company. If such exposure did not result in workable compromise, arbitration might have to be tried. Sometimes, however, matters arose that the employer considered so fundamental that arbitration would not work; the union's demands would destroy the business. Then Brandeis's sixth principle would have to be invoked: "Lawless or arbitrary claims of organized labor should be resisted at whatever cost." Brandeis would not defend what he saw as hooliganism, but neither did his condemnation of union violence stem from blindness to its cause. "If labor unions are arbitrary or lawless," he told the assembled employers, "it is largely because employers have ignominiously submitted to arbitrariness or lawlessness as a temporizing policy or under a mistaken belief as to their own immediate interests." Only anarchy would result if law were ignored in either industry or politics. His six rules, "by which alone the labor problem can be satisfactorily solved," concluded Brandeis, were "broad, indeed"; for they were derived from "the eternal principles of LIBERTY, FRATERNITY, JUSTICE, HONOR."[30]

Brandeis's emphasis on law, order, and capitalism (or, as he preferred, small business) was thoroughly conservative. Unions were a force for conservatism, which was defined as the prevention of socialism and of the trusts, both of which were to be avoided because of the way in which they concentrated power. It is no wonder that Boston found him radical or that he was bewildered by its finding him so: he was attempting to preserve Brahmin values and the small business way of life characteristic of nineteenth-century capitalism when Boston had moved into the era of financial trusts and the exploitation of labor.[31]

Brandeis wanted more than conservatism, however, and although it took some time for his ideas to develop, his passionate concern for individual liberty and fulfillment was leading toward the eight-hour work day and the whole new world of worker-participation. Back in 1894 when Brandeis was involved in a crusade to change the way Boston treated its paupers, he had made three points that were rather astonishing coming from a Brahmin putting together his first million dollars: paupers were victims of a system that did not provide them with work; they needed both work and meaningful leisure in order to function as human beings, as well as to provide for themselves; and society had an obligation to solve the problem of pauperism that it had created. "These people are not machines," he told the public officials responsible; "these are human beings . . . [with] emotions, feelings, and interests . . . They should have entertainments, they may be literary, they may be musical." He brought this same view of humanity to the area of labor, and one of the results was his emphasis on the need for a work day of reasonable length. Democracy, education, and self-fulfillment went hand in hand, and all demanded leisure.[32]

It was important that labor make leisure one of its priorities, for "no people ever did or can attain a worthy civilization by the satisfaction merely of material needs, however high these needs are raised . . . The welfare of our country demands that leisure be provided for . . . We need leisure, among other reasons, because with us every man is of the ruling class. Our education and condition of life must be such as become a ruler. Our great beneficent experiment in democracy will fail unless the people, our rulers, are developed in character and intelligence." It was necessary that people live as well as subsist. This meant that they had to have bodily health, which implied "outdoor recreation," as well as mental development, which meant education. And education had to go on throughout life, necessitating leisure: "leisure does not imply merely a time for rest, but free time when body and mind are sufficiently fresh to permit of mental effort." Education could take many forms: classes, listening to political speeches, discussion groups, reading; but for each "freshness of mind is imperative; and to the preservation of freshness of mind a short work day is for most people essential." Normally that meant an eight-hour day. While the working day for "most professions, many positions in business, and some in trades" might reasonably be longer, because those jobs brought the joy that came from development of faculties as well as financial profit, the eight-hour day was the correct norm "in most occupations and for most people" and particularly in "most industrial occupations." As Brandeis admitted, "in the unskilled trades and in many so-called skilled trades" within the industrial world, "the limits of development . . . are soon reached." Although he did not realize it in 1906, when he made that declaration to the Civic Federation of New England, the "limits of development" inherent in industrial jobs would become an intellectual problem for him. Reconciling the individual who spent his or her leisure time reading, engaging in discussion of civic matters, and continuing formal and informal education well into adulthood, with the mindless automaton demanded by the assembly line would become another thread leading him to worker-participation, in which the individual would work at a job that to some extent he or she controlled.[33]

His desire to discover solutions and his hope that others would find it as central a concern as he did led Brandeis to spend much time on the labor problem during the early years of the century. He was immersed in the problem as part of his practice, writing to his brother, "Upon each return to the city some new labor strike looms up requiring immediate attention." He wrote after the successful resolution of a strike in Syracuse, New York, "I am experiencing a growing conviction that the labor men are the most congenial company. The intense materialism and luxuriousness of most of our other people makes their company quite irksome." He not only found that he enjoyed the company of labor leaders; he also began to refine his thinking so that two major ideas emerged. One would prove unpopular with labor, the other with management. The first idea was that the closed shop should be avoided, because nonunion workers in any business would prevent labor from becoming as tyrannical as the employer. Unions, of course, believed they would remain powerless as long as the open shop existed. The germ of the second idea was to be found in his speech to the Boston Central Labor Union: "Labor unions should strive to make labor share all the earnings of a business except what is required for capital and management." "Capital" included shareholders, and Brandeis said that they should be given a fair return on their investment; but once that and the needs of the business itself had been taken care of, anything left over belonged to the workers. Brandeis was working his way toward the idea of profit sharing. As usual, he recognized the need for information if he was to hone his ideas. Thus, in 1907 he joined the newly founded American Association for Labor Legislation, requesting "as promptly as possible the English Bulletin of the International Labor office at Basle."[34]

Brandeis wanted to see a world of small unionized businesses, each operating under conditions that contributed to the self-respect and well-being of both employer and employee, who would work together for the prosperity of the business from which they derived their income. The employer, while in too frequent contact with the workers to forget their humanity, would still be primarily interested in profit, which might lead to the temptation to minimize wages or extend hours; this, however, would be offset by the power of the employees, whose union would concern itself with limiting hours and raising wages. When both sides recognized that the only way to achieve the prosperity about which they cared was to act jointly, they would do so. Enlightened self-interest would then rule. Brandeis was not so naive as to believe that people always behaved virtuously, particularly in the world of business. As Madison had, Brandeis substituted interest for virtue. It was necessary to make each interest equal in power; hence, the need for unionization. But once the interests were equalized—and they would be, if the trusts were broken and competitive small businesses were permitted to flourish—they could be counted upon to fight for themselves.

And fighting for themselves was a necessity, particularly for the workers. Benevolent employers were nice but irrelevant. People had to have control over their own lives if they were to maintain self-respect, and self-respect and dignity were paramount goals. Brandeis had not yet dealt with the problem that a worker able to elect someone to bargain on his or her behalf about hours and wages achieved a measure of economic security and perhaps a vague sense of enhanced power, but did not have much to say about the important company decisions that would affect his or her well-being. Neither was such a worker freed of the mind-stifling demands of the assembly line.

Perhaps Brandeis had not yet dealt with this problem because it took time for the son of a small businessman and the attorney for other small business people to work out what would become a radical approach to the labor problem; or, perhaps, there was an unwillingness to deal with a problem that could be solved only if the Brahmin was convinced that the amorphous entity known as "the workers," with whom he never really came into contact, had the ability to participate intelligently in decision-making. Could there have been a residual trace of social Darwinism in Brandeis—a suspicion that workers remained workers because of lack of intelligence and ability rather than because of circumstance?

Brandeis had grown from the bright youth in Louisville, to the law student and fledgling lawyer enchanted by the sophistication of Boston society, to the more assured and successful attorney who could afford psychologically to criticize and even eschew the Brahmin culture when he felt it ran counter to its intellectual underpinnings, to the concerned citizen whose evolving beliefs led him to fight for a decent life for those who could never hope to become part of Harvard or Boston and all they implied. But to be of Boston, and to take of it what one would—its money, its status, its opportunities for fulfilling work and stimulating conversation—while rejecting some of its mores—its emphasis on material wealth, its concern for social niceties, its smugness—was quite different from rejecting Boston or the idea that most of the world was doomed to remain other-than-Boston. Brandeis's evolving economic views gradually made him anathema to much of Brahmin Boston, but, seen with a wider lens, all that had happened could be likened to a family squabble about such matters as how to treat the servants and what standards of morality should prevail in the family business. Now, however, Brandeis was about to have a whole new series of experiences, and the lessons derived from them would move him from intellectual Brahminism to progressivism and beyond.

8 | The Brandeis Brief

In 1908 Brandeis submitted to the Supreme Court a brief that changed the course of American legal history. The occasion was a case called *Muller* v. *Oregon*. With only a few sentences connecting hundreds of pages of supporting statistics, Brandeis argued for the constitutionality of a state law limiting working hours for women.

> Long hours of labor are dangerous for women primarily because of their special physical organization. In structure and function women are differentiated from men. Besides these anatomical and physiological differences, physicians are agreed that women are fundamentally weaker than men in all that makes for endurance: in muscular strength, in nervous energy, in the powers of persistent attention and application. Overwork, therefore, which strains endurance to the utmost, is more disastrous to the health of women than of men, and entails upon them more lasting injury.
>
> Such being their physical endowment, women are affected to a far greater degree than men by the growing strain of modern industry.
>
> The evil of overwork before as well as after marriage upon childbirth is marked and disastrous.
>
> When the health of women has been injured by long hours, not only is the working efficiency of the community impaired, but the deterioration is handed down to succeeding generations ... The overwork of future mothers thus directly attacks the welfare of the nation.

In order to establish enforceable restrictions upon working hours of women, the law must fix a maximum working day.

We submit that in view of the facts above set forth and of legislative action extending over a period of more than sixty years in the leading countries of Europe, and in twenty of our States, it cannot be said that the Legislature of Oregon had no reasonable ground for believing that the public health, safety, or welfare did not require a legal limitation on women's work in manufacturing and mechanical establishments and laundries to ten hours in one day.

Louis D. Brandeis,
Counsel for State of Oregon

[W]e are of the opinion that it cannot be adjudged that the act in question is in conflict with the Federal Constitution.

Mr. Justice Brewer, for the
Supreme Court of the United States[1]

On February 19, 1903, the state of Oregon passed a law establishing a maximum of ten hours' work a day for women employed in manufacturing, mechanical establishments, and laundries. Joe Haselbock, overseer of Curt Muller's Grand Laundry in Portland, broke the law on September 4, 1905, by requiring Mrs. Elmer Gotcher to work more than ten hours. Muller was charged on September 18, found guilty of the misdemeanor, and fined ten dollars. (The statute provided that violators be fined no less than ten and no more than twenty-five dollars). Muller appealed to the Supreme Court of Oregon, which affirmed his conviction, and then to the Supreme Court of the United States.[2]

When Florence Kelley, the secretary general of the National Consumers' League, and Josephine Goldmark, Brandeis's sister-in-law and Kelley's associate in the league, discovered that the case was to be argued before the United States Supreme Court, they were eager to ensure that the best possible case be made on behalf of maximum hours for women, a cause the league had long espoused. Mrs. Kelley had already decided that the best course of action would be to prove that overwork adversely affected the health and safety of women, and she hoped to present the Court with factual evidence to support that claim. However, while she was out of town, the league made an appointment for her with Joseph H. Choate, a former ambassador to Great Britain and one of the leaders of the New York bar. Although the league thought it would be a great advantage to have such a distinguished advocate representing it in the case, Mrs. Kelley thought Choate would be neither sympathetic nor capable of doing the kind of job she wanted. Much to her relief, Choate refused to take the case. He told Mrs. Kelley and Miss Goldmark that he considered it entirely appropriate that "a big husky Irishwoman should . . . work more than ten hours a day in a laundry if she and her employer so desired." Delighted, Kelley told Goldmark they could now travel to Boston to talk to her first choice, Brandeis.[3]

Kelley was convinced of Brandeis's support for workers' rights, in part because they shared a network of friends active in the field: Elizabeth Glendower Evans, Mary Kenney, and Henry Demarest Lloyd, as well as Josephine Goldmark. When Kelley and Goldmark approached Brandeis in Boston, he agreed to come into the case, provided that Oregon make him its official counsel, and that the league provide him within a fortnight with the kind of extensive documentation he felt he would require. He was particularly insistent that he serve as official counsel, because the official counsel determines the line of argument to be followed and presents it to the Court in both written and oral form. Had Brandeis gone into the case only as an *amicus curiae,* he would not have been permitted to participate in either the oral argument or the decision about how Oregon should organize its case, which was all-important to his strategy. He felt he had to control Oregon's defense, because he was going to attempt a new kind of argumentation (and also, perhaps, because he was more comfortable being in control). He needed a vast collection of facts about the effects of long working hours on women, because that would be the heart of his approach. Both Oregon and the league were pleased to meet his demands. Thus, as of November 14, 1907, Brandeis had a new *pro bono publico* case; Florence Kelley, Josephine Goldmark, her sister Pauline Goldmark (secretary of the New York City Consumers' League), and a few others had the job of combing the Columbia University and New York Public Libraries for every bit of material they could find.[4]

The legal context in which *Muller* v. *Oregon* would be argued was complex. The Fourteenth Amendment to the Constitution prohibits the deprivation by state governments of "life, liberty, or property without due process of law." The Supreme Court had defined the word *liberty* in the due process clause to include liberty of contract and had declared that liberty of contract was violated when the government interfered with the employee-employer relationship. The Court assumed that the employee had not only the liberty to sell his or her labor but the power to negotiate a just bargain with a prospective employer. If this was ever true before the industrial revolution, it was far from the case by 1908 when small mercantile businesses had been replaced by giant corporations, and unionization was in its infancy. Workers in the early part of the twentieth century had the option to take or leave the offer made by employers—but rejecting it frequently meant unemployment. Nonetheless, the Court could see no reason for the government to define for employers and employees the parameters within which they could contract with one another. Limitations on workers' hours were thus seen to violate the liberty of both worker and employer. Of course, should the government be able to demonstrate that such a limitation was directly related to protection of the health or safety of the general public, the Court would uphold the statute. However, the Court had seen no such relationship in a law establishing a maximum ten-hour day for bakers, and lower courts had similarly found no relationship between eight-hour days for women and the public welfare.[5]

"Liberty of contract" had first been enunciated by the Court in *Allgeyer* v. *Louisiana* (1894), which nullified a Louisiana attempt at regulation of marine insurance companies. Justice Rufus W. Peckham wrote for a unanimous Court that the statute violated "the right of the citizen to be free . . . to earn his livelihood by any lawful calling; to pursue any livelihood or avocation, and for that purpose to enter into all contracts which may be proper, necessary and essential to his carrying out to a successful conclusion the purposes above mentioned." (It is noteworthy that what would become the very important "liberty" negating labor legislation is to be found in a case that did not involve workers at all but that resulted from the state's attempt to control insurance contracts.) However, Justice Peckham did not assert that the liberty was absolute; in fact, he said, it was subject to the regulatory powers of the state. Proper exercise of these powers was a matter to be decided by the courts on a case-by-case basis.[6]

Four years later the Court upheld a Utah law limiting miners to an eight-hour work day. Justice Henry B. Brown wrote for the six-judge majority in *Holden* v. *Hardy* (1898) that the Fourteenth Amendment restricted the states' power to act in two areas: those in which a particular group of citizens (for example, nonwhites or women) were singled out, and those in which the state had altered rules governing criminal proceedings. Neither area was involved in *Holden*. What was, as the Utah Supreme Court had held, was a judgment by the legislature "that a limitation is necessary for the preservation of the health of employes, and there are reasonable grounds for believing that such determination is supported by the facts." Brown noted that the Court made no determination as to the legitimacy of other laws regulating hours. He traced the history of the mining industry in the United States and the passage of protective laws in other states as indication that the reasonableness of the Utah statute was clear. Nonetheless, in a portent of things to come, Justices Peckham and David J. Brewer dissented (without an opinion).[7]

Had the Court upheld subsequent hours laws, using *Holden* v. *Hardy* as a precedent, the Brandeis brief might never had been invented. But in *Lochner* v. *New York* (1905) the Court took another tack. Justice Peckham's opinion for a five-judge majority seemed to emulate *Holden*, for it held that if New York had proved its assertion that overly long hours affected the health of bakers or the public, the Court would have validated the statute. However, said Peckham, the state had failed to demonstrate the existence of such dangers, and the law was an arbitrary violation of liberty of contract.[8]

Peckham differentiated the *Lochner* case from *Holden* in a number of ways, including the lack of a provision for "emergencies" in which the statute would not apply (the Utah mining law included such a clause) and the fact that the New York courts had divided on whether baking was unhealthful, whereas the Utah Supreme Court had had no such doubt about mining. But his real concern was that the New York statute represented creeping labor protectionism. Baking was no more unhealthful than lots of other jobs, Peckham declared; in fact, "it might be safely affirmed that almost all occupations more or less affect the health." Indeed, if every occupation that affected health could be regulated, the state could interfere with the hours of "a printer, a tinsmith, a locksmith, a carpenter, a cabinetmaker, a dry goods clerk, a bank's, a lawyer's or a physician's clerk, or a clerk in almost any kind of business . . . No trade, no occupation, no mode of earning one's living, could escape this all-pervading power." In fact, "interference on the part of the legislatures of the several States with the ordinary trades and occupations of the people seems to be on the increase." And Peckham continued, "It is impossible for us to shut our eyes to the fact that many of the laws of this character, while passed under what is claimed to be the police power for the purpose of protecting the public health or welfare, are, in reality, passed from other motives." Such labor legislation would alter the nature of employment in a manner unacceptable to the Court. The Constitution guaranteed workers the right to labor as many hours a day as they chose, and the state could not interfere with that right without proving that intervention was necessary for the public welfare. With this interpretation, five justices showed plainly that they intended to use "liberty of contract" to nullify legislation affecting hours and wages.[9]

Peckham and the colleagues who agreed with him clearly viewed labor legislation *per se* as unconstitutional, whether or not health or welfare was protected by it. Their attitude was based on deeply felt values, which meant that no purely legal argument, however well made, would cause them to change their votes. Justice John Marshall Harlan, writing a dissent for himself and Justices Edward Douglass White and William

Rufus Day, chided, "It may be that the statute had its origin, in part, in the belief that employers and employees in such establishments were not upon an equal footing, and that the necessities of the latter often compelled them to submit to such exactions as unduly taxed their strength . . . Whether or not this is wise legislation it is not the province of the court to inquire." Whatever the motivation, Harlan argued, the state had cited enough experts to support its claim that baking for too many hours was unhealthful and that therefore it was exercising its police power reasonably.[11]

Justice Oliver Wendell Holmes, as usual, was blunter. Thus, in *Lochner,* he scolded, "This case is decided upon an economic theory which a large part of the country does not entertain," that is, the social Darwinist belief that economic and general well-being could be best achieved by lack of government intervention in labor relations. A Constitution, however, "is not intended to embody a particular economic theory . . . It is made for people of fundamentally differing views, and the accident of our finding certain opinions natural and familiar, or novel, and even shocking, ought not to conclude our judgment upon the question whether statutes embodying them conflict with the Constitution of the United States." It was not the Court's role to get in the way of the people of a state when they decided to experiment with a new "truth." This was all the more so because, sooner or later, "every opinion tends to become a law." The words in the Constitution were "perverted" when judges used them "to prevent the natural outcome of a dominant opinion, unless it can be said that a rational and fair man necessarily would admit that the statute proposed would infringe fundamental principles as they have been understood by the traditions of our people and our law." Such could not be said about maximum hours laws; "A reasonable man might think it a proper measure on the score of health." The real question at issue, to Holmes, was "the right of a majority to embody their opinions in law," and it was with this constitutionally protected right that the *Lochner* verdict had interfered.[11]

Clearly, a majority of the Court was hostile to labor legislation. The only hope of getting that majority to sustain a statute was to flood it with such an overwhelming mass of statistics that it would be hard pressed to conclude that the state had not met its burden of proof. A mild attempt at this had been made by Julius M. Mayer, the attorney general of New York, in his brief in *Lochner.* But since the basic problem was the values of the judges rather than the quality of the argument made by counsel, this was not enough. However, if only women were affected by the statute, and if enough data could be presented to make the justices believe that the welfare of the weaker sex lay in their hands, then they could uphold labor legislation without feeling that they had altered employee-employer relations in the real world of men.[12]

Brandeis found three facets of the *Lochner* decision worth noting. The first was that, although the judges were wrong in assuming that workers actually enjoyed liberty of contract in the United States of 1905, the lawyers who argued the case were partly to blame for the judges' ignorance. "The judge came to the bench unequipped with the necessary knowledge of economic and social science, and his judgement suffered likewise through lack of equipment in the lawyers who presented the cases to him. For a judge rarely performs his functions adequately unless the case before him is adequately presented." In order to bring social realities into the courtroom, of course, the lawyer had to know what those social realities were. Brandeis approvingly quoted Charles Henderson, a professor of practical psychology at the University of Chicago, who had said, "One can hardly escape from the conclusion that a lawyer who has not studied economics and sociology is very apt to become a public enemy."[13]

Second, Brandeis noted that the judges had reversed their traditional policy of assuming that legislation was constitutional unless proven otherwise. This violated the notion that the people were best governed by those closest to them and substituted for the judgment of elected legislators that of federal judges who were removed from both social facts and the voice of the people. It also meant, again, that the lawyer defending social legislation in 1908 had to meet the heavy burden of proof now placed on his or her shoulders by the Court.

Finally, Brandeis realized that although judges had systematically struck down social legislation, they had done so because they had seen no relationship between the statutes and public health. Thus, without contesting the rationale that underlay *Lochner* (and it was clear that the 1908 Court was not about to abandon liberty of contract as a principle), a lawyer could argue that a specific law did indeed have an effect on public health. To prove a public health effect with respect to the Oregon law, Brandeis required masses of data on the correlation between hours worked by women and the health of women and their families. The legislative history of the Oregon law provided no such data; the National Consumers' League would have to find it.

Brandeis's approach was particularly suited to a law regulating hours of work for women because social "science" data was available to show that women were indeed the weaker sex. For the first time, Brandeis devoted only two pages of his brief to legal precedents, almost all of them taken from *Lochner* itself. Instead of fighting *Lochner's* assertion of the liberty of contract as a constitutional right, Brandeis cited it as one of his authorities. He also, however, cited *Lochner* to affirm that the right could be abridged by a state in order to protect health, safety, morals, and the general welfare. He reminded the Court of its statement in *Lochner* that "when the validity of a statute is questioned, the burden of proof" is on the questioners, rather than on the state. In the Court's own words, unless it found "no 'fair ground, reasonable in and of itself, to say that there is material danger to the public health (or safety), or to the health (or safety) of the employees (or to the general welfare), if the hours of labor are not curtailed,' " it had to sustain the statute. In other words, unless the Court was ready to say that Oregon had no reasonable basis for concluding that there was danger to health, safety, and welfare unless hours were curtailed, the Court's own logic forced it to sustain the law as constitutional.[14]

That was the sum of Brandeis's legal argumentation—two pages' worth. Then, to prove that Oregon was not alone in its conclusion, Brandeis added fifteen pages of excerpts from state and foreign laws limiting women's hours, noting that in "no instance has any such law been repealed." That completed the first part of the brief. The second, entitled "The World's Experience upon which the Legislation Limiting the Hours of Labor for Women is Based," was ninety-five pages long. It had numerous subtitles ranging from "The Dangers of Long Hours," to "The Reasonableness of the Ten-Hour Day" and "Laundries." Each subtitle introduced a collection of statistics on the point. Under the "Bad Effect of Long Hours on Health," for example, Brandeis quoted from the British *Reports of Medical Commissioners on the Health of Factory Operatives* (1833), testimony before the Massachusetts House, *Reports of* (the Massachusetts) *Commissioners on the Hours of Labor,* a report of the Massachusetts Bureau of Statistics of Labor (1872), the 1873, 1893, 1901, 1903, and 1906 *Reports* of the British Chief Inspector of Factories and Workshops, the 1875 report of the British Factory and Workshops Act Commission, the 1888 Report of the Maine Bureau of Industrial and Labor Statistics, the 1895 Report of the Select Committee on Shops Early Closing Bill of the House of Commons, the 1901 Reports from a similar committee of the House of Lords, the British *Journal of Royal Sanitary Institute* (1904), the German Reports of Factory Inspectors (1905), the French District Inspectors' *Reports upon the Question of Night Work* (1900), Lloyd's *Twentieth Century Practice of Medicine* (1895), the *Journal of the American Medical Association* (1906), and Arlidge's *The Hygiene, Diseases, and Mortality of Occupations* (1892). The quotations were no less copious for any other subsection. In fact, there were relatively few sentences in Part 2 that were not direct quotations. This does not denigrate the amount of work Brandeis did. Describing his oral argument before the Court, which replicated the format of his brief, Josephine Goldmark wrote, "In hours of preparation beforehand, submerging himself first in the source material, he was determining the exclusion or inclusion of detail, the order, the selectiveness, the emphasis which marked his method. Once determined upon, it had all the spontaneity of a great address because he had so mastered the details that they fell into place, as it were, in a consummate whole." Brandeis let the "facts" speak for themselves.[15]

The technique worked. The Court upheld the law and specifically credited Brandeis and his approach. It is rare for the Court to mention an advocate by name, but Justice Brewer, writing the majority opinion for the Court, commented, "It may not be amiss, in the present case, before examining the constitutional question, to notice the course of legislation as well as expressions of opinion from other than judicial sources. In the brief filed by Mr. Louis D. Brandeis . . . is a very copious collection of all these matters, an epitome of which is found in the margin." The marginal note listed the laws Brandeis had cited and mentioned that he had quoted over ninety reports. "It would of course take too much space," Justice Brewer said, "to give these reports in detail," but they could be summed up by one quotation to the effect that women's physiology, maternal role, and homemaking function " 'are all so important and so far-reaching that the need for such reduction [that is, of the working day] need hardly be discussed.' " Justice Brewer denied that constitutional questions could be settled "by . . . a consensus of present public opinion," but admitted that "a widespread and long continued belief" about a question of fact "is worthy of consideration. We take judicial cognizance of all matters of general knowledge."[16]

Brandeis had managed to create an entry to the Court for social facts, making an important impact on both labor legislation and the much larger arena of American law in general. The Court could not admit that that was what had happened in *Muller,* but by praising Brandeis's presentation, it declared publicly that it was ready to be persuaded by compilations of social facts. It thus unwittingly left the door open for precisely what happened in *Bunting* v. *Oregon* in 1917: confronted with a brief of almost a thousand pages of statistics demonstrating that it was reasonable to believe that the general welfare would benefit from limiting the hours of workingmen, the Court found itself accepting the state's (and Brandeis's) claim.[17]

Thus, the import of the *Muller* brief was that lawyers arguing on behalf of labor legislation now knew that if they could get the courts to take "judicial notice" of the social facts that had generated the legislation and to agree that reasonable legislators might well have concluded on the basis of those facts that the statute was wise, they had a chance of saving it. Brandeis had shown them a way to get around the "liberty of contract" stance of *Lochner* and similar decisions without attempting the futile task of getting the judges to back away from their own predilections.

The impact of *Muller* was tremendous. Unions, lawyers, and universities all over the country sent for the National Consumers' League's reprint of the brief and the decision. Illinois promptly reenacted a women's maximum hours law that the Court had struck down in 1895. When the new statute was attacked in court, the league called upon Brandeis to defend it. He did so in a brief of six hundred pages, which included both much of the *Muller* data and additional material from Europe and the British Empire. The women of the league did an incredible amount of work in amassing statistics, and Brandeis acknowledged the importance of the work involved in the collection of data by putting Josephine Goldmark's name on the title page of his brief as his assistant, in spite of the fact that she was not a lawyer. He had wanted to do as much in the *Muller* case, he told her, but decided that he had already made that brief unconventional enough. He and the league won the case before the Illinois Supreme Court. Similar legislation was passed in Virginia, Michigan, and Louisiana, and in 1910 all three were litigated. The league equipped the defense teams involved with their Illinois brief, and all three laws were upheld. In 1912 cases involving maximum hours laws for women were brought in Ohio, California, Washington, and Illinois (which had extended its coverage to women working in mercantile establishments).[18]

Goldmark worked again with Brandeis in defending New York's statute preventing women from being forced to work at night. The Triangle Shirtwaist Factory fire in 1911 had led to a Factory Investigating Commission. In addition to investigating fire hazards and suggesting reforms, it investigated and issued a comprehensive report on the hazards of overwork and night work for women, leading to New York's 1913 statute. Defending it in court, New York's attorney general used much of the commission's report in a Brandeis-type brief. This was not good enough for either Goldmark or Brandeis, who submitted an additional four hundred pages of information containing data drawn from outside New York. When it came to the New York minimum wage case, in which a manufacturer of boxes sought an injunction against an $8.64 minimum wage *per week* for women, Brandeis submitted a brief of two hundred pages. He and Goldmark worked for the six months before his appointment to the Supreme Court on their brief on behalf of the Oregon law setting maximum hours for men; then Brandeis turned over his role with the league to Felix Frankfurter.[19]

If the Brandeis brief placed a new burden on lawyers defending labor legislation, requiring them to learn how to do research among statisticians' reports and sociological tomes as well as in law libraries, it also represented an important step in a new theory of what law was all about and what judges were supposed to do. Brandeis had learned from Christopher Columbus Langdell that the best way to master law was to study actual cases and the opinions judges wrote when deciding them. Statutes represented solutions to factual problems that had arisen at specific historical moments, and if the spirit as well as the wording of any law was to be properly understood, its historical underpinnings had to be examined. The implication for the present was that current law, in order to be both relevant and legitimate, first had to be responsive to current social facts. Thus, laws embodied not eternal truths but views of what the felt necessities of the moment were and opinions about how those necessities should be met. The role of the lawyer was to inform judges of the larger social facts that lay behind any dispute, and to show the judges how to align existing law with those facts.[20]

Dean Roscoe Pound of the Harvard Law School, along with Oliver Wendell Holmes, had been writing the manifestos of what would come to be called sociological jurisprudence, telling the legal world and anyone else who would listen that laws were the product less of logic than of experience and that it would be improper for them to be anything else. That meant to them, as it did to Brandeis, that courts had to exercise a measure of self-restraint in the face of legislative innovation and uphold legislative experimentation unless there was a clear constitutional prohibition against it. Since the Constitution is a collection of undefined generalities that can be read to mean almost anything the reader wishes, the logic of Pound and Holmes's argument meant that judges would have reason to strike down very few attempts at bringing the law into line with social realities. The presumption was that legislation was constitutional.[21]

Brandeis went further, perhaps because, as a practicing attorney, he was faced with getting this new approach to jurisprudence accepted by the courts. If judges rejected the new orthodoxy of sociological jurisprudence, the lawyer had to show the judges how the law at issue could be considered by reasonable legislators as responding to social facts and thus, since the Constitution provided leeway for the "felt necessities," fit within constitutional guidelines. Brandeis was so insistent that intelligent action could follow only after accumulation of facts that the approach was a completely logical one for him, but it was not at all the norm in American law. As he said, "In the past the courts have reached their conclusions largely deductively from preconceived notions and precedents. The method I have tried to employ in arguing cases before them has been inductive, reasoning from the facts."[22]

This was the new sociological jurisprudence espoused by Brandeis. To find out what a law means one must first find out what it should mean, given the current needs of society. Thus, judges had to base their decisions on facts.

But if sociological jurisprudence made demands on judges, it also made demands on lawyers. Brandeis recalled with nostalgia the days when lawyers were generalists, practicing all the kinds of law needed by their communities and participating fully in the political activities around them. They were in daily touch with the community and its changing needs. Moreover, they were the lawyers for diverse elements in society, and "the same lawyer was apt to serve at one time or another both rich and poor, both employer and employee." They thus experienced the needs of all segments of society and could bring their knowledge to the aid of judges.[23]

This had changed with the industrial revolution, the growth of corporations, and corporations' need for attorneys who spent their time doing nothing but working out and defending the corporations' interests. Brandeis deplored this kind of specialization, not only because it confined lawyers to the practice of only one area of law, but because it meant specialization as well in the "character of clientage." Corporation lawyers were ignorant of many aspects of society. Their intense involvement with their professional lives tended to leave them no time for public affairs, "and thus the broadening of view which comes from political life was lost. The deepening of knowledge in certain subjects was purchased at the cost of vast areas of ignorance and grave danger of resultant distortion of judgment." Brandeis himself had made it a point to practice virtually every possible kind of law. His partner Edward McClennen recalled, "the practice which came to him was a general one, unusually diversified. It did not fall into a single class. It broadened rather than narrowed with the lapse of time. He acted for manufacturers, for merchants, for investors, for brokers, for associations of these different ones, for labor unions, for the injured, for the successful, for the unsuccessful, and for benevolent institutions. There was no field not included unless it be in the defense or prosecution of alleged criminals, the department of patents, and admiralty. Even in these unaccustomed fields he worked occasionally." Thus, Brandeis stayed in touch with all segments of the community, and, doing so, was convinced that he understood the society's needs.[24]

Brandeis lived in an age when it was taken for granted that problems could be solved through the application of science, whether the problem was how to build a better automobile, how to treat paupers, how to run schools, or how to make government work. There had to be scientific answers for the problems involved in human relationships, at least those human relationships that interacted with the economic sector. Economists and sociologists had to be drawn into the law-making process, for they were the ones with the scientific facts. When Holmes wrote that "for the rational study of the law the black-letter man may be the man of the present, but the man of the future is the man of statistics and the master of economics," he surely did not realize that the future would go beyond statistics and economics to sociology and psychology. Neither, presumably, did Brandeis, but it was his "Brandeis brief" that led the way. With his wide acquaintance among social workers, reformers, journalists, and academicians, Brandeis was prepared to accept facts from many sources not normally legitimized by American courts. This does not imply that his sources were necessarily as "scientific" as he would have liked to or did believe; certainly, the quality of his data can be questioned when its conclusion is that women are inherently inferior to men. Whatever the state of social science at the time, however, its findings suddenly became part of the legal process.[25]

The Brandeis brief, then, attempted to alter the focus of legal argumentation from Talmudic or Jesuitical treatises on the meaning of legal precedents to collections of social facts designed to educate judges about current needs. It also displayed Brandeis, the lawyer, at his best. Roscoe Pound wrote of the *Muller* brief, "The real point here is not so much his advocacy of these statutes as the breadth of perception and the remarkable legal insight which enable him to perceive the proper mode of presenting such a question." One of the qualities his former partner Edward McClennen saw as contributing to the greatness of Brandeis as a lawyer was "his fertile imagination"; that is amply demonstrated by the creation of the Brandeis brief. Another quality, and one that his partner considered to be "the prime source of his power," was his "intense belief in the truth of what he was saying." Although Brandeis did relatively little litigating as his firm grew, his brilliance in the courtroom surely had much to do with his success in gaining the courts' acceptance of the Brandeis brief. When he argued the minimum wage case before the Supreme Court, a friend wrote to Felix Frankfurter: "I have just heard Mr. Brandeis make one of the greatest arguments I ever listened to, and I have heard many great arguments . . . Holmes is the only one among them [the justices] who had any of the light of the morning left, but even he joined in bombarding the deaf and dumb man who spoke before Brandeis. When Brandeis began to speak, the Court showed all the inertia and elemental hostility which Courts cherish for a new thought, or a new right, or even a new remedy for an old wrong, but he visibly lifted all this burden, and without orationizing or chewing of the rag he reached them all . . . He not only reached the Court, but he dwarfed the Court . . . It was so clear that something had happened in the Court today that even Charles Henry Butler [the Court reporter] saw it and he stopped me afterwards on the coldest corner in town to say that no man this winter had received such close attention from the Court as Brandeis got today." Frankfurter, sending a copy of the letter to Brandeis, commented, "I wish I had heard it." Assistant U.S. Attorney-General Charles Warren told the *Boston Herald* that Brandeis's argument was "one of the most eloquent pleas heard in the supreme court room for a long time. And it was as logical and powerful as it was eloquent. It held the closest attention of the justices from start to finish and others in the court room were almost spellbound." When Brandeis's allotted hour and a half ran out, the chief justice took the highly unusual step of telling him the Court would give him the extra time needed to complete his argument. On another occasion, a lawyer commented about a hearing, "It began in the habitual way but it had not gone far before, as usual, Brandeis was in full command by common consent."[26]

What excited Brandeis about the law was not outmoded principles but the possibilities for experimentation, for growth, for making truly lasting principles live in new social circumstances. In 1911 he sent Norman Hapgood a quotation from Goethe's *Faust*:

> All rights and laws are still transmitted
> Like an eternal sickness of the race—
> From generation unto generation fitted
> And shifted round from place to place.

A year later he wrote to Hapgood, "In connection with the Goethe quotation on the laws which I sent to you last year, you will be interested (if perchance you do not already know it) in the following of Lowell's

> 'New times demand new issues and new men,
>   The world advances, and in time outgrows the laws
> That in our father's time were best;
>   And, doubtless, after us some purer scheme
> Will be shaped out by wiser men than we,—
>   Made wiser by the steady growth of truth.' "

Or, as Brandeis stated more mundanely to the Supreme Court, "In view of the facts above . . . it cannot be said that the Legislature of Oregon had no reasonable ground for believing that the public health, safety or welfare did not require a legal limitation on women's work . . . to ten hours in one day."[27]

Although they rejoiced in the labor victory, the actual Court decision could not be comforting to feminists, because it classified women as weak, dependent, and subordinate. Women were not merely different; they were both different and "not upon an equality." Therefore, "without questioning in any respect the decision in Lochner v. New York," the Court upheld the Oregon law. The damage done to the status, self-image, and independence of women under the guise of "protective legislation" is incalculable. Preventing women from being forced to work in steamy, airless laundries for more than ten hours a day in order to earn a bare subsistence wage is not the same as upholding a state law preventing women from becoming lawyers, but the objection to protective legislation in principle does not change. Brandeis's motivation thus must be understood in light of the very factor he would consider most important: the social facts.[28]

The major social facts, of course, were industrialization, urbanization, growing concentration of capital, the appalling condition of labor, and the subjection of women laborers to particularly low paid and onerous employment. Small wonder, then, that such determined suffragettes as Kelley and Goldmark would welcome the opportunity to set a precedent allowing states to pass legislation that sought to redress, however minimally, the balance between labor and employers. Much of the data in the *Muller* brief applied to both men and women, although obviously the emphasis there was on the way women were affected by overly long hours. Josephine Goldmark turned up much data that Brandeis did not consider appropriate for inclusion in the brief, largely because it showed that the sex of the worker did not alter the fact that he or she was adversely affected by excessive hours of labor. Hoping that it could be used to encourage maximum hours laws for both men and women, Brandeis successfully urged the Russell Sage Foundation to publish all of her findings, "accompanied by a proper introductory essay and copious indices." The foundation did so, producing a book entitled *Fatigue and Efficiency* in 1912. Thus, Brandeis made a tactical decision to emphasize only those "facts" that would speak to the values of the Court at that time. However, Brandeis himself was becoming increasingly aware of the equal value and responsibility of women as citizens.[29]

In 1910 Brandeis accepted appointment to the Association for Labor Legislation's Commission on Women's Work. His appointment was logical, for by then Brandeis had won in *Muller*. What might seem less logical, given Brandeis's early speechmaking against women's suffrage, was his enrollment in the cause of female political equality. Actually, it was quite logical, for a man who learned more from experience than from books and who found himself surrounded by strong female colleagues.

Brandeis's friend Elizabeth Glendower Evans threw herself into numberless reform causes, introducing Brandeis to interesting people like Mary Kenney whom she met along the way. His wife's sister Josephine Goldmark, the consumer activist, was responsible for his participation in the Oregon women's hours case. After working with Goldmark on *Muller,* he wrote to her, "I count it among the best fruits of our joint work, that we have had you with us so much, and that the children have had the rare privilege of your noble presence. It must prove an inspiration to them." In his office he had the example of Alice Grady, the secretary-become-Insurance Commissioner, and Louise Malloch, who began as a secretary but who was so trusted by Brandeis that he gradually gave her control over his extensive investments. Jane Addams was one of the strong, reform-minded women he had come to admire, and he gladly presided over a meeting of the Boston Equal Suffrage Association at which she was the main speaker.[30]

Brandeis thus saw strong women at work, but his involvement in industry also showed him the particular powerlessness of women. He described his experiences in 1912:

I came to the conclusion after a good deal of effort in that direction that if we were to improve the working condition of the people, it would have to be done by the people themselves, and in the effort to give the people this opportunity I found that the large part of those who needed it most were women workers, because they were less experienced, less protected by organization and because the demands of industry bore more heavily on them. I saw they needed not only protection but a knowledge of affairs. They needed much to uplift them out of the smallness and trivialities of life, and I saw that nothing would be more potent in that direction than the privilege of the ballot. Women often have greater opportunities than men to bring about social reform, for which all of us are working. They have the desire, enthusiasm and understanding. I learned much from them in my work. So from having been of the opinion that we would advance best by leaving voting to the men, I became convinced that we needed all the forces of the community to bring about this advance.

He applauded the efforts of the National Women's Trade Union League's monthly journal, *Life and Labor,* "in presenting the story of the working woman, and in putting before the working woman and the general public the need of organization of the women workers."[31]

He did not think of women's suffrage as a gift. On the contrary, he stated that "much that is required to be done to improve social and industrial conditions can be done only with women's aid. We cannot relieve them from the duty of taking part in public affairs." Women, in other words, had the same obligation to be good citizens as men. And because men's obligations as citizens required their participation in the causes they believed just, Brandeis added his voice to those openly calling for women's suffrage.[32]

As usual, Brandeis retained his own perspective when embracing a cause and would not go as far in extolling the expected virtues of women's suffrage as some of its supporters would have had him do. Asked by Alice Stone Blackwell—the suffragette, peace activist, and editor—for his comments on why there would be fewer wars if women voted, Brandeis replied, "Of course I am strongly in favor of women voting, but I am not so sure that votes for women would make an important difference in the frequency of wars. The causes of war lie I think far deeper than the absence of the franchise for women." Nevertheless, he agreed to act as a judge, along with Jane Addams and suffragette Carrie Chapman Catt, of a contest sponsored by Alice Stone Blackwell's *The Women's Journal* for a design to become the symbol of the suffrage movement. When asked on another occasion for a statement of support, Brandeis emphasized that he had learned from experience: "My own experience in various movements . . . converted me . . . The insight which women have shown into problems that men did not and perhaps could not understand, has convinced me not only that women should have the ballot, but that society demands that they exercise the right."[33]

His older daughter, Susan, graduated from Bryn Mawr and determined to spend a year campaigning for women's suffrage. Her father joined in, emphasizing to audiences at Boston's Tremont Temple and Fanueil Hall that his support was the result of his experiences with the political talent demonstrated by women involved in causes he shared. He felt that women had a particular right to share in the determination of the conditions under which their children, as well as they themselves, would live, and that they had a concomitant duty to bear responsibility for those conditions. Both right and duty necessitated the vote.[34]

Alice Brandeis was apparently converted to the cause as Brandeis was—through meeting admirable women. The only time she broke her rule about remaining a private person came in 1913, when she gave the *Boston American* an interview and permitted it to photograph her for a long Sunday article on suffrage. "I have followed the movement in several States for seven or eight years," she was quoted as saying, "and I know that such women as Jane Addams and Florence Kelley have taken up the suffrage stand because they feel that it is the only way now to accomplish certain reforms for women and children." Answering the contention that "woman's place is in the home, not at the polls," she said, "The home argument can hardly be used effectively to influence anyone who knows that there are more than 6,000,000 women wage earners in the United States today. If in business why not in politics?" She tied the vote to women's activities in a way that carried echoes of her husband but was slightly different: "The social philosophy of the past has been a failure; the laissez faire notion that things will come out all right if not interfered with is nonsense. Women have been for years the constructive philanthropists and now that governments are taking up the social side of economics, the women must, as the only logical conclusion, be made a part of the government." And she added, "We are not going to change human nature all at once, but I do think that women would array themselves very definitely upon vital ethical matters like temperance and schools, about which they feel strongly . . . They could do things here in Massachusetts that the men as a whole have neglected." At the same time she deplored the "militant methods" of the English suffragettes, while acknowledging that they were "thoroughly in earnest" and that their tactics "represent the sacrifice and martyrdom of many a well bred and delicately nurtured woman." The fact that the daughters raised by the Brandeises were encouraged to become respectively a lawyer and an economist in the days when "ladies" did not adopt professions is evidence that Brandeis's commitment to female equality was practiced at home as well as preached in public.

It was, of course, political and economic equality that concerned him; as a Progressive, he was a supporter of suffrage, not a feminist. His brief in *Muller* v. *Oregon* is sufficient proof of his belief that protective laws for women were good, and his emphasis on women's special role in determining the environment of children indicates the way he would have spoken, had he been asked, about motherhood. But no one asked him, nor would they have had any reason to; the suffrage movement ended for him, and for most of its supporters, with the passage of the Nineteenth Amendment in 1920.[35]

9 | Progressivism

Brandeis arrived at New York's Harvard Club on January 12, 1910; he emerged two weeks later. During that time he sat alone in his bedroom, surrounded by mountainous stacks of books, documents, memoranda, and letters. Occasionally, he would journey to the dining room, where, at various times during the day, he could be found thoughtfully snacking on shredded wheat, grapes, mutton chops, or hot chocolate. Then he would return to his room and the period of isolated study that was designed to familiarize him completely with the workings of the Department of the Interior, conservation, public land laws, the vocabulary of land management, and the geography of Alaska. When he felt he had mastered names, dates, figures, and concepts, he took the train down to Washington, and to instant national fame as counsel for *Collier's Weekly* in the Pinchot-Ballinger affair.[1]

Gifford Pinchot was a leading Progressive and one of Theodore Roosevelt's tutors in conservation. He served as chief forester of the Department of Agriculture during Theodore Roosevelt's administration, built up the Forestry Service, and made conservation a national issue. In 1908 when Richard A. Ballinger was running the Land Office, the Morgan-Guggenheim syndicate had sought to gain control of five thousand acres of coal and timber land in Alaska. Louis R. Glavis, then in his early twenties, was the Land Office's Seattle field agent. Disturbed by his suspicion that the government-owned lands were being improperly clearlisted (the first step in turning over control to a private group), Glavis communicated with Ballinger, who dismissed his fears—but, shortly thereafter, Ballinger resigned and went to work for the syndicate. Then in 1909 William Howard Taft appointed him Interior Secretary, and Ballinger announced in August that certain coal fields in Alaska (the "Cunningham Claims") were up for sale. As these had been taken off the market by Roosevelt in the name of conservation, Glavis was led to believe that the Taft administration would undo Roosevelt's conservation effort. He again went to Ballinger, who again brushed him off. Glavis then turned to Pinchot, still chief forester.

Pinchot had his own suspicions about Taft's lack of commitment to conservation, and his battles with Ballinger had gained national publicity. Pinchot, therefore, advised Glavis to go directly to Taft. Glavis did so, interrupting Taft's golfing at the Beverly, Massachusetts summer White House to give him extensive documentation to support the charges of misdoing. Taft asked for Ballinger's response, which was presented in a 730-page report on September 6. Taft spent much of September 6 and 7 reading the report and conferring with Ballinger and Oscar Lawler, an assistant attorney general assigned to the Interior Department who had accompanied Ballinger to Beverly. Taft then asked Attorney General George Wickersham to investigate and report on the matter. Wickersham submitted a 74-page report six days later. The result was a letter from Taft to Ballinger on September 13, authorizing Glavis's dismissal "for filing a disingenuous statement, unjustly impeaching the official integrity of his superior officers."[2] Taft also wrote to Pinchot, asking him to drop the matter, and wrote again to Ballinger, warning him to keep Pinchot's name out of public discussion of the issue. Taft was concerned that Pinchot's credibility with conservationists might undermine his own.

However, the outraged Glavis arranged to have his report read by Norman Hapgood, editor of Collier's Weekly. The report was published by Collier's on November 13, under the title "The Whitewashing of Ballinger." The cover of the magazine showed a picture of Ballinger in the clutches of a grasping hand and asked the question "Are the Guggenheims in charge of the Department of the Interior?" A hue and cry of course followed, and it became clear that the only possible result was a congressional investigation. Collier's learned that the special investigating committee would be stacked with Taft men and that a libel suit against Collier's might be brought at the conclusion of the hearings. In response to a demand from the Senate, the major parties to the dispute had submitted documents. Pinchot included a letter attacking the firing of Glavis and declaring that the issue went beyond conservation to the question of an honest and democratic government. Taft responded by firing Pinchot. Clearly, the hearings were going to be volatile. Concerned that Glavis, Pinchot, and Collier's would all need solid legal representation at the hearings, Hapgood called a strategy meeting at which it was decided that *Collier's* would retain Brandeis as its attorney in the matter for $25,000 and expenses. Shortly thereafter, Brandeis settled in at the Harvard Club for his course of study.[3]

The congressional committee consisted of four Republican senators, two Democratic senators, four Republican representatives, and two Democratic representatives. Republican senator Knute Nelson of Minnesota, the chairman, proved to be anti-Pinchot, anti-Glavis, and, above all, anti-Brandeis, repeatedly refusing Brandeis's demands for relevant documents and addressing such nasty comments to him that even the stacked committee was embarrassed. The hearing room was always packed, primarily with the press and the principals' families. The latter became increasingly vocal as the hearings progressed, shouting comments and cheering and hissing. Brandeis evoked amusement by bringing his papers in the green flannel bag he had used at Harvard, but little else about the hearings was lighthearted. They began on January 26, 1910, and closed on May 20, lasting from 10 A.M. until 5 P.M. with only a short break for lunch. They were highlighted by a great deal of vitriolic language, frayed tempers, outbursts of rage, legal theatrics, and, for Brandeis, detective work and dramatic "courtroom" exposures.[4]

It was obvious from the start that the committee would not be convinced by anything he proved, but that the public might be. So Brandeis played to the press, much to the annoyance of the committee and of his adversaries. Ballinger's lawyer, John J. Vertrees, accused him of it; so did Senator Nelson. Brandeis was unperturbed. Each evening he and the Washington correspondents of various newspapers would meet in his room at the Hotel Gordon, and he would explain to them what he considered important in the day's testimony and why. The newsmen in turn gave him whatever information they picked up. *Collier's* of course cooperated closely, taking his suggestions for articles and sending him proofs of editorials for his comments. Indeed, the journalists made Brandeis's reputation by drawing verbal pictures of his methods for their readers. Describing the repeated attacks upon him by the Republican senators, the *Boston Journal* correspondent wrote, "After each attempt, Mr. Brandeis bobs to the surface with a smile that is the most exasperating facial expression ever encountered by a discontented body of men. Instead of soothing the ruffled feelings of the men before whom he is trying his case, Brandeis deliberately continues to rub the fur the wrong way." The *New York Tribune,* which appears not to have been among Brandeis's admirers, added to the picture:

He finds the weakness of an opposing witness with unerring accuracy and plays upon it. With some he uses a robust voice, shouting his questions in tones which completely upset the unfortunate on the witness stand. With others, not to be discomfited by thunderous tones, he puts his questions in an oily insinuating tone calculated to arouse the anger of the witness and cause rage to blind him to the purpose of the questions. And, finally, Brandeis possesses the rare sense of knowing when to stop . . . when he has exasperated the members of the committee to the extreme limit of their endurance he grows gentler than a suckling dove and more persuasive than a second-hand clothes dealer trying to sacrifice himself to give you a bargain.[5]

It was the newspapers that helped produce the single most important piece of information used by Brandeis. In the course of the hearings, he became convinced that the seventy-four-page memorandum Attorney General Wickersham had prepared for Taft, and on the basis of which Taft supposedly made his decision to exonerate Ballinger and order the firing of Glavis, could not have been written as early as the date on which Taft claimed to have read it, and so it must have been fraudulently predated. Brandeis examined Wickersham's activities during the time he was reportedly writing the memorandum; Wickersham had clearly been too busy with other matters to read Ballinger's report of more than half a million words, digest all the relevant material, and write the memorandum. He hammered away at this theme in questioning various administration officials and noted their discomfort, but the committee blocked his attempts to subpoena the documents that might have proved his point. Brandeis was furious. He now believed that he was fighting not only to save the reputation of Glavis, an honest and mistreated public servant, but to uncover deception at the highest levels of government.

His brother Alfred, reading the newspaper accounts of Brandeis's increasingly acrimonious exchanges about the documents with committee members and Ballinger's lawyer, wrote to ask whether Brandeis had not better lower his tone. Brandeis replied, "Your remarks are entirely pertinent—but I think not sound. There is nothing for us to do but to follow the trail of evil wherever it extends . . . In the fight against special interest we shall receive no quarter and may as well make up our minds to give none. It is a hard fight. The man with the hatchet is the only one who has a chance of winning in the end. This chance is none too good. There is a chance—but a chance merely—that the people will now reverse all history and be able to control. The chance is worth taking, because there is nothing left for the self-respecting man to do." He was positive he was right about the predating. "Wickersham & White House continue their silence which confirms our conclusions, I think." He not only knew what Wickersham was doing when he was supposed to be writing his memorandum; he had compiled, largely from newspaper accounts, a day-by-day and almost hour-by-hour account of the movements of Ballinger, Wickersham, and Taft during the period in question. But he still lacked absolute proof that Taft had not studied the facts before clearing Ballinger of the charge of working for outside interests.[6]

One of the thousands of people following the hearings was Frederick M. Kerby, a twenty-four-year-old stenographer in the Interior Department. Kerby knew that Taft had made his decision on the basis of a short memorandum prepared by Assistant Attorney General Lawler, rather than on the basis of either the Ballinger or the Wickersham report; in fact, it was Lawler, rather than Taft, who had written much of Taft's letter exonerating Ballinger. Lawler had done so in consultation with Ballinger and had made sure that every scrap of the draft letter had been burned. Kerby had told his story to James Garfield, the former interior secretary, and had repeated it to Brandeis. But neither Brandeis nor Garfield felt he could urge Kerby to repeat the story in public because it would clearly cost him his job. The committee continued to refuse Brandeis's requests for the Lawler memorandum, however, and Kerby felt pangs of conscience. After agonizing with his wife about the proper course of action, he took his tale to a reporter. A newspaper syndicate thereupon decided it wanted the story so badly that it promised Kerby a job if he lost his position, and on May 14 the newspapers blazed his account. Wickersham immediately "found" Lawler's memorandum and gave it to the committee, saying it had previously been overlooked. He did so, however, without notifying either Ballinger or Taft. As soon as Kerby's story broke in the newspapers Ballinger rushed to the White House and managed to get Taft, then in Chevy Chase, on the telephone. Together, they agreed to issue a press release branding Kerby's tale a lie and maintaining that the president had written the letter himself after a thorough examination of the documents. The press, however, had already carried the story of Wickersham's admission. Taft issued another statement, attempting to make light of the deception, but the damage had obviously been done.

Neither the administration nor the committee could believe that Brandeis had uncovered the deception through the meticulous gathering of facts. How could he have known, as he had demonstrated he did in cross-examining Ballinger, exactly what train Ballinger had taken to Beverly, the name of his hotel, with whom the president was playing golf when Ballinger arrived in Beverly, where Lawler had been when, and so on? Members of the committee finally asked if he had had detectives following the principals. Brandeis then explained his "perfectly simple way" of combing newspapers so as to gather "what appears to be very extraordinary intimate knowledge." Brandeis had proved once again, to himself and others, the importance of marshaling one's facts. Norman Hapgood later reminisced in his autobiography that the only person other than Brandeis who came to understand all the intricacies of the affair and of the workings of the Interior Department was a civil servant named Finney, who appeared as a witness for Ballinger. Brandeis cross-examined Finney, after which the latter walked over to Hapgood and exclaimed, "Mr. Hapgood, I have no respect for you. I think you are doing this to make circulation for your paper. But I want to say you have a wonderful lawyer. He knows the business of the department today as well as I do."[7]

Brandeis was frequently angry during the five-month-long hearing, but he enjoyed the courtroom-like battle nonetheless. He wrote to his mother-in-law about the hearing, "The people are led to think about conservation, are learning what it means; and the investigation must prove a very helpful education." He was charmed by Glavis, whose phenomenal memory was the equal of his own. Brandeis described Glavis as "an extraordinary witness. Have never seen his equal . . . Der junge Mensch is only 26." Glavis was particularly adept at answering whatever was asked of him and then adding, "I wish to explain my answer"—thus getting whatever information he considered important into the record. Brandeis's special courtroom skills emerged in cross-examination. When Vertrees, Ballinger's counsel, put Adolph Behrens, a Seattle real estate speculator, on the stand, Brandeis cross-examined him so mercilessly that his memory failed, and he was then shown to be connected with fraudulent Alaskan land claims. Brandeis wrote cheerfully to Alfred, "I hope our last 2 days of Ballinger hearings were well reported. The enemy fell into every trap set . . . But no report can give you an adequate idea of our fun on X-ex of Vertrees first witness, Adolph Behrens . . . Keith's Continuous Vaudeville couldn't compete a minute." After the hearings ended Brandeis returned to Boston to work with George Rublee, one of his associates, on the written brief Glavis would submit to the committee. He exulted to Alfred, "I am in excellent shape. Everybody seems to say: 'Was der lebt noch?' [Is he still alive?], but for a man who would rather fight than eat, the surprise is unwarranted."[8]

Brandeis went back to Washington to elaborate upon the brief to the committee. The issue, to him, was democracy. "The loyalty that you want is loyalty to the real employer, to the people of the United States. This idea that loyalty to an immediate superior is something commendable when it goes to a forgetfulness of one's country involves a strange misconception of our government and a strange misconception of what democracy is . . . We are not dealing here with a question of the conservation of natural resources merely: it is the conservation and development of democracy; it is the conservation of manhood. This is what this fight into which Glavis enters most unwillingly means. That is what the disclosure which Kerby made most unwillingly means. It proves that America has among its young men, happily, men of courage." Had it not been for the courageous men involved and the public spirit of the press, "there would have been done in this country an act of injustice as great as that done Alfred Dreyfus in the Republic of France, and for very similar reasons. The reason here is that the men in exalted station must be protected at all hazards, and if they cannot be protected by truth then suppression and lies must be resorted to."[9]

In fact, Brandeis found the lies, coupled with his ability to uncover them, useful. In a comment to Norman Hapgood that might lead today's readers to think of Watergate, he said, "It was the lying that did it. If they had brazenly admitted everything, and justified it on the ground that Ballinger was at least doing what he thought best, we should not have had a chance. Refusal to speak the truth is the history of many a downfall." He was sincerely outraged by the lies nonetheless, and even more so by what he regarded as Taft's misuse of office.[10]

Not surprisingly, the committee voted 7 to 5 to exonerate the administration (with two strong minority reports). Brandeis, having expected the result, was undisturbed by it and certain that he could count upon the press to keep up the fight. He sent hundreds of copies of the brief to newspapers and magazines and urged action upon those who were with him. To Ray Stannard Baker, for example, who had written about Taft in the July 1910 issue of the *American Magazine,* he sent a letter calling the article "an admirable piece of work" that "must do much to make his character clear to our people. I should like very much to have your supplemental interpretations of Taft's acts in connection with ante-dating of the Attorney General's report and the suppression of the Lawler draft of letter . . . Under separate cover a copy of our brief goes to you." He told Finley Peter Dunne, also on the staff of the *American,* "As I said to you the other evening, your interpretation of the Pinchot-Ballinger controversy would aid immensely in securing a proper understanding of it by Americans. You said that you found difficulty in getting at the facts. I am therefore taking the liberty of sending you a copy of our brief, and have also asked the Clerk of the Committee to send you a copy of the oral arguments."[11]

The Pinchot-Ballinger affair confirmed for Brandeis that the press was not merely useful to him; it was an absolute necessity in a democratic system. *Collier's* magazine had originally printed Glavis's story, the popular press had printed daily reports about the hearings; the Scripps-Howard chain had offered Kerby a job and got his story out. In spite of the committee's vote, the press reports had stirred public criticism of Ballinger, and on March 7, 1911, after the hearings had ended, Ballinger resigned. He was succeeded on March 13 by Walter L. Fisher, a lawyer active in public causes and one of Brandeis's friends. Brandeis wrote to him, "My dear Walter: I am simply delighted . . . It is great to have Ballinger out, and of much greater reason for congratulations to have you come in. Now we shall have real conservation." Henry L. Stimson, who had taken no active role in the affair since the meeting at which Brandeis became the lawyer for *Collier's,* wrote to him in June, "I am rejoiced to see the way in which sober second considerations . . . by the public and the press—tend more and more to vindicate Mr. Glavis and to substantiate the justice of his position." Brandeis believed that he had won the public battle, and that the press had been his irreplaceable ally. Moreover, thanks to the national publicity he received, he had become the nation's most famous lawyer.[12]

The affair also turned Brandeis's attention to what was for him a new area of concern—natural resources—and brought him a new friend and ally—Senator Robert La Follette. Brandeis had been invited to the La Follette home when he arrived in Washington on January 25, 1910, the day before the Pinchot-Ballinger hearings were scheduled to begin. Elizabeth Glendower Evans, who was a mutual friend, had spoken so highly of the men to each other that there were no formalities, and the two immediately began an unaffected and warm relationship that grew to encompass their families. La Follette was intensely interested in the Pinchot-Ballinger proceedings, Mrs. La Follette went to the hearings every morning, and Brandeis dropped in at the La Follettes' frequently to discuss what was going on. He soon had a standing invitation for dinner.[13]

Before leaving Washington in 1910, Brandeis sent Belle La Follette a bouquet of roses. She wrote in her thank you letter, "Every day since you left Washington I have thought I would write you—not just to thank you for the roses which were indeed lovely and lasted a long, long time, but to tell you how much we missed you, and how glad we were that this had brought you to us. The other day Robert said: 'Mother, I believe I like Mr. Brandeis the best of any one we know.' Then he qualified it— 'Of course not better than Mr. Steffens but better than almost any one else.' And that is the way we all feel."[14]

Brandeis and La Follette shared a variety of interests. Both loved horses; both were concerned with the public interest; both vehemently opposed the trusts; both approached all policy issues by accumulating masses of facts. Their personal relationship became one of great warmth; however, they disagreed about some aspects of domestic policy. La Follette was more interested than Brandeis in such "direct democracy" reforms as the initiative, referendum, and judicial recall. Brandeis felt the existing machinery of government would prove sufficiently democratic if the devices by which special interests put it to their own uses were eliminated. Otherwise, however, they were in complete agreement about the evils of the trusts and worked together to pass antitrust legislation. The other issue on which they were completely united was that of public control of land.[15]

Ballinger's replacement by Walter Fisher in March 1911 did not immediately quiet concern about Alaska's future. The *Philadelphia North American* of April 20, 1911, charged that on October 28, 1910 (after the Pinchot-Ballinger investigation had ended), President Taft had granted sole rights to Controller Bay, Alaska, to the same Morgan-Guggenheim syndicate that had been at issue in Pinchot-Ballinger. Controller Bay was an outlet from the Alaskan coal fields to the sea, and the only other outlet from the Bering coal fields, Cordova Bay, was already in the hands of the Morgan-Guggenheim group. La Follette immediately introduced a congressional resolution calling for a complete investigation, and Secretary Fisher promised to comply with the request and to do whatever was necessary to prevent a monopoly of control.[16]

It seemed as if once again the "interests" had been at work and President Taft involved in another cover-up. Myrtle Abbott, an enterprising young journalist, charged that a postscript to a letter to Ballinger from a purported representative of the syndicate said that Charles Taft had gone to his brother at the behest of the syndicate and that Taft's prosyndicate decision followed. When her story appeared in a number of newspapers, Interior Department officials of course looked for the damning letter, which, mysteriously, could not be found.[17]

A House Investigating Committee, chaired by Representative James M. Graham, requested that Brandeis be counsel, and Brandeis conducted his usual thorough investigation. But eventually, he and Secretary Fisher each concluded that although Taft had withdrawn 12,800 acres on Controller Bay from the Chugah National Forest and had opened the land for bidding by the Controller Railway and Navigation Company (supposedly the "front" for the Morgan-Guggenheim interests), he had neither acted illegally nor, as far as could be ascertained, conspired directly or indirectly with the syndicate. Fisher made various recommendations about control of the land, causing the syndicate to withdraw its claims, and the matter died down.[18]

Before the affair ended, however, Brandeis had recognized that the real question was not what had or had not been done with a relatively small part of Alaska, but how policy about the huge territory was to be made. He therefore turned himself into an expert on land development in general and Alaska in particular. On August 2, 1911, he wrote to the librarian of Congress, asking for a bibliography of Alaska "if it exists," or at least "a list of all the government publications on the subject." He collected maps and reports. He compiled information on Alaska's railroads, wagon roads, trails, soil, independent coal operators, telegraph and telephone systems, and harbor facilities—everything in short, that might be necessary before developing a comprehensive policy. In addition, he had reporter John Lathrop sent to Alaska by the *Portland Evening Journal* to gather "authentic and recent information"; eventually Gifford Pinchot went as well. Secretary Fisher decided to see Alaska for himself, spending two months canoeing and sledding over the disputed territory with fifty journalists clamoring in his wake. Fisher and Brandeis came to much the same conclusions as to what should be done, which accounted for the disappearance of the matter from the public view.[19]

Brandeis had obviously been thinking about Alaska earlier, for on July 29, long before the results of all his inquiries and researches were in, he sent La Follette a lengthy letter outlining his ideas and summarizing a discussion the two men had had two days before. In it Brandeis took note of the "vastly rich" nature of the territory and attributed the fact that most of it still remained in government hands partly to the efforts of Roosevelt, Garfield, Pinchot, and Glavis, but more importantly to its inaccessibility and the difficulties and costs involved in developing it. Inaccessibility and government ownership would no longer provide sufficient protection, however, for more and more people were becoming interested in its development, and it was proper for them to do so: "The people of the United States are entitled to begin to get the benefit and the comfort of a reduction in the cost of living which will come from the utilization of Alaska's treasures." Those who had moved to Alaska were similarly entitled "to exercise to the full the opportunities which their own courage and self-sacrifice ought to open to them." Brandeis was impressed by the hardiness shown by the pioneers, but he was even more concerned about the general welfare. That welfare would best be served by development of Alaska, which in turn depended upon a transportation system and utilities. It was of the utmost importance that they be developed by the government: "Development of transportation and other facilities by the capitalists would, in a way, seriously impair development, because to give them a return which would seem to them adequate would entail rates which would be oppressive to the people of Alaska, and would, in themselves, tend to retard development and the opening up of opportunities to the sturdy, courageous men who are willing to take up their residence in the territory . . . The money raised by the people can be raised at less than three per cent interest."[20]

Brandeis was concerned that there be no repetition of the pattern he had seen in twentieth-century New England, that is, control of transportation and utilities by the "capitalists." It is interesting to note how Brandeis, convinced capitalist, hurled that title in opprobium at others of whose activities he disapproved. The small businessman, to Brandeis, was always a businessman, never a "capitalist," a word with which he described those who used other people's capital to undermine economic democracy. In addition to charging too much, capitalists would gradually squeeze out small independent operators, "and we would have in the most aggravated form the system of discrimination and rebates and corruption which have characterized the worst period of our railroad operation." Drawing on his experience with state legislatures, Brandeis predicted that local officials would provide no protection, but "would prove helpless against the pressure and power of the capitalists."[21]

Brandeis wanted to keep speculation, not development, out of Alaska. "There is no justification whatever in allowing capitalists, as such, who are not developing Alaska, to secure large tracts of its land." The government therefore had to "protect from the grasp of the capitalists" coal mines, other mines (Alaska had already been found to contain valuable minerals), "and to a large extent other properties. In other words, we must devise some system by which those who are willing to go to Alaska, with a view to working there and developing its resources, shall have not only the assurance of fair treatment, but the opportunity of operating without undue oppression through monopolistically inclined competitors." The system he suggested was government ownership of land under conditions which "should be extremely liberal in the terms which it gives to those who use the property. Only an extremely small return, at least for a long period in the future should be required . . . Our obligation to the Alaskans is to give them, and to all newcomers liberal and equal opportunities, to make what their brains and character entitle them to." Initially the government might have to do more than accept ownership of all transportation and utilities. It might even be necessary for the government to operate the coal mines and to run a line of steamships between Alaska and Seattle. But these actions should be resorted to for only a short period of time, and there should never be extensive government mining; however, "government ownership of a mine there would always be valuable as a regulator, and particularly valuable as an experiment station to instruct the government as to the conditions and terms upon which the vast coal fields should be leased." As soon as the government set up a minimal transportation system, it could offer leases for further development on terms that would attract private enterprise.[22]

The two groups of people about whom Brandeis was concerned, then, were Americans in general, for whose benefit Alaskan resources should be administered, and Alaskan pioneers. Government ownership of resources should protect the first group. The interests of the second group would be served by members of the group itself: "matters dealing with social and political conditions of the Alaskans ought to be determined by the Alaskans themselves. They should have in the highest degree, home rule . . . once we remove the temptations incident to the possibility of grabbing the Alaskan wealth, there is no reason why the officials of Alaska should not prove as loyal and honest as officials elsewhere." The American presence should be maintained in Alaska through the establishment of a "Department of Public Works and Domain" with cabinet status or, if that was not possible, a "bureau of Alaskan domain and works." To Gifford Pinchot, Brandeis added that the terms on which the government issued public franchises "probably should not be fixed for more than a generation." This would permit the constant experimentation and adjustment to changing necessities that characterized Brandeis's philosophy of politics and law.[23]

Brandeis considered his plan as no more than "a rough and bare suggestion," which should be implemented with regard to railroads, for example, only after examination of what had been done in Australia, New Zealand, South Africa, and Europe. Nonetheless, he urged La Follette to offer a congressional resolution embodying much of his plan. Repeating his ideas to Pinchot, Brandeis warned, "It seems to me most important that when the plan is presented, it should be broad, bold, and comprehensive. It should deal with the whole problem in a way to make clear; first, that Alaska is to be developed; second, that the development of its resources is for the people of the United States; third, that the opportunities of earnings of the settlers in Alaska will be the most liberal conceivable." He sent La Follette an afterthought:

My dear Bob: How would this do for the Progressive slogan:
"Alaska; the Land of Opportunity.
Develop it by the People, for the people.
Do not let it be exploited by the Capitalists,
    for the Capitalists."

La Follette did offer a resolution embodying the idea of government ownership, but after lengthy debate it was tabled. Secretary Fisher, however, returned from his trek through Alaska convinced that public ownership was necessary and said so in a speech before the American Mining Congress on October 27, in which he also advocated construction and operation of a government-owned coal mine as well as the leasing of other coal mines.[24]

In 1912 the Senate considered a bill authorizing the leasing of Alaskan coal mines and mineral lands. Joseph Robinson, Representative from Arkansas, consented to fight for the bill only if Brandeis approved of it. Brandeis also conferred with Senator Joseph Bristow and H. R. Harriman about getting the bill through, as well as one offered by Senator William Smith of Michigan that would have permitted private interests to lease and operate part of a government-constructed railroad. The Smith bill was killed in committee. When the coal mines bill reached the Senate floor, La Follette attempted to tack onto it an amendment providing for the construction of a government-operated railroad. In spite of the efforts of Robinson, La Follette, Bristow, and the others, the bill was defeated by the Senate. There was one victory, however: on June 26, 1911, the Cunningham Claims that had led to the Pinchot-Ballinger affair were cancelled by the Land Office. Brandeis sent letters of congratulation to Hapgood and the Pinchots.[25]

The way in which Brandeis handled the Controller Bay affair was an example both of his usual procedures and of his beliefs. First he collected all possible data. Second, he assumed throughout that "bigness" and the power that comes from using "other people's money" was bad and to be avoided. As he wrote to Hapgood in a note accompanying a copy of the plan he sent to La Follette, "As you know, I consider the concentration of the money power our greatest menace and problem. This project for dealing with the Alaskan problem would solve largely, pro tanto, the money problem in that connection." Government's role was to balance the large forces that used other people's money as their major weapon. Experimentation was to be encouraged; no irrevocable policy was to be permitted; reassessment was to occur. All of these themes were integral to Brandeis's theories after his experiences in New England.[26]

What New England could not teach him, however, was how to go about managing land and resources that had not already been developed. Alaska forced him to think through the problem, and, having considered it, he rejected the approach that had typified much of American land and resources policy. Brandeis could not foresee the discovery of oil in Alaska and its importance to the United States in the second half of the twentieth century, but he did realize that land and resources were finite and that control of them was a central problem for a democratic society. Land and resources meant profit, which in turn meant power; too much concentrated power was to be avoided, as was the use of land and resources for any purpose other than the enrichment of all the people. Government operation of land and resources, however, would have meant concentration of power, albeit public rather than private power. Its role, therefore, was to preserve land and resources for the people and to turn over decision making about the utilization of land and resources as well as about other political and economic matters to the people most immediately concerned.

What mattered was that the profits went to those who had earned them through their labor. The ideas of fairness and relative equality that underlie socialist theory were in no way antithetical to the Brandeis who earned his living by charging high fees and then invested his earnings in bonds, nor was the idea of the good of the community unacceptable to the man who refused to charge fees for his public interest work and who believed that every citizen had an obligation to participate actively in the body politic. What Brandeis disliked about socialism was its bigness: a big governmental bureaucracy, however well-intentioned and devoted to the public interest, must of necessity fail, for no one institution run by fallible human beings could hope to solve the problems of any society. But Brandeis did not advocate wasteful individual control alternating with equally destructive private corporate exploitation as American policy toward natural resources. He envisioned small-scale communal responsibility. The land might be utilized by individuals or by groups, and the profits could be distributed to individuals or to groups, but the basic decisions about land use had to be made communally if the consequences of individual selfishness and anarchic development on the one hand and human limitations and corporate greed on the other were to be avoided. This was twentieth-century Jeffersonianism labeled progressivism, under whose banner Brandeis and La Follette would fight side by side.

In December 1910 La Follette sent Brandeis a confidential letter about the creation of the National Progressive Republican League for "the promotion of popular government and progressive legislation." The league's Declaration of Principles stated,

> Popular government in America has been thwarted, and progressive legislation strangled by the Special Interests which control caucuses, delegates, convention, and party organizations . . . Under existing conditions legislation in the public interest has been baffled and defeated. This is evidenced by the long struggle to secure laws, but partially effective, for the control of railway lines and services, the revision of the tariff in the interest of the producer and consumer, statutes dealing with trusts and combinations, based on sound economic principles as applied to modern industrial and commercial conditions, a wise, comprehensive and impartial reconstruction of banking and monetary laws, a non-subsidized merchant marine, the

conservation of coal, oil, gas, timber, waterpowers and other natural resources belonging to the people, and for the enactment of all legislation solely for the common good.

La Follette asked Brandeis to join other "progressives of national reputation" in becoming a member of the league, whose primary goal was to amend state constitutions so as to establish initiatives, referenda, and judicial recall, as well as direct nomination of officials and direct election of senators and of delegates to party conventions. Brandeis did not agree with the moves for direct democracy but did approve of the general philosophy that had led to the group's creation, and he quickly joined Governor Hiram Johnson of California, Senator Albert Beveridge of Indiana, Gifford Pinchot, William Allen White, James R. Garfield, Charles R. Crane, Senator Jonathan Bourne, Jr., of Oregon, Representative George Norris of Nebraska, Frederic C. Howe, and others in the league.[27]

On May 15, 1911, the Supreme Court handed down a decision finding that the Standard Oil Company had violated the Sherman Act. However, instead of holding that all combinations in restraint of trade were illegal, as Progressives had understood the Sherman Act to mean, the Court said that only those trusts engaged in "unreasonable" restraints of trade were acting illegally. As the definition of "unreasonable" depended in great measure on who was sitting on the Court, this was unacceptable. La Follette sent Brandeis a telegram saying "We need you to consider next important step in view of decision of yesterday come immediately if possible." Brandeis replied the next day, "Telegram received. Leaving Boston tonight. Due Washington Thursday afternoon." Seeing a crisis in the antitrust movement, they met with Progressive members of Congress. Representatives Francis J. Heney of California and Irvine Lenroot of Wisconsin along with Brandeis were delegated to draft a bill that would correct the Court-created deficiencies, and others, in the Sherman Act. Brandeis returned to Boston, and the ensuing correspondence made it clear that he was doing most of the drafting. On August 19, La Follette introduced the La Follette-Stanley Antitrust bill in the Senate (the "Stanley" was Representative Augustus O. Stanley of Kentucky). Lenroot introduced a similar bill in the House. In the meantime, Senator Moses Clapp of Minnesota, an anti-Taft Progressive and chairman of the Senate Committee on Interstate Commerce, had written to Brandeis, urging him to draft amendments to the Sherman Act before weaker measures could be introduced and passed. Brandeis replied by describing the bill he, Heney, and Lenroot were putting together. Calling it six "perfecting amendments," Brandeis told Clapp that he would be glad to come to Washington to testify about the proposals before Clapp's committee. Clapp then arranged an investigation into trusts and federal policy toward them, and Brandeis went to Washington in December 1911 to testify.[28]

The La Follette-Stanley bill, for which Brandeis had been largely responsible, first attempted to spell out exactly which kinds of combinations were acceptable and which were in restraint of trade. It provided that any combination controlling more than 40 percent of a trade was to be assumed to be in unreasonable restraint of it. Proof that such trusts were not in restraint of trade was shifted to the trusts, making government prosecution easier. Competitors hurt by trusts would be able to bring civil suits, asking for triple damages, as would individuals claiming to have been damaged. The bill, in short, was designed to close the door opened by the Court to "reasonable" restraints of trade and to give teeth to the Sherman Act, particularly in permitting competitors to receive damages.[29]

Brandeis spent a day at the Clapp hearings listening to George W. Perkins, a partner in J. P. Morgan & Company and the representative of the Morgan interests and Big Steel. Perkins argued that trusts were good, that they had grown precisely because they were efficient, and that since they were inevitable the government should attempt to regulate rather than to destroy them. Brandeis showed no emotion as he listened, but his reaction appeared in a letter: "I listened to Perkins for a day before I began to talk, and you can imagine my temperature." On December 14-16, Brandeis presented his rebuttal, arguing that trusts were neither inevitable nor efficient, that in fact they were absentee landlords; they slowed progress; and they were inhumane.[30]

Brandeis's ideas about trusts, as expressed during the Clapp and other hearings and in articles and speeches, were viewed as radical because trusts by that time were perceived as something close to acts of God. Their existence was taken as both inevitable and good. It was inevitable that the most efficient businesses would gradually drive out competitors and seek to gain control over their share of the market; it was good that they did so, for the efficiencies made possible by trusts would provide improved products at lower costs. Even many Progressives accepted trusts as inevitable. But Brandeis refused to accept the inevitability of trusts, insisting that they would not have come into being had the laws of the United States not been skewed in their favor and had the financial interests not manipulated the economy. He was certain that the artificiality of the laws could be undone and that the money trust and others could be disbanded. The law had permitted seemingly unconnected businesses to agree among themselves on high prices; the law could remedy the situation by forbidding price fixing. Low prices existed only temporarily, when they were sustained through injections of money into the trusts by the monied interests; once competitors had been driven out, prices rose.

It was not efficiency that created trusts; it was not fair competition; it was artificial manipulation of credit. Brandeis maintained flatly that "there are no natural monopolies in the industrial world."[31]

He also denied that trusts were efficient. He pointed to the lack of success of the Newspaper Trust, the Writing Paper Trust, the Upper Leather Trust, the Sole Leather Trust, the Wool Trust, the Paper Bag Trust, the International Mercantile Marine Trust, the Cordage Trust, the Mucilage Trust, and the Flour Trust. Those trusts that were still in business and seemingly successful—the Oil Trust, the Shoe Machinery Trust, the Tobacco Trust, the Steel Trust—were successful only because they had acquired a virtual monopoly over their areas of the market and were therefore able to raise prices high enough to cover their costs. Brandeis's opposition to bigness can be understood in the context of the great importance he placed on the finite capabilities of the human mind and the human body. "When . . . you increase your business to a very great extent, and the multitude of problems increase with its growth, you will find, in the first place, that the man at the head has a diminishing knowledge of the facts, and, in the second place, a diminishing opportunity of exercising a careful judgment upon them. Furthermore—and this is one of the most important grounds of the inefficiency of large institutions— there develops a centrifugal force greater than the centripetal force. Demoralization sets in; a condition of lessened efficiency presents itself." Chief executive officers of trusts were as limited as any other human beings; "Nature sets a limit to their possible accomplishment." Firmly believing that an accumulation of facts was the necessary precondition to the solution of any problem, Brandeis argued that when the sheer volume of facts became too unwieldy, true efficiency was impossible. He did not deny that some degree of bigness could make for efficiency; the problem was to find the size at which efficiency was maximum and human abilities were still capable of control: "Whatever the business or organization there is a point where it would become too large for efficient and economic management, just as there is a point where it would be too small to be an efficient instrument. The limit of efficient size is exceeded when the disadvantages attendant upon size outweigh the advantages . . . Organization can do much to make larger units possible and profitable. But the efficiency even of organization has its bounds; and organization can never supply the combined judgment, initiative, enterprise, and authority which must come from the chief executive officers."[32]

Because the trusts were inefficient, they would inevitably collapse if they were not artificially supported by government laws. "I am so convinced of the economic fallacy in a huge unit," Brandeis declared, "that if we make competition possible, if we create conditions where there could be reasonable competition, these monsters would fall to the ground." Trusts were created through the manipulation of capital, which was utilized to put competitors out of business. Far from being efficient, they lost money. Brandeis cited figures showing that the Whisky Trust, the Cordage Trust, and the Malting Trust were not profitable because, in spite of being trusts, they had not achieved monopoly. It was monopoly, rather than efficiency, that enabled some trusts to survive; first they drove out competitors, and then they permitted their products to deteriorate in quality. Brandeis noted the Department of Agriculture's investigation into the poor quality of fence wire made for farms, the declining percentage of the market held by the supposedly efficient Steel Trust, the turning of foreign purchasers to non-American sources of steel: trusts were incapable of operating properly, because they were too big, and they became lazy. They discouraged invention, they made little attempt to reduce costs, because they felt their profits were secure. The result was that consumers were hurt.[33]

Competition would not be completely efficient. It would undoubtedly involve waste; "What human activity does not?" But just as the inefficiencies of democracy were more than compensated for by other advantages, so the minor inefficiencies involved in competition would be more than offset by the incentives and progress fostered by competition. Human beings were indeed limited, but within their limits they could achieve much, and incentive helped them to do so: "The margin between that which men naturally do and which they can do is so great that a system which urges men on to action, enterprise, and initiative is preferable in spite of the wastes that necessarily attend that process."[34]

Perkins had asserted that the trusts were public businesses, owned by numerous stockholders. Brandeis found this no defense at all; "To my mind this is a condition to be regretted . . . Such numerous small stockholding creates in the corporation a condition of irresponsible absentee landlordism; that is, the numerous small stockholders in the steel corporation, in the tobacco company, and in the other trusts occupy a position which is dangerous to society. They have a certain degree of wealth without responsibility. Their only desire is dividends . . . They have no power or responsibility; they have no relations to the employees . . . Thus we have reproduced in history the precise conditions which brought all the misery upon Ireland and upon other countries where absentee landlordism has prevailed."[35]

Trusts, built through the misuse of credit to kill competition, also killed incentive and hopes for better and cheaper products. Ten years after the Steel Trust completed its takeover of the steel industry by absorbing the Carnegie Company, the United States had fallen five years behind Germany in iron and steel metallurgy, creation of updated machinery, and methods of production. The nmber of deaths and injuries due to derailments of trains had led the Interstate Commerce Commission to investigate. It found that derailments due to broken rails had increased drastically since the Steel Trust had taken over. Only part of the cause was the introduction of heavier trains; the trust was too inefficient to keep pace with the innovations in transportation, as a result of which there had been 2,059 derailments involving death and injuries to 106 people in the decade of the trust. Similarly, when confronted with a more efficient system of shoe manufacturing, the Shoe Machinery Trust bought out the system and killed it. Trusts and rapid progress did not coexist.[36]

An additional criticism of the trusts was their treatment of their workers. Perkins had boasted of the Steel Trust's profit-sharing system, and Brandeis went after that claim with statistics. The wages paid by the Steel Trust had gone down, in absolute terms. Although steel workers' wages had increased by 18 percent from 1892 to 1907, the cost of living had increased by 22 or 23 percent. Perkins had noted that the Steel Trust had distributed $12 million to its workers over a ten-year period; Brandeis pointed out that that meant an average of six dollars a year per worker. At the same time, "the hours of labor have been shockingly increased": steel workers were on the job seven days a week, twelve hours a day. Brandeis flourished a newspaper reporting that Elbert H. Gary, the steel magnate, was planning to give his wife a string of pearls valued at half a million dollars for Christmas. He pointedly added that Perkins's firm, J. P. Morgan & Company, received $7 million as a member of the Steel Trust and $12.5 million for managing it. "Here," Brandeis declared, "is what would seem to me a perfect sham of profit-sharing which has been paraded a great deal over this country. See what that means to the social unrest. Isn't it [Gary's present] the same sort of thing that brought on the French Revolution, and which may suggest to everyone in this particular connection the damage which the queen's necklace did in those days?" (Gary issued a press release lamenting, "that he has come down to such cheap talk.")[37]

There was no real profit-sharing for workers, Brandeis said; there was little profit in their wages; their hours were inhumane; and the one mechanism that might have struck a balance between labor and capital, the trade union, was being destroyed by the trusts. There were no unions at all, for example, under the Oil and Tobacco Trusts, but there was a great deal of labor unrest. A little over a year before, on October 1, 1910, James and Joseph McNamara had dynamited the Los Angeles *Times* building, killing twenty-one workers, because of the antiunion stance of the *Times'* publisher. Brandeis saw the antiunion activities of the trusts as the primary reason for union violence. As long as men like the McNamaras believed that their only recourse was to dynamite, labor unrest would find its expression in criminal acts, and American liberty would suffer: "you cannot have true American citizenship, you cannot preserve political liberty, you cannot secure American standards of living unless some degree of industrial liberty accompanies it. And the United States Steel Corporation and these other trusts have stabbed industrial liberty in the back . . . This social unrest is what is really the matter with business. Well-founded unrest; reasoned unrest; but the manifestations of which are often unintelligent and sometimes criminal . . . Until we had these great trusts, for the great corporations which preceded them, workers could secure justice through their unions. Abuses of the trade unions have been innumerable . . . It is one of the most promising symptoms in American democracy that with all the difficulties attending such positions the labor leaders on the whole have done so little that is wrong. And you, gentlemen, Members of the Senate and Members of the House who are called upon to consider questions affecting 'big business,' must weigh well" the mistakes made by labor leaders, for "by their by-products shall you know the trusts."[38]

Brandeis's was a coolly calculating mind when it came to matters of facts and economics. But when it came to human beings Brandeis was far from cool. He opposed the trusts not only because they were inefficient but because they were also inhuman. Their control of large segments of the economy meant that many skilled and unskilled laborers would have no choice but to work for them. They treated their nonunionized employees in a manner that shocked Brandeis, forcing them to work seven days a week, twelve hours a day, for minimal wages. Such schedules turned people into automatons rather than human beings with the leisure to fulfill and educate themselves and to participate in the political process. Small wonder, said Brandeis, that there were sporadic incidents of violence by workers; they saw no other recourse. The trusts had created wage slaves in the midst of what was supposed to be a free country. They had made the United States undemocratic.

It has been argued, far more recently than the time of Brandeis, that the large corporations against which he fought have indeed become efficient through the training of a managerial class and the internalization and rationalization of a multiplicity of functions and administrative chores. It is unlikely that Brandeis would have accepted any of the evidence offered as sufficient, for he would have found it off the point. His focus today would be on two series of questions. The first would begin, how much creativity has been suppressed through the centralization of economic power? Has Max Weber's argument that bureaucracies engender an uncreative bureaucratic mind proved to be true? What has been the cost to the consumer? What are the implications for "efficiency" of cars that must be recalled because of serious defects; electrical appliances that appear to be programmed to fall apart within a relatively short time; the financial collapse of the Pennsylvania Railroad, Lockheed, and Chrysler; the polluting of the environment, the production of foods that have a profitable shelf life only through the inclusion in them of chemicals harmful to human health; the inability of American industry to provide jobs for tens of thousands of would-be workers? His second series of questions would revolve around industrial and political democracy. To what extent is it possible to involve workers in the decision-making process of huge corporations? Does lack of worker-participation give the workers a sense of alienation? Has it made them dependent wage slaves, however high their wages may be? Are workers encouraged to think of themselves as creative participants in the economic process? Does the financial power of huge corporations affect the workings of government? Are the "special interests" perceived as controlling government so completely that large sections of the population have become too apathetic or too cynical to vote?[39]

It is highly doubtful that Brandeis would accept the ability of American agribusiness to produce square tomatoes and the turning away of Americans from the purchase of American-produced cars in favor of human-sized and more environmentally (as well as economically) sound foreign automobiles as proof that he was wrong about either the economic liabilities of the trusts or their detrimental effect upon the American democracy.

The beginning of a solution to the problem of the trusts, Brandeis told the Clapp Committee, was to be found in the La Follette-Stanley bill. The Supreme Court had held Standard Oil to be in restraint of trade but had given no redress to those businesses that had been destroyed by the trust. Brandeis warned, "You will realize the danger of letting the people learn that our sacred Constitution protects not only vested rights but vested wrongs." The La Follette bill was necessary, so was a federal trade commission empowered to investigate and publicize the facts about trusts, and so were consumers' cooperatives. All were designed to cut things back to the proper size. In a statement that might have been made in the 1980s instead of in 1911, Brandeis concluded, "There used to be a certain glamour about big things. Anything big, simply because it was big, seemed to be good and great. We are now coming to see that big things may be very bad and mean."[40]

Brandeis's testimony ended two and a half days and 145 closely printed pages after it had begun. He told friends he had had a great time putting a dent into the steel corporations' armor. But in spite of his efforts and those of others, the La Follette-Stanley bill did not pass. Still, Brandeis and the other Progressives did not give up. Representative Stanley was put in charge of a House committee designated to look into the United States Steel Corporation, and Brandeis went back to Washington in January 1912 to testify once again about the dangers of the trust. But neither the House nor the Senate took action. Meanwhile Brandeis's attention and hopes had turned elsewhere, because Robert La Follette was running for president.[41]

In April 1911 a number of Progressive Republicans in Congress had asked La Follette to become their candidate for president. This had been the real purpose of the National Progressive Republican League. Brandeis was of course aware of the endeavor, because he was both a member of the league and had been in constant communication with La Follette about Alaska and trust policy throughout this period. He officially endorsed La Follette on September 22, 1911, in the *Boston Journal,* causing confusion among Massachusetts Democrats, who had hoped that Brandeis would write their platform. They were further confused by Brandeis's statement that he also endorsed the Democratic Governor for reelection. Brandeis showed no discomfort at the confusion and went off to "stump" for his friend.[42]

Brandeis publicized La Follette's views, seeking permission to send copies of his proposed antitrust bill "to each of those who are members of the Western Shoe Manufacturers' Alliance, say 75;" he wrote to those who might support La Follette. On September 19, 1911, Brandeis had sent a letter to the editor of the *Boston Post,* contrasting a speech of President Taft's about the Sherman Act (Taft had declared himself against any amendment of the law) with La Follette's proposed bill, saying that the speech "places in striking contrast the mere lawyer with the constructive statesman." The day before, Brandeis had written to the editor of the *American Magazine,* which was about to publish a serialized version of La Follette's autobiography. Giving the editor permission to make use of his comments, Brandeis wrote that the publication of the autobiography at that moment was "a matter of vital importance," and added, "no man in public office today expresses the ideals of American democracy" as fully as La Follette. "He is far-seeing, of deep convictions and indomitable will; straightforward, able, hardworking; persistent and courageous. His character is simple, yet is often misunderstood. Sometimes he is called intolerant; but he is tolerant of everything save of wrong done to the people. Sometimes he is called a demagogue and is declared insincere; but it is by those who cannot conceive of his passionate love for the people and of his faith in them. So he is called radical; but it is mainly by those who are unable to realize that 'nothing is abiding save only change'." The description might well have been written by La Follette about Brandeis. The letter was not published, but it makes clear Brandeis's support of La Follette's candidacy. He contributed money, sending the campaign $100 (its managers estimated that the campaign needed $12,500 in Massachusetts "up to and including the Presidential election") and pledging an additional $400 if the campaign organization managed to raise the entire $12,500 by February 1, 1912. (Brandeis frequently gave money in a manner that would encourage what today would be called "matching funds.")[43]

Walter L. Houser, La Follette's campaign manager, asked him to tour the Midwest; Brandeis telegraphed back, "Think I might help cause more by working further on anti-trust bill and arranging to speak in Eastern cities, invitations for which are numerous . . . If you conclude to have me go to Ohio send me full directions including Bob's platform and points I should particularly discuss." The manager said he still wanted Brandeis in the Midwest, so Brandeis agreed to make speeches in Columbus, Ohio; Muskegon, Michigan; Chicago; and one other city to be added; but he wrote to Houser, "As I wrote you, I have had no experience in political campaigning; and for this reason among others I trust you have arranged, or will arrange, so that my speaking is in conjunction with others. And I should prefer to have it arranged so that in each instance I speak after one or more of the other speakers, which will enable me to better get the feel in an unfamiliar situation." Once on the campaign trail, Brandeis apparently hit his stride. The *Cleveland Plain Dealer* called a speech Brandeis gave in that city "quiet but highly remarkable . . . there was a gripping, throbbing appeal" for La Follette; the reporter added, "Had the question been put to a vote after these speeches it would have been a runaway for the Wisconsin man." Brandeis, however, had to leave the meeting, and a resolution supporting La Follette was then defeated. In Chicago, he equated the struggle "for social and industrial justice" with the nation's struggle for independence, and La Follette with Lincoln.[44]

He wrote to his brother about Chicago, "Had a fine luncheon meeting there & two fine ones at Minneapolis Thursday. Besides talked at Madison Wednesday night & a few words at a private luncheon in Chicago Friday given by Charles R. Crane. So you see there was much 'talkee.' In fact the list must be supplemented by a talk Tuesday evening (9^{50}) in a Chicago outlying district & in Canton, O. Monday evening and Columbus Monday morning. Isn't that worse than a one night stand?"[45]

He had begun learning the arts of the politician, and he was ready for more, writing to his assistant, "I have promised . . . the Harvard Committee . . . to speak there some time. Please reach Mr. Henderson (or the right man) immediately & say to him that if it entirely suits them I will talk for them afternoon and evening, next week Friday, January 19th." The Harvard Committee was of course delighted, and Brandeis spoke at Harvard's Emerson Hall on antitrust matters.[46]

By the time Brandeis's stumping was over, it had become clear that Theodore Roosevelt was going to run for the presidency. Brandeis, La Follette, and other leading Progressives met in Washington on January 29 to reassess La Follette's candidacy. Although several of his previously staunch supporters urged him to withdraw in favor of Roosevelt, La Follette refused. The Pinchot brothers and Medill McCormick, the Chicago publisher, withdrew as backers. La Follette pushed on nonetheless, and pushed himself too hard. His daughter was due to undergo a serious operation on February 3, and his backers were deserting. In spite of exhaustion and bitterness, he insisted on going ahead with a speech before the Magazine Publishers' Association on February 2 in Philadelphia. He became nauseated before the speech but rose to speak nonetheless. The speech itself was a repetitive and incoherent attack on the influence of the money power on the press (this in an address to publishers), and a lament about the way the press had treated him. His nerves had given out, and he secluded himself for the next few weeks amid rumors that he had had a nervous breakdown.

Brandeis, reading of the crisis in the newspapers, wrote to Belle La Follette, "My thoughts have been much with you and Bob and the children, and I long to be East where I may hear something authentic. Only make Bob take the rest he needs . . . When he comes back we will take up the good fight again together." At the same time he wrote to his brother, "The news from La Follette is of course distressing, but if the smash is not a bad one, it may be all for the best to have him completely out of the Presidential race. I was sorry when he concluded to enter it. Personally I shall be glad to have no political obligations." The reference to "political obligations" presumably reflects Brandeis's unwillingness to take further time from his other work to campaign; certainly he would have been under no obligations had La Follette actually gotten into the White House. Brandeis had believed from the first, however, that that would be impossible. He was certain that Roosevelt had manipulated such apparent La Follette backers as Gifford Pinchot, Garfield, and McCormick, and that their support was part of Roosevelt's scheme to divide the Republicans and seize the nomination. He told this to La Follette at the time, and was probably correct, given the rapidity of the defections as soon as Roosevelt announced his candidacy.[47]

In spite of his collapse, La Follette refused to withdraw formally. Amos Pinchot, apparently relying upon newspaper reports that La Follette had withdrawn, announced publicly that it was now time for Progressives to join forces with Roosevelt. He was embarrassed to discover that La Follette was still a candidate and wrote to Brandeis on February 9 asking him to use his influence to get La Follette to withdraw. Brandeis's cold reply did not even mention the request: "I have not seen Senator La Follette since January 29th, and have not heard from him. The situation is certainly an unfortunate one." Roosevelt announced on February 21 that "My hat is in the ring." Virtually all of La Follette's early coterie deserted him, and George Rublee wrote Brandeis asking him, on behalf of Roosevelt, to stay overnight with Roosevelt at Oyster Bay. Brandeis refused, saying that although he would be glad to talk to Roosevelt about "social and industrial questions," he feared that La Follette might construe the meeting as another desertion. "At present I am nearly the only one of the original Progressive group which surrounded La Follette, in whom he has confidence . . . I may be able to aid in restoring cooperation between the discordant factions, if La Follette retains his confidence in my loyalty." Brandeis's tactic worked, although not on behalf of Roosevelt. Brandeis soon became convinced that Woodrow Wilson was the best candidate, and urged La Follette to support him. La Follette felt he could not overtly support a Democrat, but used his influence with friends and Wisconsin newspapers on Wilson's behalf. Wilson praised La Follette in many of his campaign speeches, and after Wilson's victory Brandeis wired La Follette, "All true Progressives owe you deep gratitude for yesterday's victory."[48]

La Follette's candidacy of 1912 never officially ended. Belle La Follette wrote to Brandeis in May 1912, asking for ideas for the La Follette delegation to take to the Republican convention in June (and urging Brandeis to run for the Senate). Many of Brandeis's proposals went into the La Follette platform. Brandeis telegraphed pro–La Follette messages to Nebraska and California and continued to speak for him in Massachusetts. The Republican convention, however, rejected both La Follette and his platform in favor of Taft, and La Follette's candidacy was over in all but name.[49]

His insistent loyalty to La Follette is perhaps the best indication of the warmth of which the sometimes cold-sounding Brandeis was capable. Believing as he did that the principled, uncompromising La Follette would serve himself and the country better by remaining in the Senate, Brandeis, nonetheless, threw himself into La Follette's campaign, because La Follette chose to run and Brandeis loved him enough to accept his decision. The families remained close and supportive of each other. *La Follette's*

Weekly (later *La Follette's Monthly*) became a regular outlet for Brandeis's essays on industrial democracy. Belle La Follette, the first woman to be graduated from the University of Wisconsin Law School, did much of the work involved in the editing and publication. La Follette's 1916 campaign for the Senate was underwritten in part by Alice Brandeis. He won his nomination in the Republican party primary in September by a vote of 100,396 to 66,569. (He would go on to win the general election in November 251,303 to 135,144). Brandeis wrote, "The country is to be congratulated and Alice and I are selfish enough to think also how much it will mean to us to have you and Belle in Washington 'for good.'" By then, of course, Brandeis had been installed on the Supreme Court. The La Follette-Brandeis loyalty continued to flow in both directions. Brandeis did not know it until long after LaFollette's death, but La Follette was the only Senator approached by Wilson before he nominated Brandeis to the Court, and La Follette gladly agreed to canvass members of the Senate before the nomination was made, to see if it could get through. In 1917 La Follette's return to the Senate was marred by a move to have him expelled because of his antiwar views. Alice Brandeis wrote to Belle La Follette that the Brandeises were shocked and outraged and found the attacks on him almost incredible. It was more than a year later before the Privileges and Elections Committee finally voted to resolve the issue by dismissing the charges against La Follette. Brandeis sent congratulations that La Follette would now be free to take his "place of leadership in the struggle for democracy in America."[50]

In 1924 La Follette was nominated for president by the Conference for Progressive Political Action and sent Gilson Gardner to ask Brandeis to be his running mate. Brandeis refused to leave the Court or, because of his position, to give more than quiet support to La Follette. He wrote to his brother, however, "The Senator will have (if he keeps his health) a grand fight. If I had several watertight compartment lives, I should have liked to be in it." Alice assured Belle La Follette, "He will help, I feel sure—in his own way when the opportunity offers. It is a thrilling & great moment & full of hope . . . With unfailing love from us both." But there were no constraints on Alice's freedom of political action. Alice came out publicly for La Follette, writing an article supporting his record on foreign affairs (under attack because of his opposition to American involvement in World War I).[51]

The alliance between Brandeis and La Follette lasted until the latter's death in 1925. Brandeis wrote of him to Alfred, "He knew not fear." The relationship between the families continued for years, with the Brandeises encouraging Belle La Follette's biography of her late husband and then, after Belle's death, subsidizing Fola La Follette's completion of it.[52]

Through his involvement in the Alaskan matters, proposed antitrust legislation, and La Follette's candidacy, Brandeis had become firmly entrenched as a leading member of the Progressives. Woodrow Wilson acknowledged as much by sending word shortly after his nomination by the Democrats in July 1912 that he was interested in Brandeis's ideas. The two men met for the first time on August 28, and although no one realized it at the time, both a new alliance and the "New Freedom" were born.[53]

The Brandeis family in Louisville, Kentucky, shortly before Louis's birth:
Amy, Adolph, Alfred, Frederika, Fannie

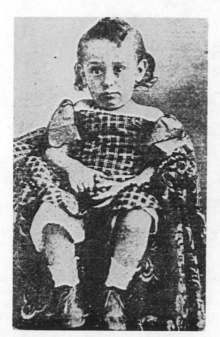

Louis at age two (1858) in Louisville

Louis at age fifteen (1871) in Louisville

Brandeis at age thirty (1886) in Boston   Brandeis at age thirty-eight (1894) in Boston

Brandeis in 1914, during the New Haven Railroad fight

Brandeis in 1913 at his summer home in
Chatham, Massachusetts

Brandeis in his office, July 1915, being interviewed on Zionism

Associate Justice Louis D. Brandeis,
Washington, 1916

Brandeis reading a letter from Lord Reading
congratulating him on his appointment to the
Supreme Court, 1916

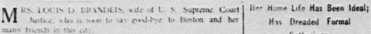

MRS. BRANDEIS SORRY TO LEAVE BOSTON FOR NEW CAPITAL HOME

MRS. LOUIS D. BRANDEIS, wife of U. S. Supreme Court Justice, who is soon to say good-bye to Boston and her many friends in this city.

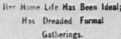

Her Home Life Has Been Ideal; Has Dreaded Formal Gatherings.

When Mrs. Louis D. Brandeis closes her Boston home to establish her family at their Summer place at South Yarmouth she will say good-bye to Boston. Mr. Brandeis' duties as Supreme Court Justice making it desirable for them to reside at Washington.

What the uprooting of associations will mean to the wife of Justice Brandeis can scarcely be appreciated. Those who know the Brandeis family intimately say that Mrs. Brandeis especially dreads the kind of formal existence which is expected of one of her position in Washington. The calls, the afternoon teas and receptions will all be foreign to the woman who has lived for twenty-six years with her husband in absolute simplicity.

BOSTON HOME IS SIMPLE.

The Boston Brandeis home is almost severe in its freedom from bric-a-brac and cumbersome furniture. There is nothing to impede nor delay effective thinking and action.

While much has been written about Mr. Brandeis and his achievements, less is known of his wife, whom neighbors maintain is peculiarly essential to her husband in everyone of his projects.

Her early history is even more dramatic and filled with interest than is that of her famous husband. Mrs. Brandeis' father, Adolph Goldmark, came to America a fugitive from persecutions following an uprising in Vienna in 1848. He became

Rare photograph of Alice G. Brandeis before leaving Boston in 1916

Brandeis at age seventy-four (1931)
in Washington

The United States Supreme Court, 1937. *Top row*: Benjamin Cardozo, Harlan F. Stone,
Owen J. Roberts, Hugo Black. *Bottom row*: George Sutherland, James C. McReynolds,
Chief Justice Charles Evans Hughes, Louis D. Brandeis, Pierce Butler.

Composite picture of Supreme Court justices walking in Washington, ca. 1926: Brandeis, Edward T. Sanford, James C. McReynolds, Harlan F. Stone, Chief Justice William H. Taft, Oliver Wendell Holmes, Pierce Butler, Willis Van Devanter, George Sutherland

10 | Worker-Participation

Brandeis was extremely busy during the summer and fall of 1910. On July 28 he agreed to chair the negotiating sessions to resolve the New York garment industry strike. During the following month he took the job of counsel for the Committee of Commercial Organizations, a group that was fighting a proposed increase in railroad rates. By the time the garment industry protocol was signed on September 2, he was already deep into preliminary hearings about the railroad rates, so he was juggling the two matters simultaneously (as well as cleaning up remaining chores from the Pinchot-Ballinger hearings, supervising the savings bank life insurance system, and conducting his private practice).

His involvement with railroad rates was part of a nine-year war Brandeis waged against the New Haven Railroad. The war had begun in 1905, when the Boston & Maine Railroad (B&M) asked the Massachusetts legislature to pass a bill permitting it to own street railways. Brandeis's view since the days of the Boston subway fights had been that railroads should not be permitted the wide-spread control of transportation they would gain if they owned trolley lines as well. He, and others, opposed the B & M's proposal. The B & M replied that it was only trying to do legally what the New Haven was already doing illegally, for the New Haven had bought up about a third of Massachusetts's trolley mileage through holding companies. Then it was discovered that the New Haven was quietly buying enough stock in the Boston & Maine to give it control. Brandeis was hired to fight the takeover by William Lawrence, whose father had about two million dollars invested in the B & M.

Although he quickly accepted the job, Brandeis soon decided that since the merger was "a matter of public interest in which I am undertaking to influence the opinion of others, I do not want to accept any compensation for my services."[1]

The battle that raged from then on makes a complicated story. Brandeis lost a number of rounds, including prevention of the New Haven–B & M merger, but eventually won the war in 1914 when President Wilson's attorney general forced the New Haven to give up both the B & M and all its trolley and steamship lines. The fight was an ugly one. The New Haven not only bought votes in the Massachusetts legislature; it also paid for anti-Brandeis articles in newspapers and magazines and the services of a Harvard Law School professor who delivered supposedly "scholarly" lectures on the virtues of the New Haven. Brandeis countered by turning himself into an expert on the financial details of the New Haven and railroads in general. His studies convinced him that more was involved than a monopoly. The New Haven was controlled by J. P. Morgan, who manipulated it and other endeavors to gain the largest possible return for his banking house. Decisions about the New Haven and its subsidiaries were not even made by railroad men, whose motives, to Brandeis, were bad enough; they were made by financiers with no interest in or understanding of transportation. The New Haven was issuing factually incorrect financial statements. Far from being the thriving, efficient endeavor publicly extolled by its officers, it was actually losing money and was being kept alive only as a mechanism for stock watering and high dividends.[2]

Brandeis's fight with the New Haven led to his involvement with petitions by it and other railroads to increase rates in 1910. His investigation of the New Haven's finances and the way in which it was being run showed him that the railroads were being operated inefficiently and that the increased rates for which they were asking could be prevented if they instituted more rational forms of management. It was thus largely through his immersion in railroad matters that Brandeis came to the idea of scientific management, which in turn became of great importance to his thinking about the labor problem.

In 1903 a journal called *Transactions of the American Society of Mechanical Engineers* had published "Shop Management," a lengthy explanation of scientific management by the father of the movement, Frederick W. Taylor. Brandeis read it shortly after it was published and became sufficiently intrigued by scientific management to read the series of articles on its application to the Atchison, Topeka and Santa Fe Railroad written by efficiency engineer Harrington Emerson and published in the *American Engineer and Railroad Journal* in 1906. Emerson's book

Efficiency as a Basis for Operations and Wages appeared in 1909, and Brandeis recommended it to friends along with Henry L. Gantt's five-part series on scientific management in the *Engineering Magazine*. One of the things that impressed Brandeis was Emerson's contention that the railroads could save a million dollars a day if only they would practice scientific management.[3]

Emerson's figures immediately came to mind when a number of railroads asked the Interstate Commerce Commission (ICC) for permission to raise freight rates. Shippers in the Northeast, whose costs would have risen by millions of dollars, organized in opposition and established a Committee of Commercial Organizations with David O. Ives, manager of the Boston Chamber of Commerce's Transportation Department, as its head. Ives immediately asked Brandeis to represent the shippers in hearings before the ICC. Preliminary hearings were held in New York's Waldorf-Astoria Hotel during August and September 1910 before two ICC special examiners. On October 12 hearings were convened in Washington before the ICC itself.

He summarized his points in a ninety-four-page brief submitted to the commission on January 3, 1911, approximately half of which dealt with scientific management and was reprinted in book form by *Engineering Magazine*. Incorporated into the brief was some of the testimony that Brandeis had elicited from various scientific management experts such as Frank B. Gilbreth, Henry L. Gantt, and Emerson, as well as from executives of businesses that had successfully introduced scientific management: Henry V. Sheel, supervisor of the Brighton Mills; H. K. Hathaway of the Tabor Manufacturing Company; and James M. Dodge, president of the Link Belt Company. The leaders of the movement met with Brandeis in his office and at Gantt's home to plan the presentation of evidence. Clearly, Brandeis had decided to use the forum of the hearings not only to make the railroads listen to reason but also to teach the public about the new "science."[4]

The function of the efficiency engineer, Brandeis explained, was to treat business "as an intricate machine. He analyzes each process into its ultimate units, and compares each of the smallest steps of the process with an ideal of perfect conditions. He then makes all due allowance for rational and practical conditions and establishes an attainable commercial standard at every step. Then he seeks to obtain continuously this standard." Because engineering meant "the planning in advance of production so as to secure certain results," scientific management permitted businesses to know before work was begun how much work would be done during what period of time in what way and what the costs would be. Brandeis brought to the stand various efficiency engineers who testified, for example, that the Brighton Mills, with 600 employees, rationalized its procedures, instructed individual weavers for over a month on how the new system would work, trained inspectors to oversee and maintain the process, and cut costs dramatically. The Tabor Manufacturing Company had brought in a team of 20 engineers to "functionalize" its business, and the expert in charge testified at length about exactly how he and his colleagues determined the best way of performing every step in the construction of machines and then put this scheme into action.[5]

The gains to the employer included the reduced labor costs that came with greater productivity, continual and efficient use of machinery, smaller stocks of materials needed, and the ability to predict exactly when work would be completed. Reduced costs were passed on to the consumers everywhere that scientific management had been introduced, and a true competitive situation existed, because businesses whose costs fell naturally reduced prices in order to get a greater share of the market. The average fall of prices after the introduction of scientific management was 10–15 percent. And, perhaps most important of all, labor benefited.[6]

Brandeis and his witnesses compared the usual factory situation, in which workers had to put up with whatever methods and conditions prevailed, with the scientifically managed factory in which management "assumes the responsibility of enabling the employee to work under the best possible conditions of perfect team play," including instruction in how best to do the work; provision of the best tools, machines, and materials; and elimination of those aspects of a job that could be done by less-skilled workers and that were presumably boring. What was more, wages went up because of greater productivity, which came not from "speeding up" but from "removing the obstacles to production which annoy and exhaust the workman" and which were not his fault, such as malfunctioning machines and periods of over- or under-work. Wages in the Brighton Mills rose 45–75 percent; in the Tabor Manufacturing Company, 25–30 percent; and in the Link Belt Company, 25–35 percent. In addition, job satisfaction and self-respect increased: "Eagerness and interest take the place of indifference, both because the workman is called upon to do the highest work of which he is capable, and also because in doing this better work he secures appropriate and substantial recognition and reward. Under scientific management men are led, not driven. Instead of working unwillingly for their employer they work in co-operation with the management for themselves and their employer in what is a 'square deal.'" Scientific management was frequently accompanied by a bonus system as well as by the discovery that, with training, workers at relatively unsophisticated jobs could become adept at more skilled work, which again added to both satisfaction and wages.[7]

Furthermore, scientific management and unionization were compatible. One of the issues for collective bargaining, for example, would become the size of the bonus and the point at which it would begin for individuals able to exceed the average work load. In the Manhattan Press of New York, which was not only a union shop but parts of which were virtually closed shops (then a rarity), bonuses were handed out on a day other than payday, so that "earnings" were spread throughout the week. One unionized factory in Philadelphia that employed principles of scientific management found that when its competitors' workers went out on strike, its own workers refused to join in.[8]

The immediate aftermath of all the testimony about scientific management was amusing. Realizing that their insistence that only a rate increase could keep them in business was becoming less credible, a number of railroad presidents had sent Brandeis a telegram which they also gave to the press: "It is reported you have stated before the Interstate Commerce Commission that American railways are wasting $1,000,000 daily. If you can point out a practical way by which a substantial portion of this amount may be saved several western railways would be pleased to tender you employment, allowing you to name your own salary. This proposition is made to you in the same spirit of sincerity in which you rendered your statement to the Commission." The railroads were obviously attempting to counter the "People's Attorney" image and call Brandeis's bluff. He replied a few days later with a serene telegram of his own, saying in part,

> I am convinced that such saving is possible through the introduction of scientific management and shall be glad, as a public service, to arrange for conferences with these Western presidents at an early date and point out how scientific management will accomplish these results. I suggest that the Eastern presidents be also invited to attend the conferences.
>
> I must decline to accept any salary or other compensation from the railroads for the same reason that I have declined compensation from the shipping organizations whom I represent—namely, that the burden of increased rates, while primarily affecting the Eastern manufacturers and merchants, will ultimately be borne in large part by the consumer through increasing the cost of living, mainly of those least able to bear added burdens. I desire that any aid I can render in preventing such added burdens should be unpaid services. Kindly suggest date and place for conference.[9]

The railroads did not bother to answer. All they had accomplished was to get the million-dollar figure onto the front pages of the country's newspapers. The *New York Times* commented about the railroad presidents, "Those somewhat too humorous gentlemen will probably regret the levity, not to say the impudence that characterized their communication . . . Their hilarious incredulity revealed a surprising ignorance of Mr. Brandeis's record and reputation as a man honestly and disinterestedly devoted to the public service." The *New York Tribune* was convinced that the railroads had to institute "new economies." Newspapers around the country suddenly featured articles about Brandeis, unwittingly aiding his educational effort. He wrote to Al, a few days after the exchange of telegrams had hit the newspapers, "I suppose you occasionally see the New York papers. I have been very pleasantly surprised at the support which we have had here in the East. I rather expected support from the West, and worked hard with some of the New York papers myself, but we have had solid support from many which I did not approach, and from whom I only had expected to have sneers and abuses."[10]

The commission ruled that scientific management as described by Brandeis lowered costs and that the burden was now on the railroads to show why they could not employ the new techniques. Brandeis promptly relieved them of that burden, bringing in witnesses to testify that scientific management could be and had been applied to railroads, that is, to large corporations. The Atchison, Topeka and Santa Fe, as well as the Canadian Pacific Railroad, had tried scientific management in their machine and locomotive shops, and labor costs had fallen dramatically. Other less enlightened railroads were operating with incredible inefficiency; their methods of loading and unloading were "substantially the same as those used in the days of the Pharaohs." It would be exciting, Emerson testified, if the ICC required the railroads to get accurate statistics about all aspects of railroad costs and management and made these available to both the railroads and the public, just as the Department of Agriculture collected and organized statistics and information which individual farmers could not hope to get for themselves elsewhere. And then, if the railroads actually instituted scientific management on the basis of the information gathered, the savings would be enormous. Brandeis had Emerson repeat and document his opinion that this would result in a savings of at least one million dollars a day.[11]

Brandeis was satisfied with the ICC decision and told Felix Frankfurter that the commission had done even more with the efficiency argument than he had expected. Daniel Willard, president of the Baltimore and Ohio had told the *New York Times,* "As I see it, there is only one thing for us to do—to put into effect the Brandeis greater efficiency system." Brandeis commented to Frankfurter that the commission had "accepted the fundamental principles that improvements in economy and management were possible, and that they must be made before the need would be recognized. Scientific management will follow that inevitably, as President Willard's remarks have already indicated."[12]

The publicity surrounding the hearings led to a spurt of interest in scientific management. At the time of the hearings, no journal of general appeal had broached the subject, but in 1911 alone there were twenty-six such articles. Progressives in general turned to scientific management as a way of reforming business without the intervention of government. Walter Lippmann and Herbert Croly both espoused it, although their interpretations of it varied somewhat from Brandeis's. In 1912 Brandeis emphasized his continuing enthusiasm for the idea by writing the foreward to his friend Frank B. Gilbreth's *Primer of Scientific Management*.[13]

But of greater ultimate importance than Brandeis's temporary victory over the railroads or than the public enthusiasm for scientific management was a defeat. Brandeis completely failed to convince the unions of the advantages of scientific management. The unions' concern was that if scientific management permitted greater production per worker and if no industry could expand indefinitely, the net result would be a loss of jobs. In addition the unions were worried about the standards that would be imposed upon workers. If some workers exceeded the quota, it would be logical for management to require all workers to meet what would in effect become the new quota. The result would be harder work for the same wages. This kind of "speed-up" would lower the wages of those who did piecework and cause the unemployment of those who were paid daily but could not keep up with the new standards. All of Brandeis's witnesses had testified that, once a "scientific" quota for piecework was established, they never raised it but instead gave bonuses to those few workers able to exceed the quota. But unions, fighting for their very existence, were naturally unconvinced that employers would suddenly develop a public conscience and use the new system to raise the workers' standard of living as well as their own. The history of labor-management relations gave them every reason to fear any system that might be used to justify eliminating jobs or lowering wages. Brandeis's old acquaintance Samuel Gompers opposed the system in the *American Federationist;* John Mitchell of the United Mine Workers expressed similar sentiments, as did Upton Sinclair.[14]

Brandeis was untiring in his attempt to convert the labor leaders. John Mitchell told the *New York Times* that Brandeis was "a valued friend of labor" and "a deep thinker," but he was mistaken in advocating scientific management and the bonus system. Brandeis promptly wrote to Mitchell, "I am convinced that upon a full understanding of what scientific management seeks to accomplish you and the other labor leaders would be the strongest supporters that the movement could have." He told Mitchell he wanted to discuss the matter with him, sent Mitchell a copy of his opening statement before the ICC, and added, "I trust . . . that you and our labor friends may not feel called upon to make any public statements until I shall have had an opportunity of going over the ground with you." The two men spoke on the telephone on December 28, and Brandeis sent Mitchell a copy of his brief before the ICC, instructing him, "I trust that you will have time to read very carefully the ninety pages dealing with scientific management; that you will make notes as you read of all points as to which you may have any doubts, in order that you may subject me to the promised cross-examination." There is no indication that Mitchell was convinced.[15]

The gulf that separated Brandeis and the workers on the question of scientific management was illustrated by the reaction to his speech, "Organized Labor and Efficiency," before the Boston Central Labor Union on April 2, 1911. His relationship with the union was a warm one. His 1905 address to its members, supporting unionism, had been received so enthusiastically that Brandeis was persuaded to have it published. The union worked hard on behalf of Brandeis's savings bank life insurance legislation, and took a stand with Brandeis against the New Haven–Boston and Maine merger.[16]

Having had his address to the New York Economic Club a few days earlier rebutted by James Duncan, a vice-president of the AFL, Brandeis was well aware of worker opposition to scientific management and set out to defuse it. He told the workers that scientific management was the answer to the need for economy in production, which was in turn created by the new "great ethical movement for real brotherhood of man" which showed that workers had to be treated decently. The assertion by the ignorant that scientific management was hostile to labor was "absolutely unfounded," he said. Scientific management meant conservation: of materials, of plant, of working capital, and of labor, including the labor of managers and other officials as well as that of wage-earners. It meant that employers had to train their workers, "and the employer's investment involved in that training creates a special incentive to the employer to retain his employee and to conserve his powers." It meant shorter hours and regularity of employment, as well as higher wages. It meant continued employment, in spite of increased production, for "if goods can be purchased cheaper, more can be bought for the same money. And more will be bought; at least if wages remain the same or increase . . . The demand for labor grows because the demands of the people grow with the ability to supply them." Unions would have to work with management, through the collective bargaining mechanism, to set a minimum wage, hours and conditions of labor, and arrangements about bonuses. The opportunity thus to help determine how to utilize scientific management so as to benefit the workers was "the supreme opportunity for organized labor." And Brandeis asked his audience, "Will you utilize it to the full?"[17]

The answer was a resounding no. One union woman shouted, "You can call it scientific management if you want to, but I call it scientific driving." Brandeis shot back, "There is nothing scientific in what you say." But even on friendly territory, he could not sell scientific management to the trade unions.[18]

Brandeis did not take into account in evaluating scientific management that he had seen it under extraordinary circumstances. His experts and their business clients displayed a most unusual sense of social responsibility. Most employers could not be counted on to emulate them, as Brandeis's own jousts with the New Haven and later with the trusts should have shown him. If he thought about it, he probably reasoned that the answer was to keep businesses small. Owners would then be in regular communication with their workers and would remember the humanity of their employees. Certainly, this kind of thinking lay behind his advocacy of mechanisms for on-going employee-employer communication. Once again, however, his distance from the union struggle both gave him an objectivity that benefited his thinking and prevented him from understanding why labor leaders would not hasten to embrace his ideas. Brandeis assumed that business would eventually accept (or be forced to accept) unionization, so he could postulate unionization as a given when he advocated scientific management. Union leaders, however, were far from certain that they would win their struggle for recognition of the legitimacy and rights of unions; they had to treat employers as adversaries if they were to have any chance of victory. They could not reasonably accept an innovation that carried the potential for further abuse of labor.

Despite its disagreement with some of Brandeis's ideas, mainstream labor considered Brandeis to be its ally—to the dismay of more radical labor elements. There is an interesting, unidentified typescript in the Library of Congress's Frankfurter papers, which appears to be a draft of a speech or article. Referring to the leader of the radical Industrial Workers of the World (IWW), it says,

A few years ago Big Bill Haywood made a study of the protocol in the garment industry. "This fellow Brandeis," he said, "is the most dangerous man in the United States." He was asked to explain. "Brandeis is the kind of a man the I.W.W. has got to look out for. Brandeis knows something about capital and labor. He isn't one of these highbrow reformers who is sure to make a fool of himself. That's why I say he is in our way. The workers trust him even when he goes against them. Think of it. He tells them they're wrong here and wrong there, he defends the manufacturers more than half the time, and still they believe him. They even say he was right sometimes when he decided against them. They're a pretty sentimental lot in the working class, and I think they'd follow Brandeis to Kingdom Come because they say nobody can buy him, that he's not in this for himself, and that he's the whitest man who ever mixed up in the class struggle. That's what makes him so damned dangerous. If he were a fool, if he didn't know all about everything, if he were in it for Brandeis, if there were only something the matter with him, he wouldn't be messing things for the I.W.W. wherever he goes."[19]

Haywood was right: Brandeis wasn't "in it for Brandeis"; nor, of course, was he "in it" to create the socialist society that Haywood and the IWW saw as the future. Mainstream labor understood this, even as it rejected Brandeis's insistence on the preferential shop and scientific management. Brandeis, however, could no more comprehend labor's disregard for such ideas than he could understand its concentration on wages and hours rather than on the far more important issue (in his eyes) of regular employment—or, later, as his theories became more sophisticated, its ignoring his belief that unions ought to have a share in the management of corporations.[20]

Ultimately labor's adversarial attitude toward business proved short-sighted, as did that of business, which prized growth above all, and of government, which encouraged unlimited growth. The collapse or extreme difficulties of segments of American industry in the 1970s and 1980s (Lockheed, the Penn Central, the automobile industry), indicates that mindless growth was feasible only as long as materials and markets were limitless. Scientific management, efficiency at all levels of corporate management, limitations on corporate size, encouragement of the kind of competition that would have made American corporations more amenable to innovation and thereby more competitive with foreign manufacturers—all were advocated by Brandeis in the early decades of the century and might have altered the American business picture of the 1980s.

Brandeis saw scientific management as a way of achieving conservation: of machines, of capital, and above all, of labor. His particular approach to the system appears to have been affected by his involvement in Pinchot-Ballinger and the whole question of land conservation. He wrote to Gifford Pinchot, during the ICC rate hearings, "You have so thoroughly trained the American mind to conservation that this new form as presented in railroad efficiency has found a relatively easy path." Further, he thought that the conservation implied in scientific management could be extended to nonindustrial fields of endeavor. However, when Felix Frankfurter shared current suggestions that the system could be adopted to legislative drafting, Brandeis replied that in the field of social legislation, "as in other fields of human enterprise, the successes are few and the failures are many." The successes were rarely the work of one person or one group, and Brandeis therefore could not support the idea of a small group of people being charged with evolving social reform. "On the other hand," he wrote, "it seems to me that a small group of able, disinterested, well-equipped men, who could give their time to criticism and discussion of legislative proposals, discouraging those which appear to be unsound, and aiding those that appear to be sound, would be of great assistance in the forward movement."[21]

Efficiency was not aided by irregularity of employment, which remained one of Brandeis's primary concerns. In urging the head of the Massachusetts Bureau of Statistics to make his reports more sophisticated, Brandeis indicated as early as 1905 that "unemployment" as a category gave no information; one had to know whether the unemployment reflected sickness, weather, or irregularity of employment. If the cause was the last, something should be done. "As one of my clients put it," Brandeis wrote to the statistician, " 'If the amount of time voluntarily not worked is large, my employees must explain; if the amount of compulsory idle time is large, I must explain.' " That particular client had clearly been well tutored by Brandeis. In 1914 Henry Ford announced a profit-sharing plan and a minimum wage (of a dollar a day), as well as an attempt to see that lay-offs occurred during the harvest season, when workers might well find temporary jobs. Brandeis wrote to the editor of the *New York Times Annualist* about Ford's plan, "In connection with unemployment, don't fail to discuss the even more important question of regularization of employment. The amount of waste and suffering in times of good business, due to seasonable industries and the jaggedness of employment in even all year business is the most serious blemish on our industrial system." And he reminded the newspaper that McElwain should be given the credit due a pioneer in employment regularization. A volume published in 1916 on unemployment brought Brandeis's congratulations to the author for publicizing "the greatest of the causes of waste and suffering." The mental connection he made between efficiency and industrial democracy was reflected in his comment that the book "should have the attention alike of those who seek industrial efficiency, and those who strive for social justice."[22]

But "The Road to Social Efficiency," as Brandeis called it in a 1911 paper presented to the National Conference of Charities and Correction and published in *The Outlook,* required more than regularity of employment. Brandeis brought the paper to the attention of such social reformers as the La Follettes, Hapgood, E. A. Grozier, Oswald Garrison Villard, and many others. His thesis, accompanied by a full array of facts and figures and references to the German, French, and English systems, was that the United States had to have workers' insurance to cover "accident, sickness, invalidity, premature death, superannuation and unemployment." This, Brandeis argued, was necessary if the political freedom supposedly available to the American working class was to be a reality. "Can any man be really free who is constantly in danger of becoming dependent for mere subsistence upon somebody and something else than his own exertion and conduct?" Brandeis told his audience, "Men are not free while financially dependent upon the will of other individuals." Brandeis was certain that because the costs would be high, a system that required compensation would result in minimization of the need for compensation. He cited a model factory village in England which had reduced the death rate by studying the causes of work-related deaths; businesses that had cut their accident rates in a similar manner; and the reduction of factory fires as a result of discovering and eliminating potential fire hazards. Irregularity of employment would also be eliminated; "In the scientifically managed business irregularity tends to disappear."[23]

Brandeis was particularly concerned, as his work in organizing the Massachusetts savings bank life insurance system indicated, about old-age annuities. In testimony before a congressional hearing in 1912, he said that the government ought to mandate pension systems that would be paid for entirely by employee and employer contributions. He was insistent that pensions had to be "movable"; that is, the worker would not lose protection by leaving one employer for another; and that employers could not be counted upon to set up such a plan voluntarily. A few months later he suggested to an employer that "much is to be said in favor of distributing profits among employees in the form of paid up annuity insurance policies." In 1909 he had put together a pension system for the Boston & Maine Railroad, which required employer and employee to contribute equal amounts per year and provided that employees who wished to contribute more than the fixed amount (and thus to secure a larger pension) could do so. The program was embodied in a statute passed by the state of Maine, which established an employee-employer Board of Trustees to manage the plan but gave the state sufficient supervisory powers to ensure the fund's stability. He designed the program at the request of the employees and with the cooperation of the railroad. Everything he wrote and said indicates that he was torn between hoping that unions would become strong enough to demand and achieve such programs and fearing that government intervention would be necessary if the programs were to be instituted by industry. In either event, however, he did not anticipate participation by the government in the program itself.[24]

His thoughts about profit sharing in general were expressed in hearings before the Senate Committee on Interstate Commerce in 1911, when his primary purpose was to testify in favor of Robert La Follette's bill to create a federal trade commission. Attacking the claim of J. P. Morgan's George Perkins that U. S. Steel had distributed profits to employees, Brandeis gave examples of what he considered to be true profit sharing. The Dennison Manufacturing Company of Massachusetts paid an 8 percent return on its stock (Brandeis considered this too high) and distributed remaining profits to its workers in proportion to their salaries. The workers also owned common stock in the corporation (only preferred stock was entitled to the 8 percent dividend). The Connor grocery business, also in Massachusetts, returned 6 percent on capital and divided additional profits between the executive officers and the workers. A Lynn, Massachusetts, grocery and provision business divided 25 percent of its profits among its non-stock-owning employees. Brandeis reminded the senators that the Boston Gas Company also raised wages in exact proportion to raises in dividends, and that the Filene Company had another kind of profit-sharing plan. He reported that when profit-sharing was introduced into the Connor business, the managers told the employees, " 'We expect a greater efficiency; we feel that when we give you half of all the profits earned the remaining half taken by the managers will be largely increased through your increased efficiency.' " And, Brandeis added, "that expectation was fulfilled."[25]

Brandeis reported that clients had told him that they thought their families were not entitled to their businesses' profits; " 'I think I am entitled to the profits of it, because I am giving it my brains and I have worked it up and I ought to be able to get out of it, and when I am gone the persons who are making that business a success, whatever their position in that business, they ought to share in it.' " Such clients discovered that "they got out of the very same men infinitely better results when the men were working for themselves than when they were merely doing work for others . . . the feeling is growing so rapidly in this country of resentment at being a hired man, of working for somebody else, that the wise business men are seeing if they want to get the best they can out of the men, the men must work for themselves." Although Brandeis mentioned that "the idea becomes contagious" and that from time to time other businesses were encouraged by the example to start their own profit-sharing plans, he also admitted that most of he businesses he referred to were owned by his clients. One can legitimately assume his influence.[26]

He was inclined to support a women's minimum wage law, cautiously. In 1911 Cornelia Lyman Warren, sister of Brandeis's first law partner, asked Brandeis whether she should aid the Massachusetts Minimum Wage Board, which was investigating the desirability of such a law. He replied that the investigation should be pursued, adding, "I have an absolutely open mind as to whether or not it would be advisable to establish by law a Minimum Wage." Brandeis's friend Elizabeth Glendower Evans was a member of the board, and in writing to her Brandeis indicated that his thinking had gone beyond his comments to Warren. "Providing for the determination of minimum wage scale for women and minors, is a conservative measure which deserves the support of all good citizens," he wrote. "If in any business the women workers are receiving wages which are inadequate to meet the necessary cost of living and to maintain the worker in health, it is inevitable that serious burdens which the Commonwealth will have to bear are being developed." He then hinted that he considered the maximum hours provision at issue in *Muller* v. *Oregon* as no more than the first step: a minimum wage for women "is a natural supplement to the Massachusetts legislation limiting the hours of labor for women and children, and it is fitting that Massachusetts which led the movement to protect its women workers from excessive hours of labor should also lead in the movement to protect them and the Commonwealth from the evil of inadequate wages." Brandeis was still thinking in terms of protective legislation for the weaker sex.[27]

On September 18, 1912, while campaigning for Woodrow Wilson, he gave a speech to the Massachusetts chapter of the AFL entitled "Labor and the New Party Trust Program." In the course of it he referred to the possible legal difficulties entailed in passage of a minimum wage law. An attorney who saw the speech printed in *La Follette's Weekly* asked whether such a law would not fall within the power of the commerce clause. And Brandeis replied that although he still thought there might be difficulties with the federal and state constitutions, he was "personally disposed to a very liberal construction of police power." Because "police power" is the term used to denote government control over matters affecting health, safety, education, and welfare and because it was used in the early part of the century to refer primarily to state (as opposed to federal) power, the letter would seem to indicate that Brandeis was thinking as a federalist interested in legislation on the state level. This is borne out by another letter written in 1912, admitting that "grave constitutional questions would be presented by any attempt to secure effective Federal legislation" mandating minimum wages for women. He urged collection of data from the states and other countries about the need for such a bill. "We are still in the initial stages of the consideration of the minimum wage question, and we ought to get the full benefit of experiments in individual states before attempting anything in the way of other Federal action. There is a great advantage in the opportunity we have of working out our social problems in the detached laboratories of the different states." In 1913 Brandeis won an Oregon court ruling that legitimized Oregon's law setting minimum wages for women.[28]

He was still not in favor of a minimum wage for men, however. When a Nebraska legislator proposed one, Brandeis expressed disapproval: "No minimum wage legislation should be passed which undertakes to fix as a general law an exact minimum wage [that is, without reference to the kind of work done and the cost of living] . . . It seems to me unwise at the present time to provide for any minimum wage law which extends to adult male workers." Brandeis urged acceptance of an alternate proposal, which was that an investigatory commission be established. This, he had pointed out in his argument in the Oregon case, had been done in that state before passage of the law, and the wage set reflected the actual cost of living. He also noted that the minimum wage law in Oregon increased efficiency and regularity of employment, because "in fixing minimum wages, the trade boards had to consider not only the rate of wages, but also the average number of days in which the employee works; and employers are thereby induced to seek to regularize employment." He did not deal with the obvious objection, that presumably the same happy effect would be derived from minimum wage legislation for men.[29]

All of Brandeis's thinking about peripheral if important labor questions—regularity of employment, hours and wages legislation—did not get to the heart of the labor-management relation, and he knew it. Such reforms and legislation might improve labor's position, as would recognition of trade unions, but it would not keep the two sides from remaining adversaries. Perhaps more important, it would not give workers the sense of independence and control over their lives necessary in a democratic society. Unions would help, but Brandeis eventually came to believe they were not enough. Something more would have to be done.

As early as 1900, Sam Warren's sister, Cornelia Lyman Warren, had spoken to Brandeis about the reforms she was introducing in the family's mills and the profit-sharing plan she was trying out with her domestic help. Even earlier, he had written of the equal relationship he thought should exist: "A manufacturer is no longer the master of his employee, but an associate. History records first master and slave, then master and servant, then employer and employee, and now they are associates or contractors." This in 1895 was no more than a hope, but it lay behind his support of labor unions. Just as the world and all its businesses would benefit from competition among businesses, so each business would benefit from competition "from within, which can exist only where the ownership and management, on the one hand, and the employees, on the other, shall each be alert, hopeful, self-respecting, and free to work out for themselves the best conceivable conditions." But unionization proved not to be gaining recognition with sufficient rapidity; hence the need for laws regulating minimum wages and pensions. And yet even with such laws, the problem was not solved. There were two contradictory strands in Brandeis's thinking. One was the Madisonian pitting of interest against interest: making the workers' power strong enough to equal the employers' power. The other was a conviction that the ultimate interests of workers and employers were intertwined and that their relationship should be cooperative rather than adversarial. As long as Brandeis's thinking sought a balance of power, he was a true Progressive, seeking to conserve traditional capitalism by keeping businesses small and labor both content and well treated. But the other strand in his thinking was more radical.[30]

The 1910 garment worker's strike gave Brandeis an opportunity to put some of his theories into action. The garment industry was an example both of individual capitalism and of the horrors it could inflict on workers. Hordes of would-be business tycoons had managed to secure the few hundred dollars necessary to rent space and machines and to hire a handful of workers. They then became entrepreneurs, producing their own designs or, frequently, serving as subcontractors or even subsubcontractors for slightly larger firms. Because it took so little capital to get a foothold in the garment industry, literally hundreds of such small enterprises existed—Brandeis's estimate was 1,500—paying their workers as little as possible, forcing them to work under unbearable conditions, and desperately fighting the prices of the competition while attempting to stave off bankruptcy. The workers, and their employers, were largely Jewish immigrants from Eastern Europe, although there were also many from Germany and Austria. Workers' families were crammed into tenements and faced lives of endless labor and economic insecurity. However, they were literate; their religion demanded, as had that of the Pilgrims, that at least the men be able to read the Bible and the commentaries on it. So although they were poor and suffered all the concomitant agonies, they also lived in a world of intellectual ferment.

Leaders of the International Ladies' Garment Workers Union had tried unsuccessfully to organize them directly into the ILGWU and continued their efforts in part through the monthly *Garment Worker*. Instead the workers joined locals, which were linked under the Joint Board of Cloak,

Suit & Skirt Makers of New York (in turn a part of the ILGWU), ignoring the *Garment Worker* in favor of the Joint Board's cheap, weekly, and more radical *New Post*. The labor leaders fought each other; the employers competed fiercely; enough of the more outspoken workers espoused socialism to make the employers certain that capitalism itself was under attack from the workers; and in all the volatile in-fighting, workers continued to toil for long hours during the week and on Sundays and holidays, to take work home to their tenements so that entire families could help out, to labor through the night when a big order had to be finished, to pay their employers for the thread and electricity they used, to be paid only when the employers could afford to do so, and to run the risk of being blacklisted and losing their jobs if they became involved in union activities.[31]

The local union leaders, who had managed to enlist only about ten thousand of the roughly sixty thousand workers in the industry, had long supported the idea of a general strike, which the International authorized in June 1910. Coordinated with the Joint Board, it began on July 7 and lasted throughout the hot, humid summer—with almost all of the sixty thousand workers participating. The employers hastily organized a Cloak, Suit & Skirt Manufacturers' Protective Association to help them stand firm against the strikers. There were riots; factories were closed; thousands of workers, treating the strike as a political uprising, were determined not to return to work until their demands were met.[32]

Into the volatile situation went A. Lincoln Filene of Boston. Filene's Department Store was of course affected by the lack of clothes, although the Filenes would have been able to supply their needs through contracts with the employers who had managed to keep their shops open. Filene found this unthinkable, however, having been a union sympathizer for long enough to have earned the trust of New York labor leaders. He, along with Henry Moskowitz, a social worker and activist in the settlement house movement, and Meyer Bloomfield, an attorney, social worker, and settlement house activist, set out to see what they could do. Both Moskowitz and Bloomfield were trusted by the workers; indeed, Bloomfield had helped set up the ILGWU.[33]

They got nowhere. The workers were demanding recognition of their union, a contract, and a closed shop. The manufacturers refused even to speak with the union until it gave up the closed shop as a demand. Filene suggested to both sides that Brandeis be called in, and both sides "responded heartily." Brandeis had earlier told Filene, when the latter had invited Brandeis to go to New York with him, that he would have nothing to do with a closed shop, because it was coercive and would give tyrannical power to unions. The idea was for unions to balance the power of the employers, not to replace it. With the assurance that both sides wanted him, however, Brandeis agreed to enter the fray. "Was called to N.Y. Saturday P.M. to try to settle the N.Y. Garment Workers' strike," he wrote to Al from New York on July 24. "I am trying to bring the parties into conference. It remains to be seen whether my power was as futile as that of the French King & his 40,000 men. I go home at midnight with thermometer out of sight."[34]

By this time, it was Brandeis's habit to bring workers and employers into immediate contact through a conference. But Brandeis was as adamant as the employers that the closed shop could not be considered. In spite of Brandeis's pleas the workers refused to waive this demand, and he went back to Boston. Samuel Gompers, president of the AFL, rushed up from Washington and talked the union into recalling Brandeis. The union's lawyer, Meyer London, and the employers' counsel, Julius Henry Cohen, signed a joint telegram asking him to return and assuring him that the closed shop would not be one of the matters at issue. Brandeis thereupon repeated the trip to New York, and from July 28 through the evening of July 30 he and representatives of the two sides labored in a room in the Metropolitan Tower.[35]

Brandeis and the ten representatives of each side began, at his prodding, with the least contentious of the twelve issues, and gradually whittled down the list. Just when Gompers was so confident of a settlement that he left for Washington, the negotiations broke down over the issue of the closed shop. Brandeis then introduced his own idea, the preferential shop. Employers would have to give preference to union workers if equally skilled union and nonunion workers applied for jobs, but a worker would not have to belong to the union in order to be employed. Questions about competency, or equality of skills, would be decided by a board created for that purpose. The manufacturers agreed; many of the union men, however, felt they could not, and once again the negotiations collapsed. There were a number of backings and fillings during the next few weeks, but eventually, after tumultuous discussion by the workers, the securing by the manufacturers of a temporary injunction forbidding the strikers to keep nonstrikers out of the shops, the continued destitution of workers' families, and much hard work by Filene, Bloomfield, Moskowitz, financier Jacob H. Schiff, and lawyer and Jewish leader Louis Marshall, the settlement suggested by Brandeis was adopted on September 2, 1910.[36]

The agreement was known as "the Protocol," and included much more than recognition of the preferential shop. Brandeis designed it as an experiment in the kind of industrial self-government he was beginning to espouse. The protocol included the normal features of a labor contract: maximum hours, minimum wages, holidays. It also included features peculiar to the garment industry, such as abolition of the charge to workers for electricity and establishment of price committees to fix rates for piecework. Breaking ground, the protocol provided for a seven-member Joint Board of Sanitary Control, whose job would be to oversee and standardize working conditions. (In 1910 factories were rarely inspected by government officials.)

Most important, in addition to establishing the preferential shop, the protocol banned all strikes and lockouts and set up a system for the settlement of disputes. Its lower rung was a Board of Grievances, which was to be called in when union-management shop committees could not solve problems. Its higher rung was a three-person Board of Arbitration, whose members included a representative of the public. Brandeis was immediately asked to be that representative and to chair the board. He accepted but did not expect to do much; his idea was that the shop committees and the Board of Grievances, by bringing labor and management into communication, would obviate the need for outside assistance and would prove that reasonable people exposed to each others' points of view would be able to reach agreement. After some initial malfunctioning by the Board of Grievances and a few changes in the machinery, the system began working fairly well.[37]

Brandeis was delighted. The "tyranny" of the closed shop and the no less onerous tyranny of the open shop had been avoided, and the garment industry was proving that industrial self-management could work. Others thought so as well. When the Chicago garment workers went on strike in November, Jane Addams asked Brandeis to come to Chicago to explain the preferential shop to the workers. (He was too busy to do so, but suggested Filene, Moskowitz, and Bloomfield instead.) A strike in New York in September 1911 led to the establishment of a similar protocol for the Ladies' Tailors and Dress Makers' trade; again, Brandeis was chosen to chair the arbitration board. The same thing occurred in January 1913, after a strike by the Waist and Dress Makers' local.[38]

No sooner had the first protocol been signed than Brandeis began his usual campaign to inform the public. He suggested to Lawrence Abbott of *The Outlook* that Moskowitz be asked for an article about the protocol, with emphasis on the preferential shop. He himself wrote an article entitled "The Spirit of Get-Together" for the September 1911 *American Cloak and Suit Review*. (Furthermore, having achieved credibility with the garment industry, he began propagandizing it about scientific management. Two interviews with him about the subject appeared in the *Cloak and Suit Review* in 1911.) In February 1912, unsatisfied that the preferential shop idea was getting enough media attention, he sent letters to Lincoln Steffens, Ray Stannard Baker, other prominent editors, and various journals, telling them, "This seems to be the time to commence the campaign of education . . . This could be made into a great human story. Would it not be possible for you to take it up?" *La Follette's Weekly* had published an article in December 1911 discussing the report of the Joint Board of Sanitary Control; in January 1913 Brandeis persuaded Frederick Mackenzie, its editor, to ask Moskowitz for an article exploring the preferential shop in more detail.[39]

Brandeis described the protocol as an "essay in industrial democracy." But it was an experiment that in the long run failed. Brandeis's much-vaunted preferential shop gave both management and labor the sense that there was something more for which each could fight: management, for less interference from labor; labor, for the union shop.The protocol sought to bring management and labor together, but counted on "reasonableness" to minimize the conflict. "Reasonableness" collapsed with the economic downturn of 1914–1915. The former secretary of the International, who had initially opposed the preferential shop as a giveaway to the employers, now endorsed the manufacturers' charge that the unions were impossible to work with and called them an "undisciplined *kampflustige* mass whose power can only be a powerful evil" and who were not sufficiently educated for democracy. John A. Dyche's charge of lack of discipline within the unions was correct, but Brandeis replied, "Discipline is not common in democracies, and it is particularly difficult to introduce it where the privates are largely composed of thinkers . . . I am confident that the Jewish workers, with their many good qualities, intellectual and moral, will in time learn discipline also." Brandeis attributed the protocol's difficulties in larger part to the country's bad economic situation. "Criticism, however well founded, if allowed at this time, will do harm, and may prove fatal. The protocol needs nursing." What it got, instead, was attack by both sides; a large-scale lockout in April 1916, followed by an even larger strike, signaled the protocol's demise.[40]

Brandeis had envisaged the protocol as one step on the road to industrial democracy. What the protocol obviously did not do was bridge the divergent interests of employer and employee that were at the heart of labor unrest. When the initial garment industry strike occurred in the summer of 1910, Brandeis was also honing and publicizing his theories of scientific management. For him, there was no question of achieving industrial democracy without scientific management. But Brandeis did not try to force scientific management and the bonus system on the incredulous, Bible-quoting radical workers of New York's sweat shops. He viewed the protocol as an experiment. Praising workers and employers for adopting it, he said, "Both parties recognized that means and methods for improving the difficult relation of employer and employee were proper subjects for study, for invention, and for experiment." It was his wont to fight hard for his ideas and then to heap lavish praise and credit upon those who accepted them. Now he called the garment workers and employers "large-minded" and complimented them for acting "courageously" and with "sympathetic, pains-taking, and able consideration of the practical difficulties arising from day to day in the introduction of a new system." The fact that the experiment failed was not to be taken as an indication of ill will on anyone's part; experiments would not be considered such, after all, if success were certain.[41]

Nonetheless, he believed that the protocol might have continued to work if he or another arbitrator like Judge Julian Mack could have been on the scene constantly; still, he reminded Mack, "the whole purpose was to make resort to the Board of most infrequent occurrence." He was saying, in effect, that if the two sides had received a continuing education in management-labor negotiations, the protocol might have succeeded; the difficulty lay in the newness of the idea rather than in its value. But by the time the protocol collapsed, Brandeis's thinking had changed. He had long opposed compulsory arbitration and had attempted to avoid voluntary arbitration, recognizing that while (as in the garment industry) arbitration might occasionally be needed, problems could best be solved through open discussion and exposure of facts. Now he began to think that the assumption of "mutual concession" that underlay both arbitration and conciliation was wrong, that when a problem appeared, the best way to deal with it was through "invention" or "constructive improvement," that is, an idea that had been thought of by neither side. The preferential shop was such an idea, and he attributed what success the protocol had had to its adoption.[42]

But where were new solutions to be found? Brandeis was attempting to deal with this problem at the same time that his attitude toward workers was changing. He had been enormously heartened by the high level of intelligence and reason he had found among the garment workers. He saw in them the kind of openness to democratic procedures and tolerance for each other's viewpoints that he considered necessary for self-governance. He also discovered them to be democratic in their attitude toward themselves and others: workers and employers shouted at one another with equal abandon in moments of annoyance, and it was clear that the workers did not consider their employers to be their betters and would not treat them as such. He heard a disgruntled worker thundering at his employer in the words of Isaiah 3:3:

> It is you who have devoured the vineyard,
>   the spoil of the poor is in your houses.

What do you mean by crushing My people,
     by grinding the face of the poor?
     says the Lord God of hosts.[43]

Brandeis spent the evenings during the negotiations relaxing with the negotiating committee. Here, at last, were the workers who could still whatever doubts the Brahmin had about the democratic skills of the working class. (The impact they had on Brandeis's Jewishness is a story that will be told later.) Perhaps the bond of Jewishness that he began to feel affected his picture of laborers; perhaps his mental picture of workers from that time on was of the literate, articulate Jews he found in the garment industry; perhaps his theories of industrial relations were postulated on the assumption that such workers would be the norm, and perhaps his intellectual sympathy for the worker was reinforced by the emotional tie he felt with these fellow Jews. Be that as it may, it is clear that Brandeis was impressed by the garment workers and had no difficulty imagining them in conditions of industrial democracy. When the protocol collapsed in 1915, he was ready to draw upon his experience with laborers in the Massachusetts textile, paper, and merchandising industries and in the New York garment industry, as well as his knowledge of railroads and their inefficiencies, for a theory of worker management that would be joined with ideas of "scientific" solutions to business problems.[44]

In 1912 the editor of a magazine called *Human Engineering* had sent Brandeis some back copies, which so impressed him that he sent for a year's subscription and wrote a long letter to the editor. In it, he reiterated his belief that "we can never secure real efficiency without a full development of the individual." Brandeis went on to postulate "two lines of development consistent with industrial democracy." One was unionism; the other, cooperation. And Brandeis's definition of the latter was quite radical. He did not mean "mere profit sharing"; that much he took for granted. In addition to profits the worker had to be given "a share of the responsibilities and management, and a utilization of the latent powers in him." Brandeis then abruptly dropped the topic and turned to a long discussion of the advances made by unionism, the unacceptability of the closed shop, and the advantages of the preferential shop, ending by telling the editor, "I hope that you will take up the subject." (In fact, the entire letter was printed under the title "The Preferential Shop: A Letter from Louis D. Brandeis.") Brandeis had not yet developed the ideas about cooperation that would enable him to explain it in detail. Clearly, it had something to do with the educated garment workers he had found to be such good candidates for the new industrial democracy. It also had to do with profit sharing, but with a vague something else as well.[45]

In May 1913 Brandeis was still feeling his way. He wrote to an advocate of profit sharing that "unless it [could] be combined with a real labor co-partnership," it was bound to be a disappointment. "To attain real efficiency we must overcome the sense of injustice; and I doubt whether a sharing of profit, without a sharing of responsibilities,—in other words, without real cooperation,—will accomplish what we long for. In the end, industrial democracy must attend political democracy." But what did democracy mean? At the very least it meant the opportunity to participate in policymaking. He was thinking in these terms in November 1913, when he wrote to an attorney interested in social reform as a way of staving off socialism, "It seems to me that the prevailing discontent is due perhaps less to dissatisfaction with the material conditions, as to the denial of participation in management, and that the only way to avoid Socialism is to develop cooperation in its broadest sense." Control over one's life was at least as important as material things. He wrote to another corresondent a few days later, "It has seemed to me that you do not lay sufficient stress upon the importance of industrial liberty. No amount of material well-being can make up for the lack of that."[46]

Many of Brandeis's experiences were coming together in a general theory of labor relations. In the testimony he gave on January 23, 1915, before the Commission on Industrial Relations he declared that large corporations did not tend to produce "a higher grade of workman and citizens"; that they interfered with the growth of unions; that they tended to be dominated by financial interests unable to deal intelligently with the problems of corporations because of human limitations; that wide-scale distribution of stock to members of the community was a form of absentee landlordism and thoroughly irresponsible; that the preferential shop presented fewer opportunities for the abuse of power than did the closed shop; that scientific management was the hope of the industrial future; and that fixing minimum wages for an entire state, without reference to the occupations and varying costs of living in different localities, would be unscientific and uneconomic ("the minimum wage in a department store, for instance, ought to be higher than the minimum wage in a factory, because the girl in the department store has to dress well all the time and that costs money"). But most of all he emphasized the need for industrial democracy, and in doing so he began to spell out the idea of worker-management.

Unrest, to my mind, never can be removed—and fortunately never can be removed—by mere improvement of the physical and material condition of the workingman. If it were possible we should run great risk of improving their material condition and reducing their manhood. We must bear in mind all the time that however much we may desire material improvement and must desire it for the comfort of the individual, that the United States is a democracy, and that we must have, above all things, men. It is the development of manhood to which any industrial and social system should be directed. We Americans are committed not only to social justice in the sense of avoiding things which bring suffering and harm, like unjust distribution of wealth; but we are committed primarily to democracy. The social justice for which we are striving is an incident of our democracy, not the main end. It is rather the result of democracy—perhaps its finest expression—but it rests upon democracy, which implies the rule by the people. And therefore the end for which we must strive is the attainment of rule by the people, and that involves industrial democracy as well as political democracy."[47]

So far, Brandeis might have been echoing the words of any labor leader who argued that it was a denigration of human beings to have them at the whim and mercy of other human beings. However, his next words, envisioned much more than negotiations over wages and hours:

[Democracy] means that the problem of a trade should be not longer the problems of the employer alone. The problems of his business, and it is not the employer's business alone, are the problems of all in it . . . The problems which exist are the problems of the trade; they are the problems of employer and employee. Profit sharing, however liberal, can not meet the situation . . .
   There must be a division not only of profits, but a division also of responsibilities. The employees must have the opportunity of participating in the decisions as to what shall be their condition and how the business shall be run. They must learn also in sharing that responsibility that they must bear to the suffering arising from grave mistakes, just as the employer must. But the right to assist in making the decisions, the right of making their own mistakes, if mistakes there must be, is a privilege which should not be denied to labor. We must insist upon labor sharing the responsibilities for the result of the business.[48]

Brandeis insisted that the employees should participate not only in decisions "as to what shall be their condition," which presumably could mean no more than hours and wages, but also in decisions about "how the business shall be run." One of the commissioners sought clarification:

Commissioner Weinstock: Let us be sure, please, that we understand alike the meaning of industrial democracy. I understand by industrial democracy a condition whereby the worker has a voice in the management of the industry—a voice in its affairs. Do we agree on that?

Mr. Brandeis: Yes, sir; and not only a voice but a vote; not merely a right to be heard, but a position through which labor may participate in management.[49]

Brandeis explained that the making of a contract and the introduction of collective bargaining was "a great advance," but no more than the "first step." The process had to "go further and create practically an industrial government." The example he chose was that of the garment trade protocol, which he described as "the most promising indications in the American industrial world." He portrayed the protocol as creating a system "as continuous as our political Government," in which employers and employees "come together to determine the problems of the trade in precisely the same way that members of the legislatures and the judges of the courts come together to decide the matters for the Nation or of the State or of the city." Brandeis praised the process as leading employees and employers to realize that "conscious fault or wrongdoing on either side is rather uncommon" and that their problems were no more than "condition[s] to be remedied" through cooperation. He cited an employer who had come up to him during one of the bitter quarrels of the preceding year and said, " 'We can not do this thing that the union wants; but if I were the union representative, I should ask for the same thing.' " Brandeis was immensely heartened by this demonstration of rationality.[50]

His view of the alteration in attitudes within the garment industry may have been overly rosy, but more important is what Brandeis thought the protocol system might lead to. Asked by the same commissioner if he was saying that "there is an earnest and sincere effort on both sides to find equity," Brandeis replied, "I think we have gotten past the point" of merely seeking equity: "They have reached now a desire to solve industrial problems, and the recognition that the problems of the employer can not be solved by shifting them onto the employee, and that the problems of the employee can not be solved by shifting them onto the employer; that some way must be found to arrive at the cause of the difficulty, to remove that cause . . . That is a hopeful attitude."[51]

Brandeis did not consider the protocol perfect. For one thing, it did not incorporate scientific management. But the constant communication minimized lack of understanding. Turning to other industries, Brandeis commented that workers tended to overestimate the amount of money a company was making and that a solution was to open the books to the workers. Any employer, he said, needed to have labor understand the real situation of his business. "Put a competent representative of labor on your board of directors; make him grapple with the problems whether to do or not to do a specific thing, and undertake to balance the advantages and disadvantages presented, and he will get a realizing sense of how difficult it is to operate a business successfully and what the dangers are of the destruction of the capital in the business." Let labor have the facts and remove labor from the arbitrary power of the employer; that would come close to ending labor disputes.[52]

This, then, was the beginning of Brandeis's answer to the problem of how to make workers economically as well as politically independent in an industrial society. By all means better the working conditions, the hours and wages, but consider that as no more than a first step, as even union recognition and the acceptance by employers of collective bargaining were no more than a first step. Speaking of the unions' success in exercising some control over wages, hours, and conditions, and in eliminating children from the coal industry, Brandeis said, "They are all gains for manhood; and we recognize that manhood is what we are striving for in America. We are striving for democracy; we are striving for the development of men. It is absolutely essential in order that men may develop that they be properly fed and properly housed, and that they have proper opportunities of education and recreation. We can not reach our goal without those things. But we may have all those things and have a nation of slaves."[53]

Once again, Brandeis returned to his first principle of human dignity and control over one's existence. He could not applaud the paternalistic employer who gave his employees all the material benefits a union might have won but kept out the union, for nonunionization denied the workers self-determination. Even with a union the primary goal might not be achieved if each worker did not participate in finding solutions to mutual problems. Brandeis was particularly enthusiastic about the early stages of scientific management, because they required the joint efforts of labor and management. Scientific management advocates had not yet shifted their emphasis from concern for the individual to the needs of administrators as they did in the 1920s; they put a premium on the cooperation of labor in helping discover which tasks were performed inefficiently and what steps had to be taken to rectify the errors. It was the perceived mutuality of interest, as well as the increased profits for both labor and management, that made Brandeis so enthusiastic about the system.[54]

Taken to its logical conclusion, the idea of making industrial workers independent meant more than permitting them to establish strong unions. Both the relatively successful Filene example (Chapter 7) and the doomed protocol took negotiations about wages and hours as a given and went on to provide methods for dealing with disputes over other conditions of labor. But neither the members of the Filene Association nor the garment workers covered by the protocol had any control over decisions that might be every bit as important to them as wages: merchandising techniques; decisions to relocate, which would cause unemployment, and which in fact became widespread later in the century as much of the garment industry moved to the nonunionized South; selection of products to be manufactured or sold; and so on. Scientific management presumably would mean that workers and employers would agree on production goals, as well as distribution of extra profits made from the business's functioning in excess of expectations. This implied that the union's involvement in decision making would be increased, as did Brandeis's suggestion that every board of directors include a representative of labor. It can be argued that putting a union member on the board would constitute a move away from the traditional differentiation between management and labor, for labor would then become part of management. But the step would be such a small one as to be insignificant, and the fact that the newcomer to the board would first have to be a laborer would make the step seem even smaller. Still, if enough laborers were included in a profit-sharing plan *and* participated in policymaking beyond the issues usually considered to be union matters, the differentiation would have begun to break down.

At this point Brandeis unknowingly hovered between Progressivism and radical worker-management. Progressivism was in many ways a conservative movement, aimed at protecting the world of the small business and at limiting new areas of government involvement to those that would aid in this endeavor, for example, trust-busting and reinvigorating small-scale competition. If Brandeis was to go beyond the notion of opposing the strength of one faction with the force of another, and completely embrace the Jeffersonian insistence that the economically dependent citizen could not be politically independent, he would have to opt at the least for a severe limitation on the differences between labor and management. And, cautiously, he did.[55]

Brandeis did not advocate a specific system of worker-management, not only because the idea flouted all existing preconceptions about social and economic roles but also because worker-management had not undergone sufficient experimentation. In 1913 Brandeis in effect told an interviewer how far away from such a scheme the United States was: "We already have had industrial despotism. With the recognition of the unions, this is changing into a constitutional monarchy . . . Next comes profit-sharing. This, however, is to be only a transitional, half-way stage. Following upon it will come the sharing of responsibility, as well as of profits. The eventual outcome promises to be full-grown industrial democracy." Then he added, "As to this last step the Socialists have furnished us with an ideal full of suggestion."[56]

In his reference to the Socialists, Brandeis surely was not speaking of their example of bureaucracy and centralization, because he loathed both. Nonetheless, he said the Socialists had a lesson to teach about industrial democracy and indicated that it had something to do with the sharing of responsibility. This must have meant more than the settlement of grievances, for had it been only grievance machinery that was in his mind, there was every reason for him to cite the then-functioning protocol and no reason whatsoever to wave the red flag of socialism. Fortunately, other events and statements give clues to his exact meaning.

Cooperatives of various kinds were feeding into Brandeis's approach to labor. He first learned of cooperatives from Beatrice Potter's *Cooperative Movement in Great Britain,* a history of the workers' cooperative movement in Great Britain and an argument for the important role trade unions would have to play if the movement was to succeed. Potter described factories and workshops with "a brotherhood of workers controlling the organization and retaining the profits of their own labour"; mills "owned and governed by the men and women who actually worked" there; and the fifty-four manufacturing associations and five agricultural associations that existed at the time the book was written. She argued that the failure of many worker-run enterprises, or their gradual conversion into traditional capitalistic businesses, was attributable to insufficient democracy within the enterprise, lack of support from without, and too little understanding of economics and market forces. She insisted that small worker-managed enterprises had to be linked through a Cooperative Union that would also include consumer cooperatives.[57]

Potter and her husband Sidney Webb were leading members of the socialistic Fabian Society, and their goal was the evolution of a Socialist state. Brandeis could not accept the massive bureaucracy he was certain would follow, but it is extremely important to note his praise of Potter's book and his continuing interest in the writings of the cooperative-minded English Socialists. In 1923 he read the Webbs' newly published *Decay of Capitalist Civilization* and recommended part of it to Felix Frankfurter's wife. Later that year he told his economist daughter Elizabeth, "Perhaps some day you may conclude to do for the Massachusetts textile industry—with its Lowell and Lawrence and Fall River—what the Hammonds have done in 'The Town Labourer,'—an admirable book,—or the Webbs in The Cooperative Movement." His reference to Potter's book (Brandeis was inaccurate in attributing the book to both Webbs; Potter had written it alone, although the Webbs collaborated on a book about consumer cooperatives) as a work for his daughter to emulate indicates his acceptance of the book's scholarship and veracity. When complimenting Harold Laski on his *Recovery of Citizenship,* Brandeis wrote, "In most instruments of social-economic advance the credits have set against them debits—sometimes heavy ones. In the Cooperatives there are only credits;—and the problem is merely one of occupying the field, and of overcoming defects, of perfecting the instrument." That was precisely Potter's point.[58]

Brandeis came to believe that the consumers' cooperatives of Sweden, Denmark, Switzerland, and England both reduced the cost of living and eliminated in part "the evil of capitalistic exploitation," because sufficiently large cooperatives could force the trusts to lower prices. He also advocated producers' cooperatives (as well as cooperative banks and credit unions), which by distributing responsibility were a force for democracy and individual development. In addition "the producer's cooperatives to large extent, merge into consumers' cooperatives, that is, the consumers through their cooperatives should become also producers, as they already are to a considerable extent." Speaking of cooperatives, he said that when people were good enough to become good Socialists they would not need socialism. He told associates of his admiration for the Scandinavian countries, where he saw the so-called Socialist governments as not socialistic in action. They did not have to be, Brandeis said; independent groups worked out the answers. He was particularly taken by Denmark, which had cooperative factories as well as consumers' cooperatives; in fact, he was so interested in small-scale Denmark and its social experiments that he later encouraged his wife and his sister-in-law to publish a volume entitled *Democracy in Denmark*. The first part was an essay by Josephine Goldmark called "Democracy in Action"; the second, Alice Brandeis's translation of a work on Danish folk high schools. He was well versed in the literature about cooperatives, subscribing to the *International Cooperative Bulletin*. In an interview given to the Sunday *Boston Post* shortly after he appeared before the Commission on Industrial Relations in 1915, Brandeis showed that he was beginning to think about workers' cooperatives in the United States.[59]

He spoke of the American protocol-type boards as "a large step toward industrial democracy, but of course only a step." Going even further, Brandeis envisioned the end of the employer-employee distinction: "In a democratic community we naturally long for that condition where labor will hire capital, instead of capital hiring labor." This, he said, could occur either through a rather vague system in which the community was served by "laborers who hire capital" or through "co-operative enterprises, private or public, by which the community undertakes to provide itself with necessaries." The example of the latter that he discussed at length was England's Co-operative Wholesale Society. The society encompassed flour mills, England's largest shoe factory, apparel factories, manufacturers of prepared food and household articles, creameries, printing plants, coal fields, a bacon factory in Denmark, a tallow and oil factory in Australia, and a tea plantation in Ceylon. Its annual gross of $150 million made it bigger than most American industries. What impressed Brandeis even more than the low prices made possible by the society was its method of choosing leaders. They were not selected "by England's leading bankers or other notables supposed to possess unusual wisdom, but democratically, by all the people interested in the operations of the society, and the number of such persons who have directly or indirectly a voice in the selection of the directors of the English Co-operative Wholesale Society is 2,750,000, for the directors of the wholesale society are elected by vote of the delegates of the 1899 retail societies, and the delegates of the retail societies are in turn selected by the members of the local societies, that is, by the consumers, on the principle of one man, one vote, regardless of the amount of capital contributed." Thirty-two full-time directors were selected in this way. Their combined salaries were less than that of many an American executive: in 1915, each director was paid about $1500 a year. "That," Brandeis commented with obvious satisfaction, "shows what industrial democracy can do."[60]

Brandeis had been advocating for years a system of profit sharing that would enable workers to own stock in the companies for which they worked. Combined with the Co-operative Wholesale Society's "one man, one vote" procedure, the result would be worker selection of management; and, as Brandeis added, the directors chosen by the society were frequently "men who have risen from the ranks." He insisted, "We in America must come to the co-operative idea." That he meant workers as well as consumers when he spoke of those involved in cooperatives was clear from his discussion of the psychological and "scientific" benefits involved. He spoke of American employers complaining that they worked harder than their employees and agreed that this was often true. But, he added, "there are few things so interesting in life as work, under proper conditions"; and the fact that employers worked so hard proved that they were "having the satisfaction which comes from work." The workers were not. "The men who are denied participation in the business are denied that satisfaction, and therefore do not in many instances exert themselves to the utmost, although they may be working the full number of hours allotted, and maybe more . . . however much they may wish to get the most out of themselves, they cannot possibly do so unless the conditions are such as to give them satisfaction in what they are doing, and they cannot get satisfaction except through freedom." In those societies, like the United States, where citizens were "accustomed to democratic ideas," there could be no hope for the greatest possible efficiency "until the workingman feels that he is working, not for somebody else, but for himself and others jointly."[61]

Then, too, Brandeis was overseeing the Jewish kibbutzim in Palestine, which were experiments in cooperative living. All of a kibbutz's land, equipment, and possessions were owned jointly; all decisions were made in meetings of kibbutz members; all the kibbutzniks' needs were filled by the kibbutz. Obviously, this was not a system that could be transported to the United States: it was based on small agricultural settlements (although, since Brandeis's day, kibbutzim have branched out into light industry); the workers lived communally, eating their meals together and putting their children to sleep in the children's quarters; and the workers had no need of money since their legitimate wants were supplied by the community. Although none of these elements could or would be transported to the United States, the kibbutzim gave Brandeis a concrete example of communal, nonbureaucratized, democratic living, in which there was no differentiation between management and labor. He began learning about the kibbutzim as early as 1914, when he assumed leadership of the American Zionist movement, and his enthusiasm for them as essays in democratic life was evident in all the speeches he made about them thereafter.

In addition his friend Norman Hapgood and Hapgood's two brothers owned an Indianapolis manufacturing plant, the Columbia Conserve Company, run primarily by Hapgood's older brother Hutchins. In 1917 Hutchins Hapgood began bringing labor into the management of the company. He did this without pressure from labor; indeed, union organizers were given free access to the plant but met a cool reception from workers who considered themselves better off under the Hapgood regime. Hutchins Hapgood found the workers surprisingly conservative. At one point, when the cost of living had risen, he suggested that the workers might want to give themselves a raise. They responded that it was too early to tell whether the business could afford it and waited six months before raising their wages. The Hapgoods were concerned that the experiences of the working class did not inspire self-confidence but habituated it to await decisions from above. Nonetheless, Hutchins began to wonder whether the workers, whom he had been guiding to make company policy, ought not to own the business. He discovered that as the workers increased their participation in management, efficiency was also increased; perhaps the process would continue if they owned the business outright. He therefore met with them over a period of time to settle upon the dividend rate that should be paid and the amount of money each share of stock was worth. It was agreed that if the company continued its growth, all profits above the established dividend (7 percent) would be used to buy the stock for the workers. By 1930 this plan had enabled the workers to buy the majority of the stock, owning it not as individuals but in the form of a trust, the proceeds of which were divided among those working the business.

Although other business people were hostile initially, Hutchins was beginning to interest them in his scheme. By 1930 he was being asked to give more talks about his experiment than he had time for and found that he met friendly skepticism rather than hostility. Norman Hapgood explained the change in attitude thus: "The basic fact that the company makes more money under its humane policy than it did under the conventional business regime preceding it gives a firm foundation for discussion, since Americans are suspicious of moral-sounding theories that give no indication of being adjustable to the world in which we live." Brandeis approved of the experiment and followed it with interest; indeed, he may have helped it along, since he was on good terms with both Norman and William Powers Hapgood, the third of the brothers and president of the Columbia Conserve Company.[62]

It therefore seems clear that Brandeis saw the desired wave of the future as some kind of worker-management or worker-participation: workers owning a business and voting democratically to elect management. Brandeis was not entirely clear about ownership. Whether stock would be held by workers alone, or by both workers and consumers, or even by the public in its collective capacity, as in his reference to public as opposed to private cooperatives (and in keeping with his belief that utilities and land should be owned by the public), was not specified. It was in keeping with Brandeis's general method not to opt for any one possibility until experiments in all had been made and factual data collected. He might look forward to the disintegration of the dividing line between labor and management, but the man who in 1933 still hoped that not too many states would institute his own plan for savings bank life insurance until the experiment had had more time to prove itself (and the experiment had been in existence since 1908!) would not speak as if the disappearance of "labor" and "management" as separate entities was about to occur. It was clearly his firm hope for the future, but, for the moment, intermediate steps had to be taken. Just as the creation of savings bank life insurance did not lead Brandeis to stop his attempts to get insurance companies to lower their rates for industrial life insurance, his theorizing about worker-management did not slow his continuing efforts to bring labor and management together in a more cooperative relationship. He therefore went on using the terms "labor," "capital," and "management," thereby possibly misleading some commentators that he was no more than a basically conservative Progressive. He was not; the logic of his own ideas, coupled with his capacity for brilliant creativity, led him to more radical dreams.[63]

They of course remained no more than dreams. Even when Brandeis was directly or indirectly advising President Franklin Roosevelt on his economic program, he did not suggest legislation that would have begun a movement in the direction of worker-management. Again, this was typically Brandeisian. Worker-management was still in its experimental stages in England, and so was scarcely ready to be transferred to the United States. Had Brandeis proposed government-encouraged worker-management at all in the 1930s, it would no doubt have taken the form of a suggestion that a state rather than the federal government take on the experiment.

Not too long after Brandeis's testimony about the future of industrial democracy before the Commission on Industrial Relations and his subsequent interview, Woodrow Wilson nominated him for the Supreme Court. His career as an innovator in industrial relations necessarily came to an abrupt end. His thinking, however, did not, and the years after 1916 brought evidence that it was still running along the line of the workers' assuming full responsibility for their workplaces in some collective manner. This perhaps emerges most clearly in the 1922 letter he wrote to Robert Bruère. Once he had joined the Court, Brandeis rarely spoke in public about anything other than Zionism, but Bruère and others had persuaded him to speak informally to a group connected with the Department of Research and Education of the Federal Council of Churches in America. He later sent a summary of his remarks to Bruère. Alpheus T. Mason has called the letter a statement of Brandeis's "creed." Indeed, it brings together his combination of conservatism and creativity, his high sense of morality, his belief in slow progress, his insistence upon experimentation and rationality, his ideas about labor, and, above all, his emphasis on democracy and the individuals for whom it was designed.

> Refuse to accept as inevitable any evil in business (e.g. irregularity of employment). Refuse to tolerate any immoral practice (e.g. espionage). But do not believe that you can find a universal remedy for evil conditions or immoral practices in effecting a fundamental change in society (as by State Socialism). And do not pin too much faith in legislation. Remedial institutions are apt to fall under the control of the enemy and to become instruments of oppression.
>
> Seek for betterment within the broad lines of existing institutions. Do so by attacking evil in situ; and proceed from the individual to the general. Remember that progress is necessarily slow; that remedies are necessarily tentative; that, because of varying conditions, there must be much and constant enquiry into facts (like that being

made by your Bureau) and much experimentation; and that always and everywhere the intellectual, moral and spiritual development of those concerned will remain an essential—and the main factor—in real betterment.

This development of the individual is, thus, both a necessary means and the end sought. For our objective is the making of men and women who shall be free—self-respecting members of a democracy—and who shall be worthy of respect. Improvement in material conditions of the worker and ease are the incidents of better conditions—valuable mainly as they may ever increase opportunities for development.

The great developer is responsibility. Hence, no remedy can be hopeful which does not devolve upon the workers' participation in, responsibility for the conduct of business; and their aim should be the eventual asssumption of full responsibility—as in cooperative enterprises. This particiaption in and eventual control of industry is likewise an essential of obtaining justice in distributing the fruits of industry.

But democracy in any sphere is a serious undertaking. It substitutes self-restraint for external restraint. It is more difficult to maintain than to achieve. It demands continuous sacrifice by the individual and more exigent obedience to the moral law than any other form of government. Success in any democratic undertaking must proceed from the individual. It is possible only where the process of perfecting the individual is pursued. His development is attained mainly in the processes of common living.[64]

The letter could stand as a testament to human dignity, but it is also an indication that Brandeis had come to believe that workers should assume "full responsibility" for the conduct of business, "as in cooperative enterprises." By the time Brandeis wrote his letter to Bruère the Russian Revolution had occurred and he, like many others, was excited by the promise of equality it seemed to hold in its early years. That may have been another source of his belief that workers could run their own businesses. In the early 1920s he told Felix Frankfurter that the "wage system is doomed"—that the loyalty workers might once have had to owners they knew had been made impossible by the introduction of public corporations and the unseen stockholder. He added that consumers ought to go without goods if they could not buy them through cooperatives. He wrote to George Soule, a *New Republic* editor and writer on economic and social matters:

Teach the public
1. To buy through consumers cooperatives
2. To refuse to buy any nationally advertised brand & to look with suspicion upon every advertised article

3. Start a buyers' strike at any rise in price of any staple article of common consumption.

The Consumer is servile, self-indulgent, indolent, ignorant. Let the buyer beware.

Three years later he wrote to Frankfurter again and demanded, "Isn't there among your economists some one who could make clear to the country that the greatest of social-economic troubles arise from the fact that the consumer has failed absolutely to perform his function? . . . He gets no worse than his desserts. But the trouble is that the parallelogram of social forces is disrupted thereby. It destroys absolutely the balance of power & lets producers and distributors "trim the balance of the world" as C C [presumably Calvin Coolidge] would say." Worker-participation and consumers' cooperatives were integral parts of the same vision.[65]

Brandeis never lost faith in his vision. He continued to urge on the fight for regularity of employment, and during the New Deal he supported laws to legitimize labor unions, establish unemployment insurance, and regulate minimum wages and maximum hours. But his hope was that government intervention with employers would ultimately be unnecessary, for the employers would be the workers themselves. It was an incredibly bold vision, especially coming from a multimillionaire Supreme Court justice in 1922.

It may also have been one of the few serious and competent efforts to bring Jeffersonianism into the industrial era. If liberty was dependent upon economic independence, but participation in the twentieth-century American economy implied factory work for great masses of citizens, then a concept that would encompass both liberty and the factory had to be found. To Brandeis, it was the liberty to participate in industrial decision-making. Reformist innovations, however, are rarely undertaken to promote profits. Brandeis told the Commission on Industrial Relations about a New York real estate tycoon who had lamented that the fire legislation enacted in New York after the tragic Triangle Shirtwaist Company fire in 1911 "required changes in factories so extensive as to rob much property of its earning power." Brandeis cited the comment as indicating that if legislation, whether building codes or minimum wage laws, were necessary for the public welfare, it would have to be passed regardless of its impact on corporate well-being. Although he was the attorney of businessmen, he was far more interested in the well-being of individuals than in that of corporations. Had the United States, particularly under as charismatic a leader as Franklin Roosevelt, chosen to make the political decision that individual liberty in the industrial era necessitated scaling down the size of business and beginning the introduction of worker-management, the business community would have howled with outrage and then would have coped—as it did with the abolition of child labor, the institution of minimum wages and maximum hours, the legitimization of labor unions, and a host of other reforms that it claimed at the time would destroy the economy. Whether the political influence of the giant corporations was so great during the New Deal that even a president of Roosevelt's stature would have found it impossible to legislate such a program is another question. But no such attempt was made; the Brandeisians lost the battle for Roosevelt's ear, and what might have been the solution to the problem of protecting economic liberty and independence in an industrial society never received full-scale discussion or meaningful experimentation. The "People's Attorney" was busy with the work of the Supreme Court and constrained both by its limitations on his activities and by his age and flagging energies. The experiment would have had to be taken up by others, and they were too busy elsewhere.[66]

If the Roosevelt administration missed an opportunity to experiment with Brandeis's ideas, so did the labor movement, for labor's mainstream insistently retained its posture as an adversary of business and concentrated on working conditions rather than on bringing labor into management. The result, seen from the vantage point of the 1980s' is exactly what Brandeis feared: the part of the work force that is unionized (and the insufficient "pull" of purely material objectives may be one factor in the extremely low percentage of laborers who are union members) has made enormous economic gains and enjoys a level of material well-being that would have been impossible without the organization of unions. At the same time, however, labor suffers from a sense of alienation and anomie, continues to feel threatened and ill-treated, and is as far from enjoying industrial liberty and equality as it was in Brandeis's day. None of this is to denigrate the efforts of the unions, which forced a major redistribution of wealth in the United States. But they did not see past wealth to the democratic process. One might remember Brandeis writing, "Improvements of material conditions are merely incidents of better conditions, valuable mainly as they may ever increase opportunities for development." It is questionable whether the unions have achieved opportunities for nonmaterial development, whether the United States has proved "that as we have in the political world shown what self-government can do, we are to pursue the same lines in the industrial world," whether American capitalism has put labor in the position of "sharing the responsibilities for the result of the business." Brandeis's dramatic warning that workers may have material things and remain "a nation of slaves" may seem to be an overstatement of today's situation, but if the United States is not a nation of slaves, neither is it an industrial democracy.[67]

11 | Wilson and
   the New Freedom

Brandeis did not know Woodrow Wilson when the former political science professor, president of Princeton University, and governor of New Jersey was selected to run for president at the June 1912 Democratic convention. He did know, however, that the same convention had adopted William Jennings Bryan's resolution renouncing "the privilege-hunting and favor-seeking class." This was a slap at the financiers Brandeis had been fighting for years, and Brandeis rejoiced that the Democrats were determined "to drive the money-lenders out of the temple." Brandeis credited Bryan with running the convention so as to put the Democratic party solidly on the road toward progressivism. Given what he had heard of Wilson, "particularly his discussion of economic problems" and the program Wilson had endorsed, Brandeis felt certain that the thing for Progressives to do was to rally behind him.[1]

On July 10 Brandeis issued a statement calling Wilson's nomination "among the most encouraging events in American History." Initially, he had hoped that Roosevelt would withdraw and throw his support behind Wilson at the National Progressive Convention, scheduled for August 5. Brandeis, who had retained his close ties with Gifford Pinchot in spite of the latter's secession from the La Follette camp and who had spent several days during the summer yachting with Pinchot, attempted to enlist his aid in getting Roosevelt to withdraw. Two days before he came out for Wilson, Brandeis told Pinchot, "It is in the power of the Progressives today to make complete their control of the Democratic organization; and [attain] the great march of Progressive legislation for which you and

I long." However, Roosevelt did not drop out of the race, and Brandeis reported sadly to his brother, "Most of my progressive friends will stand by T.R."[2]

The exchange of ideas between Brandeis and Wilson began on August 1, when Brandeis wrote complimenting Wilson on his proposal to lower tariffs by 5 percent a year. He called the plan "true statesmanship," commenting to Hapgood that it showed the Progressives were right to support Wilson. In fact, months before Wilson made his statement, Brandeis, who had been convinced of the necessity of tariff reduction for years, had discussed just such a plan with Representative William C. Redfield of Brooklyn, one of Wilson's advisers. Wilson of course knew who Brandeis was; by 1912, everyone in national politics recognized him as one of the Progressive spokesmen. Wilson replied that the letter had given him "a great deal of pleasure," and expressed his hope that the coming months would "give me the benefit of many conferences with you." On August 26 Charles Crane sent Brandeis a telegram saying that Wilson wanted to see him. Brandeis promptly took a night train from South Yarmouth, where he was vacationing, to New York and the next morning proceeded on to Sea Girt, New Jersey, and his meeting with Wilson. The two men lunched together on August 28 and spent three hours afterward talking, primarily about trusts. Brandeis replied to reporters' questions about what they had discussed that the topic was "a number of bills," all having to do "with our industries." He added that they were in complete agreement. Wilson praised Brandeis as knowing more about both the economics and politics of corporations than anyone else he knew. He declared their joint object to be "the prevention of monopoly," which is "created by unregulated competition, by competition that overwhelms all other competitions, and the only way to enjoy industrial freedom is to destroy that condition." Brandeis then returned to New York for dinner, took the night train to Boston, and arrived back in South Yarmouth the following morning.[3]

He was "very favorably impressed" with Wilson. "He is strong, simple, serious, openminded, eager to learn and deliberate." Wilson was certainly openminded where Brandeis was concerned, recognizing fairly quickly that Brandeis had clear answers to what should be done about the trusts. A confirmed capitalist, Wilson was also a moral Calvinist. Good and evil were clearly defined; moral compromise was impossible. His Calvinism permeated his capitalism. Both, he believed, were based on the importance of the individual. The Calvinist sign of the chosen was morality; the reward for morality in business was prosperity. The trusts were bad, because they made it impossible for individual moral capitalists to reap the rewards that were their due. Thus, Wilson was certain that the trusts were wrong, but he did not know how to deal with them. As Wilson's most authoritative biographer has noted, Brandeis became the "chief architect of the New Freedom" and the "man whose opinions on economic questions he [Wilson] respected above all others."[4]

Brandeis's statement to the reporters that he and Wilson were in complete agreement was not accurate, for what had happened was less a meeting of minds than the acceptance by Wilson of Brandeis as his tutor. Wilson could not agree or disagree with Brandeis because he did not yet understand his approach to the economy. Wilson's attitude toward the trusts only four years before had been one of admiration for their efficiency, although he had been inveighing against the money trust for years. He rejected the idea of government regulation as socialistic and leading inevitably to government ownership. Even though he recognized that there were evils attendant upon big business, his preferred solution was to open corporate meetings to the public, to direct the individuals involved away from sin and to punish them if they erred, but to do nothing about the institutions as such. As late as mid-1912, his campaign speeches called only for application of the criminal provisions of the Sherman Act.[5]

Because Wilson feared big government and was unable to see any way of controlling big business other than by balancing it with big government, he considered the cure fully as bad as the malady. If the price of restraining the trusts was the growth of government, then it was better for the trusts to remain unfettered and for citizens to hope that goodness would triumph in the hearts of corporate leaders. Brandeis would gradually show Wilson that government could create the conditions for the renewal of competition without itself becoming too big.

Clearly, the lessons began at the very first meeting at Sea Girt, for Wilson's attack on "competition that overwhelms all other competitions" and must be destroyed was both completely new for him and thoroughly Brandeisian. Within days, Wilson was urging restriction of the kind of competition that results in monopoly. There was no indication in his speeches, however, that he knew how to go about creating the necessary restrictions on monopoly until his speech in Boston on September 27. Wilson drove through the streets in an open automobile, Brandeis seated beside him, on his way to give a noon address at Tremont Temple. There he told his audience that corporations could become so big that they became inefficient. He now expounded two Brandeisian themes: unrestricted competition was bad because it resulted in monopoly, and monopolies were inefficient. Brandeis had presented Wilson with a program on which he could campaign, convincing him that the most important question confronting the American people in 1912 was that of economic freedom.[6]

Wilson left Boston after giving the speech but immediately telegraphed Brandeis, asking him to "please set forth as explicitly as possible the actual measures by which competition can be effectively regulated. The more explicit we are on this point," he explained, "the more completely will the enemies guns be spiked." They had talked about the matter during their car ride, so the request did not surprise Brandeis. Wilson's telegram suggested urgency but Brandeis was busy testifying before the Interstate Commerce Commission about the sins of the New Haven Railroad and could not reply for two days. In the interim he forwarded to Wilson copies of suggestions he had given to Hapgood for articles entitled "Concentration" and "Trusts and the Interstate Commerce Commission." On September 30, he sent Wilson "suggestions for the letter, about which we talked, dealing with the difference between your attitude and Roosevelt's on trusts and the remedies you propose to apply." The suggestions took the form of a lengthy summary of the problems with the Sherman Act and the virtues of La Follette's (and Brandeis's) proposed amendments. He discussed the emphasis of the "New Party" (Brandeis refused to call Roosevelt's party by its preferred title of Progressive) on accepting monopoly as long as it was regulated, as opposed to the insistence of the Democratic party that monopoly had to be prevented. Brandeis urged Wilson to "make clear to the Country that, in respect to natural resources, as well as human resources, you are quite as determined as the New Party leaders that a broad policy of conservation shall prevail." Brandeis was of course concerned that Roosevelt, widely viewed as a friend of conservation, would take that issue away from Wilson. And he emphasized the point he hoped Wilson would hammer home: the difference between the economic policies exposed by the two parties "is the difference between industrial liberty and industrial absolutism."[7]

Wilson and William Gibbs McAdoo thought that Brandeis's letter of September 30 was too detailed for use in speeches, although Wilson told McAdoo how much he liked it. McAdoo then suggested that Brandeis put the details into the form of articles. He did so, sending Hapgood articles called "Trusts, Efficiency and the New Party" and "Trusts, the Export Trade, and the New Party" for *Collier's*. As Brandeis wrote to his brother, "*Entre nous* I have Norman supplied with editorials—through the October 19th number & shall probably add two more to make the full measure." Wilson read the articles and editorials carefully; again, they were quickly echoed in his speeches, and he was soon proclaiming that "what this country needs above everything else is a body of laws which will look after the men who are on the make rather than the men who are already made." Both Wilson and Brandeis were firm believers in the pioneer as well as the capitalist ethic; indeed,

Brandeis had demonstrated this in his concern over policy toward Alaska.[8]

In addition to the articles for *Collier's,* Brandeis wrote a lengthy letter to the *Boston Journal* comparing the two parties' attitudes toward labor. By permitting the continued existence of the trusts, Brandeis told the *Journal*'s readers, the New Party menaced labor; the trusts of course prohibited unions. Brandeis dismissed the New Party's fourteen planks on labor as no more than a few paternalistic measures to lighten the load of the worker, "who, if given a fair field, could, in the main, take care of himself." This was the basis for Brandeis's assertion in the article and in letters to Progressive friends, whose support he was attempting to win for Wilson, that the Roosevelt platform promised industrial justice but overlooked the necessity for industrial democracy. The New Party ignored the right of labor to organize and that was "an omission which I have some reason to think is not accidental." Without that right, "social and industrial justice in unattainable," so the New Party was promising something that its own policies would make impossible. Brandeis did not trust Roosevelt's progressivism. He spoke publicly of "that cursed party of despotism, the New Party," and wrote to Hapgood that whereas "the law we want to enforce is the law of competition," Roosevelt had opted for "the law of monopoly." Comparing Wilson to Roosevelt, he added, "We need now a careful constructive statesman more than we do an agitator." That was the way Brandeis would always think of the two men. Toward the end of his life he said, "President Roosevelt spoke forcefully and persuasively on liberal issues. President Wilson spoke logically and convincingly." Wilson, furthermore, was trustworthy: "I have no question as to either the character or intelligence of Governor Wilson. He is not only firm and pure-minded, but he is extremely intelligent and open-minded, and he possesses that quality of careful scrutinizing thought which to my mind is more valuable in a statesman than emotionalism."[9]

Having urged Wilson's cause in the press and in his correspondence, Brandeis turned to the podium. At the request of William Gibbs McAdoo, Wilson's manager (and later his Secretary of the Treasury, as well as his son-in-law), Brandeis sent a memo listing where he proposed to speak:

Oct. 2, Springfield, Mass., Economic Club.
Oct. 4, Portland, Me., Economic Club.
Oct. 5, Boston. Twentieth Century Club.
Oct. 7, Providence Town Criers.
Oct. 8, Boston. Economic Club.
Oct. 10, New York City. West Side Y.M.C.A.
Oct. 10, New York City, Social Workers.
Oct. 11, Brooklyn. Young Republican Club.

Oct. 12, Rochester, N.Y. Ad Club.
Oct. 13, Cincinnati. Grand Opera House.
Oct. 15, Cleveland, Chamber of Commerce.
Oct. 16, Canton, Ohio. State Convention, Ohio Federation of Labor.
Oct. 17, Cleveland, Ohio. Progressive Legislation League.
Oct. 18, Detroit, Mich. Chamber of Commerce.
Oct. 19, Buffalo, N.Y. Chamber of Commerce.
Oct. 20, Pittsburgh, Pa. The Open Forum.
Oct. 22, Chicago, Illinois Manufacturers Club.
Oct. 23, Chicago City Club.
Oct. 24, Reserved for St. Paul.
Oct. 25, Omaha, Neb. Commercial Club of Omaha. (tentative)[10]

He enjoyed the tour and was not perturbed by his heavy schedule. Waiting for the evening lecture he was to give at Brooklyn's Young Republican Club, he took an eight-mile walk through Central Park and thought about "Regulation of Competition," an editorial he was helping Hapgood write. In Cleveland he had "a great night's sleep" and managed to spend three hours walking "despite numerous callers and Interviews." He spoke in Cleveland on October 15, the day after Theodore Roosevelt was shot and wounded by a fanatic. As he told his brother, the talk "was apparently a great success. I gave them a real sermon on respect for law apropos the T.R. incident, working it around to the trusts & I think I rather had them." Brandeis told the Cleveland Chamber of Commerce that the shooting was symptomatic of the decline in respect for law and argued that Americans had lost faith in the law because it expressed the will of the special interests instead of the will of the people. "To secure respect for law, we must make the law respectable," he declared and suggested that a good start would be amendment of the Sherman Act. He altered his schedule somewhat to speak in Minneapolis. He also lectured at the Economic Club in New York on November 1, and then expressed relief that "the talkfest" was over. But it was fun, and it was also important.[11]

Brandeis's vigorous campaigning had one unexpected result. His unsigned editorials in *Collier's Weekly* in favor of Wilson angered Robert J. Collier, the owner of the magazine, as well as Mark Sullivan, its chief correspondent, both of whom were Roosevelt supporters. On October 14, the day Roosevelt was shot, Collier fired Norman Hapgood and immediately published an editorial endorsing Roosevelt. Brandeis, of course, felt responsible for the debacle, initially attempting to heal the rift between Hapgood and Collier; then, when Hapgood was fired, Brandeis worked out an agreement whereby Hapgood bought *Harper's Weekly* with a loan from Charles Crane. *Harper's* then became Brandeis's press vehicle. In addition, Brandeis helped subsidize the magazine in its early days through the purchase of subscriptions.[12]

Arthur Holcombe, a Harvard political scientist and secretary of the Massachusetts branch of the American Association for Labor Legislation, had sent Brandeis a letter saying that he thought Brandeis ought to run for office. Brandeis replied, "I had been disposed to think that the path of duty for me does not lead to any public office, and I as yet see no reason for changing that opinion. On the other hand, I feel that the duty is very clear that I should utilize that insight which participation in practical affairs has given me, to prevent well-meaning progressives from being led into the belief that private monopoly is desirable or permissible, provided it be regulated." Brandeis declined to view his activities as "what would ordinarily be termed 'political campaigning' "; instead, he said, "my speeches . . . were directed to the trust issue." He had planned his itinerary to include almost no groups other than "Economic Clubs & Chambers of Commerce & the like" and to consist of speeches on nothing other than the trusts. Before his stumping began he had written cheerfully, "I think it will be rather a unique political campaign." Whenever audiences or the press asked about his political affiliations he replied smilingly, "I like to think I am a economist and not a politician. I don't know that anyone would call me a Republican. I am a LaFollette Republican or a LaFollette Democrat or a LaFollette Progressive." He insisted that he represented only himself. His motives were clear, and they did not include elective office or participation in Wilson's government as an officer. Ever since his August meeting with Wilson, there had been speculation that Brandeis would become attorney general, but in the same letter in which he confided to his brother that he was writing editorials for Hapgood, he indicated that he was not interested in the job. He was campaigning out of belief; to Hapgood he wrote, although not for publication, "The Roosevelt position on the trust question is rather that of a pervert than a reactionary." The Progressives and other citizens had to be saved from those deluded Roosevelt followers who would fool them into thinking that trusts could ever be controlled or prevented from doing evil. Perhaps part of the bond between Brandeis and Wilson was the tacit recognition of each other by two adamant moralists.[13]

In fact, most Progressives supported Roosevelt. Some did so because of the pressures of local politics. When Henry Moskowitz, Brandeis's friend from the days of the garment industry dispute, endorsed Roosevelt, Brandeis concluded that "T.R. is pretty near irresistible." He wrote Moskowitz that he could not understand social workers' support of Roosevelt, whose trust program "seems to me one that is directly opposed to industrial democracy . . . social workers have been so fascinated with the superstructure as to forget the need of industrial democracy as a safe foundation." Roosevelt's key aide and the chairman of his party's Executive Committee was Brandeis's old adversary in the savings bank life insurance and trust fights, Morgan's partner George Perkins. Brandeis admitted that there were some reactionaries in the Democratic party but insisted, "I know of no man in the Democratic Party who is a greater menace to the country than [Perkins] . . . who appears to have the full confidence of the party's chief, not only personally, but as an expert on our business needs." Brandeis told one Roosevelt follower, "My protest has been not so much against your leader as against the prime minister. Isn't the Progressive Party trying to serve both God and Mammon?" he added. "Think of Jane Addams on the one hand and George Perkins on the other,—'two props of virtue for a Christian prince to stay him from the fall of vanity'." But many of his friends were not convinced. He informed his brother that his own colleague in Washington, George Rublee, had been writing the Roosevelt platform on social questions, along with Herbert Croly, Judge Learned Hand, and Gifford Pinchot.[14]

Nevertheless, Brandeis refused to give up on his friends in the Roosevelt camp, inviting Pinchot to let him know what conservation matters Pinchot wished Wilson to consider and writing to another Progressive, "Fortunately I don't believe, like some distinguished members of your party, that everybody who disagrees with me must either be a fool or a knave." Brandeis's unwillingness to permit politics to endanger his personal relationships would make him a valuable bridge later on between Wilson and those who had supported Roosevelt.[15]

On November 5, Wilson won the race for the presidency. He had received only a plurality of the popular votes (6,286,214 to 4,126,020 for Roosevelt, 3,483,922 for Taft, and 897,011 for Eugene Victor Debs) but an overwhelming majority of the electoral votes (435, as compared with 88 for Roosevelt and 8 for Taft). Brandeis wrote to Wilson, "Every American should be congratulated except possibly yourself. May strength be given to bear the heavy burden." Wilson replied, "You were yourself a great part of the victory." To his brother, Brandeis exulted, "What pleases me most is T.R.'s defeat in the really progressive strongholds— Oregon, California, Iowa, Nebraska, Kansas, Wisconsin, the Dakotas & our eastern Progressive New Hampshire. Most of the Progressives who went over to T.R.—little Governors & the like—are left without support." Brandeis would not forgive either Roosevelt for his "misguided" brand of progressivism or most of the former La Follette supporters who had so precipitously deserted him, but he would act as a bridge among Progressives nonetheless. When Gifford Pinchot sent Brandeis an expression of his concern that Wilson might not be a good enough conservationist, Brandeis replied that although he did not know whether Wilson had given conservation much thought, "I have no doubt that he will be found to be on the right side whenever he is called upon to act." And he ended, "I hope that I may see you soon." Pinchot wrote again about a rumor that an anticonservationist might be made Secretary of the Interior. Brandeis counseled Pinchot to write to Wilson after the latter returned from his postelection trip to Bermuda, asking to speak with him about conservation, and added his certainty that Wilson would be "only too glad . . . to get the benefit of your great experience in conservation matters."[16]

It was time to heal the election wounds and bring Progressives together in the service of new legislation and Progressive policies. Wilson agreed, land after resting in Bermuda from the rigors of the campaign, the president-elect began to seek the support of all Progressives. Brandeis went to hear him speak before a dinner of the Southern Society of New York on December 17, and reported, "It was a noble utterance—worthy of the man & the cause . . . It could leave no man in doubt that he proposes to carry out his promises in letter & spirit, without fear or favor." Wilson had railed against the money trust and had appealed to his audience to "conceive of yourselves as trustees of those interests of the nation with which your personal interests have nothing to do." It was a plea calculated to stir Progressives, and it certainly impressed Brandeis: "It was all simple & conversational, almost as if he were talking to his intimates—the people of the U.S." A sense of *noblesse oblige* characterized Wilson, as it did Brandeis and most leaders of the Progressive movement.[17]

As soon as the election was over speculation increased regarding Wilson's choice of attorney general, which would show whether he indeed meant to curb corporations. The assumption that the office was Brandeis's for the asking was reflected in a request sent him by a number of retail tobacconists who had supported his attacks on the tobacco trust that they be allowed to begin circulating a petition on his behalf. Brandeis replied, "I should much prefer that no action be taken." A former Department of Agriculture official sent Brandeis an article from *Good Housekeeping*, backing Brandeis as attorney general. Brandeis commented in reply, "I am sure you must have found, since retiring from office, what has been the experience of myself, who have never held any office, that there is great opportunity for helping the people as a public private citizen. Indeed I have been disposed to think that I could best serve the people in that humble capacity."[18]

Brandeis's position on not desiring or accepting public office was consistent. Massachusetts Republicans had hoped that he would run for office. But when he decided to support Wilson, he told his brother, "I declared my views to . . . local progressives who wanted me for Governor or Senator & ended that agony." The talk of his running for office had reached as far as Detroit, where the *Detroit Times* commented that he was "bigger than a senatorship" and unlikely to win in any case because he was too honorable for machine politics. His potential lack of victory in the electoral sphere, the editorial went on, "is not . . . of great consequence to Brandeis himself. As a private citizen he weighs more than a carload of Murray Cranes. [Winthrop Murray Crane was the Republican governor of Massachusetts from 1900 to 1902 and one of its senators from 1904 to 1913.] Anyone who has ever heard him hurling the thunder at a public hearing, with Crane and others of his kind shriveling up in their chairs before him, must realize how little the senatorial toga would add to the stature of a real statesman, patriot and lover of his kind."[19]

Whether or not Brandeis agreed with the *Detroit Times*' assessment, he clearly enjoyed the role of elder statesman. As his tutelage of Wilson during the campaign and presidency indicates, Brandeis was able to influence those who made policy; indeed, in writing the Clayton Antitrust Act as well as much of the language for other pieces of legislation, he actually designed the policies himself. He was able to jump into whatever fray appealed to him. He could continue to read whatever caught his fancy at the moment, moving from economic reports and Greek history to biographies and tracts on social reform. He could spend the leisure time that he enjoyed so much with his family, rigorously limiting his work hours and safeguarding his August vacations. He could indulge himself in jousts with nature, which were both fun and necessary to his continued good health. For example, two days after his first meeting with Wilson, he was happily ignoring politics in favor of family and nature: "The children, Joe January & I paddle[d] into Stage Harbour Chatham yesterday, returning by road, the Canoe & some or all of us at times in Joe Baker's Expresswagon, & some walking at times. Time going just 6 hours; returning 3 hrs & 20 minutes. The canoeing would have been done readily in 5 hours but for hard N.W. wind which called at times for the full exercise of skill & strength." He knew that he would have to give up these activities if he ran for or accepted office; moreover, he would have to abandon the legal practice he loved. Furthermore, no politician could accomplish as much as he or she wished, but the drive to do so might well lead to disaster. As Brandeis told one of his law clerks years later, Wilson's breakdown was attributable to his having attempted to do too much.[20]

The possibility of a cabinet seat was a temptation nonetheless. On the one hand, Brandeis's achievements and reputation were formidable—

from his beginnings at Harvard Law School to his becoming the adviser of legislators and the president. But he had never gotten the kind of official recognition that comes with appointment to a high government office. And although this was ultimately to prove less important to him than his freedom of action, the prestige of office naturally had its attractions. More important than the prestige, however, would have been the power to do those things he believed should be done. As attorney general, he could not only have begun antitrust action against the New Haven Railroad and other conglomerates he found unacceptable, but he could also have demanded from them, either on the threat of litigation or in the course of it, the kind of detailed information that he was certain would damn the trusts while proving his charges of inefficiency and mismanagement. When he sought that information as a private citizen, every piece that he got took a major fight, and there was much to which he could get no access at all. His power as attorney general might have enabled him to wrest concessions in favor of the unions from corporations. Or if he had been made secretary of commerce, he could have begun redesigning the government stance toward currency, credit, and the money trust. He would have been a member of the cabinet, with frequent access to the other cabinet members whose bailiwicks were also of interest to him.

The net result was that he was in conflict with himself. He wanted a cabinet seat, but he had equally weighty reasons for not taking it. Unable to resolve the internal conflict, he did nothing. He could have told Wilson that he would accept no position. He could have joined La Follette and the other Progressives who were campaigning actively on his behalf. But while the Progressive forces were urging Wilson to appoint him and the big business forces were fighting equally hard to keep him out, Brandeis sat back and awaited the outcome. Once the political forces arrayed against him had triumphed, and Wilson had made the decision not to offer him a cabinet position, he wrote to his brother, "As you know I had great doubts as for it's [sic] being desirable for me; so I concluded to literally let nature take its course and to do nothing either to get called or to stop the talk, although some of my friends were quite active." Brandeis analyzed Wilson's decision as being influenced by Brandeis's old foes: "State Street, Wall Street and the local Democratic bosses did six months' unremitting work; but seem not to have prevailed until the last moment." His opponents' charges of unprofessional conduct, which they would repeat when Wilson named Brandeis to the Supreme Court in 1916, led the president to ask Norman Hapgood to undertake a thorough investigation of the charges. "Not that I believe in any of them," Wilson told Hapgood, "but I need to have the facts." Hapgood's exhaustive investigation enabled Wilson to threaten Brandeis's critics, "I am willing to hear your arguments from political expediency and party harmony. But if you make any more charges against Mr. Brandeis's character I shall appoint him regardless of other considerations."[21]

But Wilson did not offer him the appointment, and Brandeis commented, "The local Democratic bosses were swayed partly by their connections in the financial district, partly by the fear of being opposed in job-seeking." Agreeing with Brandeis's assessment, one of the editors of his letters adds that local party chieftains had been important to Wilson's election, and "he could not afford to antagonize" them. Arthur Link, Wilson's most authoritative biographer, lays the major responsibility for Wilson's decision at the door of Colonel House. Link cites House's diary as saying that Brandeis was not a real Democrat, too controversial, and too antagonistic to business. Link also takes note of the influence of "the Irish politicians of Boston, and spokesmen of the great financial interests," as well as the fact that Brandeis was perhaps the American most hated by big business, financial leaders, and the railroad interests. He quotes Wilson as saying later that "in the position of Attorney General I simply could not appoint a radical—that is I could not support a known radical. [The Attorney General] cannot be a person of the crusader type in public life."[22]

Brandeis saw as "further evidence that the Massachusetts opposition to my going into the Cabinet was not in its essence political," the fact that George Anderson, a past Democratic nominee for Massachusetts attorney general and a Public Franchise League man, along with a Democratic labor leader, "both good friends," soon urged him on behalf of the state Democratic machine leaders to run for attorney general. He declined, but understood the overture as meaning that it was not the Democratic party as such that had opposed him but the "interests" that dominated it.[23]

Wilson's great admiration for Brandeis, as indicated by his continued reliance upon him; his gratitude for Brandeis's help in the campaign; the friends Brandeis had around Wilson; Brandeis's ability to manipulate men and media; and the hard time his opponents had in talking Wilson out of the appointment all seem to indicate that had Brandeis decided to fight for a cabinet position, he would have gotten it. Instead, he became an éminence grise.

Within days of the decision against giving him a cabinet post, Brandeis was in the White House lobbying for his favorite causes. He had sent messages of congratulations to James McReynolds, the new attorney general, and to William Cox Redfield, the new secretary of commerce. Indeed, he had no reason to be dissatisfied with the men Wilson had

named. McReynolds was known as the assistant attorney general who
had resigned from Theodore Roosevelt's administration, charging that
antitrust policies were not being pursued with sufficient vigor. Brandeis
referred to that event in his letter, noting that McReynolds's history
would "assure the country that the President's trust policy will be carried
out promptly and efficiently, and business be freed at last." Redfield was
a congressman and former businessman whose "wise and enlightened"
business policies (Brandeis's words) had been spelled out in a book called
The New Industrial Day: A Book for Men Who Employ Men. Mc-
Reynolds had not yet demonstrated the extreme anti-Semitism he would
display when both he and Brandeis served on the Supreme Court, and
no one could predict that Redfield would prove to be a thoroughly in-
effective secretary of commerce.[24]

Brandeis's messages made clear that he did not expect his lack of
position to limit his influence. To McReynolds he wrote, "I intend to
call upon you soon, and hope you will have time to talk over our special
New England needs" (a reference to Brandeis's ongoing dispute with the
New Haven); to Redfield, "There is much to talk over with you, and I
hope to have the pleasure of calling on you soon." Five days later he
told his brother, "Had a good private talk with the President this evening
for an hour—and with [Secretary of the Interior Franklin K.] Lane,
Redfield, [Secretary of State William Jennings] Bryan, and McReynolds
today—inter alia pushing along New Haven and Shoe Machinery matters." To Hapgood he reported, "All were extremely cordial, and expressed themselves as eager for all help which can be given them." Then
he set to work advising Wilson and his cabinet about executive and
judicial appointments. Wilson offered Brandeis the chairmanship of the
Commission on Industrial Relations, but Brandeis declined. Instead, he
suggested other possibilities for personnel, including a Wobbly (member
of the IWW), and "reminded" Wilson that one of the three representatives
of the general public on the commission should be a woman.[25]

Brandeis continued to meet frequently with cabinet members and other
administration members. Two letters give a sense of the breadth and pace
of his activities. On June 8 he wrote to Alfred from New York, "Arrived
here this A.M. Shall spend the day on Zionism and the evening with
Norman H & Crane. Leave for Washington at midnight and expect to
stay there until Wednesday noon, then to speak in Baltimore and be back
in Boston Thursday or Friday. Was here last Wednesday at Conference
on Price Maintenance . . . The Supreme Court is all wrong in declaring
price maintenance agreements on trade-marked goods illegal, & I want
to set machinery in motion to get this straightened out. Also want to see
I.C.C. people; & Dept. of Justice on New Haven matters & LaFollette

on some legislation." He did reach Washington on June 9 as planned and conferred with Commissioner of Corporations Joseph E. Davies. Davies asked for Brandeis's suggestions about businesses that could be investigated in order to show the relative efficiency of small and large units. Brandeis replied, "I think the comparison of the Department Store with the small or specialty business would afford a particularly interesting and fruitful subject of investigation. The impression prevails generally that the Department Store operates at a lower average cost than the smaller stores. I am informed that this is a mistaken view; that, on the whole, the operating expenses,—including interest upon capital—is larger in the department stores than in the smaller stores." As usual, he had for Davies the name and address of someone with more information about the matter. Brandeis also responded to requests from administration members for names of possible officials and to requests from would-be office-holders or their friends that he exercise his influence in their behalf. Most important of all, he kept up his tutoring of Wilson on Progressive issues, although they met only sporadically.[26]

In April 1913 Brandeis went to the White House with John Purroy Mitchel (soon to be elected mayor of New York City) and Henry Bruère (a Progressive, and director of the New York Bureau of Municipal Research) for a conference on government economy and efficiency. He talked to the president about scientific management and the need to adopt a federal budget. Other than that, however, he saw little of Wilson for some months. Brandeis was occupied with the Interstate Commerce Commission's hearings about the New Haven Railroad. Wilson was initially busy with tariff reform, but he soon turned his attention to currency and banking reform, to which he had promised to give his "most serious and immediate attention." Brandeis had already studied the matter and had followed closely the hearings held by the House Banking and Currency Committee (the Pujo Committee) between May 1912 and January 1913 to investigate the money trust. Unimpressed by the extent of the committee's investigations or its recommendations, Brandeis began his own inquiry. His knowledge of the New Haven had indicated that there was indeed a money trust and that the concentration of control over money and credit was one of the major problems of the economic system. His interest was paralleled by that of Representative Carter Glass, who now chaired the House Banking and Currency Committee, and who was working on a way to undo the money trust, and Henry Parker Willis, the economist advising Glass.[27]

Wilson had written about currency reform as early as 1896 and in 1911 had called the money trust "the most pernicious of all trusts." After his election he had declared, "You must put the credit of this country at the disposal of everybody upon equal terms." It was an issue of such great importance that he was prepared to overcome his distaste for big government and put banking under government supervision.[28]

Glass and Willis presented Wilson with a plan to establish a reserve system that would be privately controlled and decentralized, with a maximum of twenty independent banks participating. Wilson added to the proposal the creation of a Federal Reserve Board that would supervise the system. When Secretary of State Bryan learned of the plan, he quickly joined forces with Senator Robert L. Owen, a leading Progressive from Oklahoma; Samuel Untermyer, the attorney who had served as counsel to the Pujo Committee during its investigation of the money trust and who had actually orchestrated the hearings; and Secretary of the Treasury William McAdoo. They regarded the Glass-Willis plan as a giveaway: the issuing of currency would still be in private hands, and the members of the proposed Federal Reserve Board would be elected by bankers. Not only would the bankers still control currency, they would now do so with the blessing of the government. McAdoo proposed a government-owned-and-operated central bank, but the Bryan faction realized this was so radical that neither the business community nor Wilson could possibly accept it. Instead, the group argued that there had to be a system that was controlled (but not owned) by the government, through government appointment of members of the Federal Reserve Board, and that its notes had to be government obligations. The banking community of course favored the Glass-Willis plan; the Progressives, with McAdoo among them, were fighting strenuously for their own plan. Wilson had to make a choice.[29]

On June 11, 1913, Wilson called Brandeis to the White House. In doing so he was turning to someone who was convinced that the money trust was worse than any other because it was responsible for the manipulation of credit that enabled syndicates to put competition out of business and create monopolies. Brandeis therefore told Wilson that he had to support the Bryan position. First, he said, "the power to issue currency should be vested exclusively in Government officials," and the bankers should be strictly limited to an advisory role. "The beneficent effect of the best conceivable currency bill will be relatively slight, unless we are able to curb the money trust." It was only the banking interests that argued otherwise, Brandeis explained; businesses other than the trusts would be reassured to know that "whatever money is available, will be available for business generally, and not be subject to the control of a favored few." Big business, including the money trust, was by nature hostile to the aims of the Wilson administration, so that its advice should not be followed "even in a field technically [its] own." In addition a bill such as Glass's, passed now, would simply strengthen the money trust to the point where the success of later, stronger legislation would be doubtful. At Wilson's request Brandeis put his arguments in writing three days later on June 14. Wilson was convinced. On June 18, he told all concerned that he would propose Bryan's plan: there would be a Federal Reserve Board appointed by the government, with bankers brought in as advisers; there would be regional banks, but all currency would be issued under the control of the board. Bryan was ecstatic; the banking community, outraged. A group of bankers took their objections to Wilson, who asked calmly, "Which of you gentlemen thinks the railroads should select members of the Interstate Commerce Commission?" The bankers may not have been convinced by that approach but Glass was, and he agreed to manage the bill in the House. The Federal Reserve bill passed both houses and was sent to Wilson on December 23, 1913. It was surely one of the most important laws produced by the Wilson administration.[30]

The experience confirmed Wilson's belief that he could rely on Brandeis's advice about money matters. In 1913 Brandeis had written a series of articles about the money trust and its evils, published in *Harper's Weekly* and then in book form as *Other People's Money* in 1914. Wilson read and annotated these articles.[31]

Next to the money trust, Brandeis found the general trust issue most interesting. He began urging Wilson and his administration to push ahead with new antitrust legislation. But members of the cabinet disagreed, urging that no new legislation be attempted until the business community had adjusted to the Federal Reserve Act and the tariff laws, and arguing that forecasts of a depression meant that the government should move with caution. Brandeis interpreted the lesson of the coming depression quite differently. On December 9, 1913, before the Federal Reserve bill had been sent to the president, he met with Secretary of the Interior Franklin K. Lane; on December 12, he wrote to Lane that an antitrust law was "not only essential to carrying out the policy of New Freedom, but . . . politically necessary to satisfy the demands of the very large number of progressive Democrats and the near Democrats, who are already beginning to express some doubt whether the administration will have the courage (in view of indicated business depression), to carry out the policy which it has hitherto declared." (As was his habit, Brandeis put this political advice in the last paragraph of the letter. His letters to Wilson and cabinet members advocating specific pieces of legislation were devoted largely to a summary of the existing situation and the way in which the statute would remedy it. Then, either because he felt it was appropriate when dealing with politicians or in order to give them additional ammunition, he added a final paragraph explaining the political benefits of his suggestions.)[32]

In the struggle over whether there should be an attempt at antitrust legislation, Brandeis had the advantage of possessing a fully thought-out program. He did not advocate antitrust action; he advocated *his* antitrust action, and he spelled out the details in his letter to Lane. As he had done with Wilson, he emphasized that the enemy was not business but the trusts, and particularly the money trust with its desire for "industrial and financial absolutism." Brandeis told Lane, "We want industrial democracy. The conflict between us is irreconcilable." But the New Freedom would be good for the business community at large; to make this clear and to negate opposition from business "an affirmative constructive policy must be adopted; one which will show that the business man is as much the subject of governmental solicitude as are the farmers and the working man." The first constructive step would be the establishment of an Interstate Trade Commission "with substantially the powers suggested by me in paragraph third of my article in Harper's of November 8." Throughout the letter Brandeis cited the eight-part series he had published in *Harper's* between November 22, 1913 and January 10, 1914. There were no longer references to the La Follette policy or the La Follette bills; the brain behind the economic legislation of the New Freedom was Brandeis's, and there was no point in attempting to camouflage that within administration circles. The powers suggested by Brandeis in the article referred to (actually spelled out in the third section rather than the third paragraph) were those of investigation, utilization of information to aid the Justice Department in litigating against the trusts, and action to secure compliance with the law at the request of injured parties.[33]

Brandeis's second step was similar to the fourth section of his article: to empower the proposed Federal Trade Commission (called Interstate Trade Commission earlier in the letter) to investigate trade agreements in restraint of trade, as differentiated from monopolies. "In the absence of such data," he wrote, we "cannot deal . . . intelligently" with trade agreements. The third step, which Brandeis had first suggested in 1911, was to establish "industrial experiment stations and other bureaus for research and for the dissemination of education in industry." This was necessary to secure equality of opportunity for smaller businesses, who would gain the information currently available only to large corporations able to maintain research laboratories. The fourth step was to repeal the law prohibiting price fixing of trademarked merchandise by its producer or distributor, as it tended to discourage competition. Here Brandeis cited his November 15 article "Price Maintenance, Competition That Kills." In it, he differentiated price maintenance by the producer of an article, who had a stake in the reputation of the article and an interest in maintaining its quality, from price cutting and price fixing. Price cutting was "the most potent weapon of monopoly—a means of killing the small rival to which the great trusts have resorted most frequently." Price fixing was the device used by monopolies to force consumers to pay whatever prices the monopolies chose, whereas price maintenance restored a true market situation: the "independent producer" had to be careful not to set a price so high that consumers would not buy or that excessive profits would draw competitors into the field. Brandeis claimed that the consumer who paid the price established by the independent producer did so "voluntarily . . . because he deem[ed] the article worth that price as compared with the cost of other competing articles." A consumer forced to buy staple articles at a price fixed by a trust did so under compulsion. The *Harper's* article did not include the criterion by which trusts would be differentiated from independent producers; presumably, however, the criterion was the over-40 percent of the market that Brandeis had suggested to La Follette.[34]

The next series of suggestions had to do with amending the Sherman Act to make its application and enforcement easier; here Brandeis referred Lane to the November 8 article (which embodied the provisions of the La Follette-Stanley bills). Then Brandeis turned to the need to abolish interlocking directorates, citing the December 4 article, called "Endless Chain," and that of December 13, entitled "Serve One Master Only!" Essentially, Brandeis argued that no man could serve two masters, first because he could not act in one capacity without considering the effect of that action on his other interests, and second because to do so strained the resources and abilities of any one individual beyond human limitations. No one could possess enough facts to make intelligent decisions about a multiplicity of businesses. Brandeis gave an example of the dishonesty inherent in interlocking directorates:

J. P. Morgan (or a partner), a director of the New York, New Haven & Hartford Railroad, causes that company to sell to J. P. Morgan & Co. an issue of bonds. J. P. Morgan & Co. borrow the money with which to pay for the bonds from the Guaranty Trust Company, of which Mr. Morgan (or a partner) is a director. J. P. Morgan & Co. sell the bonds to the Penn Mutual Life Insurance Company, of which Mr. Morgan (or a partner) is a director. The New Haven spends the proceeds of the bonds in purchasing steel rails from the United States Steel Corporation, of which Mr. Morgan (or a partner) is a director. The United States Steel Corporation spends the proceeds of the rails in purchasing electrical supplies from the General Electric Company, of which Mr. Morgan (or a partner) is a director. The

General Electric sells supplies to the Western Union Telegraph Company; and in both Mr. Morgan (or a partner) is a director. The Telegraph Company has an exclusive wire contract with the Reading . . . the Reading buys its passengers cars from the Pullman Company . . . The Pullman Company buys . . . locomotives from the Baldwin Locomotive Company . . . The Reading, the General Electric, the Steel Corporation and the New Haven [also] buy locomotives from the Baldwin . . . The Steel Corporation, the Telephone Company, the New Haven, the Reading, the Pullman and the Baldwin Companies, like the Western Union, buy electrical supplies from the General Electric. The Baldwin, the Pullman, the Reading, the Telephone, the Telegraph and the General Electric companies, like the New Haven, buy steel products from the Steel Corporation. Each and every one of the companies last named markets its securities through J. P. Morgan & Co.; each deposits its funds with J. P. Morgan & Co.; and with these funds of each, the firm enters upon further operations.

In every one of the companies mentioned, Brandeis indicated, J. P. Morgan (or a partner) was a director. And this example had to be multiplied "many times and with many permutations" if the extent of interlocking directorates in the country was to be fully portrayed.[35]

Finally, Brandeis urged upon Lane laws that would embody the legislation recommended in the report of the Interstate Commerce Commission on its hearings about the New Haven Railroad. The proposed laws would in effect keep the railroads from expanding into other businesses and prevent abuses of their monopoly over transportation.[36]

By the time Wilson delivered a special message to Congress on January 20, 1914, all of Brandeis's *Harper's* articles on the money trust had been printed. The presidential message outlined administration proposals about monopolies and trusts: outlawing interlocking directorates and price cutting that would destroy competition, creating a Federal Trade Commission (FTC), giving the Interstate Commerce Commission the power to regulate railroad financing, and amending the Sherman Act to provide penalties for individuals engaged in the restraint of trade and to allow private individuals to recover damages from a combination judged by the courts to have operated in restraint of trade. Brandeis wrote triumphantly to his brother that Wilson's message "has paved the way for about all I have asked for & some of the provisions specifically are what I got into his mind at my first interview."[37]

Wilson came under fire from the Progressives over the FTC bill, which would have created an information agency rather than a regulatory one. Brandeis was asked to redraw the bill, but was so busy with the Interstate Commerce Commission's hearings on railroad rates that he asked George

Rublee to work with a number of associates on the redrafting. He did find the time to complain to Attorney General McReynolds about the proposed antitrust law, to spend most of a day going over the bill with him, and to write a stronger provision on interlocking directorates.[38]

Rublee and Representative Raymond B. Stevens, who had written a proposed bill turning the FTC into a regulatory rather than a purely investigatory body, were scheduled to take their bill to the president on June 10. Rublee asked Brandeis to go along, even though Brandeis did not approve of such extensive government regulatory involvement, because Rublee believed they would receive a more serious hearing if Brandeis were present. To the surprise of Rublee and the others, Brandeis not only accompanied them but, when the president sought his advice, persuaded Wilson that they were right. Although Brandeis had not changed his principles, he told the president he had become convinced that it was not possible to write a law covering all possible violations of antitrust policy. Instead, an agency with the power to expand upon basic legislative policy should be created. Brandeis testified to that effect before the Senate Interstate Commerce Committee; he also testified before the House Committee on Interstate and Foreign Commerce and the House Judiciary Committee about the trust and FTC bills. In addition, at Wilson's request, he lobbied a number of senators for the FTC bill.[39]

The bills passed the Congress, although the Clayton Antitrust Act was watered down somewhat, and Wilson signed the FTC bill into law on September 10, 1914. The next problem was personnel; as Brandeis wrote to Colonel Edward House, "The success or failure of the Commission will depend largely upon the quality of men selected." Wilson did not choose activist Progressives for the commission, and as a result the commission did not function as Brandeis had hoped. Although he attempted to influence the commission through letters to Rublee and a letter to Commissioner Edward N. Hurley about the FTC's powers, sent at his request, Brandeis's efforts had little effect. He and the other Progressives viewed the FTC appointments as a major defeat, and privately, Brandeis held Wilson responsible for ruining the FTC. They were also horrified at Wilson's appointment of bankers to the Federal Reserve Board, a move that delighted the business community. The only possible conclusion was that Wilson was turning from "real progressives" and beginning to woo the business community—and indeed, such was the case. A business depression had begun in late 1913 and was to last until 1915. Its effect on both business and employment worried Wilson, who, thinking as well about the 1916 election, began to seek closer ties to businessmen and bankers. Furthermore, he was distracted from the goals of progressivism by a virtual civil war that erupted in Colorado at the climax of a coal strike; by the war that had begun in Europe; and by his wife's illness, which soon led to her death.[40]

Brandeis understood that the Wilson of the summer of 1914 was not as devoted to Progressive concerns as he had been. Replying to a request to talk to the president about regularity of employment, Brandeis lamented, "I suppose that it would take some time to bring the President to a full realization of the problem if he has not yet given it attention." But he added stoutly, "If he became convinced of the urgency, he might be willing to send in a special message."

Thoroughly disheartened by Wilson's attitude, Brandeis left Washington for his usual August vacation in 1914 ready for activity in a new sphere. Within weeks, he had plunged into leadership of the Zionist cause.[41]

His relations with Wilson, however, remained extremely cordial. He was disappointed by some of Wilson's failures, but that did not alter his respect for either the man or his accomplishments. "Perhaps the most extraordinary achievement of Mr. Wilson's first administration," Brandeis wrote ten years later, shortly after Wilson's death, "was dissipation of the atmosphere of materialism which had enveloped Washington for at least forty years, and probably since Lincoln's days. The rich man—the captain of industry—was distinctly at a disadvantage. One breathed the pure, rarified air of mountain tops." He concluded that Wilson "should be judged by what he was and did prior to August 4th, 1918, the date of the paper justifying the attack on Russia. That was the first of his acts which was unlike him; and I am sure the beginning of the sad end." Although Brandeis supported Wilson fully on American entry into World War I, he clearly regretted that Wilson's involvement first with the war and then with the League of Nations took him away from progressivism and overtaxed the strength given to any human being. But he had no desire to blacken Wilson's memory; he said of his own negative comments, "It is better that I should not be quoted."[42]

Brandeis felt free to call upon Wilson and members of his administration after the summer of 1914, particularly for support of Zionist activities and of the Balfour declaration that would create a Jewish homeland in Palestine. Gratitude for Wilson's role in the Zionist cause may have helped overcome Brandeis's disappointment at Wilson's turn from progressivism. Rabbi Stephen S. Wise, one of Brandeis's closest colleagues in Zionism, could "hardly think of a Jewish supporter of Wilson, who failed to stand at his side with utter disinterestedness and limitless devotion to the end of his terms of office."[43]

Wilson, for his part, showed continued friendship for Brandeis and belief in his talents. In 1915 Wilson used his influence to get Brandeis membership in Washington's exclusive Cosmos Club, where he had been opposed as too dangerous a radical. The following year Wilson took the politically courageous step of nominating Brandeis to the Supreme Court. Almost as soon as the ensuing battle was won, Wilson demonstrated that he wanted to continue using Brandeis for government purposes: he appointed him to a commission to investigate a border dispute with Mexico. Brandeis, after consulting with Chief Justice Edward White, replied that the business of the Supreme Court was too demanding to permit him to engage in additional activities. There is no indication that Brandeis was particularly interested in serving on the commission; his letters to White indicate that he had turned to the chief justice for a suggestion as to how to decline the appointment gracefully, rather than for a true consultation.[44]

Wilson continued to seek Brandeis's advice. Wilson's secretary, Joseph P. Tumulty, and the president disagreed about the appointment of a director general of the railroads. Tumulty wanted Wilson to appoint McAdoo as director general and felt that Brandeis could win the day with Wilson. Brandeis agreed to try but refused to go to the White House, believing that to undertake such a political errand would be inappropriate for a member of the Court. If Wilson asked him to go, however, Brandeis told Tumulty, he would regard it as a command and would obey. This kind of ethical hair-splitting probably indicates better than any other incident during the Wilson administration (or during the New Deal Administration, which Brandeis also advised), how torn Brandeis was between the judicial ethics he acknowledged and accepted and the attractions participation in policymaking held for him. If it was inappropriate for Brandeis to call upon Wilson on a political errand, it was equally inappropriate for Brandeis to offer the president political advice. The excuse that a presidential invitation constituted a "command" was nonsense: as a member of the federal judiciary, coequal with the executive branch, Brandeis did not have to respond to commands from the White House. Nor did he have any obligation to do so as a citizen, the Constitution and laws of the United States giving the president no power to command the appearance of a citizen. And Brandeis, much concerned with protecting the image of the judiciary, knew this as well as he knew that the judicial canons of ethics required judges to maintain the reality as well as appearance of avoiding political affairs.

But Brandeis was eager to overcome the president's scruples against naming his son-in-law to the post, for he had long held McAdoo in high regard (although Brandeis told Tumulty that McAdoo would have to resign as secretary of the treasury, consistent with Brandeis's belief in human limitations). Tumulty therefore promised Brandeis that the president would invite him to call. Instead, Wilson appeared unannounced upon the justice's doorstep on December 9, 1917, saying "I could not request you to come to me, and I have therefore come to you to ask your advice." The conference was held in Brandeis's study, which Alice Brandeis described as book-covered: books on the walls, the desk, chairs, the floor. As always, the lighting was dim; Brandeis carefully protected his eyes from glare. "Here," Mrs. Brandeis wrote to her sister, "was the scholar, the student at his work. And yet it is as a practical man of affairs, a statesman, that Louis's advice is so much sought."[45]

The general perception of Brandeis, in fact, was of a statesman rather than of a jurist, and this became all the more true when World War I seemed to demand that officials ignore formal job descriptions and make themselves available for whatever task needed to be done. "I need Brandeis everywhere but I must leave him somewhere," Wilson told Rabbi Wise, when the latter urged Wilson to name Brandeis to the Peace Commission. Wilson lamented to Robert Woolley, an interstate commerce commissioner and friend, "When a seemingly impossible war emergency task looms, I am urged to draft Brandeis to tackle it. At least twice I have put it up to him. Very properly he replied he would take it up with the Chief Justice. In each instance Chief Justice White held that a member of the Supreme Court should confine his endeavors to the work of that Court. I readily agreed. Whereupon Brandeis would offer to resign, which was characteristic of him. My reply was: 'Not on your life. On that Bench you are more important to the country than you could possibly be elsewhere. It was too difficult to get you there to take a chance on losing you through a temporary appointment.' " Brandeis's name was urged upon Wilson for the position of national labor administrator and chairman of the War Labor Policies Board. Although Brandeis may have been willing to assume such a post temporarily, for example, during the Court's summer vacation, there is no reason to assume that his offers to resign from the Court or his conferences with Chief Justice White were more than window-dressing. He cared deeply about the country and the problems it encountered as the war progressed, and it was clear that he thought at length about solutions, but there is no evidence that he was ever tempted to leave the Court. He shared Wilson's view that it was on the Court that he could make his greatest contribution.[46]

However, he continued to advise Wilson, and Wilson took his advice. McAdoo was appointed as director general but, ignoring Brandeis's admonition, kept his position as secretary of the treasury. Brandeis forgave him for his lapse, writing when he resigned from both positions on November 23, 1918, "Your retirement is a measureless misfortune; but I rejoice that you have determined upon a complete rest." He was also brought into the rivalry between the military services and the War Department to secure labor and material. Wilson, beset by advisers disagreeing about how to stop the jousting, which was driving up the costs of both labor and materiel, had House ask Brandeis for his opinion. Brandeis replied with a lengthy letter, saying that "betterment" in the work of the War Department and the War Industry Board and Committees "can come only through radical changes in system." He suggested seven changes, the most important of which was that the "powers of the munitions administration shall be vested in a single head with full power of delegation," and that the munitions administration should be separate from the War Department. Wilson adopted the suggestion, soon creating the War Industries Board and bestowing extensive powers upon its chairman, Bernard Baruch. Wilson seemed, in the War Industries Board matter, to have needed the assurance of the advocate of small government that it was legitimate to create strong centers of power in the government during wartime. Brandeis advised lesser members of the administration as well. In June 1917 he spent two evenings talking with Secretary of Labor Newton D. Baker about the need to remember the conditions of the workers in the rapidly expanding munitions industry.[47]

On the day the Armistice was signed, Brandeis sent Wilson his congratulations along with several lines from Euripides' *The Bacchae*. Shortly thereafter, Attorney General Thomas W. Gregory called Brandeis in to look at the notorious "Protocols of the Learned Elders of Zion," a tract purporting to be the plan for a Jewish takeover of the world, which was then being widely distributed by Henry Ford. Gregory promised Brandeis to investigate the source of what he agreed was clearly not a document written by Jews. Contacts with the members of the Wilson Administration continued, largely on Zionist matters. But Brandeis also found some of the cabinet congenial. He wrote to his wife on December 3, 1918, "The A.G. came in to dine with me alone last evening & was fine as usual." When Wilson suffered a stroke in 1919 after campaigning across the United States for ratification of the Versailles Treaty, Brandeis regretted the secrecy with which the Wilsons (or at least the second Mrs. Wilson) surrounded the matter. Referring to the recent resignation of Secretary of War Lindley Garrison, for which Garrison had offered no public explanation, Brandeis wrote to Felix Frankfurter, "Our general American trouble is that we make public what should be private & treat as private what is strictly a public matter, e.g. the degree & nature of the President's illness."[48]

Wilson continued to think of Brandeis as one of the few men on whom he could rely, and he left the White House convinced that the Democrats had lost the election of 1920 because they had been untrue to Progressive principles. Although in private law practice with Bainbridge Colby, his last secretary of state, Wilson remained concerned about the future of progressivism. He soon asked Brandeis, Colby, and Thomas Chadbourne, a lawyer and friend, to join with him in working out a platform for the 1924 Democratic convention. Brandeis agreed, initially conferring with Colby and Chadbourne in New York during the summer of 1921. He and Wilson began an extensive correspondence on the subject of "The Document," as the proposed platform was called by its authors.[49]

The correspondence is particularly interesting for the light it sheds on the difficulty Brandeis had confining himself within the traditional boundaries of judicial ethics. The writing of "The Document" constituted a clear involvement in partisan political matters; the point was to steer the Democratic party toward progressivism to help it win the next national election. The platform Brandeis and Wilson put together reflected the concerns of each. For example, following a meeting between the two men, Wilson wrote Brandeis a suggestion for a "broadside" condemning the rejection by the Senate of the Versailles Treaty and "the influence of men who preferred personal and party motives to the honor of their country and the peace of the world . . . [they were] the most partisan, prejudiced and unpatriotic coterie that has ever misled the Senate of the United States." Wilson expanded upon this theme in a later communication redefining the "America First" slogan to mean "that in every international action or organization for the benefit of mankind America must be foremost." (Rather pathetically—and in great contrast with the kind of staff now provided former presidents—Wilson wrote in a postscript: "Please excuse the bad typewriting of the document enclosed; I have the use of only one hand, fortunately the right one.") He also sent suggestions about the merchant marine and about access to energy supplies, apologizing for the frequency of his letters but explaining that his ideas "form themselves somewhere in the hidden recesses of my system and I am uneasy until I get them out." As the correspondence went on, Brandeis sent Wilson copies of Court decisions he thought would interest him because they dealt with matters, such as the rights of labor, women's suffrage, and federalism as an antidote to big government, with which Wilson had been concerned as president. Wilson replied in letters addressed to "My dear Brandeis" or, occasionally, "My dear Friend," although he sometimes used the form "My dear Mr. Justice."[50]

Wilson expressed his satisfaction to Brandeis that "you and Mr. Colby have generously assumed the laboring oars in the all important enterprise." Brandeis was circumspect in his own letters, frequently acknowledging the former president's suggestions in language that gave no indication of Brandeis's own part in the project. He would say, "Thank you for the noble and penetrating note," or send a comment such as, "I am very glad that you are turning your thoughts to the railroad problem." But the correspondence also documents Brandeis's continuing work with Colby, and Wilson's letters were less discreet. On January 7, 1922, Wilson offered his reply to Brandeis's question, sent the day before, "as to whether it would be best to omit paragraphs three and four from the memorandum of suggestions just sent you." The following year he thanked Brandeis "for the statement which you were kind enough to write and send me . . . It will admirably suit the purpose which I had in mind." Wilson also asked for Brandeis's opinion about sending the platform to the head of the Democratic National Committee for transmittal to the party's candidates for Congress in 1922, "with the intimation that they select from it the declarations of policy and intention they were to include in their manifestos to the voters of the districts. In that way the thoughts of the party might, it seems to me, be drawn into common channels before the big tasks of nineteen hundred and twenty-four demand immediate performance." However, the preparations for 1924's "big tasks" were never completed; they ended abruptly with Wilson's death on February 3, 1924.[51]

Woodrow Wilson owes part of his place in history to Brandeis. Without Brandeis, there would have been no New Freedom. Wilson had disliked the trusts before he met Brandeis, but he accepted them as being as inevitable as original sin. It was Brandeis who convinced Wilson that something could be done about the trusts; that it was possible for government to regulate big business without itself committing the sin of becoming too big; that an attack on the money trust would benefit the average business and open the door for citizens to prove themselves in the marketplace. Brandeis and Wilson initially used Wilson's presidency, and the potential power it gave him, to teach the nation about the ideals of Brandeis and the Progressives and to enact some of them into law. Wilson was a Progressive before he knew Brandeis, but he was a Theodore Roosevelt Progressive by another name: he would accept and regulate trusts, not seek to abolish them. And, beset by the exigencies of politics, he eventually lost his enthusiasm for the Brandeisian approach. For a while, however, in the early days of the Wilson administration, the Brandeis philosophy permeated Washington. The belief that small-scale businesses and competition could be resurrected, the insistence on federalism in preference to big government, the assumption that people given true freedom could provide for themselves both economically and politically—all were part and parcel of the New Freedom; all were elements of the Brandeis credo.[52]

Brandeis also owed a great deal to Wilson. It was Wilson who gave him the opportunity to put some of his economic ideas into effect. The general knowledge that Brandeis was one of Wilson's trusted advisers added enormously to Brandeis's prestige and, ultimately, to his power. For example, the relationship with Wilson was one of the reasons that Brandeis was asked in 1914 to participate in the Zionist movement, which he immediately took over. Brandeis's access to Wilson and his cabinet then made it possible for him to gain crucial American support for the Balfour Declaration and the creation of a Jewish homeland, Brandeis's main goal as a Zionist. And most important of all for Brandeis's career, Wilson appointed him to the Supreme Court.

The two men shared a moment in American history and benefited mutually from their relationship. Much of what Wilson did was undertaken without reference to Brandeis, and vice versa. Nonetheless, had the two men not met, Wilson's approach to the economy would have been completely different, and Brandeis would almost certainly not have become a member of the Court. They lived at a time when it was still possible to alter the direction, and perhaps the essence, of the American economy, and together they made a strong attempt to do so. In retrospect, it is clear that they were only partly successful. They prevented the total control of the economy by the money trust, but the major role played in the American and world marketplaces by a few American banks proves that concentration of capital, even without total monopoly, is sufficient to achieve the kind of enormous economic and political dominance that Wilson and Brandeis sought to prevent. The ties between the Federal Reserve System and the business community, as well as those between the Federal Trade Commission and business, reflect the continuity between government and big business. The Federal Reserve and the FTC have achieved some of their objectives of regulation, but they have not been used as the cutting edges of an attack on giant corporations and banks. The Clayton Antitrust Act has been used to prevent some combinations; however, the phenomenon of combination is still the most important element in the American economic system. The Depression of 1929 was only the most dramatic example of how dependent the economy was—and is—on the forces Brandeis tried to combat; indeed, his intense involvement in the economic policies forged by the New Deal indicated his realization that much of the battle remained to be fought.

Nonetheless, Wilson and Brandeis were a formidable team that changed the terms of political debate. They would have liked the country to ask "How can the trusts be destroyed?" instead of "Should the trusts be controlled?" Instead, they got the country to ask "How should the trusts be regulated?" Although it was not as much as they wanted, persuading the electorate to question earlier unarticulated assumptions about the desirability of the trusts was a major accomplishment.

They were not friends, in spite of Wilson's addressing Brandeis as such after the presidential days were over. At times they were teacher and pupil; at others, comrades-in-arms. They recognized and appreciated each other's cold, objective intelligences and the sense of moral certitude that gave them each the courage to fight for unpopular causes. The bond between them was their strict sense of morality. When Brandeis said after Wilson's death that Wilson "knew not fear," he was bestowing the highest possible praise: Wilson was a citizen who was not afraid to do what had to be done. Whatever internal doubts or fears either of them may have had were not visible. Singly and together, they defined "right," and then worked tirelessly to bring it into existence. Neither could do less; it was their duty.[53]

12 | The Making of
    a Zionist

In 1914 Brandeis's life took a completely unexpected turn when he was invited by American Zionists to an emergency conference on August 30. World War I, which had broken out during the summer, closed Europe's borders, and European Zionists were unable to meet and to continue financial assistance to Zionist communities in Palestine. To make matters worse, the colonists' earnings from the export of citrus fruits and wine were cut off by a naval blockade. Henry Morgenthau, American ambassador to Turkey, had contacted American Zionists. Morgenthau's plea reached the United States at the same time that Shmaryahu Levin of the Actions Comité, the major world Zionist organization, found himself stranded in the United States after a speaking tour. As a result of the situation in Europe and Levin's willingness to work with American Zionists, leadership of the Zionist movement would shift from Europe to the United States. The August emergency conference then, began this transfer of leadership and had as one of its aims the collection of fifty thousand dollars for the immediate relief of the Palestine settlers. To the great surprise of those present, perhaps including Brandeis himself, it also led to Brandeis's leadership of American Zionism.[1]

How and why did Brandeis become a Zionist? Although his family never denied its Jewishness, it did not seem to consider being Jewish particularly important. Neither Brandeis nor his parents practiced any religion. Brandeis's donations to Jewish charities were minimal, well below his contributions to other causes: up to 1912 he had given less than $1,500 to

Jewish organizations; between 1912 and 1939, in contrast, he donated over $600,000 to Jewish organizations, with most of the money directed toward Zionism. "When I entered upon the Jewish work," he wrote in 1941, "I concluded that my contribution, financial and otherwise, should be concentrated on Palestine." Contributions to non-Zionist Jewish organizations were made only when he felt personally involved with the people running them. One of his daughters has declared emphatically that the pre-1912 contributions are useless as evidence of a tie between her father and the Jewish community. He used his German-Jewish connections in Boston as a source of business, and kept a Jewish law clerk in his firm to handle the Jewish clients. Seemingly, he did not feel impelled either to socialize with his German-Jewish clients or to deal with their business himself; indeed, his insistence on economic independence was designed in part to free him from the social pressures of wooing clients. He played no role in Boston Jewish society, and the *Jewish Encyclopedia* did not even mention his name. Brandeis was invited to the August 1914 meeting because he had gained a national reputation as a reformer and a confidant of President Wilson, not because he had shown great interest in Zionist affairs.[2]

A number of reasons have been offered for what became Brandeis's total commitment to Zionism. It has been suggested that Brandeis was a "marginal man"; that is, one who had been "rebuffed by the majority in his efforts to identify with its culture" but managed to achieve "partial adjustment by identification with his subordinate ethnic group." The rebuff was Brandeis's exclusion from Wilson's cabinet. Another view is that Brandeis was catapulted into Zionism by his exclusion from Boston Brahmin society. An additional explanation is that Brandeis understood his rejection as a possible cabinet member to be the result of blackballing by influential Jews, whom he was now determined to cultivate.[3]

There are problems with those interpretations. In order to be a marginal man, one must feel excluded by the majority and different from it in important negative respects. Nothing in Brandeis's conduct, his letters, or the memories of his family indicates such to have been the case. On the contrary, his letters from the time show him to be a self-assured, dynamic man at peace with himself. He was both self-reliant and gregarious, able to throw himself with zest and enormous energy into legal and public affairs and equally able to put them aside for periods of relaxation with a loving and much-loved family; and, above all, he enjoyed life. He was not "rebuffed . . . in his efforts to identify with [the majority's] culture"; his separation from the Brahmins came long after that cultural identification was a *fait accompli*. Norman Hapgood wrote, "Brandeis had abandoned hosts of charming friends in Boston, and cut himself off from clients he would have needed had he cared for riches, when he began to reshape some of the ideas and practices prevailing around him." He aroused a particularly great "fury" by his attack on the New Haven Railroad and exacerbated it by his participation in the Pinchot-Ballinger affair: "The attacks on Mr. Brandeis in privileged and conventional circles, the slanders against him, were increased; but the public confidence was increased also." The philosopher Horace Kallen, who worked on Zionist causes with Brandeis, said repeatedly that Boston "society" turned against Brandeis because he had decided to "repre-sent . . . the little people."[4]

Far from feeling like a "marginal man" victimized by anti-Semitism, Brandeis considered himself to be the bearer of the torch of true Amer-icanism, and had more than adequate proof that he was so considered by others. His commitment to reform grew out of his education in the Puritan and Brahmin ethics and his understanding of American history. Brandeis's ideas, like those of the Brahmins, had European-American roots in Jefferson, Emerson, Goethe, and Euripides. Furthermore, his version of Americanism had served him well: not only was he the best-known lawyer in the United States, and by far one of the richest; not only was he regularly called upon to testify before congressional and administrative bodies; not only was he the valued adviser to an American president, and key architect of much of Wilson's domestic policy; but he also numbered among his callers, admirers, dinner companions, and friends the intellectual and political elite of the United States: Robert M. La Follette, Norman Hapgood, Florence Kelley, Jane Addams, Lincoln Stef-fens, Ray Stannard Baker, Mary K. O'Sullivan, Roscoe Pound, Charles Crane. Had he any doubt about his enormous influence as the "People's Attorney," the reaction to his exclusion from Wilson's cabinet would have eliminated it. Progressives expressed outrage and the press specu-lated that Wilson had hurt himself far more than Brandeis.[5]

It is true that after having been a fair-haired boy of Harvard and Boston, he found himself shunned by many of the Brahmins who he had thought shared his ideas. But they were not motivated by Brandeis's Jewishness, though some may have felt a measure of anti-Semitism; rather, they perceived that *he* had rejected *their* world. In attacking the insurance companies and the New Haven Railroad, in espousing the causes of labor and consumers, Brandeis was seen by the Brahmins as attacking the financial basis of their lives and society. Among the most vicious of Brandeis's detractors was Colonel Henry Lee Higginson, exemplar of Brahmin society, a banker and philanthropist, son of a Cabot, and close personal friend of Theodore Roosevelt and Henry Cabot Lodge. When Woodrow Wilson was considering Brandeis for a cabinet seat, Higginson urged one of Wilson's closest friends, Cleveland H. Dodge, to use his influence against Brandeis. He portrayed Brandeis as unscrupulous and untrustworthy. Dodge reported this to Wilson, and it became a factor in Wilson's decision against the Brandeis appointment.[6]

But either Higginson based his opposition on other factors or it took him an extraordinarily long time to discover that Brandeis was Jewish. When Brandeis married, Higginson's wife was the first person to call on the couple. Brandeis was Higginson's guest at his Lake Champlain house on July 4, 1890. In 1897, when Brandeis led the fight against the Boston Elevated Railway Company, his interest paralleled those of Higginson's firm so closely that Brandeis had to deny that Lee Higginson & Company had retained him. Brandeis numbered among the members of a group of like-minded Bostonians, who had offered to lease the subway for a $7/_8$ percent profit, Francis Lee Higginson, Colonel Higginson's brother. And Brandeis's Public Franchise League received at least one major contribution from Joseph Lee, the son of Henry Lee of Lee Higginson. Further, in 1905 Brandeis became involved on behalf of the Civic Federation in a dispute between the Boston Symphony Orchestra and its musicians' union. When the American Federation of Musicians attempted to organize a closed shop, Colonel Higginson, who had founded the orchestra and paid all its expenses, insisted that the orchestra "be subject only to the rules laid down by me." Eventually, a compromise established union minimum wages but not a closed shop. The settlement pleased Brandeis, and the correspondence between Higginson and Brandeis was amiable.[7]

However, Higginson's opinion of Brandeis, and that of the Boston banking community in general, changed suddenly in 1907. Brandeis was in the thick of the fight for savings bank life insurance. Higginson had proposed an alternate plan, the main purpose of which was to protect the interests of the existing insurance companies by undercutting SBLI. Ultimately, of course, Brandeis's plan triumphed over Higginson's. But a year later, when Brandeis was fighting the proposed merger of the Boston & Maine Railroad with the New Haven Railroad, Higginson joined forces with Senator Henry Cabot Lodge to oppose him. Higginson wrote of Brandeis, "He had attacked and lied . . . Brandeis is not to be trusted . . . I should consider him a most dangerous man . . . I certainly should not believe Brandeis . . . on oath." Higginson also wondered aloud where the money for Brandeis's antimerger campaign was coming from. Brandeis, commenting on the source of Higginson's antagonism, wrote that the acquisition of Boston & Maine stock by the New Haven had been "engineered by Lee, Higginson & Company under an arrangement which is reported to be that the brokers get $1.50 per share for putting the transaction through. All of State Street is of course in favor of the merger."[8]

Higginson's change in attitude, then, can clearly be traced to the divergence between his financial interests and what Brandeis thought of as the public interest. This was typical of the reaction of the Brahmin community to Brandeis's transformation from a socially acceptable, Harvard-trained, corporation lawyer to a radical political innovator. It is true that Higginson later joined the Immigration Restriction League and became a member of its Advisory Committee, agitating against the immigration of "undesirable" races. He also supported a right-wing magazine, misnamed *Truth*, which printed anti-Semitic diatribes against Brandeis, but its circulation was so negligible that it lasted for only two years. After the turn of the century Brahmin Boston was becoming increasingly nativist, racist, and anti-Semitic, but this attitude toward newcomers is insufficient to explain Boston's animus toward the man to whom it had so eagerly opened its doors only a generation earlier. Brandeis's economic reformism, not his religion, put him on a collision course with the brokers of State Street. He acknowledged that the financial interests opposed him in a letter to his brother written after the Wilson cabinet had been chosen. In it he said, "It is almost, or indeed, quite amusing how much they fear me—attributing to me power and influence which I in no respect possess." Arthur Link's examination of the reasons for Wilson's decision makes no mention of Brandeis's religion; instead, it emphasizes the antagonism of the financial interests and notes the extent to which Progressives saw the question of Brandeis's appointment only as "a test of Wilson's sincerity." Robert La Follette's daughter reported that Wilson's failure to appoint Brandeis attorney general "raised doubts among the Progressives as to the policy of the new Administration" about such matters as trusts and control of capital.[9]

Brandeis evinced no regrets at Wilson's decision, writing to La Follette's son-in-law, "I am inclined to think that so far as I personally am concerned the disposition which has been made of the Cabinet matter is best. The Senator and I are planning to do some legislative work together, of which we are very hopeful." He was angry at the political power demonstrated by the "interests," but he was already hard at work with La Follette to overcome them.[10]

The evidence that has been accumulated to prove that Brandeis was never truly a part of Boston "society," and therefore was a victim of anti-Semitism, misses the point. The situation must be seen from Brandeis's point of view. He chose his companions for their brains, not for their bank accounts or ancestry, and it is clear that, with the exception of his first heady introduction to a society more cosmopolitan than that of Louisville, he was always thoroughly bored with "society." There is no indication that he saw anti-Semitism as having anything to do with him; he discussed the phenomenon with both Kallen and Solomon Goldman without once mentioning any personal experience of it.[11]

It is inconceivable that had Brandeis perceived Wilson as knuckling under to the forces of prejudice, he would have remained in close contact with him. Brandeis was a whole-hearted believer in the dignity of the individual. Among the attributes always mentioned by those who knew him were his strict sense of morality, and his insistence that moral imperatives could never be ignored. Bigotry was unacceptable, and he could not have worked closely with a man he saw either as bigoted or as granting victory to the forces of bigotry. Yet Brandeis was so convinced of Wilson's ethnic pluralism that he continued to advise President Wilson and worked with him up until his death in 1924.[12]

The argument that Brandeis turned to Zionism for political reasons is equally unacceptable, for, aside from its being out of character for him to have done so, it would have served no purpose. To Brandeis, Zionism came to mean a belief in the need for a Jewish state and the concomitant duty to "educate" the American public about its necessity. The idea of a Jewish state, however, was anathema to the politically important Jews of the period. Almost entirely of German background and well assimilated into the American society and its economy, they viewed Zionism with horror as an attempt to create divided loyalties among American Jews. Those who espoused the need for a Jewish homeland, they warned, were playing into the hands of anti-Semites, who would point to Zionism as proof that American Jews did not fully pledge their allegiance to the United States. This was the belief of such leading Jews as Jacob Schiff, Felix Warburg, Louis Marshall, Adolph Ochs (publisher of the *New York Times*), and Felix Adler (Brandeis's brother-in-law, who in addition to heading the Ethical Culture Society taught ethics and morals at Columbia University). Far from placating them, Brandeis's new-found interest in Zionism put him in opposition to them—scarcely a way to curry favor! Furthermore, one of the leading historians of Zionism points out that until 1914 "the Zionist Organization in America was weak, in financial distress, and with no influence in the Jewish community." It was Brandeis who eventually turned the German-Jewish aristocracy into Zionists.[13]

Before 1910 Brandeis had only a vague knowledge of Zionism's existence. Sometime in the 1890s he had read in the *North American Review* about Theodor Herzl and the colonization movement in Palestine. There is a possibly apochryphal story that upon reading about the first Zionist Congress at Basle in 1897, he told his wife, "Now *there* is something to which I could give myself." However, in 1905, speaking before the New

Century Club on the occasion of the 250th anniversary of the first settlement of Jews in the United States, he condemned ethnic separatism: "There is room here for men of any race, of any creed, of any condition in life, but not for Protestant-Americans, or Catholic-Americans, or Jewish-Americans, nor for German-Americans, Irish-Americans, or Russian-Americans." This was the attitude typical of assimilated German-American Jews.[14]

Why, then, did Brandeis, a secular humanist, become a fervent Zionist? Although the most important factor may have been his humanism and the knowledge of classical Greece that was an important part of it, other parts of the explanation lie in his relationship with his uncle Dembitz, his mediation of the 1910 garment workers' strike, an extraordinary meeting with an English Zionist, and another one with a Palestinian Jew.

Lewis Naphtali Dembitz was Brandeis's role model. He was, first of all, an outstanding lawyer. Already an adult when he arrived in the United States, he became so knowledgeable about the law of his new land that his *Kentucky Jurisprudence* was considered authoritative. He combined law with public service, both as Louisville's assistant city attorney and as a sufficiently active Republican to be sent to the 1860 convention. In 1888 he drafted the first "Australian" ballot law ever to be adopted in the United States. He also devised a new tax collection system for Louisville, combining levies on personal property, garnisheeing of rents, and equity suits. And he was eclectic, equally at home in linguistics, mathematics, and astronomy. Dembitz was considered a "walking encyclopedia" and "an authority on any and all questions" by Louisville's intellectual circles as well as by his nephew. Here, perhaps, was the source of Brandeis's determination never to be wrong on a question of fact. Dembitz loved to share his knowledge, and particularly delighted in teaching children. He was the intellectual center of his extended family and a source of informal education for all its members.[15]

With the alteration of details, this description fits Brandeis: outstanding lawyer, legal writer, public servant; someone thoroughly immersed in the intellectual process and eager to teach those around him. They were even alike in their health problems: Dembitz was so nearsighted that he had to hold anything he read only inches from his eyes, and he was unable to understand the American game of baseball because he could see neither the players nor the ball. Nonetheless, Dembitz, like Brandeis, loved the outdoors and swam and rowed regularly.[16]

The one great difference between them was religion. Dembitz had become an orthodox Jew when he was thirteen, apparently due to the influence of a classmate at his Prague boarding school. He faithfully observed orthodox practices during his years in Louisville, refusing to write, open letters, or do anything else that he believed constituted work on the Sabbath. He was a charter member of the Adath Jeshurun Congregation in Louisville, wrote a book entitled *Jewish Services in Synagogue and Home* (1898) as well as articles for the *Jewish Encyclopedia*, served as a member of the commission that established the curriculum of the Hebrew Union College and as a vice-president of the Orthodox Jewish Congregational Union of America, and was awarded the first honorary title (Doctor of Hebrew Literature) ever conferred by the Jewish Theological Seminary.[17]

The young Brandeis was inevitably aware of his uncle's religious concerns but seems not to have given them much conscious thought. It is clear from his mother's *Reminiscences* that his parents were extremely skeptical of any religion, other than a vague deism, and that any involvement by Brandeis in his uncle's religious practices would have created a conflict between the values of his adored mother and his equally idolized uncle. So Brandeis remembered his uncle as a "university" and as an abolitionist lawyer, rather than as a Jew. Yet near the end of his life Brandeis could still remember not only the awesome serenity of his uncle on the Sabbath, but the details of his observances.[18]

Brandeis's own memories were enhanced in 1912 by those of Jacob de Haas, who had been secretary to Theodor Herzl, the father of Zionism, and had later come to the United States, where he became editor of Boston's *Jewish Advocate*. Brandeis had met him briefly in 1910, while conferring with local editors in hopes of eliciting their support for savings bank life insurance. At the time, Brandeis was unaware of de Haas's Zionist background and activities. However, in August 1912 they met again when de Haas visited Brandeis in South Yarmouth at William G. McAdoo's request, to consult about funds for Wilson's campaign. When their conversation was over, Brandeis took de Haas to the train station. Along the way de Haas asked Brandeis if he was related to Lewis Dembitz. Brandeis replied that he was, and de Haas commented that Dembitz, who had died in 1907, had been a "noble Jew." When Brandeis questioned him, de Haas replied by describing Dembitz's interest in Zionism and sketched his own background as a Zionist. Fascinated, Brandeis took de Haas back to the cottage for lunch to learn more, and the whole family heard de Haas talk about the origins and urgency of the Zionist movement, and what de Haas called the "epic story of Theodore Herzl." The two men had additional conversations about Zionism during the following winter.[19]

The meeting with de Haas had an enormous impact on Brandeis. One leader of Hadassah recalled Brandeis as being "eternally grateful" to de Haas, whom he credited with "unfold[ing] the Zionist cause to him."

Chaim Weizmann remembered that Brandeis called de Haas his "teacher in Zionism." Brandeis told Felix Frankfurter that it was de Haas who had gotten him interested in Zionism. And he wrote to Julian Mack, "I consider de Haas the maker of American Zionism."[20]

Brandeis was undoubtedly more receptive in 1912 to de Haas's tales of Zionism than he would have been a few years before because of his experience with the Jewish garment industry in 1910. Brandeis had found the workers and owners both rational and tolerant, fully aware of each other's problems. They reminded him of lawyers: "They have the same respect for one another which opposing lawyers have for each other. Their conflict does not create enmity. The men, though contending for exactly the opposite results, became friends." He came away convinced that they were idealistic and shared his passion for justice and democracy. These were Eastern European Jews, far removed from the upper- and upper-middle-class German Jews with whom Brandeis was more familiar. But Brandeis found that he and the garment men got along well. In the evenings, after negotiations were over for the day, they would drink beer together (this in itself made the evenings extraordinary, for Brandeis was not normally a drinker), and Brandeis would regale them with tales of the Ballinger affair.[21]

Brandeis came away from the negotiations with the important realization that he had much in common with the lower-class Eastern European Jews, in spite of the difference in life styles—perhaps more in common with them than with the German Jews he knew. He met some of their leaders: Julius Henry Cohen, an attorney for the employers; Henry Moskowitz, who later became an adviser to Governor Al Smith; Meyer Bloomfield, lawyer, union man, and head of the Civil Service House, a settlement house for workers; and Meyer London, counsel for the union. These were people who, Brandeis felt, could understand his dreams of self-government. They had made him understand not only the degradations that had led them to emigrate from Eastern Europe, but also the problems they faced as immigrants in the United States. Thus, Brandeis was both reinforced in his belief in the possibilities of trade unionism and worker-participation and made aware of the Jewishness he shared with people he had considered alien. His sense of identification with his new acquaintances is all the more striking considering the difference in style between the austere, controlled Bostonian and the emotional, verbose New Yorkers. One participant in the labor negotiations described "how the picturesque, exotic, often powerful personalities involved in the strike, would burst into thunder-claps of oratory while Brandeis sat by silently, thinking. When the debate was at last spent, he would quietly point to irrelevancies in fact and render a seemingly obvious decision." Nonetheless, the identification was there. Benjamin V. Cohen was convinced that the garment strike made Brandeis "conscious of the fact that he was dealing with an immigrant industry consisting mostly of Jews and that he himself was a Jew." Louis E. Kirstein thought the strike not only gave Brandeis "faith in the Jewish masses" but also reinforced his belief that "equity, righteousness, justice and good will could settle any controversy."[22]

Not surprisingly, shortly after the garment workers' strike, he spoke publicly for the first time about Zionism. During an interview that December with a reporter for *The American Hebrew*, he was asked for his reaction to "those Jews who are working for the revival of a Jewish state in Palestine." Brandeis replied, "I have a great deal of sympathy with the Zionists. The movement is an exceedingly deserving one. These so-called dreamers are entitled to the respect and appreciation of the entire Jewish people." But he continued to warn against hyphenated Americans, adding that "habits of living, of thought which tend to keep alive difference of origin or to classify men according to their religious beliefs are inconsistent with the American idea of brotherhood and are disloyal." He now began noticing references to the history of Zionism. His friend Elizabeth Glendower Evans wrote years later, "The profound emotional experience that gave birth to his realization of himself as a Jew grew out of the dress and waist-makers' strike . . . There he saw foreign-born Jews trying to gain a foothold in a new world, with no background in the old world to which they could look with pride and whose greatness should eke out their own insignificance. He determined to acknowledge these downtrodden men as his own blood brothers." This undoubtedly overstates the case a bit; certainly, however, the garment strike signaled a potential new road for Brandeis. He acknowledged this in 1915, telling two interviewers, "I now saw the true democracy of my people, their idealistic inclinations and their love of liberty and freedom." But as Felix Frankfurter pointed out, it would take Brandeis "deep searching" and "long brooding" before he found a Zionism to which he could commit himself.[23]

It would be a mistake to think of his Jewishness as a key part of Brandeis's identity before 1910. He was Jewish in the same way that he came from Louisville: both were acknowledged as making up part of his background; both were relatively unimportant to his present. Perhaps Louisville was of greater importance than Judaism, for his family ties in Louisville led him to return there for visits; he was conscious of no such ties to Judaism.

This gradually changed as a result of Brandeis's experience in the garment trade and de Haas's tales of Dembitz and Zionism. Suddenly,

Brandeis was reminded that he did have family ties to Judaism and Zionism. He found the society of democratic unionization for which he had been seeking, among the garment workers; he learned what Zionism was about. He also learned about anti-Semitism, which the workers had experienced first in Europe and then in the United States. Gradually, he came to see it as representing the failure of liberalism, which shielded individuals but not groups and therefore provided less than total protection. He began to notice anti-Semitism around him. In October 1914, shortly after he became leader of the American Zionists, he wrote to his brother from Detroit: "By the way, Anti-Semitism seems to have reached its American pinnacle here. New Athletic Club with 5000 members and no Jews need apply." This is the first mention of anti-Semitism in any of his letters. In November he received a letter from a young lawyer in Philadelphia who felt himself the victim of anti-Semitism and wondered if he should move elsewhere. Brandeis replied that anti-Semitism existed in most cities and that the answer was "to endeavor to meet such feelings as you may find to exist in the place in which you are working." Cautiously optimistic, he believed that in spite of anti-Semitism, talent would be recognized in the United States "even if not necessarily at 100 per cent of its value."[24]

Thus, for the first time in his life, Brandeis began to grapple with the problem of anti-Semitism in the United States. As a Zionist he fought European anti-Semitism, which had reduced Jewish communities to a pitiful condition, but he felt directly challenged to find a solution to the dramatic waste of human potential caused by American anti-Semitism. Henry Moskowitz wrote, "He was tremendously impressed by the selfless idealism of the Jewish labor leaders and of their teachers and intellectuals. As he thought about it his mind played upon the frustration and waste involved in the dying out of many of the spiritual and intellectual qualities of a gifted people. They should be consciously cultivated as a distinctive contribution to world civilization of a small, but gifted race." Moskowitz saw the strike as having more influence than any other experience on Brandeis's becoming a conscious Jew. Waste of any kind—but particularly waste of human potential—was anathema to him.[25]

Brandeis viewed the problem as two-pronged: establishing equality for American Jews and securing Jewish talent for the benefit of the United States and the world. Jews and Gentiles alike had to be convinced that Jews had an important contribution to make and that identification of Americans as Jewish in no way impaired their loyalty as Americans. In addition, an opportunity had to be found for foreign Jews, who would clearly not be permitted to fulfill their potential in many of the anti-Semitic communities abroad, to do so elsewhere. Brandeis would eventually reach the conclusion that Zionism could be used to teach Americans about the values of Judaism as well as to establish a small democratic society to which persecuted Jews could emigrate.[26]

By 1912 the garment workers and their difficulties were real to Brandeis, but Palestine was not. However, while he was in Chicago campaigning for La Follette in January 1912, he was taken to a lecture on agriculture; there he met Aaron Aaronsohn, a Palestinian Jew who had discovered wild wheat. Brandeis later described Aaronsohn, head of the Jewish Agricultural Experiment Station in Palestine, as "one of the most interesting, brilliant and remarkable men I have ever met," and called his achievement "one of the most remarkable and useful discoveries in recent years, and possibly of all times." Zionism began to appear in a new light: in fact, Hapgood thought that Aaronsohn's tale of his discovery and its possible impact on life in Palestine planted the first "seed of Zionism" in Brandeis's mind.[27]

In 1912 he joined the Federation of American Zionists (FAZ), and soon became a member of its Associate Executive Committee. He also joined the Zionist Association of Greater Boston, the Menorah Society, and the advisory board of the Hebrew Sheltering & Immigrant Aid Society. Then he shocked his relatives, who were unaware of his new interest, by speaking at a Zionist meeting in Boston. The occasion was a reception at the Plymouth Theatre for Nahum Sokolow, a leading European Zionist and member of the Actions Comité. Brandeis introduced Sokolow with a few sentences, speaking of "the idea of the Jew for centuries—social righteousness, the war against iniquity, relief for the burdens of the oppressed, and the lessening of the toil of the poor." This was in March 1913. Brandeis sent Sokolow to Secretary of State William Jennings Bryan and urged Norman Hapgood to have Aaronsohn write for *Harper's Weekly* about Zionist idealism. Sokolow was impressed by Brandeis and reported on their meeting to the Zionist Congress in Vienna where Brandeis's membership in the Federation of American Zionists had been reported at its convention in 1912. Now publicly recognized as a Zionist, he gave a number of speeches before Jewish and Zionist groups, and the 1913 convention of the FAZ elected him as a delegate to the Zionist Congress meeting to be held in Vienna that summer. There was even a rumor that he would be elected head of the Zionist movement. Brandeis was unable to go but sent a message that was read before the congress. In it, he firmly advocated Jewish immigration to Palestine and the creation of new colonies, as well as creation of a corporation that would enable some industrial development to begin.[28]

The publicity his new activities generated also led some members of the press to attack him. An editorial in the *Atlanta Constitution*, of

September 16, 1913, calling Zionism an un-American endeavor, added that if Brandeis was sincere in his Zionism he could "put himself right by catching the first boat for the Mediterranean." It is important to note that overt press attacks on Brandeis as a Jew followed his public conversion to Zionism; they did not precede it and can scarcely be called a cause of it. After he became a Zionist, he was attacked for his Zionism, which was perceived as dangerously divisive of American loyalties. The attacks came from anti-Zionist Jews as well as from non-Jews; those of the former were perhaps blunter and nastier. It would be naive to mistake anti-Zionism for anti-Semitism. While there were no doubt those who were of both persuasions, there was genuine concern among Jews and Gentiles alike that the United States could not survive if Americans indulged themselves in what Theodore Roosevelt called "hyphenated Americanism." Ethnic identity was to disappear in the melting pot; a search for ethnic and racial "roots" and an articulated ethnic consciousness would not become acceptable to mainstream America until decades later.[29]

Although the press was somewhat excited by Brandeis's Zionism, and Zionists were clearly delighted to have the wealthy and famous "People's Attorney" join their ranks, the new convert himself spent little time on Zionism. From 1912 until early 1914 he was busy with Wilson and Wilsonianism—first with the campaign and then with efforts to hammer out the legislation of the New Freedom. Some Zionists may have thought of him as one of their own, but he was not; although a member of the FAZ's Associate Executive Committee, for example, he attended no meetings and did not go to the 1913 Vienna Congress.[30]

This situation changed during the summer of 1914 when Wilson began to lose interest in antitrust and other Progressive measures. Brandeis's influence was waning. In June, over the adamant opposition of Brandeis and other Progressives, Wilson had named businessmen to the Federal Reserve Board, and Brandeis, already discouraged by what he saw as Wilson's inattention to "real progressives," left Washington.[31]

He decided to spend his summer vacation reading intensively in Zionism and Jewish affairs. As usual, any new field of endeavor had first to be researched thoroughly: one had to ascertain all the relevant facts before formulating ideas. So Brandeis was immersed in Zionist books when, in August, the call came to attend the emergency meeting of Zionists in New York. Exactly what Brandeis read that summer is not known. His letters and speeches in the following months show a familiarity with Herzl, the Hebrew philosopher Ahad Ha'am (Asher Ginzberg), Edward A. Ross's *The Old World in the New*, Arthur Ruppin's *The Jews of Today*, Israel Cohen's *The Zionist Movement*, Abraham Geiger's *Judaism and Its History*, Ignatz Zollschan's *Jewish Question*, and Leopold Zunz's *The Sufferings of the Jews During the Middle Ages*. The most important book Brandeis read, and one he quoted throughout his life and made certain that all the members of his extended family read, was not about Zionism: it was Alfred Zimmern's *The Greek Commonwealth*.[32]

Brandeis did not read Zimmern's book immediately upon its publication in 1912, and probably got to it when he could because of his lifelong habit of reading widely in Greek history. He was familiar with Zimmern's name, writing to Felix Frankfurter in another context that "in the Roman survey . . . Ferrero (Zimmern's translator) was my entree." It is notable that he read the book immediately before the crucial summer during which he immersed himself in Zionism, emerged with a coherent theory of Zionism, and became leader of the American Zionist movement. A 1917 letter to Zimmern states that Brandeis read the volume during the winter of 1913–14, while he was investigating the New Haven Railroad. It constituted, Brandeis wrote, his only recreation during that period, and he added that the book gave him more pleasure than almost anything else he had read in recent years, except for Gilbert Murray's *Bacchae*. His future fellow worker in Zionism, Horace Kallen, later told him that Zimmern was interested in Zionism, and that, Brandeis reported, gave him the sense that Zimmern was much more involved in the same cause than he had realized. The letter also suggests that Brandeis's close fiend Norman Hapgood was in contact with Zimmern.

Zimmern's political views paralleled those of Brandeis, and the idea of the Greek city-state matched the possibilities of Palestine. Zimmern may have been the catalyst for the ideas already circulating in Brandeis's mind, or he may have offered Brandeis a new way of looking at Zionism. Whatever the case, the book was one of the few that Brandeis considered central to his life and one that reflects perfectly his approach to Zionism.

In order to understand the importance of Zimmern for Brandeis, one must first appreciate the high esteem in which Brandeis held the Greeks of fifth-century Athens. The highest tribute that Brandeis could give his uncle Dembitz was that "he reminded one of the Athenians." Brandeis also compared the Founding Fathers to the Athenians in his most eloquent defense of free speech and the democratic process, his concurrence with the majority opinion in *Whitney* v. *California*. He wrote, in part, "They believed liberty to be the secret of happiness and courage to be the secret of liberty." Paul Freund, who was first Brandeis's law clerk and then his lifelong friend, has identified the sentence as coming from Pericles' "Funeral Oration." Zimmern shared Brandeis's high regard for the "Funeral Oration"; the premise of his book is that the oration reflects the greatest heights ever reached by democracy. Other indications of Brandeis's interest in ancient Greece include the comment of the reporter who followed Brandeis around for two days in 1916 and wrote wryly, "Euripides, I now judge, after having interviewed Brandeis on many subjects, said the last word on most of them." Jacob de Haas noted, "Greek and Roman history are as clear to him as though they were part of the morning's news." His favorite and most often quoted poem was from Euripides' *The Bacchae*; he clearly felt it expressed his view of citizenship and public service. In short, to discover how the model political human being would function in the model political society, Brandeis turned to the Athenians.[34]

Zimmern was a political scientist, sociologist, and classicist at Oxford University, who put more than ten years' work into the original version of *The Greek Commonwealth* and then annotated it as it went into each successive edition. He initially wrote the book in "an attempt to make clear to [himself] what fifth-century Athens was really like," but he believed the book took on a new significance by the time of the publication of the second edition in December 1914. He wrote in the new preface, "Greek ideas and Greek inspiration can help us to-day, not only in facing the duties of the moment, but in the work of deepening and extending the range and the meaning of Democracy and Citizenship, Liberty and Law, which would seem to be the chief political task before mankind."[35]

Zimmern was enraptured by Pericles' Athens: "For a whole wonderful half-century, the richest and happiest period in the recorded history of any single community, Politics and Morality, the deepest and strongest forces of national and of individual life, had moved forward hand in hand towards a common ideal, the perfect citizen in the perfect state." Creation of the perfect citizen in the perfect state was of course Brandeis's goal and the object of his insistence on education, democracy, and self-fulfillment. Each of the elements that Zimmern discussed as basic to the heights attained by Athens was in turn one of the elements central to Brandeis's concerns. Brandeis, for example, insisted on decentralization and local self-government; Zimmern wrote of the Greeks and local independence, "They grew up unable to conceive of any other state of government." Brandeis advocated efficiency, both as scientific management in industrial affairs and in the activities of Zionists; Zimmern attributed the Greeks' creation of cities to their need for efficiency. Brandeis feared centralization of power, not only because it would end local experimentation, but because it would mean that all-too-limited human beings would falter and be corrupted by an excess of responsibility; Zimmern wrote, "The record of civilized States seems to show that no sub-division of the community . . . is sufficiently well informed or wise or tolerant or unselfish to be entrusted for long, without control or responsibility, with the powers and temptations of government." And as Brandeis fulminated against the inefficiency of big business and big government, Zimmern commented, "Public business is much the same as private: and men are not able to transact business in hordes. Large companies are much the same as small, only more uncomfortable. No one likes to sit for hours listening to other men talking . . . Hence the atmosphere of boredom and languor so conspicuous . . . in most modern Parliaments." Brandeis argued that only a passionate concern for justice and public affairs would safeguard democracy; Zimmern agreed that "it is only in a state where men are jealous for the maintenance of justice that the freedom of the individual can permanently be secured." He added that "it was Pericles' boast that his fellow-citizens found time to do justice both to public and private responsibilities, that they were at once (what is nowadays considered impossible) the most active political workers and the most many-sided individuals of their time." And Zimmern himself believed that "democracy is meaningless unless it involves the serious and steady co-operation of large numbers of citizens in the actual work of government."[36]

Brandeis found his own ideas paralleled in many ways in Zimmern and the Greece that he described. Wealth was useful only to ensure "social well-being." Conspicuous consumption was corrupting. Civilization meant more than material possessions; the Greeks were "people for whom comfort meant something very different from motor-cars and arm-chairs, who, although or because they lived plainly and austerely and sat at the table of life without expecting any dessert, saw more of the use and beauty and goodness of the few things which were vouchsafed them— their minds, their bodies, and Nature outside and around them." Brandeis, with his love of simplicity, the intellect, outdoor sports, and long walks, would have fit in well. When he spoke of the meaning of leisure, he referred to the Greeks: "In other words, men and women must have leisure, which the Athenians called 'freedom' or liberty."[37]

Brandeis was concerned that factory work turned human beings into robots. Zimmern wrote: "Our modern industrial system . . . has contrived to take the joy out of craftsmanship . . . It has replaced . . . the independent thought of the human brain by 'soulless organization'. It has removed the maker or producer from all association with the public for whom he works, and substituted a deadening 'cash-nexus' for the old personal relationship or sense of effort in a corporate cause. Above all, it has taken from him his liberty, and forced him to work for a master who is no artist, and to work fast and badly." Brandeis fought for industrial reform. Zimmern, too, viewed labor conditions as untenable: "Any system of labour which is organized on the assumption that man is no more than one among many other machines and implements, and is to be treated accordingly, is inhuman and unnatural: it does violence, that is, to the true nature of man . . . Slavery, in the broader sense of the term, i.e. treating labourers as soulless instruments . . . needs to be faced anew under our more complicated industrial system at home, where exploitation can take a thousand shapes, as any one familiar with working-class conditions knows only too well." To Brandeis, every problem was capable of solution; one had only to examine it in sufficient depth to find the answer, and then "educate" the human beings involved into acceptance. Zimmern's words were: "There is no such thing as a problem of material organization. All problems, from gas and tramways to education and women's rights, are human problems, concerned with people rather than with things."[38]

Brandeis's fights on behalf of workers and consumers led to his being branded a "radical." Zimmern called the Athenians "Natural Radicals . . . as all men who are fond of exercising their intellect on political questions are tempted to be." But Athens' acceptance of "hot-headed Radicals" was one of the things that made it great; "when Pericles delivered his Funeral Speech their foremost communities were, in most essential respects, more civilized than ourselves."[39]

The similarity of Brandeis's and Zimmern's attitudes toward such things as society, politics, modern life, participation in democracy, and material well-being is remarkable. Had there been nothing more, Brandeis might well have read the book, enjoyed the endorsement it gave to his deepest beliefs, and forgotten it. But Zimmern not only spoke of Greece; he spoke of Palestine.

Zimmern was a classicist; he was also a half-Jew. Which of these factors accounts for his sprinkling his book about Greece with references to Palestine, Jewish history, the Old Testament, and the Prophets is unknown; the two factors may have been equally responsible. He saw early Jewish civilization in Palestine as lesser than that of the Greeks, but the analogies he made between the two societies suggested that a civilization as great as Athens could be built in Palestine.

Geography, Zimmern thought, was a major factor in the rise of the Athenian city-state, and therefore he began his book with a description of the Mediterranean area. One "can only understand Mediterranean life," he wrote, "whether in Greece or Palestine, by a deliberate effort of the imagination." He emphasized the geographical similarity of Greece and Palestine: "Greece, like Palestine, relies for its moisture on the unsettled weather of winter and the big rainfalls in the autumn and spring, the 'former' and 'latter' rains of the Bible." Greece has distinct geographic areas. "This threefold division is as true of Palestine as of Greece. Compare the Parable of the Sower, with its 'rock', 'thorns' (i.e. pasture), and 'good soil'." One of the consequences of the fortunate climate of Mediterranean lands was equality: "Wherever life is easy and open there is a certain natural equality . . . this equality will tend to create a constant and vigorous public opinion and an interest in public affairs." This was not to argue that the Greek and Palestinian societies had been similar: "Palestine has fared very differently at the hands of her rulers from Greece." But there was certainly hope for the future: "Still it is true to assert of all these regions that, even if they have not preserved their independence or attained to popular government, they yet provide conditions which will prove helpful at any time to their successful exercise."[40]

So one vital element in the rise of the near-perfect state, that is, geography, was present in Palestine. Again and again, Zimmern compared Palestine with Greece, sometimes to show their similarities, sometimes to show their divergences. He likened the Greek "nation" to the ancient Jewish "tribe"; Greek legends and poems, passed on from generation to generation, to "Jewish scriptures"; the Greek princes who served as farmers or shepherds to the David of the Old Testament; the prophets of Delphi and the innovations they made in Greek religion to the Israeli prophets Amos and Isaiah. Elsewhere, he mentioned the similarity of the complaints made by Greek and Jewish tenant-farmers; compared the Greek poet Archilochus with Hosea and Amos on the subject of drinking in newly commercial societies; spoke of the juxtaposition of craftsmen and farmers in Greece and Palestine; and cited "2 Kings xviii.16; showing that the temple of Jerusalem was a treasure-house just like the Parthenon." He saw the Greek code of Elis and the book of Deuteronomy as forming "a double link in the chain of gold which ends in the Declaration of the rights of Man." At one point, Zimmern touched upon both the assimilationist dilemma that was so crucial to American Zionism and one of the philosophers Brandeis seems to have read in 1914: "The fifth-century Greeks had none of the post-Exilic Jews' fear of assimilating foreign elements. This conflict is still being fought out in Jewry; cf. a remarkable volume of essays by Achad Haam . . . The writer preaches substantially the same doctrine as Herodotus." Was it this footnote, or de Haas, that sent Brandeis to Achad Ha'am?[41]

Zimmern's thesis, stated simply, is that there were three causes of the decline of Pericles' Greece: a lack of attention to details, such as the treatment of health problems; the plague; and the simultaneous arrival of the Lacedaemonian enemy's armies. The plague was the beginning of the end; it killed a quarter of the citizens. "Athenian idealism broke for the first time under the strain, and the snapped ties were never again securely reunited." Brandeis was already sensitive to health problems, and he was especially wary of malaria. When he assumed leadership of the Zionist movement, he made one of his first priorities the eradication of malaria in Palestine, because it interfered "with self-support and the building up of the country" as well as with "the joy of life"; until it was gone a workable civilization could not be developed in Palestine.[42]

In summary, Zimmern shared Brandeis's political and economic views; he extolled the Athens of Pericles as the closest human beings had come to achieving the ideal of the perfect citizen in the perfect state; and he emphasized the historical analogies between Athens and Palestine, as well as the similarity in their geography, which he considered a major factor in the course of civilization. The chronological record certainly suggests that Zimmern enabled Brandeis to bring together his political beliefs, his love of ancient Greece, and his new-found interest in Zionism. The suggestion is bolstered by the fact that Brandeis urged Zimmern upon everyone—colleagues, family, friends, law clerks—throughout the remainder of his life. Brandeis would quote whole passages from Zimmern. Dean Acheson, Brandeis's law clerk for two years, remembered that "two interacting themes seem to have dominated the Justice's talk—the Greek Genius (he was an admirer of Alfred Zimmern's *The Greek Commonwealth*) and the Curse of Bigness."[43]

There is an even more important piece of evidence linking Brandeis and Zimmern, and indicating that Brandeis considered Zimmern in large measure responsible for his Zionism. Although the two men had not met before, in 1919, when Brandeis set sail for his only trip to Palestine, he chose Zimmern as one of his two companions.

Brandeis left New York for London on June 14, 1919. His companions on board the R. M. S. *Mauretania* were his daughter Susan and Mr. and Mrs. de Haas. Part of the trip, he wrote to his wife, was spent rereading Paul Goodman's "little history of the Jews, which accompanied us to Quebec in 1913," as well as the Book of Daniel.[44]

Brandeis arrived in London on June 20 and, after various sessions with Zionists (including his first one with Chaim Weizmann), left for a day in Paris. There he met with many of those involved in the Versailles Conferences as well as with leaders of the World Zionist Organization and with Lord Balfour. On June 25 he sailed from Marseilles to Port Said. With him was Alfred Zimmern, who apparently joined him in Paris.[45]

Jacob de Haas was an obvious choice of traveling companion because Brandeis thought that "all that was done by the American Zionists" was due to de Haas, "the central man." But why Zimmern? Clearly, the answer lies in the similarity of Brandeis's and Zimmern's ideas. And yet Zimmern was not a Zionist. Although he sympathized with the Zionist cause and occasionally advised Chaim Weizmann, Zimmern was primarily a World Federalist. In a 1916 *New Republic* article Zimmern had insisted, "We are slowly moving towards a single World-State." He thought of Jews as having enriched the common culture: "the world is the richer for them in more senses than one." Zimmern spoke not of nationalism but of "nationality," and differentiated it from loyalty to a nation-state. He saw national consciousness as manifesting itself in education and literature, not as an obstacle to international organization. As various nationalities came to interest themselves in each other's culture, they would be drawn together.[46]

Here Brandeis and Zimmern differed. Although Brandeis fulminated against "the false doctrine that nation and nationality must be made coextensive" and that the nationality of Jews interfered in any way with their loyalty to the United States, he came to see Jewish nationality as culminating in the establishment of Palestine. Zimmern's focus on the abolition of national boundaries prevented his calling himself a Zionist, but his emphasis on the role of national consciousness as a step toward a world state made him sympathetic to the revival of Jewish culture and history that was implicit in Zionism. In any event, *The Greek Commonwealth*, written long before his article, pointed the way to a melding of Zionism, the love of ancient Greece, and the political ideas that he shared with Brandeis.[47]

By the time Brandeis left Marseilles, Susan and Mrs. de Haas had gone their own ways and Brandeis's only companions were de Haas and Zimmern. Brandeis wrote on June 27, from the ship *Malwa*, that he and de Haas were "reading and talking Palestine and much else with Zimmern who is not only interesting but a congenial, gemutlich travelling companion." After reaching Port Said, the three men traveled to Cairo, where they were greeted by a twenty-three-piece band of Zionists playing "Hatikva." "They bore their heads high and the backs were straight and they bore the blue and white like a free and independent people," Brandeis wrote to his wife. The band followed the men to their luxurious apartments at Shepheard's and again played the Zionist anthem in their honor. The next day, Brandeis had brief meetings with the English top command in Palestine, and he and Zimmern did a bit of sightseeing. They then boarded a train for Alexandria, where they sat for some days awaiting the return from Palestine of Viscount Allenby, High Commissioner for Egypt (whose jurisdiction included Palestine until 1920). So many people wanted to see Brandeis that he felt justified in splitting his little group up, sending Zimmern to tea with Sir Percy Amos (a judicial advisor to the Egyptian government) and de Haas to a commencement at a local Jewish school—while Brandeis himself took a nap. It is clear from two of Brandeis's comments about Zimmern, the one made on the *Malwa* and one in Alexandria, that neither he nor Alice had met Zimmern before: "My two companions are most agreeable . . . Zimmern is like one of the family, more Jewish in looks than a half-gentile is entitled to be."[48]

Brandeis and his party left for the Suez Canal on July 6, traveling there by train, crossing it by boat, retraining for Lod, and then motoring to Jerusalem. They were late arriving in Lod, for a reception committee waited from seven in the morning until the afternoon to greet them. In addition to British authorities and representatives of various Zionist groups, the reception committee included some doctors from Hadassah and Lieutenant Vladimir Jabotinsky with forty members of his Jewish Brigade. Their subsequent arrival in Jerusalem was a warm one; indeed, the trip became a virtual triumphal procession for Brandeis.[49]

He was greeted in the settlement of Motza by singing children and an honor guard. Told that a tree Herzl had planted there had been destroyed during the war, he immediately promised to replace it. He was eulogized at a reception at the Lemel School in Jerusalem, with another honor guard and the presentation of a silver-cased parchment praising him. He apologized for not speaking Hebrew and proclaimed his complete commitment to Zionism. The combination of the intrinsic excitement of Palestine and the tumultuous welcome was reflected in his ecstatic letters home. After only forty-eight hours in Palestine, he wrote to his wife from Jerusalem, "It is a wonderful country, a wonderful city. Aaronsohn was right . . . The ages-long longing, the love is all explicable now . . . The marvellous contrasts of nature are in close juxtaposition . . . It was a joy from the moment we reached it at Rafia . . . even in the hot plains the quality of the air was bracing . . . It is indeed a Holy Land." He added, "What I saw of California and the Grand Canyon seemed less beautiful than the view from the Mount of Olives upon the Dead Sea and the country beyond. And yet all say that northern Palestine is far more beautiful, and that in this extra-dry season we are seeing the country at its worst . . . To my surprise, I have experienced no inconvenience from altitude (about 2500 feet) here, and I have seen nothing in the country yet which should deter even such lovers as you of the cool to avoid summering here. The nights are always cool. In Jerusalem it is comfortable at mid-day in the shade, and there is almost constant breeze."[50]

His enthusiasm kept pace with the trip. Boy Scouts, Girl Scouts, and other children lined the road to Tel Aviv, awaiting his arrival, and in Jaffa, people dressed in their holiday best crowded along Herzl Street, "even on the roofs and the fences," waving flags. At Rishon LeZion, he was again greeted by the entire population of the *moshav* and by its singing children. It was the first day of the grape harvest, and Brandeis was given grapes to throw into the pressing machine. At Zichron Yaacov, where a special gate was built in his honor, he pledged to return to Palestine soon and to remain longer. He went so far as to break a lifelong habit of staying away from synagogues, visiting the synagogue in Rehovot and going twice to the synagogue in Zichron Yaacov (where Aaron

Aaronsohn lived), praying with the congregation on Saturday morning and giving a speech at the end of the service. (The only other time he ever set foot in a synagogue was during a 1916 Zionist convention in Pittsburgh.) He reported to his wife that he was even "converted to the food and found long auto travel agreeable and not fatiguing." And from Haifa he wrote to Weizmann, with members of whose family he was staying, "Palestine has won our hearts . . . It is no wonder that the Jews love her so."[51]

The paucity of ships from Egypt back to Europe forced Brandeis to cut his trip short and rush from Palestine to board a steamer at Port Said. He had had "16½ days" in Palestine, during which he visited "practically all the country; all the cities and 23 of the 43 Jewish Colonies." He did not consider his stay too short for full understanding, and left convinced that it was only in Palestine that the Jewish tradition could flourish. "All my previous reading has become vitalized," he wrote as he journeyed back to Europe, "so that the 16 days represent in some respects years of acquisitiveness." De Haas wrote that "years of reading" had thoroughly familiarized Brandeis not only with the history of Palestine and its Jewish settlements but with its geography and topography. The travelers had carried "a Hebrew Phrase Book, Bible, Baedeker of Palestine and George Adam Smith's Historical Geography of the Holy Land, Ellsworth Huntington's Palestine and its Transformation, and The Holy Land, by John Kelman." The choice indicates the extent to which Brandeis thought of Palestine in terms of its history as well as of its potential future. By contrast, Egypt seemed both exotic and undesirable. He wrote of the colorful flowing gowns worn with grace even by "blackened coal loaders," the "ever picturesque Arabs and Egyptians," the enchanting mixture of "the ass and the camel amidst Victorias and Motor Cars." But the "primitiveness" of the average Egyptian's life was "almost inconceivable," and he judged the reed and mud shacks no more than five minutes' walk from his Alexandria hotel to be "such as the poorest American Negro would not be content with even for a night's lodging." It seemed to him that "the climate, the unearned wealth, the plethoric population would demoralize if they didn't disgust," and that the concomitant squalor and degeneracy represented "the forces that made Cleopatra and overcame Anthony and Caesar." He recognized the responsibility of the British and the wealthy Egyptians for the conditions that appalled him, commenting, "This country makes one pretty doubtful of the blessings of civilization, and superimposed good government." The only "higher class" people of any race he found attractive were the Egyptian Jews. Examining some ancient strawless bricks, he suggested to de Haas that "probably such labor saved the Jews from complete demoralization," and that the Jews had been fortunate to leave a place of such luxury and corruption. In short, Brandeis's short experience of Arab civilization offended his Puritan sensibilities, and on the day he left for Palestine he wrote to his wife, "Our Egyptian bondage is to end today."⁵²

The comparison Brandeis made between what he considered the decadence of Egypt and the young hope of Palestine is reminiscent of the contrast many of the Founding Fathers saw between Europe and the American colonies. Its greater significance is that from then on Brandeis shared the unconscious vision of other early Zionists of Palestine as a Westernized entity rather than as an integral part of the Middle East. Because the assumption of Westernization was unarticulated, it could not be examined and was to have tragic consequences for the new state of Israel and its neighbors.

But in 1919, the state of Israel was still a dream, and Brandeis considered Palestine the appropriate place for its realization. The trip became one of the great events of his life. He would refer to its impact upon him in his subsequent speeches. "Palestine has affected me deeply," he told an economic conference on Palestine in 1929, "though I have lived most of my life apart from the Jewish people." He added, "I acquired on my visit to Palestine the faith which the experience of years has deepened." He told another audience, "I had read much about it, heard much about it . . . and reasoned much about it. But it was only by going there that I could convince myself in fullness how much was open to us and why we should endeavor to work out the problem, not as a dream, but as a beautiful reality . . . If . . . persistence, devotion and ingenuity, readiness of self-sacrifice and self-control . . . is manifested by those who have an interest in it, there is nothing worthy which cannot be realized there."⁵³

By 1914, Brandeis had undergone a number of experiences that would lead him to Zionism. He had discovered the Eastern European New York Jews, who had three lessons for him. The first was that something in their backgrounds and lives—and he considered that "something" to be Judaism—had prepared them to be the natural citizens of the democratic society he had spent so long seeking. The second was that he shared their values, but if their values were derived from their Judaism, the logical conclusion was that his own Jewish heritage might be of more importance than he had hitherto realized. It was de Haas's clear impression that the story of Herzl, "coupled with the capacity for the ideal which he had found in the needle workers of New York, opened to Brandeis new vistas." The third lesson was an awareness of the anti-Semitism that surrounded and isolated them, depriving the community at large of their ideals.⁵⁴

Then came the meetings with de Haas and Aaronsohn. De Haas reported that Brandeis was "suddenly and unexpectedly confronted" by "the whole problem of Jewish existence" as well as the idea of Zionism. "Here," de Haas wrote, "was something of which he knew nothing and yet of which in a remote way he was a part. The how and the why merited exploration, and so from that first interview he began an earnest quest for knowledge." De Haas's account might be considered self-serving were it not for Brandeis's repeated assertions that de Haas was his "teacher in Zionism" and for the fact that Brandeis was reading a great deal about Jews and Zionism by 1913.[55]

It is therefore not surprising that by 1914 Brandeis, disillusioned with the Wilson administration and the possibility of achieving the perfect state through the federal government, was willing to turn to the problem of saving the jeopardized Jewish communities in Europe. He was almost fifty-eight years old, which is not an unusual age for a person to reexamine his or her origins and the values implicit in them. He discovered that he could unite his new ideas and his new interest with his overriding passion: creation of a society which would be small, self-governing, and worthy of the dignified self-made citizens he considered ideal. There was a place where the mistreated Jews of Europe could develop. There was a place that could exemplify the values and lessons of Judaism and that could then be pointed to as a model for Americans in their quest for a just society—and which, in turn, would lead non-Jewish Americans to appreciate the potential contributions of the American Jews who lived among them. There was a place that was underdeveloped and where there were no old, misguided institutions or entrenched power centers to fight against: a place for American-style pioneers armed with their Jewish idealism. And there was every reason to hope that it could recreate its geographically close but unhappily extinct predecessor, Pericles' Athens.

There are relatively few references to Athens in Brandeis's speeches about Zionism. This is hardly surprising, since Brandeis's goal was to demonstrate that Zionists were completely loyal Americans, not that they sought inspiration in such exotic locales as ancient Greece. But his battles within the Zionist movement are comprehensible only if it is remembered that Brandeis's goal for Palestine was a latter-day Athens. And as soon as he assumed leadership of American Zionism, he left no doubt that he would fight to make *his* ideas those that would prevail in the development of Zionist Palestine.

13 | Zionist and American

When Brandeis attended the 1914 emergency conference of 150 Zionists at New York's Hotel Marseilles, he was the least experienced in Jewish activities, but his was the only name likely to be recognized by large masses of both Jews and non-Jews. De Haas and others therefore asked him to become chairman of the new Provisional Executive Committee for General Zionist Affairs (PC) created that day. Brandeis was to head the organization in name only, becoming involved solely to urge some of his wealthy friends to contribute to the cause. An administrative committee of eleven people was to do the actual work.

Brandeis's remarks in accepting the chair of the PC were brief. He acknowledged his "disqualification for this task," and added, "Throughout long years which represent my own life, I have been to a great extent separated from Jews. I am very ignorant in things Jewish." This unusually modest statement was true, but it was also politically wise, for it diffused possible grumblings that he was not sufficiently knowledgeable to exercise real leadership over the movement. While maintaining that he felt "unable to bring to this task the knowledge, the experience, and the ability which it requires," he noted, "In the last few weeks, since the need of American aid became probable I have endeavored to acquaint myself with what has been accomplished." More significantly, he said, "Recent experiences, public and professional . . . have taught me this: I find Jews possessed of those very qualities which we of the twentieth century seek to develop in our struggle for justice and democracy; a deep moral feeling which makes them capable of noble acts; a deep sense of the brotherhood of man; and a high intelligence, the fruit of three thousand years of civilization." He ended by exhorting the Zionists, "Let us work together! Carry forward what others have, in the past, borne so well! Carry it forward to the goal for which we all long!"[1]

The program continued according to plan: Brandeis announced the establishment of an Emergency Fund, to which he would contribute one thousand dollars; Nathan Straus pledged five thousand dollars; and, with the fund now an entity and the American Zionists having taken on both the leadership of and the responsibility for world Zionism, the delegates prepared to call it a good day's work and go home. Then Brandeis changed the scenario. He said he knew nothing of the many organizations represented at the conference or of their leaders, their memberships, and their techniques. He asked the delegates to stay and educate him; they did, and throughout that evening and all through the next day, Brandeis sat in his hotel suite while the Zionists explained what their organizations were and how they were run. When they finally left, late on August 31, Brandeis had absorbed enough to know how he wanted to begin, and American Zionism had a new leader.[2]

Brandeis threw himself into the work of organization with his usual energy and concern for detail. In his first letter to Chaim Weizmann, written in October 1914, he summarized what had been accomplished. He reported that the PC had given priority to communication (with the Actions Comité, the Zionist federations in countries that were nonbelligerents, and with Palestine), fund-raising for the Palestinian communities and for continuation of the administrative work previously done by the Actions Comité, and establishment of a relationship with the American Jewish Committee (AJC). "Less than two weeks after the formation of the Provisional Executive Committee," he wrote to Weizmann, "it appeared, greatly to our satisfaction, that the central office of the Zionist organization was in a position to conduct its affairs." The Actions Comité had authorized the PC to proceed with its task of supporting the colonies. The PC had agreed with Shmaryahu Levin that $100,000 was the minimum sum necessary to achieve its goals during the next two years. "Collections are now in progress in all cities and towns in the United States in which there are societies affiliated with the Federation of American Zionists. In the large centers mass meetings have been held." In a letter to its president, Louis Marshall, the American Jewish Committee had been asked to join in organizing a conference of the more than seventy large Jewish organizations in the United States to discuss the situation created by the war and to decide on actions. Brandeis added seven appendices to the letter, thereby giving Weizmann copies of correspondence, fund-raising appeals, and memoranda.[3]

In spite of its length and its appendices, the letter did not begin to give a picture of the problems Brandeis encountered or the extent of his activities. A letter dated August 31, printed in both English and Yiddish, had gone out to hundreds of individuals, announcing the formation of the PC and calling upon Zionists to "put the machinery of all your organizations into motion without delay" in order to meet the goal of $100,000. Benjamin Perlstein, an accountant, was installed in New York as the PC's administrative secretary. Within days, Brandeis began bombarding him with an endless stream of communiqués concerning the details of organization; frequently, Perlstein would receive up to half a dozen letters from Brandeis in one day. No detail was too small to receive Brandeis's attention. After speaking at a few meetings during the cross-country lecture tour on which he immediately embarked, Brandeis cabled Perlstein, "Request [Louis] Lipsky to caution organizers of my meetings to select rather small halls. Overcrowded small hall meeting better than large hall nearly full. Every man turned away for lack of room is worth two who get in." And the pace of his activity, if possible, increased in the following months.[4]

Norman Hapgood, Brandeis's close friend and the editor of *Harper's Weekly*, was enrolled in the cause and advised by Brandeis on what to read about Zionism and what kinds of articles in *Harper's* would be most helpful. Hapgood responded immediately with "Zionism's Crisis" in the September 26 edition, and from August 1915 through January 1916 ran an entire series on Zionism and Jewish problems. Indeed, although not Jewish, Hapgood was so excited by Brandeis's vision of a "Progressive" Palestine that he became a fervent Zionist. He was only the first of many editors to be persuaded to write about Zionism. Brandeis, managing to get Zionism far more coverage than it would otherwise have received, naturally turned to the journals with which he was familiar and which had Progressive leanings, since his Zionism was so much an extension of progressivism into a new sphere. For example Lawrence Abbott's *Survey* published an entire symposium on Zionism in January 1916—and although Abbott's own contribution was an endorsement of the anti-Zionist position, the symposium began with an article by Brandeis.[5]

The details with which Brandeis concerned himself were both organizational and substantive. On October 5, 1914, he wrote to Arthur Ruppin, head of the Zionist Organization's office in Palestine and the man responsible for the purchase of new land, "I agree with you entirely as to the importance of acquiring when possible, additional tracts of fertile land. It seems to me that money available could not be put to better use." The same day Brandeis wrote to Nathan Kaplan, a leading

Chicago Zionist, concerning his forthcoming trip to Chicago, the advance work he wanted for it, and the amount of money he thought appropriate as Chicago's contribution. Urging that in addition to a banquet, an address to the congregation of a sympathetic rabbi, and a mass meeting, Kaplan organize "a large number of small meetings . . . at each of which a collection could be taken up," Brandeis "venture[d] to suggest that the collections from Chicago ought to reach in the aggregate $20,000 . . . Considering the large Jewish population in Chicago," this struck Brandeis as "a fairly modest demand." After all, one meeting in Boston had raised $7,000, and continued work there was expected to raise the total to at least $15,000. But Chicago would contribute its share only if plans were well laid: "I am quite sure that you will agree with me that the only way to make our November meetings a success is for all of our Chicago friends to undertake very persistent missionary work in advance, and secure contributions in advance, of which reports can be made at the meeting. It was such intensive work, carefully planned, and persistently carried out, which made the Boston meeting so great a success; I have no doubt that the month intervening before the meeting will be put by you to the best possible use."[6]

The letter, typical of many Brandeis was to send, shows the organizer at work. He had been the head of the Zionist movement for only a month, but he already knew the size and fiscal possibilities of the major Jewish communities. He understood the uses not only of advance publicity but of the technique of creating a "snowball" effect by announcing to potential contributors the donations made by their colleagues. Having been told in effect that Boston's leaders would fulfill Brandeis's expectations, how could Chicago's leaders bear to do less? Two weeks later he wrote to de Haas, who had become his lieutenant, "I agree fully with the opinion which you express that there has been a great lack of organization in the western and southern country and that there is opportunity for extensive development there. My conviction, however, was and is that the most fruitful of all territory is Massachusetts, and that . . . we should obtain most by thoroughly developing the Massachusetts field, for its own sake and as an example to others; and not only as an example but as affording a basis of experience which could be applied elsewhere." This was of course in keeping with Brandeis's problem-solving approach, which relied on initial, small-scale experimentation. The Massachusetts "experiment" was carried out, and, as Brandeis had planned, was used to educate and goad elsewhere.[7]

Nathan Kaplan of Chicago again received advice. Writing in November 1915, after "practically a year's experience in Massachusetts and Northern New England," Brandeis informed him that the Chicago Knights of

Zion, then responsible for ten states, attempted to cover too much territory and could not expect effective results. The Massachusetts and Northern New England organization covered "a territory of nominally 58,030 square miles." But the Jewish population of the five states covered by the New England Bureau was "little more than one-half of the Jewish population of the State of Illinois alone." The solution, therefore, was to make Illinois a separate state unit, enabling the Knights of Zion "to so intensify the work as to secure in the State of Illinois alone, within a relatively short time, at least four times as many members as there are now in the societies of the Knights of Zion in all of the ten States." State organizations should also be created elsewhere, for "the very fact that State leaders are created, and responsibility placed upon them, will tend to develop men and activity." Then dues should be raised "to not less than $3.00 a year"; otherwise, the Illinois group would not be able to offer its members Zionist bulletins and newspapers, as well as once-a-month meetings in each large city. "In the most successful of the New England societies,—the Zionist Society for Great Boston,—(which has a membership of about 425), the dues are $5.00 a year." And Brandeis enclosed a memorandum describing the work of the Boston Bureau. A keen understanding of human nature underlay Brandeis's organizing efforts. He knew that "to be effective a Zionist Society must offer something to its members"; he had also learned in non-Zionist endeavors that "it is only the intensive work which is effective . . . Individual efforts, not intensive, are like drops of rain—the benefit of which is lost by early evaporation." After telling Kaplan in effect that his whole organization was a mess, Brandeis assured him of his belief that if Kaplan took his advice, "you could do the best possible that could be done for the cause," and asked him for his suggestions about possible leaders for other state organizations.[8]

A carrot was thrown in here, and elsewhere, because Brandeis was a natural politician. He was also a natural teacher. Students who have been criticized will respond best if they are then assured of the teacher's confidence in their ability to do well in the future. Nevertheless, on the surface, Brandeis saw no great need for the carrot. It was his firm conviction that human beings were infinitely educable and that they thirsted for knowledge and truth. He loved books because he loved to learn, and he could not assume less about his fellow human beings. His letters sometimes seem cold because they simply laid out what was to be done as concisely as possible. Writing letters that way saved the time that helped enable him to do so many things. It was also an appropriate way to communicate with other intelligent people. Brandeis's language became flowery only with people he did not know very well and whose intelligence he had therefore not yet tested, with those for whom he had contempt and, occasionally, with those who held high office, for he was aware of the kind of language to which they had become accustomed. On the whole, however, he chose his words for clarity rather than style. His belief in the rationality of human beings cannot be overstated; it illuminated everything he did.

When Brandeis was in a one-to-one relationship, as in his letters, he assumed that a frank recital of the truth would suffice. When he could not be certain of his audience, as was the case when he lectured to masses of people, his language became somewhat more hortatory. Even there, however, the reprinted addresses do not reflect his persuasiveness, for much of it lay in his method of delivery. There seem to have been astonishingly few people who did not succumb to his charm, fluency, sincerity, and passion. It is possible that his personality was as responsible for his enormous impact on American Zionism as were his ideas.

One element of that personality was self-assurance. Brandeis never began a course of action until he had studied the situation and gathered data, and he continued to accumulate and evaluate data at least as long as each endeavor lasted. He thus embarked upon each course of action only after he was convinced that it was the most proper and effective approach, and he had difficulty understanding the failure of others to reach the same conclusions. If they were ignorant, he was willing to educate them. He could circulate his "propaganda" with total equanimity, because he did not view it as a way of acquiring followers and increasing the strength of what had by then become *his* movement, but rather as an educational tool. Since he was right, his propaganda was truth. If rational human beings did not see that, their motivations and sincerity were open to question.

Brandeis became the prophet for so many of the people around him and for so many of the people he met that he never fully comprehended the role his personality rather than his ideas played in the process. This is not to deny the brilliance of his ideas, but the particular magic that turned such an unusually high proportion of the people who heard him into converts was as much the product of his personality as it was of his thoughts. On one level, he was aware of this, for after he began lecturing for Zionism his letters to his brother tacitly admitted that it was his presence that had made all the difference. In general, though, something made him draw back from the obvious conclusion. He could report his successes and enjoy them, but he insisted that it was his ideas that had triumphed. So as he turned his attention to Zionism, he was serenely confident that success was a simple, if energy-consuming, matter of organization and education.

To further his own education, Brandeis demanded endless streams of information. On October 5, 1914, he asked a PC member for information about "the Turkish Law, regulations and practices . . . in regard to the admission and the treatment of Jews in Palestine, and specifically to what extent, if any, they are subjected to discriminations in comparison with the Musselmans or Christians," as well as for similar information about Palestine in the previous "thirty or forty years" and about treatment of Jews elsewhere in the Ottoman Empire. De Haas was told to "arrange that I receive not later than the 5th of each month a report covering the activities of the Zionist Bureau during the preceding month" and to see that the format of the reports be consistent so as to facilitate comparisons of progress from month to month. He also wrote to de Haas that local Zionist organizations should be made to see "the necessity of monthly reports" about their fundraising efforts, and said, "We should resolutely insist that all of our men who are working away from the office should send in daily reports; if the report says nothing more than 'I did nothing', we must have it on file and the monthly report made up in the office to be ready on the 20th of the month should embody a report of the activities separate of each of our workers in the field." The only thing that could prevent Brandeis's examining these reports was, after 1916, his work on the Court, and then he ignored them only temporarily: "Except for the examination of the daily financial reports which I want to have come to me regularly, it is imperative in view of my judicial duties that I should not be interrupted by or called upon in anyway to consider any matters relating to the Jewish Problem before August 21, when I should like to have sent me to S. Yarmouth all of the reports referred to above." South Yarmouth, of course, was where he spent his vacation. He also besieged Robert Kesselman with demands for daily financial reports, and he did not mean that he wanted only the larger picture. "What is done about the checking up of stamps?" he demanded, referring to postage stamps. "If any appreciable amount of stamps are held over from day to day ought they not to appear in the daily report?"⁹

Brandeis's eyes missed nothing. He congratulated Lipsky on having improved the format of the *Maccabean*, the official publication of the Federation of American Zionists, but complained about the small print, because "Zionists are great readers, and we ought to preserve their eyes." He similarly urged Henrietta Szold to adopt larger type for the Hadassah Bulletin. Later Brandeis thanked her for a report and added, "If it would be agreeable to you to adopt the 10 point leaded for your Bulletin, I shall be glad to pay personally the extra expense for a year, which I understand to be at the rate of $4.00 a month for 1,000 copies." These letters can be attributed to Brandeis's difficulties with his own eyes, but he was no

less concerned about all other details. He wanted each Zionist head-
quarters to have a "working library" and to get Zionist materials into
public and university libraries; he wanted to have the PC choose the
"hour and duration" of its meetings "after the evening meal" and institute
"a fine for absence or tardiness"; to organize college Zionist societies;
to "improve the form of notice" about an essay contest for college students about Jewish life and culture in Palestine; to have local Zionist
membership committees meet "at least as often as once a week"; to have
Rabbi Stephen Samuel Wise serve as the chairman of the PC's Finance
Committee, because he would find less opposition among New York
Jews with financial connections than would Brandeis, "on account of the
persistent attitude that I have taken in regard to the financial practices
of Wall Street and allied interests." Brandeis also disapproved of Yiddish
and applauded the Palestinian Jews' resurrection of spoken Hebrew. He
asked de Haas, "Wouldn't it be wise to begin very gradually a reformation
of the Yiddish Volk [a newspaper] by introducing each week (a) A small
section in English, e.g. incorporating excerpts from the English weekly
'Palestine' (b) A small Hebrew excerpt—from some foreign Hebrew
paper."[10]

Brandeis's style and organizational abilities were entirely new to Zionists. To their utter amazement, he installed a timeclock in the Zionist
offices. He introduced a card system that, by August 1917, held 250,000
names. When 523,048 people signed a petition to President Wilson in
1919, urging creation of a Jewish homeland, he had the petition card-
indexed as well. His personal style was as much of an innovation as was
his sense of organization. A Hadassah leader described him as a "new
phenomenon—a leader in Zionist life who was a listener instead of a
speaker, one who had respect for punctuality, regard for time and pre-
cision, a dislike for personal publicity. I recall how on occasions when
speakers took too much time, Brandeis would omit his part of the program and tell the audience he would come back some other night and
speak at a more appropriate hour." Marvin Lowenthal's observations
about PC meetings portray the style common to Zionists and suggest
why Brandeis was perceived as being so different: "Oratorical thunder
and forked-lightening filled the Committee rooms with noise, fire and
occasional light . . . Brandeis acted by sitting and doing the thinking while
others talked. He dominated every tempest by a smile and by the last
word. As debate waxed hotter, he had a trick of encouraging each speaker
with a nod and a beam. And when the storm was spent, he gently placed
the debaters back on the ground of facts . . . One wondered what the
storm had been about." Brandeis commented laconically, "Zionism suffers from a superfluity of orators and a dearth of statesmen."[11]

In spite of his seeming contempt for oratory, his own oratorical talents and national reputation were immensely important to the movement. His presence and speaking ability brought potential Zionists to meetings all over the country; his name as chairman brought immediate attention to the PC. Brandeis and Shmaryahu Levin spent much of the fall and winter of 1914 criss-crossing the country. He spoke at Symphony Hall in Boston, where Mrs. Evans "heard the cries: 'The new Moses, the new Moses!' resound through the building." Mrs. Evans thought that when he spoke his face "shone with an inner light that transformed his whole being." And audiences, of course, felt the force of his charisma. Four thousand people heard him in Cleveland and gave him a five-minute ovation. He spoke in Cincinnati, New York, Chicago, Milwaukee, New York again, Rochester, Buffalo, Philadelphia, Pittsburgh, St. Louis, Springfield (Massachusetts), Boston again, New York over and over again. He was overwhelmingly successful. In Chicago one wealthy Jewish leader, "who had been quite anti-Zionist in his inclinations . . . insisted that the donors should bind themselves to continue contributions, and he rose and stated that he would give $1,000 a month during the war and for twelve months thereafter . . . The general feeling was that we had captured the town." From Milwaukee Brandeis wrote, "The leader of the German community . . . stated to me at the dinner that he was opposed to Zionism, and no argument could move him; but when I got through with my talk, he said that I had converted him, and I think that was true of some of the others."[12]

The pace of his lecturing continued into 1915. He spoke in Portland, New Haven, Atlantic City, Salem, Baltimore, Washington, Louisville. In February he wrote to his brother from Boston, "I am off for N.Y. tonight, after more than a fortnight here. My longest stay since—well it must be more than a year. Expect to spend Thursday in N.Y., Friday in Washington, Saturday again in N.Y. Sunday I speak in Providence & Monday am due here again. Activities are now quite largely Jewish relief." And again, "Things Jewish have been occupying my time largely . . . Zionist affairs . . . are really the important things in life now." He even broke his rule about working only eleven months out of twelve; in 1915 "practically every day of my supposed vacation has been invaded by Zionist emergencies," and this was true of 1916 as well. There could be no letting up, however, at least as long as the war lasted: "You cannot possibly conceive of the horrible sufferings of the Jews in Poland & adjacent countries. These changes of control from German to Russian & Polish anti-semites are bringing miseries as great as Jews ever suffered in all their exiles . . . Terrible stories of suffering in Palestine & generally. The Jews are having a bad time."[13]

As he read during the summer of 1914 and as he worked with the Zionist organization, Brandeis developed a philosophy of Zionism for himself. He had argued in the past that the United States had no room for hyphenated Americans. He had placed no great importance on his Jewishness; indeed, as he admitted to the PC, he was ignorant of what it meant. Now he had to convince others that being a Jew was special and that the specialness had to be preserved through the creation of a Jewish state. By 1914 the two years since his conversation with de Haas and the month of intensive reading had already resulted in what was at least the germ of a philosophy.

The themes of Brandeis's Zionism were sounded in his acceptance speech as chairman of the PC. Zionism was a struggle for justice, democracy, and a moral society. This was what the Athenians had had; this was what he hoped industrial democracy would achieve in the United States; this would be the future of Palestine. A very clear thread runs from Brandeis's interest in classical Greece, through his Jeffersonianism, and into his reformism, his view of the law, and his Zionism. Human beings were limited animals; given institutions of reasonable size, however, they were infinitely susceptible to development. They could organize and manage businesses, governments, unions, and other entities in such a way as to provide all members of society both with the material necessities of life and with the dignity that made life worth living. They were infinitely educable; when given the facts, they would make wise decisions. With education would come both knowledge and involvement; enlightened human beings would take control of their own affairs and participate actively in a democratic system, whether that system was political or economic. Human beings were "capable of noble acts" and could comprehend that civilization was possible only if it was built upon a belief in "the brotherhood of man." This was the civilization that modern Jews would create in Palestine; for Palestine had become, for Brandeis, the small, politically aware, well-educated society of which Jefferson had dreamed. It was, in his vision, the recreation of Periclean Athens.[14]

Brandeis was impressed by the national character and historical contributions of the Jews. "Jews gave to the world its three greatest religions, reverence for law, and the highest conceptions of morality . . . Our teaching of brotherhood and righteousness has, under the name of democracy and social justice, become the twentieth century striving of America and of western Europe. Our conception of law is embodied in the American constitution which proclaims this to be a 'government of laws and not of men.' " The proper way to treat this inheritance, he argued, was with a sense of "noblesse oblige" that would affect not only one's individual conduct but also one's conduct toward other members of the community; that is, respect for others (Jew and non-Jew alike) and participation in the realization of Zionism. Kallen often heard Brandeis speak of noblesse oblige, arguing that educated Jews had a "special responsibility for the maintenance and the defence of the democratic principle." In this sense, Zionism was no more than an extension of the citizen's obligation to work for the public welfare, and the goals of Zionism were so similar to those of the United States that a commitment to Zionism would make one a better American.[15]

In 1914, Brandeis told an audience at Boston's Symphony Hall that "practical experience and observation convinced me . . . that to be good Americans, we must be better Jews, and to be better Jews, we must become Zionists . . . The Jewish Renaissance in Palestine will enable us to perform our plain duty to America. It will help us to make toward the attainment of the American ideals of democracy and social justice that large contribution for which religion and life have peculiarly fitted the Jews." In fact, the parallels helped explain why Jewish emigrants from Russia, "the most autocratic of countries," quickly became good Americans: "twentieth century ideals of America have been the ideals of the Jew for more than twenty centuries. We have inherited these ideals of democracy and of social justice . . . We have inherited also that fundamental longing for truth on which all science, and so largely the civilization of the twentieth century, rests."[16]

But Jewish ideals were in danger of being lost, for as "ghetto walls are falling, Jewish life cannot be preserved and developed, assimilation cannot be averted, unless there be re-established in the fatherland a center, from which the Jewish spirit may radiate." Typifying assimilation as something to be "averted" was an astonishing *volte-face* for the man who had argued only a few years before that hyphenated Americans were not true Americans. However, the articulation of an approach that would enable American Jews to appreciate their "differentness" while maintaining absolute loyalty to the United States was to be one of Brandeis's main contributions to American Zionism. His American Zionism would insist that ethnic awareness and an understanding of the unique contributions of each group of Americans could enrich American life.[17]

The possibilities for ethnic enrichment of American society were spelled out in the speech he made in Boston's historic Faneuil Hall on July 4, 1915. The July 4 oration was a major event in the Independence Day celebration, and Brandeis was the first Jew ever given the honor of being orator. Mayor James Michael Curley, the Irish-American who asked him to make the speech, may have been flouting the Brahmins by selecting a foe of State Street or by honoring a hyphenated American; Brandeis qualified on both counts. In any event, Brandeis must have recognized that a city where the Brahmins were being displaced by Irish-American political leaders and where there was sharp division over the merits of the Anti-Immigration League would be watching to see whether a Jew and Zionist could be as thoroughly "American" as the WASP speakers who had delivered the oration in years past. His speech did not include the word Zionism, but its thrust makes it clear that Zionism, and the opportunity to persuade Americans that Zionism was not an anti-American endeavor, was much in his mind.

Horace Kallen described the scene: the "hot afternoon . . . the stratified audience—Beacon Hill and the Back Bay; the West and the North Ends; South Boston and East Boston, distributed duly and in good order according to cash, caste and sect; the stuffy smell of the hall, the gaunt figure and the Lincoln-like mask of the orator, his vibrant voice and the measured yet passionate delivery."[18]

Brandeis began with the motto of the United States, "E pluribus unum," reminding his listeners that the founding fathers "were . . . convinced, as we are, that . . . under a free government, many peoples would make one nation." He devoted the speech to immigration and "Americanization," which he defined as more than the superficial adoption of costume and customs. It was acceptance by the immigrant of American ideals. He asked, "What are the American ideals? They are the development of the individual for his own and the common good; the development of the individual through liberty, and the attainment of the common good through democracy and social justice."[19]

The constitution guaranteed individuals life, liberty, and the pursuit of happiness. "Life, in this connection, [meant] living, not existing," which in turn meant a reasonable income, regular employment, and working hours that would not undermine health. Liberty implied "freedom in things industrial as well as political . . . Industrial liberty on the part of the worker cannot . . . exist if there be overweening industrial power. Some curb must be placed upon capitalistic combination. Nor will even this curb be effective unless the workers cooperate, as in trade unions." Reaching the last of the American trinity of rights, Brandeis declared, "Happiness includes, among other things, that satisfaction which can come only through the full development and utilization of one's faculties." Working hours had to be short enough to permit leisure for self-fulfillment; education, the prerequisite for intelligent citizenship, was a life-long process and depended upon available time, or leisure. "Leisure, so defined, is an essential of successful democracy."[20]

Brandeis then asked, "What is there in these ideals which is peculiarly American?" and answered, "Inclusive brotherhood." Unlike other nations that were also interested in developing the individual, America "has always declared herself for equality of nationalities as well as for equality of individuals." Using "race" as a synonym for "nationality" or "national origin," Brandeis described America's uniqueness as its recognition that "racial equality [is] an essential of full human liberty and true brotherhood, and that racial equality is the complement of democracy." In contrast, aristocracy's "arrogant claim of superiority" of some nationalities had led to "the Russianizing of Finland, the Prussianizing of Poland and Alsace, the Magyarizing of Croatia, the persecution of the Jews in Russia and Roumania" and it was also the "underlying cause" of the war in Europe. (This was Brandeis's only specific mention of Jews in the speech.)[21]

Brandeis argued for differentiation, as opposed to subordination, on the grounds of nationality. He deplored "the misnamed internationalism which seeks the obliteration of nationalities or peoples." Then he stated the credo that brought his Zionism into thorough compatibility with his progressivism and Americanism: "The new nationalism adopted by America proclaims that each race or people, like each individual, has the right and duty to develop, and that only through such differentiated development will high civilization be attained. Not until these principles of nationalism, like those of democracy, are generally accepted will liberty be fully attained and minorities be secure in their rights. Not until then can the foundation be laid for a lasting peace among the nations." And he closed with the admonition, "And let us remember the poor parson of whom Chaucer says:

> 'But Christe's loore, and his Apostles twelve,
> He taughte, but first he followed it hymselve.' "[22]

Brandeis's description of the "new nationalism," which he found so quintessentially American, led logically to his insistence that Jews had to become Zionists. If it was "only" through the development of each nationality that civilization could be attained, Jews clearly had to develop their nationality; thus, Zionism meant not only the goal of a Jewish state but the revitalization in the United States of Jewish culture and values. There was, for the moment, no other place in which the Jewish tradition could both be preserved and develop freely. Later, Brandeis changed his definition of Zionism to mean what it commonly does today—support for the Jewish homeland, without necessary reference to Jewish life elsewhere. In 1915, however, his goal for himself, as well as for his audience, was the reconciliation of Zionism with Americanism. He always said, "My approach to Zionism was through Americanism." Significantly, the July Fourth address begins a book of Brandeis's Zionist speeches. The address shows how Brandeis convinced German-American Jews that democracy and Zionism was intertwined; it helps explain how he converted such non-Jews as Norman Hapgood and former President Eliot of Harvard into supporters of Zionism, going so far as to secure Eliot's services as a consulting editor of the Harvard student-run *Menorah Journal*. And there was no doubt that Brandeis considered the speech to be an important and persuasive articulation of his beliefs.[23]

Brandeis showed how thoroughly he equated the Jewish tradition with the American dream in a letter to the *Menorah Journal*. "America offers to man his greatest opportunity—liberty amidst peace and natural resources," he wrote. "But the noble purpose to which America is dedicated cannot be attained unless this high opportunity is fully utilized ... To America the contribution of the Jews can be peculiarly large." Brandeis argued that the Jews' religion and afflictions "have prepared them for effective democracy. Persecution made the Jews' law of brotherhood self-enforcing. It taught them the seriousness of life; it broadened their sympathies: it deepened the passion for righteousness; it trained them in patient endurance, in persistence, in self-control, and in self-sacrifice. Furthermore, the widespread study of Jewish law developed the intellect and made them less subject to preconceptions and more open to reason." Both the Calvinist Pilgrims and the Jews had been required to read their theological laws, and this resulted in both groups placing a heavy emphasis on education. The first group built Harvard, the second studied the Torah and the Talmud; both were thereby made more "reasonable." As the Pilgrims had given the best in their heritage to the United States, so must the Jews: "Patriotism to America, as well as loyalty to our past, imposes upon us the obligation of claiming this heritage of the Jewish spirit and of carrying forward noble ideals and traditions through lives and deeds worthy of our ancestors." However, if Judaism was to continue to contribute its particular strengths to civilization, Judaism itself had to be preserved. In the strongest possible statement, Brandeis declared, "Assimilation is national suicide ... The Fruit of three thousand years of civilization and a hundred generations of suffering may not be sacrificed by us." Speaking of the drive for self-determination that he saw as a vital part of World War I, he exhorted, "Let us make clear to the world that we too are a nationality striving for equal rights to life and to self-expression."[24]

In a similar vein Brandeis wrote to Norman Hapgood, "The democratic doctrine of equality of opportunity involves the assumption that the common weal will be most advanced by allowing all classes and individuals the opportunity of full development. Lasting peace must rest not upon the basis of toleration of unlike nations, but upon the belief that civilization will be most advanced through permitting each nation and race to develop." One of the nations that had to be permitted to develop, both to preserve the Jewish heritage and to aid in the advance of civilization, was a Jewish Palestine.[25]

Brandeis thus saw his task as persuading American Jews to become active Zionists. "Your own self-respect, your own duty demands that you join a Zionist organization because without organization, without a great and perfected organization," a Jewish homeland could not become a reality. Jews had to understand what Zionism meant: "Learn, study, read what has happened in the Zionist world. There isn't a thing that should be more interesting to a Jew today than the events of Zionism as they are occurring from week to week . . . Learn about Zionism, and there will be no doubt as to your own interest, or your desire to move others to follow your example and to become members of the Zionist organization." Education would develop good citizens and would enable them to proselytize. "It is our proud boast (if boast there be on the part of the Jewish people) that we have been a literate people, accustomed for thousands of years to use the mind, and use it especially for study, learning and intellectual pursuits. We may ask, therefore, of each and every Zionist that he make study a part of his daily work; study of Zionist facts, not merely of the theory of Zionism . . . Every Zionist should make it a part of his business to read at least one of our Zionist papers and to read it, not cursorily as he reads and throws away the daily papers morning and afternoon, but to read it diligently and digest its contents. Read and master the facts and you will be able to overcome the indifference and the opposition which surround you." Brandeis took his own advice. In February 1913 he had begun subscribing to the *Jewish Advocate*; he later added a subscription to the *Immigrants in America Review* and joined the American Jewish Historical Society. And he continued reading such books as Adolf Friedemann's *Das Leben Theodor Herzls* and Albert M. Hyamson's *Palestine: The Rebirth of an Ancient People*. Kallen commented that Brandeis made himself "expert on every aspect of the being of Palestine."[26]

As suggested by his July Fourth speech and *Menorah Journal* letter, Brandeis's vision of Palestine had solidified by 1915. His major Zionist address that year contained many of the elements of what would later become the Pittsburgh Program and indicated that all the blessings that Jefferson thought would flow from agrarianism were to be found in Brandeis's Palestine. He repeated Aaronsohn's report that there was no crime among the settlers: "The new Palestine Jewry produces instead of criminals, scientists like Aaron Aaronsohn . . . pedagogues . . . craftsmen . . . intrepid Shomrim, the Jewish guards of peace, who watch in the night against marauders and doers of violent deeds." (The marauders were of course not Jewish; the Shomrim voluntarily protected the settlements because the Ottoman government refused to do so adequately.) Education, that key to democracy, flourished, because to the Jews "civilization without education is inconceivable . . . And so they have established in Palestine a school system almost complete. But for this war [World War I], it would have been capped with the establishment of the first department of the University of Jerusalem . . . as well as the opening of the Institute of Technology at Haifa." Even before the war the high schools took both Palestinian Jews and immigrants from Eastern Europe and educated them so thoroughly "that they could enter on equal terms with the European students any of the great universities of Austria, Gemany and France." Both sexes benefited, Brandeis added in a subsequent speech: "In their self-governing colonies . . . the Jews have pure democracy, and since those self-governing colonies were establishing a true democracy, they gave women equal rights with men, without so much as a doubt on the part of any settler. And women contributed, like the men, not only in the toil of that which is narrowly called the home, but in the solution of broader and more difficult problems." The settlers understood the evils of unemployment and, when war ended the export trade and created unemployment, the Palestinians created jobs through public works, loans to industries with numerous workers, and voluntary pay cuts.[27]

However, the establishment of a Jewish homeland did not mean that all Jews were expected to move there. Brandeis never perceived Palestine as a homeland for American Jews. He exhorted American Jews to learn all they could about Palestine, to work for the creation of a Jewish state there, to open their pocketbooks, but not to move there. He explained that Zionism was "essentially a movement to give to the Jew more, not less freedom," rather than a movement to compel mass emigration. Zionism sought "to establish in Palestine, for such Jews as choose to go and remain there, and for their descendants, a legally secure home, where they may live together and lead a Jewish life, where they may expect ultimately to constitute a majority of the population, and may look forward to what we should call home rule." Only there could Jewish life be "fully protected from the forces of disintegration," and the Jewish spirit "reach its full and natural development." But as a practical matter, Palestine could not become the home of all the world's Jews, for, as Brandeis pointed out in 1915, "there are 14,000,000 Jews, and Palestine would not accommodate more than one-third of that number." Zionism was therefore not only a movement to establish a homeland, but a means by which Jews living elsewhere could participate in the continuation of the Jewish heritage and in the rebirth of the Jewish nation.[28]

Once American Jews understood what Jewish culture was all about, once they understood the ideals that would be incorporated into Palestine, they could begin to demonstrate the importance of the Jewish heritage to a more democratic United States. Zionism was a means whereby American Jews could establish their particular identity without turning to religion. A secularized version of Judaism, similar in Brandeis's version to the Brahmin credo, would bind Jews to each other, to their history, and to the United States, because nothing could be more American than the Judaic ethic. In a sense, Brandeis sought both to prove to Jews that there was no contradiction in being an American Jew and to make the United States more Jewish in its values. Within the context of the United States, Brandeis's Zionism was conservative; he used it to remind Americans of the ideals on which the country had been built.

Later, Brandeis's emphasis would change. After the Balfour Declaration of 1917 had committed the British to establishing a Jewish homeland in Palestine, Brandeis became impatient with attempts to revitalize Jewish culture anywhere else, including the United States. Jews had recognized themselves as an identifiable group and would act as such when it became necessary to do so, for example, to combat anti-Semitism and to support the Jewish state. There was no reason for them to continue concentrating on their Jewishness: they had to become not more Jewish, but more Zionistic. This put him at odds with the American Jews of Eastern European background, whom he had formerly treated as the guardians of the Jewish tradition. But Brandeis had thought of them as precisely that, guardians. Once the Jewish tradition had its own home, he saw no further need for guardians. Judaism was of no importance to his life; Zionism was. Brandeis never really understood the Judaism of the Eastern Europeans, and they never understood his Zionism. Nor did the European leaders of the Zionist movement, like Chaim Weizmann. To Brandeis, Zionism was the transformation of progressivism into a Jewishness that could recreate Athens—progressivism and its ideas came first. Zionism simply helped solve the problem of anti-Semitism and made a small-scale Progressive state possible. To Weizmann and the other Eastern European Jews, however, Zionism began with Judaism, and was its logical culmination and embodiment. "To feel like a 'Jew' meant for me . . . to be a Zionist," Weizmann wrote, "and to express in the Zionist movement the ethical as well as the national spirit of our Jewishness . . . The environment I was born into . . . the upbringing which I received, made Jewishness—the Jewish nation, nationalism, as others term it—an organic part of my being. I was never anything but Jewish, I could not conceive that a Jew could be anything else." Weizmann recognized Brandeis as "an ardent Zionist" but correctly understood the American's Zionism as "an intellectual experiment, based on solid foundations of logic and reason." Eventually this difference in points of departure, and their inability to empathize with each other, would open an unbridgeable gap between Brandeis and Weizmann.[29]

14 | Zionism Reconsidered

By 1919 Brandeis had transformed American Zionism from the belief of a minority of Jews into a large-scale movement. In 1914 the Federation of American Zionists, the umbrella organization for Zionist groups, had some 12,000 members; by 1919 its membership was 176,000, and many thousand more American Jews were members of smaller Zionist groups. But Brandeis was never satisfied; his constant cries were "Members! Money! Discipline!" and "Organize! Organize!" until every American Jew was active in the Zionist cause. To Zionist well-wishers who had sent congratulations upon his appointment to the Supreme Court in 1916, he replied with a standard short sentence of thanks along with a longer paragraph exhorting them to keep up the fund-raising and membership drives. When the British army captured Jerusalem in 1917, thereby "liberating" it from Turkish rule and making a Jewish Palestine a real possibility, Brandeis wrote to de Haas, "I note your telegram, fall of Jerusalem creating 'Big Sensation.' Is it creating big 'Money & Members'?"[1]

The idea that Jewish and Zionist organizations (although Zionist organizations were obviously Jewish, leading Jewish organizations were largely anti-Zionist) ought to be mass organizations did not receive universal acceptance. Reform Jews were least likely to be Zionists. Their theology and liturgy adhered less rigidly to the orthodox laws and customs, and they were therefore able to move into the mainstream of nineteenth and early twentieth-century American life far more easily than were Orthodox Jews. This assimilation was important to them, and they rejected anything that they felt brought their Americanism into question.

Thus, most Reform Jews rejected Zionism in favor of "indivisible" loyalty to the United States. For these and many other reasons organized American Jewry, dominated by Reform assimilationists, was anti-Zionist.[2]

The American Jewish Committee had been organized in 1906 by members of the German-Jewish aristocracy—such men as Oscar Straus, Jacob Schiff, Julius Rosenwald, Mayer Sulzberger, Cyrus Adler, and Louis Marshall. What amounted to a handful of men exercised total control over the committee and its activities, which included philanthropy (aimed particularly at the Jewish immigrants arriving from Eastern Europe), the Jewish Theological Seminary (a non-Orthodox institution), and a conservative Yiddish newspaper. Their money helped shape American Judaism in a Reform Jewish, assimilationist, pro-business, and anti-Progressive image. There were thus many differences between AJC views and Brandeis's. The AJC version of assimilationism deemphasized ethnic identity; Brandeis became the champion of cultural pluralism and outspoken Zionism. They were not only allies but members of the big railroad and banking interests, which had been the objects of Brandeis's Progressive reform for over a decade. Their attitude toward the Eastern European Jews alternated between embarrassment and paternalism; Brandeis saw the vitality and intellectualism of the same Jews as a force for democracy.[3]

The AJC also represented an established, well-financed force in American Judaism. Brandeis and the PC were newcomers. When war broke out in Europe, the AJC organized the American Jewish Relief Committee (AJRC); shortly thereafter, the PC established the Palestine Relief Fund. The two competed, and the Zionists acknowledged the greater ability of the AJRC to raise money by asking for its help. Eventually, the two groups united their efforts in the Joint Distribution Committee. It was controlled by AJC loyalists, however, and as soon as the relief effort was well underway the Zionists in effect withdrew from the relief field and turned to improving their organizational efforts to help the colonization of Palestine.[4]

Brandeis was exasperated by the existence of a variety of Zionist groups and by the sloppiness of their bookkeeping. The Federation of American Zionists (FAZ) was about as effective an umbrella agency as the American government had been under the Articles of Confederation. Just as colonists saw themselves as Virginians or New Yorkers rather than Americans, so Zionists gave their loyalty to numerous small lodges and benevolent associations rather than the federation, which had no coercive power and could only plead with its constituent groups for cooperation. These weaknesses had led top Zionists to ignore the federation in 1914 and create the PC. By 1915 Brandeis had decided that it was necessary to bypass the local organizations and clubs as well and to tie individual Zionists directly to one national Zionist organization to which all would belong; it, in turn, would draw upon local groups to carry out policy and to deal with local problems. This was the genesis of the American Jewish Congress.

The attempt to found such an organization was actually precipitated not by Brandeis and the Zionists but by the AJC. American Jews from Eastern Europe wanted to organize a drive to emancipate Jews still in Eastern Europe; the AJC decided to retain control by leading a movement that it had not wanted. It therefore announced a congress to be held in Washington in the fall of 1915, which would be attended only by 150 delegates of the organizations it selected and in numbers it arbitrarily apportioned. It invited the Federation of American Zionists to attend.

The Zionists were outraged, charging that the AJC wanted to pack the congress. Meeting in June, the Zionists charged the PC with calling its own, more democratic congress. This would presumably include members, numbering in the hundreds of thousands, of the Yiddish-speaking groups (*landsmanschaften*) from Eastern Europe functioning as mutual aid societies. The specter was unsettling to the AJC, which delegated Cyrus Adler to meet with Brandeis and someone who belonged to both the AJC and the PC. Brandeis chose Felix Frankfurter, the Harvard law professor he had come to know and respect during his Zionist work.

Brandeis suggested that there be a preliminary conference of a dozen or so mutually acceptable groups to decide how delegates were to be chosen by every Jewish organization in the United States. The inevitable result would be domination of the congress by the *landsmanschaften*. Adler countered by suggesting a prepreliminary committee to choose the organizations for the preliminary meeting, which would then shape the congress, and Brandeis withdrew for consultations.[5]

Before the shape of the congress had been decided upon, Brandeis took to the stump, telling a mass meeting in New York's Carnegie Hall, "The Congress is not an end in itself. It is an incident of the organization of the Jewish people, an instrument through which their will may be ascertained . . . In order that their will may be ascertained truly the Congress must be democratically representative." The decision should embody the wisdom "not of the few, however able and public-spirited, but the thought and judgment of the whole people . . . It must be the support of the million, not of the few generous, philanthropic millionaires." To Brandeis the fight was between democracy and aristocracy, but he knew that the financial contributions of the aristocrats were important. He reported telling one Jewish leader, concerned about the leadership that might emerge from such democratic involvement, "My conviction was that if they adopted democratic methods, they would find the Jewish masses not only willing but eager to have the best in leadership that was available, and that whatever good there was in Jews of longer American life and greater education would be readily adopted, if offered in the proper spirit." The "Jews of longer American life and greater education" obviously meant the German-American Jews and the remark was designed to quiet fears, but it also reflected Brandeis's belief that the masses could be relied upon to choose well. There was certainly no doubt that they would choose him.[6]

The convolutions of the events that followed are best left to a history of the American Zionist movement. In effect the stance of the AJC made it vulnerable to the charge of Brandeis and the Zionists that it was undemocratic, and the AJC-proposed congress was eventually called off. This did not mean the simple victory of the Zionists, however, for the mass of Eastern European Jews ignored both organizations and went ahead with a preliminary conference in Philadelphia in March 1916. The Eastern European Jews saw the fight over the congress as a struggle for power between themselves and the Western European Jews, involving all the differences in life style and ideology between the two groups, and they realized that they had the numbers. The American Jewish Congress, therefore, held its first meeting on March 26 and 27 with Brandeis's blessing and the participation of PC officers but without the attendance of the AJC. It remains a force in American Zionism to this day. The American Jewish Committee, which is also still a powerful presence in American Jewry, achieved a kind of revenge. While all the wrangling was going on, President Wilson had appointed Brandeis to the Supreme Court, and the Senate, after its own wrangling, had confirmed him. The AJC and its ally, the *New York Times*, launched a campaign to force Brandeis to resign from the Zionist movement, claiming that his continued leadership of it while a justice would violate propriety. Brandeis recognized that the claim had merit, and on July 21, 1916, resigned his offices in the American Jewish Congress, the PC, the AJRC, and the Joint Distribution Committee. Nevertheless, although others technically headed these organizations in the following years, he remained the effective leader of the American Zionists until 1921.[7]

Zionism gave full play to Brandeis's organizational talents. It also made use of his ties with President Wilson and his administration. These ties were important even at the beginning of Brandeis's leadership of the movement when the first major objective of the PC was to get relief funds to Jews in Palestine and Europe. Until the United States entered the war in 1917, neither the Allies nor the Central Powers objected to the activities of American charitable organizations behind their lines. The problem, however, was to set up workable conduits. Henry Morgenthau, U.S.

Ambassador to Turkey, helped with the distribution of funds to Palestine; obviously, this could not have been done without the consent of the administration he served. He, along with three leading Palestinian Jews, constituted the committee which received funds from the United States, and it was he who arranged for an American war ship to take the initial $50,000 raised by the PC to Palestine. On February 8, 1915, Brandeis cabled Morgenthau that about three thousand acres of Palestinian orange groves were in jeopardy unless $120,000 was spent immediately on their maintenance. He proposed to borrow the money in the United States, using the groves as security, and asked, "Would you be willing to lend your supervisory aid to securing lenders greatest protection possible?" Morgenthau promised "to render every assistance." When the military governor of Palestine stopped checks drawn on the Anglo-Palestine Bank, Brandeis rushed to Washington. His trip, he wrote Rabbi Wise, "certainly proved of value. The recent messages are more reassuring, and particularly so in that Ambassador Morganthau is brought into such direct touch with the problem." Morgenthau had intervened with the Turkish government, which overrode the governor's action. When de Haas conceived the notion of permitting Americans to transmit funds directly to relatives or other individuals in Palestine and Europe, Brandeis first checked with the State Department, and, having received its permission, wrote asking Morgenthau to "act as the first intermediary" in the transmission of the funds. The transfer of funds to individuals which resulted in the distribution of millions of dollars, was undertaken on behalf of Jews and non-Jews alike, with the PC paying all incidental charges.[8]

Brandeis acknowledged Morgenthau's contribution by expressing to him "the very high appreciation of the Zionists, and generally of the Jews in America, for the devoted and efficient aid which you are giving to our bretheren in Palestine. Scarcely a communication, oral or written, comes to us from Palestine, or from Alexandria, which does not express in some form gratitude for the untiring work which you are doing." Brandeis's praise was not merely politic; he wrote to Arthur Ruppin, one of the Palestinians on the distribution committee, that the American Zionists' relief efforts were made possible by "the friendly attitude of the American government, and the great zeal of Ambassador Morganthau at Constantinople . . . Too much in praise cannot be said of the assistance to us by the Federal Government in this connection."[9]

Morgenthau extended his efforts to fund-raising, securing $25,000 from the non-Zionist Daniel Guggenheim. His involvement ultimately became so extensive that Brandeis took to using the code name "Ezrah" when referring to Morgenthau in letters to others. Brandeis used him as a conduit for messages as well, telling Nahum Sokolow that Morgenthau would "facilitate communication" if Sokolow, then in Europe, wanted to send cables to Brandeis. Although Morgenthau was kindly disposed to the Palestinian Jews, he was not a Zionist, and his intervention with Turkish officials on behalf of the Jews was based on a combination of his own humanitarianism and his adherence to administration policy.[10]

Morgenthau was not the only member of the administration through whom Brandeis worked. At one point in 1915 the Zionists realized that remission of funds alone to Jews in Palestine was insufficient, for too few consumer commodities were available for purchase there. They therefore decided to send the colonists a ship loaded with food and medicine. It proved to be impossible to charter a ship, but at that juncture "the American Government was induced to grant us, without compensation, the opportunity of sending 900 tons of food to Palestine on the Vulcan." The U.S.S. *Vulcan*, a Navy collier, was already scheduled for a trip to Alexandria when Brandeis persuaded Secretary of the Navy Josephus Daniels to permit the ship to carry the food and medical supplies in addition to its regular cargo. At various times Brandeis saw Secretary of State William Jennings Bryan or communicated with him or Acting Secretary of State Robert Lansing (who became secretary of state after Bryan's resignation in June 1915) about such matters as permission to use Morgenthau and American consuls in Palestine for the transmission of funds. Bryan came to think so highly of Brandeis that after the Balfour Declaration seemingly insured the creation of a Jewish state and Brandeis's name was being mentioned as its first president, Bryan wrote supporting what he thought was Brandeis's candidacy and added, "I would be pleased to vote for you as President of the United States." Bryan not only urged Morgenthau on in his efforts, but also sent copies of State Department communications about Palestine to the PC.[11]

The State Department permitted the PC to use its cipher facilities and generally helped the Zionists in a variety of ways. This was not applauded by the department bureaucrats, who were motivated by, among other things, their concern about seeming American interference with the internal affairs of Turkey. Once the United States entered the war and Turkey became an enemy, this motive no longer existed, but State Department hostility to Zionist aims continued. Brandeis began a report to the PC, nonetheless, by declaring that "without the aid given by officials of the Department of State and of the Navy Department, it would have been impossible to render the assistance which has preserved the Palestinian colonies . . . help has been given, generously and graciously, by every official of the United States, highest or lowest, whenever help was possible." It is doubtful that Brandeis was unaware of the anti-Zionist advice being offered by the bureaucrats in the State Department; he probably recognized that giving thanks where due and making no mention of official opposition was the best course to take if quiet cooperation by those willing to give it was to continue. The only official thanked by name, "because he is a Jew," was Morgenthau.[12]

After the United States entered the war on April 6, 1917, and the Zionists began their agitation for a Jewish state in Palestine under British control, interaction greatly increased between the Wilson administration and Brandeis (along with other Zionist leaders such as Rabbi Stephen Wise). It was assumed that Britain would seize Palestine from Turkey, as indeed happened in December. Brandeis, Wise, and others met frequently with Wilson and House about the matter and believed they had secured Wilson's agreement to the idea long before the president was prepared to make such agreement public.[13]

The matter of a British protectorate also brought Brandeis into contact with Arthur James Balfour, the author of the Balfour Declaration, foreign secretary of Great Britain from 1916 to 1919, and a former prime minister. Brandeis and Balfour first met at a reception in Washington on April 23, 1917. According to Brandeis, "As soon as he heard my name, his face brightened up and he said: 'I have heard much of you and I want to have a talk with you.' I told him to summon me when he had the time & I shall probably hear from him soon." On May 7, Brandeis discussed Palestine with Balfour and reported, "He said in terms 'I am a Zionist' . . . It is clear that B will do all he can to advance our cause." They met again on May 10. Then, during the last crucial moments before the Balfour Declaration announcing the British acceptance of a Jewish homeland in Palestine was officially released on November 2, 1917, they telegraphed each other about the homeland's boundaries, Brandeis urging Balfour to hold firm (as he did) on the boundaries that had been promised. On his way to Palestine in 1919, Brandeis had an interview with Balfour in Paris, which Brandeis described to his wife as "very delightful and satisfactory," and he also spoke with Colonel House and Georges Clemenceau's chief aide, André Tardieu. Balfour gave Brandeis a letter of introduction to Viscount Allenby, the British High Commissioner in Egypt responsible for the military administration that then ruled Palestine. Brandeis and Balfour met again on Brandeis's return trip from Palestine in August.[14]

Balfour, too, became one of Brandeis's admirers. His niece and biographer, Blanche E. C. Dugdale, remembered Balfour's saying after his trip to the United States that Brandeis "was in some ways the most remarkable man he had met" there. She added, "It seems from such notes of these conversations as survive, that Balfour pledged his own personal support of Zionism." The record clearly indicates that Brandeis's ability to intervene with Balfour, as well as with the Wilson administration, was significant in the creation of the Jewish homeland. Chaim Weizmann, who had no love for Brandeis by the time he published his autobiography in 1949, nonetheless said that Brandeis's 1917 meeting with Balfour enabled Brandeis "to throw the full weight of his remarkable personality onto the scales" in support of a Jewish homeland. Weizmann also credited Brandeis with carrying on "a general work of clarification" with leading American Jews, thereby securing their aid and influence.[15]

In gratitude to Balfour the Zionists proposed the establishment of a *moshav* named after him. Brandeis was tireless in pushing the project. No doubt he felt it was the least owed to Balfour, but the wording of his letters about it indicate that he was also thinking of possible future benefits. In 1920 he wrote to a key Zionist, "As you know, I feel that we must make a success of Balfouria whatever the cost." In February 1921 he listed "put[ting] Balfouria on the road to success" as one of his first priorities for immediate action. The colony, named Balfouriya, was actually founded in 1922.[16]

Virtually nothing could have been of greater importance to Brandeis than his success in helping to establish the Jewish homeland in Palestine. He had had a specific vision of it since the beginning of his involvement with Zionism, and his Zionism revolved completely around the idea of the Jewish state. Aaron Aaronsohn, accounting for the lack of crime among Jews in Palestine, had reportedly told Brandeis, "Every member of those communities is brought up to realize his obligations to his people. He is told of the great difficulties it passed through, and of the long years of Martyrdom it experienced. All that is best in Jewish history is made to live in him, and by this means he is imbued with a high sense of honor and responsibility for the whole people." The words "all that is best in Jewish history is made to live in him" would have been sufficient to interest the man of whom de Haas reported that Greek and Roman history was as clear as the morning's news. He promptly cast Zionism in a historical mode, seeing it as the living culmination of thousands of generations of Jewish history. Palestine would become the place where the Jews would achieve their age-old dream of democracy and social justice. In Brandeis's eyes, it became a Jeffersonian dream. He waxed poetic over the land, "treeless a generation ago," which the Jewish settlers had shown "to be capable of becoming again a land 'flowing with milk and honey.' "[17]

Brandeis always thought of Palestine as agrarian. He called it "a miniature California," and said that although "there must of course be industries established there . . . our hope is that they may be incidental to agriculture." He cautioned Weizmann, "Our pursuit must be primarily of agriculture in all its branches. The industries and commerce must be incidental merely, and such as may be required to ensure independence and national development." Brandeis realized that not all the immigrants would be farmers, but even the urban middle-class immigrants would be transformed: "We can also give to those who have not yet accustomed themselves to the peculiarities of the country, a certain amount of education in agriculture. We can let them have land practically free without exacting interest or returns for a considerable period while they are accommodating themselves to the new situation." The agrarian nature of Palestine was so important to Brandeis that he occasionally came close to speaking about the future Hebrew University in Jerusalem as no more than a means of turning out sophisticated farmers. This was an aberration, but when priorities in Palestine were being discussed, agriculture did not lag far behind education. He wrote to Weizmann about the university, "I assume we are also in accord—substantially—as to the order in which the several faculties should be developed. Academic should come first, with the great work of sanitation. [To Brandeis, this meant elimination of malaria and creation of a healthful environment.] Then agriculture should take the commanding place."[18]

Brandeis's desired land policy for Palestine was scarcely a surprise, given the attitude he had taken about the development of Alaska. On June 25, 1918, his statement of "the principles which have guided the Zionist Movement since its inception," and which he hoped would similarly guide the Jewish homeland promised in the Balfour Declaration, was unanimously adopted at the FAZ's convention in Pittsburgh. It consisted of six points, known thereafter as the "Pittsburgh Platform."

First: We declare for political and civil equality irrespective of race, sex, or faith of all the inhabitants of the land.

Second: To insure in the Jewish National Home in Palestine equality of opportunity we favor a policy which, with due regard to existing rights, shall tend to establish the ownership and control by the whole people of the land, of all natural resources and of all public utilities.

Third: All the land, owned or controlled by the whole people, should be leased on such conditions as will insure the fullest opportunity for development and continuity of possession.

Fourth: The cooperative principle should be applied so far as feasible in the organization of all agricultural, industrial, commercial, and financial undertakings.

Fifth: The system of free public instruction which is to be established should embrace all grades and departments of education.

Sixth: Hebrew, the national language of the Jewish people, shall be the medium of public instruction.

Earlier, Brandeis had written to Weizmann, "The utmost vigilance should be exercised to prevent the acquisition by private persons of land, water rights or other natural resources or any concessions for public utilities. These must be secured for the whole Jewish people. In other ways, as well as this, the possibility of capitalistic exploitation must be guarded against . . . And the encouragement of all kinds of cooperative enterprise will be indispensable."[19]

The platform may seem, at first reading, to be a strange one for a confirmed capitalist and Jeffersonian. But Brandeis was concerned not only with bringing Jeffersonianism into the twentieth century, but also with making it applicable to the specific territory. Palestine was not the United States: its land and natural resources were limited; the history of its settlements was one of communal ownership rather than capitalist enterprise. Any realistic program had to take these facts into account. The first point, political and civil equality for all, was Jefferson's "all men are created equal." In Brandeis's version, however, men and women were to share political and civil rights, as were members of all races and religions. The phrase, "all the inhabitants of the land" necessarily begged the question of citizenship, for inhabitants were presumably British, rather than Palestinian, citizens. Nonetheless, the civil liberties stance taken in his judicial opinions leads to the assumption that Brandeis advocated political and civil equality for all inhabitants of Palestine, whatever their faith or citizenship status. Land would be owned or controlled by the entire people, but would be "leased," primarily to cooperative entities such as the *kibbutzim* and *moshavim*, as well as the consumers' cooperatives in which Brandeis believed. The control of natural resources and utilities by the people was a reflection of Brandeis's progressivism and of his fights in Boston and in the Pinchot-Ballinger affair. The Jewish National Home was meant to be a true democracy, so public education had to be established; it was to be a unified nation, so Hebrew had to be the common tongue of the immigrants who would arrive from many lands.

Brandeis was clearly pleased that a country could be created in which the worst excesses of capitalism could be avoided. This did not mean, however, that he had turned his back on Jeffersonian economic self-reliance. The specifics of his economic program were detailed in a memorandum he wrote while sailing home from the 1920 meeting of world Zionists in London. Known as the Zeeland program, after the name of the ship on which he drafted it, his statement said in part, "We are compelled by the present conditions of the country and political requirements to create ourselves those new conditions under which self-support can alone become possible. But in doing so we must be careful to go no step further, otherwise we shall demoralize our settlers and make success not only impossible, but also develop a population of undesirables . . . We cannot attain our objective of a manly, self-supporting population unless the settlers are made to realize that they must, and unless they actually do incur, in some form, hardships equivalent to those incurred by hardy pioneers in other lands . . . The slogans must be 'No easy money in Palestine,' and 'No easy living' for any human being." Later, Brandeis compared the Palestinian settlers to the Pilgrims in one of his Zionist speeches: "The pilgrims had faith, we should have it. Like our early Palestinian pioneers, they did not allow themselves to be discouraged . . . Disease, death and sore trials were borne and put behind them. For the Pilgrims had the indomitable spirit . . . The same spirit which brought the Pilgrim west is the spirit which has sent many a Jew to the east." He cited four "conditions essential to successful democracy." The first, "an all-pervading sense of duty in the citizen," had also been found "in the early days of the colonies and states of New England, when American democracy reached there its fullest expression; for the Puritans were trained in implicit obedience to stern duty by constant study of the Prophets." The second, "relatively high intellectual attainments," was fully appreciated by early New Englanders, as demonstrated by their immediate founding of a school system and their creation of Harvard College only six years after Boston was settled. The Puritans were not mentioned by Brandeis in conjunction with the third trait, "submission to leadership as distinguished from authority"; this he saw as the outcome of the Diaspora and the turning of Jews in their suffering to leaders who were "highly endowed, morally and intellectually." The fourth trait was "a developed community sense," described by Achad Ha'am as appearing "when the individual . . . values the community as his own life, and strives after its happiness as though it were his individual wellbeing." Brandeis demanded, "Is not that the very essence of the truly triumphant twentieth-century democracy?"[20]

In part, all this achievement was made possible by the size of Palestine. "To my mind," declared the critic of bigness, "the smallness of the country contributes greatly to the probability of complete success. The problems are all compassable. None is so big in bulk, so complex as to make man seem inadequate for the task." In 1924 he spoke of the proposed Jewish population of Palestine as being "at least, many hundreds of thousands"; clearly, the country's area was expected to keep the population relatively small. In 1941, shortly before his death, Brandeis reiterated his hope that "Palestine, when the Jews constitute the majority there, may, because of its very smallness, serve as a laboratory for some far-reaching experiments in democracy and social justice."[21]

Brandeis had no doubt that the majority of citizens in the Palestinian state would be Jewish. There is no indication that he knew much about the existing Arab population, but he assumed that Arabs would continue to live in the Jewish state and thought they could do so amicably. During the summer of 1929 he discussed with other Zionists the possibilities of including Arabs in cooperatives, labor unions, and industries. He was certain the Arabs would come to appreciate the beneficial effects for them of the Zionists' medical and antimalaria work. Although he spoke at a time of Arab attacks on Palestinian Jews, he noted that "Jews lived among [the Arabs] in perfect amity before and during the war. I have confidence they will again do so." Some of his confidence may have had its genesis in the warm relationship that was established during 1918 and 1919 between Weizmann and Frankfurter and Emir Feisal, who agreed that such enmity as existed between Arabs and Jews was an artificial creation of the British, and that the two groups of people could each attain their national goals. Brandeis concurred: "The available material affords also ample evidence in support of the argument that with a proper British attitude Jews can live in harmony with the Arabs; that friendly relations are being developed in many places; and that raising of the level of Arab existence has been, and is, not only a necessary incident of the Jewish upbuilding of P.[alestine]—but the Jewish desire."[22]

Brandeis's attitude toward Jewish-Arab relations was simple—some might say simplistic. It was based on the dignity of every human being that underlay all of his views, including Zionism. The Jews needed Palestine and could bring Western technology to the Arabs, but that did not mean that the Jews could not learn from the Arabs. "I should think it presumptuous for any people in this century to assert that it alone had a mission for all peoples, but that none of the other peoples had any mission for it," he told Solomon Goldman. "Every people . . . has its own character. And insofar as it has a character of its own it has a mission . . . In the realm of things material one people may be a solitary benefactor and not a beneficiary. In the realm of the spirit there is no such solitary philanthropist. Here all peoples give and take, some more and some less, each giving what it has, and if it is wise it takes what it needs." He added, "Let us teach all peoples that they are all chosen, and that each has a mission for all." Brandeis's vision of Palestine was of a state in which Jews would constitute the majority and would share the benefits of full citizenship with all non-Jews who chose to live there. Shortly before he died, he made a special contribution to Hadassah for playgrounds to be used jointly by Jewish, Moslem, and Christian children. Playgrounds as such may be insignificant, but Brandeis was supporting a larger scheme: the ability of different peoples to live together amicably would be fostered by educating their children to assume that such co-existence was completely natural.[23]

Brandeis's perception of life in Palestine was both realistic and opti-mistic. "We can best live in amity with the Arabs by not living too near them," he wrote in 1929. "That is a common experience among blood relations." He realized that "Jewish industrialists" counted on a higher standard of living among Arabs "to enlarge the home market." He was insistent that Jews not take advantage of the Arabs' lower standard of living; again, partly because to do so would be immoral and partly because Jews had to be self-reliant pioneers rather than overseers. He wrote in 1940, "We should promote Arab stockholding in Jewish en-terprises and proportionate employment of Arab labor, but never more than such proportionate employment and never for the purpose of em-ploying labor at lower rates." "Proportionate" presumably referred to the proportion of citizens in the Jewish state who were Arabs.[24]

Brandeis can perhaps be faulted for not recognizing that a generalized good will would not overcome the problem of Arabs living in a Jewish state. However, his model was the United States, where the Jews existed comfortably and with full liberties in what was essentially a Christian state. His expectation of amity in the face of land claims was more problematic. Brandeis had assumed from the time of the Balfour Dec-laration that Transjordan would be part of what would otherwise be an unviably microscopic state. His letters throughout the 1930s reflect his growing belief that the British would do nothing to secure Transjordan for Zion, and in 1933 he sent Emanuel Neumann to negotiate with King Abdullah Ibn Hussein for the purchase of Jordanian land. The mission failed, but Brandeis remained adamant about the need for more land. His feelings were strengthened later in the 1930s by the rise of fascism in Germany and his recognition that European Jews would need a place to which they could escape. How his demand for more Arab land fit into his scheme for Arab-Jewish peace is unclear, unless he thought the Pal-estinian land-purchasing entities he helped establish eventually would succeed where Neumann had failed. Given the desire of the newly in-stalled Hashemites to hold onto the kingdom they had received as a gift from the British, it is difficult to understand Brandeis's optimism.[25]

The seemingly unrealistic optimism and determination of many Zi-onists such as Brandeis, however, helped bring Israel into existence. It was reinforced for him by the experience of seeing the Jewish communities in Palestine. Until he went to Palestine in 1919, Brandeis had merely accepted the decision of other Zionists to recreate Zion there. During his trip with de Haas and Zimmern, however, all of his dreams about the new Zion seemed to spring into reality. He began to urge his audiences to visit Palestine, assuring them, "If you do that you will enjoy the greatest experience of your life."[26]

"The greatest experience of your life" is strong language for a man used to choosing his words carefully, even given the context of an oratorical appeal for Zionist support. Brandeis admitted that only through his trip had he become convinced "in fullness" of the possibilities of the Jewish state in Palestine. He was equally certain that as a result of the trip he really knew "the main problems and the difficulties and possibilities." His belief in his own ability to find correct solutions, never limited, was reinforced and would lead to his final fight with Weizmann. Paradoxically, the trip that made Brandeis a fully confirmed Zionist also resulted in his fall as the Zionist leader.[27]

Now that he was doubly certain of the answers, Brandeis was anxious to see them implemented. After his return from Palestine to Paris and the consultations with Balfour, he went to London to meet with the European Zionist leaders. The Europeans talked endlessly, examining every possible detail and taking what to Brandeis seemed too little action. He wrote to his wife, "The East Europeans have much to learn in practical affairs." He had told them that the eradication of malaria was of the first importance; Weizmann said it was too early to concentrate on that and brushed off the suggestion. But Brandeis's boyhood memories made him press ahead, saying, "I lived as a small boy in a malarial region, and I have some idea how this disease can hamper and frustrate the efforts of farmers." He was insistent that malaria was a very basic problem, for it made many areas unworkable, seriously reduced the ability of settlers to function, and would deter skilled Jews from moving to Palestine. Undaunted by Weizmann's response, Brandeis gave $10,000 to Hadassah, which was concentrating on health problems under the leadership of Henrietta Szold, and persuaded Baron Edmond-James de Rothschild to contribute another £12,000. The money was used for an experimental program in a small area (near Lake Huleh, in Galilee)—the typical Brandeis approach; the malaria rate was cut by over 95 percent within a year. Settlers in other areas asked that the program be extended to them. Within four years, malaria had almost been eradicated in the country. Brandeis interpreted this success, and Weizmann's disapproval of the program, as proof of Weizmann's inability to grasp fundamentals; Weizmann took Brandeis's absorption with the malaria problem as another indication of *his* inability to understand the things, like a revival of Jewish culture, that were of key importance to the Jewish people. The argument over malaria alone did not account for the break between the two men, but the issue confirmed each in his impression of the other's unsuitability for leadership.[28]

The issues that separated the two leaders were numerous, but they fell roughly into four areas of concern. The first, as indicated by the dispute over malaria control, had to do with priorities. Brandeis insisted that Palestine, dominated by Arabs (in 1919, there were 80,000 Jews and over 600,000 Arabs living there), had to be made healthful and attractive to potential immigrants if it was to become a viable Jewish state. Weizmann argued that the Americans, with all the money available to them, should concentrate on problems of schools, administration, and land reclamation. The second area of contention lay in Weizmann's desire for *gegenwartsarbeit*, the revitalization of Jewish culture throughout the Diaspora. Brandeis argued that Zionists should be concerned only with building the physical Zion, that is, Palestine. The Americans were clearly afraid of what the notion of Jewish separatism within the United States would do to their support from the wealthy assimilated American Jews. In addition, Brandeis, who felt no need of non-Zionist Judaism himself, could not comprehend what he considered a wasteful tangent. Weizmann's reaction was that Brandeis and the other American Zionists lacked a true understanding of Jewish history and had no true Jewish national consciousness. A third problem was administrative. The Americans were raising most of the money but the Europeans were spending it, and Brandeis was appalled (in the same way that he had been when he assumed leadership of the American movement) at what he considered unforgiveable sloppiness in the management of money. The Europeans saw American attempts to "rationalize" the accounting system as a manifestation of American obsession with money.

The fourth issue was personal involvement. When the British had asked the Zionists to send a commission to Palestine in 1918, Weizmann had given up his job as a matter of course and other European Zionists had done the same. Brandeis did not leave the Supreme Court and was unable to persade other American Zionist leaders (Frankfurter, Rabbi Stephen Wise, Judge Julian Mack) to leave their jobs. The Europeans could not understand, and were contemptuous of, Americans who gave primacy to their jobs and took care of Zionist activities only in their spare time. When they met again in 1920, Weizmann offered Brandeis the leadership of world Zionism; Brandeis turned it down in favor of remaining on the Court. Weizmann naturally saw this as a lack of real commitment to Zionism, and Brandeis, for his part, could not conceive of leaving the Court and his life in the law. He also feared that his departure from the Court would be viewed as a repudiation of his oft-proclaimed belief that, for American Jews, Zionism was not in conflict with Americanism, that it would be a defeat for progressivism, and that he could not work well with the European Zionists whose methods and procedures he found so alien. Weizmann ultimately accused Brandeis, not without a measure of truth, of wanting the power to direct the world Zionist movement but not the responsibility of leading it.[29]

Felix Frankfurter, who liked and admired Weizmann, and who was also Brandeis's protegé and representative in some of the battles that took place between the two men, saw the clash resulting from differences in background and temperament. He described the "divergence . . . between the rigorous, economically oriented outlook of Justice Brandeis and the entire consequence of the disciplined, even if inspired, mind that he was, and the kind of passionate, romantic, quasi-messianic temperament of Weizmann." Weizmann viewed Palestine as an adventurous dream that "required something more and beyond the careful calculation of an enterprise influenced by economic considerations, or the kind of hard-headed regard for details that was so characteristic" of Brandeis. In addition, Frankfurter suggested, there was a sense of rivalry. Weizmann had become the leader of Zionism, and then, "out of the West comes . . . a judge with a composed temperament, a non-oratorical temperament, and almost inevitably challenges Weizmann's predominance, Weizmann's position of leadership." The situation was exacerbated by de Haas, who seems to have alienated everyone in the movement except Brandeis, Frankfurter, and Mack. Brandeis refused to remove deHaas as his lieutenant out of loyalty and because he felt indebted to de Haas for introducing him to Zionism. Unfortunately, Weizmann and de Haas had an old feud which predated Brandeis's Zionism. Frankfurter agreed with at least part of Brandeis's estimate of Weizmann, commenting that "Weizmann was no administrator at all."[30]

The disagreement came close to an irrevocable split at the June 22, 1920, meeting of world Zionist leaders in London's Memorial Hall. Brandeis (and the twenty-eight other members of the American delegation) wanted a restructuring of the operative leadership of world Zionism, which would then include both Zionists like himself and Weizmann and wealthy non-Zionist Jews like Baron James de Rothschild. If Palestine was to have a firm economic base, he thought, it needed the involvement of non-Zionist Jews, and not only Americans; fund-raising in the United States had become difficult. The actual day-to-day operations would be transferred to Palestine and a group of Zionists with economic expertise. Weizmann and his allies who disliked the idea of putting power into the hands of non-Zionists, suggested a separate organization that would include non-Zionists (eventually the Jewish Agency), and were horrified at Brandeis's assumption that economic ability rather than a proven concern for Jewish culture and history was the natural criterion for leadership. Out of respect for Brandeis, however, they met with him to consider his ideas; however, he would discuss only economic development, not resurrection of the Hebrew language or establishment of an educational system that would foster it. Weizmann, pressed by his followers, then made a unilateral decision to alter Brandeis's proposal for organization of the top leadership; Brandeis, who had believed that he had Weizmann's agreement, felt betrayed. He offered an economic plan, which he hoped would help attract small businessmen to Palestine. Weizmann disagreed with the plan, which would have limited the funds available for *gegenwartsarbeit*, but was willing to try it if Brandeis would assume actual leadership of the movement. Brandeis not only refused but, charging Weizmann with duplicity over the change in the proposed organization of the leadership group, also threatened to leave the leadership entirely if any American accepted a position on the executive committee that was to be created.

Although his ultimatum was successful in its immediate aim and the executive committee was set up without an American member, his insistence that the organization follow his economic plan at the same time that he rejected active leadership antagonized members of the American delegation. But Brandeis was convinced that he was right. Weizmann had gone back on his word and had even taken his new organizational structure to de Rothschild and the other non-Zionists before Brandeis knew anything of it. Weizmann had been dishonest; therefore, Brandeis would refuse to serve on the European-dominated executive committee that Weizmann had created, and so should any other American, both to demonstrate their anger and to deny the appearance of American endorsement to the decisions that would be made by the executive committee. The other Americans appreciated Brandeis's anger and his charge that the Europeans operated amid administrative chaos, but they could not forgive what they perceived as his abdication of responsibility.

The tension was not eased by the European proposal to create a new financial agency to be called Keren Hayesod, which would collect money for the development of Palestine and would accept both contributions for general purposes and money loaned for specific projects. Brandeis could not accept the pooling of outright gifts with loans; it was the kind of imprecise fiscal management he abhorred. The Europeans would not believe that his objection was to the way Keren Hayesod would be managed rather than to the agency as such and accused him of disloyalty to the cause. Brandeis, who had fought much of his adult life against organizations whose sloppy fiscal techniques had hidden irresponsible use of money, did not see why others could not appreciate the sophisticated fiscal niceties of his objections. The majority went ahead and established the Keren Hayesod in spite of his protests. Thus, when he was elected

Honorary President of the World Zionist Organization, the appearance of unity was only cosmetic. The conference ended, or, rather, disintegrated; and Brandeis sailed for home on the S.S. *Zeeland.*[31]

As a result of the London conference, Brandeis knew that questions would be raised at the annual convention of the Zionist Organization of America (ZOA) in November 1920 in Buffalo. Furthermore, discontent had surfaced in the Yiddish press, in which Brandeis was alternately depicted as a tyrant and begged to assume active leadership of world Zionism. A letter he wrote to Wise, who was to present the Brandeis point of view, reflects the mixture of belief in democracy and attention to tactical detail that permeated all Brandeis's battles: "I am convinced that if the facts and the arguments to be deduced therefrom are clearly and fully presented . . . our party must prevail;—provided only that proper preparation is made and results or tactics are not left to chance." He then pointed out, "In legislative assemblies as in the courts, most cases are won before the parties appear on the field of contest," and instructed Wise: "What is needed primarily is full and free discussion with the general convictions that no attempt is made to suppress or intimidate . . . It is, of course, desirable that discussion should proceed on the basis of the actual facts and that misstatements should be corrected and that misapprehensions be dispelled." He would not be present at the convention "because my presence could not fail to curtail in some measure full discussion and would naturally embarrass those who desired to express freely their views on what I have wrongly done or omitted, or am believed to have so done or omitted." The strategy was to be aggressive pedagogy: "Our case should not be defended . . . We should be the attacking party . . . And by attack, I mean merely that we should take the aggressive, seize the ball at the outset and cling to it throughout the game. And by attack I mean further, clear exposition of our plans, purposes, and methods and the weaknesses of the methods and lack of feasible plans of our adversaries . . . I think it extremely important with reference to the long future of our organization that we undertake to educate our members. They are capable of understanding . . . we should try to convince them, not merely to get their votes. Of course we must have adequate Yiddish speaking men on the floor, fully posted and able to meet arguments." Referring to the criticisms that would be made about his "anomalous position in the organization"—that is, leading it without being willing to accept the title of leader and using others to present his decisions as their own—he wrote that he did not "resent them in any way so far as they are based on facts. Indeed, knowing well the ability of men to misunderstand, I am entirely patient even with misrepresentations. The only remedy is telling the simple truth to the objectors."[32]

The Brandeis group continued in power, winning a resounding endorsement. Brandeis and his administration of the ZOA were endorsed partly because there was no other available leader and partly because they still wanted him; in fact, they wanted more of him than he was willing to give. Here his inability to distinguish between his own charismatic appeal and the strength of his ideas surfaced once again. American Zionists wanted Brandeis, and if he would lead, they would accept his ideas; he wanted the Zionists to support his ideas because they understood and agreed with them. He could not accept the notion that his own presence was vital.

With the ZOA convention safely behind them, the Americans invited Weizmann to come to the United States. The Brandeis group hoped he would gain a better understanding of the fund-raising problems they faced, although relations had deteriorated to such a point that they simultaneously dreaded his visit; Weizmann was certain that they were not doing their best but hoped to heal the breach for the sake of the movement. He arrived on April 2, 1921, and toured the country, receiving enormous grateful acclaim from the Jewish masses and meeting with Brandeis's lieutenants. The two groups were unable to reach an accord and parted with the rift having been widened further. Brandeis, however, was busy with the Court, wanted as little to do with Weizmann as possible, and initially felt confident that Weizmann would be unable to win the masses away from him.

He was wrong. Weizmann told his huge audiences that the Brandeis group was hiding behind the matter of the Keren Hayesod and financial niceties, when the real issue was their refusal to accept responsibility and go to work in Palestine. The climax of his visit came on June 5, 1921, at the annual ZOA convention, held that year in Cleveland. When Weizmann entered the hall, the delegates cheered him and sang "Hatikvah." They then heard Judge Mack present the Brandeis view of the dispute, emphasizing the lack of good faith shown by the Europeans, the need for proper fiscal management, and the rejection of Diaspora nationalism. The majority rejected his arguments; when he was nominated as permanent chairman of the convention, he lost by a vote of 139 to 75. A motion was made to establish an American Keren Hayesod, in which donations and investments would be mixed and which would be under the control of the World Zionist Organization headed by Weizmann rather than under the ZOA. It was debated in a tumultuous and lengthy session which ended with a vote at one-thirty in the morning. The motion was passed 153 to 71.

The Brandeis forces had realized in the weeks immediately preceding the convention that they might lose, but Brandeis's determination not to involve himself personally in the fray remained firm. They had, therefore, prepared a message of resignation, and as soon as the vote on the Keren Hayesod was taken, Mack announced those who were giving up their positions in the organization: Brandeis, Mack himself, Frankfurter, de Haas, Wise, Robert Szold (Henrietta Szold's nephew), Nathan Straus, Abba Hillel Silver—in all, thirty-six people, constituting the bulk of both leadership and administrative staff. The delegates were stunned; many wept. Mack pledged that they would all remain faithful Zionists and members of the ZOA, but when the convention ended at 2 A.M., so did Brandeis's leadership of American Zionism.[33]

During the meetings of the Brandeis and Weizmann groups at the beginning of May, a compromise on Keren Hayesod appeared to have been worked out, but Weizmann came under intense pressure from extremist colleagues, rejected the compromise, broke off the talks, and without telling the Brandeis group in advance proceeded to announce the establishment of the Keren Hayesod in the United States. When the compromise seemed certain, Brandeis had written to Frankfurter, a member of the negotiating team, with congratulations. Brandeis subsequently realized that matters were hopeless, and that the outcome of the battle at the ZOA convention the following month was inevitable. He was furious and bitter. Frankfurter sent him a telegram asking him to talk with Weizmann himself. Brandeis replied that it was inadvisable and that "anyone's talk with him" was "dangerous." It was dangerous in part as a tactical matter, because the appearance of a willingness to compromise would undermine appreciation of the principled stance taken by the Brandeis group. "Our strength within the Organization will exist & be appreciated only if it is once understood that when we take a position— we are immovable. We cannot hope to have votes enough at any Congress or Conference to overcome the Easterners—as they will practically stuff ballot-boxes as they did in effect in London last summer." "The Easterners," as he went on calling his opponents, "will not listen to argument & emotional oratory—subsidized to occupy the time—will prevail . . . We must therefore, by passive resistance, protect our standard." He quoted, in German, Martin Luther's statement, "I can not do other," and said that that "must be our stand." They would protect their standard through this kind of "passive resistance." They had no choice; at the bottom of the argument was Weizmann's "utter untrustworthiness," which made joint participation in conferences impossible. "We Westerners are not, in spite of plenitude of knowledge, able to protect ourselves in any conference under such conditions." He wrote shortly thereafter that Weizmann "gives new proof that 'Character is the thing' and his, bad as it was, is worsening under the strain."[34]

This vitriolic language, with its echoes of Western jingoism, indicates how deeply Brandeis felt the hurt. For seven years he had worked long and hard for a cause in which he had come to believe completely. His activities would have constituted an entire career for most human beings, but he performed them in addition to his huge volume of work first as a lawyer and then as a Supreme Court justice. He had made the American Zionist movement viable; he had played an active role in bringing about the Balfour Declaration and, thus, in the very creation of a Jewish homeland. In 1916, on his sixtieth birthday, Zionists had presented him with a testimonial signed by 10,000 people, a clear endorsement of his leadership.[35] And then, suddenly, he faced rejection. He was certain his ideas were right; he knew that thousands of American Jews had agreed to follow them and that he had been greeted as a hero by the Palestinian settlers; he was, in spite of his refusal to participate actively, Honorary President of the World Zionist Organization, which implied that non-Americans had also recognized the legitimacy of his ideas. His early experiences in New England gave him every reason to believe that determined opponents remained so out of self-interest; this had been the case with his adversaries in the subway fight, and in those involving the gas company, the insurance companies, and the railroads. Their particular interests obviously made them impervious to his teachings. Judging from his earlier battles, he concluded that his Zionist opponents, too, suffered grievous faults of motive or character, or more charitably, that they required more of an education than he, with his duties as a Supreme Court justice, could supply. Until 1914 he had undergone no defeats other than the one in the New Haven Railroad case, and there he could rightfully argue that Big Money had bought the decision. The only reason he could find for Weizmann's success was the man's evil genius, which enabled him to close the ears of the masses to reason and to lead them astray. There was no other possible explanation.

He was not only embittered; he was despairing. Brandeis had come to see the intelligent, well-read, politically involved Zionists as a proof that democracy was possible. Half a year earlier, when writing to Mack before the Buffalo convention, he had noted, "If we can't make Zionists reason, we Americans & the rest of the world might as well renounce our hopes of democracy." Nevertheless, he managed to put a good face on the defeat, writing to his brother on June 12, "The result of the Cleveland convention is satisfactory to us, as it enables us to carry on our work under more favorable conditions." But his letters to Frankfurter and Mack a few weeks earlier made the depth of his feeling clear. It would have been crisis enough for him to be defeated; he was not used to defeat and could not but have suffered the pangs of self-doubt that accompany a debacle. Even worse than the blow to his *amour propre* was the temporary damage done to his ideology. Could he have been wrong about democracy? education? the strength of the Jewish intellectual tradition? There must have been uncomfortable hours. But, typically, he got himself through the experience by taking action.[36]

He and his loyalists, firm in the belief that "the road to a Jewish Palestine is economic," put together a host of economically oriented groups: the Palestine Development Leagues, the Palestine Co-operative Company, the Palestine Development Council, the Palestine Endowment Fund, the Palestine Economic Corporation. The Palestine Endowment Fund supported the creation of Hebrew University and raised the money for the purchase of what is now the city of Eilat. The Palestine Development Council, which enabled business people to invest in Palestine, was merged with the Joint Distribution Committee's Palestine Committee and became the Palestine Economic Corporation in 1926—a signal that American Zionists were gradually returning to the Brandeisian fold. He turned his attention to loans for small industry, consumers' cooperative societies, and low-cost housing. He helped finance the Rutenberg plan, which harnessed the waters of the Jordan River to produce electricity and irrigate land. He still talked to Jewish groups and urged them, with as much vigor as ever, to aid the Zionist cause. Between 1914 and 1921 he had given $171,538 to Zionist organizations, a yearly average of $21,442, with contributions ranging from $3,160 in 1914 to $53,614 in 1919. His donations between 1922 and 1939 totaled $440,984, a yearly average of $24,499; in 1937 alone, he gave $77,325. As he had done in the past, he continued to send stipends to such needy allies in Zionism as de Haas and Henrietta Szold. His will left half of his $3,000,000 estate, after $800,000 was deducted for trusts for his family, to the Palestine Endowment and Hadassah.[37]

His relationship with Hadassah, the one Zionist organization that remained steadfastly loyal, became even closer, as indicated by his legacy to it. He rewarded loyalty with loyalty; in addition, he was endlessly impressed by Henrietta Szold and the activities of the women she recruited. One of the early Hadassah leaders, lamenting the fact that women were only theoretically equal to men within the Zionist movement, has pointed to Brandeis's relationship with Hadassah as an indication of his willingness to treat women as equals. He aided its emergence from the ZOA as an autonomous organization—which, in the years after 1921, enabled him to exercise greater control than he would have had it remained under the ZOA umbrella. He established its bookkeeping procedures, received and read all of its minutes, reports, and financial statements, and gave it unceasing streams of advice. Small wonder that he told the same Hadassah leader that "of all the organizations he knew, Jewish and non-Jewish, he considered Hadassah the best organized and most efficient." Certainly, his will indicated that, among Zionist organizations, he trusted only Hadassah and the Palestine Endowment Fund that he had created to use his money properly.[38]

Brandeis's commitment to Zionism would last for the rest of his life. He had resigned as Honorary President of the World Zionist Organization on June 19, 1921, in a letter that promised that he and his fellows would take their places "as humble workers in the ranks, where we may hope to hasten by our struggle the coming of the day when the standards which we seek to establish and maintain will be recognized as indispensable to the attainment of our great end." Referring to Louis Lipsky, an American Zionist leader who had allied himself with the Weizmann faction, he wrote in 1928, "The Romans of the great days occasionally lost a campaign. They never lost a war . . . because they never permitted a war to end until they won . . . The terrible demoralization wrought by the Lipsky administration cannot be overcome without teaching Zionists the wages of sin. There must be no suppression in the supposed interest of Palestine—or to 'save the movement.' The cause cannot be served without saving the souls of American Jewry." Brandeis did not normally speak of either sins or souls. He was casting himself, verbally at least, in the mold of the Biblical prophets, unhonored in their time but ultimately unwavering in their faith. He had lost the leadership war to Weizmann in large measure because their cultural differences led them to different immediate goals and made understanding between them impossible. The American "Yiddishkeit" was foreign to him, as was the need of Eastern European-American Jews to maintain a culture and tradition linked with those that would emerge in Palestine and stemming from the same history and values.[39]

Typically, however, he persevered. He continued to spend part of every day, and particularly large parts of his vacation days, on Zionist work. Two of the three pictures on his study wall in Washington were of Herzl (the third was of Langdell). An oil painting of Herzl decorated his study in Chatham, as did a small metal relief map of Palestine. De Haas portrayed Brandeis ruminating on Zionism during the summers: "in an old sweater, under his heavy tweed jacket, cap on head, he saunters through the berry paths that lead from his Chatham home to the river inlet." And his perseverance paid off. It was not very long before he regained leadership of the movement.[40]

In 1929 a conference on economic aid for Palestine was organized by a group of non-Zionists: Felix Warburg, Cyrus Adler, Lee K. Frankel, and James Marshall. Brandeis was asked to speak, and, presumably because the conference was approaching Palestinian problems in a manner of which he approved, he agreed to send it a message of encouragement. Since it was his first public pronouncement about Palestine since the 1921 debacle, it was news: it was reported by the *New York Times* and led to renewed interest in his services on the part of the Zionists. In June 1930, the ZOA convention adopted a reorganization plan that put the faction devoted to Brandeis back into power. He sent a letter to the convention, regretting "that added years make it impossible for me to assume now the official responsibilities of leadership as I did prior to 1921" (thereby tacitly admitting that his lack of official office from 1917 to 1921 had in no way interfered with his leadership of the movement). The "added years" seemed to make little difference; although the pace of Brandeis's activities decreased slowly as he aged, after 1930 he was again in full control of the American Zionist movement. He acknowledged birthday greetings from the ZOA covention of 1931 in his usual brief, hortatory style: "Please express to the delegates my deep appreciation and my hope that each will vow not to let pass within the next twelve months a single day without furthering in some way the upbuilding of Palestine."[41]

In late 1937 a small group of American colonists associated with the Hashomer Hatzair youth movement began building a new kibbutz, enabled to do so in part by the unheralded donation by Brandeis of $50,000. Eleven months later, the kibbutz laid the cornerstone of its first permanent building, embedding in it a scroll dedicating the kibbutz, called Ein Hashofet (Spring of the Judge), to Brandeis. A year later they sent him a model of the kibbutz, carved out of plywood by one of its members, and until his death the kibbutz also sent him part of each harvest.[42]

Brandeis had been called "the Chief" since the formation of the PC in 1914; he was still "the Chief" when he died in 1941. He had turned American Jews into Zionists, even if he was not always successful in getting them to understand his fiscal conservatism; he had dealt as no other Zionist could with Wilson and Balfour and had thus helped bring the Jewish homeland in Palestine into existence; he had wiped out malaria in Palestine and aided in the creation of industries and housing in places malaria had made inaccessible, proving in the process that he was right about the need for a healthful environment and a strong economic base. He was pleased that "Palestine has developed Jewish character." The Jewish Palestinians had drawn upon centuries of Jewish suffering and its lessons about "will, courage, pertinacity to succeed under all circumstances and amidst all difficulties" to overcome such tests as malaria and massacres: "Our representatives in Palestine have been tested; and they stood the test superbly well." They had blossomed in "spiritual and social development," which was aided by what was "perhaps the most extraordinary achievement of Jewish nationalism," the revival of Hebrew as "the living mother tongue" that united immigrants who arrived speaking a bewildering variety of languages.[43]

Brandeis was too much of a civil libertarian to be sanguine about many aspects of the Israel of today: the enforcement of orthodox religious beliefs transformed into civil law; the systematic legalized mistreatment of Israeli Arabs; the inequality of women; the military expansionism and violation of the rights of captive populations. The first plank of the Pittsburgh Platform was, "We declare for political and civil equality irrespective of race, sex, or faith of all the inhabitants of the land." This was echoed in Israel's 1948 Declaration of Independence, which proclaimed in part that Israel "will ensure complete equality of social and political rights to all its inhabitants irrespective of religion, race or sex." Like many of the other early Zionists, Brandeis's vision was libertarian and egalitarian; he did not live to see the negation of much of his vision by successive generations.[44]

The fault, however, lay partly with Brandeis's generation of Zionists, whose understandable preoccupation with the goal of a Jewish homeland blinded them to questions that remain unanswered: What should be the relationship between religion and state in a Jewish state? What would become of the Arabs displaced by the Jews? What would the response of the state be if non-Jews grew to be a majority? Did the creation of a Jewish homeland give it the status of *the* Jewish homeland? The answers, or lack thereof, have profound implications for the recognition of individual dignity that was so central to Brandeis's thought.

But Brandeis would be pleased by the existence of a Jewish state that, although as prone to human error as any other, holds both intellectuals and farmers in high regard, benefits from an impressive degree of citizen participation in public life, calls its leaders by their first names and declines to surround them with pomp or mystique, and cherishes history and education. Brandeis got his Athens.

15 | Mr. Brandeis Goes to Washington

When Supreme Court Justice Joseph R. Lamar died on January 2, 1916, speculation immediately erupted in Washington and elsewhere about President Wilson's likely nominee. Some assumed that since Lamar had come from Georgia, his successor would have to be Southern; others saw an opportunity to put former President Taft on the Court. Labor and Democrats vehemently opposed Taft; newspapers overflowed with conflicting advice for Wilson; and politicians sought out members of Wilson's cabinet to lobby for one person or another.[1]

Wilson serenely ignored it all. He spoke quietly with his son-in-law, Secretary of the Treasury William McAdoo, and with Attorney General Thomas W. Gregory. Both enthusiastically suggested Brandeis, although Gregory, while calling Brandeis "the greatest lawyer in the United States," warned the president that his nomination would result in a "tempest." Wilson, who may already have thought of Brandeis, discussed the matter only briefly with a few members of his entourage and almost not at all with anyone else. He asked Senator Robert La Follette whether Progressive Republicans in the Senate could be counted on to cross party lines and vote to confirm Brandeis; La Follette enthusiastically said yes. Wilson also checked with Samuel Gompers and received an equally strong assurance of labor support. The only step remaining was to secure the favored candidate's consent to the nomination. George W. Anderson, who had worked on Boston public affairs with Brandeis, was now a U.S. district attorney and a Brandeis admirer. Wilson and Gregory dispatched him to contact Brandeis, who was traveling up and down the East Coast organizing the American Jewish Congress. Brandeis and Anderson eventually met in Bridgeport, Connecticut, where Brandeis immediately agreed to the nomination.[2]

Brandeis's meeting with Anderson on January 24, 1916 occurred just ten months before his sixtieth birthday. Although he was still vigorous and active—leading the Zionists, creating a whole new Zionist organization, working on minimum wage and maximum hours cases with the Consumers' League, heading the garment workers' Arbitration Board, shuttling between New York and Washington with such frequency that he had virtually set up a second home for himself in the Hotel Gordon— he had been having problems with his health. He was far too dynamic and involved to give up his professional life—and yet he simply could not maintain the physical pace of years past. To both Brandeis and his wife, who had been concerned by the way he pushed himself, a position on the Court seemed a good solution. Alice wrote to Alfred, once the nomination was announced, "I had some misgivings for Louis has been such a 'free man' all these years but as you suggested—his days of 'knight erranting' must have, in the nature of things, been over before long . . . The great excitement in the newspapers is amusing, is it not? . . . I tell Louis, if he is going to retire, he is certainly doing it with a burst of fireworks." Three days earlier Brandeis had thanked Alfred for a congratulatory telegram, saying, "I am not entirely sure that I am to be congratulated, but I am glad the President wanted to make the appointment & I am convinced, all things considered, that I ought to accept." Two weeks later he added, "As you correctly divined, I should have preferred to be let alone until sixty-five." Brandeis regretted that his freedom of action in public causes would be so soon limited, but clearly he considered a Court seat appropriate for his "retirement" years. Only one hurdle remained. "I can see now," his partner Edward McClennen wrote, "the expression of terror in his face when I told him that he would have to wear a silk hat. It lasted until inspiration brought him relief, and he said: 'Holmes wears a soft one.' " McClennen also reported that Brandeis saw accepting Wilson's offer as his duty as a citizen.[3]

The fireworks Alice wrote of began exploding on January 28, the day Wilson announced the nomination. They went on exploding for six months, while the nomination was fought over by a subcommittee of the Senate Judiciary Committee (established on January 31), the Judiciary Committee itself, the entire Senate, the newspapers, and a host of combatants pulling one way or another behind the scenes. Testimony before the subcommittee alone filled more than a thousand pages. There are entire scrapbooks of press clippings in the Brandeis archives, and they probably include only a portion of the vehement debate. Brandeis's nomination was one of the most controversial in the history of the Supreme Court. The public charges by those opposed, the counter-charges by Brandeis supporters, the speculation about behind-the-scenes maneuvering to affect Senators' votes—all make a lengthy and dramatic tale, which has been told elsewhere. A friend wrote to Taft, "When Brandeis' nomination came in yesterday, the Senate simply gasped . . . There wasn't any more excitement at the Capitol when Congress passed the Spanish War Resolution."[4]

Brandeis and his allies agreed that a major fight would be mounted on his behalf, but that he would play no overt part in it. On January 28, Brandeis went to a previously scheduled dinner for Wilson at the McAdoos'. Present were Justices Charles Evans Hughes, Mahlon Pitney, and James McReynolds, to whom Wilson cheerfully presented Brandeis as their next colleague. The press rushed to question him, but he said, "I have nothing whatever to say; I have not said anything and will not." Returning to Boston, he gave up lunching at the Union Club, refused to take on any new clients, and maintained a steadfast silence—athough he was far from inactive in the battle. For example, after the subcommittee hearings were over, La Follette insisted that Brandeis answer all the charges made at the hearings. "Take the hearings and make a brief for me just as if I was the man to be confirmed," La Follette urged Brandeis. "Don't ask anybody else to do this. You do it—send it to me on plain paper typewritten without any signature." Thus, in spite of his silence and although he did not complete the "brief," Brandeis's analysis of the reasons for the fireworks survives.[5]

> The dominant reasons for the opposition to the confirmation of Mr. Brandeis [wrote Brandeis] are that he is considered a radical and is a Jew. The reasons stated are mainly (1) an alleged lack of "judicial temperament," (2) an alleged undesirable "reputation" at the Boston Bar, and (3) certain alleged acts of "unprofessional" conduct. An examination of these specific acts of alleged unprofessional conduct will show not only that his action was consistent with the highest professional standards, but affords striking evidence of the possession of judicial temperament and of the high reputation in which Mr. Brandeis was perhaps universally held until malicious libels undertaken for business purposes, and in spite of them he is now generally held at the Boston Bar as well as elsewhere.[6]

Brandeis recognized that the prospect of the first Jewish Supreme Court justice inevitably brought out a good deal of latent anti-Semitism. George Wickersham, for example, who stirred up the opposition forces, included anti-Semitic remarks in his letters to Taft. But Wickersham did not need anti-Semitism as a motive; he was the attorney general whose fraudulent statements Brandeis had exposed during the Pinchot-Ballinger hearings. Taft's own letters said nothing that can be construed as anti-Semitic and, in spite of their doctrinal differences, he and Brandeis became fairly good friends during the years they served together on the Court. Some of Brandeis's Jewish opponents, professing fear that the nomination could exacerbate anti-Semitism, urged Wilson to withdraw it. Perhaps coincidentally, they were the same people—Louis Marshall, Jacob Schiff— who opposed Brandeis's organization of the American Jewish Congress.[7]

Brandeis, in fact, realized that his Jewishness had relatively little to do with the extent and depth of the outcry: a Jewish Wall Street lawyer who worked for J. P. Morgan would not have met with opposition nearly as bitter. He wrote to Alfred about the attacks on his record as a lawyer, "It is not as unpleasant to us as would seem to the outside. This attack continued throughout nine years has quite accustomed us to it and we are glad to have it out. At all events the country including Boston will know what I have been 'up against.' " The "nine years" referred to the beginning of Brandeis's assault on the New Haven. "The purpose of that stream of abuse," he wrote to his partner McClennen, "was to break down the good reputation which I had, and which was recognized as an important factor in carrying through the policies which I advocated." Senator Thomas J. Walsh of Montana, a member of the subcommittee and a key Brandeis supporter, concurred: "The real crime of which this man is guilty is that he has exposed the iniquities of men in high places in our financial system. He has not stood in awe of the majesty of wealth. He has, indeed, often represented litigants, corporate and individual, whose commercial rating was high, but his clients have not been exclusively of that class. He seems to have been sought after in causes directed against the most shining marks in it. He has been an iconoclast."[8]

Basically, the nomination became a confrontation of interests and ideologies rather than a display of prejudice. (In fact, some of Brandeis's congressional opponents feared that their opposition would be perceived incorrectly as anti-Semitic.) There is some evidence that the anti-Brandeis campaign was financed by Brandeis's old Boston foe Henry Lee Higginson. One anti-Brandeis petition, circulated by Harvard President A. Lawrence Lowell, bore such staunch Brahmin names as Adams, Sargent, Gardner, Grew, Peabody, Thorndike, Putnam, and Coolidge. Austen George Fox, a Wall Street attorney, offered to aid the subcommittee without fee, and his help was accepted. (So, in the name of fairness, was that of Brandeis partisan George Anderson.) A letter against the nomination was sent to the subcommittee by seven of the sixteen living former presidents of the American Bar Association.[9]

The other side was equally impressive. Nine of the eleven Harvard

Law School professors supported Brandeis, one opposed him, and one refused to comment. Dean Pound came out in favor of Brandeis; so did Harvard President Emeritus Eliot, who wrote to the committee that rejection of Brandeis "would be a grave misfortune for the whole legal profession, the Court, all American business, and the country." ("Next to a letter from God," McClennen said of Eliot's letter, "we have got the best.") In support of Brandeis 713 Harvard students countered Lowell's petition with one of their own. Writing to the committee or testifying before it on Brandeis's behalf were Newton D. Baker, reform mayor of Cleveland, president of the National Consumers' League, and future Secretary of War; Frances Perkins, later Franklin Roosevelt's Secretary of Labor; Henry Moskowitz; Norman Hapgood; Charles Crane; Paul Kellogg; Rabbi Stephen Wise; Amos Pinchot; and Walter Lippmann.[10]

The Reverend A. A. Berle said of the Brahmin community, "Long and unchallenged control of everything in the Commonwealth has given many of these gentlemen the perfectly natural feeling that whoever is not approved by them is ipso facto a person who is either 'dangerous' or lacking in 'judicial temperament' . . . They simply cannot realize, and do not, that a long New England ancestry is not prima facie a trusteeship for everything in New England. That is in my judgment the real spring of most of the opposition." Of the 620 letters the committee received from Massachusetts lawyers, only 8 of those originating outside of Boston were negative, and the White House got a continuing stream of pro-Brandeis mail from unions and their members. Ironically, Senator Henry Cabot Lodge, who encouraged the Bar Association to fight against the nomination, was lobbied on Brandeis's behalf by his own nephew, Ellerton James, who had worked with Brandeis during the Washington Street subway fight. The differing opinions of uncle and nephew were symbolic: Lodge exemplified the past; James's support of Brandeis represented the future of both American politics and American law.[11]

But the future is sometimes brought about only with great difficulty. The fight was brutal, and although he took no public part in it, Brandeis was very much at its center. By February 1 he had begun to mount his campaign. One of his first actions was to fire off two letters to Hapgood, the first naming prominent lawyers and jurists around the country who could be counted upon to write favorable letters, the second listing sympathetic "prominent Jews." Hapgood, La Follette, and Gregory had become an informal campaign committee, which would gradually be complemented and to some extent supplanted by Brandeis's partner Edward McClennen, George Anderson, and Felix Frankfurter. McClennen moved to Washington for the duration of the battle and acted as an information conduit. He told Brandeis that Progressives like La Follette and Hapgood would have to maintain a low profile. Attorney General Gregory was insistent that the nomination appear as a Democratic move, not a Progressive one. He was equally certain that Southern Democrats would be offended by organized Jewish action. Brandeis went to Washington on February 2 and conferred with Anderson and Gregory. They decided that Brandeis should stay out of Washington during the hearings. From Boston on February 12 Brandeis wrote Alfred a thoroughly misleading letter: "I am leaving the fight to others . . . But the fight that has come up shows clearly that my instinct that I could not afford to decline was correct. It would have been, in effect, deserting the progressive forces. Now my feeling is rather—'Go it husband, Go it bear' with myself as 'interested spectator.' "[12]

Far from emulating the wife who loved a good fight so much that she remained impartial, Brandeis was already fighting hard for himself. On the same day that he wrote to his brother, Brandeis, at Anderson's request, sent McClennen a letter about some of the litigation in which he had been involved. On the previous day he had sent McClennen three detailed letters with information about his handling of three other cases. His actions in them had been criticized before the subcommittee by a hostile witness, whom Brandeis identified to McClennen as having received funds in the past from the New Haven. On February 13 Brandeis asked his office "to ascertain to what extent I personally have had any professional relations with each & any of the 55 alleged signers of the [Lowell petition] within the past 20 years" and to follow his partner Nutter's suggestion that the identity of each as a Boston Brahmin be made public. As other matters came up in testimony, Brandeis wrote to McClennen as often as four times a day. He also kept Louise Malloch busy pulling out files and supplying ammunition to Anderson and Frankfurter.[13]

To his supporters from all over the country who asked what they could do, Brandeis wrote as he did to efficiency expert Harrington Emerson: "The circumstances are such that it has seemed proper for me not to take any part in the present fight at Washington. I understand that many men who think as you do have written letters to Senator William E. Chilton, Chairman of the Sub-committee, expressing their views." The recipients of such letters were of course expected to do likewise. Felix Frankfurter worked with former Governor Robert P. Bass of New Hampshire on a letter-writing campaign. Frankfurter would surely have checked with Brandeis first; indeed, at one point Brandeis vetoed a suggestion by Bass that the Progressive Republican appear at the hearings.[14]

Brandeis had learned too much about the power of the press to ignore its possibilities during the battle for the Court seat. Frankfurter wrote unsigned editorials for the *New Republic* urging confirmation. The *New*

Republic, in fact, published a steady stream of support for Brandeis, who told editor Herbert Croly, "I feel almost as if you and your associates must carry the responsibility." Walter Lippmann charged in the *New Republic*, following Lowell's petition, that Brandeis had been found untrustworthy only by "the powerful but limited community which dominated the business and social life of Boston. He was untrustworthy because he was troublesome. He was disloyal, if at all, to a group. All the smoke of ill-repute which had been gathered around Mr. Brandeis originated in the group psychology of these gentlemen." Lippmann's article was prompted in part by an analysis made in Brandeis's office of the interlocking business and social connections among the signers of the Lowell petition; Brandeis saw that Lippmann (addressed, by the man who rarely used first names, as "My dear Walter") received a copy of the analysis and of a newspaper article in which some reputed signers denied having been involved with the petition.[15]

When Taft and the other former Bar Association presidents issued their statement, Brandeis saw an opportunity to remind the public of what he considered to be Taft's hypocrisy in the Pinchot-Ballinger affair. Frankfurter talked with Lippmann, who promptly wrote a devastating editorial for the *New Republic*, and he urged Hapgood to work with others "to bring out these matters clearly in the dailies as well as the periodicals." The result, within two weeks, was a slew of hard-hitting editorials in Hapgood's *Harper's Weekly*, an article by Florence Kelley in Paul Kellogg's *Survey*, and a syndicated article by Gilson Gardner. Brandeis and McClennen considered writing a "brief" to counter one sent out by Austen Fox. Recognizing that it should not appear to be his own work or that of his associates, Brandeis suggested that it appear in *Harper's* or the *New Republic*. The plan was abandoned, but Brandeis's partner George R. Nutter did write a long statement that was published by the *New York World*, a newspaper sympathetic to Brandeis since the days of the insurance investigations. Another source of support was the *Independent*, whose managing editor Hamilton Holt had worked with Brandeis on savings bank insurance and on the garment workers' protocol. When Brandeis's confirmation was finally voted by the Senate he wrote to Holt, "The struggle was a long one, and in it you and The Independent played a notable part."[16]

Hapgood, Rabbi Wise, and Henry Morgenthau had strategy sessions in New York almost every day. Morgenthau, looking toward the Senate with which Wilson would have to work after the 1916 election, at one point came up with the amazing idea that Brandeis should reject the Court appointment after confirmation and run for the Senate against Henry Cabot Lodge. But he worked tirelessly for the confirmation and became a conduit to Colonel House, who told Morgenthau that some Southern senators were afraid that Brandeis would try to undo the separate but equal doctrine.[17]

On April 1, the subcommittee voted favorably, 3–2, but the issue quickly became bogged down in the full committee. It was composed of ten Democrats and eight Republicans, which meant that two defections from the Democratic side would be fatal. Both sides, unsure of how the voting would go, acted to delay. This infuriated Brandeis who was well aware that Congress would adjourn before the Republican national convention on June 3. Accordingly, he went to New York on May 4, supposedly for a Zionist meeting, and met with Hapgood, Wise, and Nutter. Anderson had urged Attorney General Gregory two days before to solicit a statement from President Wilson. Now Hapgood traveled to Washington to push for the statement. Gregory gave Wilson a three-page memorandum, and it was arranged that Senator Charles A. Culberson, head of the Judiciary Committee, would formally ask Wilson to explain his reasons for making the nomination. On May 8, Senator Culberson read Wilson's nine-paragraph letter into the committee record. "I am profoundly interested in the confirmation of the appointment," Wilson had written. Rejecting the charges against Brandeis as "intrinsically incredible," praising the "singularly enlightening, singularly clear-sighted and judicial" advice, "full of moral stimulation" that he had gotten from Brandeis, citing Brandeis's "extraordinary ability as a lawyer," his "fairness and love of justice," and his "impartial, impersonal, orderly, and constructive mind," Wilson reminded the committee (and particularly its Democrats) that he was thoroughly committed to the nomination and had a personal interest in its fate: "I knew from direct personal knowledge of the man what I was doing when I named him for the highest and most responsible tribunal of the nation." On May 14, when it appeared that the votes of two Democratic members of the committee might be decisive, Hapgood invited them to his Washington apartment for an informal Sunday evening. Brandeis unexpectedly met them there, and the previously uncommitted Senators were persuaded to vote for him.[18]

On May 24 the Judiciary Committee voted for confirmation on a strict party basis, 10–8. The full Senate followed suit on June 1, 47–22, with only one Democrat leaving the fold. And that evening, when Brandeis got home from the office, Alice conveyed the good news with "Good evening, Mr. Justice Brandeis."[19]

Brandeis's behavior during the Court confirmation fight differed considerably from his behavior while he was being considered for the Wilson cabinet in 1912. In both instances he claimed, even to his brother, to be sitting back and letting events take their course. But although in 1912

he did precisely that, in 1916 he did not. Brandeis wanted to go on the
Court, but he had been ambivalent about a cabinet position. Becoming
a Justice would not take him away from the law; it would not limit his
activities in Zionism and in policymaking; but it would enable him to
assume the slower pace that his always worrisome health and his age
now seemed to demand. Ultimately, it would also permit him to implement his ideas about what law was and should be. Coincidentally, it was
on the day after Justice Lamar died that Brandeis had given his speech
on "The Living Law" to the Chicago Bar Association. He had spoken
of how he thought lawyers could make the law relevant; now he could
show the country a judge's contribution.[20]

Wilson was also pleased by the confirmation. "I never signed any
commission with such satisfaction as I signed his," he told Morgenthau.
Wilson's naming of a leading Progressive to the Court would help placate
Progressives disappointed with the performance of Justice McReynolds—
Progressives whose votes would be needed in the November election. In
addition, Wilson admired and relied on Brandeis and would continue to
do so. Hapgood reported going to see Wilson about the Court's next
vacancy (when Justice Hughes resigned to run for the presidency). "I can
never live up to my Brandeis appointment," Wilson told Hapgood. "There
is nobody else who represents the greatest technical ability and professional success with complete devotion to the people's interest."[21]

On June 5 Brandeis left the Lafayette Hotel in Washington to ride to
the Supreme Court's chambers (then in the Senate building) with Chief
Justice Edward Douglass White. In the justices' private robing room
White administered the oath of allegiance to the Constitution; the justices
then proceeded into the packed courtroom. Brandeis's wife, daughters,
and brother were among the spectators who watched him recite the
justices' oath of office. He had embarked on a new career; and a new
era of jurisprudence had begun.[22]

There were numerous details to be seen to as Brandeis took his seat on
the Court. He answered the congratulatory letters and telegrams that
had poured in—two hundred on the day of his installation alone. He
resigned from membership in organizations that might conflict or give
the appearance of conflicting with his new office: the National Economic
League, the Utilities Bureau, the garment trade's Conciliation Council,
the Hebrew Sheltering and Immigrant Aid Society. He also resigned from
many Boston-based organizations: the City Club, the Exchange Club,
the Union Boat Club, the Social Law Library, the Boston Bar Association,
the Massachusetts Bar Association, and the Massachusetts Civil Service
Association. Initially he retained his membership and offices in Zionist

organizations, but criticism from Jewish opponents quickly made him realize the impossibility of that course (although he retained his position of leadership in the movement).[23]

Brandeis was concerned that his investments (worth two million dollars) might present a conflict of interests and discussed the matter with Chief Justice White as they rode to the Capitol for the installation ceremonies. Brandeis had always insisted on investing his money in "safe," relatively low-yield railroad and public utility bonds, in part because he treated his fortune as a trust to be managed conservatively during his lifetime and passed on to public causes after his death. He also saw such investments as freeing him from any potential conflict when he became interested in a private case or public matter. Brandeis proposed to leave management of his money in the capable hands of Louise Malloch, where it had been for some time. The chief justice agreed that this would present no ethical problems. Brandeis, of course, resigned from his law firm, collecting his 30.47 percent of the fees charged by the firm up until June 1.[24]

The Court adjourned a week after Brandeis was sworn in. He returned to Boston, took a month to see to various details, attended the July 16 Zionist conference in New York, then vacationed with his family in South Yarmouth. Early in October the Brandeises moved to Washington, renting an apartment on fashionable Connecticut Avenue in a large complex called Stoneleigh Court. The street, with its broad sidewalks and double rows of sycamore trees, had, according to Dean Acheson, the feel of "a small, gangling southern city." The basement of Stoneleigh Court boasted a barber shop, where Brandeis went surreptitiously twice a week for an "invisible haircut"; Mrs. Brandeis preferred his hair long. Justice Holmes lived a bit more than a block away, and Brandeis and Holmes would go walking together regularly until Holmes's age turned their walks into automobile rides through Virginia. Mr. Justice Brandeis had begun to settle into Washington.[25]

"It is hardly likely that anyone came to the Supreme Court with a more closely articulated set of convictions than those which Brandeis held," a former law clerk and leading Brandeis scholar has written. Wilson's appointment of Brandeis was both a part and a symbol of what they hoped was the changing of the old order. Brandeis took to the Court not only many of the tenets of progressivism but also a new jurisprudence and set of convictions forged by his experiences as the "People's Attorney." Theodore Roosevelt had commented that the presidency was a "bully pulpit"; now Brandeis would demonstrate that the Court could also be an effective educational forum. He would use Court opinions to

educate legal and political policymakers. First, however, he had to develop a working relationship with his colleagues, so that the movement
for the "living law" and industrial democracy could be spearheaded by
the Court. His years on the Court would find him drawing upon his skills
as an educator, advocate, and politician.[26]

It would be misleading, however, to give the impression that Brandeis
ignored judicial proprieties in service of his goals for society. Brandeis
joined the Court determined to instruct the justices and the country in a
key element of sociological jurisprudence: judicial restraint. Such judge-
made doctrines as liberty of contract, which Brandeis had had to wrestle
with in the minimum wage and maximum hours cases, were, in his eyes,
undemocratic; social policy should be made by legislatures, not judges.
If Brandeis read a case as asking the Court to render an abstract opinion
on a matter not ripe for decision—one, for example, in which there was
no real conflict between litigants—he insisted that the Court had to be
silent. For example, when Arizona sued to prevent the construction of
the Boulder Dam, claiming that it might lead to Arizona waters being
diverted to California, construction of the dam had not yet begun. "Years
must elapse before the project is completed . . . There is no occasion for
determining now Arizona's right to interstate or local waters which have
not yet been, and which may never be, appropriated," Brandeis told
Arizona. But when a case did present a real controversy that could be
decided on either constitutional or statutory grounds, Brandeis demanded
that the Court follow its own rule and render a decision on the basis of
a statute unless a constitutional determination was absolutely necessary.
Where litigation involved interpretation of state and local laws and the
lower courts had not rendered such an interpretation, it was improper
for the Supreme Court to do so; the case had to be remanded to the local
courts, which the Court believed to be in the best position to understand
local law.[27]

Judicial restraint also required judges to consider the consequences of
creating new rights—a matter preferably left to legislatures. In 1918 the
Associated Press challenged the right of the International News Service
to copy its foreign news dispatches, claiming that it had a property right
in the dispatches. No such property right had been recognized by American legislatures, and Brandeis disagreed with the Court's decision that
such a right existed. What, he asked, were the limitations on such a right?
Under what conditions should news gathered by a private agency be
considered "affected with a public interest" and thereby subject to government regulation? The Court ruling, in other words, created an undefined right, usurping the legislative function: "the creation or recognition
by courts of a new private right may work serious injury to the general

public, unless the boundaries of the right are definitely established and wisely guarded . . . Courts would be powerless to prescribe the detailed regulations essential to full enjoyment of the rights conferred or to introduce the machinery required for enforcement of such regulations. Considerations such as these should lead us to decline to establish a new rule of law in the effort to redress a newly-disclosed wrong, although the propriety of some remedy appears to be clear."[28]

It might be argued that Brandeis's dissent in the Associated Press case reflected his prejudice in favor of the widest possible dissemination of news. His dissent from what amounted to the Court's creation of a new category of untaxable property stock dividends might similarly be viewed as a reflection of his bias, particularly as his opinion attacked the machinations of the money trust (in *Eisner* v. *Macomber*). But he opposed unnecessary judicial intervention even when it clearly ran counter to his beliefs, which helps explain why even those who disagreed with Brandeis considered him a great lawyer. ("My, how I detest that man's ideas," said Justice George Sutherland, one of Brandeis's opponents on the Court and the author of the Court's opinion in *New State Ice Company* v. *Liebmann*. "But he is one of the greatest technical lawyers I have ever known.")[29]

In *New State* a 1925 Oklahoma law required that, before any new ice company could begin manufacturing and selling ice, it had to acquire a certificate of public convenience and necessity from the state, in order to limit wasteful duplication of plants and delivery service, which resulted in higher costs passed on to consumers. The New State Ice Company obtained such a certificate; Liebmann ignored the statute and set up a competitive plant without a license. When New State sued Liebmann, the state courts ruled that the statute violated the Fourteenth Amendment, depriving citizens of their property without due process of law.

The majority of the Supreme Court agreed. The ice business, Justice Sutherland wrote for the majority, was not "affected with a public interest," and Oklahoma's law was no more than a device for creating monopoly. In light of Brandeis's consistent support of competition, it seemed logical that he would agree. Instead, in a brilliant dissent, he argued that the law represented legitimate state experimentation that should not be undermined by the Court. In fourteen heavily footnoted pages he explored the social conditions that had led Oklahoma to pass the law (and other states to enact similar legislation). Oklahoma was hard-struck by the Depression; employment and prices had both plummeted. There were more goods being produced than consumers could afford to buy. Brandeis quoted the mean normal temperature each month in Oklahoma, showing the need for ice; the dependence of industries and retail dealers on ice; the lack of refrigerators and their cost as against the lower cost of ice.[30]

"The people of the United States are now confronted with an emergency more serious than war," he declared. "Some people believe that the existing conditions threaten even the stability of the capitalistic system. Economists are searching for the causes of this disorder and are re-examining the basis of our industrial structure." Slipping in his own view, he went on, "Most of them realize that failure to distribute widely the profits of industry has been a prime cause of our present plight." But, his own view notwithstanding, "rightly or wrongly, many persons think that one of the major contributing causes has been unbridled competition. Increasingly, doubt is expressed whether it is economically wise, or morally right, that men should be permitted to add to the producing facilities of an industry which is already suffering from over-capacity." He repeated another of his strongly held beliefs: "All agree that irregularity in employment—the greatest of our evils—cannot be overcome unless production and consumption are more nearly balanced." There were many plans for achieving this goal, one of which was embodied in the Oklahoma law. "Whether that view is sound nobody knows." The only indication that Brandeis disliked the Oklahoma "experiment" was a paragraph noting that the law had its dangers, including the demands of the project on human intelligence and character. "Man is weak and his judgment is at best fallible."[31]

It was clear that the great technological advances of the past two centuries were due to experimentation. "Some people assert that our present plight is due, in part, to the limitations set by courts upon experimentation in the fields of social and economic science . . . There must be power in the States and the Nation to remould, through experimentation, our economic practices and institutions to meet changing social and economic needs." Brandeis was not ready to insist that others share his faith in competition and profit sharing as basic remedies for economic distress, nor did the Court have the right to choose among remedies. The limitations of the human mind meant that there could be no progress without experimentation: "To stay experimentation in things social and economic is a grave responsibility" which might be "fraught with serious consequences to the nation." The glory of federalism was the ability of a state to serve as a laboratory for social change. "This Court has the power to prevent an experiment . . . But in the exercise of this high power, we must be ever on our guard, lest we erect our prejudices into legal principles." And Brandeis ended with one of his most cherished beliefs: "If we would guide by the light of reason, we must let our minds be bold."[32]

At every major point, Brandeis cited a host of sources: thirty-seven books, articles, reports, scholarly papers, and congressional hearings, including articles from *New Republic,* the *Survey Graphic,* The *Yale Review,* the *Political Quarterly,* the *Yale Law Journal, Mechanical Engineering, The Nation's Business, Christian Century,* and the *Saturday Evening Post.* If legislatures had accumulated enough evidence to argue that they had acted reasonably, the Court should not interfere, even if it meant revising its category of "business affected with a public interest."[33]

There were other cases in which Brandeis's insistence on the Court's respect for federalism and experimentation led him to decisions which conflicted with his expressed beliefs. Thus, he wrote an opinion saying the Court could not interfere with a state law that prevented an orphan from receiving support from her father; joined in another that prevented an injured workman from receiving workmen's compensation; and wrote a third that prevented a widow from collecting her deceased husband's insurance policy. In each case, the part of the Constitution involved was the section of Article IV that requires each state to give "full faith and credit" to the laws of other states. Brandeis viewed the clause as a means of strengthening the ties among states while retaining the individuality of each and felt that it had to be upheld by the Court in service of a harmonious federalism.[34]

It was Brandeis's strong conviction that the rules regarding the Court's jurisdiction—the circumstances under which it could hear and decide cases—were of great importance, because they kept that body from overstepping its legitimate boundaries. Members of the Court had been elected by no one; they were not accountable, in the sense of not having to run for reelection; they were more removed than the other branches of government from the public and its wishes. This was as it should be, if the Court was to render objective and occasionally unpopular opinions, but it also meant that the Court had to restrain itself from undue involvement in the policymaking process. If judicial self-restraint meant that judges had to vote against their political predilections when a case came before them, then they were doing no more than their duty. If democracy was to survive, jurisdictional rules had to be followed meticulously.

Under the American system of judicial review, the constitutionality of laws is frequently in question until the Supreme Court renders a decision, so various artificial devices for bringing laws before that body have been devised. For example, if a corporation opposes a tax, it may arrange to have itself sued by one of its own stockholders, who asks the courts to enjoin the company from misusing his or her money to pay an allegedly unconstitutional tax. Or a business opposing legislation designed to protect labor (for example, a minimum wage law) may have an employee ask the courts to enjoin enforcement of the law on the grounds that it violates his or her right to contract freely with the employer. Brandeis considered such "friendly" proceedings an unacceptable fiction, in violation of the requirement that the Court hear only cases involving real controversies. He adhered to this rule even when it meant destruction of a law he supported.[35]

Such was the situation with federal child labor laws. In 1918 when the Court held unconstitutional the federal law prohibiting the shipment in interstate commerce of articles produced by child labor (*Hammer* v. *Dagenhart*), Brandeis joined in Justice Holmes's dissent. Congress attempted to circumvent the 1918 decision by enacting a statute that imposed a 10 percent tax on all profits of businesses that employed children under sixteen for more than eight hours a day, six days a week, or at night. A Mr. Johnston and his son, between fourteen and sixteen years old, asked a federal district court to enjoin the Atherton Mills from discharging the boy, which the mills were allegedly about to do in order to avoid the tax. The Johnstons claimed that by depriving them of the son's earnings, the new law was unconstitutionally taking their property in violation of the Fifth Amendment. The lower court agreed that the law was unconstitutional, and the case was appealed to the Supreme Court.[36]

Brandeis promptly wrote a "Memorandum," arguing that the Court had no jurisdiction over the case because it was trumped-up; the parties were in collusion. In *Hammer* v. *Dagenhart*, the earlier child labor case, government officials had been threatening to enforce the statute by confiscating the business's goods; here, no threatened government action was involved, and the Court had long held that federal courts could not interfere with the right of an employer to dismiss an employee. By the time the Court's decision was handed down in 1922, Chief Justice Taft could call it moot: the boy had turned sixteen and the Act could no longer be a reason for discharging him. In the interim, however, another case, *Bailey* v. *Drexel*, had been properly brought under the Act, and the Court had declared the Act unconstitutional. Brandeis's Memorandum was never published by the Court.[37]

As Alexander Bickel has shown in his brilliant examination of some of Brandeis's unpublished opinions for the Court, early drafts of Brandeis's Memorandum make it clear that he considered the Act constitutional. One sentence read, "If I believed that this Court had jurisdiction . . . in this proceeding . . . I should have no difficulty in holding the act valid . . . for the reason expressed in the dissent by Mr. Justice Holmes in Hammer v. Dagenhart . . . in which I joined." And of course his pre-Court history in the labor movement indicates his personal distaste for the use of child labor. Nonetheless, judicial self-restraint was more important than any immediate social gain, and the Court should not decide the case.[38]

Brandeis knew that Progressives saw the Court as a bastion of entrenched privilege. He had long been disturbed by the growing disrespect for law and courts and recognized that to a great extent the courts had created the disrespect by refusing to acknowledge "felt necessities" and by substituting their own judgments about social policy for that of the people and their legislatures. However, he disagreed with La Follette, who had earlier espoused recall of judges and who, in response to the child labor decision, called for a constitutional amendment stripping the lower federal courts of their power of judicial review and permitting Congress to override Supreme Court decisions. (The extent of the Progressives' disaffection with the Court may be seen in the support of the La Follette proposal by such Brandeis allies as Florence Kelley and Samuel Gompers.) Brandeis understood the discontent and viewed it with the objectivity of the historian. Writing to Frankfurter after the Court handed down *Bailey*, he commented, "About every really important decision (at least in the early days), gave rise to some proposal of the disappointed class to amend the Constitution." A few months later he added,

> The remedy for the prevailing discontent with USSC must be sought:
>
> 1. In refraining from all constitutional dicta.
> 2. In refusing to consider a constitutional question except in "cases" or "controversies"—"initiated according to the regular course of judicial procedure"
> 3. In refusing to pass on constitutional questions if the case can be disposed of on any other
> 4. In refusing to hold an act void unless it clearly exceeds powers conferred etc.[39]

Judicial restraint would not only make the Court more fit to take its place in a democratic system, but it would also enhance respect for law and legal institutions, without which a society was condemned to anarchy and injustice.

There were other dramatic examples of Brandeis's adhering to jurisdictional rules even when doing so forced him to an uncomfortable position. For example, in *Whitney* v. *California* Brandeis penned an eloquent defense of freedom of speech and association in a democratic society (see Chapter 15). But because Whitney's attorneys had not raised in the trial court the question of whether her actions constituted the "clear and present danger" to society that Brandeis accepted as the only circumstance permitting the government to interfere with the rights of speech and assembly, Brandeis said, "Our power of review in this case is limited not only to the question whether a right guaranteed by the Federal Constitution was denied . . . but to the particular claims duly made below, and denied." Because the Court lacked the power to correct such "vital errors" made in state trial courts, Brandeis felt himself forced to concur with the Court's decision, upholding the conviction.[40]

The most explicit statement by Brandeis of what he considered to be the limits on judicial review of constitutional matters came in another concurrence in 1936. The specifics of the case, involving the power of the Tennessee Valley Authority to construct the Wheeler Dam were less important to Brandeis than that the case was gotten into court by a stockholder's suit. The Court held the project to be constitutionally valid. Brandeis concurred, saying that he would not have reached the constitutional issue because the plaintiffs had no real standing to sue. Then, quoting earlier Court decisions, he spelled out what he believed to be the rules the Court had developed (and should adhere to) when constitutional questions were raised:

The Court will not pass upon the constitutionality of legislation in a friendly, non-adversary, proceeding . . . The Court will not "anticipate a question of constitutional law in advance of the necessity of deciding it" . . . The Court will not "formulate a rule of constitutional law broader than is required by the precise facts to which it is to be applied" . . . The Court will not pass upon a constitutional question . . . if there is also present some other ground upon which the case may be disposed of . . . The Court will not pass upon the validity of a statute upon complaint of one who fails to show that he is injured by its operation . . . The Court will not pass upon the constitutionality of a statute at the instance of one who has availed himself of its benefits . . . "When the validity of an act of the Congress is drawn in question . . . this Court will first ascertain whether a construction of the statute is fairly possible by which the question may be avoided."[41]

The praise Sutherland expressed for Brandeis's legal capabilities was echoed by other members of the bar. Walton Hamilton, for example, wrote that Brandeis "is probably the best technical lawyer on his bench." But Brandeis knew more than legal niceties. Holmes had predicted that the lawyer of the future would be the master of economics and statistics, and as Felix Frankfurter commented in 1932, "Hardly another lawyer had amassed experience over so wide a range and with so firm a grip on the details that matter." The admiration of lawyers for Justice Brandeis was enhanced by his impact upon such seemingly arcane fields as railroad regulation, the evaluation of utilities, depreciation rules, the basis on which the Court would calculate appropriate rates to be charged by railroads and utilities, and administrative law. The legal profession was stirred by his jurisprudence; the public, by the concrete results of it. His jurisprudence was based on utilization of facts in service of the "living law"; the results were support for federalism, unionization, protective social legislation, government involvement in the economy, and civil liberties.[42]

16 | Law and Civil Liberties

Justice Oliver Wendell Holmes, Jr., was delighted when Brandeis donned the robes of the Supreme Court. At last, another advocate of sociological jurisprudence would join him in attacking the Court's interference with legislative experiments (see Chapter 8). Holmes and Brandeis did vote together far more often than not, and the phrase "Holmes and Brandeis, dissenting" quickly became a feature of Court decisions. The friendship between the two men and the similar votes they cast led Chief Justice Taft to exclaim, "I am very fond of the old gentleman, but he is so completely under the control of Brother Brandeis that it gives to Brandeis two votes instead of one." Holmes seems to have been aware that Taft's view was generally shared, for just a few months before Taft made his comment, Holmes had written to Frederick Pollock about Brandeis, "I am glad that he dissents from the only opinion I have to deliver. It will indicate that there is no preestablished harmony between us."[1]

Taft's comment was unfair to Holmes; and the general perception that Holmes and Brandeis shared an approach to law and society was quite wrong. Brandeis found the key to jurisprudence in facts. Holmes found it in philosophy. Brandeis recalled having told Holmes "that if he really wants to 'improve his mind' (as he always speaks of it), the way to do it is not to read more philosophic books . . . but to get some sense of the world of fact. And he asked me to map out some reading—he became much interested—and I told him that I'd . . . get some books, that books could carry him only so far, and that then he should get some exhibits from life. I suggested the textile industry, and told him in vacation time he is near Lawrence and Lowell and he should go there and look about. He became much interested . . . but very unfortunately it was the time when Mrs. Holmes was very sick, and he had her on his mind . . . And so he reported to me, very apologetically, in the fall his inability to pursue the study." Holmes's version of the incident was entirely different in tone. He wrote to Pollock, "Brandeis the other day drove a harpoon into my midriff with reference to my summer occupations. He said 'you talk about improving your mind, you only exercise it on the subjects with which you are familiar. Why don't you try something new, study some domain of fact. Take up the textile industries in Massachusetts and after reading the reports sufficiently you can go to Lawrence and get a human notion of how it really is.' " But then Holmes grumbled to Pollock, "I hate facts. I always say the chief end of man is to form general propositions—adding that no general proposition is worth a damn . . . I have little doubt that it would be good for my immortal soul to plunge into them [facts] . . . but I shrink from the bore."[2]

The difference in the accounts reflects the difference in the way the two friends saw law and life. Brandeis was always the educator, certain that progress could be made—in this case, in the education of his colleague—through mastery of data. Holmes considered such data irrelevant to both law and individual beliefs. What mattered were great philosophies that transcended specific circumstances. Brandeis told Frankfurter, "[Holmes] has said many things in their ultimate terms, and as new instances arise they just fit in." For Brandeis philosophy was "the cyclone cellar for finer souls" as the monasteries had been during the Dark Ages; that is, philosophy was a hiding place: "In our Democracy, the hopeful sign would be recognition of politics & government as the first of the sciences & of the arts." He considered it "a very bad sign" that Will Durant's *Story of Philosophy* was a best seller. Holmes, in turn, told Frankfurter, "I have just received a typewritten report of the U.S. Coal Commission. Brandeis would be deep in it at once. I turn to Sainte-Beuve."[3]

Holmes had once said that the life of the law is not logic, it is experience—but he saw no reason to involve himself in the experiences that culminated in new laws, feeling that most of them were a waste of time. He was a social Darwinist who believed that, left to themselves, the "fittest" human beings would survive, propagate, and bring about progress. He wrote to Brandeis, "Generally speaking, I agree with you in liking to see social experiments tried but I do so without enthusiasm because I believe it is merely shifting the pressure and that so long as we have free propagation Malthus is right in his general view." Holmes viewed American democracy as the right of the people to do whatever they wanted, within the generous confines of a largely vague Constitution. He would, therefore, oppose judicial interference with experimentation but did not care particularly what the experiments were about. Writing again to Frankfurter, he said, "[Brandeis] always desires to know all that can be known about a case whereas I am afraid that I wish to know as little as I can safely go on." Confronted with a case of legislative experimentation, Holmes asked only whether there was anything in the Constitution that reasonable people would agree explicitly prohibited it. Brandeis asked instead whether reasonable people, looking at the factual context, would agree that it was a rational (if not necessarily a good) approach to the problem.[4]

Holmes was the detached, cynical observer; Brandeis, the deeply involved reformer. While clerking for Brandeis, David Riesman said that Holmes's opinions "merely told how not to interpret the Constitution," whereas Brandeis "has tried . . . to lay the ground work of a pattern of constitutional interpretation." Riesman told Frankfurter that "Holmes was skeptical of action and thought but seemed to have faith in the inevitable,—Brandeis is skeptical of power and of human abilities but he does not believe that things are inevitable. With Holmes, actions are paralyzed, nor would he try to prevent the action of others which are merely the inevitable coming to pass. Justice Brandeis is not so absolute,— he does not believe that human beings are the prey of unconquerable forces. As you say, he puts his trust in reason but a skepticism of power and human limitations lies at the bottom of his constitutional philosophy." It was perhaps Brandeis's belief in the possible—his insistence that people and their actions could make a difference—that made him an acceptable prophet both to his young law clerks and to the reformist New Freedom and New Deal administrations. Although Brandeis's roots were in part European, while Holmes was the quintessential Boston Brahmin, Brandeis's pragmatism was much closer to the mainstream of American political thought and Holmes's detachment more reminiscent of the European penchant for ideology.[5]

Although Holmes insisted that the "felt necessities" were the true stimulus of law and that judges had to recognize that truth, he did not show judges how to ascertain the felt necessities. This was Brandeis's role. He taught judges that it was their duty to undertake independent fact-gathering before they rendered constitutional judgments. The reasonableness of state regulations, Brandeis wrote, "can ordinarily be determined only by a consideration of the contemporary conditions, social, industrial and political, of the community to be affected thereby. Resort to such facts is necessary, among other things, in order to appreciate the evils sought to be remedied and the possible effects of the remedy proposed." The competing claims of public needs and private desires were to be weighed in light of the experiences of other states and nations, as well as the context in which the law was passed.[6]

Counsel frequently did not provide the justices with the requisite facts, so the Court had to accumulate such material for itself. Brandeis disagreed with the Court's overturning of a Nebraska law that set weight standards for commercially sold loaves of bread on the ground that it took bakers' and dealers' property without due process of law and lectured his brethren on how they should have gone about making their decision: "Unless we know the facts on which the legislators may have acted, we cannot properly decide whether they were . . . unreasonable, arbitrary or capricious." Here, Brandeis said, the Court had "merely to acquaint ourselves with the art of breadmaking and the usages of the trade; with the devices by which buyers of bread are imposed upon and honest bakers or dealers are subjected by their dishonest fellows to unfair competition; with the problems which have confronted public officials charged with the enforcement of the laws prohibiting short weights, and with their experience in administering those laws." And Brandeis set about performing this "mere" task with his usual gusto, presenting the Court with fifteen pages of information about the baking industry, most of it in lengthy and forbidding footnotes. Holmes would have told the Court no more than that the statute violated no constitutional provision on its face and therefore had to be presumed constitutional, without feeling the need to immerse himself in data about the baking industry.[7]

Brandeis used facts to sustain laws with which he agreed. Arguing in another opinion that a state could seek to control the cutthroat competition that existed in the lumber business, Brandeis praised the encouragement of exchange of information among lumber mills—a function he had maintained that the Federal Trade Commission ought to perform for industry on a national level. A case involving a producer of gramophones became the occasion for Brandeis's reiteration of his contention that the setting of prices by a small manufacturer prepared to stand behind his product might be necessary to prevent his being driven out of business by trusts and was not comparable to the unacceptable collusion on prices by large corporations. A challenge to Oklahoma's law favoring farmers' cooperatives over individuals in the competition to receive a cotton gin license led Brandeis to write a short history of the cooperative movement in the United States and praise its aim of "economic democracy on lines of liberty, equality and fraternity." But even when he disliked a state's action, as in Oklahoma's limitation on competition so as to achieve economic health in the ice industry, he reluctantly concluded that social facts could lead reasonable lawmakers to consider the legislation necessary. He would use facts to encourage state experimentation; not to strike it down.[8]

Holmes and Brandeis usually voted the same way on the Court because Holmes read the Constitution as precluding very few experiments, and Brandeis tried to read the experimental statutes with the eyes of their writers. However, they sometimes disagreed; for example, when the Court was asked to consider the constitutionality of Pennsylvania's Kohler Act, which forbade the mining of anthracite coal in such a manner as to cause the subsidence of a home. A coal company, which had sold land on which a house was subsequently built, had reserved its rights under the land. The company, decades later, gave notice that it wished to mine under the house, but was enjoined by the state courts on the grounds that to do so would violate the recently enacted Kohler Act. The company argued that the state was in effect taking its property without compensation, in violation of the Fourteenth Amendment's due process clause. Holmes, writing for the Court, agreed. Brandeis, sole dissenter, wrote that such protection of individual safety was a legitimate exercise of the state's police power. Holmes replied that the state had made a contract when it awarded mining rights to the company, and that if the public's representatives "have been so short sighted as to acquire only surface rights without the right of support," that was the public's problem. The state was choosing to elevate one person's property right over that of another, which it could not do without compensation. Brandeis disagreed that the problem was the state's taking sides in a dispute between two private interests. Rather, the state was invoking its power to protect its interest in maintaining private as well as public buildings (which were also covered by the Act).[9]

To Holmes, the due process clause was controlling. And clearly, Holmes's disdain for the property buyer's failure to look ahead when signing his contract was a factor influencing his decision. Brandeis wrote to Frankfurter, "There are indications that Benjamin is accentuating the tendency of age to conservatism." He added in a later conversation that he accounted for Holmes's opinion "by what one would think Holmes is last man to yield to—class bias. He came back to views not of his manhood but childhood . . . Here is Holmes in a case where you would have thought he above all men could be insured against reaching the result he did." A "heightened respect for property," Brandeis concluded sadly, "has been part of Holmes's growing old." But it was not Holmes's age that led to their differing votes; it was Brandeis's inclination to validate legislative experimentation in the area of the police power when the facts led him to believe the legislation could be considered reasonable.[10]

Similarly, although they both dissented, the approaches of Brandeis and Holmes to *Truax* v. *Corrigan*, which involved state injunctions against picketing in labor disputes, were quite different. Brandeis asked whether the law was reasonable and based his answer on fourteen pages of citations showing that others had found similar laws reasonable under similar circumstances. Holmes's two-page dissent was a legal argument, not a factual one, and ended, "There is nothing that I more deprecate than the use of the Fourteenth Amendment beyond the absolute compulsion of its words to prevent the making of social experiments that an important part of the community desires, in the insulated chambers afforded by the several States, even though the experience may seem futile or even noxious to me and to those whose judgment I most respect." At a first glance, this might sound like Brandeis. Brandeis's tactic, however, was to show that those whose judgment he respected might not label the experiment "futile." This tactic led Holmes to call Brandeis's opinions those of an advocate. Indeed, they were the opinions of an advocate of state experimentation. Holmes did not advocate it, he put up with it.[11]

A major area in which Holmes and Brandeis tended to reach the same conclusions was civil liberties, but their principles were totally different, particularly when the rights of speech and the press were involved. Holmes's attitude toward speech was based on his social Darwinism. He believed that idea should clash with idea in the "marketplace of ideas"; he enjoyed watching competing ideologies being stretched to their conclusions and rising or falling in popularity as the public will decreed. Thus, on the Massachusetts Supreme Judicial Court and during his early days on the United States Supreme Court, Holmes had no difficulty in sustaining violations of free speech. Basically, and in spite of his own penchant for reading philosophy, he felt ideas would make no difference; the "fittest" human beings would survive and shape society in their image. "I am so skeptical as to our knowledge about the goodness and badness of laws that I have no practical criterion except what the crowd wants," he wrote. "Personally I bet that the crowd if it knew more wouldn't want what it does—but that is immaterial."[12]

To Brandeis, ideas made a great difference. The experiments that would enable public and private institutions to adjust themselves to changing societal needs were based on ideas. Without the free exchange of ideas it would be impossible to discover and refine those institutions and practices that would best serve society. People had to be able to explore all available ideas in order to learn, to stretch their own intellectual horizons, and to fulfill their individual capabilities. The subject of Brandeis's philosophy was human beings; the object, their development. He had, as Riesman said, "an extraordinary faith in the possibilites of human development." He had known laborers and labor leaders who, with little formal education, had impressed him as being far more rational and intelligent than many of the well-educated people of Boston: what, given exposure to the ideas produced by history and training in analyzing them, might such people not achieve? To be sure, there were limits to the capabilities of any human being. That was why there had to be federalism, for no one person could know and understand all ideas, and there had to be laboratories in which different people with different skills and opinions could experiment. Although Brandeis constantly emphasized human limitations, he also insisted that human possibilities had not begun to be tapped. Giving full play to the minds of people would benefit both the individuals themselves and the society that all good citizens sought to improve. In *Myers* v. *U.S.* (1926), Brandeis condemned excessive presidential power by saying that the doctrine of separation of powers was designed "not to promote efficiency but to preclude the exercise of arbitrary power." Given a choice between efficiency and liberty, Brandeis would opt for liberty, but he did not think that a choice was necessary. In the long run liberty of speech and of ideas would be efficient, because by enabling human beings to educate themselves, free speech would lead to the development of the ideas needed by society.[13]

The Court's problem in defining permissible limits on free speech stems from the wording of the First Amendment: "Congress shall make no law . . . abridging the freedom of speech, or of the press." This would seem to leave no room whatever for congressional limitations on speech, but the Court has found this reading untenable. What, for example, is Congress to do if soldiers make inflammatory speeches during wartime, criticizing the war effort and urging that their comrades refuse to fight? What if someone tells an enemy about deployment of forces or the nature and workings of armaments? Is Congress to have no power to punish such speech? As Holmes wrote for the Court in 1919, "We venture to believe that neither Hamilton nor Madison, nor any other competent person then or later, ever supposed that to make criminal the counselling of a murder within the jurisdiction of Congress would be an unconstitutional interference with free speech." When the Court held in 1925 that the clause of the Fourteenth Amendment that prohibits states from depriving citizens of "life, liberty or property without due process of law" incorporated the First Amendment's prohibition on interference with liberty of speech, the question became even more complicated. Again, as Holmes said in another case, "The character of every act depends upon the circumstances in which it is done . . . The most stringent protection of free speech would not protect a man in falsely shouting fire in a theatre and causing a panic." So, with the exception of Justice Hugo Black and occasionally of Justice William O. Douglas, the justices have refused to read the First Amendment as an absolute prohibition on government laws abridging speech and have then had to face the dilemma of what the permitted abridgments should be.[14]

The "clear and present danger" doctrine was an attempt to deal with the problem. Speech that was distasteful, demonstrably false, or infuriating still had to be allowed if the government was unable to prove that the words were likely to result in any real danger occurring to society in the near future. Holmes (and Brandeis) believed that this was the sole area in which judges should not assume that legislation is constitutional unless proven otherwise, because the free exchange of ideas had to be allowed if democracy itself was to be maintained. The burden of proof that a statute making speech a crime was constitutional was shifted to the enacting legislature, which had to prove that the law was necessary, and to enforcement officials, who had to prove that the specific speech presented a "clear and present danger." Brandeis could not encourage the states to experiment with placing limitations on free speech, because democracy and progress required that there be experiments by individuals with new ideas.[15]

Holmes created the "clear and present danger" rule, and Brandeis is commonly considered to have agreed with Holmes's formulation. He did not. Brandeis approved of "clear and present danger" as the criterion, but interpreted it rather differently. Holmes first enunciated the doctrine in *Schenck* v. *United States* when a trial court had used the 1917 Espionage Act to convict a Socialist party official for sending leaflets to draftees urging them to oppose the draft. Writing for the Court, Holmes upheld the conviction, saying that whether or not speech was permissible was "a question of proximity and degree. When a nation is at war many things that might be said in time of peace are such a hindrance to its effort that their utterance will not be endured so long as men fight and that no Court could regard them as protected by any constitutional right." Thus, the fact that a nation was engaged in war had a direct effect on the Court's decision about whether certain speech was permissible; the pamphlets would have been protected by the First Amendment had the nation been at peace.[16]

Holmes spoke for a unanimous Court, and included the "clear and present danger" criterion, with which most of his colleagues would soon indicate they did not agree, in the Court's opinion, where it carried more weight than it would have had it been included only in a dissent. Brandeis later regretted having voted to uphold the conviction, telling Frankfurter, "I have never been quite happy about my concurrence . . . I had not then thought the issues of freedom of speech out—I thought at the subject, not through it." Presumably, the same was true in the case of *Frohwerk*

v. *United States*, decided a week after *Schenck*, in which Holmes, for the unanimous Court, upheld a conviction of journalists for articles printed in a German-language newspaper that attacked the purposes of the war and the legality of and need for the draft.[17]

However, in *Abrams* v. *United States*, decided by the Court in the same year as the *Schenck* and *Frohwerk* cases, Holmes and Brandeis dissented from the upholding of a conviction, under the Sedition Act, of two pamphleteers who opposed sending American troops to Russia and urged a strike in the munitions industry. Holmes's dissenting opinion is justly famous for its insistence on the free flow of ideas: "When men have realized that time has upset many fighting faiths, they may come to believe even more than they believe the very foundations of their own conduct that the ultimate good desired is better reached by free trade in ideas,—that the best test of truth is the power of the thought to get itself accepted in the competition of the market; and that truth is the only ground upon which their wishes safely can be carried out. That, at any rate, is the theory of our Constitution. It is an experiment as all life is an experiment."[18]

Two things might be noted about Holmes's words. First, in likening free speech to the "competition of the market," he based his approach on claims of utility, not of morality. There was nothing necessarily good about speech as such; what was good was the fight among competing ideas. Second, Holmes argued that the Constitution embodied his own view: there was no such thing as absolute truth; all one could do was experiment and hope for the best. Brandeis, however, saw free speech as being an end as well as a means and did believe that he had discovered certain absolute truths: that humans were educable, that power corrupted, that power therefore had to be balanced by power, that bigness was bad, that the ultimate test of institutions was their impact on human dignity, and that no institutions would work properly unless they were predicated upon the limited abilities of each human being.

Brandeis had had a chance to think through the problem of speech, and particularly of speech in wartime, when he wrote three dissents in free speech cases decided in 1920. The first case was *Schaefer* v. *United States*, which involved five men convicted under the Espionage Act for printing misleading articles about the war in two German-language newspapers. The basis for the charge was that they copied articles from other newspapers in less than their entirety, and that if they had printed the complete articles, the message they carried would have been more discouraging to the enemy. The articles themselves were contemptuous of the American war effort and hinted that the war was entirely the doing of the American president. Thus the president, treasurer, business manager, chief editor, and managing editor of the *Philadelphia Tageblatt* and the *Philadelphia Sonntagsblatt* were found to have obstructed recruiting and to have promoted the success of the enemy. The Court upheld their conviction.[19]

Brandeis, writing for himself and Holmes, could not see that the clear and present danger test had been met. He called the test "a rule of reason" that could be applied "only by the exercise of good judgment," for which calmness was "as essential as fearlessness and honesty . . . If the words were of such a nature and were used under such circumstances that men, judging in calmness, could not reasonably say that they created a clear and present danger that they would bring about the evil which Congress sought and had a right to prevent," then the words had to be allowed. Justice McKenna's opinion for the Court had quoted some of the material from the newspapers. Brandeis protested, "The nature and possible effect of a writing cannot be properly determined by culling here and there a sentence and presenting it separated from the context. In making such determination, it should be read as a whole." So Brandeis took eight pages to reprint the relevant articles in their entirety. He found it impossible to believe that a jury "acting in calmness" would find that the articles created a clear and present danger of obstructing recruiting or promoting the success of the enemy. Prosecution for the printing of such harmless disagreements with government policy would stifle criticism of government policy in the future; how, then, was democracy to work?[20]

Perhaps the most telling lines of the opinion were the following: "The constitutional right of free speech has been declared to be the same in peace and in war. In peace, too, men may differ widely as to what loyalty to our country demands; and an intolerant majority, swayed by passion or by fear, may be prone in the future, as it has often been in the past, to stamp as disloyal opinions with which it disagrees. Convictions such as these, besides abridging freedom of speech, threaten freedom of thought and of belief." It was precisely in time of war that "an intolerant majority" was most likely to be "swayed by passion or by fear." Brandeis was beginning to move away from the *Schenck* and *Frohwerk* decisions, which had not shown that the offending words had had any real effect on the war effort. Thus, he was also beginning to reject the *Schenck* notion that the mere fact of war might make some speech illegal.[21]

His position became clearer in the second case, *Pierce v. United States*, another Espionage Act case, in which the Court upheld convictions for the distribution of leaflets that had allegedly interfered with the operation of the war effort and had caused insubordination. Again, Brandeis reprinted an entire leaflet, distributed by the Socialist party and entitled "The Price We Pay." The leaflet said in part, "Into your homes the recruiting officers are coming. They will take your sons of military age and impress them into the army." To Brandeis's combined amusement and dismay, the government had actually had a major with twenty-eight years' experience in the regular army testify that recruiting was voluntary and that gangs of recruiters did not break into homes to impress soldiers. The government's purpose had been to prove that the distributors were guilty of conspiring to cause insubordination by spreading false information. But in fact the leaflet had been distributed to civilians, not to military personnel, and so it could not possibly be proved to have caused insubordination; it described "lurid and perhaps exaggerated pictures" but also pointed to the "hopelessness of protest" against the "irresistible power of the military arm of the Government," counseling acquiescence. "It is not conceivable," Brandeis wrote, "that any man of ordinary intelligence and normal judgment would be induced by anything in the leaflet" to commit the serious crimes of insubordination and mutiny; "Certainly there was no clear and present danger that such would be the result."

Brandeis saw the case in light of the need for speech as an aid to experimentation: "The fundamental right of free men to strive for better conditions through new legislation and new institutions will not be preserved, if efforts to secure it by argument to fellow citizens may be construed as criminal incitement to disobey the existing law." He did not differentiate between peace and wartime. And he could think of only one explanation for Justice Mahlon Pitney's opinion for the Court. He attributed it to "Pitney's Presbyterian doctrine of freedom of will," which led Pitney to assume he understood the real cause of war: "Those individuals having free choice of right and wrong, choose wrong"; therefore one could not permit them to be exposed to wrong ideas. Brandeis thought Pitney "very kindly, though in many ways naive and wholly without knowledge."[22]

Some years later, during Herbert Hoover's presidency, when Brandeis spoke of his opinions in *Schaefer* and *Pierce*, he told Frankfurter that Hoover believed that "criticism should end at water's shore . . . I felt just opposite—wrote those long dissents in Schaefer and Pierce cases to put on permanent record what we were not allowed to say." He added, "Not until I came to write the Pierce and Schaefer cases did I understand" the issues of freedom of speech. It was all right for the government to enact espionage (but not sedition) legislation that would be "confined to war"; "in peace the protection against restrictions of freedom of speech would be unabated . . . in Schaefer and Pierce cases I made up my mind I would put it all out." He spoke also of *Debs v. U.S.*, another 1919 case in which Holmes wrote for a unanimous Court, upholding the Espionage Act conviction of the radical leader Eugene Victor Debs on the grounds that the probable effect of his speech had been to prevent recruiting. Brandeis was unhappy that he had remained silent in that case, too, and said, "I would have placed the Debs case on the war power—instead of taking Holmes' line about 'clear and present danger.' Put it frankly on war power . . . and then the scope of espionage legislation would be confined to war." In other words, Brandeis would have gone even further than "clear and present danger" in protecting the liberties of the people.[23]

It can be argued that while Brandeis's approach might have worked during the 1920s, when he held his conversations with Frankfurter, it became less realistic in the period that began after World War II. Whether or not that is true, however, is irrelevant. The point is that Brandeis had come to disagree with Holmes about the extent to which the government could plead military necessity in curbing the liberties of the people. This became even more apparent when Holmes and Brandeis voted differently in the third 1920 case, *Gilbert* v. *Minnesota*.[24]

A Minnesota law prohibited any interference with the military enlistment effort. Joseph Gilbert, manager of the organization department of the Nonpartisan League, was sent to jail under the act for making the following statement at a public meeting of the league in 1917: "We are going over to Europe to make the world safe for democracy, but I tell you we had better make America safe for democracy first. You say, what is the matter with our democracy . . . Have you had anything to say as to whether we should go into this war? You know you have not. If this is such a great democracy, for Heaven's sake why should we not vote on conscription of men. We were stampeded into this war by newspaper rot to pull England's chestnuts out of the fire for her. I tell you if they conscripted wealth like they have conscripted men, this war would not last over forty-eight hours." Justice McKenna, speaking for the Court, upheld the conviction. Justice Holmes concurred without an opinion.[25]

Brandeis, dissenting, felt strongly enough to violate his own rule against deciding constitutional issues when doing so was unnecessary. He made the point, with which Chief Justice White agreed, that the war power belonged exclusively to Congress, which had already exercised it by passage of the Espionage Act. That, as the chief justice pointed out, was enough to negate the law. But Brandeis went further, calling the Minnesota statute "an act to prevent teaching that the abolition of war is possible." Because it remained in force whether or not the country was at war, "the restriction imposed relates to the teaching of the doctrine of pacifism and the legislature in effect proscribes it for all time." It prohibited public statements that the armed forces were inefficient or that young men might more wisely choose a civilian career. More, it made it illegal "to teach in any place a single person that a citizen should not aid in carrying on a war . . . Thus the statute invades the privacy and freedom of the home. Father and mother may not follow the promptings of religious belief" by teaching their children that their religion considered participation in war to be wrong. Brandeis caught himself; because he had already found the statute an interference with federal power, he saw "no occasion to consider whether it violates also the Fourteenth Amendment." But he went on to blast the Court: "I have difficulty in believing that the liberty guaranteed by the Constitution, which has been held to protect against state denial the right of an employer to discriminate against a workman because he is a member of a trade union . . . the right of a business man to conduct a private employment agency . . . does not include liberty to teach, either in the privacy of the home or publicly, the doctrine of pacifism . . . I cannot believe that the liberty guaranteed by the Fourteenth Amendment includes only liberty to acquire and to enjoy property."[26]

This is an issue to which Brandeis would return and about which he and Holmes differed. Holmes considered the states to have less than absolute power to experiment with limitations on property rights. Thus, he disagreed with Brandeis over the Kohler Act and its restrictions on mining. However, Holmes voted more often than not to permit such limitations. In 1921 Holmes wrote the Court's opinion upholding a District of Columbia law that restricted the power of landlords to evict tenants without cause, arguing that the District could define rental practices as clothed with a public interest and regulate them accordingly. The four dissenters claimed that the law violated the landlords' due process rights. Brandeis concurred with Holmes, writing to Frankfurter that the dissent should be compared "by the reflecting student" with the Court's opinions in *Schaefer* and *Gilbert*.[27]

Brandeis reiterated the theme in *United States ex rel. Milwaukee Social Democratic Publishing Company* v. *Burelson*. The Espionage Act gave the postmaster general the right to deny the use of the second-class mails to newspapers he found unacceptable under the Act. The Court upheld the prohibition as applied to *The Milwaukee Leader*. Brandeis dissented, employing statutory construction: according to his reading of the Act, the postmaster general had the power to prohibit second-class mail that was subversive but not to enjoin future mailings on the basis of past articles that he considered to be subversive. Again, Brandeis added *obiter dicta* on the Court's willingness to use the Constitution to protect property but not speech. He pointed out that there was a property right involved: "The right which Congress has given to all properly circumstanced persons to distribute newpapers and periodicals through the mails is a substantial right . . . It is of the same nature as, indeed, it is a part of, the right to carry on business which this court has been jealous to protect against what it has considered arbitrary deprivations." Holmes dissented separately, saying that while his initial reaction had been that the action was valid, he had had "the advantage of reading the judgment of my brother Brandeis in this case" and had come to agree "in substance" with him. The only apparent reason for Holmes's penning his own opinion was to disassociate himself from Brandeis's slap at the Court's use of the due process clause to protect property but not civil liberty.[28]

Because of the way the Court used the Fourteenth Amendment to limit the power of states to experiment, Brandeis favored its repeal. As long as it existed, however, he argued, it should be restricted to procedural regularity and "to things that are fundamental," among which he included "Right to Speech. Right to Education. Right to choice of profession. Right to locomotion." He added, "There may be some aspects of property that are fundamental," but that did not include the right to be free from legislative limitations, "whereas right to your education and to utter speech is fundamental *except* clear and present danger." In other words, the Court should have been busy protecting free speech and education rather than property rights.

Brandeis made these comments while discussing *Meyer* v. *Nebraska* with Frankfurter. Reacting to World War I hysteria, Nebraska had forbidden the teaching of German in public schools, ostensibly to make English the mother tongue of all residents. (Iowa and Ohio enacted similar legislation.) Brandeis concurred in Justice McReynolds's opinion, which held that punishing Meyer (a parochial school teacher) for teaching a ten-year-old to read German deprived Meyer of his liberty under the Fourteenth Amendment. Holmes, however, dissented, saying that this "experiment" to get all citizens to "speak a common tongue" was not unreasonable and was within the powers of the state. Although Brandeis wrote no opinion of his own, probably in the name of harmony on the Court, he said to Frankfurter that the right to an education was such a fundamental right that any impairment of it had to be judged by the "clear and present danger" test. In other words, Brandeis put education on the same high plane as speech, beyond the reach of most state experimentation. He and Holmes had apparently discussed the matter, for Frankfurter's notes of the conversation continue, "Holmes says doesn't want to extend XIV."[29]

The two civil liberties opinions for which Brandeis is properly best known are his dissent in *Olmstead* v. *United States* and his concurrence in *Whit-*

ney v. *California.* Together, they constitute his clearest and most eloquent explanation of the importance of civil liberties in a democratic society.[30]

The background of Brandeis's lengthy dissent in *Olmstead* can be found in *Casey* v. *U.S.*, in which a Seattle attorney was convicted of violating the Harrison Anti-Narcotic Law. The warden of a county jail informed federal narcotics agents of his suspicion that attorney Casey was supplying his clients with drugs. The federal agents induced two prisoners to offer Casey money for morphine and then recorded the jailhouse conversations between the prisoners and Casey. A relative of the prisoners testified that she picked up the drugs from Casey's office.[31]

Holmes wrote the Court's opinion sustaining the conviction. Brandeis dissented: "The prosecution must fail because officers of the Government instigated the commission of the alleged crime." Brandeis argued that the evidence admitted in *Casey* would not have existed otherwise. The government was permitted to "set decoys to entrap criminals," but here the government had done more; "the act for which the Government seeks to punish the defendant is the fruit of their criminal conspiracy to induce its commission . . . [The Government] may not provoke or create a crime and then punish the criminal, its creature." In contrast to the opinion he would deliver in *Whitney*, when the failure of the defendant to raise in the trial court the point that Brandeis considered relevant led him to concur in upholding her conviction, Brandeis dismissed the fact that Casey had not pleaded entrapment as irrelevant: "This prosecution should be stopped, not because some right of Casey's has been denied, but in order to protect the Government. To protect it from illegal conduct of its officers. To protect the purity of its courts."[32]

The Court then immediately considered the *Olmstead* case, in which Brandeis again found government action unacceptable. For almost five months the government had tapped the home and office telephones of a group of men suspected of violating the National Prohibition Act, and had made 775 pages of notes. The men were convicted over their protest that the evidence obtained by wiretapping violated the search and seizure clause of the Fourth Amendment.

Chief Justice Taft, writing for the majority of five, upheld the convictions. There had been no search of the men's homes and offices, Taft said; no official had actually entered the premises; and nothing physical had been seized. There had been no trespass, and no one had forced the defendants to talk over the telephone. Therefore, the Fourth Amendment had not been violated.[33]

Brandeis found wiretapping an incredible invasion of privacy. "Whenever a telephone line is tapped, the privacy of the persons at both ends of the line is invaded, and all conversations between them upon any subject, and although proper, confidential, and privileged, may be overheard. Moreover, the tapping of one man's telephone line involves the tapping of the telephone of every other person whom he may call, or who may call him." Writs of assistance and general warrants had been outlawed by the Constitution, but such devices "are but puny instruments of tyranny and oppression when compared with wire tapping." James Otis had said, "of much lesser intrusions than these, that they put 'the liberty of every man in the hands of every petty officer.' " Lord Camden had called "a far slighter intrusion . . . 'subversive of all the comforts of society.' " Brandeis asked, "Can it be that the Constitution affords no protection against such invasions of individual security?"[34]

The writers of the Fourth Amendment had not specifically mentioned wiretapping, because wiretapping had not been invented when they wrote. Brandeis reminded his colleagues of Chief Justice Marshall's famous admonition, "We must never forget that it is a Constitution we are expounding," meaning that the Constitution, as the basic law of the land, had to have its specific meanings (but not its spirit) altered as societal circumstances changed. The Court had altered the specific meaning of many parts of the Constitution, Brandeis pointed out; it had even done so in interpreting the search and seizure clause. Most important was the spirit behind the amendment, which was to ensure privacy: "The makers of our Constitution undertook . . . to protect Americans in their beliefs, their thoughts, their emotions, and their sensations. They conferred, as against the Government, the right to be let alone—the most comprehensive of rights and the right most valued by civilized men. To protect that right, every unjustifiable intrusion by the Government upon the privacy of the individual, whatever the means employed, must be deemed a violation of the Fourth Amendment." It made no difference that the government had violated the Constitution in the name of law enforcement. "Experience should teach us to be most on our guard to protect liberty when the Government's purposes are beneficent . . . The greatest dangers to liberty lurk in insidious encroachment by men of zeal, well-meaning but without understanding."[35]

Furthermore, the government had misused its role as an educator. "Our Government is the potent, the omnipresent teacher. For good or for ill, it teaches the whole people by its example. Crime is contagious. If the Government becomes a lawbreaker, it breeds contempt for law: it invites every man to become a law unto himself; it invites anarchy. To declare that in the administration of the criminal law the end justifies the means—to declare that the Government may commit crimes in order to secure the conviction of a private criminal—would bring terrible retribution. Against that pernicious doctrine this Court should resolutely set its face."[36]

Brandeis circulated a memorandum to the Court, pleading that the case be decided not on the constitutional question of the legality of the Volstead Act but on the grounds that the government should not profit from an illegal act. The point had not been considered during the conference in which the justices considered the case and cast their initial votes; indeed, some of the justices told Brandeis they had not even thought of it. Nevertheless, the majority stayed with Taft. Brandeis was so shocked at the Court's endorsement of government criminality that he persuaded Holmes to write an additional dissent. Speaking to his niece about the case, he insisted that "lying and sneaking are always bad, no matter what the ends," and added, "I don't care about punishing crime, but I am implacable in maintaining standards." "I suppose," he lamented to Frankfurter, "some reviewer of the wire tapping decision will discern that in favor of property the Constitution is liberally construed—in favor of liberty, strictly."[37]

Privacy had of course been a major concern of Brandeis's for years. He and Sam Warren had written the definitive statement on privacy in their article "The Right to Privacy" in the 1890 volume of the *Harvard Law Review*. In that article, which combined the issue of privacy with a conception of the law as a changing entity, Brandeis and Warren first used the phrase "the right to be let alone," which they attributed to Judge Thomas M. Cooley. Warren and Brandeis had warned that new inventions brought their dangers to privacy: "instantaneous photographs and newspaper enterprise have invaded the sacred precincts of private and domestic life; and numerous mechanical devices threaten to make good the prediction that 'what is whispered in the closet shall be proclaimed from the house-tops.' " Similarly, almost fifty years later Brandeis wrote, "Discovery and invention have made it possible for the Government, by means far more effective than stretching upon the rack, to obtain disclosure in court of what is whispered in the closet . . . The progress of science in furnishing the Government with means of espionage is not likely to stop with wire tapping. Ways may some day be developed by which the Government, without removing papers from secret drawers, can reproduce them in court, and by which it will be enabled to expose to a jury the most intimate occurrences of the home." One of Brandeis's working folders for *Olmstead* contains a 1928 clipping reporting on the development of something called television. Brandeis was a great believer in progress—but not all progress was good.[38]

Fulminating about government law-breaking and "spying," Brandeis sent a series of letters to Frankfurter the year before *Olmstead* was handed down: "Couldn't you get started through your men a series of the HLR covering the danger of arbitrariness etc. in the several federal Depts. & Bureaus? I omitted to ask you what progress is being made in the effort to reduce the appropriations for spies in the public service. It may take a generation to rid our country of this pest, but I think it probably can be done . . . The temper of the public at some time in conjunction with some conspicuous occurrence will afford an opportunity . . . Wouldn't it be possible to interest . . . [Harvard Law School teachers and students in writing for the *Law Review*] articles bearing on the redress for the invasion of civil and political rights through arbitrary, etc. governmental action, by means of civil suits? I think the failure to attempt such redress as against government officials for the multitude of invasions during the war and post-war period is . . . disgraceful . . . Americans should be reminded of the duty to litigate . . . Wouldn't it be possible to have some one in Congress move for a Claims Commission to make reparations to American citizens for the outrages incident to the Jan 20 Palmer raids? An article on the Sedition law reparations would prepare the way . . . I have grave doubt whether we shall ever be able to effect more than superficial betterment unless we succeed in infusing a sense (A) of the dignity of the law among a free, self-governing people and (B) of the solemnity of the function of administering justice. Among the essentials is that the government must, in its methods, & means, & instruments, be ever the gentleman."[39]

Brandeis considered government "espionage" to be "un-American. It is nasty. It is nauseating." He persuaded an editor of the Scripps-Howard newspapers to campaign against it and asked Frankfurter to help by having the "very competent young woman" who had produced a series of articles for the newspaper chain to go through material in the files of the American Civil Liberties Union. He suggested creating a coalition of those "wets indignant at prohibition practices," anti-administration forces (presumably opposed on political grounds to government spying), and administration forces concerned with the size of the budget, to get appropriations for internal spying cut. Brandeis was willing to use all available resources in the service of eliminating illegal and unethical intrusions by government into the lives of the people. Ironically, neither Brandeis nor Frankfurter knew that throughout the period of their correspondence about government spying, the Massachusetts state police, concerned about the Sacco-Vanzetti case in which Frankfurter was playing a major role, maintained a wiretap on Felix Frankfurter's telephone.[40]

It was not privacy but the free exchange of ideas that was at issue in *Whitney* v. *California*. Anita Whitney had been convicted of helping to organize, being a member of, and assembling with the Communist Labor party. That, in 1919, was a felony in California. Whitney argued that the conviction violated the liberty guaranteed her by the Fourteenth Amendment.[41]

Brandeis said in his concurrence in *Whitney* that he regretted the Fourteenth's due process clause being applied to the substance of laws as well as to the procedures by which they were passed. If it was going to be used to protect liberties, however, it should be used to protect civil liberties. "All fundamental rights comprised within the term liberty are protected by the Federal Constitution from invasion by the States," Brandeis wrote. In fact, the Court had not gone that far; all it had done by 1928 was to declare that the rights of speech, teaching, and assembly were fundamental and were included in the Fourteenth Amendment's guarantee of liberty. Brandeis simply assumed that similar protection was given to other fundamental rights.[42]

Although the rights of speech and assembly were fundamental, they were clearly not absolute. Brandeis pointed out that the Court had not yet defined exactly what "clear and present danger" meant, but he was inaccurate in implying that the doctrine had been adopted by the Court as a guide. Although Holmes's opinion enunciating the doctrine had been written for a unanimous Court, the majority of the justices had not employed it in deciding subsequent cases. This was true not only of earlier cases—*Abrams* v. *United States*, the *Schaefer, Pierce, Gilbert,* and *Milwaukee* cases, *Gitlow* v. *New York*; it was also true of the *Whitney* case itself, in which a majority of the Court upheld California's right to enact the Criminal Syndicalism Act because the passage of the statute reflected the judgment of the California legislature that a grave danger to the state existed whenever a society to advocate criminal syndicalism came into being. Thus the Court deferred to California instead of applying the clear and present danger test itself. The Court would not set the boundaries of "clear and present danger" because it chose not to use that standard as its criterion for judgment.[43]

But Holmes and Brandeis did, and so Brandeis wrote in *Whitney* that in order to determine what "clear and present danger" meant, it was necessary to consider why the right to free speech existed at all; why, as he put it, a state was "ordinarily denied the power to prohibit dissemination of social, economic and political doctrine which a vast majority of its citizens believes to be false and fraught with evil consequence."[44]

His statement of the rationale behind the right to free speech is a reflection of Brandeis's strongest beliefs:

Those who won our independence believed that the final end of the State was to make men free to develop their faculties; and that in its government the deliberative forces should prevail over the arbitrary. They valued liberty both as an end and as a means. They believed liberty to be the secret of happiness and courage to be the secret of liberty. They believed that freedom to think as you will and to speak as you think are means indispensable to the discovery and spread of political truth; that without free speech and assembly discussion would be futile; that with them, discussion affords ordinarily adequate protection against the dissemination of noxious doctrine; that the greatest menace to freedom is an inert people; that public discussion is a political duty; and that this should be a fundamental principle of the American government . . . they knew that order cannot be secured merely through fear of punishment for its infraction; that it is hazardous to discourage thought, hope and imagination; that fear breeds repression; that repression breeds hate; that hate menaces stable government; that the path of safety lies in the opportunity to discuss freely supposed grievances and proposed remedies: and that the fitting remedy for evil counsels is good ones.[45]

This, Brandeis said, was the reason that "those who won our independence" amended the Constitution to protect free speech and assembly. But how far did that protection extend? "Fear of serious injury" resulting from speech was insufficient to justify government repression, Brandeis argued; for example, in America's own history "men feared witches and burnt women. It is the function of speech to free men from the bondage of irrational fears." Fear could not justify suppression of speech; instead, there must be "reasonable ground to fear that serious evil will result . . . there must be reasonable ground to believe that the danger apprehended is imminent. There must be reasonable ground to believe that the evil to be prevented is a serious one." It was perfectly true that when laws were denounced, the probability of their being broken was increased, and that advocacy of law-breaking made the probability even greater. But the "wide difference between advocacy and incitement, between preparation and attempt, between assembling and conspiracy, must be borne in mind. In order to support a finding of clear and present danger it must be shown either that immediate serious violence was to be expected or was advocated, or that the past conduct furnished reason to believe that such advocacy was then contemplated." The time element was crucial. Again, Brandeis cited the beliefs of the Founding Fathers:

Those who won our independence by revolution were not cowards. They did not fear political change. They did not exalt order at the cost of liberty. To courageous, self-reliant men, with confidence in the power of free and fearless reasoning applied through the processes of popular government, no danger flowing from speech can be deemed clear and present, unless the incidence of the evil apprehended is so imminent that it may befall before there is opportunity for full discussion. If there be time to expose through discussion the falsehood and fallacies, to avert the evil by the processes of education, the remedy to be applied is more speech, not enforced silence.

"Imminent danger" alone was not sufficient. Even the likelihood that speech would result in "some violence or in destruction of property is not enough to justify its suppression. There must be the probability of serious injury to the State. Among free men, the deterrents ordinarily to be applied to prevent crime are education and punishment for violations of the law, not abridgment of the rights of free speech and assembly."[46]

How far Brandeis was willing to go in support of speech has not been fully understood. Speech was to be permitted even if it led to "some violence" or "destruction of property." Only if there was a real danger to the state itself could speech be suppressed. People could be punished for violence or destruction of property, but, except in the most extreme cases, they could not be silenced.

Passage by a state of a statute limiting speech or assembly did no more than create "a rebuttable presumption" of a clear and present danger. Anyone convicted under the statute had the right to ask whether in fact such a danger was real, produce the evidence, and let the judge or jury decide. The California legislature's conclusion that criminal syndicalism constituted a threat did not automatically make an individual's advocacy of revolution illegal: "I am unable to assent to the suggestion in the opinion of the Court that assembling with a political party, formed to advocate the desirability of a proletarian revolution by mass action at some date necessarily far in the future, is not a right within the protection of the Fourteenth Amendment."[47]

Brandeis understood the power of ideas; indeed, it was precisely because ideas could bring about change that they were so important to a democratic society. Democracy, to Brandeis, was not an end; it was a means, and as such it was a continuous process in which all citizens had to participate. Alvin Johnson called Brandeis an "implacable democrat"; Dean Acheson called him an "incurable optimist." Both were right. Fully aware of human limitations, Brandeis nevertheless had endless faith in human possibilities. He was more than a democrat and an optimist: he was a civil libertarian.[48]

An examination of all of Brandeis's opinions and concurrences in civil liberties cases would require a volume of its own. However, brief examination of three more areas will give a sense of the range of his views.

In his opinions involving prohibition and the Volstead Act, as Alpheus Mason has written, the prophet stumbled. Since the days when his brother kept him supplied with Kentucky bourbon, Brandeis and his wife had given up alcoholic beverages. Early in his career, he had testified before the Massachusetts legislature against the law that prohibited the sale of liquor except as part of a meal, saying, "The use of liquor is not a wrong. It is the abuse and not the use which is wrong . . . No law can be effective which does not take into consideration the conditions of the community for which it is designed; no law can be a good law—every law must be a bad law—that remains unenforced." License the sale of liquor, Brandeis told the legislators, so that the liquor business will be in the hands of respectable men rather than criminals and so that liquor dealers would stop bribing politicians to keep from having the law enforced.[49]

Justice Brandeis seemed to have forgotten Advocate Brandeis's comment that unenforceable laws were bad; worse, he did not merely uphold the prohibition laws as a regrettable but legitimate government experiment, but permitted enforcement even when it violated civil liberties. It was Brandeis who held that the double jeopardy clause did not prevent the federal government from convicting a person for possessing liquor and then convicting him again for selling the same liquor; he found nothing wrong in the government's confiscation of a motorcar on the grounds that a passenger in it had a small flask of whisky with him; he spoke for the Court in permitting the government to close breweries and distilleries without compensating the owners for their losses. It was only when the government went so far as to wiretap in order to secure convictions against bootleggers that Brandeis decided that enforcement effort had gone too far.[50]

Brandeis's civil liberties record was also disappointing with regard to the rights of black and Asian citizens and resident aliens. Essentially, the Court's actions toward nonwhites during the Brandeis years reflected three motivating beliefs: that *Plessy* v. *Ferguson* had settled the issue of whether or not separate-but-equal treatment of nonwhites violated the Constitution; that the Fourteenth Amendment prohibited only state discrimination, not that by individuals; and that the Fourteenth Amendment required states to give blacks at least the appearance of equal rights in the courtroom and in elections. For example, in 1917 the Court unanimously struck down a Louisville statute mandating block-by-block housing segregation. In 1926, however, the Court upheld a private restrictive covenant, under which whites agreed not to sell homes in a residential area to nonwhites. The reasoning of the unanimous Court was that no state action was involved. *South Covington* v. *Kentucky* in 1920 upheld the separate but equal doctrine in transportation, and *Gong Lum* v. *Rice* in 1927 upheld a state's right to insist that a Chinese student go to a black rather than a white school, the Court relying on a state's right to choose the method by which it educated its students.[51]

Brandeis wrote the opinion of the Court in *Wan* v. *United States*, overturning the conviction of a Chinese man who had been held and interrogated by the police under circumstances that made his "confession" highly questionable. The case involved the federal government rather than the states, over whose courts the Supreme Court was then declining to exercise much supervision. Still, the Court was not willing to validate extreme instances of injustice for blacks in state courts. In 1923 Holmes's opinion for the majority, including Brandeis, overturned the murder conviction of a black man, obtained under highly pressured circumstances from an all-white jury. The famous Scottsboro trial, in which black youths were sentenced to death for the alleged rape of two white girls, became the occasion for the Court's holding that under certain circumstances an indigent accused of a capital crime had a right to a state-provided attorney. The Court overturned the second conviction of the youths three years later, this time on the ground that a persistent pattern of excluding blacks from juries in Alabama precluded a fair trial by their peers. The Court restated its holding later in 1935 and again in 1938.[52]

Holmes wrote for a unanimous court in 1927 when it struck down the Texas law excluding blacks from participation in the Democratic party primaries (at that time, nomination by the Democratic party in Texas was tantamount to election). The Court split 5–4 five years later when it overturned Texas's subsequent law permitting the Democratic Executive Committee to decide who could vote in its primaries. Again, the action of the state (rather than of a private party) was determinative, and Brandeis voted with the majority. Texas avoided the consequences of the Court's ruling, however, by passing a law allowing a party convention control over the franchise in primaries; this law was unanimously upheld, as, according to the Court, it gave control over primaries to private parties rather than to the state.[53]

In 1938 the Court (Brandeis again voting with the majority) held that the Norris-LaGuardia Act covered a labor dispute in which the New Negro Alliance picketed to persuade the owners of a District of Columbia store to hire blacks in their large chain of stores. The lower courts had read the Act as applying only to disputes involving wages, hours, unionization, and working conditions. Justice Owen J. Roberts, however, noting that the Act did not classify disputes according to motive, stated that the "desire for fair and equitable conditions of employment on the part of persons of any race, color, or persuasion, and the removal of discrimination against them by reason of their race or religious beliefs is quite as important to those concerned" as was any other labor dispute. He added that "race discrimination by an employer may reasonably be deemed more unfair and less excusable than discrimination against workers on the ground of union affiliation." (Justices McReynolds and Butler exclaimed in dissent, "Under the tortured meaning now attributed to the words 'labor dispute,' no employer . . . who prefers helpers of one color or class can find adequate safeguard against intolerable violations of his freedom if members of some other class, religion, race or color demand that he give them preference.")[54]

In 1938 the state of Missouri argued that the system by which states, desiring to keep their law schools entirely white, offered to pay out-of-state tuition for would-be law students who were black satisfied the equal protection clause; the Court, by a 6–2 majority (in which Brandeis joined), said it did not. This was the first in a series of decisions that eventually led the Court to declare in *Brown* v. *Board of Education* (1954) that separate schools for the two races could never be equal.[55]

Felix Frankfurter, whose public service activities were funded in part by Brandeis, was a leading advisor of the National Association for the Advancement of Colored People and a mentor for a series of outstanding black Harvard Law School students. There were few black lawyers during Brandeis's years on the Court, and it was clear that most law schools were not likely to begin welcoming black students. The incoming president of Howard University was advised by Brandeis in the late 1920s: "I can tell most of the time when I'm reading a brief by a Negro attorney. You've got to get yourself a real faculty out there or you're always going to have a fifth-rate law school. And it's got to be full-time and a day school." President Mordecai Johnson soon named Charles Houston dean of the Law School. Houston, a disciple of Frankfurter's, had earned a place on the prestigious *Harvard Law Review* and had stayed at Harvard for a fourth year to work for a graduate degree with Frankfurter. Houston argued the Missouri law school case and wrote the first of the NAACP's Brandeis-style briefs some years later in *Shelley* v. *Kraemer*, the case in which the Court struck down private restrictive covenants. By that time, Brandeis had died, but Frankfurter was on the Court to hear his protegé's argument.[56]

Frankfurter and Brandeis both encouraged Nathan Margold, a Harvard student who later taught at the Law School for three years. Brandeis's efforts to keep Margold in the teaching profession were unsuccessful. Margold argued and won the second Texas primary case for the NAACP and designed the legal strategy the NAACP followed in its ultimately successful effort to negate the separate but equal doctrine.[57]

Brandeis almost certainly knew about Frankfurter's work with the NAACP and his encouragement of black students at Harvard, and Brandeis's abolitionist upbringing would have made him sympathetic to these efforts. The implication of his letter to President Johnson of Howard was that he thought that a black law school *could* be first-rate. In other words, there is no evidence of racism on Brandeis's part; it is likely that his insistence on merit made him relatively indifferent to color.

Brandeis's attitude toward Asians living in the United States was more obvious in his letters than in his votes on the Court. Congress had made Japanese immigrants ineligible for citizenship; California had gone further and made them ineligible to own land or to become sharecroppers. The Court upheld the California statute, with Brandeis and McReynolds noting that they felt the cases should have been dismissed for want of a justiciable question. Brandeis's comments to Frankfurter reflect indignation at the plight of the Japanese.

> In connection with the Japanese Alien Land Cases, following matter arising incidentally should receive separate appropriate comment—
> The Jap. get $^1/_2$ the crop—only;
> The owners get $^1/_2$ for furnishing, practically, only the land (paying taxes thereon)
> I think throughout history you probably could not find such rackrenting as we have made common in America.[58]

In 1927 the Court decided two cases concerning admission of Chinese to the country and the rights of naturalized Chinese. Brandeis may have been referring to these cases when he again wrote to Frankfurter, "These Chinese cases present food for Civil Liberties Assn activity. Some steps should be taken, through Chinese minister, consuls or otherwise, to help Chinese to better counsel. Some way should be pursued to make the Federal official suffer for such illegal acts. And to make sure, through Congress or otherwise that illegalities such as here condemned do not go unnoticed." As the editors of the Brandeis letters note, it is unclear whether Brandeis was referring to instances of federal mistreatment of Chinese that were before the Court or to incidents that were being handled elsewhere. But the letters make clear that he disapproved of the way Asian immigrants were being treated, did not think the Court the proper body to deal with the problem, and was urging Frankfurter to use his relationship with such journals as *The New Republic* and the *Harvard Law Review* as well as with the American Civil Liberties Union to attempt reform through political action.[59]

This, unfortunately, does not explain his acquiescence in the Court's perpetuation of the separate but equal rule. It is true that race relations had not yet become a priority for most civil libertarians; but Brandeis was not usually limited by other peoples' priorities. He had before him the example of the first Justice John Marshall Harlan, whose dissent in *Plessy* provided a strong argument that legally mandated segregation violated civil rights. Brandeis's support for state experimentation does not solve the problem, for he voted against such experiments when they violated rights of speech, press, and assembly. It might be argued that he disliked the Fourteenth Amendment and was loathe to use it even to strike down segregation, but, he was willing to go along with the Court's use of the Fourteenth to overturn state action in the voting and criminal procedure cases mentioned above. Brandeis could have written a dissent echoing Harlan's when a case like *South Covington* v. *Kentucky* or *Gong Lum* v. *Rice* presented the constitutional question of whether the separate but equal doctrine violated the Fourteenth Amendment. But he may have believed, as all the justices between 1916 and 1954 (the year of *Brown* v. *Board*) seemingly did, that the Fourteenth did not in fact prohibit state segregation, however much he may have disliked racism. The letters about Asian-Americans and his encouragement of Frankfurter's work with the ACLU and the NAACP make it unlikely that protection of the rights of nonwhite Americans was as low on Brandeis's agenda as it was on the agenda of most whites of his era. Respect for state sovereignty and federalism may account for the absence of any manifestation of his concern in Court opinions; the precise explanation, however, remains a mystery.[60]

Brandeis was much quicker to protect freedom of the press. For example, in *Near* v. *Minnesota*, the state had enjoined publication of the *Saturday Press*, which Near published. The newspaper had its disreputable side, including scandal-mongering and anti-Semitism, but the issue which led to the injunction was accusing public officials by name of being participants in a gambling ring. Minnesota law permitted the enjoining of periodicals which were "malicious, scandalous and defamatory." When Minnesota's Deputy Attorney General was presenting his oral argument before the Court, Brandeis interrupted. Stating that it was common knowledge that "just such criminal combinations" involving public officials did exist, "to the shame of some of our cities," Brandeis said that he could not tell whether such was the case in Minnesota. However, Near and his partner had attempted to expose what they thought was such a combination. "Now, is that not a privileged communication, if there ever was one?" he asked. "How else can a community secure protection from that sort of thing, if people are not allowed to engage in free discussion in such matters? . . . You are dealing here not with a sort of scandal too often appearing in the press, and which ought not to appear to the interest of any one, but with a matter of prime interest to every American citizen." The attorney general responded that this was fine if the article was correct, but that it had been defamatory. "Of course there was defamation," Brandeis replied. "You cannot disclose evil without naming the doers of evil. It is difficult to see how one can have a free press and the protection it affords in the democratic community without the privilege this act seeks to limit. As for such defamatory matter being issued regularly or customarily, how can such a campaign be conducted except by persistence and continued iteration?" He praised the publishers for their "campaign to rid the city of certain evils." "So they say," the lawyer commented. "Yes, of course," Brandeis agreed, "so they say. They went forward with a definite program and certainly they acted with great courage. They invited suit for criminal libel if what they said was not true. Now, if that campaign was not privileged, if that is not one of the things for which the press chiefly exists, then for what does it exist?"[61]

The difference in the ideologies of Holmes and Brandeis, masked by their almost identical voting patterns, was significant in two ways. It was important for the protection of civil liberties. Had Holmes been on the Court without Brandeis, there probably would have been a "clear and present danger" doctrine. Without Brandeis, however, there would have been no soaring early-twentieth-century explications of the democratic value of free speech and an unrestrained press, nor any excoriation of a government that was threatening to corrupt the people by teaching that ends justified any means. And it is Brandeis's belief that unlimited human advancement can be furthered by legislation and that the probable relationship between the legislation and advancement can be demonstrated through the accumulation of factual data that has come to illuminate American law.

Thus, Brandeis played at least as important a role as Holmes in making sociological jurisprudence the American approach to law in the second half of the twentieth century. Holmes enunciated the principles in his pre-Court writings and in his opinions, but Brandeis, while admiring them enormously, had not needed them for his own jurisprudence. Brandeis had already gotten the essence of that approach during his student days at Harvard under Professors Langdell and Thayer, when he had become convinced that the law was a dynamic entity. His knowledge of state legislatures, gained primarily from his public interest fights in Massachusetts, had taught him that what appeared to be a reasonable piece of legislation might be no more than a giveaway to vested interests. He was therefore unwilling to accept the legislature's judgment of rationality; he had to prove to himself that a statute was reasonable. At the same time, his conviction that federalism and state experimentation were the keys to the progress of the political system made him bend over backward to demonstrate that state experimentation met his criterion. And so, paradoxically, in spite of his suspicion about the motives of state legislators, he ended up supporting greater police powers for the states than did Holmes. He used his compilations of facts to shore up the claims of the legislatures rather than to undermine them. In so doing, he gave to lawyers and judges, living through an era of great skepticism about the state legislatures, a methodology for differentiating "private interest" legislation from the kind of social experimentation favored by Progressives and, later, New Dealers.

Law schools began teaching the techniques of sociological jurisprudence. Johns Hopkins University established an Institute of Law in 1928 to study the relationship between law and society and the way lawyers might use such disciplines as psychology, psychiatry, sociology, and criminology. The law schools at Columbia, Yale, and Harvard added social science theory and data to their curricula and political scientists, economists, and sociologists to their faculties. Legislators learned to preface their statutes with an explanation of the factual need that had led to them. As the federal government began enacting increasingly larger numbers of social experimentation statutes during the New Deal and the decades thereafter, federal legislators followed the new procedure adopted by their colleagues in state legislatures. It became common to create a legislative record replete with facts to sustain claims of constitutionality. In passing the 1964 Civil Rights Act, for example, Congress held hearings that enabled it to preface the Act with the assertion that segregation interfered with interstate commerce and that the Act was therefore a legitimate exercise of the undoubted congressional power to regulate such commerce. The Court, in turn, upheld the Act on those grounds.[62]

Similarly, the Court itself established new factually oriented legal doctrines. When a state law is alleged to have violated the Fourteenth Amendment's equal protection clause, the Court normally uses one of two criteria for its decision. The first possibility is whether the law bears a rational relation to a legitimate state goal, which is usually not difficult to prove. The second is whether the state has a "compelling interest" in achieving whatever it is the law seeks to accomplish; this criterion is harder to meet than the first and is dependent upon a showing that the state could not deal with the factual situation without the aid of the statute. A third criterion is used by the Court primarily in cases involving categorization of people by race. The Court calls that categorization a "suspect classification," which triggers suspicion of unconstitutional bias. Utilization of the "suspect classification" criterion almost invariably results in a declaration that the state has not met the heavy burden of alleviating the justices' suspicion and that the action is unconstitutional. When racial classifications are employed remedially, however, as when a school district takes note of the racial composition of its student body in order to maintain integrated classrooms, the justices usually uphold the action.[63]

Thus, the Court's decision has frequently rested on its assessment of the factual situation. It has become less necessary than it was in Brandeis's day for the Court to seek facts not included in the brief provided by counsel for the parties, both because the parties in a case now routinely provide the Court with the factual material and because major constitutional cases are likely to generate *amici curiae* briefs. The justices then choose among the facts; and, because the opposing parties have disagreed about or emphasized different facts, the justices in the majority and those who dissent can all point to "facts" when writing their opinions. In recent years various justices have used as the basis for their opinions what they consider to be facts: for example, that women have assumed new roles in modern society, that minimizing the availability of legal abortions will result in the deaths of poor women from illegal abortions, that black medical students tend to return to their own communities when they go into practice, that black children do not learn as well in segregated schools as in those that are integrated, that putting two prisoners in a sixty-three-square-foot cell designed to house only one is not inhumane, and that the death penalty deters would-be murderers.[64]

It is notable that these cases involve civil liberties rather than the kind of economic policymaking which led to the creation of the Brandeis brief. Beginning in 1937, the Court once again began to view social legislation as presumptively constitutional. (Since John Marshall's day, the Court had formally adhered to a rule that legislation was constitutional unless proven otherwise, but in practice the Court of the late nineteenth and early twentieth centuries almost always found against the constitutionality of socioeconomic legislation.) It therefore became less necessary for defenders of legislative experimentation to present the justices with a plethora of facts in their support. Beginning with the Warren Court and the mid-1950s, however, federal courts rather than the state legislatures became the major policy innovators, mainly in civil liberties issues. In order to justify its role, the Court started to present its opinions as no more than logical conclusions drawn from "facts," which in turn have been supplied to the Court by those arguing for broadened definitions of liberties. Whether these "facts" are correct or not, the Court has rendered constitutional decisions that have altered the balance of power between competing groups and values in American life on the strength of its belief that reasonable legislators could consider certain facts to warrant particular legislation, rather than on the basis of purely legalistic argumentation. That, for better or worse, is Brandeis's legacy; and those who consider the law to be a dynamic entity and the involvement of American courts in the policymaking process an ineluctable reality can only consider the justices' access to and recognition of the human situations that underlie their decisions a welcome innovation.

17 | The Curse of Bigness

Brandeis was central to the growth of modern American public law; his major contributions were in sociological jurisprudence and civil liberties (see Chapter 16) and in his Progressive critique of orthodox assumptions about American society. By telling Americans over and over again that bigness was not necessarily good, that corporations were less than perfect institutions, that unionization was both legitimate and desirable, that experimentation in the economic sphere was to be encouraged, that legislation designed to protect individuals from the consequences of economic crises was constitutional, that democracy was a continuing process that had to be nurtured rather than a goal to be attained and then forgotten—by reminding Americans, in short, of the realities of twentieth-century life and placing them in a constitutional context, he both stimulated and reflected the alterations that were occurring in the American system. His role as a prophet of change, reflected in his clerks' (and Franklin Roosevelt's) references to him as "Isaiah," was demonstrated by the dwindling number of dissents he wrote during his last years on the bench. By the time Brandeis retired, public policy had begun to catch up with many of his ideas.

Throughout his adult life one of Brandeis's major concerns was bigness; a book of his collected papers was entitled *The Curse of Bigness*. Anything that ignored the limitations of human nature and the difficulty human beings experienced in ascertaining the most successful patterns of life was to be avoided. Above all, human beings had to be wary of the evil of bigness, in government as well as in business. For with their complex combination of creativity and limited intellect, human beings could create institutions that were too big for them: too big to monitor for efficiency and effectiveness, too big to assess for value or liability to society, too big to control.

In the economic sphere, the Court's duty was to reinforce governmental efforts to return American businesses to the size they would have been had the money trust and the laws its power produced not artificially created giant corporations. The Court had the responsibility not to interfere with experimentation in limiting bigness (antitrust laws) and to encourage the growth of nongovernmental forces (unions) that would help curb the power that flowed from bigness.

Brandeis brought the whole force of his new jurisprudence to bear in support of federalism and economic experimentation by the states. His belief in experimentation and his equally strong faith in competition found expression when the Court decided *Liggett* v. *Lee* in 1933. A Florida law imposed heavier license fees on stores that were part of multicounty chains than on independent shops: there were different annual license fees, depending on whether stores were independently owned ($5 per store), part of an intracounty chain (up to $40 per store), or part of an intercounty chain (up to $50 per store). Clearly, Florida was seeking to discourage chain stores. Justice Roberts, speaking for a majority of five, held that the law was an unconstitutional violation of the equal protection and due process clauses of the Fourteenth Amendment, because there was no reasonable basis for such classification of stores. Dissenting, Brandeis reminded the Court of its own rule that statutes were presumed to be constitutional and argued that there was no reason not to apply that rule to the Florida law. It was well established that states had the right to use tax laws to promote or burden businesses for social and economic purposes. The wisdom of Florida in enacting this particular law was not the business of the Court; the only question for the Court was whether the power exercised was a legitimate one and precedent indicated that it was.[1]

Having made the traditional argument, Brandeis then drew on facts to show that a state was correct to consider the discouragement of bigness a "felt necessity." First, he attacked corporations: "The prevalence of the corporation in America has led men of this generation to act, at times, as if the privilege of doing business in corporate form were inherent in the citizen; and has led them to accept the evils attendant upon the free and unrestricted use of the corporate mechanism as if these evils were the inescapable price of civilized life." But although the states had begun early in their histories to grant corporate charters to religious, educational, and charitable organizations, they had initially denied the right of incorporation to businesses. "It was denied because of fear. Fear of encroachment upon the liberties and opportunities of the individual. Fear of the subjection of labor to capital. Fear of monopoly . . . There was a sense of some insidious menace inherent in large aggregations of capital, particularly when held by corporations." These fears led states to reduce limitations only gradually, even after "the desire for business expansion created an irresistible demand" for charters. And as each state's limitations were gradually removed, it became all too clear that the early fears had been warranted. Citing, among other studies, Adolph A. Berle and Gardiner Means's *The Modern Corporation and Private Property* and Thorstein Veblen's *Absentee Ownership and Business Enterprise*, Brandeis drew a picture of the results of corporate growth: "Through size, corporations, once merely an efficient tool employed by individuals in the conduct of private business, have become an institution . . . which has brought such concentration of economic power that so-called private corporations are sometimes able to dominate the State . . . the lives of tens or hundreds of thousands of employees and the property of tens or hundreds of thousands of investors are subjected, through the corporate mechanism, to the control of a few men." The great impact on the workers and the public led scholars to compare corporatism with feudalism and to "the rule of a plutocracy." Now a few hundred people controlled the 200 nonbanking corporations that in turn directly controlled one quarter of the country's wealth and indirectly controlled much more. This was a "negation of industrial democracy" and meant that "there has occurred a marked concentration of individual wealth; and that the resulting disparity in incomes is a major cause of the existing depression." Brandeis added, "Such is the Frankenstein monster which States have created by their corporation laws."[2]

It just happened, Brandeis went on, that 5 of the 12 plaintiffs in the case were among the 200 nonbanking corporations he had mentioned, each with assets of more than $90,000,000. They had a total of $820,000,000 worth of assets and 19,718 stores throughout the United States; one of the corporations operated almost 16,000 stores. Against this Goliath were pitted the brave Davids of Florida: the individual retailers, who were fighting for their very existence. Florida's motive might have been only preservation of competition, it might also have been "broader and deeper": "They may have believed that the chain store, by furthering the concentration of wealth and of power and by promoting absentee ownership, is thwarting American ideals; that it is making impossible equality of opportunity; that it is converting independent tradesmen into clerks; and that it is sapping the resources, the vigor and the hope of the smaller cities and towns."[3]

There was nothing new about a justice using an opinion to express his beliefs. But it was unusual for a twentieth-century justice to attack rather than defend corporate giantism. It was equally unusual for a justice to cite, in support of his description of huge corporations as inhumane, elitist, and subversive of American ideals, volume after volume by economists and sociologists. But Brandeis cited numerous books, their authors (in addition to those already mentioned) ranging from Stuart Chase, J. A. Hobson, and Arthur Dahlberg to I. Maurice Wormser (*Frankenstein, Incorporated*); articles in such journals as *Editorial Research, Labor, American Economic Review, Annals* of The American Academy of Political and Social Science, and *Retail Ledger*; and a variety of congressional hearings, speeches, and government reports. All contributed to Brandeis's conclusion that if the citizens of Florida believed that bigness had to be undone in order to stop a paralysis of individual initiative and creative power, to reopen opportunities for leadership, and to "secure the moral and intellectual development which is essential to the maintenance of liberty," there was nothing in the Constitution to stop them from imposing discriminatory license fees on corporate chains: "To that extent, the citizens of each State are still masters of their destiny."[4]

It is clear why Brandeis on the Court was as admired, revered, hated, and feared as was Brandeis the public-spirited attorney. His hard-hitting language in *Liggett*, written when he was seventy-six years old, showed undiminished passion and eloquence; his lambasting of the abuse of corporate power marked his judicial career. Dissenting when the Court overturned a Pennsylvania statute that taxed corporations more heavily than individually owned businesses and partnerships, Brandeis had proclaimed:

> there are still intelligent, informed, just-minded, and civilized persons who believe that the rapidly growing aggregation of capital through corporations constitutes an insidious menace to the liberty of the citizen; that it tends to increase the subjection of labor to capital; that, because of the guidance and control necessarily exercised by great corporations upon those engaged in business, individual liberty is being impaired and creative power will be lessened; . . . that the evils incident to the accelerating absorption of business by corporations outweigh the benefits thereby secured; and that the process of absorption should be retarded.[5]

It is easy to hear echoes in these opinions of Brandeis's pre-Court writings and testimony before congressional committees. His ideas were forged by the combined experiences of home, Harvard, Boston, his legal practice, and his days as the "People's Attorney," and they did not change one iota once he reached the Court. A comprehensive summary of Brandeis's 528 judicial opinions would be as repetitive as it would be lengthy, because he kept hammering at the same finely honed ideas he had espoused in the decades before he ascended the bench. It is therefore unnecessary to delve at length here into even all of those opinions that might be labeled "major." Felix Frankfurter commented, "To quote from Mr. Justice Brandeis' opinions is not to pick plums from a pudding but to pull threads from a pattern." Brandeis himself, asked after he had left the Court whether he had plans to write his memoirs, responded, "I think you will find that my memoirs have already been written." The history of his ideas moves with no break from his days as an attorney to his years on the bench.[6]

Brandeis's attitude toward labor unions was no less consistent than his other beliefs. For example, a year after he joined the Court, he dealt with the case of a coal company that had made its employees agree not to join a union. When the union began fighting against these "yellow-dog contracts," the company sought an injunction against the union organizers. The Supreme Court found the union guilty, in effect, of threatening to coerce the company to accept unionization. Brandeis dissented, pointing out that the union was attempting to put the company on an equal footing with its employees. Said Brandeis, "The employer is free either to accept the agreement or the disadvantage. Indeed, the plaintiff's whole case is rested upon agreements secured under similar pressure of economic necessity or disadvantage. If it is coercion to threaten to strike unless plaintiff consents to a closed union shop, it is coercion also to threaten not to give one employment unless the applicant will consent to a closed non-union shop." Although Brandeis considered at length the need of the mine workers to unionize if they were to achieve security and economic independence, the dissent was not merely an emotional reaction on Brandeis's part. He had long disapproved of the injunction as a method of coping with labor agitation and, of course, he approved of unionization. But Brandeis, as his debate with Gompers had indicated, was absolutely opposed to the closed shop as a form of labor despotism. Nonetheless, his duty as a judge was to make liberty of contract a reality by establishing the legal equality of the two parties, not to say what the union should fight for once such equality had been attained.[7]

As an advocate he had urged business and labor to find a forum for resolving their differences, and that forum would not come into existence until unionization forced business to recognize its desirability. As a judge, he saw prolabor legislation as encouraging at least the first step in the process, unionization. That step should not be negated by lower court judges issuing injunctions against attempts at unionization. Such an injunction, for example, was issued when the Duplex Printing Company claimed that damage would result from a union's efforts to force it into unionization through a boycott of its products. The Court decided that the injunction was permissible under the Clayton Act. Brandeis disagreed. Recounting in some detail the history and intentions of the Clayton Act (Brandeis did not have to remind his brethren that he had been much involved in that history), he argued that the purpose of the Act was precisely to indicate that Congress did not want judges interfering with such union activities as sympathetic strikes.[8]

Brandeis did not merely cite statutes, legislative background and law reviews. It has long been axiomatic among teachers of constitutional law that if creatures from Mars with no knowledge of human affairs landed on Earth and read through the hundreds of volumes of Supreme Court decisions, they would come away with a sound understanding of what had happened during two hundred years of American society. Almost all the phenomena, clashes, and values of the American system are reflected in Supreme Court cases. As Alexis de Tocqueville wrote with his usual discernment, "Scarcely any political question arises in the United States that is not resolved sooner or later into a judicial question." Tocqueville was correct, but in order for Court opinions to serve as history lessons, they must include not only legal-philosophical analyses but a reflection of the human conflicts that lie behind cases. This was one of the services Brandeis rendered to the country in the dissents he penned between 1916 and 1939.[9]

It would be difficult to comprehend the nature of the labor struggle from reading the opinions of justices such as Pitney, Taft, and Sutherland, who saw the labor movement as no more than an unprincipled attack by lawless ruffians on the sacred doctrines protecting private property. Brandeis, however, used his opinions to summarize the situations at issue: not merely who was suing whom but why. He pointed out in *Duplex* v. *Deering* that there were only four companies in the United States manufacturing newspaper printing presses; that three had been unionized and had agreed to such progressive measures as the eight-hour day and payment of a minimum wage; that when Duplex refused to recognize the union, two of the other companies threatened to withdraw from their agreements with the union. The union, whose very existence was thus in jeopardy, not only called out its workers at Duplex but asked other workers to refuse to install, repair, or work on Duplex machines. "May not all with a common interest," Brandeis asked, "join in refusing to expend their labor upon articles whose very production constitutes an

attack upon their standard of living and the institution which they are
convinced supports it?"[10]

While explaining the plight of the union, Brandeis returned to his theme
of the limited role the judiciary ought to play in a democratic society.
"All rights are derived from the purposes of the society in which they
exist; above all rights rises duty to the community." Should conditions
in labor relations develop to the point "that those engaged in it cannot
continue their struggle without danger to the community," the rules might
have to be altered. "But it is not their function to set the limits of permissible contest and to declare the duties which the new situation demands. This is the function of the legislature which, while limiting individual
and group rights of aggression and defense, may substitute processes of
justice for the more primitive method of trial by combat."[11]

Limits could be drawn by the federal legislature, as in the Clayton
Act, or by the state legislatures. For example, Arizona had forbidden its
courts to issue injunctions against strikes and picketing. Nonetheless,
when the cooks and waiters at the English Kitchen on Main Street in
Bisbee, Arizona, went on strike and encouraged a boycott of the restaurant through picketing and leafleting, the restaurant asked the local courts
for an injunction. The Cochise County Superior Court denied the injunction; the Arizona Supreme Court denied it; the English Kitchen then
took its case to the Supreme Court, where it found a more sympathetic
hearing. Chief Justice Taft held the Arizona law to constitute a violation
of the equal protection and due process clauses of the Fourteenth Amendment. Brandeis, predictably, asked whether the statute might not be considered a reasonable exercise of the police power. He wrote fourteen
pages drawing upon similar statutes in England, the British dominions,
the federal government, and the states, all to show that reasonable people
might well agree with Arizona's experiment. The test, in dealing with
the equal protection and due process clauses, was whether the classification or right established by a statute could be considered reasonable.
Brandeis's dissent (with which three other justices concurred) was designed to demonstrate that there was nothing unreasonable about a state's
decision to permit picketing. It also cautioned, "The divergence of opinion
in this difficult field of governmental action should admonish us not to
declare a rule arbitrary and unreasonable merely because we are convinced that it is fraught with danger to the public weal, and thus to close
the door to experiment within the law."[12]

The distinction made by the Court between combinations of employers
and combinations of workers continued to exasperate Brandeis. When
the Journeymen Stone Cutters' Association, attempting to unionize the
Bedford Cut Stone Company, asked all local unions not to handle stone

cut by nonunion labor, the Court held that this "combination in restraint of trade" was a violation of the Sherman Antitrust Act. Brandeis was furious: "If, on the undisputed facts of this case, refusal to work can be enjoined, Congress created by the Sherman Law and the Clayton Act an instrument for imposing restraints upon labor which reminds of involuntary servitude." He pointed out that the Court had found nothing in the Sherman Act to deter the steel trust, which enabled a single corporation to dominate the steel trade; it had found nothing in that law to deter a corporation that controlled "practically the whole shoe machinery industry of the country"; where, then, did the Court find in the Act a congressional intention "to deny to members of a small craft of workingmen the right to cooperate in simply refraining from work, when that course was the only means of self-protection against a combination of militant and powerful employers"?[13]

Thus, although Brandeis supported unionization, his opinions were couched in terms of judicial self-restraint. Courts through the late nineteenth and early twentieth centuries had set ample antilabor precedents. Most experimentation undertaken by the states or Congress, therefore, would necessarily be prolabor. Brandeis could thus lambast judicial activism and support the union cause at the same time. When the logic of the law demanded, however, he cast his judicial vote against his beliefs (see Chapter 15). The occasions when he concurred in seemingly antilabor decisions that had implications beyond those for the individuals concerned have been misconstrued; invariably, as Alexander Bickel has shown, he went along with the majority as a way of avoiding a more damaging decision or to gain allies for later victories.[14]

Holmes, unimpressed by Brandeis's professed restraint, wrote to Harold Laski, "He is affected by his interest in a cause, and if he feels it he is not detached." Holmes returned one of Brandeis's draft opinions with the comment, "Yes, forcibly put—but I cant think it good form to treat an opinion as an essay and put in footnotes." Holmes's view was apparently shared by Roscoe Pound. Laski reported to Holmes, "Pound and I agreed yesterday that if you could hint to Brandeis that judicial opinions aren't to be written in the form of a brief it would be a great relief to the world. Pound spoke rather strongly as to the advocate in B. being over-prominent in his decisions just as in his general philosophy." Justice Harlan Stone also criticized Brandeis on these grounds. After reading Brandeis's dissent in *Liggett* v. *Lee*, Stone sent him a letter chiding, "I think you are too much an advocate of this particular legislation. I have little enthusiasm for it, although I think it constitutional. In any case I think our dissents are more effective if we take the attitude that we are concerned with power and not with the merits of its exercise."

Frankfurter, however, understood that although Brandeis's work on the bench "may accurately be described as a continuation of devotion to the solution of those social and economic problems of American society with which he was preoccupied for nearly a generation before his judicial career," part of Brandeis's solution was to insist, "as the great men of law have always insisted, that law must be sensitive to life." It was unthinkable for the man who had said, "I abhor averages. I like the individual case," to deal with a case in any way other than to start with the relevant facts.[15]

Just as Brandeis insisted that all solutions began with facts, he also maintained that each individual was a "wee thing," so it was necessary to see what others who had dealt with similar situations found to be the facts. Then, it became Brandeis's responsibility to help educate those who read his opinions by demonstrating how and on what basis he had reached his conclusions. Paul Freund has recalled Brandeis's comment when the first opinion on which Freund worked as Brandeis's clerk "had gone through what seemed the last possible revision. 'The opinion is now convincing,' he said, 'but how can we make it more instructive?' " Willard Hurst remembers Brandeis's "strong moral impulse that he had an obligation to . . . interpret the action of which he was part." Dean Acheson and Calvert Magruder made reference to Brandeis's desire to educate both the other justices and the general public. When Brandeis found the Court intractable, he put his hope in the people. Thus, while working on his dissents in *Schaefer, Pierce,* and *Gilbert* he told Acheson, "The whole purpose, and the only one, is to educate the country. We may be able to fill the people with shame, after the passion cools, by preserving some of it on the record. The only hope is the people; you cannot educate the Court." Acheson was certain Brandeis meant that the Court could not be educated on the particular subject.[16]

Brandeis invariably advocated what his thorough investigation of the facts had led him to believe was the proper course of action for the Court. Occasionally, as in *New State Ice*, that course was to give judicial legitimation to a law of which he disapproved. He would have considered himself irresponsible had he not explained why he had to support a law that minimized competition; hence his extensive examination of the ice industry in Oklahoma and the "reasonableness" of the statute. Because Brandeis as a judge urged judicial self-restraint in a day when that was far from the norm, he felt it incumbent upon him to explain why legislatures should be permitted to experiment. He also advocated utilizing the judicial opinion as an educational device, unlike the laconic Holmes, who seemingly expected the eloquence of his pronouncements to substitute for persuasion. In a sense, the very length of Brandeis's opinions bears testimony to his faith in democracy. If all the facts were known and understood, people would choose the wisest course of action. And so the Brandeis brief, created to circumvent the Court's decisions against maximum hours statutes (by educating the judges), was transformed into a judge's opinions designed to educate the people.

Brandeis saw federalism and separation of powers, in part, as the Constitution's solutions to the problem of governmental size, and it was the Court's duty to adhere to both. Jurisdictional rules helped keep the Court itself within the boundaries prescribed by the Constitution and prevented it from intervening in social problems that were too big for any nine justices to solve. Part of the Court's function, in turn, was to maintain the narrow margin of separation between the federal executive and Congress. Further, the Court's role was to protect the powers of the states from the encroachment of the central government—while keeping "states' rights" from limiting creative national solutions to new problems. That is why Brandeis dissented passionately from the Court's decision in *Myers* v. *U.S.* (1927) that a president could unilaterally fire a civil servant even though a statute required Senate advice and consent before such a removal. Brandeis assumed that the Founding Fathers feared bigness and concentration of power as much as he did. "The doctrine of the separation of powers was adopted by the Convention of 1787 not to promote efficiency but to preclude the exercise of arbitrary power. The purpose was not to avoid friction, but, by means of the inevitable friction incident to the distribution of the governmental powers among three departments, to save the people from autocracy." Separation of powers meant that no one branch would become so big that it would be both unmanageable and unaccountable.[17]

With the advent of the New Deal, Brandeis saw many of his socioeconomic concerns being shared by the federal government and many of his ideas enacted into legislation. This did not, however, alter his attitude toward bigness. He could support the Banking Act (1933) and the Securities Act (1933), which embodied his belief that banks had to be kept out of the stock brokerage business and that securities houses had to make full disclosure to potential investors. He approved of the 1935 Social Security Act (including provisions for unemployment compensation) and the Wagner Act (1935) that created the National Labor Relations Board and gave labor the federally protected right to unionize. He liked the Miller-Tydings Act (1937), strengthening fair-trade laws; the Walsh-Healy Act (1936), requiring federal contractors to follow minimum wage and maximum hour guidelines; the statute creating the Tennessee Valley Authority (1933), so similar to the solution he had proposed in 1911 for the Alaskan problem; the Bituminous Coal Act (1935); the Fair Labor Standards Act (1938); the Wealth Tax Act (1935); the Robinson-Patman Act (1936); and the Public Utilities Holding Company Act (1935). Although rarely going as far as Brandeis would have liked, all were in keeping with his principles.

But he could not tolerate turning large and amorphous areas of power over to federal officials, as in Brandeis's view, was done by the National Industrial Recovery Act of 1933 (NRA). It gave exemption from antitrust laws to industries adopting codes providing for specific wages, hours, conditions of employment, and prices. But it provided no guidelines for the substance of the codes, leaving it to the president to approve or disapprove them. He was also skeptical about the Agricultural Adjustment Act (1933), which attempted to keep farmers solvent by paying them to restrict production. The result of both acts was creation of big, regulatory bureaucracies of the kind that Brandeis had always warned about. He wrote to his daughter on April 22, 1934, "As you may have imagined, I see little to be joyous about in the New Deal measures most talked about, N.R.A., and A.A.A. seem to be going from bad to worse." He was not ready to give up on the NRA, writing to Hapgood on October 27 that it "seems to be tending toward . . . the lowering of prices, which is essential to lessening unemployment." But he began to see all his fears of big bureaucracy and centralization of power validated when the first case involving the NRA came before the Court.[18]

The president had promulgated a code for the oil industry, and officials of two companies had been prosecuted for ignoring it. The counsel for one company told the Court on December 10, 1934, that his client had not known the law existed. The only copy of the code that the client knew of, he said, was in the "hip pocket of a government agent sent down to Texas from Washington." Brandeis immediately asked the government's lawyer, "Who promulgates these orders and codes that have the force of law?" The lawyer replied, "They are promulgated by the President, and I assume they are on record at the State Department." Brandeis pressed: "Is there any official or general publication of these executive orders?" "Not that I know of," the lawyer answered. "Well," demanded Brandeis in exasperation, "is there any way by which one can find out what is in these executive orders when they are issued?" The most the government lawyer could say was, "I think it would be rather difficult, but it is possible to get certified copies of the executive orders and codes from the NRA." The answer was not good enough; Brandeis joined seven of his colleagues in striking down this use of the NRA.[19]

Nevertheless, many were taken by surprise when Brandeis joined the unanimous Court a few months later in declaring the NRA unconstitu-

350   LOUIS D. BRANDEIS

tional. (Roosevelt, stunned by the unanimity of the vote, asked, "What about old Isaiah?") Chief Justice Hughes wrote for the Court that the massive delegation of power to the president violated the separation of powers. Hughes's second point, which caused Justices Cardozo and Stone to concur rather than add their names to Hughes's opinion, was that the Act sought to regulate activities having only an indirect effect on interstate commerce. Under Article I, Congress is given the power to regulate interstate (but not intrastate) commerce, and the difference between inter- and intrastate commerce, and between activities with a "direct" rather than an "indirect" effect on interstate commerce, had been used by the Court to strike down remedial economic legislation enacted by the federal government. Brandeis was on record as disagreeing with the Court-related distinction. He had written to Frankfurter in 1923 that "my own opinion has been that it was wise (1) to treat the constitutional power of interstate Com. as very broad & (2) to treat acts of Congress as not invading State power unless it clearly appeared that the federal power was intended to be exercised exclusively (3) to rectify the tendency to hold federal power exclusive by applying the Webb-Kenyon doctrine" (which lent federal enforcement power to state laws regulating commerce). It would have been logical for Brandeis to go along with Cardozo's argument that the facts in each case had to be considered before the Court could decide whether a direct or indirect effect on interstate commerce was involved. He did not.[20]

Hughes announced the verdict against NRA on May 27, 1935. The Court had begun its noon sessio with Justice Sutherland announcing his opinion for the unanimous Court in the case of *Humphrey's Executor* v. *United States*. The Court in effect overturned its earlier ruling in *Myers* v. *U.S.* and adopted much of Brandeis's dissent in that case, holding that the president could not remove members of independent regulatory commissions. Brandeis followed Sutherland with his own bombshell: his opinion in *Louisville* v. *Radford*, again for a unanimous Court, holding unconstitutional the Frazier-Lemke Act (1933), which had permitted farmers to defer mortgage payments and had established a procedure under which a bankruptcy court could take over the mortgage for five years, set and collect rent for those years, and then charge the farmer whatever he still owed of the price of the property. Brandeis and the Court found this to be a violation of the Fifth Amendment, for the Frazier-Lemke Act took title to the property from the bank which held the mortgage, infringing the substantive rights of the property owner. What should have been done, Brandeis said, was to use the power of eminent domain, pay the banks for their property, and put the cost of the burden on the taxpayers.[21]

Brandeis did in *Louisville* the very opposite of what he had done in *Pennsylvania* v. *Mahon* (1922), where he had argued that the state had the right to declare a category of property to be affected with a public interest and to prevent it from being used without reimbursing the property holder. The difference for Brandeis, however, was twofold. First, the *Mahon* case had involved state rather than federal legislation. Brandeis had told Frankfurter that what some of his fellow justices didn't understand was that "recognition of Federal powers does not mean denial of State powers. I have not been against increase of federal power, but curtailment of State's powers." (The most explicit statement of his position would come in 1938, when, speaking for a unanimous court, he overruled the court-made doctrine that federal common law was binding on the states.) Now, in *Louisville*, he pointed out that the Act, as applied in this case, completely destroyed property rights hitherto protected by Kentucky law. The second difference between the two cases had to do with Brandeis's approach to economics and big business. After quoting the Act's definition of farmers as those "the principal part of whose income is derived from farming operations," Brandeis suddenly changed the style of his opinion. He had used his earlier text and footnotes to refer to purely legal matters, but he now turned to economic facts. "We have no occasion to consider either the causes or the extent of farm tenancy; or whether its progressive increase would be arrested by the provisions of the Act," he wrote. "Nor need we consider the occupations of the beneficiaries of the legislation." He considered both factors nonetheless. One of the motives behind the Act had been to stop tenancy, the process by which farmers lost ownership over their land and remained employed on it as tenants. Brandeis noted the suggestion that the growth in tenancy was completely unrelated to mortgage foreclosures; that is, he had doubts about the utility of the Act. Moreover, the definition of farmer in the Act included "persons who are merely capitalist absentees." And if there was anything Brandeis disliked more than concentrations of power, it was the "capitalist absentees"—whether owners of land or of stock—whose concentrations of money gave them excessive power. Most of the compilations of facts in Brandeis's opinions were used to argue that legislation should be upheld, not struck down; *Louisville* was the exception, but Brandeis used it to overturn a federal law that permitted the federal government to curb state power.[22]

Brandeis viewed the three decisions handed down by the Court on "Black Monday" as indicating the rational limits on federal power. The reason he chose not to join the Cardozo concurrence in the NRA case but went along with Hughes's blast at federal interference in what could be seen as local commerce was apparent in a comment he made to Thomas

G. Corcoran, a Frankfurter protegé, a former clerk for Justice Holmes, and one of Roosevelt's most important aides. Summoning Corcoran to the justices' robing room, Brandeis told him, "This is the end of this business of centralization, and I want you to go back and tell the President that we're not going to let this government centralize everything. It's come to an end. As for your young men, you call them together and tell them to get out of Washington—tell them to go home, back to the states. That is where they must do their work." "Black Monday" for Brandeis was a signal that bigness in government could be every bit as oppressive as bigness in business. The assumption that a big government could control big business had been embodied in Theodore Roosevelt's New Nationalism program and challenged by Brandeis during the 1912 presidential campaign. Franklin Roosevelt, in Brandeis's eyes, was making the same mistake—accepting big business as inevitable rather than scaling it down to size. Brandeis had no qualms about taking Roosevelt to task, and, for a short while, even managed to persuade Roosevelt to support Brandeisian legislation.[23]

Brandeis, however, would not fall into the trap of supporting an all-powerful Court to deal with big government. Thus, he agreed to join Justice Stone's dissent when the Court struck down the Agricultural Adjustment Act. Much as he disliked the AAA, he did not agree with the Court that it was an unconstitutional use of the taxing power. As if to prove that judges, too, were fallible, Justice Roberts, speaking for the majority, wrote an opinion that embodied all the jurisprudential axioms that Brandeis had exposed and battled against. When a statute was challenged as unconstitutional, Roberts proclaimed, "all the court does" is carry out its duty "to lay the article of the Constitution which is invoked beside the statute which is challenged and to decide whether the latter squares with the former." Roberts denied that the Court had any power beyond "the power of judgment. This court neither approves or condemns any legislative policy. Its delicate and difficult office is to ascertain and declare whether the legislation is in accordance with, or in contravention of, the provisions of the Constitution; and having done that, its duty ends."[24]

This apparently was too much for Brandeis. If the Court could not uphold New Deal legislation, at least it could be honest about the nature of its function. Unchecked judicial power was just as bad as unchecked power of any other kind, so Brandeis concurred in Stone's acid attack on what they (and Cardozo) saw as Robert's belief that courts are "the only agency of government that must be assumed to have the capacity to govern." Since that was not Brandeis's assumption, although he had his doubts about various pieces of New Deal legislation, he voted to strike down only two (the NRA and the Frazier-Lemke Act).[25]

Brandeis could not consider the Court "the only agency of government that must be assumed to have the capacity to govern," but he did think it was a first-rate institution. He urged Frankfurter to include in the latter's *Business of the United States Supreme Court* (1928), written with Brandeis's former clerk James Landis, a full discussion of the factors that made the Court a good one:

A.   Encouragement of oral argument. Discouragement of oratory. Socratic method at argument applied through the judges . . .

B.   Assignment of cases to the J[ustice]s by the C. J. after discussion and vote at conference.

C.   Distribution of opinions in print, and consideration at subsequent conference. Ample time thereafter for writing dissents & at conferences for suggestion & then recirculation of revised opinion.

D.   Consideration of every case . . . by every judge before the conference . . .

E.   Limiting, by means of certiorari, the number of cases by the human limitation of 9 judges' working time.

F.   Discouraging rehearings.

G.   Importance of length of service, as distinguished from method of selection of judges.

H.   Team play, encouraging individual enquiry (and dissent) as distinguished from subservient ignorant unanimity.

I.   Tradition.

J.   The play of public opinion upon the Court's performance . . .

K.   And the extraordinary service through longevity & loyalty in the Clerks & Marshal's office . . .

Frankfurter and Landis incorporated this language into their "Preface" almost verbatim.[26]

The "team play" of which Brandeis spoke was in large part due to the size of the Court; a "team" of ninety would have been more difficult to work with than was a team of nine, and once again Brandeis's emphasis on smallness appeared to him to be validated. What he did not mention in his letter to Frankfurter (but what did emerge in private conversations held by the two men during the 1920s) was that Brandeis was able to work well with the team in spite of his ideological differences with most of its members, because of one of the talents he took to the Court. Brandeis took to the Court his jurisprudence, his emphasis on education, his love of liberty, his belief in experimentation, and his hatred for bigness. He also took his skill in politics.[27]

18 | Style and Politics on the Court

Brandeis discovered in 1916 that it was customary for each new justice to "inherit" his predecessor's messenger, in his case a man named Poindexter; to be given a copy of the federal court reports; and to be permitted to hire one additional employee. Most justices used this allotment for a stenographer-typist. Brandeis, however, had already decided to write his judicial opinions in longhand. He adopted Holmes's innovation of hiring a law clerk instead of a secretary, agreeing that the enthusiasm and knowledge of young law school graduates would provide him with stimulation and the kind of assistance his approach to the law required. Therefore, each year Frankfurter sent him the Harvard Law School graduate he considered most impressive. A partial list of his clerks includes Calvert Magruder, his first clerk, later a federal appeals judge; Dean Acheson, the highest of whose many later offices was secretary of state; James M. Landis, later dean of Harvard Law School: Harry Shulman, later dean of Yale Law School; Henry J. Friendly, later a federal judge; David Riesman, who became a renowned sociologist; H. Thomas Austern, senior partner in the politically prominent Washington law firm of Covington, Burling; and several who would become the country's most important law professors—William G. Rice, William F. McCurdy, Henry M. Hart, Paul Freund, Louis Jaffe, Nathanial Nathanson, and Willard Hurst. The reminiscences of these men enable one to get a picture of Brandeis at work.[1]

He had joined the Court in the days when the courtroom was still in the Capitol building. There was no space for offices for the justices or for their aides; the Court's library was in the Capitol basement. Brandeis eventually came to feel that a wing should be added to the Capitol for court offices, but Chief Justice Taft lobbied vigorously and successfully for construction of the building that now houses the Court. Brandeis, who was opposed to the opulence of the new building and to its isolation from Congress and the White House, refused to move into the building. He ignored his right as a senior justice to pick one of the better three-room suites, saying he would take whatever was left over: he had no plans to use the suite in any case.[2]

Two rooms in the Brandeis household were set aside as offices: one for Brandeis, the other for his clerk. In 1926, when the Brandeises moved to Florence Court West on California Street, they rented a two-room apartment above their own where Brandeis spent much of his working day. Willard Hurst found the office apartment overflowing with papers and books. The bathtub was filled with folders of clippings and references to bits of irrelevant information Brandeis came across while doing research, information that interested him as well as data that might prove useful some day in a case before the Court. When, for example, *Liggett* v. *Lee* reached the Court, Brandeis delved into his bathtub for the background facts he would use in his dissent. There were two folders with factual material, two with bibliographies, two with copies of the Federal Trade Commission's hearing on chain stores, plus a wealth of other material. The kitchenette was piled with manuscripts and corrected proofs.[3]

The clerks went to Brandeis each year in trepidation, worked with exhilaration, and left in exhaustion. He was as demanding of them as he was of himself; he after all was not only functioning as a justice, but was also leading the American Zionist movement and advising presidents. His clerks found themselves spending endless hours in libraries: not only in the Court library, seeking legal precedents, but also in the Library of Congress, where they sought out the innumerable citations to sociological material that Brandeis demanded. His photographic memory astounded them. While working on a patent case, he told one clerk, "There is a book in the Library of Congress published about 1870; a small volume with a green cover; and in chapter three the point in this case is discussed." The amazed clerk found the book, the green cover, and the point in chapter three. He had Dean Acheson collect footnotes for a minor prohibition case; when published, the footnotes covered fifteen pages. Two of them referred to two particular state cases. Brandeis looked at the footnotes, had a page bring him the relevant volumes, and demanded of Acheson, "Did you read all the cases cited in the footnotes?" When Acheson replied that he had, Brandeis said, "Suppose you read these two again," and walked out. Acheson discovered with horror that he had made an error in his notes and that the two cases were totally irrelevant. He apologized and was told by Brandeis, "Please remember that your function is to correct my errors, not to introduce errors of your own." To Brandeis, of course, few things were more important than facts and accuracy.[4]

Brandeis insisted on doing that portion of the work he believed only justices should do. Some justices turn over to their clerks the initial reading of petitions for *certiorari*—petitions for the Court to hear a case—each one requiring a vote from each justice before the petition can be accepted or rejected. Brandeis wanted to make his decision on the basis of the petition alone, not the suggestion of his clerk, and so his clerks had nothing to do with the petitions. Similarly, he would not permit his clerks to write a summary of briefs submitted to the Court. In Dean Acheson's words, "To Justice Brandeis, one of the great advocates of the American bar, this was a profanation of advocacy. He owed it to counsel . . . to present them with a judicial mind unscratched by the scribblings of clerks." But the clerks scarcely lacked for work. When counsel did not present all relevant facts, his clerks were expected to compensate for the deficiency. A patent case involving six oil corporations had Brandeis's clerk working for six months, putting together background material on petroleum, natural gas, cracked gas, and cracking processes.[5]

His insistence on facts and accuracy stemmed not only from his desire for truth but also from his belief that Supreme Court opinions were great educational mechanisms. One clerk remembers Brandeis making sixty changes in a draft opinion of ten pages, with some of his opinions going through as many as twenty or thirty versions. The drafts, now in the Harvard Law School library, show continuing, painstaking attention to niceties of style and thought. Brandeis always delivered his opinions from the bench without a single note, while journalists sitting in the courtroom followed the printed version in an unsuccessful attempt to catch him misquoting himself. They, of course, knew neither about the training in memorization that he had given himself during his law school days when his eyes were so troublesome, nor about the number of times he rewrote each opinion before it was handed down. Brandeis rewrote because if the Court was to teach, it had to speak clearly. And it had always to be factually correct, which in Brandeis's opinions was a burden the clerks carried.[6]

His relationship with a particular clerk seemingly determined the degree of the clerk's independence. To some, Brandeis merely gave drafts to check and flesh out with citations; others Brandeis encouraged to write first or later drafts, and the two would engage in mutual criticism of each other's ventures. Calvert Magruder, clerking in 1916–1917, wrote to Frankfurter, "Honestly, I think I'm liking the job—I can't recall ever having been the victim of such terror as L.D.B. caused at first. The earliest memorandum handed in—well, my hand very nearly shook the words off the paper as I placed it on his desk . . . But that has passed, and I'm beginning to feel quite normal . . . he puts me at trying to disagree with his opinions." Similarly, James Landis disagreed with Brandeis in memoranda written during the course of the *Whitney* case (1927), as did David Riesman in a memo detailing his "Doubts and Hesitations" about "our position" in *Carter* v. *Carter* (1936). But the basic function of all clerks was research.[7]

When Dean Acheson clerked for Brandeis in 1919–1921, he realized that Brandeis's working papers had historical value and received Brandeis's permission to collect them; each successive clerk continued the practice. Thus, the notes of William F. McCurdy, Brandeis's clerk in 1922–1923, survive for *Shafer* v. *Farmers Grain Co.*: "I have your memorandum and I am at present engaged in collecting the material from the Federal Trade Commission and from the Department of Agriculture and am looking through the reports and debates." Later notes conveyed that "the Department of Agriculture is now getting together the publications which you listed . . . The Hearings on the 1916 bill I will check up and send." When *McGrain* v. *Dougherty* was before the Court in 1926, Landis prepared endless pages of research, but carefully noted that they were "not so much to portray a particular line of argument as to set forth suggestive methods of approach and to put the material before you so that, whatever line of argument you may adopt, it will be valuable for this purpose."[8]

Brandeis demanded this kind of research before and after he voted in a case and whether or not he wrote an opinion in it. He did not write in *McGrain*, for example, but he did dissent in *Myers* v. *U.S.* Landis's notes on *Myers* fill a huge folder. Warren Ege, the clerk who preceded him during the Court's initial involvement in the case, left a memorandum saying, "This is the net result of fifteen books on Constitutional Law and Political Science—and of all the digests and legal periodicals . . . Tomorrow morning I will seek further Political Science references." A number of clerks report the experience of working through the night in the upstairs office on a memorandum or opinion the justice particularly wanted. Each tiptoed to the front door of the justice's residence at about 5:30 in the morning and slipped his papers partway under the door, only to watch as a mysterious hand pulled the papers from the other side.

Each concluded that Brandeis, too, had been working all night. However, the justice was scrupulous about getting to bed by 10 P.M. But when work demanded it, he was up promptly at 5 A.M. to begin the day.[9]

Most of the clerks left Brandeis's service with admiration bordering on adulation. One, describing him as looking "like a combination of a Hebrew prophet and Abraham Lincoln," summarized Brandeis's charisma by saying, "I never understood Jesus Christ until I met Brandeis." Their recollections are complemented by newspaper accounts, written primarily when Brandeis was in his seventies. The journalists spoke of "the gray hair, drawing back from the fine forehead, yet still abundant . . . the nose is large and straight, and the cheeks, like Lincoln's, are creased . . . he is more than six feet tall and strongly built." One wrote, "His face is stamped by sincerity. There is a quiet friendliness about it." Another observed, "He is charged with a nervous energy which makes it difficult for him to sit still." Again, "He views his fellow men with wide tolerance and with a kind of humor which expresses itself in apt comments rather than in anecdotes. When he is ironic he redeems his irony by his smile . . . he loves to deal in analogies, and to measure the America of 1931 by medieval Venice or ancient Rome and Greece. Because he does thus measure the contemporary scene he is patient and hopeful." One writer noted that in 1932 Brandeis had finally stopped horseback riding, but still took regular long walks. Particularly relevant to his clerks' reactions were the comments about Brandeis's "affection for youth that youth repays with the most enthusiastic devotion."[10]

Some of the clerks remained in Washington, and Brandeis became their friend as well as their mentor. Acheson consulted Brandeis on an ethical matter when the former was serving as Roosevelt's under secretary of the treasury. When he was appointed assistant secretary of state for economic affairs, Acheson chose to be sworn into office by Justice Brandeis at the latter's apartment. A letter from Brandeis's first clerk is indicative of the respectful but warm relationship the young men had with Brandeis. Sending birthday greetings in 1926, Calvert Magruder (by then teaching at Harvard Law School) still addressed Brandeis as "My dear Mr. Justice," but wrote, "It is hard to believe that 10 years have gone by since we began our judicial labors together. In my whimsical mood I sometimes tell myself that the distinction which you have since earned as one of the truly great judges of that historic court is in some degree due to the fortunate start you had with me. The danger is, that if I say that to myself too often, I'll begin to believe it!" Letters to Magruder from Brandeis and his wife indicate the warmth they felt for him. In 1945 nineteen of his former clerks presented Harvard Law School with a bronze head of Brandeis, and Magruder, speaking for them, recalled

Brandeis's "almost parental concern" for and continuing interest in "his boys."[11]

But Brandeis stayed rather aloof from his clerks while they worked for him, expecting from them hard work ("perfection as a norm, to be bettered on special occasions") rather than companionship. Willard Hurst has described the relationship Brandeis had with his clerks as a "working partnership" or a "two-person team." The clerk was expected to check in with Brandeis each morning, but was free to set his own hours. He used the clerks' time with him to continue their education. His deliberate pedagogy was in keeping with his "hidden agenda" for them: they were to constitute a new pool of Jewish law professors.[12]

After 1923 the overwhelming majority of Brandeis's clerks were Jewish. Although encouraging Frankfurter to "act as usual on your own good judgment" in picking law clerks, Brandeis told him that "other things being equal, it is always preferable to take some one whom there is reason to believe will become a law teacher." For example, Brandeis thought highly of Harry Shulman, his clerk in 1929–1930. He reported to Frankfurter that Shulman was "too good in mind, temper, and aspirations to waste on a New York or other law offices" and asked, "Can't you land him somewhere in a law school next fall? You will recall that Yale needs men; and Hamilton thinks that the right man there would find no opposition on the score of anti-Semitism." (Hamilton was Walton H. Hamilton, a Yale Law School professor.) That triggered a thought in Brandeis's mind. He went on to say, "It seems to me that a great service could be done generally to American law and to the Jews by placing desirable ones in the law school faculties. There is in the Jew a certain potential spirituality and sense of public service which can be more easily aroused and directed, than at present is discernible in American non-Jews." Typically practical, he added, "The difficulty which the Law Schools now have in getting able men may offer opportunities, not open in other fields of intellectual activity." He was disappointed that both Robert Page and Henry Friendly, his clerks for 1926–1927 and 1927–1928, respectively, had gone into private practice but thought it possible that "they, or at least Friendly, may reform and leave his occupation." He had had a good deal of trouble with Irving Goldsmith, his clerk for 1928–1929, and passed the ultimate judgment upon him: "It would have been possible to divert Goldsmith from the private practice, but he lacked the qualities which would have made him desirable in a law school."[13]

Brandeis had met Felix Frankfurter in 1905, when Frankfurter, then a student at Harvard Law School, went to hear Brandeis deliver his lecture, "The Opportunity in the Law." The two men came into closer contact when Frankfurter moved to Washington in 1910 to work in

Henry Stimson's Department of War and Brandeis was traveling to Washington regularly for the Pinchot-Ballinger hearings. By 1914, when Frankfurter was offered a job by the Harvard Law School, Brandeis had come to think so highly of him that he urged Frankfurter to leave government for academia; he was virtually alone among Frankfurter's advisers in recommending the move.[14]

Brandeis himself had struggled in deciding between an academic career and private practice. His adored parents and Uncle Dembitz had encouraged him to make teaching his life's work, and he had expressed mixed feelings at rejecting their advice. It may be that Brandeis's encouragement of academic careers (mixed with public service) for Frankfurter and for his own law clerks was something of a substitute for the life Brandeis would have led had he been a more obedient son and followed his parents' wishes. Of course, it can be argued that the high value Brandeis placed on education was sufficient reason for his wishing Frankfurter and his clerks to become educators. In that case, however, why would a man who put such priority on education and whose teaching efforts proved quite successful, not at some point give up private practice in order to teach law? The answer seems to be, simply, that he liked the excitement of practice much more than the quieter life of the academic. Nevertheless, he must have been somewhat concerned that he had not followed his own advice and become a teacher. He might have argued that a professor's salary would not have given him the "luxury" of serving the public, although that seemed not to bother him when he tried to steer his clerks into teaching. However he justified his role, Brandeis seems to have been able to meet a psychological need by training young men to do that which he consciously considered important.[15]

Be that as it may, Brandeis's use of his clerks tended to further their education. He would sit in his office, reading and writing by the light of his gooseneck lamp, which Brandeis preferred for his sensitive eyes, while the clerk (when not burrowing through musty tomes in the Library of Congress) worked in his own office next door. When they conferred, the clerk would occasionally hear examples of Brandeis's quiet, wry sense of humor, or get glimpses into the dynamics of the Court. When Willard Hurst told Brandeis that he thought the Court was about to make the wrong decision in one case, Brandeis told him that if he (Brandeis) pointed out the fallacy in the chief justice's reasoning, the "Chief" would simply find another reason to reach the same decision. Hurst objected to the granting of *certiorari* in another case, involving bank directorships. Brandeis replied that the Court had taken the case in order to teach a lesson about directorships. Brandeis put into *Senn* v. *Tile Layers Protective Union* (1937) an important sentence declaring that picketing by unions was part of the speech constitutionally protected by the First Amendment. Hurst spent days attempting to find a citable precedent; there was none. When Hurst despairingly reported as much to Brandeis, the latter merely smiled and said, "I think we'll let it stand anyway." He told both Hurst and Nathanial Nathanson, an earlier clerk, that Justice Holmes employed a simple rule of thumb for judging the constitutionality of statutes, summed up in Holmes's question, "Does it make you puke?" He never gossiped with the clerks about the other justices (clearly, he considered such discussions unethical) but he taught them a great deal about the law, his jurisprudence, and his approach to life. The clerks were in their mid-twenties and, depending upon the specific year, Brandeis was in his sixties or seventies or eighties and known not only as the creator of a new jurisprudence and a public advocate but also as the confidant of those in power. With his Lincolnesque appearance, his asceticism, his high moral standards, his brilliance, his incredible memory, he could not but make a marked impression on his young clerks, many of whom referred to him as "Isaiah." Even a clerk such as David Riesman, who considered Brandeis less than responsive to his clerk's needs, wrote immediately after his service with Brandeis, "I have made his character a test of my own."[16]

The reaction of Brandeis's clerks is helpful in understanding the profound impact that he made on almost everyone who came in contact with him. Paul Freund describes him as a "source of spiritual strength" to those who knew him. His awesome intellect and standards help explain the respect in which he was universally held, but he also inspired great affection. The common perception of Brandeis as cold and brilliant is mistaken. He was as demanding as he was brilliant, but he was far from cold, as his clerks and others who knew him realized. Thomas Austern describes him as "a thoroughly passionate man, but absolutely and completely under control." He apportioned his time precisely and would brook no interference with it; he refused to suffer either fools or foolishness gladly; he was exasperated when the world did not live up to his standards.[17]

There are numerous examples of his eclecticism and his disgust with "experts" who knew less than he. He told Dean Acheson that the title of his brief in *Muller* should have been "What Any Fool Knows." David Riesman remembers William Bullitt, then ambassador to the Soviet Union, being asked by Brandeis at one of the Sunday teas about cotton production in Turkestan. Although Brandeis considered Soviet production of great potential importance to American cotton farmers, Bullitt knew nothing about it. Brandeis later expressed his contempt for the ambassador's lack of knowledge. A similar incident occurred with a Danish ambassador. Brandeis was much taken by Denmark's small size, its democratic system, the wide participation of its citizenry in politics, the relative lack of extremes in citizens' wealth, and the education it offered adults in the traditions of their localities. In the 1930s, when people frequently expressed a desire to visit the Soviet Union, he asked them why they didn't go to Denmark instead. At his request the Library of Congress updated its bibliography on Denmark each year, and Brandeis made a point of knowing each Danish ambassador to the United States and of inviting him to tea. Freund remembers one Danish ambassador being flabbergasted when Brandeis turned to him over tea and said that he had noticed that during the last week Denmark's exports to Great Britain had fallen. How, Brandeis asked, did the ambassador account for it? The ambassador left in embarrassment.[18]

This was the kind of intellectual standard Brandeis set for his clerks, most of whom nonetheless found him warm and caring and humorous. Dean Acheson, for example, commented that Brandeis was tolerant of "a large segment of humanity—which did not include his law clerks." At the same time, however, Acheson recounted Brandeis's response to questions about why his one-year rule for clerks had been broken in Acheson's case. Whenever Brandeis was queried about it in Acheson's hearing, the latter recalled, "He would speak of a concern for my prospective clients." Such wryly affectionate remarks must have given his clerks a sense that Brandeis respected and cared more about them than he otherwise showed. Many of them remember that although he demanded hard work, he was also solicitous of their health. Perhaps they learned of his feelings from Frankfurter, with whom they tended to remain in contact and to whom Brandeis would occasionally express such praise as "Magruder is proving very helpful" or "Landis did notable work on the Myers case."[19]

One of the functions of the clerks was to help arrange and assist at what became the famous Brandeis Sunday or Monday teas. The presence at these teas of participants in one administration after another enabled Brandeis to retain close ties with acquaintances in government, to accumulate "inside" information, and to make his influence felt in Washington. One of the clerk's first jobs was to see that all the women in the room were sitting down, because the courtly justice would insist on standing if any woman was doing so. Mrs. Brandeis, ever aware of his limited physical strength, instructed each clerk in turn about this duty and let him know that if necessary, he was also to make conversation with any wallflowers. Furthermore, she had learned how seriously people in Washington took their titles, and the clerk was admonished to be certain to get them right.[20]

Their "household" role, which gave the clerks access to the conversations of the mighty also showed them the household's austerity. Judge Julian Mack, Brandeis's coworker in Zionism and a self-styled gourmet, took to telling people that whenever he went to the Brandeis's for dinner, he ate before and afterward. Felix Frankfurter's wife once refused to accompany her husband and Learned Hand to the Brandeis home in Chatham, complaining, "He has nothing beautiful in his house. His food is awful too." Brandeis's clerks found his home modest or "shabby," the food "frugal," the record collection terrible. After his year of clerking, David Riesman told Frankfurter that Brandeis's principle of life seemed to be asceticism. Some years later he added drily, "Asceticism makes one a hero, but it is hard on those around one." No doubt Judge Mack would have agreed. So, too, would the Court printer, who printed the justices' initial opinions for private circulation among them. The combination of Brandeis's virtually indecipherable, old-German-style handwriting and his habit of correcting his drafts so that there were almost more words scribbled between the lines than on them meant that the burden of his decision against a typewriter fell on the printer, who, Dean Acheson commented, "must have employed a gifted cryptanalyst." An unsigned typed note in the Brandeis papers, possibly inserted by a clerk, reads, "Justice Brandeis wrote his opinions in long hand and sent them directly to the printer without having them typed. The typesetter was reputed to be a man of extraordinary intuition." On one occasion Brandeis wrote a note to the printer on the back of one of his drafts: "Please work so far as necessary at night on this as I must distribute this tomorrow as early as possible."[21]

One of the sources to which Brandeis sent his clerks for information was law reviews, which he was wont to read himself. Brandeis saw the periodicals as both stimulating discussions in themselves and as potential educators of the legal community. He was of course a faithful reader of the *Harvard Law Review*, which he had helped create, and he occasionally read others as well. In a letter to Frankfurter, he noted that two articles on recent Court cases continued the *Review*'s "function of enlightened public opinion" about the Court. "With 20 such organs, & the service continued throughout 10 years, we may hope to see some impression made. There must be persistence." He was eager for the Court to begin using the reviews to ascertain both factual data and the thinking of leading legal scholars. On the pre-Brandeis Court the dominant theory of jurisprudence had been that justices looked only at laws, not social situations or others' perceptions.[22]

Brandeis first used citations of law review articles in his dissent in *Adams* v. *Tanner*, handed down in 1917. None of the reviews mentioned by him there was cited in the briefs. Later, he was most likely to use the reviews in those opinions which altered the law significantly, such as *Erie Railroad* v. *Tompkins*, in which he cited twenty-eight articles. He had a two-way relationship with the reviews, and particularly with the *Harvard Law Review*, frequently suggesting to Frankfurter topics or Court decisions that merited coverage. His ideas often found their way into the *Review* in this manner. For example, Brandeis bombarded Frankfurter with ideas for articles on diversity of citizenship jurisdiction and on what he considered to be the misuse by the Court of the idea of a federal common law; then, when Brandeis persuaded the Court to let him announce that there was no such thing as federal common law, his opinion cited one of the Frankfurter articles on the subject. The law reviews reciprocated his admiration: on his seventy-fifth birthday the *Columbia Law Review*, the *Yale Law Journal*, and the *Harvard Law Review* all devoted issues to Brandeis and his jurisprudence.[23]

At first the other justices found the practice of citing law review articles unacceptable. Willard Hurst tells how he and Brandeis worked on the best way to formulate their reference to notes in two law reviews for one opinion. Brandeis decided not to say that the notes "showed" that a certain rule was established but to mention merely that "the cases are collected in Notes in" the reviews. " 'Mr. Justice McReynolds,' Brandeis remarked with his own private twinkle, 'did not favor Law Review citations.' " As the "nine old men" were gradually replaced by Roosevelt, however, the citing of law review articles became the norm. Indeed, by 1957 in one Court term alone sixty-six articles were mentioned in twenty-four opinions. The relationship thus formed between the Court and the law reviews was another of Brandeis's contributions to sociological jurisprudence and to the modernizing of the judicial and legal processes.[24]

The deference Brandeis showed to McReynolds's sensibilities was typical both of his awareness of his colleagues' judicial proclivities and of the diplomacy he exercised within the Court. It was inevitable that he would pay due attention to the brethren's proclivities. The justices of the Supreme Court have an ongoing relationship that outlasts the consideration of any one case. Each justice who writes the opinion of the Court recognizes that his words will be more authoritative in direct proportion to the number of other justices he can carry with him. Although every justice comes to the Court with intellectual and psychological "baggage," he does not have an automatic answer for every case that will be heard by the Court while he is on it. Judges are frequently in doubt as to how to vote in various cases, and they are open to persuasion from their brethren. Thus, although it is possible to discern a justice's political beliefs from a perusal of a large number of his opinions and votes, it is not at all possible to predict accurately how he will vote in every case. Many cases do not involve issues central to each justice's value system. Others are complicated by factual circumstances or may involve more than one issue and force a choice among the justice's values. Thus, in any given case, a justice whose feelings are particularly strong may be able to persuade others to his point of view. A justice must know the other judges' propensities and psychologies well enough to frame his arguments in such terms and in such a style as to make them most attractive to potential allies. Similarly, a justice who refuses to compromise with his brethren will find that he has lost most of his ability to influence them. The justices most successful in affecting the actions of the others are those who understand the art of politics.[25]

Brandeis insisted, even to Frankfurter, that he did not "play politics" on the Court—but he did, most obviously in the choices he made about whether or not to dissent. The phrase "Holmes and Brandeis, dissenting" became widely known because their dissents were in major cases that received much attention. But in spite of the degree to which Brandeis differed ideologically with a majority of justices during most of his years on the Court, 454 of his 528 opinions were written for the majority; only 74 out of 528 were dissents or concurrences. Brandeis dissented when he considered it important to do so, but only after extensive attempts to bring the Court around to his way of thinking and only in carefully chosen cases.[26]

"Of course there are all sorts of considerations that affect one in dissenting," Brandeis told Frankfurter; "there is a limit to the frequency with which you can do it, without exasperating men; then there may not be time, e.g. Holmes shoots down so quickly and is disturbed if you hold him up; then you may have a very important case of your own as to which you do not want to antagonize on a less important case etc. etc." Brandeis went along with Holmes's opinion in *United Zinc & Chemical Co. v. Britt* (1922) although he disagreed with it. "I was rushed with other work," he explained, "and so would have had to hold up Holmes if I was going to write a dissent and to hold him up from firing off is like sending an executioner after him. I had dissented recently in a number of cases, Holmes cared a good deal about his opinion, he had gone with me in my dissent so I let it go—without dissenting." To avoid such situations, Brandeis suggested to the Court that "no case is to go down until eight days after opinion is circulated except by unanimous consent in special cases." Holmes was vehemently opposed to the idea:"he would be miserable for eight days—he'd worry all the time. He can't wait after he circulates his opinions, to have them back and 'to shoot them off.' "[27]

"Great difficulty of all group action of course," Brandeis confided to Frankfurter, "is when and what concessions to make. Can't always dissent—may have dissented much just then" or the case might be so unimportant that it was not worth expending limited time on writing a dissent. "After all there are various reasons for withholding dissent—so that silence does not mean actual concurrence. (1) All depends on how frequent one's dissents have been when the question of dissenting comes, or (2) how important case, whether it's constitutionality or construction. So that I sometimes endorse an opinion with which I do not agree, 'I acquiesce.' " Brandeis was not too uncomfortable withholding a dissent in a case involving statutory construction, but there was a "special function of dissent in constitutional cases. In ordinary cases there is a good deal to be said for not having dissents—you want certainty and definiteness and it doesn't matter terribly how you decide so long as it is settled. But in these constitutional cases, since what is done is what you [Frankfurter] called statesmanship, nothing is ever settled—unless statesmanship is settled and at an end." And always, one came back to group dynamics and the personality of the justice writing for the majority, remembering that one would have to go on working with him. In one case in which Pitney wrote for the Court, Brandeis wished to dissent. He knew, however, that once Pitney had written his opinions "he was all worked up until they were disposed of or delivered. I said to him 'I have some suggestions to submit as to that'. He said in the nicest way 'do it quick—until you will I'll have no peace'. Well it would have spoiled his European trip etc—so I contented myself with registering a formal dissent" and wrote no opinion.[28]

When possible, Brandeis used persuasion, especially with Holmes. "Had . . . $1/_2$ hour at Justice Holmes on a dissenting opinion I want him to write," he told Alice in 1918. On another occasion, Brandeis noted, "It happened to be recess time so that (1) I had time to think out the problem in my own mind—which takes me long time (2) I had time to go over to Holmes and talk things over with him at length and modify his views." The other justices recognized Brandeis's influence with Holmes. When the conference vote was taken in *Hamilton* v. *Kentucky Distilleries & Wine Company* (1919) Chief Justice White and Brandeis were in the five-man majority, Holmes in the minority. "Then," according to Brandeis, "White met Holmes on the street. H. told him he had doubts about his vote and he was ready to have it written the other way to see how it would go. White then came to see me and asked me to write it, because he thought I could get Holmes more easily." Frankfurter noted in the margin, next to this quotation, "L.D.B. influence with Holmes," but in fact the outcome of the case indicates much wider influence: Brandeis wrote for a unanimous Court, holding that the War Time Prohibition Act remained in effect during the period after the cessation of hostilities but before the signing of a peace treaty.[29]

"Talk[ing] things over" with his fellow justices was just one of the techniques Brandeis used on the Court. When he disagreed with the majority vote or opinion, he frequently circulated what he called a "Memorandum" or "Report" to the Court which indicated that he had not decided to dissent and that he was willing to negotiate—on the wording of the Court's opinion, the grounds for decision, or whatever. Occasionally, postconference thought changed Brandeis's mind about his own vote, and he was able to use a "Memorandum" to change the minds of the other justices as well. In *McCarthy* v. *Arndstein* (1923), for example, Brandeis circulated a memorandum saying, "The vote of the conference was to reverse and the case was assigned to me for opinion. Upon further study I have concluded that the entry should be judgment reaffirmed and have prepared the annexed memorandum which embodies my views." This became the opinion for the Court. Similarly, in *St. Louis, Brownsville and Mexico Railroad Company* v. *United States* (1925), Brandeis attached a note to one of his draft opinions: "The vote of the conference was to affirm also as to the third claim. Upon closer study of the record I concluded that as to this claim my vote was wrong. With the approval of the Chief Justice, I have put my views in the form of an opinion." Again, his draft convinced the Court and eventually became its opinion. In such cases, Brandeis carefully took the other justices' views into consideration in writing his next drafts.[30]

Sometimes the series of memoranda did not convince the brethren and were turned into dissents, as happened in *Pierce, Duplex, Gilbert, New State Ice,* and *Liggett,* among others. Occasionally, when his views were rejected, he refrained from writing an opinion, presumably for the tactical reasons mentioned above. For example, he circulated a memorandum in the *Truax* case but commented later that it reached the brethren "too late: by the time [of] my memo their backs were up and wouldn't change." However, in an extremely important case involving the right of unions to strike (*United Mine Workers* v. *Coronado,* in 1922), Brandeis distributed a strong dissent to the brethren. As Alexander Bickel has suggested, Brandeis changed the argument of his dissent as it went through the usual multiple drafts until he found the grounds that he thought most likely to appeal to the Court. In this case Chief Justice White had planned to write the opinion of the Court, but he died before this could be done. The case was reargued after Taft took his seat, and Taft intended to hold against the union. When Brandeis explained his views, Taft changed his mind, as did the others who had initially agreed with him. Taft then handed down the opinion for a unanimous Court, upholding the right of the union. Brandeis was pleased, and the now unnecessary dissent was not published. He cared much less about who wrote the opinion than about its substance. "They will take [a pro-union decision] from Taft but wouldn't from me," Brandeis said of the brethren; in fact, Taft's opinion drew upon the logic of Brandeis's dissent.[31]

The threat of a dissent by Brandeis was taken seriously, as Brandeis's dissents were strong, literate, and likely to receive newspaper coverage. It would be a mistake, however, to assume that it was only Brandeis's politicking or his great public reputation that enabled him to carry his colleagues along. They respected him as a judge, as a craftsman, and as someone able to work his way through masses of economic data. Taft noted on one of Brandeis's memoranda (in *McCarthy* v. *Arndstein*), "I am inclined to go with you because I don't know where else to go"; on another (*Atlantic Coast Line Railroad* v. *Watts*, in 1923), "I concur with terror at and respect for your progress through the maze." But they had a reciprocal relationship. Taft wrote to Brandeis to congratulate him on his opinion in *Southern Railway Company* v. *Watts* (1923), commenting, "It is admirable, compact forcible and clear. It relieves me greatly to get rid of such a case so satisfactorily. Thank you for your promptness." Then he added, "There are a couple of suggestions I would like to make," and proceeded to make them at length. (Their relationship can be glimpsed in the remainder of the letter, in which Taft sent Brandeis and his wife "warm and cordial season's greetings" and complained that McReynolds had written an opinion in which "it seems to me that he is weighing evidence in reaching his conclusions as if we were a Jury or a Chancellor— What do you think of it?")[32]

Other Brandeis drafts were returned by his colleagues with such comments as "Yes—Simply, clearly and admirably well put" (White); "Yes, A great opinion. Note a few suggestions as to form in margin" (Clarke); "Yes—This is a most excellent piece of Judicial work" (Day); "Good— You have convinced me" (Clarke); "I was inclined to be [with] the others—but you cannot speak with reason to the Dane and lose your voice" (McKenna); "Yes sir. Well done." (Sutherland); "Yes. Fairly done" (Sanford); "This is a fine, first class piece of work" (Holmes); "I have suggested numerous changes in the text, but none, I think, that impairs in the least the substance of your very able argument" (Pitney). The high opinion in which most of the justices held Brandeis made his occasional requests for advice flattering, as when he sent a copy of a draft to Justice Stone with the note, "May I trouble you to look this over *before* I circulate it and let me have your suggestions?" or when he wrote to Van Devanter, "The ground you recommend was not the one on which I voted 'no'—

But I think that, as a matter of policy, you are clearly right; and I am engaged in redrafting the opinion on that line. May I trouble you to formulate the rule of law, which you think should be established? And I should be very glad to have any authorities or arguments in support of the construction recommended."[33]

Brandeis was usually meticulous in not discussing the other justices with outsiders (clerks were not considered outsiders, but the extent of his comments to them about the other justices was limited). Happily for posterity, however, he broke his self-imposed rule during a series of conversations with Frankfurter during summers in Chatham in the early 1920s. It is highly doubtful that Brandeis was aware that Frankfurter kept notes or that he would have approved of the practice. From Frankfurter's notes of these conversations one learns that Brandeis did not think Taft or Holmes always thought things through; if they had to write an opinion every time they voted, he believed, they might reach quite different conclusions. Van Devanter and Clarke would not be moved by threatened dissents: "Clarke practically never changes his views." Day was not to be bargained with: "Day couldn't be persuaded by anybody but himself. He does change his own views; he is a fighter, a regular game cock." Brandeis had a high opinion of Van Devanter, saying at one point that he was running the Court: "he is like a jesuit general: he is always helpful to everybody, always ready for the C. J. [Chief Justice]," worked hard, and was knowledgeable, although he occasionally made what Brandeis considered to be mistakes. Brandeis recalled that in *Jay Burns Baking Co.* v. *Bryan* (1924), Van Devanter " 'got busy,' in his personal way, talking and laboring with members of Court," and finally persuaded two of the justices not to dissent. Van Devanter "would have been the last of the Cardinals" during the Middle Ages, Brandeis commented: "He is indefatigable, on good terms with everybody, ready to help everybody, knows exactly what he wants and clouds over difficulties by fine phrases and deft language." He continued, about Van Devanter, "One can achieve his results by working for them—but I made up my mind I wouldn't resort to finesse and subtlety and 'lobbying'." "He never fools himself," Brandeis said; and if that was true, it was more than could be said of Brandeis. Although his tactics differed from Van Devanter's, Brandeis excelled at "finesse and subtlety and 'lobbying'."[34]

He made a point of maintaining cordial relations with his colleagues (with the exception of McReynolds, who consistently slighted him), even when he thought little of them; he held his fire when a dissent might hurt his bargaining position; and he used the threat of a dissent as a way of "lobbying." There was one case in which McReynolds circulated a majority opinion that Brandeis "couldn't stand for." Brandeis warned the chief justice that McReynolds's opinion had "glaring errors" that would haunt the Court in the future. As a result, "Van D. worked with McR. and made changes and Chief asked me whether that will remove my sting—I had written a really stinging dissent—they didn't want the Court shown up that way, and corrections weren't adequate and finally the Chief took over the opinion . . . and I suppressed my dissent because after all it's merely a question of statutory construction and the worst things were removed by the Chief." Brandeis credited Van Devanter with taking McReynolds, the Court's "enfant terrible," in hand, and with successful "strong lobbying with the members individually" to minimize the number of dissents.[35]

Taft, it will be remembered, had opposed Brandeis's nomination to the Court. The two men were nonetheless quite cordial after Taft became chief justice, as Taft's comments quoted above indicate. "Things go happily in the Conference room with Taft," Brandeis told Frankfurter. Taft "does about two men's work," running the Court, assigning cases fairly, and going through *certiorari* petitions. He was a much better chief justice than White had been: he smoothed out difficulties, he was personally admirable, as well as a good administrator; in fact, "It's astonishing he should have been such a horribly bad President, for he has considerable executive ability." Perhaps Taft had "cared about law all the time and nothing else . . . He is a first-rate second-rate mind." He had an "open mind" but "poor judgment" and was busy "with legislative matters"— presumably a reference to Taft's involvement with the Harding administration. The "open mind" was useful; Taft had drawn upon Brandeis's thinking not only in the labor union case but elsewhere as well; for example, Brandeis said of Taft's opinion for the Court in *Sonneborn Brothers* v. *Cureton* (1923), "That's my opinion—Taft wrote it on basis of memo in which I analyzed all cases." He added that Taft, having taken over one of the late Chief Justice White's opinions although he "knew practically nothing about it . . . was very nice in the suggestions he took from me." Brandeis considered Holmes and Taft the only members of the Court worth talking with. It was "a pleasure to talk with Taft—you feel you talk with a cultivated man. He knows a lot, he *reads*, he has wide contacts." Yet he also said that Taft "looks like many a benevolent, good-natured, distillery drummer I used to see in the days when I was counsel for some distilleries. His face has nothing in it—it's so vapid."[36]

Brandeis commented on the other justices as well. He loved Holmes, considered him the "best intellectual machine" on the Court, and thought him "as wonderful in character as in brain." Yet he spoke disparagingly of Holmes's dislike of the Sherman Antitrust Law and his inability to understand the threat of big business. These views, according to Brandeis, indicated Holmes's "deep prejudice." Holmes had "no realization of what moves men," did not "understand or appreciate facts," wrote such loose opinions that he left "more loopholes for rehearing petitions than anyone else." With regard to jurisdictional restraints, Brandeis reported proudly that "Holmes is beginning to learn—intellectually he is beginning to appreciate our responsibility, though not emotionally."[37]

If Brandeis was coolly objective about people he liked, he was devastating about those he did not. Sutherland was "a mediocre Taft"; Sanford "thoroughly bourgeois"; McReynolds "lazy," moved by the "irrational impulses of a savage," a man who "would have given Balzac great joy" and who looked at times like "an infantile moron"; Pitney was "much influenced by his experience and he had had mighty little" (although he had "real character" and "welcomed correction"—from Brandeis); Pierce Butler had "given no sign of anything except a thoroughly mediocre mind." Worst of all was Joseph McKenna: the "only way of dealing with him is to appoint guardians for him."[38]

None of these judgments was reflected in his conduct toward his colleagues. All human beings, even justices, were educable; therefore, Brandeis was respectful, cordial, and willing to compromise when necessary. When White was chief justice, he would visit Brandeis at home for chats. Brandeis invited Justice Clarke to dinner, begged Van Devanter not to resign because of the important contributions he made in conference, and treated the justices who disagreed with him and their arguments with great deference and respect. He considered himself "nonpolitical" because he would not emulate Van Devanter's style of lobbying, but in fact his courtesy and self-restraint served the same end, getting the other judges to alter or moderate their views. On the Court, as elsewhere, Brandeis was a first-rate teacher and politician.[39]

19 | Isaiah's Extrajudicial Activities

Brandeis, during his pre-Court days, had been deeply involved in public issues, in legislation, and in the policies of the Wilson administration. However, involvement in policymaking is incompatible with the disinterested stance of Supreme Court justices that is implied in the Judicial Canon of Ethics and is the basis for much of the respect paid to the Court. Brandeis never resolved this incompatibility.

His initial posture was scrupulous. He cleared the propriety of his investments with the chief justice and resigned from all organizations with overtly political purposes or with interests that might involve litigation before the Court. He resigned his Zionist positions (but not his authority) in order not to embarrass the Court. He turned down all invitations to speak, to write, to attend meetings (always excepting Zionist meetings), or to accept honorary degrees; such activity would not have been appropriate for a member of the Court. Brandeis's respect for the Court is unquestionable. He spoke of it with solemnity as "Our Court," which had to be kept separate from the political process. He was glad that Charles Evans Hughes lost when he left the Court in 1916 to run for president, because he believed that the Court should not become a "stepping stone" to political office.[1]

Nonetheless, almost as soon as he joined the Court, Brandeis arranged to maintain contact with politics and public causes. He began to finance Felix Frankfurter's activities on behalf of matters that interested them both. In November 1916 Brandeis sent Frankfurter a check along with a letter saying, "You have had considerable expense for travelling, telephoning and similar expenses in public matters undertaken at my request or following up my suggestions & will have more in the future no doubt. These expenses should, of course, be borne by me." Frankfurter returned the check, but Brandeis sent it back with another letter:

> In essence this is nothing different than your taking travelling and incidental expenses from the Consumers League or the New Republic—which I trust you do. You are giving your very valuable time and that is quite enough. It can make no difference that the subject matter in connection with which expense is incurred is more definite in one case than in the other.
>
> I ought to feel free to make suggestions to you, although they involve some incidental expense. And you should feel free to incur expense in the public interest. So I am returning the check.

Frankfurter kept it and eventually accepted regular payments amounting to $52,250. Most of the money was paid directly into Frankfurter's bank account by Brandeis's financial secretary.[2]

The arrangement was flexible. Brandeis expressed "some concern" in 1923 that Frankfurter must have incurred "incidental expenses which in the aggregate are pretty large" and said that he would forward a check for $1,000. In 1925 Frankfurter wrote to Brandeis of "personal needs," and Brandeis replied, "I'll send the $1500 now or in instalments as you may prefer. Your public service must not be abridged." The amount involved kept pace with inflation: $2,000 in 1927; $3,500 in 1934.[3]

The causes in which they participated remained of great importance to Brandeis, who continued to look upon Frankfurter as his protegé and as the professor Brandeis had never been. Although Frankfurter had taken over the minimum wage and maximum hours cases that Brandeis had been working on at the time of his Court appointment, Brandeis was most interested in the education of the public—an effort Frankfurter could be counted upon to continue. And Brandeis was pleased with the results. He wrote to Harold Laski in 1925 that there was "an ever widening appreciation of [Frankfurter's] rare qualities. His students are becoming teachers. Given another twenty years of such activity, and he will have profoundly affected American life." He added in 1928 that Frankfurter "seems to me clearly the most useful lawyer in the United States." When Frankfurter was approached in 1932 about a position on the Massachusetts Supreme Judicial Court, Brandeis counseled that there might be "some reason to leave the law school" only if the appointment was to the United States Supreme Court and Frankfurter was "old enough" to give up active public service and teaching. Then Franklin Roosevelt asked Frankfurter to become his solicitor general in 1933, as a step toward the Supreme Court. Brandeis, along with Holmes and Frankfurter's wife, advised him to turn down the appointment; Brandeis wanted Frankfurter able to participate actively in "their" causes.[4]

Brandeis thought of Frankfurter as a son as well as an ally in public causes. Judge Henry Friendly recalls that the relationship between the two men "seemed like father and son," and Brandeis wrote to Frankfurter, "Marion [Frankfurter's wife] knows that Alice and I look upon you as half brother, half son." Norman Hapgood recalled Brandeis remarking about "the personal freedom needed especially by a reformer. As long as a person is in need of money he is not in a position to challenge . . . the community around him." So Frankfurter, completely dependent upon his small professorial salary and taking Brandeis's place in various reform movements, would need a modicum of financial independence.[5]

It was not unusual for Brandeis to subsidize those who were in need and to whom he felt emotional ties. He and his brother had sent money to needy relatives for years. Later, Brandeis helped de Haas and Henrietta Szold with living expenses. Similarly, when Hapgood took over *Harper's Weekly*, Brandeis sent him $822 to cover subscriptions for 274 Massachusetts libraries, arranged for subscriptions for all public libraries in New England, asked Alfred to do the same for Kentucky; and got others to cover various other states. None of these gifts implied an obligation on the part of the recipient.[6]

The arrangement Brandeis made with Frankfurter was not secret, nor did either man consider it unethical. Late in 1929 Lewis H. Weinstein, a student in Frankfurter's federal jurisdiction seminar, asked Frankfurter's advice about obtaining a $500 loan to get him through graduation. Frankfurter regretted that he could not lend the money, reminded Weinstein that he himself was receiving an annual stipend from Brandeis, and arranged a loan from the Littauer Foundation. Frankfurter had mentioned his own stipend earlier to the seminar, while talking about the difficulties of living on a professor's salary. Knowledge of the arrangement was common at the Harvard Law School, and it seems not to have been viewed as unethical. John P. Frank has noted that "I have personally been aware of the contributions to Frankfurter for as long as I can remember, not from any inside source but simply as a matter of common knowledge." Since so many members of the Law School community, and particularly Frankfurter's students, went to work for the New Deal, it is conceivable that people outside Cambridge knew about the stipend as well.[7]

Brandeis himself told others that he was giving money to Frankfurter. He wrote to Julian Mack in 1922 that any funds Frankfurter accepted for Zionist activities "should come from me . . . I think it may be consistent with what is best to put $1000 into his hands this year to pay expenses incident to his public work." He added, "Of course, anything that I can do for Felix, which is best for him and for the causes he so generously serves, I am more than glad to do." Surprised that Frankfurter was having difficulty raising the funds for a 1934 trip from England to Palestine, Brandeis wrote to Mack, "Of course, he has spent much on cabling, telegraphing and the like—but I have for years made him an allowance of $3,500. a year for public purposes." He also mentioned the stipends and special payments in letters to de Haas and to Edward McClennen.[8]

Having made certain that Frankfurter could afford public work, Brandeis bombarded him with suggestions concerning Zionism, articles for the *Harvard Law Review* and the *New Republic*, the Harvard Law School, and many public service matters. He urged Frankfurter to work for specific pieces of legislation, some of which were pending in Congress. These included laws to bring the railroads under the workers' compensation acts, to prohibit injunctions against unions, to make reparations for government wrong-doing, and to limit federal court jurisdiction. He advised Frankfurter to have the *New Republic* (N.R.) "take up a continuous campaign against espionage" (meaning domestic spying); to cultivate "Congressmen & other publicity makers"; to investigate the development of strike insurance; to write about a host of other matters.[9]

On September 30, 1922, Brandeis wrote Frankfurter a lengthy missive entitled "What to do about Capitalism," which he introduced by saying,

Re N.R. policies I am enclosing as my last will & testament before opening of term memo as follows—of course not for publication— but for your study or consideration:

(1)   On Prohibition
(2)   On Capitalism
(3)   On the spread
(4)   On fear
(5)   On transportation (supplemental)
(6)   Labor Saving devices.

His thoughts on capitalism included encouragement of consumer cooperatives, producers' cooperatives, cooperative banks and credit unions; municipal ownership of utilities and transportation; graduated income, inheritance, and corporation taxes; unionism; and life insurance. The "spread" was of trusts using nationwide advertising. (Unfortunately, the memorandum "On fear" has been lost.) At other times, Brandeis sent messages to Herbert Croly, editor of the *New Republic*, or met with him directly. Two scholars have correctly commented, "Brandeis was more than just an anonymous contributor to the *New Republic*; he was very nearly a member of its editorial staff *in absentia*." In addition, Brandeis gave Frankfurter advice about staffing *The Nation*.[10]

Similarly, Brandeis used Paul Kellogg's *Survey* and *Survey Graphic* as his "faithful torchbearer," particularly on the subject of unemployment. During the prosperous year of 1920, Brandeis wrote to Kellogg, "We shall soon have had a year of freedom from what have been regarded as the main causes of misery:—unemployment, low wages and drink." He urged Kellogg to "prepare a survey of the gains from the first year of this freedom," suggesting study of the three factors as they affected a small city and a village. Kellogg sent two reporters to Grand Rapids, Michigan, and printed the resultant articles later that year. In his letter of praise to Kellogg, Brandeis indicated another theme he would later hammer home to the New Dealers:

> I was particularly glad to find the phrase which you used referring to [Grand Rapids]. "Nor is a typical American city undistinguished by characteristics peculiarly its own." The great America for which we long is unattainable unless that individuality of communities becomes far more highly developed and becomes a common American phenomenon. For a century our growth has come through national expansion and the increase of the functions of Federal Government. The growth of the future—at least of the immediate future—must be in quality and spiritual value. And that can come only through the concentrated, intensified striving of smaller groups. The field for special effort should now be the State, the city, the village . . . If ideals are developed locally—the national ones will come pretty near taking care of themselves.

Kellogg printed Brandeis's comments as an introduction to the articles. Presumably, Brandeis felt his thoughts were general enough not to violate his usual rule against permitting quotation.[11]

Brandeis sent Kellogg further suggestions. In 1924, noting that the downturn in business might generate serious discussion of economic matters ("In the heyday of prosperity, Americans never think. In suffering, they sometimes do."), he urged three special editions on irregularity of employment, the preservation of timber, and soil preservation. Kellogg demurred. Brandeis, undeterred, wrote again in 1928 in a letter marked "Private," "Now that unemployment has been forced upon public attention, would it not be possible for the Survey to take up vigorously and persistently the musts of Regularity in Employment?" Brandeis urged Kellogg to put Robert Bruère and Morris L. Cooke (with whom "I have discussed this subject much") to work on some articles, and Kellogg asked Brandeis how to "drive home to people's consciences and imaginations the right to regularity in employment" and for a paragraph spelling out the right. Brandeis replied with an analysis of unemployment statistics. At the same time, he was writing about the subject to Beulah Amidon, a friend of his daughter Susan and an associate editor of the *Survey Graphic*, linking employment with scientific management and pointing out the success of William H. McElwain. Amidon later interviewed Brandeis on savings bank life insurance as well. Brandeis was so pleased with the *Survey* that he wrote it into his will, leaving it a quarter of the estate remaining after provision had been made for his family.[12]

The bulk of Brandeis's letters to Frankfurter about the *New Republic* (as well as his letters to Kellogg) were written between 1920 and 1929; in other words, toward the end of the Wilson administration and before the New Deal when Brandeis's connections with the Harding, Coolidge, and Hoover administrations were minimal. He reemerged as a leader of American Zionism at a meeting on November 24, 1929. During the next three years he was particularly busy with Zionism. Then, with the advent of the New Deal, he had more immediate access to policymakers.[13]

Brandeis had been active in the Wilson administration through the first half of 1914. The move to Washington and the Court meant that he was able to see his administration friends at his own home, to hear from them about the politics of the moment, and to influence those politics. Norman Hapgood later noted that the most important members of the cabinet were Secretary of the Navy Josephus Daniels, Secretary of the Treasury William McAdoo, Secretary of Labor Newton D. Baker, and Secretary of Agriculture David F. Houston. The first three were Brandeis's close acquaintances and former comrades-in-arms. Daniels, who described Brandeis as "having the finest mind in America dedicated to the Common Weal," acted as an intermediary between the justice and the president. The system worked so well that in 1934 Daniels urged it on Franklin Roosevelt.[14]

Hapgood was another intermediary; through him, Brandeis urged that all enforcement of the prohibition laws except with regard to interstate commerce be left to the states. Brandeis approved of prohibition, but he disapproved of the federal government's overreaching itself. Hapgood used his relationship with Wilson and Brandeis to secure the appointment of Herbert Hoover as food administrator during World War I. Hapgood, out of the country, wrote to Wilson, to Houston, and to Brandeis. Brandeis, who had gotten to know Hoover and who thought highly of him, called McAdoo to say that Wilson should be told that Hoover was "too valuable a force" to be lost and that the appointment, complete with ample powers, should be made immediately; Hoover was soon installed in office. Brandeis also advised Baker (who had testified on his behalf during the Court confirmation hearings) about workers' conditions in the munitions industry. At Wilson's request, the justice wrote a lengthy letter to Colonel House detailing the way the War Industries Board should be organized. And various members of Wilson's war government saw Brandeis regularly, seeking his advice and frequently passing it along to the president.[15]

In 1917 Wilson asked Brandeis to work with Colonel House to compile ideas for a peace treaty, particularly concerning the rights of minorities. Brandeis, therefore, immersed himself in geographical, ethnic, and historical data. Charles Crane sent his old friend Thomas G. Masaryk, a leader of the Czechoslovakian independence movement and eventually the first president of Czechoslovakia, to see Brandeis, who later gave him suggestions for the Czechoslovakian declaration of independence. A memorandum to Hoover, then a delegate to the Versailles peace conference, from his secretary, Lewis Strauss, says, "As arranged, I had a talk with Justice Brandeis, during the course of which he expressed his views as to the proper handling of the British question, it being understood that I would repeat them to you . . . The urgency of the Russian question, and the fact that upon its settlement rest inevitably the proper functioning of economic interdependence in Europe, indicates to him the necessity that it should be the first matter to be settled by the Powers at the forthcoming Conference in Paris." Brandeis clearly saw no ethical problem in helping the administration with personnel matters and war-related policies during a national emergency, and his advice was most unlikely to result in a case before the Court.[16]

Even after Wilson had left the White House, officials, politicians, labor leaders, journalists, and activists of various kinds still flocked to the Brandeis apartment for a short chat, for one of the famous teas, or for a dinner of ham shipped from Louisville by Alfred Brandeis. Their conversation inevitably focused on government activities. From such conversations Brandeis was able to report to his brother the probable makeup of Harding's cabinet and to Frankfurter that the ambassador to Mexico and President Coolidge were both unhappy with the Department of State's policies toward Mexico and Nicaragua but that Coolidge would replace the secretary of state only if he could muster up the necessary courage. The flow went in both directions; Brandeis was able to keep his concerns alive in the minds of his guests. Senator Thomas J. Walsh, who had championed Brandeis during the confirmation fight, read parts of the *Survey Graphic* issue on unemployment into the *Congressional Record* and called for a government building program as a partial antidote. When the Court based its decision in *Black & White Taxi Co.* v. *Brown & Yellow Taxi Co.* on the doctrine of diversity of jurisdiction that Brandeis disliked so much, he wrote to Frankfurter that a bill eliminating the doctrine should be drafted and sent to Walsh. Then during dinner at the Brandeises' on March 1, 1928, Representative R. Walton Moore of Virginia mentioned the possibility of such a statute. In the ensuing discussion "it was suggested" that Frankfurter and his associates might draft the bill. Brandeis advised Frankfurter to send a copy of his *Business of the Supreme Court* to Moore and let Moore then request Frankfurter's help. Later, Brandeis asked Frankfurter to draw up two additional bills affecting jurisdiction and send them to Moore. It was Moore who had given Brandeis the information about Mexico, Nicaragua, and Coolidge. Among other visitors during the 1920s were Andrew Furuseth, head of the Seamen's Union; Samuel Gompers; George Rublee, legal advisor to the American Embassy in Mexico; Vernon Kellogg, an assistant to Hoover in the Food Administration and later permanent secretary of the National Research Council; Hoover, by then Harding's secretary of commerce; the La Follettes; Senators Davis Elkins, Henrik Shipstead, John Blaine, and Burton K. Wheeler; Representative John M. Nelson; Father John Augustine Ryan, Director of the National Catholic Welfare Council's social action department and a Jesuit theologian; Governor Henry Allen of Kansas; Robert Woolley and Mark Potter, members of the Interstate Commerce Commission; Anna Bird, a feminist active in the Republican Party; Grace Abbott, chief of the United States Children's Bureau; Edward Keating, a member of the House of Representatives until 1919 and thereafter editor of *Labor*, the magazine of the railroad brotherhoods; Leo Rowe, assistant secretary of the Treasury: Richard Boekel, head of a national news service; Lowell Mellett, editor of the Scripps-Howard newspapers; journalist Drew Pearson; Ernest Gruening, managing editor of the *Nation*; and George Milton, editor of the *Chattanooga News*.[17]

Brandeis pulled his guests, Frankfurter, and his causes together. Brandeis learned one evening that his sometime guest Andrew Furuseth had drawn up Senator Henrik Shipstead's bill prohibiting labor injunctions. Brandeis told Frankfurter that if it was "not drawn as it should be, you can doubtless get it changed . . . For the subcommittee of the judiciary consists of Tom Walsh, [George W.] Norris and [John]Blaine. Furuseth is also intimate with the LaFollettes—breakfasts there every Sunday." The subcommittee later called Frankfurter in to redraft the bill. Brandeis went on to indicate the usefulness of his interlocking circle of acquaintances: "Senator Blaine was in the other day. I took occasion to talk to him and Sen LaFollette jointly on restricting federal jurisdiction whenever they saw a chance. Blaine seemed entirely in accord. I guess it would be a good idea for you to write him a line accompanying 'Business'."[18]

Brandeis remained friendly with Herbert Hoover, whom he had met through Norman Hapgood, throughout the early 1920s. He told Hapgood in 1917 that Hoover "seems to me the biggest figure injected into Washington life by the war." He commented to Alpheus Mason, "In one hour, I learned more from Hoover than from all the persons I had seen in connection with war matters heretofore." Their friendship was furthered when Alfred Brandeis spoke with Hoover later in 1917 and was promptly drafted as an unpaid special assistant for the Food Administration. Brandeis regretted Hoover's turn to Republicanism in 1920 and his rejection as that party's candidate. Gradually becoming disenchanted, however, Brandeis quietly rooted for Al Smith in 1928, when Hoover ran for president.[19]

Because of their past friendship, Brandeis influenced some personnel matters when Hoover became president. One was the naming of Raymond Stevens as special adviser to Siam. Hoover also asked Brandeis for advice about potential members when organizing the National Commission on Law Observance and Enforcement. In 1929 Joseph Eastman, a friend from Boston Public Franchise League days, was up for reappointment to the Interstate Commerce Commission. Brandeis asked Justice Stone to talk to Hoover about the appointment, got George Anderson (his advocate during his own confirmation hearings) to call up James Richards (the president of Consolidated Gas in Boston) and to arouse Massachusetts politicians, and talked with a Washington lawyer who was circulating a petition for Eastman. Eastman was reappointed. Hoover also consulted Brandeis at least once on policy. In June 1931 the president sent for the justice and talked with him about what Brandeis called "specific matters." Brandeis was still disillusioned when he left the White House: "Here even in private conversation Mr. Hoover refused to recognize the most obvious facts."[20]

Frankfurter had met Franklin Roosevelt briefly in 1906 and again during World War I. By 1928, when Roosevelt was elected governor of New York, they were friends, although Frankfurter thought Roosevelt suffered from "lack of incisive intellect and a kind of optimism that sometimes makes him timid, as well as an ambition that leads to compromises." Nonetheless, the friendship was close enough for Roosevelt to ask Frankfurter to continue calling him "Frank" in 1933 (rather than the proper "Mr. President"). Brandeis began using Frankfurter as a conduit to Roosevelt before the 1928 gubernatorial election, writing, "If, as I expect, Roosevelt is elected, I should like through you to put in early two requests: (a) Far reaching attack on 'The Third Degree', (b) Good counsel in N.Y.'s cases before our Court." Frankfurter suggested that the two men meet;

Brandeis replied, "If I should chance to see Franklin Roosevelt, I should not hesitate to talk with him about my two requests. But I think it entirely unnecessary that I should see him . . . I am sure that the request from you will accomplish what we desire." When Roosevelt was nominated for president by the Democratic convention in June 1932, Brandeis wrote to his niece, "Aunt Alice and I think Franklin Roosevelt is much underrated by the Liberals. The opposition of the vested interests, who have opposed him, indicated that they fear him." And Brandeis was pleased with McAdoo's involvement in the nomination: "McAdoo, the ablest of the Democrats, is redivivus—that will mean much."[21]

In mid-October 1932 Roosevelt, seemingly certain of his election, called Frankfurter and asked if Brandeis would meet with him when he was in Washington for the inauguration. They actually met on November 23. Brandeis offered the president-elect his help and advised him to finance public works programs by taxing large estates. Later Brandeis was able to assure Frankfurter that Roosevelt seemed "well versed in most fundamental facets of the situation" and was "against the bankers."[22]

An extraordinary number of New Deal officials wanted to see Brandeis, who found Roosevelt's cabinet choices "on the whole reassuring." He was particularly glad that Frances Perkins was to become secretary of labor: she was "the best the U.S. affords; & it is a distinct advance to have selected a woman for the Cabinet." Perkins quickly went to talk to Brandeis about a public works program and staffing her department, returned to consult with Senator Hugh Black's proposed maximum hours bill, and was back within a week and a half to meet Harvard economist Oliver Sprague at Frankfurter's request.[23]

Frankfurter also arranged a visit by Secretary of the Interior Harold Ickes, who recorded in his Diary that they had discussed "government policies, particularly with relation to my own Department," and that he felt as if he had been "sitting at the feet of one of the fine old prophets." He agreed to appoint Nathan Margold, the Frankfurter protegé and NAACP lawyer in whom Brandeis had taken an interest, as his solicitor. Margold, in turn, asked Frankfurter and Brandeis for advice on how to staff his office. The staffing of the various bureaucracies with Harvard graduates was as important to Brandeis's influence during the New Deal as was Frankfurter's access to Roosevelt or the awe in which so many New Deal personnel held "Isaiah."[24]

In August 1933 General Hugh Johnson, head of the National Recovery Administration, spoke on the telephone with Brandeis about unions and regularity of employment, then visited in November when Brandeis discussed unemployment insurance. The major policy question was the balance that should be struck between federal involvement and state power.

Brandeis would have left the matter to the states but to encourage them to pass an adequate law he would have had the federal government set a date after which every employer not part of a state-sponsored plan would pay an excise tax. The monies collected would go into the general revenue fund rather than an unemployment compensation fund, "lest . . . we start national provision." He suggested that the District of Columbia follow the Wisconsin plan, created largely by Brandeis's daughter Elizabeth and her husband, Paul Raushenbush. Each corporation built up its own fund for paying workers who were laid off. The amount paid into the fund was based on an "experience rating," calculated on the corporation's previous success in maintaining regularity of employment. Companies with high rates of irregular employment paid the most. (Elizabeth explained the system in articles in the *Survey* and the *New Republic*.) Brandeis outlined both plans to Johnson and sent him a copy of one of Elizabeth's articles. "The General expressed approval of the general plan," Brandeis reported to his daughter, "but I guess he didn't understand overmuch."[25]

Johnson was gradually replaced by Donald Richberg, a labor and utilities lawyer who had been active in the Progressive party and who had written "The Industrial Liberalism of Justice Brandeis" for the *Columbia Law Review* issue dedicated to Brandeis on his seventy-fifth birthday. Richberg had gone to Washington in 1933 as general counsel for the NRA and had quickly become influential with Roosevelt. During an interview with the president in early 1934, he explained Brandeis's suggestions about utilizing the government's taxing powers as part of a recovery program, reporting to Brandeis that Roosevelt had taken notes on the ideas. Shortly after Richberg's arrival in Washington, Brandeis had written to him, "With you, Ickes and Lilienthal in seats of power it looks really like a New Deal." These three were part of the Brandeis-Frankfurter interlocking group. David Lilienthal was a director of the Tennessee Valley Authority, whose appointment Brandeis had influenced through Arthur Morgan and with whom Brandeis had spoken about soil reclamation and the necessity for a public works program during the summer of 1932. At Harvard Law School, Lilienthal had impressed Frankfurter, who sent him to Donald Richberg, then setting up a law firm in Chicago; together, they drafted the Railway Labor Act of 1926. One of Richberg's partners was Harold Ickes. In 1931 Wisconsin Governor Philip La Follette, son of Senator Robert La Follette and the man who asked Elizabeth and Paul Raushenbush to work on the Wisconsin unemployment act, tried to get Richberg to head the Wisconsin Public Service Commission. Richberg recommended Lilienthal, who accepted and had a distinguished career there before being lured to Washington.

In 1933 Ickes asked Brandeis to recommend someone to head the proposed public works administration. Brandeis suggested Philip La Follette, but Roosevelt decided to make Ickes himself head of the agency.[26]

Brandeis used a variety of conduits to Roosevelt. Samuel Rosenman, a former New York state judge and one of Roosevelt's advisers, took Brandeis's thoughts about regularity of employment and taxation to the president. As early as November 25, 1932, Huston Thompson wrote to Roosevelt, "I have had another conversation with Mr. Justice Brandeis and he suggested we should consider in our plans the very best way of checking and controlling holding companies, which would be by taxing the dividends . . . The Justice was very positive and enthusiastic about his suggestion. He asked me to forward the idea to you." In February 1933 Brandeis spoke to Raymond Moley, one of Roosevelt's Brain Trusters, about the urgent need for a public works program; in September, he talked with Moley about a number of specific proposals. Moley wrote to Frankfurter in 1935, "the reference which I deleted [from an article in *Today* magazine] as to his quiet advising from the sidelines (not as to what he or the Court were going to do, of course, but as to what he believed administrative and legislative policy should be) was true. He has been a determinant and active factor in the guidance of legislative and administrative policy. I do not object to this. I admire it. And I do not think that, *entre nous*, we should hesitate to admit it."[27]

In 1933 Frankfurter introduced Thomas Corcoran and Benjamin Cohen into the New Deal circle. Corcoran saw Brandeis regularly to consult about the drafting of such legislation as the 1934 Securities Exchange Act and eventually to tell him, for Roosevelt, about the Court-packing plan before it became public. Corcoran, Cohen, and James Landis, Brandeis's former clerk, drafted the Public Securities Act of 1933, the Securities Exchange Act of 1934, the Holding Company Act of 1935, and the Social Security Act of 1935, all of which reflected Brandeis's program for economic recovery. There was no question among Brandeis's opponents that Frankfurter, Corcoran, and Cohen were surrogates for Brandeis. Speaking of how Brandeis influenced Roosevelt, Rexford Tugwell wrote, "The first of these means was his disciples; the second was the threat of unconstitutionality. The first apostle in the Brandeis hierarchy was Frankfurter . . . Through Frankfurter, mostly, the staffing of New Deal agencies was controlled and dissenters were got rid of. And because Brandeis was, after Holmes's death, the most influential member of the court among intellectuals and liberals—and with Roosevelt—a word from him was very nearly a command . . . The blandishments of Frankfurter, the alternatives offered by Corcoran and Cohen, and the threat of judicial disapproval if they were not agreed to were sufficient . . . the results are plain enough." Tugwell, an influential member of the early Brain Trust, was one of Brandeis's ideological enemies who left the administration in disgust. He exaggerated Brandeis's influence; as he said, "the results are plain enough," and they indicate that Roosevelt frequently did not heed Brandeis's advice. But historians generally agree that these three men were Brandeis's main channels of communication with Roosevelt.[28]

Other avenues were Brandeis's nephew Louis Brandeis Wehle (an old friend of Roosevelt's), Norman Hapgood (to whom Roosevelt wrote in 1935, "Our Cape Cod friend [Brandeis] is a grand person and I hope he will help us to find ways of answering the people who can only say either 'don't do it' or 'you can't do it' whenever constructive action of any kind is proposed."), and Zionist leaders. When Rabbi Stephen Wise went to the White House for one of his periodic conferences with Roosevelt and mentioned Brandeis, Roosevelt exclaimed, "Grand man! You know, Stephen, we of the inner circle call him Isaiah."[29]

Brandeis cared passionately enough about two matters to visit Roosevelt himself. The first matter, Palestine and the plight of European Jews before the United States entered World War II, did not involve an issue likely to come before the Court; the second, a federal plan for unemployment insurance, did.

Brandeis and Rabbi Stephen Wise became aware that American German-Jewish leaders such as Felix Warburg were advising Roosevelt that German Jews were in no danger, partly because they feared publicity would harm relatives inside Germany. Brandeis, appalled, hammered away at Frankfurter to get Roosevelt to do more about the German Jews; Frankfurter, knowing Roosevelt's feelings that it was an internal German problem (although it is unclear how lowering American immigration restrictions would have interfered) was reluctant to badger him. Frances Perkins's attempts to change Roosevelt's attitude were thwarted by the State Department. The Zionists were successful in one instance, however: following a series of Arab-inspired riots during the summer of 1936, when the British government proposed to suspend all immigration to Palestine until it had a chance to study the situation, Wise rushed to see Roosevelt and successfully urged that he intervene. The State Department thereupon announced that the United States "would regard suspension of immigration as a breach of the Mandate." As a result, Prime Minister Stanley Baldwin postponed suspension until the study undertaken by the newly appointed Peel Commission was complete. The commission reported that the Mandate had become impossible and that Palestine should be divided into a Jewish state, an Arab state, and an international zone around Jerusalem. The proposed Jewish state would have encompassed only 1,554 square miles and was totally unacceptable to the Zionists.

Brandeis promptly sent Stephen Wise and Robert Szold to London, telling Szold to confer first with Benjamin Cohen. The Woodhead Commission, investigating the feasibility of the Peel recommendation, eventually reported that it was impossible.[30]

Urged on by the Zionists, prominent American Christians began lobbying Roosevelt and British officials against any cessation of immigration. But Frankfurter feared that Roosevelt did not understand the absorptive capacity of Palestine, and Brandeis decided to see Roosevelt himself. The justice then reported to Frankfurter, "F.D. went very far in our talk in his appreciation of the significance of Palestine—the need of keeping it whole and of making it Jewish. He was tremendously interested—and wholly surprised—on learning of the great increase in Arab population since the War; and on learning of the plenitude of land for Arabs in Arab countries, about which he made specific inquiries. Possible refuges for Jews elsewhere he spoke of as 'satellites', and there was no specific talk of them."[31]

Brandeis did not speak with Roosevelt again about the Jewish situation until October 24, 1939, after he had resigned from the Court and the MacDonald White Paper of May 1939, calling for an independent Palestinian state and severe restrictions on Jewish immigration and land purchases, had been issued. Brandeis spent thirty-five minutes with Roosevelt and found him "as sympathetic as in the past; and as interested in all I was able to tell him about the present in Palestine. There is reason to hope that he will say something about Palestine . . . Miss LeHand was present, and he had her take down what he wants to consider . . . I handed him the P[alestine]. E[conomic]. C[orporation]. 12th Annual Report which he glanced at in my presence." On December 4 Brandeis suggested that Roosevelt ask Secretary of Agriculture Henry Wallace for a copy of a report on "Jewish Colonization in Palestine." Roosevelt replied that he wanted to see Brandeis "right after the New Year," but the meeting did not take place.[32]

The last known letter that Brandeis sent to Roosevelt, on April 26, 1941, reflected his consternation (and that of Frankfurter, who drafted the letter) over the refusal of the British to permit the Palestinian Jews arms, even though the Nazis were moving across North Africa. "A word from you to the British manifesting your desire to be assured that the Jews in Palestine will be afforded the necessary means for self-protection would be of the greatest help," Brandeis wrote. "Nor would it be irrelevant to suggest that such a measure would help the British." Roosevelt assured Brandeis that the suggestion had been "passed on to the British Government," which ultimately permitted Jewish Palestinians to join the British army.[33]

The second matter that sent Brandeis to Roosevelt was a federal plan for unemployment insurance. He wrote to Elizabeth on September 16, 1933, explaining his view of the plan the government should adopt and adding, "F.D. indicated yesterday to F.F. a desire to talk with me generally on matters, before Court convenes. If he carries out his purpose, I want to discuss irregularity of employment with him. Let me have as soon as possible your & Paul's views as to the above; &, if you can, a rough suggestion for a bill." Thinking further about the matter, Brandeis came up with an idea for a federal payroll tax on employers, from which they could deduct whatever amount they were paying into state unemployment plans. Later that fall the Raushenbushes met with Corcoran, Wyzanski, and a number of other young New Dealers and liberal business leaders. Another meeting, arranged by A. Lincoln Filene, was held during the Christmas holidays. Frances Perkins and Senator Robert F. Wagner were present to organize a campaign in support of the Brandeis idea. Thomas H. Eliot of the Labor Department and Paul Raushenbush drew up a bill; in February 1934 it was submitted to Congress by Senator Robert F. Wagner and Representative David J. Lewis of Maryland. In April 1934 Brandeis told Elizabeth that Secretary Perkins and Senator Wagner were "working on the President to come out for" the plan, which they expected Congress to enact.[34]

Unexpectedly, however, Roosevelt asked Congress to delay consideration of the bill, largely because a variety of critics wanted a more comprehensive unemployment and old age insurance system. He then appointed Secretary Perkins as chair of a Cabinet Committee on Economic Security, which was to develop a program to submit to Congress. On the day of Roosevelt's announcement, Brandeis sent Elizabeth a letter from Boston marked "Strictly Confidential," which said in part, "Don't be discouraged by the President's message. He summoned me yesterday & when I reached him at 4:45 P.M. he had in his hands his message & started to read it to me. When he came to the part on social insurance, I stopped him, told him it was all wrong, & for about ³/₄ hours discussed that question & I think I convinced him of the error. He said the message had already gone to the Capitol & it was too late to change that; but it would not commit him as to means, etc. I have left some efficient friends in Washington, who are to work for the true faith during the summer." After a good deal of internal dissension, the Perkins Committee recommended the Wagner-Lewis approach, and a second and somewhat altered plan was introduced by Wagner and Lewis on January 17, 1935. It came under sharp attack, and Brandeis told Elizabeth that he was "trying through the faithful and efficient here to prevent F.D.'s from falling into social worker error," meaning treating unemployment compensation as a form of relief rather than as an earned right. The bill was finally passed and signed into law on August 15, 1935. Raushenbush was offered a job with the new Social Security Board, coordinating state unemployment compensation legislation, but declined in order to remain in charge of the Wisconsin program. This pleased Brandeis, who believed that the "important" work was to be done in the states. " '*In die Beschränkung zeigt sich erst der Meister* [One must first show oneself the master of limited things],' " he told Elizabeth, repeating one of his favorite quotations from Goethe.[35]

Reflecting on Franklin Roosevelt, Brandeis told an interviewer in 1940 that he thought Jefferson, Cleveland, and Wilson had been great presidents, "but none of them could match this fellow." Frankfurter reported to Roosevelt that during the last meeting Brandeis and Frankfurter ever had, Brandeis had called Roosevelt "greater than Jefferson and almost as great as Lincoln." The remarks were made long after Roosevelt had abandoned any attempts at Brandeisian control of the economy, so Brandeis's respect for him went beyond partisan appreciation.[36]

Brandeis's acquaintances ranged beyond the executive branch; there was always a "mix" of people at the dinners and at the weekly teas. As Margaret Truman wrote, "To be invited to the Justice's apartment on California Street was regarded by many New Dealers in Washington during these days as a great honor. To be invited back was an even greater honor." One might find there William Green, president of the American Federation of Labor; Father Ryan (who, for many years, was a regular Thanksgiving dinner guest); legislators; and, always, a scattering of the young people pouring into the ever-growing federal bureaucracy. According to one of the Brandeises' close friends, "The fact that there were so many young people in any gathering at his house represented his effort to reach out even into the future." Mrs. Brandeis presided over the teas, making certain that guests participated in what was almost "a game of musical chairs, designed to give the Justice ten or fifteen minutes of individual conversation with as many of the guests as could be talked to in an hour and a half." Brandeis's hospitality and his incredibly extensive correspondence resulted in "emissaries in every conceivable field—politics, universities, law schools, journalism—all of whom he kept supplied with material on his 'worth-while causes.' "[37]

Members of Congress appeared regularly. Brandeis was "a sort of father confessor" to Senator Burton K. Wheeler, who eventually became head of the Senate Interstate and Foreign Commerce Committee. In 1935 Wheeler submitted a bill that would have imposed a graduated tax on the net capital return of corporations, eliminating bigness. Wheeler did not expect his bill to pass but offered the Brandeisian proposal to begin a discussion of industrial decentralization. Two years later, when Roosevelt sent Congress his Court-packing plan, which would have permitted the president to appoint an additional justice for each one currently on the Court who was over seventy years old, Wheeler fought it. Supposedly, such elderly men could not carry a full load of work, but the plan's real purpose was to get enough New Dealers on the Court to keep it from striking down Roosevelt's legislation. Brandeis was opposed to the plan, viewing it as an unacceptable political attack on the independence of the judiciary. Wheeler went to Brandeis for help in opposing the bill, and Brandeis promptly steered him to Chief Justice Hughes, who wrote a strong letter, endorsed by Brandeis and Van Devanter, to the Senate Judiciary Committee. Wheeler then made the letter public.[38]

Senator Harry Truman was one of the members of Wheeler's Commerce Committee. The senator from Missouri described Brandeis as "a man of awesome intellect . . . he was a great old man. I went to his place very often, and we seemed to have no trouble in hitting it off. We had many a long talk . . . Justice Brandeis and I were certainly in agreement on the dangers of bigness . . . I think I've read every one of his decisions . . . I'm sure whatever he said was right. Because he was a man who always thought his way through to the right conclusion." Truman and Brandeis seem an unlikely twosome, but Dean Acheson recalled, "Mr. Truman was a good friend of Justice Brandeis, and when he was in the Senate, he used to go almost every week, I believe, to the Justice's at-homes." Acheson described Truman as possessing "an Aristotelian understanding of power. He had not only read the Greek and Roman philosophers, he understood them." Perhaps the two talked about the Greeks and Romans; certainly, they discussed transportation. Truman had learned about transportation as an official in Missouri and became expert on Wheeler's subcommittee investigating railroad finances. "For hours at a time," Margaret Truman has written, "Justice Brandeis would talk with Dad about his committee's latest discoveries in railroad wrecking and looting. Dad agreed wholeheartedly with Justice Brandeis's contention that a company's size should be limited by one man's capacity." Brandeis must have thought of his fight against the New Haven Railroad as he listened to Truman: "One of the first investigations I conducted was into the affairs of the Missouri-Pacific Railroads, and my goodness, the telegrams I got, and the phone calls and letters . . . I was threatened with political ruination of every kind you can imagine if I didn't call off the investigation . . . I was called every name in the book that they could think of, including that I was a Socialist and a Communist and an anarchist and I don't know what all." Truman's reading of history had convinced him that "the railroads have always been subsidized by the government, and they have always made enormous profits, and . . . very little looking into it is ever done . . . The railroads just keep on being looted, and the greedy do it and get away with it." Brandeis shared the sentiment. Truman also shared Brandeis's view on government wiretapping. He agreed with the *Olmstead* dissent "right down the line," adding, "Any attempt to invade the privacy of a private citizen, doesn't matter what it is, is in violation of the Bill of Rights, and those who propose such a thing are more of a danger to the country than the ones they want to listen in on."[39]

Furthermore, Truman was intrigued by Palestine. "That is one part of the world that has always interested me," he said after he left the presidency. "The whole history of that area of the world is just about the most complicated and most interesting of any area anywhere, and I have always made a very careful study of it . . . the pity of it is that the whole area is just waiting to be developed. And the Arabs have just never seemed to take any interest in developing it. I have always thought that the Jews would, and of course, they have." Given Truman's interest and Brandeis's commitment, Palestine seems a likely subject of their conversation. When Rabbi Wise went to see the newly elected President Truman to discuss American support in Palestine, Truman told him that "as far as I was concerned, the United States would do all that it could to help the Jews set up a homeland"—in spite of the fact that the State Department had already warned him against such a course. Alben Barkley, who later became Truman's vice-president, visited Brandeis frequently and credited Brandeis with *his* interest in Zionism and Palestine. Truman named James D. McDonald the first United States ambassador to Israel in 1948. McDonald had been the high commissioner for refugees of the League of Nations until 1945, keeping in contact with Frankfurter and Brandeis during the 1930s and working valiantly but unsuccessfully to get Roosevelt to aid Jewish refugees throughout the war. Although there is no proof of a Brandeis-Truman-McDonald link, it seems evident that Truman was yet another president influenced by Brandeis.[40]

Brandeis permitted neither age nor temporary setbacks to interfere with his campaigns for what he considered to be intelligent government policy. The passage of the unemployment insurance bill left open the kind of system each state would use. Brandeis, unhappy about the system subsequently adopted by many states, saw the head of the Federal Security Administration and his counsel. "I subjected them to a long discourse on the heresy of the prevailing unemployment compensation system," he reported to his daughter. The administrator "said definitely that he agreed with me; and both agreed to my statement that, in presenting the option to the several states, the Social Security officials have not done so fairly . . . We can't expect anything to result immediately, but it is worth-while to have them understand & to be really sympathetic." The counsel mentioned that he had a copy of Brandeis's 1911 memo to Lincoln Filene about regularity of employment; Brandeis, unsatisfied, recommended that Elizabeth send a copy of Paul's memo on experience rating to a Washington friend who would undoubtedly pass it on to the counsel. But "we can't expect anything to result immediately," he cautioned Elizabeth. He was just short of eighty-three; still determined, optimistic, passionate, articulate, and glad to be in the fray. It is not hard to understand why he had been dubbed "Isaiah."[41]

It has been fashionable for historians of the New Deal to dismiss Brandeis as an advocate of the good old days who had no practical program either for recovery from the Depression or for the years thereafter. They are mistaken. He certainly had one, and on the surface it appears no less workable, thoughtful, or just than the haphazard patchwork of policies that became the New Deal.

The program that he outlined in part on December 8, 1933 to his clerk Harry Shulman relied heavily on use of the federal taxing power. Taxation should be used to keep the banks from doing more than one kind of banking: "This would avoid all the evil of great concentration of financial power in the hands of bankers." The bankers had to be the first object of government action, because at the moment the government was in the bankers' hands. To supply government funds, the postal system should be used for savings accounts, checking accounts, commercial accounts, and the issuance of securities. Then, with the government freed from the control of the money trust, excise taxes would be imposed on overly large corporations of other kinds. The states would continue to regulate corporations, but the federal government would keep them small (and capable of being regulated) by taxation. Thus, the federal government would not become too big: "You must remember that it is the littleness of man that limits the size of things we can undertake. Too much bigness may break the federal government as it has broken business." Federal taxes would also curb the size of inheritances. The government would then encourage state adoption of the Wisconsin unemployment plan by taxing nonparticipating employers. Shulman asked whether reducing the size of corporation would not be "attempting to do the impossible, to turn the clock back." Brandeis's reaction was "immediate and spirited: 'Why shouldn't we turn the clock back? We just turned the clock back on a "noble experiment," which was unanimously adopted in the country and was being tried for some time [Prohibition]. At any rate whether the program can be executed or not is a separate question. To have that objection raised only confuses the proponent and directs his mind away from the real issue. First, we must determine what is desirable to do and then we can find ways and means to do it'.[42]

To deal with the immediate unemployment problem, Brandeis recommended a massive program of public works (including what became the Tennessee Valley Authority) which he thought could get two million people to work within two months. He also urged credit for small businesses, help for small farmers and sharecroppers, and elimination of holding companies and interlocking directorates. But he was equally concerned that measures be taken by the states. When Elizabeth and other La Follette Wisconsinites wanted to issue a policy statement, Brandeis elaborated on some of his ideas in a letter to her:

> Curb of bigness is indispensable to true Democracy & Liberty. It is the very foundation also of wisdom in things human
>
> "Nothing too much"
>
> I hope you can make your progressives see this truth. If they don't, we may get amelioration, but not a working "New Deal." And we are apt to get Fascist manifestations. Remember, the inevitable ineffectiveness of regulation, i.e. the limits of its efficiency in regulation.
>
> If the Lord had intended things to be big, he would have made man bigger—in brains and character . . .
>
> My idea has been that the Depression can be overcome only by extensive public works.
> (a) that no public works should be undertaken save those that would be effective in making the America of the future what it should be,
> (b) that we should avail [ourselves] of the present emergency to get those public works which Americans would lack the insight & persistence to get for themselves in ordinary times.
> These public works are, for every state,
> (1) afforestation
> (2) running water control
> (3) adult education
> (4) appropriate provision for dealing with defectives and delinquents . . .
> It is absurd to permit either floods or droughts, or waste of waters. We should so control all running waters, by reservoirs, etc., so
> (a) as to prevent floods & soil erosion

(b)   to make it possible to irrigate practically all land
(c)   to utilize the water for power & inland navigation
(d)   & for recreation[43]

Brandeis, like Keynes, emphasized government spending, but only during emergencies. Brandeis now added slum clearance and adult education to land use and natural resources as potential targets for federal money. But spending was to be temporary and limited to the kinds of programs that would help solve problems that would otherwise remain after the Depression had been overcome, and the income derived from federal taxation had to be shared with the states. If the money trust was broken up, government could begin to deal intelligently with public land and resources and other matters. The workers needed for initial projects would be paid through the federal and state public works programs. Brandeis was opposed to early New Deal attempts to limit production and raise prices; the approach, he believed, should be to lower prices and make jobs and goods available to workers, who would be able to take care of themselves once they had regular employment and unions. Smaller corporations would become manageable, creative, efficient laboratories for scientific management; small businesses would be permitted to set prices on the products they chose to stand behind.

Brandeis was not advocating a return to nineteenth-century laissez-faire economics. The role of the state governments in setting minimum wages and maximum hours (necessary until the workers slowly learned how to involve themselves in the running of corporations), in operating transportation and banking systems, in preventing the overaccumulation of wealth and power through taxes on estates and profits, in forcing corporations to bargain collectively with employees, in extending credit to small businesses and farms, in accumulating and disseminating information about industries and agriculture, in encouraging the growth of workers' and consumers' cooperatives, in limiting the activities of bankers and stockbrokers so that the money trust was not resurrected—none of this had anything to do with laissez-faire government but everything to do with correcting past mistakes while keeping each government relatively small. Brandeis was fond of saying, "Many men are all wool but none is more than a yard wide," and that even the tallest man is not very much taller than the ordinary man. Institutions had to be cut down to human scale: that would help prevent depressions and the twin evils of fascism and socialism.[44]

Brandeis gave a confidential interview to two journalists at his summer home in Chatham on June 23, 1935, one month after the Court had struck down major New Deal programs on what he considered " 'the

most important day in the history of the Court and the most beneficent,' "
because it had " 'compelled a return to human limitations.' " Saying that
progress had to take place in states and localities and in particular industries, Brandeis reiterated some of his ideas: the federal government
had to impose heavy taxes on out-of-state corporations, on directors who
did business with their own corporations, on intraorganization transactions within a holding company, and on public utility holding companies. The object of all the taxes was to end the practices and institutions
taxed.[45]

Brandeis told the same thing to New Deal officials and, for a while,
it looked as if Roosevelt was listening. When the first two years of the
New Deal had ended and the "second New Deal" began, a coalition
between "lawyers in the school of Brandeis and economists in the school
of Keynes" began to hold sway. A Brandeisian use of the taxing power
may be seen in the Walsh-Healy Public Contracts Act; the Public Utility
Holding Act; the 1936 Revenue Act; the Guffey Coal Act; and the new
versions of the Agricultural Adjustment Act, the NRA codes, and the
farm-foreclosure moratorium act. However, these policies affronted those
who saw salvation in a large central government, and they began to
pressure Roosevelt. Norman Hapgood summed up the situation in a letter
to the president on February 20, 1936:

> If Tugwell happens to remember a dinner of 7 or 8, given by
> Robert Lord O'Brien when the N.R.A. was young, he may also
> remember a fragment of conversation, that ran something like this,
> Tugwell having been speaking:
> O'Brien: "As Hapgood is the only person from outside, I think
> we ought to hear from him."
> Hapgood: "I doubt it. I fear I have not been able to learn anything
> since 1912."
> Tugwell (evidently understanding the implication): "I do not see
> why your crowd and ours cannot work together;" then, in a par-
> enthesis: "not Brandeis."
> In other words, inside the group of movements we call the New
> Deal, are two philosophies, both wishing to curb the power of plu-
> tocracy, but one wishing to do it with a few basic changes, the other
> believing in a mass of new administrative activities from Washington.
> If we can win our fight in November (and I am sure we can if
> there is not a big scare about solvency) we can probably bring the
> two groups of reformers a bit nearer together in the following two
> or three years.

Roosevelt replied, "I always hate the frame of mind which talks about
'your group' and 'my group' among Liberals. For instance . . . I can move

only just so fast during any given period, lest a political barrier be thrown up to retard or stop our progress. In the same way with monopolies, Brandeis is one thousand per cent right in principle but in certain fields there must be a guiding or restraining hand of Government because of the very nature of the specific field."[46]

The last sentence shows Roosevelt's refusal to meet head-on the argument between the two groups of New Dealers. Brandeis's position was predicated on keeping the size of institutions compatible with human limitations. With certain exceptions (in transportation, utilities, and land development), government regulation of industry was only to keep businesses small enough to prevent absentee ownership and to enable workers (and consumers) to meet employers as equals. Having done that, however, government was to leave the groups to their own devices, eliminating the need for a huge, uncontrollable federal bureaucracy.

Those in the other camp (Tugwell, Moley, Adolph Berle, Jr., and eventually Richberg) were convinced that big business was inevitable and that the only way to counteract its power was by setting up an equally powerful regulatory government. They assumed that the government would be filled with people like themselves who could be trusted to behave properly. But Brandeis cautioned Robert Bruère, "Do not pin too much faith in legislation. Remedial institutions are apt to fall under the control of the enemy and to become instruments of oppression."[47]

The approaches of the two New Deal groups were absolutely incompatible. Roosevelt declined to recognize this or be concerned with theoretical underpinnings. As C. Herman Pritchett has noted, the New Deal's chief failure was the lack of "any consistent social and economic philosophy to give meaning and purpose to its various action programs." James MacGregor Burns describes Roosevelt as "disdain[ing] elaborate, fine-spun theories . . . He hated abstractions." Arthur Schlesinger notes that Roosevelt "wriggled away" when confronted with the differences between the two camps and said to Adolph Berle, "This country is big enough to experiment with several diverse systems and follow several different lines. Why must we put our economic policy in a single systemic strait jacket?" According to Schlesinger, Roosevelt defined the New Deal as the " 'satisfactory compromise' " between the New Nationalism of Theodore Roosevelt and the New Freedom of Woodrow Wilson. As Brandeis could have told him, such a compromise was impossible.[48]

There was also an unarticulated disagreement between the two camps about the nature of the political process. To Brandeis, democracy was impossible without continuous citizen participation, and he did not mean only by the Washington elite. He had written to Frankfurter in 1921 that "too much stress cannot be placed upon the futility of knowledge unless people care enough to apply it. Men must be induced to set to work to do those things public which are within their immediate grasp and within their capabilities of performance. In that way possibly they may also be taught to love their community enough to make it livable." Speaking of a survey that Frankfurter and others were undertaking of crime, Brandeis said, "The chief difficulty, I fancy, will not be in discovering the cause of evil conditions or in devising legal and administrative remedies or even in getting them adopted—on paper. It will be in securing continuous, exacting application of the accepted remedy. To ensure patient, persistent and fearless application, support of a strong, earnest, stable public opinion will be necessary. To obtain that the public interest must be deep-seated. It must be fed by something more than the understanding however enriched by knowledge. Probably love of the city or at least local pride will be indispensable. Unless the citizens can be made really to care for Cleveland as an entity—to feel joy in its achievements and shame at its shortcomings—I don't see how one can expect more than mere temporary cleansing." Were Brandeis running the country, he would educate the citizens about the need for their day-to-day participation in the body politic. That had been one of the themes of all his public battles.[49]

But the other camp of New Dealers and Roosevelt himself were essentially elitists. Although they cared about inequality and injustice and economic opportunity, they did not believe that citizen activity was a prerequisite for the society they wanted to create. There was no effort at mass mobilization by the New Deal; the electorate was asked only to vote for New Dealers, wait for them to solve the country's problems, and try to avoid fear in the interim. The big government created by and in Washington signaled an end to meaningful federalism and to real experimentation by the states. Increases in federal taxes on individuals and corporations meant a draining of fiscal resources from the states. Having seen, as Brandeis had seen, the corruption of state legislatures and the inability of the states to solve the economic crisis of the Depression, the New Dealers understandably concluded that only centralized policymaking would work. Brandeis's reaction was just the opposite: too many creative people were being lured to Washington, and it was precisely because the states were in such trouble that the well-educated had an obligation to work there. He counseled horrified young New Dealers to return to the "provinces" from which they had gratefully escaped. One young man exclaimed, "But Mr. Justice—Fargo, North Dakota!" To the protest of another that "I have no hinterland. I'm from New York City," Brandeis replied implacably, "That is your misfortune."[50]

Brandeis's formula for recovery and industrial democracy might have worked, or it might not have. Certainly, it was more carefully thought through than were the plans of most of the pragmatic New Dealers, including Roosevelt. Brandeis's proposals, when they were considered at all, were considered *seriatim* rather than as interlocking parts of a general scheme. His comprehensive program was therefore never seriously evaluated by those in power; he was not, except in a few instances in 1935, asked to spell out the specifics of his proposed policies; thus, his alternatives were rejected without ever having been examined. The effect of World War II was to put Americans to work, which both made it appear that the Roosevelt administration had solved the nation's economic problems and turned most Americans' attention away from internal matters. Only in the 1970s and the 1980s, when the consequences and dangers of big government began to be understood, was interest in Brandeis revived and the question of the possible utility of his thinking asked.

The work of a Supreme Court justice, coupled with advising the administration, would be enough for most people of sixty (as Brandeis was during the Wilson years) or seventy-seven to eighty-three (as he was during the Roosevelt years). Brandeis, however, did much more. He no longer had an office and a staff to administer after 1921, but he continued his second full-time career as a Zionist leader, organizing and masterminding the Palestine Endowment Fund and the Palestine Development Council and continuing to advise Hadassah.

In addition he retained his interest in savings bank life insurance. Throughout his first few years on the Court he was in almost daily communication with his former secretary Alice Grady, who had become executive secretary of the Savings Bank Insurance League and, in 1920, deputy secretary of Savings Bank Insurance in Massachusetts. He kept in regular touch thereafter: "This month's figures are impressive" (September 22, 1927); "Do you know Mr. Bang. Judging from what La Follette's [Magazine] says he ought to be one who would not only appreciate S.B.I., but might become an effective ally" (November 18, 1927); "Your February record is fine" (March 9, 1929); "I suggest for your consideration: A. An effort through publicity to increase the monthly growth in outstanding insurance to One Million Dollars. B. A renewal of tactful efforts to increase the number of SBI banks. C. An educational campaign." (March 25, 1928); "I think I laid yesterday a solid foundation on which you can build a powerful ally" (May 9, 1928); "Let me know what the present attitude & what the past has been, of the Springfield Republican on S.B.I." (May 27, 1928). Brandeis was enormously proud of Alice Grady and her efforts and urged friends to help her whenever private insurance companies undertook new attempts to cripple the system. "When you have a fight on, one never knows whether to be glad or sorry," he wrote to her once. "Somehow you make the enemies of S.B.I. pay tribute & we come out a peg or two ahead." Nevertheless, he gave constant encouragement: "Of course you have been having a horrid time. But you will win . . . If anyone doesn't want you present at a conference, it is merely a dodge because he fears you . . . I know you are a 'bonnie fighter'—& with the right, for which you always battle, on your side—even the legions of the Evil ones cannot beat you." He was still sending her suggestions in 1932, talking about "the spearhead of our campaign" and "When we have succeeded there will be no town in Mass. without an S.B.I. policy." He wanted to make sure that SBLI had its own funds, so early in 1932 he arranged to have a cheap (fifteen cents per copy) edition of *Other People's Money* printed, with the royalties assigned to SBLI. The correspondence ended only with Alice Grady's death on April 19, 1934.[51]

An interest that began years before Brandeis's involvement in savings bank life insurance that never flagged was the Harvard Law School. He had helped organize the Harvard Law School Association and found the *Harvard Law Review*. He was a member of the Committee of Visitors to the Law School from 1889 to 1916, and remained interested in the curriculum of the school, its finances, and its faculty while he was on the Court. He contributed regularly and generously and was also available for special donations, such as a possible series of lectures by Eugene Ehrlich, a leading German exponent of sociological jurisprudence; a proposed Legislative Department; and chairs in criminal law and in legislation. He sent Frankfurter ideas about general fund-raising, students, and even Frankfurter's classes' examination papers.[52]

In 1913 Brandeis campaigned for Frankfurter's hiring by the Law School and helped raise the money to fund the professorship. He backed Frankfurter when the latter came under attack for being too "radical." Dean Roscoe Pound worried that the anti-Frankfurter feeling might lead, at the least, to the faculty's reassigning Frankfurter's public law courses. "Oh, don't worry about that," Brandeis reassured him. "It doesn't matter what he teaches. If he were to teach Bills and Notes, he'd be teaching himself." Brandeis similarly supported Professor Zechariah Chafee, Jr., when Chafee's belief in free speech led some alumni to attempt to purge him from the faculty. He played an important role in keeping Roscoe Pound from resigning as dean when Pound was having difficulties with the university administration and with his own faculty. He attempted to get Harold Laski to teach at the Law School, although Laski decided to be housed instead in the Department of Government. And he sent his best clerks back to teach at Harvard.[53]

The Law School was of course grateful for his efforts. He was awarded an honorary A.M. in 1891 and in 1904 membership in Phi Beta Kappa. He was enormously touched when, for his seventieth birthday, a group of friends organized by Judge Mack gave the Law School $50,000 to establish the Brandeis Research Fellowship.[54]

Brandeis commented most extensively on his vision of the Law School in 1924 when Pound decided to use increased demands for admission to build the school into the best and biggest in the nation. Pound went to Washington in October to tell Brandeis of his plans, which were already being opposed at Harvard by a group of faculty headed by Frankfurter. Brandeis sent Frankfurter his reactions: "Make frank recognition of the fact that numbers in excess of 1000, and the proposed 350 seats lecture halls & lectures, are irreconcilable with H.L.S. traditions and aims. Instead, make frank avowal of a purpose to aid in building up the lesser schools. Then aid in placing H.L.S. resources at their disposal so far as possible, i.e., create a new kind of exchange-professorships . . . Also arrange that picked students from such lesser schools may enter, not only postgraduate H.L.S. classes, but the higher undergraduate classes . . . Be the mother church for the new & worthy legal education & legislation." He discussed the matter with fellow Harvard alumni who were judges: Holmes and Edward T. Sanford of the Suprme Court, and Julian Mack and Augustus Hand of the lower federal courts. Then he sent Frankfurter his ideas about selection of students:

(a) Limitations must *not* be affected by raising tuition fees.
(b) The method must ensure national representation, geographically & in respect to colleges.
(c) Provision must be made for star men (undergraduates) of other law schools.
(d) Provision must be made for teachers of or those definitely preparing for teaching at other law schools.

He told Judge Mack that he wanted "not a bigger H.L.S., but 20 Harvard Law Schools." And he immediately set about creating at least one other Harvard, this one in Kentucky.[55]

Believing that all states should have their own scholarly faculties, the still-loyal son of Kentucky turned his attention to the University of Louisville in 1924. Characteristically, Brandeis thought first of books. He sent the College of Liberal Arts his collections on sociology, economics, fine arts, and World War I, asking for a "catalogue of the University or Programs of Instruction." (A servant inadvertently included some volumes that he and his wife "cherish[ed] as daily companions": Livingston's *What the Greek Genius Means to Us, The Legacy of Greece,* Gilbert Murray's translation of Euripides, and a volume of Plutarch's *Lives.* He immediately wrote to the niece through whom he had made the present and asked that those books be returned promptly so as to "relieve an aching void.") "To become great," he wrote to his brother, "a university must express the people whom it serves, and must express the people and the community at their best . . . History teaches, I believe, that the present tendency toward centralization must be arrested, if we are to attain the American ideals, and that for it must be substituted intense development of life through activities in the several states and localities. The problem is a very difficult one; but the local university is the most hopeful instrument for any attempt at solution." The University of Louisville had to be the creation of Kentuckians, and Brandeis considered its development "a task befitting the Adolph Brandeis family," particularly Alfred and his family in Louisville, although Brandeis and Alice would send money and suggestions.[56]

He gradually decided on helping the creation of departmental libraries and in the upgrading of the law school. Brandeis was particularly interested in nine departmental libraries: the World War, Sociology and Economics, English Literature, German Literature, Fine Arts and Archaeology, Music, Palestine and Zionism, and Classics. He explained to a Louisville nephew that since the war had wrought epochal changes, understanding it had become essential to American statesmanship. Brandeis had been impressed by Wilson's emphasis on national self-determination. Thus, it was important for the university to be cosmopolitan, to know and teach its students about other lands, in turn encouraging their integration into American society and their appreciation of the contributions of other cultures (including those from which their ancestors had come). The Jewish goal of self-determination in Palestine, along with a desire to honor the memory of his uncle Dembitz, led Brandeis to work on creation of a Zionist library named after Dembitz.[57]

Brandeis also sent the university the beginnings of a railroad library, a fund for development of a Greek department (as well as a library on Greek art and archeology), and the kinds of documents he felt crucial to a real collection of Kentuckiana: official reports at all governmental levels; annual reports of charities, schools, and religious institutions; and reports and publications of businesses and business organizations like the Board of Trade. Brandeis anticipated recent trends in historiography by writing, "It is in publications of this nature, largely uncopyrighted and usually treated as being of ephemeral, if of any value, that the real history of the Community is recorded. By their close and continuous study, the important facts, political, economic and social will evolve. And it is through an adequate study of such sources that the experience, which is to become our teacher, is to be gained." To secure for the university documents on a variety of subjects that would otherwise be unavailable, Brandeis pressed into service a member of the World War Foreign Debt Commission, the Counsel of the War Finance Corporation, the Legal Advisor of the United States Veterans Bureau, the Chairman of the Mixed Claims Commission, Dean Acheson, John G. Dudley of the Food Administration, Walker D. Hines of the Federal Trade Commission, a counsel to the United States Shipping Board, the editor of *Labor*, a commissioner of the Interstate Commerce Commission, Justice Sanford, and, of course, Felix Frankfurter. Brandeis also sent advice to the workers in Louisville on how to solicit local aid for the university.[58]

However, when Brandeis turned his attention to the law school, he found the university totally lacking in enthusiasm. Brandeis was unperturbed, and sent a long letter to Alfred about the situation. Speaking of the lack of interest of the president and trustees and of the Brandeis family's willingness to contribute funds, he said, "To give the school essential tools of trade, and a decent work room is satisfying an obvious need. To make the gift in honor of persons—partly members of the Trustees' families or fellow members of their profession is a compliment easily understood. And when this is coupled with our offer of as much as $10,000 a year for ten years—well 'money talks' . . . When I said our project is 'irresistible,' I didn't mean that obstacles would vanish in the winking of an eye, and walls tumble before the blowing of the horn. 'This sort of thing takes a deal of trimming,' of patience, persistence and tact." He added, "Indifference. Of course they are in the main indifferent. If they weren't they would have set in motion before this forces which would have relieved us of the necessity for effort . . . There is in most Americans some spark of idealism which can be fanned into a flame. It takes sometimes a divining rod to find what it is; but when found—and that means often, when disclosed to the owners—the results are often most extraordinary." He thought that the approach of building library collections in a variety of fields, as well as the law school, meant that all the trustees would eventually be persuaded: "The goods we have to offer are so varied, and the stock so large, that there is in fact probably included the particular fly to which the particular trout would rise." And of course time proved him correct: the libraries and law school are thriving, there is a Brandeis seminar room in the law school, and the ashes of Brandeis and his wife are buried close to the entrance.[59]

Brandeis's enthusiasm for the university led Alfred Lief to make an interesting comparison: "Jefferson in the retirement of his old age lay the foundations of the University of Virginia; by coincidence Brandeis undertook to further the growth of the University of Louisville." Both Jefferson and Brandeis understood that democracy could not exist without the thorough education and preparation for citizenship of the generations to come.[60]

Many of Brandeis's ideas were similar to Jefferson's, and Brandeis's thoughts about industrial democracy were in effect an updating of Jefferson. This is not to imply that Brandeis consciously modeled himself on Jefferson or that his theories were based on his reading rather than upon his experience; on the contrary, Brandeis derived almost all of his ideas, original or not, from his experiences and the thinking that accompanied and followed them. It is interesting to note, however, that Brandeis was quoting Jefferson as early as 1904.[61]

References to Jefferson were sprinkled through Brandeis's correspondence with increasing frequency in his later years. He was reading Francis W. Hirst's *The Life and Letters of Thomas Jefferson* in 1926 and quoted from it in letters to Frankfurter. July 1927 found him immersed in Fowler's edition of Jefferson's *Works*. July 1927 was one of the months in which Frankfurter's activities on behalf of Sacco and Vanzetti were coming to an unsuccessful climax. Brandeis followed the matter with great interest and sympathy, and at one point wrote to Frankfurter, "This from Bowers Jefferson and Madison p. 325—may sometimes may be of use in connection S.V." There followed a passage in which Jefferson was quoted as extolling John Adams's brave courtroom defense of the British officer charged with murder in connection with the Boston Massacre of 1770. In September the Brandeises went "to pay homage (at Monticello & the University) to Thomas Jefferson." Brandeis returned to Washington "with deepest conviction of T.J.'s greatness. He was a civilized man." He promptly told Alice Grady that Jefferson "would have had no difficulty in appreciating S.B.I." In December 1927 he was reading Albert Jay Nock's *Jefferson*. In 1929 Pauline Goldmark sent him a leather-bound book by or about Jefferson as a birthday gift. Brandeis wrote, acknowledging the gift, "Jefferson has been properly painted for many achievements and qualities—without enough emphasis on the fact that he was the most civilized of our presidents."[62]

When the American Jewish Congress boycotted German products in response to the persecution of Jews in Germany, Brandeis told Rabbi Wise that reference should be made to the Americans' boycott of British goods prior to the Declaration of Independence. "You will find reference to Jefferson's part in the boycott in Lisitzky's 'Jefferson', recently published by Viking Press, pp. 61–62," he wrote. Brandeis later suggested to Sherman F. Mittell, founder of the National Home Library Foundation, that the foundation reprint Albert Jay Nock's *Jefferson*, which he called "the worthiest account of our most civilized American and true Democrat." The foundation timed its edition for Brandeis's eighty-fourth birthday and published it with a dedication to Brandeis, putting a large number of copies at his disposal. He promptly proposed "that one copy shall go to every high school (and similar institution) in Kentucky. So far as teachers and students may be led to read the book something important may be done for the education—the culture—of the State; and the gift of the book may stimulate or develop the school library." Ever the politician, he arranged for the copies to be sent not by him but by the University of Louisville, in order to "develop relations between the University and the Schools which will be helpful to both."[63]

Brandeis obviously did not limit his activities during his Court years in any sense. Whether or not Brandeis's deep involvement in the policy-making of the executive and legislative branches can be justified by the circumstances of both World Wars and the Depression, the question of the ethics of his involvement remains. Particularly during the New Deal, he helped frame legislation that was quite likely to come before the Court for adjudication. One might argue that had he not considered such legislation constitutional, he would not have aided in creating it. But it has long been the practice of the Court not to give advisory opinions, and Brandeis had endorsed that practice in his opinion in *Ashwander*, listing the kinds of cases the Court should not hear. In addition, legislation is invariably altered as it moves through the various committees of the House and Senate, onto the floors of both houses, and through conference committee; language or provisions might be added that made the statute's constitutionality doubtful.[64]

Many justices are now known to have given advice to various presidents. Why should Brandeis's activities in this regard be questioned? First, Brandeis imposed a stern ethical code upon himself and judged others by it; that is one of the reasons the New Deal nicknamed him "Isaiah." Second, the continued power and utility of the Court depends upon the general perception of that body as being above politics. As Alexander Hamilton pointed out in *Federalist #78*, the Court has neither purse nor sword with which to enforce its decisions. Its power, and the respect it engenders, depends on the electorate's belief that the Court merely interprets the Constitution and thereby acts as a conveyor of a neutral, "higher" law. The American people see the Supreme Court as the high priests of the communal secular religion embodied in the Constitution, which is why the Court is powerful. The people may become disenchanted with Court decisions or particular justices, but the usual reaction in such instances is to call for the ousting of the justice or justices viewed as the culprits, or even for Congressional action to undo what is perceived as an incorrect reading of the Constitution—not abolition of the Court or a demand that judicial review be ended. No one really "knew" whether the Civil Rights Act of 1964, outlawing segregation in interstate commerce, was constitutional until the Court said it was; then implementation of the law began almost to be taken for granted. When the Supreme Court decided in 1974 that President Richard Nixon had to turn over tapes that showed him guilty of plotting to break the law, he had no alternative but to do so; defiance of the Court would have led to impeachment. The mystique of the Court as an apolitical body is thus part of the machinery that holds the clashing threads of American life together in a coherent social fabric.[65]

That mystique is lessened to the extent that justices are perceived as political, and there is no question that Brandeis was acting politically when he advised the Wilson administration, helped Wilson draft a Democratic party platform, and worked intimately with members of the New Deal. One may conclude, with Justice William O. Douglas, that had any of the advice given by Justice Brandeis (and, later Justice Frankfurter) "caused any collision with future judicial decisions which they had to make . . . those men would have been the first to suggest that they not sit." One certainly would like to think so, and there is an example of Brandeis doing precisely that. After Sacco and Vanzetti had been sentenced to death, Brandeis refused their lawyers' request that he hear their plea, even though he did not believe them to be guilty. His wife and their close friend Elizabeth Glendower Evans had helped the defense and the two men's families, sheltering them for a while in the Brandeis home in Dedham. It was not known at the time that Brandeis was supplying Frankfurter, one of the lawyers for the defense, with funds, and it is impossible to ascertain whether this was another factor in his restraint.[66]

One might also note, in Brandeis's defense, his scrupulous following of the rules against sitting on a case in which he had an interest. He disqualified himself from the District of Columbia minimum wage case because one of his daughters had been working on its minimum wage board and from a corporate reorganization case because he owned bonds of the railroad company involved. He also overcame his personal predilections, voting on the basis of legal principle in cases like *New State Ice, Whitney,* and *United States* v. *Butler.*[67]

Brandeis's entire adult life before joining the Court had been spent in the public service, fighting for the causes in which he believed. The controlled rationality with which he approached problems was combined with a passionate zeal for those solutions he considered best. It would have been thoroughly out of character for him to withdraw entirely from the world of politics and make no attempt to influence policy; indeed, his retention of leadership of the Zionist movement indicated that he had no intention of giving up the causes he held dear. Then in 1933, when he was past seventy-six, a president who might finally have enacted Brandeis's program entered the White House. The temptation must have been overwhelming. His friendships with dozens of members of the New Deal and its active supporters and his acquaintance with hundreds more provided easy access. He may have convinced himself that it was his duty as a citizen to give the state full use of his energy and talents, or his ethical sense may have made it impossible for him to consider the moral implications of what he was doing. On some level, however, he knew that his actions could be considered improper, for he was so careful to keep them confidential that his first biographers knew nothing of them. His approach, conscious or not, seems to have been that it was of the utmost importance to maintain propriety, but that the actuality could be somewhat different on occasion. Thus he told Hughes that it would have been improper for the chief justice to testify before the Senate committee considering the Court-packing plan, for the justices should not appear to be involving themselves in the legislative process; however, Hughes could read the committee a letter that did no more than convey the information that the Court was having no difficulty keeping up with its workload. Of course, in doing so, Hughes was undercutting Roosevelt's stated rationale for the plan, but the proprieties had been observed. Similarly, while Paul Freund was serving as Brandeis's clerk, Raymond Moley called and told Freund that Secretary of State Hull wanted to see Brandeis at his convenience to speak about policy toward Germany. Freund relayed the message, to which Brandeis responded, "I do not wish to see the Secretary; Secretary Hull wishes to see me; I will see him at *his* convenience." Freund understood the comment as Brandeis's way of pointing out that it was not he who was instituting conversations with members of the administration. The meeting was held nonetheless, and Brandeis did tell Hull his ideas, although for reasons unrelated to Brandeis they were not implemented.[68]

Brandeis seems to have been both unethical and honest: he immersed himself in the formulation of policy in a most unjudicial manner, but he judged the cases that came before him according to the legal principles he enunciated publicly. However, that does not end the matter or answer the question; even assuming that Brandeis-as-politician did not affect the decisions of Brandeis-as-judge, the ability to change roles completely is rare. The world does not produce many human beings of the calibre of Brandeis, and it is doubtful that all the other justices who have trekked periodically to the White House for consultations have been equally successful in clothing themselves in objectivity upon their return to the Marble Palace. Perhaps Brandeis's contributions to the New Deal were important (although, given the Brandeisians in the administration, it is probable that most of the Second New Deal legislation would have been enacted even had Brandeis himself remained aloof from the process). Nonetheless, one must sadly conclude that, as Brandeis said in the *Myers* case, dispersion of power is more important to a democracy than is efficiency. The great irony is that when the usually scrupulous justice ignored the spirit of separation of powers during the Roosevelt administration, he did so with little success. His vision of America was not even understood by the politicians, so there was never the slightest chance that they would implement it.[69]

20 | Possibilities and Limitations

Two major strands run through Brandeis's thought: possibilities and limitations. He believed that almost anything was possible if human beings, with their individual limitations, recognized that each could bring only so much to the achievement of a goal. Great deeds, including the creation of a civilized existence, could be done, if all citizens participated in the workings of their societies.

The most important thing individuals could do for themselves was to fulfill their own possibilities. For that, they needed the freedom to read and hear and think and speak. "I believe that the possibilities of human advancement are unlimited," Brandeis said. "Liberty is the greatest developer." Private and public attempts to curb liberty of speech and the press had to be fought. Those who would fulfill themselves also had to have both leisure and economic independence. Possibilities could not be explored if individuals lacked the necessities of life, or if they were so financially dependent on others that they were afraid to speak the truth, or if they had no time to themselves. Brandeis recognized, however, that the possibility of liberty for the majority of the people was questionable in the United States of the twentieth century. His response was to work for the beginnings of economic liberty through regularity of employment, freedom of speech and assembly, minimum wages, and maximum hours. Legitimizing labor unions was a way to start achieving these goals. The best solution, however, would be to change the fact that most adults did not work for themselves and to create systems of profit-sharing and worker-participation so that citizens could be sufficiently independent to develop their possibilities.[1]

People had to avoid concentrating so much on possibilities, however, that they forgot limitations: the limitation on one person's ability to oversee vast industrial complexes or the limited ability of a group of people in Washington to understand and respond to the needs of people in all the towns and cities and nooks and crannies of the United States. People were selfish; their "ineradicable selfishness" meant that if they were given too much power, they would "inevitably" abuse it. But, kept within their limitations, people could do wonderful things. Brandeis told Frankfurter in their last conversation "that on the whole he thought the greatest mistakes that men make derive from two weaknesses: (1) the inability to say no; and (2) the unwillingness to take a vacation when they should and therefore going on in the making of important decisions when their judgment was fatigued and not well poised." He was uneasy when even those he trusted amassed too much responsibility and too much power. He considered Roosevelt to be an honorable man; nonetheless, he wrote to Frankfurter in November 1933, "There is some comfort in the thought that each day brings Congress' convening nearer. It was a terrible thing to leave absolute power in one man—and adjourn for so long a period." The key question that Brandeis asked about any government act was not how extensive the power involved was but whether the responsibility for its exercise was diffused. Paul Freund speaks of Brandeis's "two most fundamental beliefs: that ordinary men have great capacity to grow through the sharing of responsibility, and that the limits of capacity in even the best of men are soon reached. For him, therefore, the democratic faith was grounded in urgent necessity as well as in moral duty." Thus, the greatest thing the individual could do for society was to participate actively in the political process.[2]

Alvin Johnson labeled Brandeis "a serenely implacable democrat." He was at once secure in his faith in democracy and tireless in fighting for it. Dean Acheson asked him whether police harassment of socialists and trade unionists during the early 1920s discouraged his hopes for democracy in America. Brandeis replied that he was "not discouraged: simply deeply humiliated and filled with a sense of sin that we with the greatest possibilities of any people should waste ourselves on these age-old methods of oppression." He could be optimistic as long as there were public-spirited citizens to fight and good teachers to educate. Because the well-intentioned were as apt to make mistakes as anyone else, there was a need not only for democracy today but for the unceasing education of the young so that they could carry on the development of democratic society tomorrow. "The scoundrel in politics or a political position is the result of the people in power who put him in," he told his niece. "The cure for that, like most human ill, is to have a decent population." Such a population could be attained through education, but it would be an unending process. "Moses said 'The Masters are gone but we still have the Slaves' and it was forty years before he allowed the Israelites to enter the Promised Land. The hope now is with the youngest generation."[3]

There were many things he would teach the young. In addition to having them learn about public participation in a democracy, he would have them understand the need for discipline. "Generally speaking," he declared toward the end of his life, "I should say that a human being who cannot organize himself so as to keep his appointments on time is an unorganized human being. And I do not believe that anybody or anything is at his best when in a state of disorganization. People think that poets and philosophers are notoriously absent-minded, forgetful, and disarranged. Well they may be absent-minded and forgetful, but not disarranged. There is a pattern of organization in Dante's *Divine Comedy* and Kant's *Critique of Pure Reason* which any construction engineer might envy and emulate." Discipline was a requirement for achievement. "Bear in mind," he told an admirer, "that in canoeing I have enjoyed not only floating down streams. Paddling up them was also a feature."[4]

Brandeis's self-discipline was legendary, and it was without doubt a major cause of his successes. He had learned to be independent, a fighter for his beliefs, hardworking, well organized, sociable, articulate, flexible, interested in both people and ideas, and comfortable with himself. His self-discipline was not a sign of compulsion: he usually adhered with some rigor to his established schedule, but he abandoned it when a case or cause required that he do so. Similarly, his well-defined belief system did not reflect a closed mind: he was able to alter his views, for example, of women's suffrage and Zionism. One might well ask, however, whether, with all his brilliance, hard work, and creative dedication to public service, Brandeis was correct in his optimism about democracy. When the moment for enactment of his program for government finally arrived with the inauguration of Franklin Roosevelt, that program was ignored— not entirely, to be sure—but in all the ways that would have led to fulfillment of his dreams for the country.

The phenomenon of Brandeis being hailed as "Isaiah" by the New Deal while those who so honored him paid no attention to his larger view merits close examination. It would have been more readily understandable if the New Deal had turned him into a prophet without honor, dismissing all of his ideas, but it did not. The New Dealers thought that they owed many of their important policies to him and that they rejected only those that would have attempted to return to the economics of the nineteenth century. That interpretation enabled them to amass in their own hands enormous power to do "Brandeisian" things, while paying no heed to his strictures against centralization of power. They had no notion that a truly Brandeisian policy would have revitalized the democratic process and extended it to industry. And because they misunderstood Brandeis, they may have missed a unique opportunity to create an industrialized society based as much on liberty and equality as it is today on technology and machines.

The Depression was largely responsible for the election of Roosevelt in 1932. It also made Congress and the general population more willing to rethink basic assumptions than they had been at any other time during the twentieth century. Congress was never again as willing to give Roosevelt carte blanche as it was during the famous first Hundred Days of his administration, but it could still be pushed fairly far. In fact, James MacGregor Burns has described the summer of 1935 as the "second Hundred Days" when the administration fought for and secured passage of the Wagner Labor Relations Act, the Social Security Act, the Public Utilities Holding Company Act, the Emergency Relief Appropriations Act, the Banking Act, the Revenue Act, and the Guffey Coal Act. Roosevelt's resounding victory in the election of 1936 showed that the electorate was still very much with him. Social Darwinism was rapidly losing respectability, thereby creating an ideological void; the Depression made it difficult to retain the belief that people were poor only if they deserved to be, for the middle class had been hard hit along with the poor. If ever there was a moment in American history to teach the electorate that, on the whole, individual prosperity has less to do with talent than with artificially manipulated economic forces, 1933 was it. But Roosevelt, who was a superb educator, unwittingly let the opportunity disappear; instead, he concentrated on an ill-defined welfare capitalism that regulated privately owned industry with a limited degree of government responsibility for the citizen's economic well-being.[5]

Brandeis would have had the New Deal address the paradox implicit in the linking of the terms liberty and equality and the way it could be resolved within the context of American ideals and the industrial society. Does equal mean that all human beings are presumed to be the creatures of God and hence equal in whatever "natural rights" the Deity bestows upon them, as the Declaration of Independence maintained? Does it mean the constitutional possession of natural rights, transmuted into such civil liberties as speech, religion, and privacy, along with a certain amount of equality among races and in the courtroom? Does it mean equality of opportunity, and if so, how is that to be defined, and what role should the government have in providing it? Does it mean that one person's liberty (of property) carries a lesser value than another one's equality (of access to a minimum standard of living)? Adoption of the phrase "welfare capitalism" implied that all people were equal in something, but no one knew what. And liberty is quite as difficult. It might mean the liberties of the Declaration of Independence, which again flowed from the natural rights concept; it might mean the liberties listed (but not defined) in the Constitution and amendments; it might, as the Court Brandeis joined argued, mean liberty to amass and use property without interference; it could mean, depending upon one's point of view, liberty from government taxation, or liberty to educate one's children at home, or, as Brandeis would have it, liberty to develop as an individual. The question of the extent to which liberty should be limited for the sake of equality or vice versa is not only one that has occupied philosophers for centuries; it is also one that Brandeis believed the New Deal had to attempt to answer.

The New Deal, however, chose pragmatism illuminated by a vague if sincere good will, rather than a thorough-going reexamination of first principles. This was exemplified not only by Roosevelt, but by such other figures as Adolph A. Berle, Jr., whose father, the Reverend Adolph A. Berle, was Brandeis's colleague in many of the early fights in Boston. The younger Berle's first job was in Brandeis's law firm, and he understood some of Brandeis's thinking. On Brandeis's eightieth birthday in 1936, Berle wrote for the *Survey Graphic*, "There is his passionate belief in the doctrine that men are entitled to fulfill themselves; hence democracy; hence the desire for preservation of local experimentation; hence the fear of overmastering big combination; hence also the fear of an overmastering federal government." Twenty or so years later Berle returned to the subject, saying that Brandeis "disliked bigness because he considered, rightly, that the men creating and operating it did not understand what they were doing." But then Berle went on to argue that although a certain amount of rationality might be lost in the process, the growth of gigantic economic entities and of equally huge government agencies to regulate them was inevitable.[6]

Berle was typical of the New Dealers who opposed Brandeis; they thought he had an admirably positive attitude toward democracy but no comprehension of the realities of twentieth-century economics. Yet Brandeis, the master of facts, understood those realities very well. He simply asked different questions. The New Dealers asked how, given the "fact" of corporate giantism, the government ought best to control it. Brandeis did not accept the legitimacy of the question. At age eighty-four he wrote to a political scientist and economist that "bigness was not inevitable, not merely man-made, but authorized by our corporation laws; and that which is man-made can be unmade. As Machiavelli said: 'Fate is inevitable only when it is not resisted.' " Brandeis asked what corporate and governmental giantism would do to the possibilities for liberty and equality and whether the economic benefits that would flow to a segment of the population were worth it, whether in the long run the country might not be better off economically as well as freer by making the political decision to destroy concentrations of wealth and power.[7]

There is no doubt that the Brandeisian plan, beginning with a massive public works program financed through taxation and continuing with federal taxation of wealth, would have ended such concentrations within two generations. If technological and economic creativity is engendered only by the vision of huge profit, his plan would have ended creativity as well. If, however, creativity is most prevalent in small-scale institutions and is stifled by the weight of bureaucracy in mammoth corporations, then his program would have enhanced creativity and the quality of life as well as liberty and equality. If the number of automobiles, refrigerators, and color television sets is an index of prosperity in the United States, then one may reasonably proclaim the success of welfare capitalism, American-style. If one examines the statistics showing that at least 15 percent of the American population is poor—lacking in spite of such post–New Deal programs as food stamps and Medicaid, adequate food, clothing, shelter, medical care, and educational opportunities—and that the distribution of wealth has not changed significantly since the New Deal, then one might ask whether the system really deserves applause. Given the appalling lack of personal freedom and the tendency toward totalitarianism that exist in today's socialist systems, and the futility of trying to balance the number of hungry people in one system against the victims of the police state in the other, perhaps Brandeis's disdain for both traditional capitalism and socialism and his emphasis on the individual, dispersion of power, and industrial democracy merit examination.

Brandeis was not what is ordinarily considered a philosopher. He wrote no treatises nor did he sit in the marketplace, like Socrates, to influence the young elite. He was an activist. It was therefore all too easy to assume that his thinking was not systemic. He appeared to have typically pragmatic American solutions for discrete problems. In fact, he resembled Socrates in his tireless efforts to educate: through Harvard, the University of Louisville, the press, his dinners and teas, his massive correspondence. And he did have something to teach—a comprehensive approach to politics and society.

The editors of *The Economist* have been quoted as saying, "Mr. Roosevelt may have given the wrong answer to many of his problems. But he is at least the first President of modern America who has asked the right questions." But Roosevelt did not ask all the right questions; he did not seek a philosophical base for the New Deal. Paradoxically, his success as president can be attributed in part to this lack of interest in first principles. Roosevelt went into the White House with a set of positive, humane attitudes, but no coherent scheme. He remained open to advisers with contradictory opinions and took what he considered to be the best solutions offered without reference to their source. He considered no one policy beyond compromise when legislators pressed him. James MacGregor Burns has described Roosevelt as "open to almost any idea and absolutely committed to almost none"; in short, he had the mind of "an opportunist and pragmatist." He may have leaned slightly toward conservatism, but he was willing to tilt occasionally to the left. That may help account for his accomplishments, which were considerable.[8]

What Burns has referred to as Roosevelt's "Grand Coalition"—urban laborers (many first- or second-generation immigrants), Catholics, Jews, blacks, farmers, and, to some extent, home owners, the academic and artistic communities, the elderly, and women—which hitherto had possessed only the procedural political equality embodied in the right to vote, now had access to the policymakers and the policymaking process. Enhancement of the power of the Department of Labor was a symbol both of the new power of the coalition and of the nonrevolutionary nature of the New Deal. The New Deal created the concept of a "floor," maintained by the federal government, beneath which most citizens would not be permitted to fall. Legislation (which had far from universal application) establishing a minimum wage, unemployment compensation, and welfare payments was important not only in what it did or did not do substantively but in the rejection of social Darwinism that had to precede the new policies. The belief that the continued existence of the economically unfit was a threat to the progress of the species came under serious attack. It was not, unfortunately, abandoned as an element of the national ethos, but it lost credibility among top New Deal officials and slowly began to fade from the pantheon of respectable principles.[9]

The New Deal's "welfare capitalism" was the haphazard result of the ideas of those who happened to be among Roosevelt's "inner circle" at various moments, of who in Congress demanded what or persuaded whom, of how members of the legislature and the executive assessed the popularity of those they considered to be extremists. The New Dealers battled each other furiously over policy, but not over ideology. The "First New Deal" (1933–1934) preferred centralization of economic power in the hands of the administration; the "Second New Deal" (1935) moved further toward the Brandeisian approach of breaking up concentrations of power; then the impending war gradually forced Roosevelt's attention away from domestic affairs, and there was no third New Deal. The First New Deal was not undone by the Second New Deal, and the Second New Deal was incomplete. Thus, the regulatory bureaucracy in Washington expanded by leaps and bounds, and as late as 1938 Roosevelt was contemplating reviving the NRA, which to Brandeis represented the worst of the First New Deal.[10]

The New Deal was, essentially, an attempt to pull the United States out of the Depression, avoid extremes, and divide the economic pie a bit more evenly; the ingredients of the pie were not reconsidered. Brandeis, however, did reconsider them. In so doing, he avoided the simplistic right-left political spectrum common among most Americans. Brandeis did not believe laissez-faire capitalism was possible in an industrialized society; he deplored the centralization of power that accompanied socialism. He wanted the equality of power that would come from balancing organizations of disparate interests; he wanted the individual to have the liberty of leisure and the equality of economic partnership; he wanted the central government to use its power, and particularly its taxing power, to break up concentrations of power elsewhere and to ensure that society's underdogs would be treated fairly. He did not want substitution of the power of Washington for the power of the trusts; neither did he want a return to nineteenth-century economics and government. Unfortunately, his great admirer Max Lerner reflected the view of most policymakers in describing him in 1935 as, "in the eyes of many, another Don Quixote—a gaunt and gallant but essentially helpless figure out of another era, earnestly tilting at windmills." But in the 1960s, the 1970s, and the 1980s his concern for liberty would become the theme of one group after another. His fulminations about the evils of overconcentration of power would be echoed by voices as diverse as Nixon, Carter, Reagan, Common Cause, Ralph Nader, the New Left, and the New Right. Perhaps Lerner was right: Brandeis's voice did belong to another era— a later one.[11]

Unsolved social problems reappear, in different eras and in different arenas. The problems of liberty and equality moved from one arena to another in the 1940s, the 1950s, and the 1960s; they wound up in the federal courts.

Brandeis's approach to sociological jurisprudence gradually became *the* jurisprudence of the Court and eventually of the entire federal system. The law schools, whose faculties included increasing numbers of Frankfurter's disciples and *their* disciples, taught that social and economic facts could reasonably be construed as requiring whatever kind of government intervention was at issue. If the facts required it, something in the Constitution could be found to legitimize it. The followers of this school populated not only the courtrooms, as advocates and judges, but they were also to be found in the New Deal bureaucracy, whose young lawyers fashioned much of the federal economic legislation upheld by the Court beginning in 1937.

Many of these young lawyers took Roosevelt's welfare capitalism as another part of their ideology. The Court had "followed the election returns" of 1936 and from then on upheld experimentation by the legislatures; those younger jurists who would gradually take their seats on the lower federal courts and the Supreme Court did so as well. Roosevelt was able to appoint eight of the nine justices on the Supreme Court. The "Roosevelt Court" endorsed both sociological jurisprudence and the New Deal view that Big Government was a necessary counterweight to Big Business; it also validated government's moves to protect labor as an additional counterweight. Having legitimized Big Government, the Court would eventually have to face the dangers inherent in it. Having validated the rise of the central government as the national problem solver, the Court would discover that its position at the peak of the national judiciary made it the favored arena for litigants with complaints about government action or inaction, whether the government involved was national or local. The jurists, all of whom were social activists who had long fought for government intervention in economic matters, were perhaps not likely to be attuned to the dangers to liberty presented by the growth of Big Government. As Paul Murphy has pointed out, "New Dealers generally were not . . . individualistically oriented. Nor did they place high values upon the free individual operating with maximum self-determination within society." In other words, they were not Brandeisians. Nonetheless, for a number of reasons, the Court found itself beginning to expand the definition of liberty.[12]

Holmes and Brandeis had stressed freedom of expression in their practice of sociological jurisprudence, and the new justices drew upon their precedents in deciding major litigation of the 1930s and 1940s. They used the rights to speech and association, for example, to create a constitutionally protected liberty to organize. They returned to the right to speech when confronted with questions of religious liberty; gradually, they extended the logic of *Gitlow* v. *New York* and made the religion clauses of the First Amendment binding on the states. Beginning in the mid-1930s, the Court began to hear a few cases involving criminal justice (right to jury trial, police behavior), voting rights, and the right to travel. By the 1950s, the Court had come close to supplanting the presidency as the national problem-solver wherever civil liberties and rights were concerned, and this development continued through the 1960s and into the 1970s. If advocates could amass sufficient factual material to convince the judges that government action or inaction resulted in violations of civil liberties—the right to privacy, to speech, to travel, to control one's reproductive processes, to remain master (or mistress) of one's home and to be free of official interference there and of official coercion in the station house, to join with others for political purposes, to be treated equally with other citizens by the government, to publish without prior restraint—they could win cases that proclaimed the existence of new liberties or novel applications of old ones.[13]

The actions of the Warren Court (and to some extent the early Burger Court) in race relations, criminal justice, speech, religion, reapportionment, and privacy would be applauded by the legal profession until it began to appear that judicial action was replacing political processes. The perceived primacy of the Court was best illustrated by the women's movement which, attempting to emulate the success of the civil rights movement, turned to the federal courts in its quest for eventual definitive rulings by the Supreme Court. In so doing it paid relatively little attention to political mobilization not only at the national level but at the state and local levels (where Brandeis would have been most encouraging of it). Thus, the movement was thoroughly unprepared for the success at those levels of antirights and antiabortion forces. The movement erred in viewing litigation as an end in itself rather than as part of a comprehensive educational effort.[14]

It is fair to postulate that Brandeis would have been pleased at the context of some of the Court's proliberties decisions but horrified by the activist stance adopted by the judiciary. He had encouraged Frankfurter in the latter's work for the American Civil Liberties Union and for the National Association for the Advancement of Colored People, both of which concentrated on litigation, as he would undoubtedly have supported the legal muckraking of Ralph Nader, who is in many ways his ideological heir. But Brandeis would most certainly not have approved of the courtroom's replacing the legislative committee room as the place where the most creative minds and the most creative new techniques are to be found. Brandeis had reason to know better than most that it is much harder to convince the electorate than it is to win cases in a courtroom. "Democratic methods are necessarily slow and often seem unreasonable," he had written to Hapgood in 1916. "And the fact that our instruments are man with his weaknesses and defects, is at times exasperating." Nevertheless, Brandeis believed that litigation should not flourish at the expense of dynamic political processes. A politically uneducated and quiescent electorate meant the end of democracy. Victories were slow in coming when they had to be won in the political arena, but that was precisely why they were so important: the people had to be convinced, and in the process they were educated and involved, and democracy flourished.[15]

Brandeis recognized that many civil liberties would have to be protected by the courts; because the majority controlled the legislatures and executives in a democratic society, the minority would require an advocate. But he never considered judicial protection to be a substitute for education; even his judicial opinions were designed as educational vehicles. And he never believed that the definition of liberty in a changing world should be monopolized by judges. Judicial tribunals could uphold legislation that recognized the rights of unions, but legislation had to be passed by the representatives of the people before it reached the courts. Endless experimentation accompanied by endless persuasion was the way to effect social change. The courts were meant to legitimize social change, not to fashion it. It is ironic that the factual sociological jurisprudence Brandeis created has been used by the courts as a substitute for the political processes he cherished.

Louis Dembitz Brandeis resigned from the Supreme Court on February 13, 1939, saying that at eighty-three, "years have limited the quantity and intensity of work possible, and I think the time has come when a younger man should assume the burden." He suffered a heart attack at his Washington home on October 1, 1941, and died four days later.[16]

Speaking at the funeral service on October 7, Felix Frankfurter—by then Justice Frankfurter—began, "Two dominant sources of our culture are Hebraism and Hellenism. They express the intellectual and moral impulses of man. Not often have these two streams of Western civilization been so happily fused as they were in the great man whom we are bidding farewell." Brandeis's "pursuit of reason and his love of beauty" were Hellenic, Frankfurter said; his "ceaseless striving for perfection" paradoxically combined with his "inner harmony" were Hebraic.[17]

Brandeis's thought reflected not only Hellenism and Hebraism but his family, his life in and with the law, and his experiences of a rapidly industrializing United States. His creed revolved around a belief in democracy, in education, in the ability of the people to choose wisely, in liberty and equality, in the development of a society that would enhance the possibilities and potential of human beings while remaining aware of their limitations. But American institutions have become bigger since Brandeis's death; industrial democracy, as he defined it, has not been tested; and although the Zionist state has been achieved, the Zionist dream has not.

Yet those who knew Brandeis did not believe he would think his

optimism misplaced. Dean Acheson told the mourners at Brandeis's funeral, "his faith in the human mind and in the will and capacity of people
to understand and grasp the truth never wavered or tired." Nathaniel
Nathanson, remembering Brandeis's belief that Palestinian Jews would
become a bridge between the West and Arab civilization, and wondering
whether Brandeis could have cherished that vision had he seen the Middle
East of some decades later, concluded, "I have no doubt that his confidence in the future would still be unshaken, for the Justice . . . took the
long view of history." And Brandeis himself often reminded friends of
the quotation from William James he had copied into his notebook when
still a young man: "I am . . . in favor of the eternal forces of truth which
always work in the individual and immediately unsuccessful way . . . till
history comes, after they are long dead, and puts them on top."[18]

Brandeis at seventy-one had written to his ailing older brother, "It's
just 50 years since my eyes gave out. Since then, there has never been a
time that I haven't had to bear in mind physical limitations of some sort.
The walls curbing activity were always in sight; and I had to adjust my
efforts." Yet the man who was always aware of the "walls curbing
activity" had spent hours at a time paddling furiously in a canoe on
waters that were too wild for anyone else. He was well aware of limitations. But Brandeis preferred to think of possibilities.[19]

Abbreviations Used in the Notes

BP   Brandeis Papers, University of Louisville, Louisville, Kentucky

BP-HLS   Brandeis Papers, Harvard Law School, Cambridge, Massachusetts

FDR   Franklin Delano Roosevelt

FF   Felix Frankfurter

FF-HLS   Felix Frankfurter Papers, Harvard Law School, Cambridge, Massachusetts

FF-LC   Felix Frankfurter Papers, Library of Congress, Washington, D.C.

HLS   Harvard Law School

LDB   Louis Dembitz Brandeis

Letters   Melvin I. Urofsky and David W. Levy, eds., *Letters of Louis D. Brandeis*, 5 vols. (Albany: State University of New York Press, 1971–1978)

SUNY-Albany   Brandeis Papers, State University of New York, Albany, New York

WW   Woodrow Wilson

Notes

1. Beginnings

1. The account of the families in Prague and their arrival in Cincinnati is drawn from Josephine Goldmark, *Pilgrims of '48* (New Haven: Yale University Press, 1930), pp. 178–181, which in turn is based upon Frederika Dembitz Brandeis, *Reminiscences*. The *Reminiscences* were written in German at the request of Louis Dembitz Brandeis during 1880–1886, were translated by Alice Goldmark Brandeis, and were printed privately in 1944. There are copies in the libraries of Yale University and Radcliffe College (Schlesinger Library).

2. Goldmark, *Pilgrims*, p. 181.

3. Frederika Brandeis, *Reminiscences*, p. 10, n. 1.

4. Goldmark, *Pilgrims*, pp. 183–187.

5. Ibid., pp. 187–198.

6. Ibid., pp. 195–200.

7. Ibid., pp. 207–210.

8. Ibid., pp. 169, 202. Adolph's citizenship certificate is in BP, Scrapbook I: Clippings 1889–1905.

9. Goldmark, *Pilgrims*, pp. 171–191, 208.

10. Ibid., p. 209.

11. Ibid., pp. 216–219.

12. Ibid., pp. 219–220; Alpheus Thomas Mason, *Brandeis: A Free Man's Life* (New York: Viking Press, 1946), pp. 18–19. Brandeis & Crawford is described in an untitled, undated newspaper clipping in BP, Scrapbook I: Clippings 1889–1905, as well as in Goldmark, *Pilgrims*, p. 284.

13. Quoted in Ernest Poole, "Brandeis: A Remarkable Record of Unselfish

Work Done in the Public Interest," *American Magazine*, February 1911, p. 481. Cf. Goldmark, *Pilgrims*, p. 284.

14. Brandeises as abolitionists: Goldmark, *Pilgrims*, pp. 227, 228, 284. Home in Louisville: Bert Ford, "Boyhood of Brandeis," *Boston American*, June 4, 1916, pp. 3–6; BP, Clippings Box II, citing an interview with Brandeis's secretary Alice Grady; Mason, *Brandeis*, p. 24.

15. Adolph and politics: Goldmark, *Pilgrims*, p. 285. Dinner table conversation: Alfred Lief, *Brandeis: The Personal History of an American Ideal* (New York: Stackpole, 1936), p. 15.

16. Mason, *Brandeis,* p. 23.

17. Ford, "Boyhood of Brandeis," pp. 4, 5; Mason, *Brandeis*, p. 24.

18. For pictures of Adolph and Frederika see Lief, *Brandeis*, p. 17; for Alfred, *Letters*, I; 356c; for LDB at two and at fifteen, Ford, "Boyhood of Brandeis," pp. 2, 3.

19. LDB to Frederika, September 7, 1870, BP, M 1-1.

20. Goodrich's *Reader* and the other books preserved are in BP, Addendum, Box 10; report cards, BP, Scrapbook I; graduation anecdote, Ford, "Boyhood of Brandeis," p. 6.

21. Christmas: see, e.g., Alfred to LDB, December 28, 1880, BP, Addendum, Box 1, 1-1. Frederika Brandeis, *Reminiscences*, pp. 8–9, 32–34. Alfred's marriage: Alfred to LDB, April 30, 1884, BP, Addendum, Box 1, 1-2, Allon Gal, *Brandeis of Boston* (Cambridge: Harvard University Press, 1980), pp. 4, 9. LDB on son-in-law: LDB to FF, August 15, 1925, *Letters*, V, 184.

22. Lief, *Brandeis*, pp. 15–16; Mason, *Brandeis*, p. 27; Goldmark, *Pilgrims*, p. 227; Gal, *Brandeis*, p. 2. LDB on Dembitz: LDB to Stella and Emily Dembitz, May 17, 1926, quoted in Bernard Flexner, *Mr. Justice Brandeis and the University of Louisville* (Louisville, Ky.: University of Louisville Press, 1938), pp. 36–37.

23. Quoted in Solomon Goldman, *The Words of Justice Brandeis* (New York: H. Schuman, 1953), p. 160.

24. Mason, *Brandeis*, pp. 29–30. Quote is in Lief, *Brandeis*, p. 19, and Ford, "Boyhood of Brandeis," p. 6, as well as in Mason.

25. Mason, *Brandeis*, p. 30; Lief, *Brandeis*, p. 20; Ford, "Boyhood of Brandeis," pp. 6–7.

26. Picking book: Ford, "Boyhood of Brandeis," p. 7. School stifling: LDB, *Business—a Profession* (Boston: Small, Maynard, 1914), intro. Ernest Poole, p. xi. LDB to Freund: quoted in Mason, *Brandeis*, p. 31.

27. LDB and "fire of youth": the words are LDB's, recorded as "Conversation with Uncle Louis, Friday, Sept. 15, 1939," BP, Addendum, Box 1, 1-7. The paper is headed "Ladless Hill Farm" and the notes were probably made by Alfred's daughter Fannie.

28. Adolph to LDB, October 7, 1877, and February 20, 1878, BP, Misc. 1. Again, I am grateful to Marion Lorie for the translations from the German. Alfred on hard work: variety of letters collected in BP, Addendum, Box 1, 1-1. Adolph to LDB, October 3, 1890, BP, Addendum, Box 1, 1-3. The letter is unusual in being written in English.

29. Adolph to LDB, April 2, 1882, BP, Misc. 1.

2. The World of the Boston Brahmin

1. Arthur Schlesinger, *The American as Reformer* (Cambridge: Harvard University Press, 1950), p. 12; Arthur Mann, *Yankee Reformers in the Urban Age* (Cambridge: Harvard University Press, 1954), pp. 73, 100; George Wilson Pierson, "The Obstinate Concept of New England," *New England Quarterly*, 28 (March 1955), 13, 14; Barbara M. Solomon, *Ancestors and Immigrants* (Cambridge: Harvard University Press, 1959), p. 2.

2. Richard M. Abrams, *Conservatism in a Progressive Era* (Cambridge: Harvard University Press, 1964), p. 163; Duane Lockard, *New England State Politics* (Princeton: Princeton University Press, 1959), p. 119; Mason, *Brandeis*, p. 39.

3. Barbara M. Solomon, "The Intellectual Background of the Immigration Restriction Movement in New England," *New England Quarterly*, 25 (March 1952), 48–49; Mann, *Yankee Reformers*, pp. 3, 5, 11, 12. Mark Twain, "What Paul Bourget Thinks of Us," *North American Review*, January 1895, p. 166. Bourget was a French novelist and critic who had described the United States in ways that Twain found ludicrous.

4. Emerson, quoted in Mason, *Brandeis*, p. 39.

5. Abrams, *Conservatism*, pp. 4, 11: Melvin I. Urofsky, *A Mind of One Piece: Brandeis and American Reform* (New York: Scribner, 1971), p. 5.

6. William James and hotel: Solomon, *Ancestors and Immigrants*, pp. 2, 185. Elizabeth Glendower Evans, "Memoirs," Evans Mss., folder #2, p. 3, Schlesinger Library, Radcliffe College. Schindler: Mann, *Yankee Reformers*, pp. 55–58.

7. Classmate Philip Alexander Bruce quoted in Bert Ford, "Boyhood of Brandeis," *Boston American*, June 4, 1916, in BP, Scrapbook: Clippings II, 7; Lief, *Brandeis*, p. 21; picture, Ford, "Boyhood of Brandeis," p. 4.

8. Mason, *Brandeis*, p. 29; picture of Dane Hall, Lief, *Brandeis*, p. 25; list of LDB's law school textbooks and casebooks, LDB to Elizabeth Peabody, March 15, 1917, and Peabody to LDB, March 31, 1917, BP, NMF 19-18a.

9. LDB, "The Harvard Law School," *The Green Bag*, January 1889, pp. 17–19, in BP, Scrapbook: Clippings I.

10. Christopher Columbus Langdell, *Selected Cases on Contracts* (Boston: Little, Brown, 1871), quoted in LDB, "Harvard Law School," pp. 19–20; ibid., p. 20.

11. LDB, "Harvard Law School," pp. 20, 21, 23; classmate Bruce quoted in Ford, "Boyhood of Brandeis," p. 7.

12. "Wonderful years" and "happiest of my life": LDB to Otto A. Wehle, March 12, 1876, BP, M 1-2; LDB, *Business*, p. xii. LDB to Amy Brandeis Wehle, January 20, 1877, *Letters*, I, 14; LDB to Elizabeth Peabody, March 15, 1917, and Peabody to LDB, March 31, 1917, BP, NMF 19-18a, n. 9.

13. LDB to Amy Brandeis Wehle, December 2, 1877, *Letters*, I, 19; Mason, *Brandeis*, p. 42; LDB to Alice Goldmark, October 13, 1890, *Letters*, I, 92; Gal, *Brandeis*, p. 8; LDB to Otto Wehle, March 12, 1876, BP, M 1-2.

14. LDB to Amy Brandeis Wehle, April 5, 1877, *Letters*, I, 16-17; to same,

December 2, 1877, ibid., 20; Mason, *Brandeis*, pp. 42, 48; LDB to Alfred, June 28, 1878, *Letters*, I, 24; Frederika to LDB, October 21, 1877, BP, M 1-3; LDB to Amy, December 2, 1877, ibid.

15. LDB to Amy Brandeis Wehle, April 5, 1877, *Letters*, I, 16-17.

16. Mason, *Brandeis*, p. 54. LDB to Walter Bond Douglas, August 27, 1877, November 13, 1877, January 31, 1878, July 6, 1879, March 21, 1881, July 11, 1881, and October 1, 1890, *Letters*, I, 18, 21, 36, 63, 91. LDB to William R. Richards, January 31, 1878, *Letters*, I, 21; LDB to Frederika, July 20, 1879, BP, M 1-3; cf. *Letters*, I, 18 n. 2. The argument about LDB's Jewishness is made in Gal, *Brandeis*.

17. LDB to Amy Brandeis Wehle, December 2, 1877, *Letters*, I, 20. The spelling idiosyncrasies of LDB and his correspondents have been retained in quotations throughout the text. Notebook: Mason, *Brandeis*, pp. 38–40, 43.

18. Violin: Lief, *Brandeis*, p. 22. Notebooks: Mason, *Brandeis*, pp. 39, 40. Mason claims Brandeis was accepted (p. 63) and Gal claims that he was not (pp. 37, 42–43).

19. LDB to Walter Bond Douglas, January 31, 1878, *Letters*, I, 21; LDB to Alfred, June 28, 1878, *Letters*, I, 23: Mason, *Brandeis*, p. 46; author's interview with Mary Kay Tachau, June 12, 1980.

20. Ford, "Boyhood of Brandeis," pp. 7–8.

21. Alfred to LDB, November 10, 1877, BP, Addendum, Box 1; Mason, *Brandeis*, p. 48; Adolph to LDB, October 7, 1877, BP, M 1-4.

22. LDB to Walter Bond Douglas, November 13, 1877, *Letters*, I, 18; LDB to Otto Wehle, November 12, 1876, BP, Unmarked Folder. Bursar's Record, June 20, 1877, BP, Scrapbook; Clippings I. Alfred to LDB, November 10, 1877, BP, Addendum, Box 1.

23. Portfolio: Mason, *Brandeis*, p. 48; Lief, *Brandeis*, p. 22. LDB to Alfred, June 18, 1878, *Letters*, I, 23, and July 5, 1878, ibid., 25.

24. LDB to Alfred, June 28, 1878, *Letters*, I, 23–24; Burton C. Bernard, "Brandeis in St. Louis," *St. Louis Bar Journal*, 11 (1964), 54.

25. LDB to Frederika, August 2, 1878, quoted in Mason, *Brandeis*, p. 5; Frederika to LDB, August 11, 1878, BP, M 1-3; LDB to Amy Brandeis Wehle, January 20, 1877, *Letters*, I, 14.

26. LDB to Alfred, August 11, 1878, *Letters*, I, 27; James Taussig to LDB, September 22, 1878, BP, Scrapbook: Clippings I; Mason, *Brandeis*, p. 51; LDB to Amy Brandeis Wehle, January (?) 1879, *Letters*, I, 28–29.

27. LDB to Amy Brandeis Wehle, ibid.; to same, February 1, 1879, quoted in Mason, *Brandeis*, p. 54; to Otto Wehle, February 10, 1879, BP, M 1-2; to same, April 1, 1879, M 1-2. Malaria: Mason, *Brandeis*, p. 53.

28. Warren to LDB, May 5, May 22, May 28, 1879, FF-HLS; LDB to Warren, May 30, 1879, Mason, *Brandeis*, pp. 54–55.

29. LDB to Walter Bond Douglas, July 6, 1879, *Letters*, I, 36; to Charles Nagel, July 12, 1879, BP, M 2-1; to Alfred, July 31, 1879, *Letters*, I, 44.

30. Edmund J. James et al., *The Immigrant Jew in America* (New York: B. F. Buck, 1906), intro. Charles Eliot, p. 4, quoted in Solomon, *Ancestors and*

Immigrants, p. 171. On Eliot: ibid., pp. 182, 186. On Channing: ibid., pp. 4, 5, 53.

31. Solomon, *Ancestors and Immigrants*, pp. 48, 111, 116, 135, 139, 202.

32. Ibid., pp. 90–92, 156–159, 168–171.

33. The suggestion is made in Gal, *Brandeis*, pp. 36–43. Warren F. Kellogg to LDB, December 3, 1891, and December 10, 1891, BP, NMF 7-15a.

34. Abrams, *Conservatism*, p. 56.

3. Practicing Law

1. LDB to Charles Nagel, July 12, 1879, BP, M 2-1; LDB to Frederika, July 20, 1879, BP, Misc. 1; LDB to Amy, December 4, 1879, *Letters*, I, 49; fragment, Winter 1880/81, BP, M 1-2; to Alfred, October 9, 1879, *Letters*, I, 49.

2. Mason, *Brandeis*, p. 57; LDB to Alfred, July 31, 1879, *Letters*, I, 44; LDB to Charles Nagel, July 12, 1879, BP, M 2-1.

3. LDB to Frederika, July 20, 1879, BP, M 2-1.

4. LDB to Charles Nagel, July 12, 1879, BP, M 2-1; LDB to Amy, January 2, 1881, BP, M 2-2.

5. LDB to Alfred, October 9, 1879, *Letters*, I, 48; LDB to Amy, December 4, 1879, *Letters*, I, 49; LDB to Otto Wehle, January 11, 1880, BP, M 1–2; LDB to Amy, April 6, 1880, *Letters*, I, 53; LDB to Alfred, June 19, 1880, *Letters*, I, 53; cf. n. 2. The case was *Allen* v. *Woonsocket*, 13 R.I. 146 (1880).

6. Warren to LDB, March 29, 1880, quoted in Mason, *Brandeis*, p. 61; LDB to Alfred, September 11, 1880, *Letters*, I, 55–57.

7. LDB and Harvard: to Winthrop Howland Wade, June 9, 1886, *Letters*, I, 69; to alumni of the Harvard Law School, August 9, 1886, *Letters*, I, 69-71; Lief, *Brandeis*, p. 31; James M. Landis, "Mr. Justice Brandeis and the Harvard Law School," *Harvard Law Review*, 55 (1941), 184. Jacob J. Kaplan, "Mr. Justice Brandeis, Prophet," *The New Palestine*, November 14, 1941, p. 27.

8. LDB to Charles Nagel, July 12, 1879, BP, M 2-1; Adolf to LDB, November 22, 1880, BP, Clippings I.

9. Mason, *Brandeis*, p. 61; Gal, *Brandeis*, pp. 5, 16, 17, 43–46; LDB to Amy, January 2, 1881, BP, M 2-2.

10. Lief, *Brandeis*, p. 24; LDB to Alfred, July 30, 1881, *Letters*, I, 63–64; Urofsky, *Mind of One Piece*, p. 29; Mason, *Brandeis*, p. 691; BP, Addendum, Box 5.

11. LDB to Alfred, July 31, 1879, *Letters*, I, 45; Mason, *Brandeis*, pp. 63–64; Oliver Wendell Holmes, Jr., "Trespass and Negligence," *American Law Review*, 1 (January 1880), 1–15; LDB to Amy, December 4, 1879, *Letters*, I, 49.

12. LDB to Charles Nagel, July 12, 1879, BP, M 2-1.

13. Mason, *Brandeis*, p. 6; Dembitz to LDB, April 16, 1882, quoted in Mason, *Brandeis*, p. 66; Frederika to LDB, April 2, 1882, quoted in Mason, *Brandeis*, p. 66; Adolph to LDB, April 2, 1882, quoted in ibid.

14. Lief, *Brandeis*, p. 27; Mason, *Brandeis*, p. 66.

15. Amy's illness: Mason, *Brandeis*, p. 29. Family's malarial attacks: Fred-

erika to LDB, April 11, 1878, BP, Misc. 1; Alfred to LDB, June 27, 1884, BP, Addendum, Box 2, 1-2. Bowl of pills: Jacob de Haas, *Louis D. Brandeis: A Biographical Sketch* (New York: Bloch, 1929), p. 116. LDB's "bad case": Lief, *Brandeis*, p. 24. Hemengway: *Letters*, I, 65, n. 1. LDB to Alfred, September 11, 1880, *Letters*, I, 56.

16. LDB to Adolph, May 30, 1883, quoted in Mason, *Brandeis*, p. 66.

17. Mason, *Brandeis*, p. 66; Lief, *Brandeis*, p. 28.

18. LDB to Alfred, March 21, 1887, BP, M 2-4.

19. Louis D. Brandeis and Samuel D. Warren, Jr., "The Watuppa Pond Cases," *Harvard Law Review*, 2 (1888–1889), 195; Louis D. Brandeis and Samuel D. Warren, Jr., "The Law of Ponds," *Harvard Law Review*, 3 (1889–1890), 1; Louis D. Brandeis and Samuel D. Warren, Jr., "The Right to Privacy," *Harvard Law Review*, 4 (1890–1891), 193. Roscoe Pound to Senator William Chilton, included in letters printed in U.S. Congress, Senate, Committee on the Judiciary, *Nomination of Louis D. Brandeis*, 64th Cong., 1st sess., 1916.

20. LDB to Alfred, October 31, 1884, *Letters*, I, 66. Ernest Poole in LDB, *Business*, pp. l-li; Mason, *Brandeis*, p. 79. Time sheets: BP, NMF, Box 13; "Louis D. Brandeis: Advocate of Arbitration," *Strauss Magazine Theatre Program*, March 31, 1913, in BP, Scrapbook II.

21. LDB to William H. Dunbar, February 2, 1893, FF-LC.

22. LDB, "The Practice of the Law," BP, NMF 85-3.

23. Interview, *New York Times Analyst*, January 27, 1913, p. 36, reprinted in LDB, *The Curse of Bigness*, ed. Osmond K. Fraenkel (New York: Viking Press, 1934), p. 41.

24. LDB, "The Opportunity in the Law," in *Business*, pp. 314–331.

25. LDB, *Business*, pp. 321, 324–327.

26. Poole in LDB, *Business*, p. xii.

4. Family Life

1. LDB to Laski, September 21, 1921, *Letters*, IV, 17; Mason, *Brandeis*, p. 78.

2. LDB to William H. Dunbar, February 2, 1893, FF-HLS; LDB to Alfred, October 31, 1884, *Letters*, I, 66; to Alfred, March 24, 1890, *Letters*, I, 88.

3. LDB to Alfred, March 21, 1887, and March 20, 1888, BP, M 2-4; LDB to Adolph, November 1 and November 21, 1889, BP, M 3-1; *Letters*, I, 81, n. 1.

4. Harlan B. Phillips, ed., *Felix Frankfurter Reminisces* (New York: Reynal, 1960), pp. 209, 210.

5. Lief, *Brandeis*, pp. 30, 31; Mason, *Brandeis*, pp. 76, 78; LDB to Adolph, November 21 and November 30, 1889, BP, M 3-1; Scrapbook of photographs, BP, Addendum, Box 10.

6. LDB to Adolph, December 16, 1889, BP, M 3-1; Alice's diary quoted in Mason, *Brandeis*, p. 72.

7. LDB to Alice, early November 1890, quoted in Mason, *Brandeis*, p. 75; December 9, 1890, *Letters*, I, 96; February 26, 1891, *Letters*, I, 100.

8. LDB to Alice, October 27, 1890, quoted in Mason, *Brandeis*, p. 94; LDB to Alfred, September 8, 1890, *Letters*, I, 90–91.

9. LDB to Alice, October 27, 1890, quoted in Mason, *Brandeis*, p. 94; December 4, 1890, quoted in Mason, *Brandeis*, p. 74.

10. Interview with Mary Kay Tachau. Bills and household correspondence are in BP, NMF Boxes 7–19.

11. Elizabeth Glendower Evans, "Justice Brandeis At Home," *Springfield Republican*, November 11, 1931, in Louisville Free Public Library, Kentucky Authors Scrapbook Box 8, Part I; interview with Elizabeth Brandeis Raushen-bush.

12. LDB to Alice, October 1, 1890, and December 22, 1890, *Letters*, I, 92, 96; Mason, *Brandeis*, p. 74; Lief, *Brandeis*, p. 47.

13. LDB to Alice, December 20, 1890, *Letters*, I, 96; December 5, 1890, quoted in Mason, *Brandeis*, p. 75; February 26, 1891, quoted in Mason, *Brandeis*, p. 74; December 29, 1890, *Letters*, I, 97–98.

14. Inventory, BP, NMF Box 1, Folder 503; LDB to Alice, January 7, 1891, *Letters*, I, 98–99.

15. *New York Herald*, March 3, 1912, quoted in Mason, *Brandeis*, p. 77; cf. Lief, *Brandeis*, p. 200; donations, Mason, *Brandeis*, p. 692. Letters about Gardiner, BP, WB Box 8; about relatives, BP, WB Box 11; about Szold and de Haas, BP, WB Box 19.

16. Bills, February 1, 1913, March 1, 1913, April 15, 1913, BP, WB Box 15; September 23, 1916 and October 2, 1916, BP, WB Box 17.

17. R. L. Duffus, "Brandeis, at 75, Still the Fighter," *New York Times*, November 8, 1931; Elizabeth Glendower Evans, "Louis D. Brandeis—Tribune of the People," *Springfield Republican*, May 13, 1931; William Hard, "Brandeis the Conservative or a 'Dangerous Radical'?" *Philadelphia Public Ledger*, May 12, 1916, p. 10; LDB to Alice, February 11, 1891, *Letters*, I, 99; interview with Elizabeth Brandeis Raushenbush, September 23, 1980.

18. LDB to Elizabeth Glendower Evans, March 3, 1893, *Letters*, I, 110; LDB to Amy Brandeis Wehle, February 1, 1895, *Letters*, I, 119; Mason, *Brandeis*, p. 77; cf. Hard, "Brandeis the Conservative." Bills: BP, WB Boxes 10, 13.

19. Article from *Boston American*, September 29, 1912, BP, Clippings II; Edward F. McClennen, "Louis D. Brandeis as a Lawyer," *Massachusetts Law Quarterly*, 33 (1948), 25–26; Alden L. Todd, *Justice on Trial: The Case of Louis D. Brandeis* (New York: McGraw-Hill, 1964), p. 55.

20. Letters between LDB and Alfred: BP, Addendum, Box 1, folders 1–3 and folders marked 1910–1928; BP, M 2-4; *Letters*, I, 4, n. 3; interview with Mary Kay Tachau, June 12, 1980. Although dozens remain, most of the letters were destroyed by Alfred's daughters after his death, and others were burned by LDB. In both cases, the motivation was a desire for privacy.

21. LDB to Amy Brandeis Wehle, July 9, 1891, *Letters*, I, 103; Adolph to LDB, March 27 and 30, 1893, BP, Addendum, Box 1, 1-2, Lorie translation. There is no copy of LDB's letter of March 27, but presumably the circumstances that limited his writing time were the birth of his first daughter, Susan, and Alice's difficulties in recovering from childbirth. Cf. LDB to Elizabeth Glendower Evans,

March 27, 1893, *Letters*, I, 112. LDB to Frederika, November 12, 1888, quoted in Mason, *Brandeis*, pp. 93–94; interview with Mary Kay Tachau, June 12, 1980. On Susan's letters: Elizabeth Glendower Evans, "Louis Dembitz Brandeis— Tribune of the People," *Springfield Daily Republican*, May 13, 1931, BP, Scrapbook 3.

22. LDB to Amy Brandeis Wehle, July 9, 1891, *Letters*, I, 103–104 (cf. 104–105, n. 5); LDB to Susan Goldmark, November 17, 1896, *Letters*, I, 126– 127; bills from bookstores, January 1915, March 1916, April 1916, BP, WB Box 17; LDB to Amy, February 1, 1895, *Letters*, I, 119; to same, November 19, 1898, *Letters*, I, 135.

23. Hard, "Brandeis the Conservative," p. 10; LDB interview, *Boston Traveler*, June 10, 1910, BP, Scrapbook II.

24. Evans, "Justice Brandeis at Home"; article in *Boston American*, Clippings II; interview with Mrs. Raushenbush.

25. Rent bill, 1897, in BP, WB Box 7; Benjamin F. Bray to LDB, April 27, 1909, BP, WB Box 15; LDB to Bray, July 23, 1909, BP, WB Box 15; LDB to Charles H. Brown, July 30, 1908, BP, WB Box 15. Other bills and correspondence are in BP, WB Box 17. Estate inventory, November 1, 1941, BP, WB Box 1, pp. 1, 3, 7.

26. *Louisville Herald*, February 8, 1910, BP, Scrapbook II; "A Great American," *Philadelphia North American*, February 11, 1911, quoting Ernest Poole in *American Magazine*, February 1911, BP, Clippings II; article in *Philadelphia Public Ledger*, December 4, 1910, BP, Clippings II; Ray Stannard Baker, quoted in *Literary Digest*, July 1, 1916, BP, Clippings II.

27. Susan quoted in Evans, "Justice Brandeis at Home."

5. A Public Career

1. LDB to Alfred, January 30, 1884, *Letters*, I, 66; cf. ibid., n. 1.

2. LDB to Alfred, March 20, 1886, *Letters*, I, 67–68. The case was *Train v. Boston Disinfecting Co.*, 144 Mass. 523 (1887); cf. *Letters*, I, 68, nn. 2, 3.

3. Legislation on temperance and on the poor: LDB to Alice, February 9, 1891, *Letters*, I, 98; Lief, *Brandeis*, pp. 34–37; Mason, *Brandeis*, pp. 89–91; LDB, "The Anti-Bar Law. The Twenty-Five-Feet Law. Argument of Louis D. Brandeis, Esq. before the Joint Committee on Liquor Law of the Massachusetts Legislature: Boston, February 27, 1891," BP, Clippings I.

4. Membership in New England Free Trade League: Gal, *Brandeis*, pp. 12, 14, 19, 24. Lobbyists: "Mr. Brandeis [sic] Experiences," unidentified clipping labelled 1897, BP, Clippings I. Appearance at hearing: *Boston Herald*, January 12, 1897, BP, Clippings I; Mason, *Brandeis*, pp. 91–92.

5. Outrage: *Boston Herald*, January 12, 1897; *Springfield Republican*, January 13, 1897, BP, Clippings I; Mason, *Brandeis*, p. 92. Garrison quoted in *Boston Herald*, January 12, 1897.

6. LDB speech: U.S., Congress, House, "Statement before House Committee on Ways and Means, January 11, 1897: Tariff Hearings," 54th Cong., 2d sess., pp. 2081–84; cf. Lief, *Brandeis*, p. 63.

7. Walter H. Reynolds to LDB, February 21, 1893, quoted in Mason, *Brandeis*, p. 106; cf. Mason, *Brandeis*, p. 107.

8. LDB: "The Experience of Massachusetts in Street Railways," speech to the National Convention on Municipal Ownership and Public Franchise, February 25, 1903, printed in *Boston Transcript*, February 25, 1903; also reprinted in *Municipal Affairs*, 6 (1903), 721, 727. Cf. LDB: "The Massachusetts System of Dealing with Public Franchises," address at Cooper Union, New York City, February 24, 1905, typescript BP, Clippings I; Lief, *Brandeis*, pp. 55–56.

9. *Boston Evening Transcript*, April 30, 1897, quoted in Mason, *Brandeis*, p. 107; LDB to Editor, *Evening Transcript*, April 30, 1897, BP, NMF 1-5.

10. LDB to William Ames Bancroft, May 20 and 21, 1897, BP, NMF 76-2; LDB to Albert Pillsbury, May 20, 1897, BP, NMF 76-2.

11. LDB, "Experience of Massachusetts," p. 729; Mason, *Brandeis*, p. 108.

12. Mason, *Brandeis*, pp. 109, 111; Gal, *Brandeis*, pp. 49–50, 52; LDB to Winthrop M. Crane, June 7, 1901, BP, NMF 2-5; LDB to Morton Prince, June 6, 1901, BP, NMF 2-5; LDB to Crane, June 20, 1901, BP NMF 2-5.

13. Letters to supporters: See, e.g., LDB to James R. Carter, March 24, 1900; to Laurence Minot, April 16, 1900; to Morton Prince, May 18, 1900; to Carter, January 28, 1901; to Minot, February 15, 1901; to George B. Upham, February 26, 1901; to Edward Filene, March 11, 1901; to Charles R. Saunders, June 4, 1901; to Morton Prince, June 6, 1901; all BP, NMF 2-5. Solicitations: LDB to Jerome Jones, March 24, 1900; to Edward A. Clement, April 18, 1900; to Arthur A. Maxwell, April 24, 1900; to John E. Parry, May 6, 1901; to William Schofield, May 27, 1901; to Guy W. Currier, June 8, 1901; all BP, NMF 2-5. LDB to Edward Filene, June 1, 1901, BP, NMF 2-5.

14. LDB, "Experience of Massachusetts," p. 729; LDB to Thomas L. Livermore, January 31, 1902, BP, NMF 2-5; typescript, "Some Objections to the Matthews-Livermore Terminal Subway Bill," February 17, 1902, BP, NMF 2-5; LDB to Morton Prince, January 31, 1902; to Benjamin F. Keith, February 25, 1902; to George B. Upham, February 24, 1902; to Edward Warren, February 25, 1902; to Morton Prince, February 28, 1902; all BP, NMF 2-5; LDB to Edward Filene, April 11, 1902; to Edward A. Adler, April 15 and 22, 1902; to Edwin A. Grozier, April 29, 1902; to Huntington Smith, May 1, 1902: all BP, NMF 4-2. Quoted letters: LDB to Carter, February 24, 1902; to Laurence Minot, February 24, 1902; to Warren, February 24, 1902; to Keith, February 25, 1902; to Minot, February 25, 1902; all BP, NMF 2-5.

15. Mason, *Brandeis*, pp. 113–115; Lief, *Brandeis*, pp. 68–69; LDB, "Experience of Massachusetts," p. 729. Cf. LDB to Patrick A. Collins, April 28, 1902; to Winthrop M. Crane, April 28, 1902; to Collins, May 12, 1902; to George R. Jones, May 14, 1902; to Collins, May 28, June 2, 3, 5, and 6, 1902; all BP, NMF 4-2.

16. LDB to Edward McClennen, February 17, 1916, BP, NMF 76-2; Edwin Hale Abbot to LDB, July 7, 1901, quoted in Mason, *Brandeis*, p. 112; John T. Boyd to LDB, October 21, 1902, BP, NMF 4-2; Edward A. Filene, "Louis D. Brandeis As We Know Him," *Boston Post*, July 14, 1915; McClennen, "Brandeis as Lawyer," p. 24; LDB to Louise Malloch, November 4, 1907, BP, NMF 1-H-

1; LDB interview in *American Cloak and Suit Review*, January 1911, p. 159, reprinted in LDB, *Bigness*, p. 266.

17. Samuel Warren to LDB, n.d., BP, Clippings I; Warren to LDB, July 28, 1891, quoted in Mason, *Brandeis*, p. 95; Jacob de Haas, "The People's Attorney: Justice Louis D. Brandeis," *The Jewish Tribune*, August 23, 1929, pp. 3, 9; Lief, *Brandeis*, pp. 56–57.

18. LDB to Benjamin F. Keith, November 5, 1901; LDB to William H. McElwain, June 18, 1902.

19. LDB to Edward H. Clement, July 21, 1902; LDB to John L. Bates, November 24, 1902; LDB to Edward A. Adler, January 29, 1903; all BP, NMF 3-4. Lecturing: LDB to George A. Comins, March 20, 1902; to George U. Crocker, March 20, 1903; to James H. Dodge, March 24, 1903; to the Editors of the Boston Newspapers, March 24, 1903; all BP, NMF 6-5. Cf. speech before the Boston Boot and Shoe Club, March 18, 1903, reported in full in the *Boston Post* and *Boston Evening Transcript* on March 19, 1903, and reprinted as "Address on Corruption," LDB, *Bigness*, pp. 263–265. Collecting facts: LDB to George H. Tinkham, April 2 and 6, 1903; to Edward A. Adler, March 20, 1903; all BP, NMF 6-5. LDB to William H. Gove, April 1, 1903; and to Edward A. Adler, April 7, 1903, both BP, NMF 3-4. Speeches: *Boston Herald*, March 19 and April 9, 1903, BP, Clippings I; *Boston Journal*, April 9, 1903, BP, Clippings I.

20. Brighton speech: Alice H. Grady's typescript, BP, Clippings I; *Boston Globe*, November 16, 1904, reporting speech of November 16, BP, Clippings I.

21. Organizations: Mason, *Brandeis*, pp. 118, 125; LDB to Laurence Minot, March 27, 1903, BP, NMF 6-5; *Boston Daily Advertiser*, February 28, 1903, BP, Clippings I. Speech to physicians, June 14, 1905, reported *Boston Herald*, June 14 and 15: *Boston Post* and *Boston Journal*, June 15, BP, Clippings I.

22. *Boston Daily Advertiser*, February 28, 1903, BP, Clippings I. Article in Pittsfield, Massachusetts, newspaper, February (?) 1903, BP, Clippings I.

23. Pittsfield article, February 1903; good government lecture, typescript dated December 11, 1903, BP, Clippings I; Mason, *Brandeis*, pp. 117–124; Lief, *Brandeis*, pp. 69–73.

24. LDB to Abbot L. Lowell, March 6, 1901, BP, NMF 3-2; to James P. Munroe, May 15, 1901, BP, NMF 3-2; to Thomas N. Hart, June 27, 1901, BP, NMF 2-5; to Mary B. Kehew, January 20, 1902, BP, NMF 3-2; to Edmund Billings, December 17, 1903, BP NMF 8-2; to Clara C. Park, June 19, 1911, and January 27, 1912, BP, NMF 46-4; to Committee on Prisons, February 11, 1907, BP, NMF 20-2; to Charles F. Jenney, February 7, 1907, BP, NMF 20-2. LDB's "candidacy": *Boston Herald*, April 14, 1903, quoted in Mason, *Brandeis*, p. 122; *Boston Evening Record*, September 13, 1904, and *Boston Traveler*, September 15, 1904, both BP, Clippings I; LDB to George W. Morse, April 15, 1903, and to W. Wallace Waugh, April 17, 1903, BP, NMF 6-5; LDB to Unknown, paraphrase, April 14, 1903, Alfred Lief, ed., *The Brandeis Guide to the Modern World* (Boston: Little, Brown, 1941), p. 38; LDB to Frank Parsons, July 29, 1905, quoted in Mason, *Brandeis*, p. 122.

25. LDB to Alice Goldmark, October 11, 1890, *Letters*, I, 92; Lief, *Brandeis*,

p. 31; cf. letters urging him to run from Henry Swift, October 9, 1890, and N. Matthews, Jr., November 13, 1890, BP, Scrapbook I.

26. LDB, "How Boston Solved the Gas Problem," *The American Review of Reviews*, 26 (November 1907), pp. 594–598, reprinted in *Business*, pp. 93–108; LDB to Edward R. Warren, May 2, 1904, BP, NMF 10-1: Mason, *Brandeis*, pp. 126–128.

27. Mason, *Brandeis*, pp. 78–79, 128–129; LDB, *Business*, pp. 97–98; Lief, *Brandeis*, p. 76.

28. Lief, *Brandeis*, pp. 78–79.

29. LDB to Richard L. Gray, March 2, 1905; to Massachusetts Board of Gas and Electric Light Commissioners, March 6, 1905; to Governor William L. Douglas, March 7, 1905; all BP, NMF, 10-1.

30. *Springfield Republican*, April 18, 1905; *The Outlook*, 80 (June 3, 1905), 254–255; LDB to Warren, April 17, 1905; to Morton Prince, April 24, 1905; to Samuel Bowles, May 8, 1905; to Mark Sullivan, July 27, 1906; all BP, NMF 10-1.

31. LDB to Warren, March 13, 1905, BP, NMF 10-1; testimony printed as pamphlet by Public Franchise League, "Consolidation of Gas Companies and of Electric Light Companies, argument of L. D. Brandeis on behalf of the Massachusetts State Board of Trade." Cf. LDB, "How Boston Solved the Gas Problem." LDB to John N. Cole, March 22, 1905; to Alfred S. Hall, March 22, 1905; to Harold P. Moseley, March 22, 1905; to William H. Ames, April 7, 1905; all BP, NMF 10-1; Mason, *Brandeis*, pp. 135, 137–138.

32. LDB to Morton Prince, April 24, 1905, BP, NMF, 10-1; Lief, *Brandeis*, pp. 80–81; Mason, *Brandeis*, p. 134; cf. LDB to Thomas Babson, May 3, 1905; to Solomon B. Griffin, January 24, 1906; and to Charles H. Jones, March 31, 1906; all BP, NMF 10-1.

33. Richards to LDB, April 20, 1906, and LDB to Richards, April 21, 1906; BP NMF 10-1. Quotation in *Boston Evening Herald, Boston Evening Transcript*, and *Boston Globe*, all June 6, 1905, BP, Clippings I.

34. Mason, *Brandeis*, pp. 135–139; LDB to Alfred, May 27, 1906, BP, M 2-4; cf. LDB to Norman Hapgood, May 28, 1906, BP, NMF 10-1; LDB to Horace E. Deming, June 20, 1905, BP, NMF 1-7; LDB to Joseph Walker, April 17, 1905, BP, NMF 10-1.

35. LDB to Editor of the *Boston American*, May 9, 1905, BP, NMF 10-1; LDB, *Business*, pp. 94–96; George L. Barnes to LDB, June 5, 1906, BP, NMF 10-1; LDB to Mark Sullivan, June 24, 1907, BP, NMF 16-1; to Sullivan, July 27, 1906, BP, NMF 10-1. Cf. LDB to Lawrence F. Abbott, July 1, 1907, BP, NMF 16-1.

36. LDB, *Business*, p. 102.

37. LDB, *Business*, pp. 100, 103–106.

38. *Boston Transcript*, March 9, 1905, reporting hearing same day, BP, Clippings I.

39. LDB to Henry Lee Higginson, April 26, 1905, BP, NMF 12-11; to Hayes Robbins, June 19, 1905, BP, NMF 12-11; to Leonard A. Jones, May 8, 1905,

BP, NMF 12-4; to Morris R. Cohen, May 10, 1905, BP, NMF 12-4; to Warren A. Reed, May 11, 1905, BP, NMF 7-2; to Clinton R. Woodruff, May 24, 1905, BP, NMF 1-7. To Adolph, July 9, 11, 13, 15, and 31, 1905, *Letters*, I, 334–340; to Adolph July 27, 1905, *Letters*, I, 351; to Adolph July 22, 23, and 28, 1905, *Letters*, I, 340, 346–347, 352–353. LDB to John Hinkley, BP, NMF 12-4, July 20; to James F. Jackson, July 24, BP; NMF 13-1; to Charles F. Pidgin, July 26, BP, NMF 13-1; to Massachusetts Board of Prison Commissioners July 31, BP, NMF 13-1; to Edward W. Bemis, July 25, BP, NMF 10-1; to Charles E. Nexdorff, July 27, BP, NMF 8-2; to William De Las Casas, July 31, BP, NMF 13-1; to Adolph July 23, *Letters*, I, 346.

6. **Reforming Life Insurance**

1. The account of the industrial insurance system is based on Brandeis, "Wage-Earners' Life Insurance," *Collier's*, 37 (Sept. 15, 1906), reprinted in Alpheus Thomas Mason: *The Brandeis Way* (Princeton: Princeton University Press, 1938), pp. 311–325. The book contains a complete account of the insurance battle.

2. Mason, *Brandeis Way*, pp. 83–88; Lief, *Brandeis*, pp. 94–95.

3. Brandeis's conclusions: Mason, *Brandeis Way*, p. 91; LDB to Policy Holders of the Equitable Life Assurance Society, July 22, 1905, *Letters*, I, 341. Frick report: quoted in Mason, *Brandeis Way*, p. 91.

4. Ryan's purchase: Mason, *Brandeis Way*, pp. 90–92; LDB to Adolph, July 13, 1905, *Letters*, I, 336. Recommendations: LDB to Policy Holders, July 22, 1905.

5. LDB to Policy Holders, July 22, 1905.

6. Mason, *Brandeis Way*, pp. 90–98. Quote in *New York Evening World*, May 11, 1906, Mason, *Brandeis Way*, p. 98.

7. Mason, *Brandeis Way*, p. 99.

8. Lief, *Brandeis*, pp. 97–98, 100; Mason, *Brandeis Way*, pp. 103–104.

9. Commercial Club Speech: reprinted in Brandeis, *Business*, pp. 109–153.

10. LDB to Grady: quoted in Mason, *Brandeis Way*, p. 122. LDB to N.Y. Board of Insurance Commissioners, November 22, 1906, *Letters*, I, 487; cf. *Letters*, I, 487, n. 1.

11. Armstrong Committee report and commissions on insurance: Mason, *Brandeis Way*, pp. 113–114, 171. LDB to Grady: quoted in Lief, *Brandeis*, p. 99. Elizur Wright: Mason, *Brandeis Way*, pp. 118–120. LDB to Walter Wright: November 24, 1905, BP, I, 1-1.

12. LDB to Wright, November 24, 1905.

13. Ibid.

14. LDB to John C. Pegram, November 1, 1905, BP, NMF 12-8; to Fred S. Elwell, December 8, 1905, BP, NMF 12-8; to Samuel Warren, November 1, 1905, BP, NMF 7-2; to James P. Munroe, May 9, 1905, BP, NMF 7-2; to Charles F. Libby, November 10, 1905, BP, NMF 6-7; to Ralph M. Easley, January 8, 1906, BP, NMF 12-11; to Pegram, December 29, 1905, BP, NMF 12-8.

15. LDB to Alfred, November 30, 1906, *Letters*, I, 499; to Alfred, January

3, 1907, BP, M 2-4; Poole in LDB, *Business*, p. xxvii; *Letters*, I, 529, n. 3; Lief, *Brandeis*, p. 102; Mason, *Brandeis Way*, p. 161; LDB to Adolph, July 27, 1905, *Letters*, I, 351.

16. LDB to Curtis Guild, Jr., December 2, 1905, BP, NMF 3-4; to Alfred, March 2, 1906, *Letters*, I, 408; to John N. Cole, June 4, 1906, *Letters*, I, 443; Mason, *Brandeis Way*, pp. 171–173.

17. Mason, *Brandeis Way*, pp. 188–190; Mason, *Brandeis*, pp. 159, 163; Lief, *Brandeis*, p. 101.

18. LDB to Hapgood: January 10, 1906, BP, NMF 10-5; May 28, 1906, BP, NMF 10-1; July 14, 1906, *Letters*, I, 453; June 25, 1906, *Letters*, I, 448–449. The LDB paper appeared in *Collier's*, September 15, 1906. Cf. Mason, *Brandeis Way*, pp. 311–325. LDB to Mark Sullivan: June 24, 1907, *Letters*, I, 587; June 24, 1907, BP, NMF 16-1.

19. LDB to Alice and Charles Park, July 23, 1938, BP, Addendum, Box 1.

20. LDB to Charles Hall, June 12, 1906, *Letters*, I, 446; Robert Luce to LDB, July 26, 1906, *Letters*, I, 460; LDB to Wilmot R. Evans, Jr., July 27, 1906, *Letters*, I, 462; LDB to George L. Barnes, August 2, 1906, *Letters*, I, 465; also letters noted in I, 445, n. 1. See also Mason, *Brandeis Way*, p. 178. Letters about article: LDB to A. D. Noyes, July 27, 1906, in Mason, *Brandeis Way*, p. 134; to Edwin Grozier, July 21, 1906, *Letters*, I, 457; to Grozier, July 24, 1906, *Letters*, I, 458; to Samuel Bowles, editor of the *Springfield Republican*, July 24, 1906, *Letters*, I, 458; LDB to Mark Sullivan, July 24, 1906, *Letters*, I, 458–459. Cf. Lief, *Brandeis*, pp. 100–101.

21. Criticism and facts: Mason, *Brandeis Way*, pp. 122, 134–136, 181, 188, 191, 192, 212, 222. Guild's message: January 3, 1907; Committee report: January 8, 1907; Mason, *Brandeis Way*, p. 176.

22. LDB to Henry B. Needham, December 1, 1906, *Letters*, I, 502; Roosevelt to LDB, January 14, 1907, *Letters*, I, 519, n. 1; LDB to Roosevelt, January 18, 1907, BP, NMF 16-2; *Congressional Record*, 59th Cong., 2d sess., XLI, 1603.

23. LDB to John H. Schoonmaker, April 26, 1907, *Letters*, I, 557–558; to William H. McElwain, May 1, 1907, *Letters*, I, 565; Mason, *Brandeis Way*, p. 196.

24. Hearings: Mason, *Brandeis Way*, pp. 182–190; Warren Reed to LDB, March 23, 1907, quoted in Mason, *Brandeis Way*, pp. 184–185; savings bank leaders: LDB to Reed, March 26, 1907, *Letters*, I, 534; endorsements: LDB to Norman White, March 26, 1907, *Letters*, I, 535–537; LDB to Henry Abrahams, March 28, 1907, *Letters*, I, 538. *Boston Post*: LDB to Edwin A. Grozier, March 30, 1907, *Letters*, I, 540. Individuals: LDB to Alfred G. Bookwalter, April 3, 1907, *Letters*, I, 542; to Charles W. Welch, April 3, 1907, *Letters*, I, 543–544; to George Barnes, April 4, 1907, *Letters*, I, 544; to Arthur R. Jones, April 4, 1907, *Letters*, I, 544–545; to William H. McElwain, April 16, 1907, *Letters*, I, 549; to Norman H. White, April 17, 1907, *Letters*, I, 551; to William S. Kyle, April 18, 1907, *Letters*, I, 552–553; to John T. Boyd, April 22, 1907, *Letters*, I, 555. Labor unions: LDB to Norman H. White, April 15, 1907, *Letters*, I, 548–

549; to same, April 29, 1907, *Letters*, I, 560; to Dennis D. Driscoll, May 1, 1907, *Letters*, I, 562–563. Postcards: Mason, *Brandeis Way*, p. 201; pamphlets: LDB to Norman H. White, March 26, 1907, *Letters*, I, 535–537.

25. Grozier: LDB to Grozier, May 3, 1907, *Letters*, I, 566–567; editorial, *Boston Post*, May 4, 1907; LDB to Grozier, May 6, 1907, *Letters*, I, 568–569; editorial: *Boston Post*, May 7, 1907; LDB to Grozier, May 10, 1907, *Letters*, I, 571. House and Senate Ways and Means Committees: Mason, *Brandeis Way*, pp. 210, 214–220. LDB to Alfred: June 13 and 18, 1907, *Letters*, I, 584–585; June 19, 1907, *Letters*, I, 586.

26. LDB to Guild: June 25, 1907, *Letters*, I, 588–589; June 28, 1907, *Letters*, I, 591; Mason, *Brandeis Way*, pp. 225–226. LDB to Robertson G. Hunter, December 20, 1907, *Letters*, II, 60–61; Mason, *Brandeis Way*, pp. 229–230, 233–235, 308.

27. LDB to H. C. Parson, July 8, 1907, quoted in Mason, *Brandeis Way*, p. 237; Warren Reed to LDB, December 4, 1908, and Alice Grady to Warren Reed, December 7, 1908, both quoted in Mason, *Brandeis Way*, pp. 237–238; Poole in LDB, *Business*, pp. xxviii, xxix.

28. Mason, *Brandeis Way*, pp. 239–241, 248, 308.

29. LDB to Norman White, July 6, 1907, *Letters*, II, 6–7; Mason, *Brandeis*, p. 692; LDB to Alfred, September 20, 1908, BP, M2-4; LDB to W. W. Alexander, July 21, 1908, *Letters*, II, 201–202; LDB to Lincoln Steffens, December 10, 1909, *Letters*, II, 302; cf. Mason, *Brandeis Way*, p. 252.

30. LDB to Robertson Hunter, February 27, 1909, *Letters*, II, 224–226; to George L. Perin, January 9, 1909, *Letters*, II, 217; to Colin A. Scott, January 19, 1909, *Letters*, II, 217–218; to Charles R. Towson, January 4, 1909, *Letters*, II, 215; LDB to Hunter, November 10, 1908, *Letters*, II, 214.

31. LDB to Robertson Hunter, February 15, 1909, *Letters*, II, 219; cf. to same, March 19, 1909, *Letters*, II, 241; to Argus Press Clipping Bureau, November 22, 1906, *Letters*, I, 487; to Charles F. Dole, October 10, 1908, BP, NMF 19-2; to Hapgood, October 14, 1908, BP, NMF 8-3.

32. Alfred L. Aiken to Grady, February 6, 1914, quoted in Mason, *Brandeis Way*, p. 244. Grady: Mason, *Brandeis Way*, pp. 243–244; Lief, *Brandeis*, pp. 104, 183.

33. Lief, *Brandeis*, p. 105; Alpheus T. Mason, *Brandeis, Lawyer and Judge in the Modern State* (Princeton: Princeton University Press, 1933), p. 42; Mason, *Brandeis*, p. 177; LDB to Lincoln Steffens, December 10, 1909, *Letters*, II, 303–305.

34. LDB to Ermon J. Ridgeway, August 3, 1908, BP, NMF 15-1; to Meyer Bloomfield, July 6, 1908, *Letters*, II, 196; to Warren Reed, December 3, 1906, *Letters*, I, 505.

35. LDB to John E. Pember, February 4, 1908, *Letters*, II, 73–75; cf. LDB to Gertrude B. Beeks, April 21, 1908, *Letters*, II, 129; LDB to Eben S. Draper, June 5, 1908, *Letters*, II, 176; to Lincoln Steffens, December 10, 1909, *Letters*, II, 304.

36. LDB to Lawrence Abbott, June 25, 1908, *Letters*, II, 191–193; Abbott editorial, *Outlook*, 89 (July 11, 1908), 543–544; LDB to Samuel Gompers, July

17, 1908, *Letters*, II, 198; article published as "Massachusetts Old Age Annuities" in *American Federationist*, 15 (August 1908), 595–597; "Massachusetts' Substitute for Old Age Pensions," *The Independent*, 65 (July 16, 1908), 125–128; LDB to Alfred, July 20, 1908, BP, M 2-4; "Massachusetts Savings Insurance and Annuity Banks," *The Banker's Magazine*, 78 (August 1908), 186–188.

37. LDB to John Golden, June 24, 1907, *Letters*, I, 586; to Charles R. Henderson, March 18, 1907, *Letters*, I, 526; to Ralph M. Easley, July 16, 1907, *Letters*, II, 13; to John E. Pember, February 4, 1908, *Letters*, II, 75; to Charles R. Towson, January 4, 1909, *Letters*, II, 216.

7. Trade Unionism

1. LDB to Alice, October 27, 1890, quoted in Mason, *Brandeis*, p. 94.

2. Josephine Goldmark, *Impatient Crusader: Florence Kelley's Life Story* (Urbana: University of Illinois Press, 1953), p. 153; "epoch in career" quoted in Levy S. Richard, "Up from Aristocracy," interview with LDB in *The Independent*, July 27, 1914, BP, Clippings II.

3. Lief, *Brandeis*, pp. 39–40; Gal, *Brandeis*, pp. 56–58. Notes for both sets of lectures: Abram L. Sachar and William M. Goldsmith, comp., The Public Papers of Louis Dembitz Brandeis in the Jacob and Bertha Goldfarb Library of Brandeis University (microfilm, Brandeis University, Waltham, Massachusetts), Horace Kallen, *The Faith of Louis D. Brandeis, Zionist* (New York: Hadassah, n.d.), p. 7.

4. Edward A. Filene, "Louis D. Brandeis, As We Know Him," *Boston Post*, March 4, 1916, quoted in Mason, *Brandeis*, p. 145; Lief, *Brandeis*, p. 41; LDB interview, *New York Times Annualist*, January 27, 1913, p. 36, reprinted in Brandeis, *Bigness*, p. 41.

5. See note 4, above.

6. See note 4, above.

7. LDB, "Business—A Profession," address at Brown University Commencement, 1912; published in *System, the Magazine of Business*, 11 (October 1912), reprinted as "Business—the New Profession," in LDB, *Business*, pp. 1, 6–9. Cf. Mason, *Brandeis*, pp. 145–146; Gal, *Brandeis*, pp. 63–64.

8. LDB to John Tobin, March 28, 1905, BP, NMF 8-3; in LDB, *Business*, p. 6; to Alfred, January 12, 1908, BP, Addendum; to William McElwain, June 18, 1902, BP, NMF 3-4; to Charles Henry Jones, April 13, 1907, *Letters*, I, 545–546; to McElwain, April 16, 1907, *Letters*, I, 549–550; to same, May 1, 1907, *Letters*, I, 563–565.

9. Elizabeth Glendower Evans, "Mr. Justice Brandeis, The People's Tribune," *The Survey*, October 29, 1931; LDB to Clarence Darrow, December 12, 1902, BP, NMF 5-1; to Henry Demarest Lloyd, November 24, 1902, BP, NMF 5-1; to Darrow, December 10, 1902, BP, NMF 5-1; to same, December 13, 1902, BP, NMF; to Lloyd, December 20, 1902, BP, NMF 5-1; Lloyd to LDB, December 13, 1902, and LDB to Lloyd, January 2, 1903, BP, NMF 5-1; Lloyd to LDB, January 26, 1903, and LDB to Lloyd, February 2, 1903, BP, NMF 5-1; Mason, *Brandeis*, p. 143.

10. LDB to Frank S. Brown, June 17, 1912, BP, NMF 8-3; LDB, *Bigness*, p. 41.

11. Mary La Dame: *The Filene Store: A Study of Employees' Relation to Management in a Retail Store* (New York: Russell Sage Foundation, 1930), pp. 21, 45–46.

12. Ibid., pp. 259–293.

13. Ibid., pp. 30–32, 119–120, 440; Mason, *Brandeis*, p. 147.

14. La Dame, *The Filene Store*, pp. 47, 164–188, 306–321, 441, 442. LDB to Edward Filene, June 25, 1906, BP, NMF 7-2.

15. LDB, Address before the Filene Co-operative Association, May, 1905, published in *Filene Association Echo*, May 1905, reprinted as "Industrial Co-operation" in LDB, *Bigness*, pp. 35–37.

16. Ibid.

17. Articles of Association of the Industrial League, July 21, 1903, BP, NMF 7-2; LDB to William Dembar, July 21 and 22, 1903, BP, NMF 7-2; to Warren A. Reed, May 11, 1905, BP, NMF 7-2; to Samuel Warren, November 1, 1905, BP, NMF 7-2; to Eugene Cochrane, July 8, 1906, BP, NMF 12-11; cf. to same, July 11.

18. Federation's services: e.g., Great Northern Paper Company Strike, 1906. See LDB to Hayes Robbins, July 26, 1906, BP, NMF 12-11; cf. LDB to Lewis Flanders & Co. et al., May 14, 1907, and to Edwin Ginn, May 17, 1907, BP, NMF 17-2; to Higginson, April 26, 1905, BP, NMF 12-11; to Hayes Robbins, June 19, 1905, BP, NMF 12-11; Robbins to Ralph M. Easley, June 14 and 15, 1905, BP, NMF 12-11; LDB to Robbins, June 30, 1905, BP, NMF 12-11.

19. LDB to J. W. Beatson, June 25, 1904, BP, NMF 9-2; to Amory Appleton Lawrence, January 25, 1905, BP, NMF 12-11; to Dennis D. Driscoll, January 28, 1905, BP, NMF 12-1; to Lucius Tuttle, February 6, 1905, BP, NMF 12-11.

20. LDB and Gompers as quoted in "Should Trade Unions Be Incorporated: Joint Debate Between Gompers and Brandeis on Question," *Boston Post*, December 5, 1902; (the words "enlightened self-sacrifice" are those of the article's anonymous author).

21. Ibid.

22. "Brandeis Excited: Who Is This Man, Daring to Scare a Judge So? He asks," *Boston Herald*, December 5, 1902, BP, Clippings, Scrapbook I, Folder 4.

23. Words "of the most cosmopolitan character" are in *Boston Herald* article; list of those present and mention of Durand are in *Boston Post*.

24. Gompers described in *Boston Herald*.

25. Gompers to LDB, February 4, 1905, and LDB to Gompers, February 13, 1905, BP, NMF 8-3. April 1905 discussion: *Letters*, I, 304 n. 1. LDB to Gompers, July 17, 1907, *Letters*, II, 14–15; LDB, "Savings Bank Life Insurance," *The Federationist*, 14 (October 1907); LDB to Gompers, July 7, 1908, *Letters*, II, 198; LDB, "Massachusetts' Old Age Annuities," *American Federationist*, 14 (August 1908). LDB, "Trade Unionism and Employers," published as "An Economic Exhortation to Organized Labor," *National Civic Federation Monthly Review*, 1 (March 1905), 20–24. A. L. Filene to Edward Filene, July 18, 1910, *Letters*, II, 365, n. 2. J. M. Neeman to LDB, March 9, 1912, and LDB to Neeman,

March 11, 1912, BP, NMF 8-3. The remarks had been printed in the *Green Bag* of January 1903.

26. LDB, "The Employers and the Trade Unions," delivered to the annual banquet of the Boston Typothetae, April 21, 1904, reprinted in LDB, *Business*, pp. 13–27.

27. LDB, *Business*, pp. 16–17.

28. Ibid., pp. 18–19.

29. Ibid., pp. 20–22.

30. Ibid., pp. 22–27.

31. Article in *Daily Eastern Argus*, Portland, Maine, April 19, 1905, quoted in Mason, *Brandeis*, p. 149.

32. On paupers: quoted in Mason, *Brandeis*, p. 91. LDB, "Hours of Labor," address before first annual meeting of the Civic Federation of New England, January 11, 1906, reprinted in LDB, *Business*, pp. 28–36.

33. LDB to Alfred, February 23, 1906, *Letters*, I, 407–408; to Alfred, June 18, 1907, BP, M 2-4; to Alfred, February 22, 1906, *Letters*, I, 407.

34. Closed shop: LDB in *National Civic Federation Review*, May 11, 1905, quoted in Mason, *Brandeis*, p. 150. Speech to the Central Labor Union: *Boston Post*, February 6, 1905, quoted in Mason, *Brandeis*, p. 151. LDB to Edna F. Weber, October 19, 1907, BP, NMF 21-2; to John B. Andrews, January 24, 1910, BP, NMF 21-2.

8. The Brandeis Brief

1. LDB, assisted by Josephine Goldmark, *Women in Industry* (New York: The National Consumers' League, n.d.), pp. 18, 24, 36, 47, 86, 113; *Muller* v. *Oregon*, 208 U.S. 412, 423 (1908).

2. *Muller* v. *Oregon*, 208 U.S. 412.

3. Choate quoted in Mason, *Brandeis*, p. 248. Lief, *Brandeis*, p. 136; Goldmark, *Impatient Crusader*, pp. 149–154; Todd, *Justice on Trial*, p. 159. The preface to the Goldmark book is by Elizabeth Brandeis, who completed the final revision of the book after Goldmark's death in 1940; the foreword is by Felix Frankfurter.

4. Goldmark, *Impatient Crusader*, pp. 142, 153, 155–156, 163.

5. *Lochner* v. *New York*, 198 U.S. 45 (1905): *Ritchie* v. *People*, 155 Ill. 98 (1895); *People* v. *Williams*, 198 U.S. 45 (1905).

6. *Allgeyer* v. *Louisiana*, 165 U.S. 578 (1897); ibid., 589–593.

7. *Holden* v. *Hardy*, 169 U.S. 366; ibid., 383–384, 393–398.

8. *Lochner* v. *New York*, 198 U.S. 45, 53, 58.

9. 198 U.S. 50, 54–58, 59, 63, 64.

10. 198 U.S. 64, 69, 70–71.

11. Holmes in *Lochner* v. *New York*, 198 U.S. 74–76.

12. Mayer's brief: summary, 198 U.S. 51. I am indebted to Professor John P. Roche for calling the brief to my attention.

13. LDB to Chicago Bar Association, January 3, 1916, printed as "The Living Law" in *Illinois Law Review*, 10 (February 1916), 461–471, reprinted in LDB, *Bigness*, pp. 316–326.

14. LDB, *Women in Industry*, pp. 9–10; *Lochner* v. *New York*, 198 U.S. 45–68.

15. Memorandum prepared by Goldmark for Mason, quoted in Mason, *Brandeis*, p. 250.

16. *Muller* v. *Oregon*, 208 U.S. 412, 419, 419–420 n. 1.

17. *Bunting* v. *Oregon*, 243 U.S. 426 (1917).

18. *Ritchie* v. *People*, 155 Ill. 98 (1895); *Ritchie* v. *Wyman*, 244 Ill. 509 (1910); cf. *People* v. *Eldering*, 254 Ill. 579 (1912). Ohio law: *Hawley* v. *Walker*, 232 U.S. 718 (1914). Goldmark, *Impatient Crusader*, pp. 158–164. LDB acted jointly with the state attorney-general in the California case.

19. New York law: *People* v. *Schweindler Press*, 214 N.Y. 395 (1915). Oregon hours for men: *Bunting* v. *Oregon*, 243 U.S. 426 (1917). LDB prepared the brief in *Bunting*, which duplicated the form used in *Muller*. Felix Frankfurter took over the case when LDB was appointed to the Court, apparently writing only the appendices to accompany LDB's 960 pages. The brief was printed as Felix Frankfurter, assisted by Josephine Goldmark, *The Case for the Shorter Work Day* (New York: National Consumers' League, 1915). *Muller* brief applicable to men: LDB, *Women in Industry*; see, e.g., pp. 24–32, 35–36, 42–45, 56, 61–64. Additional data: Josephine Goldmark, *Fatigue and Efficiency* (New York: Russell Sage Foundation, 1912); cf. LDB to John M. Glenn, November 30, 1909, *Letters*, II, 297–298. Goldmark, *Impatient Crusader*, pp. 164–167, 170.

20. LDB, *Bigness*, p. 325.

21. Works by Pound: "Liberty of Contract," *Yale Law Journal*, 18 (1909), 454; *The Spirit of the Common Law* (Boston: Marshall Jones, 1921); *The History and System of the Common Law* (New York: Collier, 1939); *An Introduction to the Philosophy of Law* (New Haven: Yale University Press, 1922). See works listed in George A. Strait, *A Bibliography of the Writings of Roscoe Pound* (Cambridge: Harvard Law School Library, 1960). Holmes: *The Common Law* (Boston: Little, Brown, 1951); cf. the essays and addresses published as Oliver Wendell Holmes, *Collected Legal Papers* (New York: Harcourt, Brace, 1921; New York: Peter Smith, 1952).

22. LDB interview with Ernest Poole, quoted in "A Great American," *Philadelphia North American*, February 11, 1911, BP. Addendum, Clippings I.

23. LDB, *Bigness*, p. 324.

24. LDB, *Bigness*, p. 324; McClennen, "Brandeis as Lawyer," pp. 22–23.

25. LDB, "Scientific preparation of legislation": to William O. Lewis, November 13, 1912, *Letters*, II, 718–719; Holmes, "The Path of the Law" in *Collected Legal Papers*, p. 166.

26. Pound to Sen. William E. Chilton, 1916, FF-LC Box 127; McClennen, "Brandeis as Lawyer," pp. 3, 4, 27; Judge William Hitz to FF, December 17, 1914, BP, Addendum, Scrapbook 2; *Boston Herald*, "Babbit's Column," January 3, 1915, BP, Addendum, Scrapbook 2.

27. LDB to Hapgood, April 17, 1911, BP, NMF 46-3; to Hapgood, April 6, 1912, BP, NMF 46-3, quoting James Russell Lowell's "A Glance Behind the Curtain"; LDB, *Women in Industry*, p. 113.

28. *Muller* v. *Oregon*, 208 U.S. 421–423. The decision about women lawyers is *Bradwell* v. *Illinois*, 83 U.S. 130 (1872).

29. Cf. note 19, above.

30. LDB to Josephine Goldmark, October 11, 1910, *Letters*, II, 381. For influence of Goldmark, Grady, and Malloch, cf. Lief, *Brandeis*, p. 183. LDB on Jane Addams: LDB to Arthur M. Holcombe, October 3, 1912, BP, NMF 53-2; to Charles H. Davis, October 4, 1912, BP, NMF 53-2; cf. Lief, *Brandeis*, p. 210.

31. 1912 description: Lief, *Brandeis*, p. 256; *Life and Labor:* LDB to Alice Henry, February 10, 1913, BP, NMF 8-3.

32. LDB, telegram to Caroline I. Hibbard, March 18, 1913, BP, NMF 37-3.

33. LDB to Alice Blackwell, October 6, 1914, BP, NMF 47-3. *The Women's Journal*: LDB to Agnes E. Ryan, September 30, 1915, BP, NMF 47-3. Experience: to Mrs. F. W. Wile, June 19, 1915, BP, NMF 47-3.

34. Daughter: Lief, *Brandeis*, p. 339. Rights and duties: Lief, *Brandeis*, pp. 340–341; cf. LDB to Alfred, October 22, 1915, BP, M 4-1.

35. Alice: interview, *Boston American*, February 2, 1913, BP, Scrapbook II. Her health and LDB's encouragement of his daughters: interview with Elizabeth Brandeis Raushenbush, September 24, 1980.

9. Progressivism

1. Mason, *Brandeis*, p. 257; Lief, *Brandeis*, p. 159. The next few pages draw upon the very comprehensive account in Alpheus T. Mason, *Bureaucracy Convicts Itself* (New York: Viking Press, 1941).

2. Taft's letter to Ballinger: U.S., Congress, Senate, *Hearings before Committee of Investigation of Interior Department and Bureau of Forestry*, 61st Cong., 3rd sess., S. Doc. 719, vol. 8, p. 4507.

3. Mason, *Brandeis*, pp. 256–257; Lief, *Brandeis*, pp. 156–159; Norman Hapgood, *The Changing Years* (New York: Farrar & Rinehart, 1930), pp. 184–186.

4. Mason, *Bureaucracy*, pp. 99–100; Lief, *Brandeis*, p. 162.

5. LDB and journalists: Mason, *Brandeis*, pp. 240, 280–281; Lief, *Brandeis*, p. 163; LDB to Hapgood, February 27, 1910, BP, NMF 28-3; LDB to Mark Sullivan, June 2 and June 4, BP, NMF 28-3. Proofs of editorials: Mason, *Brandeis*, p. 280; LDB to Abbot Lowell, June 16, 1910, BP, NMF 29-4. *Boston Journal*: May 19, 1910, quoted in Mason, *Brandeis*, p. 261. *New York Tribune*: Lief, *Brandeis*, p. 169.

6. LDB to Alfred, April 24 and May 1, 1910, BP, M 3-3.

7. Senate, *Hearings . . . Bureau of Forestry*, p. 4495; Hapgood, *Changing Years*, pp. 186–187.

8. LDB to Regina Wehle Goldmark, March 2, 1910, BP, NMF 28-3. Glavis: LDB to Alfred, January 31, 1910, BP, M 3-3; quoted in Hapgood, *Changing Years*, p. 187. Behrens: LDB to Alfred, March 27, 1910, BP, M 3-3; written brief: to Alfred, June 14, 1910, BP, M 3-3.

9. Oral argument: Senate, *Hearings . . . Bureau of Forestry*, vol. 9, pp. 4903–4923, 5005–5021; cf. Lief, *Brandeis*, pp. 173–175.

10. Hapgood, *Changing Years*, p. 190.

11. Copies of brief: LDB to La Follette, June 13, 1910, BP, NMF 29-3; to Felix Frankfurter, June 14, 1910, BP, NMF 29-4; to Amos Pinchot, June 14, 1910, BP, NMF 28-3; to Henry Stimson, June 15, 1910, BP, NMF 29-3. Baker: *American Magazine*, 70 (July 1910), 361–371; LDB to Baker, June 24, 1910, BP, NMF 29-4. LDB to Finley Peter Dunne, June 24, 1910, BP, NMF 29-4.

12. Stimson to LDB, June 17, 1911, quoted in Mason, *Brandeis*, p. 281. Press as ally: Belle and Fola La Follette, *Robert M. La Follette* (New York: Macmillan, 1953), p. 288. LDB to Walter L. Fisher, March 7, 1911, BP, NMF 25-4.

13. La Follette and La Follette, *La Follette*, pp. 288–295.

14. Belle La Follette to LDB, June 15, 1910, quoted in Mason, *Brandeis*, pp. 367–368.

15. *La Follette*, pp. 290–291, 295, 296, 369; Mason, *Brandeis*, p. 368; Urofsky, *Mind of One Piece*, pp. 82–84.

16. Mason, *Brandeis*, pp. 282–283.

17. Myrtle Abbott's articles appeared, e.g., in the *Philadelphia North American*, July 7, 1911. Missing letter: Mason, *Brandeis*, pp. 283–284.

18. LDB to James Graham, July 21, 1911, BP, NMF 39-1; to Graham, July 27, BP, NMF 36-8; to John Lathrop, August 2, BP, NMF 39-1; to William Colver, July 15, BP, NMF 39-1; Mason, *Brandeis*, pp. 282–289.

19. LDB to Herbert Putnam, August 2, 1911, BP, NMF 39-1; to La Follette, July 29, BP, SC 1-2; to Gifford Pinchot, July 29, BP, NMF 39-1; to Amos Pinchot, August 2, BP, NMF 39-1. Lathrop: LDB to Lathrop, July 28, 1911, BP, NMF 39-1. Pinchot and Fisher: Mason, *Brandeis*, p. 288; cf. LDB to Graham, November 27, 1911, BP, NMF 38-6.

20. LDB to Robert La Follette, July 29, 1911, BP, SC 1-2; cf. LDB to Lathrop, July 28, 1911, BP, NMF 39-1, mentioning discussion with La Follette; LDB to Gifford Pinchot, July 29, 1911, BP, NMF 39-1.

21. LDB to La Follette, July 29, 1911, BP, SC 1-2.

22. Ibid.

23. LDB to Gifford Pinchot, July 29, 1911, BP, NMF 31-1.

24. LDB to Amos Pinchot, August 2, 1911, BP, NMF 39-1; to La Follette, July 31, 1911, BP, NMF 39-1. Senate Resolution 144, *Congressional Record*, 62nd Cong., 1st sess., vol. 5, pp. 4197, 4262–4305. Fisher's speech: LDB to James Graham, November 27, 1911, BP, NMF 38-6; Mason, *Brandeis*, p. 288.

25. Senate bills: Smith bill, S. 6275; coal mines bill S. 3124, amended December 11, 1912. Cf. LDB to Overton Price, May 1, 1912, and to Joseph Bristow, May 13, 1912, both BP, NMF 44-7. Congratulations: LDB to Hapgood, June 27, 1911, BP, NMF 29-4; to Amos Pinchot, June 27, *Letters*, II, 458; to Gifford Pinchot, June 28, BP, NMF 29-4.

26. LDB to Hapgood, September 7, 1911, BP, NMF 39-1.

27. La Follette to LDB, December 30, 1910, with accompanying transcript, BP, SC 1-2.

28. *Standard Oil* v. *United States*, 221 U.S. 1 (1911). Telegrams: La Follette to LDB, May 16, 1911; LDB to La Follette, May 22; both BP, SC 1-2. LDB to

La Follette, May 26 and June 13, 1911, BP, SC 1-2. LDB to Moses Clapp, June 22, 1911, BP, NMF 43-4.

29. Details of bill: LDB to Edwin Grozier, September 19, 1911, BP, NMF 43-4; to James Studley, January 22, 1912, BP, NMF 43-3. The "Stanley" of the bill was Representative Augustus O. Stanley of Kentucky, who worked with Brandeis on antitrust matters again in 1914, and who later became a senator.

30. LDB on Perkins: to Isaac MacVeagh, December 19, 1911, BP, NMF 43-4.

31. LDB, "Competition," in *American Legal News*, 44 (January 1913), 5-14, reprinted in LDB, *Bigness*, pp. 112–124. The quotation is on p. 115.

32. LDB, "Competition," in *Bigness*, pp. 116–117.

33. LDB's comments on the bill, discussed in this and subsequent paragraphs: U.S., Congress, Senate, Committee on Interstate Commerce, *Hearings on Control of Corporations, Persons, and Firms Engaged in Interstate Commerce*, 62nd Cong., 2nd sess., 1911, vol. 1, pt. 16, pp. 1146–1291.

34. LDB, *Bigness*, p. 116.

35. LDB, "The Regulation of Competition Against the Regulation of Monopoly," reprinted in *Bigness*, p. 110.

36. LDB, *Bigness*, pp. 119–120; LDB, "Trusts and Efficiency," *Collier's Weekly*, September 14, 1912, reprinted in LDB, *Business*, pp. 198–217; LDB, "Trusts and the Export Trade," *Collier's Weekly*, September 21, 1912, reprinted in *Business*, pp. 218–235; LDB, "The Solution of the Trust Problem," *Harper's*, November 8, 1913, reprinted in LDB, *Bigness*, pp. 128–136; LDB, "Competition That Kills," *Harper's*, November 15, 1913, reprinted in *Business*, pp. 236–254. Cf. LDB to Charles Crane, November 11, 1911, *Letters*, II, 510–511.

37. Gary's comment quoted in Lief, *Brandeis*, p. 221.

38. McNamaras: LDB to the Editor of the Boston Globe, December 2, 1911, BP, NMF 8-3; Senate, *Hearings . . . in Interstate Commerce*.

39. Cf. Alfred D. Chandler, Jr., *The Visible Hand* (Cambridge: Harvard University Press, 1977). For a view closer to LDB's than Chandler's, see Rosabeth Moss Kantor, *The Change Masters: Innovation for Productivity in the American Corporation* (New York: Simon & Schuster, 1983).

40. Senate, *Hearings . . . in Interstate Commerce*.

41. Friends: Lief, *Brandeis*, p. 221. U.S., Congress, House, *Hearings before the Committee on Investigation of United States Steel Corp.*, 26th Cong., 3rd sess., 1912, Rep. 1137. Brandeis's testimony, presented on January 29–30, 1912, is at pp. 2835–2872.

42. Mason, *Brandeis*, pp. 368–371.

43. Permission: LDB to La Follette, December 19, 1911, BP, SC 1-2. LDB to Edwin Grozier, September 19, 1911, BP, NMF 43-4. *American Magazine*: LDB to John S. Phillips, September 18, 1911, BP, NMF 34-1.The autobiography ran in the magazine from October 1911 through July 1912. Contribution: LDB to Charles E. Ware, Jr., December 21, 1911, BP, NMF 34-1.

44. Campaign manager: LDB to Walter L. Houser, December 21 and 27, 1911, BP, NMF 34-1. *Cleveland Plain Dealer*, January 2, 1912, quoted in Mason, *Brandeis*, p. 371; La Follette and La Follette, *La Follette*, pp. 343–344, 374;

Chicago Tribune, January 4, 1912, and *Chicago Record-Herald*, January 3, 1912, quoted in Mason, *Brandeis*, pp. 371–372, cf. *La Follette's Weekly*, February 3, 1912, p. 5.

45. Campaigning: LDB to Alfred, January 6, 1912, BP, M 3-3.

46. LDB to Alice Grady, January 9, 1912, BP, NMF 43-1.

47. LDB to Belle, February 7, 1912, *Letters*, II, 542; to Alfred, February 7, 1912, BP, M 3-3; to Fola La Follette, August 31, 1937, quoted in La Follette and La Follette, *La Follette*, p. 366.

48. LDB to Amos Pinchot, February 13, 1912, BP, NMF 34-1, cf. Mason, *Brandeis*, p. 373. LDB to George Rublee, March 16, 1912, BP, NMF 34-1; LDB to La Follette, July 3, 1912, BP, SC 1-2. Arthur Link, *Wilson: The Road to the White House* (Princeton: Princeton University Press, 1968), p. 468 n. LDB cable to La Follette: November 6, 1912, BP, NMF 52-2.

49. Belle La Follette to LDB, May 29, 1912; LDB to Belle, May 31; LDB to La Follette, July 3; all BP, SC 1-2; cf. Mason, *Brandeis*, pp. 373–374.

50. 1916 Senate campaign: *La Follette*, p. 580; LDB to La Follette, September 6, 1916, *Letters*, II, 257; Alice to Belle, October 4, 1917, *Letters*, II, 314, n. 1; LDB to La Follette, November 24, 1918, *Letters*, II, 364.

51. LDB to Alfred, July 19, 1924, BP, M 4-4; Alice Brandeis to Belle La Follette, July 16, 1924, quoted *La Follette*, p. 1115; Alice on La Follette: *La Follette's Magazine*, October 1924, p. 146 and *New York Times*, October 15, 1924; cf. *La Follette*, p. 1116.

52. LDB to Alfred, June 20, 1925, *Letters*, V, 169, n. 1. Biography: LDB to Fola, December 30, 1937, *Letters*, V, 592; LDB to Bernard Flexner, May 15, 1941, *Letters*, V, 652.

53. LDB and WW: LDB to Alfred, August 29, 1912, BP, M 3-3; Link, Wilson: *The Road to the White House*, pp. 488–493.

10. Worker-Participation

1. LDB to E. Louise Malloch, November 4, 1907, BP, NMF 1-H-1; McClennen, "Brandeis as Lawyer," p. 24.

2. The story of the New Haven battle is told in Henry Lee Staples and Alpheus T. Mason, *The Fall of a Railroad Empire* (Syracuse: Syracuse University Press, 1947). Cf. Mason, *Brandeis*, p. 210; U.S., Congress, *Financial Transactions of the New York and Hartford Railroad*, 63rd Cong., 2nd sess., S. Doc. 543, pp. 37–38. The journal *Truth* was set up in part for this purpose and financed by Mellon. See Mason, *Brandeis*, pp. 210, 386.

3. Oscar Kraines, "Brandeis' Philosophy of Scientific Management," *Western Political Quarterly*, 13 (March 1960), p. 192; LDB to Rudolph G. Leeds, November 9, 1910, *Letters*, II, 383–385; cf. LDB to Amos Pinchot, November 14, 1910, *Letters*, II, 386. Gantt's series appeared in *Engineering Magazine*, 39 (January–June 1910).

4. Mason, *Brandeis*, p. 316; LDB brief: *Scientific Management and the Railroads* (New York: Engineering Magazine, 1911); Mason, *Brandeis*, p. 323;

Kraines, "Brandeis' Philosophy," p. 192; LDB to Horace B. Drury, January 31, 1914, *Letters*, III, 240–241.

5. LDB, *Scientific Management*, pp. 8, 9, 12–14, 17–22, 40–42.

6. Ibid., pp. 48–50.

7. Ibid., pp. 14–15, 35–36, 37–47.

8. Ibid., pp. 55, 57–60.

9. Telegram, November 3, 1910, quoted in Mason, *Brandeis*, p. 328; November 29, 1910, quoted in Mason, *Brandeis*, pp. 328–329.

10. *New York Times*, November 30, 1910, quoted in Mason, *Brandeis*, p. 330; *Tribune*, November 22, 1910, quoted in Mason, *Brandeis*, p.331; articles about Brandeis; Mason, *Brandeis*, p. 329; LDB to Alfred, December 5, 1910, BP, M 3-3.

11. LDB, *Scientific Management*, pp. 62, 63, 68, 69, 74, 76, 77, 83–88.

12. *New York Times*, February 24, 1911, *Letters*, II, 412, n. 2; LDB to FF, February 27, 1911, *Letters*, II, 412.

13. Kraines, "Brandeis' Philosophy," p. 191; cf. clippings in BP, Scrapbooks, "Advance Rate Case," numbers 2-4; Lippmann and Croly: Samuel Haber, *Efficiency and Uplift: Scientific Management in the Progressive Era 1890–1920* (Chicago: University of Chicago Press, 1964), especially p. xi and chap. 5. Frank B. Gilbreth, *Primer of Scientific Management* (New York: Van Nostrand, 1912).

14. Mason, *Brandeis*, pp. 331, 332; Lief, *Brandeis*, p. 222.

15. LDB to John Mitchell, December 12, 1910, *Letters*, II, 394–395; Mitchell in *New York Times*, December 11, 1910, quoted in *Letters*, II, 395, n. 1; LDB to Mitchell, January 2, 1911, *Letters*, II, 398.

16. LDB, "Organized Labor and Efficiency," *The Survey*, 26 (April 22, 1911), pp. 148–151, reprinted in LDB, *Business*, pp. 37–50; LDB to Ralph M. Easley, February 8, 1905, BP, NMF 12-1; *Boston Globe*, February 6, 1905, BP, NMF 12-1; "An Economic Exhortation to Organized Labor," *National Civic Federation Monthly Review*, 1 (March 1905); LDB to Norman H. White, April 29, 1907, *Letters*, I, 560; to Samuel Gompers, July 17, 1907, *Letters*, II, 14; to Mark Sullivan, March 27, 1908, *Letters*, II, 112.

17. Address to the New York Economic Club: "The New Conception of Industrial Efficiency," *Journal of Accountancy*, 12 (May 1911), 35–42; cf. LDB to Richard L. Barnum, March 25, 1911, BP, NMF 38-4. LDB, "Organized Labor," in *Business*, pp. 41–42, 47, 48, 50.

18. Lief, *Brandeis*, p. 223.

19. Typescript quoting Bill Haywood, FF-LC Box 128.

20. Interview with Elizabeth Brandeis Raushenbush, September 24, 1980.

21. LDB to Gifford Pinchot, December 19, 1910, BP, NMF 29-4; LDB to FF, January 28, 1913, *Letters*, III, 19–20.

22. LDB to Charles F. Pidgin, July 25, 1905, BP, NMF 13-1; to Editor, *New York Times Annualist*, January 5, 1914, *Letters*, III, 230; to Arthur O. Taylor, January 19, 1916, BP, NMF 56-4. The book was: Taylor, *Persistent Public Problems: Unemployment Social and Industrial Righteousness* (Boston: Vail Ballou, 1916).

23. LDB, "The Road to Social Efficiency," address, June 8, 1911, in Boston; printed in *Outlook*, 98 (June 10, 1911); reprinted in LDB, *Business*, pp. 51–64; cf. LDB to Lawrence Abbott, May 17, 1911, BP, NMF 33-3; LDB to Mary B. Sumner, March 12, 1912, BP, NMF 23-1.

24. Testimony before Stanley Committee, January 1912, published as "Our New Peonage: Discretionary Pensions," *The Independent*, 72 (July 25, 1912), 187–191; reprinted in LDB, *Business*, pp. 65–81; LDB to Henry T. Noyes, April 17, 1912, BP, NMF 47-2; Boston & Maine pension plan: LDB to Arthur P. Kellogg, May 26, 1909, BP, NMF 26-2; cf. to Hapgood, Hamilton Hodd, Oswald Garrison Villard, and Samuel Bowles, same date; printed, slightly revised, as "Boston and Maine Pensions," *The Survey*, 22 (June 19, 1909), 436.

25. Senate, *Hearings . . . on Interstate Commerce*, vol. 1, pp. 1146–1291, particularly pp. 1151–1152, 1184–1185.

26. Ibid.

27. LDB to Cornelia L. Warren, August 29, 1911, BP, NMF 69-2; to Elizabeth G. Evans, December 22, 1911, BP, NMF 69-2.

28. Speech to Massachusetts AFL: printed in *La Follette's Weekly*, October 12, 1912, cf. LDB to John J. Chapman, September 17, 1911, BP, NMF 50-3; police power: LDB to William Scallon, November 4, 1912, BP, NMF 53-1. Experimentation in states: LDB to Mary McDowell, July 8, 1912, BP, NMF 69-2. *Stettler* v. *O'Hara*, 69 Oregon 519 (1914).

29. Minimum wage law for adult male workers: LDB to John C. Barrett, February 24, 1915, BP, NMF, 69-2. LDB argument before the United States Supreme Court: *Stettler* v. *O'Hara*, 243 U.S. 629, December 17, 1914, published as "The Constitution and the Minimum Wage," *The Survey*, 33 (February 7, 1915), 490–494, 521–524; reprinted in LDB, *Bigness*, pp. 52–69.

30. LDB to Cornelia L. Warren, March 10, 1900, BP, NMF 2-2; LDB to Lorin F. Deland, February 9, 1895, paraphrased in LDB, *Brandeis Guide*, p. 161; LDB, "Shall We Abandon the Policy of Competition?" article in *Case and Comment*, 18 (February 1912), 494–496, reprinted in LDB, *Bigness*, pp. 104–108.

31. LDB to George M. Price, August 30, 1911, BP, NMF 36-1; Mason, *Brandeis*, p. 291; Lief, *Brandeis*, pp. 184–185.

32. Mason, *Brandeis*, p. 291; Lief, *Brandeis*, pp. 184–185.

33. Lief, *Brandeis*, p. 184; Mason, *Brandeis*, p. 292; Gal, *Brandeis*, p. 124.

34. Mason, *Brandeis*, pp. 291–292; Lief, *Brandeis*, pp. 183–184; LDB to Alfred, July 24, 1910, BP, M 3-3.

35. Lief, *Brandeis*, pp. 185–186; Mason, *Brandeis*, pp. 292–293.

36. Mason, *Brandeis*, pp. 294–300; Lief, *Brandeis*, pp. 186–188.

37. Mason, *Brandeis*, pp. 300–302; Lief, *Brandeis*, pp. 188–191; Edith F. Wyatt "The New York Cloak-makers' Strike," *McClure's*, 34 (April 1911), 708–711; John Bruce McPherson, "The New York Cloakmakers' Strike," *Journal of Political Economy*, 19 (March 1911), 153–187; cf. LDB to Price, August 30, 1911, BP, NMF 36-1.

38. Jane Addams to LDB, November 21, 1910, BP, NMF 33-1; LDB to Jane Addams, November 26, 1910, BP, NMF 33-1; Julius H. Cohen to LDB,

October 6, 1911, BP, NMF 42-4; LDB to Cohen, October 7, 1911, BP, NMF 42-4; Mason, *Brandeis*, p. 303.

39. LDB to Abbott, September 6, 1910, BP, NMF 33-5. Articles in *Cloak and Suit Review*: January 1911, p. 159, reprinted in LDB, *Bigness*, p. 266; March 1911, p. 106, reprinted in LDB, *Bigness*, p. 266; March 1911, p. 106, reprinted in LDB, *Bigness*, p. 191. LDB to Steffens et al.: February 26, 1912, BP, NMF 55-1; LDB to MacKenzie, January 22, 1913, BP, NMF 55-1; Belle Case La Follette and Caroline L. Hunt, "An Epoch-Making Report," *La Follette's Weekly*, 3 (December 2, 1911), 10–11; Henry Moskowitz, "An Experiment in Industrial Control," 5 (April 19, 1913), 13–14.

40. LDB to Julian Mack, October 3, 1916, quoted in Mason, *Brandeis*, p. 314; John A. Dyche to LDB, February 9, 1915, quoted in Mason, *Brandeis*, p. 312; LDB to Dyche, February 11, 1915, BP, NMF 67-2; Mason, *Brandeis*, p. 312; LDB to Dyche, February 11, 1915, BP, NMF 67-2; Mason, *Brandeis*, p. 314.

41. LDB to George M. Price, August 30, 1911, BP, NMF 36-1.

42. LDB to Mack, October 13, 1916, quoted in Mason, *Brandeis*, p. 314; to Howard White, February 6, 1913, BP, NMF 8-3; to Roy Painer, March 31, 1913, BP, NMF 55-1; to William T. Donaldson, October 1, 1913, BP, NMF 5-1.

43. Story recounted by Milton R. Konvitz, "Louis D. Brandeis," in *Great Jewish Personalities in Modern Times*, ed. Simon Noveck (Washington, D.C.: B'nai Brith, 1960), p. 300.

44. Lief, *Brandeis*, p. 187.

45. LDB, "The Preferential Shop: A Letter from Louis D. Brandeis," *Human Engineering*, 2 (August 1912), 179–181.

46. LDB to Maurice Barnett, May 26, 1913, BP, NMF 47-2; to Dix W. Smith, November 5, 1913, BP, NMF 47-2; to Arthur Williams, November 17, 1913, BP, NMF 4-1.

47. Testimony: U.S., Congress, Senate, Commission on Industrial Relations, S. Doc. 415, 64th Cong., 1st sess. Serial 6936, pp. 7657–7681, hereafter *Commission*; portions reprinted as "On Industrial Relations" in LDB, *Bigness*, pp. 70–95. Corporations: *Commission*, pp. 7658–7659; political democracy, pp. 7659–7660.

48. *Commission*, p. 7660.

49. Ibid., pp. 7660, 7664.

50. Ibid., p. 7665.

51. Ibid.

52. Ibid., pp. 7666, 7669.

53. Ibid., p. 7663.

54. Scientific management before 1920: Haber, *Efficiency and Uplift*, pp. 160–166.

55. Progressivism as a conservative movement: Haber, *Efficiency and Uplift*, p. xi; Melvin I. Urofsky, *Louis D. Brandeis and the Progressive Tradition* (Boston: Little, Brown, 1981), pp. 18, 21, 22.

56. LDB interview, *La Follette's Weekly Magazine*, May 24, 1913, p. 5, reprinted in LDB, *Bigness*, pp. 43–47.

57. Beatrice Potter, *The Cooperative Movement in Great Britain* (London: Swan Sonnenschein, 1899), pp. 118, 127, 138, 139.

58. Sidney and Beatrice Webb: *The Decay of Capitalist Civilization* (New York: Harcourt, Brace, 1923); cf. LDB to FF, April 6, 1923, *Letters*, V, 90. LDB to Elizabeth B. Raushenbush, August 7, 1923, *Letters*, V, 99. The reference is to John L. and Barbara Hammond, *The Town Labourer* (London: Longmans, Green, 1917). The Webb's book on cooperatives was Sidney and Beatrice Webb, *The Consumer's Cooperative Movement* (London and New York: Longmans, Green, 1921). LDB to Laski, November 29, 1929, BP, M 18-3. Laski, *The Recovery of Citizenship* (London: E. Benn, 1928).

59. LDB to C. H. Hubbert, December 27, 1911, BP, NMF 47-21; LDB's remarks in *Boston America*, November 19 and 23, 1911; LDB editorial in *New York American*, November 28, 1911; LDB to Albert Sonnicken, July 16, 1913, BP, NMF 59-7; cf. to Bernard A. Rosenblatt, July 24, 1913, BP, NMF 11-2. Producer's cooperatives: LDB to FF, September 30, 1922, *Letters*, V, 65–67; cf. dissent in *Liggett* v. *Lee*, 288 U.S. 517, 579 (1933). Scandinavia: Lief, *Brandeis*, p. 479. Denmark: LDB to Hapgood, March 2, 1915, BP, NMF 62-1; Alice Goldmark and Josephine Goldmark, *Democracy in Denmark* (Washington, D.C.: National Home Library Foundation, 1936). Cf. LDB to Josephine, January 8, 1932, BP, M 7-2, on obtaining information about Denmark from the Danish ambassador. Literature: LDB to Hapgood, March 2, 1915, BP, NMF 62-1; to Isaac Netzorg, February 23, 1912, BP, NMF 47-2; to Laski, November 29, 1928, PB, M 18-3. *Boston Post*, February 14, 1915, BP, Scrapbook II.

60. *Boston Post*, February 14, 1915.

61. Ibid.

62. Hapgood, *Changing Years*, pp. 290–296, 393–394; LDB to Hapgood, May 14, 1917, *Letters*, IV, 292.

63. Brandeis's interest in worker-participation was confirmed by Roger Baldwin in an interview (May 19, 1981). See also Baldwin, "Affirmation of Democracy," *Jewish Frontier* 3 (November 1936), 10.

64. Mason, *Brandeis*, p. 585; LDB to Henry Bruère, February 25, 1922, BP, NMF 15.

65. BP-HLS Box 114-7, also in FF-LC Box 224, p. 4. LDB to George Soule, April 22, 1923, BP, SC 6-2; to FF, February 12, 1926, *Letters*, V, 207.

66. On the Triangle fire: see Leon Stein, *The Triangle Fire* (Philadelphia: Lippincott, 1962). *Commission*, p. 769. LDB to Alfred, March 23, 1917 and March 25, 1919, BP, M 4-1; to Alice, March 15, 1917, *Letters*, IV, 276, and June 13, 1919, *Letters*, IV, 398; to Hapgood, May 14, 1917, *Letters*, IV, 293.

67. LDB to Bruère, February 25, 1922, BP, NMF 15; LDB, *Bigness*, p. 35; *Commission*, p. 7665.

11. Wilson and the New Freedom

1. LDB to Charles Amidon, July 3, 1912, BP, NMF 40-1; LDB to Hapgood, July 3, BP, NMF 53-2. For platform: Arthur Link, *Wilson: The Road to the White House* (Princeton: Princeton University Press, 1947), chap. 13.

2. LDB to Hapgood, July 3, 1912, BP, NMF 53-2; to Gifford Pinchot, July

8, 1912, BP, NMF 53-2; to Charles Amidon, July 3, 1912, BP, NMF 40-10; to Pinchot, July 8, 1912, BP, NMF 53-2; cf. LDB to Arthur Wray, July 15, 1912, BP, NMF 53-2; LDB to Alfred, July 10, 1912, BP, M 3-3.

3. LDB to Woodrow Wilson, BP, NMF 35-2; LDB to Hapgood, August 1, 1912, BP, NMF 53-2. On Redfield: Lief, *Brandeis*, p. 250. Woodrow Wilson to LDB, August 7, 1912, quoted in Mason, *Brandeis*, p. 377. Their discussion: *New York Times*, August 29, 1912, quoted in Melvin I. Urofsky, "Wilson, Brandeis and the Trust Issue, 1912–1914," *Mid-America*, 49 (January 1967), 7–8; cf. Lief, *Brandeis*, p. 251. LDB's trip: LDB to Alfred, August 29, 1912, BP, M 3-3; LDB to Ray Stannard Baker, September 17, 1926, BP, NMF 86-1.

4. For Wilson's thought see Alexander and Juliette George, *Woodrow Wilson and Colonel House* (New York: John Day, 1956); Arthur S. Link, *Woodrow Wilson and the Progressive Era* (New York: Harper and Brothers, 1954); William Diamond, *The Economic Thought of Woodrow Wilson* (Baltimore: Johns Hopkins University Press, 1943); for Wilson and trusts: Ray Stannard Baker, *Woodrow Wilson: Life and Letters*, 8 vols. (Garden City, N.Y.: Doubleday, Doran, 1931–1939), III, 398. LDB to Alfred, September 17, 1926, BP, NMF 86-1. New Freedom: Link, *Wilson and Progressive Era*, pp. 20–21, 28, 48.

5. Urofsky, "Wilson, Brandeis," pp. 4–6; Link, *Wilson: Road*, pp. 487–492.

6. Urofsky, "Wilson, Brandeis," p. 8; Link, *Wilson and Progressive Era*, p. 20; Link, *Wilson: Road*, p. 510. Tremont Temple: Lief, *Brandeis*, p. 254; Link, *Wilson: Road*, p. 509.

7. WW to LDB, September 27, 1912, BP, M-17; LDB to WW, September 30, 1912, *Letters*, II, 686–694; LDB to WW, September 28, 1912, *Letters*, II, 685.

8. LDB, "Trusts, Efficiency and the New Party," *Collier's*, 49 (September 14, 1912), p. 14; "Trusts, the Export Trade, and the New Party," *Collier's*, 50 (September 21, 1912), p. 10. Editorials: LDB to Hapgood, September 4, 1912, BP, NMF 46-3, September 25, 1912, BP, NMF 50-3, and October 2, 1912, BP, NMF 52-2. Speeches: LDB to Ray Stannard Baker, September 17, 1926, BP, NMF 86-1. LDB said he was told about WW's reading at the time by Wilson's aide Dudley Field Malone. See LDB to Baker, July 5, 1931, *Letters*, V, 482; Baker, *Wilson*, III, 366; Urofsky, "Wilson, Brandeis," p. 10. "Body of laws," quoted in Urofsky, "Wilson, Brandeis," p. 10.

9. *Boston Journal*, September 24, 1912, BP, NMF 49-13. LDB on WW: to Hapgood, September 14, 1912, BP, NMF 46-3; to Arthur Holcombe, September 11, 1912, BP, NMF 50-3. On Roosevelt speaking: Solomon Goldman, ed., *The Words of Justice Brandeis* (New York: Schumann, 1953), p. 159; cf. Lief, *Brandeis*, p. 253.

10. LDB to McAdoo, October 2, 1912, BP, NMF 52-2.

11. "Regulation of Competition": LDB to Alice, October 11, 1912, *Letters*, II, 702; sermon: LDB to Alfred, October 15, 1912, BP, M 3-3; Cleveland Chamber of Commerce: quoted in Mason, *Brandeis*, p. 383; Minneapolis: LDB to Alfred, October 25, 1912, Mason, *Brandeis*, p. 384; Economic Club: LDB to Alfred, November 2, 1912, BP, M 3-3.

12. *Collier's* debacle: e.g., LDB to Collier, November 3, 7, 11, and 14, 1912, all BP, NMF 52-1. *Harper's Weekly*: to Hapgood, January 2 and 28, 1913, BP, NMF 52-1; to Crane, February 15, 1913, BP, NMF 52-1.

13. Holcombe to LDB, September 30, 1912, BP, NMF 53-2; LDB to Holcombe, October 3, 1912, BP, NMF 53-2; "political campaigning": LDB to Robert Collier, November 14, 1912, BP, NMF 52-1; "unique": to Alfred, September 15, 1912, BP, M 3-3; "not a politician": quoted in Lief, *Brandeis*, p. 257; LDB to Hapgood, September 14, 1912, BP, NMF 46-3.

14. LDB to Alfred, July 28, 1912, BP, M 3-3. LDB to Moskowitz, September 17, 1912, BP, NMF 35-2. Perkins: LDB to Arthur K. Stone, September 4, 1912, BP, NMF 52-2; to Edwin Mead, September 4, 1912, BP, NMF 34-2; to Moses Clapp, September 11, 1912, BP, NMF 52-2. Jane Addams: LDB to Charles H. Davis, October 4, 1912, BP, NMF 53-2. The quote is from *Richard III*. Cf. LDB to Arthur Holcombe, October 2, 1912, BP, NMF 53-2. Rublee, etc.: to Alfred, July 29, 1912, BP, M 3-3.

15. LDB to Pinchot, August 8, 1912, *Letters*, II, 660; LDB to Charles Zueblin, October 1, 1912, BP, NMF 51-6.

16. LDB to WW, November 6, 1912, BP, NMF 52-2; WW to LDB, November 19, 1912, *Letters*, II, 709; LDB to Alfred, November 7, 1912, BP, NMF M 3-3. LDB to Pinchot, November 11, 1912, BP, NMF 51-7; LDB to Pinchot, December 5, 1912, BP, NMF 52-2.

17. LDB on Woodrow Wilson's speech: to Alfred, December 18, 1912, BP, M 3-3.

18. Arthur S. Link, *Wilson: The New Freedom* (Princeton: Princeton University Press, 1956), p. 10. Tobacconists: Vincent Farley to LDB, November 9, 1912, BP, NMF 52-2. *Good Housekeeping*: LDB to Harvey Wiley, December 9, 1912, BP, NMF 52-2. Private citizen: LDB to Mrs. Charles Edward Russell, February 14, 1912, quoted in Mason, *Brandeis*, p. 385.

19. LDB to Alfred, July 10, 1912, BP, M 3-3; cf. to Raymond Pullman, July 17, 1912, BP, NMF 53-2. *Detroit Times*, July 13, 1912, quoted in *Letters*, II, 651, n. 1.

20. LDB's reading is reflected in the following: bill from Old Corner Book Store for *Fortnightly Review, Lord Kelvin, Disraeli*, vol. 2, October 1, 1912, BP, Addendum, Box 14, folder 14-15a; bills from Old Corner Book Store for *Disraeli, Up from Slavery,* and *Pioneer Work for Women*, January 1, 1915, February 1, 1915, March 1, 1916, BP, Addendum, Box 15, folder 15-11a, and Box 17, folder 17-2b; bill from Charles E. Lauriat Co. Booksellers for *Philip the King, Cavour, Historical Geography* and *Greek Tradition*, April 1, 1916, BP, Addendum, Box 17, folder 17-12b; bill from U. Holzer, Book-Binder, for *Vu de Pasteur*, March 23, 1916, BP, Addendum, Box 17, folder 17-12c; subscriptions to the *Journal of the American Institute of Criminal Law and Criminology* (letter, May 25, 1917, BP, Addendum, Box 19, folder 19-18b), *National Municipal Review* (letter, May 24, 1918, BP, Addendum, Box 19, folder 19-18b). Canoeing: LDB to Alfred, August 31, 1912, BP, M 3-3. Wilson's breakdown: letter from Willard Hurst to author, October 3, 1980.

21. LDB to Alfred, March 2, 1913, BP, unmarked folder; to Hapgood, July

9, 1913, BP, NMF 52-1. Both quotes are in Hapgood, *The Changing Years*, p. 191.

22. LDB to Hapgood, July 9, 1913, BP, NMF 52-1. Melvin I. Urofsky, *American Zionism from Herzl to the Holocaust* (Garden City, N.Y.: Doubleday, 1975), pp. 11, 116; Link, *Wilson and the Progressive Era*, pp. 28–31.

23. LDB to Hapgood, July 9, 1913, BP, NMF 52-1; see also LDB to Alfred, March 2, 1913, BP, unmarked folder.

24. LDB to McReynolds, March 5, 1913, BP, NMF 33-2; to Redfield, March 5, 1913, BP, NMF 53-2. Approval of McReynolds: Lief, *Brandeis*, p. 261; LDB to Moses Clapp and to Gibson Gardner, March 5, 1913, BP, NMF 53-2. Redfield's book was *The New Industrial Day: A Book for Men Who Employ Men* (New York: Century, 1912).

25. Intending to call: to McReynolds, March 5, 1913, BP, NMF 33-2, and Redfield, March 5, 1913, BP, NMF 53-2; LDB to Alfred, March 10, 1913, BP, unmarked folder; to Hapgood, March 12, 1913, BP, NMF 53-2. Advising about appointments: to McReynolds, March 29, 1913, BP, NMF 53-2; to John Hobart Marble, March 4, 1913, BP, NMF 53-2; to Franklin K. Lane, March 5, 1913, BP, NMF 53-2; to Hapgood, March 12, 1913, BP, NMF 53-2; to McAdoo, April 14, 1913, *Letters*, III, 61; to McAdoo, May 12, 1913, *Letters*, III, 85; to McAdoo, May 22, 1913, BP, NMF 58-1; to WW, May 26, 1913, *Letters*, III, 97–98; to WW, May 27, 1913, *Letters*, III, 104; to La Follette, June 16, 1913, *Letters*, III, 119; to McAdoo, July 17, 1913, BP, NMF 58-1; to McAdoo, July 23, 1913, *Letters*, III, 148; to McAdoo, July 30, 1913, BP, NMF 58-1; to McReynolds, August 13, 1913, BP, NMF 58-1; to McAdoo, September 13, 1913, BP, NMF 58-1; to McAdoo, September 13, 1913, *Letters*, III, 170; to McReynolds, September 25, 1913, BP, NMF 58-1; to WW, October 10, 1913, *Letters*, III, 194; to Lane, October 15, 1913, BP, NMF 58-1; to McReynolds, October 18, 1913, BP, NMF 58-1. Commission on Industrial Relations: LDB to WW, April 29, 1913, *Letters*, III, 76; to WW, May 19, 1913, *Letters*, III, 87–88. The letters, sent a week apart, might seem to indicate that Brandeis thought seriously about the offer. In fact, however, he deferred his decision for a week after the offer was made only because he was once again busy with the ICC hearings and did not have time to write the kind of letter he wished. Cf. Lief, *Brandeis*, p. 272.

26. Meetings with administration officials: to Redfield, June 12, 1913, *Letters*, III, 112; to Joseph Davies, June 16, 1913, BP, NMF 59-7; to McAdoo, July 15, 1913, BP, NMF 51-1; to McAdoo, July 30, 1913, BP, NMF 58-1; to McAdoo, August 9, 1913, *Letters*, III, 160–1; to McReynolds, August 13, 1913, BP, NMF 58-1; to Redfield, November 17, 1913, *Letters*, III, 211–4; to Alice, December 15, 1913, *Letters*, III, 221; to Alice, December 18, 1913, *Letters*, III, 224; to Alice, December 28, 1913, *Letters*, III, 227; to Alice, December 30, 1913, *Letters*, III, 228. Also see to Redfield, May 21, 1913, BP, NMF 53-1. LDB to Alfred, June 8, 1913, BP, unmarked folder. "Norman H" is Hapgood; "Crane" is Charles Crane. His speech in Baltimore, at a meeting of the Associated Advertising Clubs, was about morality in business. The Supreme Court decision, "all wrong," was *Bauer* v. *O'Donnell*, 229 U.S. 1 (1913). Letter to Davies: June 16, 1913, BP, NMF 59-7. Responses to requests: See, e.g., to John Hobart Marble, March 4,

1913, BP, NMF 53-2; to Seeber Edwards, March 12, 1913, BP, NMF 53-2; to Garrett Droppers, April 1, 1913, BP, NMF 58-1; to Frederick Chamberlin, May 23, 1913, BP, NMF 58-1; to Augustus Owsley Stanley, October 3, 1914, *Letters*, III, 311; to Treadwell Cleveland, Jr., November 27, 1914, BP, NMF 66-3; to Charles McCarthy, December 2, 1914, BP, NMF 66-3; to James Clark McReynolds, March 28, 1913, BP, NMF 53-2; to same, August 13, 1913, BP, NMF 58-1; to same, October 18, 1913, BP, NMF 58-1. Cf. Lief, *Brandeis*, p. 298; Mason, *Brandeis*, pp. 404–406.

27. "attention": quoted in Urofsky, "Wilson, Brandeis," p. 15.

28. WW on trusts: ibid., p. 15.

29. Link, *Progressive Era*, p. 48; Urofsky, "Wilson, Brandeis," pp. 15–17.

30. LDB to WW, June 14, 1913, *Letters*, III, 113–5. Federal Reserve bill: Urofsky, "Wilson, Brandeis," p. 18; Mason, *Brandeis*, p. 399; H. Parker Willis, *The Federal Reserve System* (New York: Ronald Press, 1923), passim; Link, *Progressive Era*, p. 48.

31. Baker, *Wilson*, IV, 366.

32. LDB to Lane, December 12, 1913, *Letters*, III, 210–211.

33. The articles referred to are LDB, "A Solution of the Trust Problem," *Harper's*, November 8, 1913, and the other seven *Harper's* articles, printed together as *Other People's Money* (New York: Stokes, 1914, 1932).

34. LDB, "Price Maintenance, Competition That Kills," *Harper's*, November 15, 1913, reprinted in LDB, *Business*, pp. 236–254. For LDB on price maintenance, cf. LDB to John Commons, May 27, 1913, BP, NMF 58-1; to Redfield, May 27, 1913, BP, NMF 58-1.

35. LDB, *Other People's Money*, pp. 36–37.

36. LDB to Lane, December 12, 1913, *Letters*, III, 218–221.

37. LDB to Alfred, January 23, 1913, BP, M 4-1. The ideas were introduced to Congress as the Clayton Bill, on trusts; the Covington Bill, on the FTC; and the Rayburn bill, on the Interstate Commerce Commission.

38. LDB to McReynolds, February 22, 1914, BP, NMF 66-3.

39. George Rublee to LDB, March 13, 1914, BP, NMF 66-3; LDB to Alice, February 27, 1914, *Letters*, III, 259; to Rublee, March 14, 1914, BP, NMF 66-3; "Memorandum from L. D. Brandeis for the President, dictated over the telephone," June 10, 1914, cited in Urofsky, "Wilson, Brandeis," p. 27. Testimony: Urofsky, *Mind of One Piece*, pp. 24–25; Mason, *Brandeis*, p. 402; U.S., Congress, House, Committee on Interstate and Foreign Commerce, *Hearings on H.R. 13305*, Jan. 9, 1915, 63rd Cong., 2nd sess.; U.S., Congress, Senate, Committee on Interstate Commerce, *Hearings on Bills Relating to Trust Legislation*, 63rd Cong., 2nd sess., 1914; U.S., Congress, House Committee on the Judiciary, *Hearings on Trust Legislation*, 63rd Cong., 2nd sess., 1914, Serial VII, p. 16. LDB lobbying: Urofsky, *Mind of One Piece*, p. 27; Link, *Progressive Era*, pp. 71–72.

40. LDB to House, December 31, 1914, *Letters*, III, 393; Link, *Progressive Era*, p. 72, citing Ray Stannard Baker interview with LDB, March 23, 1929. For Brandeis's hopes about personnel and his subsequent disappointment, see also to Henry French Hollis, November 4, 1914, BP, NMF 68-2; to Charles McCarthy, December 2, 1914, BP, NMF 66-3; to WW, March 6, 1915, BP, NMF 68-2; to

NOTES TO PAGES 216–221 449

Rublee, March 20 and 29, 1915, BP, NMF 66-3; to Gilson Gardner, September 7, 1915, BP, NMF 66-3; to William Smyth, September 22, 1915, BP, NMF 66-3; to Charles Crane, October 9, 1915, BP, NMF 66-3; cf. Lief, *Brandeis*, p. 337; Mason, *Brandeis*, pp. 406–407. LDB to Hurley, December 28, 1915, BP, NMF 66-3.

41. LDB to Edwin Alderman, December 15, 1924, Alderman Mss., University of Virginia Library; LDB to Charles McCarthy, November 18, 1914, BP, NMF 11-2; WW in 1914: Link, *New Freedom*, pp. 445–460.

42. LDB to Alderman, December 15, 1924. Cf. Baker, *Woodrow Wilson*, VIII, 316, n. 1, citing LDB's comment to Baker that WW's statement of August 3, 1918, justifying American and Japanese troop involvement in the U.S.S.R., was "unnatural," and the first sign of the effects of overwork and mental strain.

43. Stephen Wise, "Battling with Wilson for Justice to the Jew," *The Jewish Tribune*, March 14, 1924, p. 22.

44. Cosmos Club: Jonathan Daniels: *The End of Innocence* (New York: DaCapo Press, 1972), p. 189. WW using LDB: LDB to WW, August 14, 1916, BP, G 1-1; cf. to Justice Edward D. White on August 9 and 14, 1916, BP, G 1-1.

45. WW's visit: Lief, *Brandeis*, p. 221; Alice Brandeis quoted in Mason, *Brandeis*, pp. 521–522.

46. WW to Woolley quoted in Mason, *Brandeis*, p. 525; WW needing LDB: quoted in Lief, *Brandeis*, p. 409.

47. LDB to McAdoo, November 23, 1918, *Letters*, IV, 364. War Industries Board; LDB to Colonel House, January 8, 1918, BP, WW 3-1; cf. Robert D. Cuff, *The War Industries Board* (Baltimore: Johns Hopkins University Press, 1973), chap. 5. Talks with Baker: Mason, *Brandeis*, pp. 522–523.

48. Bacchae: LDB to WW, November 11, 1918, *Letters*, IV, 362 (Gilbert Murray translation). Protocols of Zion: LDB to Julian Mack, November 16, 1918, *Letters*, IV, 365. LDB to Alice, December 3, 1918, *Letters*, IV, 369. LDB to FF, February 17, 1920, *Letters*, IV, 449.

49. LDB to WW, June 25, 1921, BP, M 17-3. The document is in BP, M 17-3.

50. WW to LDB, June 20, November 6, and December 6, 1921, all BP, M 17-3; LDB to WW, December 28, 1921, *Letters*, V, 40; March 3, 1922, *Letters*, V, 46-7; January 22, 1923, *Letters*, V, 86: April 14, 1923, *Letters*, V, 91. "My dear Friend": WW to LDB, December 29, 1921; February 27, 1922; April 18, 1923; all BP, M 17-3; "My dear Mr. Justice": WW to LDB, January 7, 1922; March 4, 1922; April 1, 1923; all BP, M 17-3.

51. WW to LDB, November 6, 1921, BP, M 17-3. LDB to WW, November 8, 1921, *Letters*, V, 30, and March 3, 1921, *Letters*, V, 46. Cf. December 8, 1921, *Letters*, V, 36. Work with Colby: WW to LDB, January 7 and February 27, 1922, BP, M 17-3; LDB to WW, March 3, 1922, *Letters*, V, 47, WW to LDB, April 18, 1923, BP, M 17-3. Democratic National Committee: WW to LDB, January 7, 1922, BP, M 17-3.

52. Link, *New Freedom*, pp. 95, 423, 433–439; *Wilson and Progressive Era*, pp. 70–71; *Wilson: Road*, pp. 488–489.

53. LDB to Edwin A. Alderman, May 11, 1924, Alderman Mss., University of Virginia Library. Alderman had been one of Woodrow Wilson's advisers and was to give a memorial speech at a joint session of Congress on December 15, 1924. LDB had earlier quoted admiringly to his wife Shakespeare's "Of all the wonders that I yet have heard, it seems to be most strange that men should fear." LDB to Alice, December 18, 1913, *Letters*, II, 224, quoting from *Julius Caesar*, Act II, scene 2.

12. The Making of a Zionist

1. Melvin I. Urofsky, *American Zionism from Herzl to the Holocaust* (Garden City, N.Y.: Doubleday, 1975), pp. 119–120; interview with Elizabeth Brandeis Raushenbush, September 23, 1980.

2. Jacob de Haas, *Louis D. Brandeis*, p. 135; interview with Elizabeth Raushenbush; Gal, *Brandeis*, pp. 45–46. LDB's contributions: Mason, *Brandeis*, p. 692; LDB to Henry Hurwitz, March 14 and 20, 1941, *Letters*, V, 649–650.

3. Yonathan Shapiro, *Leadership of the American Zionist Organization, 1897–1930* (Urbana: University of Illinois Press, 1971), pp, 30, 61–70, 264–268; Gal, *Brandeis*, passim.

4. Hapgood, *Changing Years*, pp. 185, 190; Horace M. Kallen, *The Faith of Louis D. Brandeis, Zionist* (New York: Hadassah, n.d.), pp. 8, 24–25. Cf. Kallen, "The Faith of Louis Brandeis," *The New Palestine*, November 14, 1941, pp. 23, 26.

5. Reaction to LDB's exclusion from Cabinet: Mason, *Brandeis*, pp. 394–395; La Follette and La Follette, *La Follette*, p. 463.

6. Lief, *Brandeis*, p. 260; Irving Katz, "Henry Lee Higginson vs. Louis Dembitz Brandeis: A Collision Between Tradition and Reform," *New England Quarterly*, 41 (1968), 67–68.

7. Mason, *Brandeis*, pp. 109, 127; Higginson's wfe: Urofsky, *American Zionism*, p. 10, citing Katz; LDB and Higginson's firm: LDB to Albert Enoch Pillsbury, May 20, 1897, BP, NMF 76-2; LDB on F. L. Higginson: LDB to Arthur Aaron Maxwell, April 24, 1900, BP, NMF 2-5; Boston Symphony Orchestra dispute: LDB to Henry Lee Higginson, April 26, 1905, BP, NMF 12-11; LDB to Hayes Robbins, June 19, 1905, BP, NMF 12-11.

8. Higginson on LDB, April 24 and 28, 1908, quoted in Gal, *Brandeis*, pp. 109–110; LDB to Edward Filene, June 29, 1907, *Letters*, I, 592–593.

9. LDB to Alfred, March 2, 1913, BP, unmarked folder: La Follette and La Follette, *La Follette*, p. 463.

10. LDB to George Middleton, March 12, 1913, quoted in La Follette and La Follette, *La Follette*, p. 463.

11. Solomon Goldman, "A Practical Idealist," *The New Palestine*, November 14, 1941, p. 5. Cf. note 4 above.

12. The federal bureaucracy became highly segregated during Wilson's administration. This is one of the pieces of evidence used to support the charge that Wilson was a racist. Ray Stannard Baker, however, has described Wilson as a foe of segregation. He depicts Wilson as having felt that the pressure from

Southern segregationists was unbearable and as having designated certain parts of the bureaucracy as the domain of blacks in order to give them access to and control over at least some federal entities. Baker, *Woodrow Wilson: Life and Letters* (Garden City, N.Y.: Doubleday, Doran and Co., 1931), IV, 220–225.

13. Urofsky, *American Zionism*, pp. 97–98, 173–194; Shapiro, *Leadership*, pp. 52–54.

14. Mason, *Brandeis*, p. 442; Lief, *Brandeis*, p. 278; de Haas, *Brandeis*, p. 51; Goldman, "Practical Idealist," p. 4; LDB's 1905 speech, "What Loyalty Demands," November 28, 1905, BP, Misc.

15. LDB to Stella and Emily Dembitz, May 17, 1926, quoted in Flexner, *Mr. Justice Brandeis*, pp. 36–37. John W. Petrie, "Lewis Naphtali Dembitz," *Louisville Courier Journal*, February 27, 1916, in Louisville Free Public Library, Kentucky Authors Scrapbook # 21; untitled typescript in same collection.

16. Petrie, "Lewis Naphtali Dembitz."

17. Mason, *Brandeis*, p. 441; *Louisville Courier-Journal*, June 4, 1922, in Louisville Free Public Library, Kentucky Authors Scrapbook #21.

18. Solomon Goldman, ed., *The Words of Justice Brandeis* (New York: Schumann, 1953), p. 160.

19. Mason, *Brandeis*, p. 443; de Haas, *Brandeis*, pp. 51–52.

20. Rose G. Jacobs, "Justice Brandeis and Hadassah," *The New Progressive*, November 14, 1941, p. 17; Chaim Weizmann, *Trial and Error* (Philadelphia: Jewish Publication Society of America, 1949), p. 248; Phillips, ed., *Frankfurter Reminisces*, p. 181; LDB to Julian Mack, December (n.d.) 1934, *Letters*, V, 549.

21. Mason, *Brandeis*, p. 442; Lief, *Brandeis*, pp. 191, 331; Goldman, *Words of Justice Brandeis*, p. 14; Urofsky, *Mind of One Piece*, p. 99.

22. Mason, *Brandeis*, pp. 442–443; Lief, *Brandeis*, pp. 198–199. Style in garment strike and identification with Jews: Rose G. Jacobs, "Justice Brandeis and Hadassah"; Benjamin V. Cohen, "Faith in Common Man"; Louis E. Kirstein, "A Personal Appreciation"; all in *The New Palestine*, November 14, 1941, pp. 13, 14, 17.

23. LDB on hyphenated Americans: *Jewish Advocate*, December 9, 1910, reprinted as "Jews as a Priest People" in de Haas, *Louis D. Brandeis*, pp. 151–152. Elizabeth Glendower Evans, "Louis Dembitz Brandeis, Tribune of the People," *Springfield Daily Republican*, May 13, 1931; Michael M. Hammer and Samuel Stickles, "An Interview with Louis D. Brandeis," *The Invincible Ideal*, I (June 1915), 7; Solomon Goldman, ed., *Brandeis on Zionism: A Collection of Addresses and Statements by Louis D. Brandeis* (Washington, D.C.: Zionist Organization of America, 1942), p. v.

24. Anti-Semitism as failure of liberalism: Horace Kallen, *Faith of Louis D. Brandeis*, pp. 24–25; anti-Semitism in Detroit: LDB to Alfred, October 10, 1914, BP, M 4-1a; LDB's advice to young lawyer: LDB to Max H. Wilensky, November 5, 1914, BP, NMF 78-1.

25. Henry Moskowitz, "An Army of Striking Cloakmakers," *Jewish Frontier*, November 1936, p. 16.

26. Horace M. Kallen, *Zionism and World Politics: A Study in History and*

452   NOTES TO PAGES 235–241

Social Psychology (Garden City: Doubleday, Page, 1921), p. 137; Goldman, "Practical Idealist," pp. 4–5; LDB, "The Jewish Problem," (in de Haas, *Louis D. Brandeis*) discussed in next chapter.

27. LDB, "To Be a Jew," in Goldman, *Brandeis on Zionism*, p. 39; Hapgood, *Changing Years*, p. 197.

28. Mason, *Brandeis*, pp. 443–444; Lief, *Brandeis*, pp. 279–280; Urofsky, *Mind of One Piece*, p. 100; LDB to Louis Lipsky, April 17, 1913, BP, Z 1-4.

29. Mason, *Brandeis*, p. 444; Gal, *Brandeis*, p. 201.

30. Urofsky, *American Zionism*, p. 126.

31. Arthur S. Link, *Wilson: The New Freedom* (Princeton, N.J.: Princeton University Press, 1956), pp. 451–69; Urofsky, *Mind of One Piece*, p. 91; Gal, *Brandeis*, p. 68; Robert M. La Follette to Belle La Follette, July 31, 1914, in La Follette and La Follette, *La Follette*, p. 500.

32. LDB to Arthur Ruppin, October 5, 1914, BP, Z 10-3; LDB to Alfred, October 18, 1914, BP, M 4-1; LDB to Louis Lipsky, November 14, 1914, BP, Z 1-4; LDB to Bloch Publishing Company, December 23, 1914; speech, "A Call to the Educated Jew," delivered at conference of Intercollegiate Menorah Association, printed in Goldman, *Brandeis on Zionism*, pp. 65–66; speech, "Dreams May Be Made into Realities," delivered at convention of the Federation of American Zionists, June 1915, reprinted in Goldman, *Brandeis on Zionism*, p. 72; Alfred Zimmern, *The Greek Commonwealth* (Oxford: Clarendon Press, 1912, 1915, 1921, 1924, 1931). Unless otherwise indicated, subsequent quotations from Zimmern are from the 1931 edition.

33. My great gratitude to attorney Burton C. Bernard, who located the 1917 letter and was kind enough to share it with me. LDB to Zimmern, July 21, 1917 (Bodleian Library, Zimmern Manuscript Collection #15, folios 46-7, 73-4.) LDB to FF, September 1, 1925, *Letters*, V, 185. Bills from the Old Corner Book Store, November 17, 1915, Janary 1915, November 30, 1915, and April 1, 1916, BP, Addendum, Box 17.

34. LDB to Stella and Emily Dembitz, May 17, 1926, quoted in Flexner, *Mr. Justice Brandeis*, pp. 36–37; Paul Freund, "Mr. Justice Brandeis: A Centennial Memoir," *Harvard Law Review*, 70 (1957), 769, 789; interview with Freund, December 5, 1977; William Hard, "Brandeis the Conservative or a 'Dangerous Radical'?" *Philadelphia Public Ledger*, May 12, 1916, BP, Clippings II; de Haas, *Louis D. Brandeis*, p. 44.

35. Zimmern, *Greek Commonwealth*, preface to 4th ed., p. 3; preface to 1st ed., p. 7; preface to 2nd ed., p. 6.

36. Zimmern, *Greek Commonwealth*, pp. 67, 84, 107, 135, 144, 160, 166, 432.

37. Ibid., pp. 131, 215, 226; LDB, "Efficiency and Social Ideals," *The Independent*, November 30, 1914, p. 327, reprinted in *Bigness*, p. 51.

38. Zimmern, *Greek Commonwealth*, pp. 63, 222, 260, 387.

39. Ibid., pp. 70, 72, 139.

40. Ibid., pp. 19, 39, 43–44 n. 2, 66.

41. Ibid., pp. 71, 76–77, 91, 106, 120 n. 1, 122, 123–134, 181–182 n. 1, 258, 280, 309 n. 1, 311.

42. Zimmern, *Greek Commonwealth*, pp. 298, 431–434: LDB, *Brandeis on Zionism*, pp. 124, 138, 146.

43. Dean Acheson, *Morning and Noon* (Boston: Houghton Mifflin, 1965), p. 50; cf. Acheson on LDB quoting Euripides, p. 96; interview with Elizabeth Brandeis Raushenbush, September 23, 1980; interview with Mary Kay Tachau, June 12, 1980.

44. LDB to Alice, June 14, 1919, *Letters*, IV, 400; LDB to Alice, June 18, 1919, *Letters*, IV, 401; cf. LDB to Alfred, June 20, 1919, BP, M 4-1.

45. LDB to Alice, June 22, 1919, BP, M 4-3; LDB to Alice, June 24 and 27, 1919, BP, M 4-3; de Haas, *Louis D. Brandeis*, p. 113.

46. Quoted in *Hadashot Haaretz*, July 11, 1919, p. 4. *Hadashot Haaretz* (The News of the Land) was the newspaper of the Jewish settlements. I am grateful to Professor Asher Arian of Tel Aviv University for locating these articles and having them translated. Alfred Zimmern, "The Meaning of Nationality," *The New Republic*, January 1, 1916, pp. 215–217.

47. LDB, "The Jewish Problem" in de Haas, *Louis D. Brandeis*, pp. 177, 184–186. Cf. Marie Syrkin, "Brandeis and Zionism," *Jewish Frontier*, November 1936, p. 29.

48. de Haas, *Louis D. Brandeis*, p. 113; LDB to Alice, June 27, July 1, 4, and 6, 1919; all BP, M 4-3; LDB to Elizabeth, July 1, 1919, *Letters*, IV, 411–412; LDB to Alfred, July 6, 1919, BP, M 4-1.

49. LDB to Alice, July 6, 1919, BP, M 4-3; *Hadashot Haaretz*, July 7, 1919, p. 3.

50. Motza: *Hadashot Haaretz*, July 10, 1919, p. 3. Jerusalem and Lemel: Ibid., July 11, 1919, p. 3; July 15, 1919, p. 5; LDB to Alice, July 10, 1919, BP, M 4-3.

51. *Hadashot Haaretz*, July 17, 1919; July 20, 1919, p. 4; July 22, 1919, p. 4; July 27, 1919, p. 3. Pittsburgh: Lief, *Brandeis*, p. 114. LDB to Alice, August 1, 1919, BP, M 4-3. LDB to Weizmann, July 20, 1919, *Letters*, IV, 418–419.

52. LDB to Alice, July 1 and 4, 1919, BP, M 4-3; to Alfred, July 6, 1919, BP, M 4-1; de Haas, *Louis D. Brandeis*, p. 114; LDB to Alice, July 7, 1919, BP, M 4-3.

53. "Palestine Has Developed Jewish Character," delivered November 24, 1929, in Goldman, *Brandeis on Zionism*, pp. 145–146; "Realization Will Not Come as a Gift," delivered June 24, 1923, in *Brandeis on Zionism*, p. 137.

54. de Haas, *Louis D. Brandeis*, p. 52.

55. Ibid., pp. 52–53.

13. Zionist and American

1. Acceptance speech reprinted as "The Jewish People Should be Preserved" in Goldman, *Brandeis on Zionism*, pp. 43–45.

2. Urofsky, *American Zionism*, pp. 120–121; Mason, *Brandeis*, pp. 444–445; Lief, *Brandeis*, p. 322; de Haas, *Louis D. Brandeis*, p. 135; LDB to Chaim Weizmann, October 11, 1914, *Letters*, III, 322–329. Horace Kallen claims LDB

became chairman "reluctantly." Horace M. Kallen, *The Faith of Louis D. Brandeis, Zionist* (New York: Hadassah, n.d.), p. 23.

3. LDB to Weizmann, October 11, 1914, *Letters*, III, 322–327.

4. LDB to Zionists of America, August 31, 1914, *Letters*, III, 291–292; LDB to Perlstein, September 8, 1914, and daily thereafter, BP, Z 3-2; LDB's cable to Perlstein, September 29, 1914, BP, Z 3-2.

5. LDB to Hapgood: see, e.g., September 24, 1914, BP, NMF 62-1; September 29, 1914, BP, NMF 62-1; October 1, 1914, BP, NMF 62-1. Hapgood, "Zionism's Crisis," *Harper's Weekly*, 49 (September 26, 1914), 289; series on Zionism, *Harper's Weekly*, vols. 61, 62. Hapgood as Zionist: Hapgood, *The Changing Years*, pp. 196–197. *Survey* symposium, January 1916; see LDB to Abbott, December 6, 1915, BP, Z 8-1.

6. LDB to Ruppin, October 5, 1915, BP, Z 10-3; LDB to Kaplan, October 5, 1914, BP, Z 3-1.

7. LDB to de Haas, October 21, 1914, BP, Z 6-1.

8. LDB to Kaplan, November 29, 1915, BP, Z 3-1.

9. LDB to Richard Gottheil, October 5, 1914, *Letters*, III, 312; to de Haas, January 25, 1915, BP, Z 6-1; to de Haas, July 5, 1916, BP, Z 20-1; to Robert Kesselman, September 27, 1916, BP, Z 14-1; to Kesselman, January 13 and 16, 1916, BP, Z 14-2.

10. LDB to Louis Lipsky, January 27, 1915, BP, Z 1-4; to Henrietta Szold, March 4 and 24, 1915, BP, Z 12-2; to Joseph L. Cohen, May 1, 1915, BP, Z 10-2; to Perlstein, March 12, 1915, BP, Z 3-2; to Horace Kallen, March 4, 1915, *Letters*, III, 460; to David Rubin, February 10, 1915, BP, Z 2-3; to Israel B. Brodie, November 11, 1915, BP, Z 12-3; to Wise, November 16, 1914, BP, Z 6-2. Yiddish Volk: to de Haas, July 12, 1918, *Letters*, IV, 348.

11. Timeclock and indexes: de Haas, *Brandeis*, pp. 63, 69, 70–71. Style: Rose G. Jacobs, "Justice Brandeis and Hadassah," *The New Palestine*, November 14, 1941, p. 17; Marvin Lowenthal, "Sat Through the Storm," *The New Palestine*, November 14, 1941, p. 27. LDB's remark: Solomon Goldman, ed., *The Words of Justice Brandeis* (New York: Schumann, 1953), p. 184.

12. Elizabeth Glendower Evans, "Louis Dembitz Brandeis—Tribune of the People—II" in *Springfield Daily Republican*, May 13, 1931. Speeches: Mason, *Brandeis*, pp. 446–448; Lief, *Brandeis*, pp. 324, 326. LDB to Alfred, November 27, 1914.

13. February 24, March 6, and April 25, 1915; all BP, M 4-1. Vacation: to Wise, August 26, 1915, BP, Z 11-1. Sufferings: to Alfred, December 8 and 12, 1914, BP, M 4-1. LDB, "The Jewish Problem," in Goldman, *Brandeis on Zionism*, pp. 22–23; Horace Kallen, *Zionism and World Politics: A Study in History and Social Psychology* (Garden City, N.Y.: Doubleday, Page, 1921), pp. 31, 34.

14. "The Jewish People Should Be Preserved," in Goldman, *Brandeis on Zionism*, pp. 43–45.

15. "The Jewish Problem," in Goldman, *Brandeis on Zionism*, pp. 12–13.

16. Reprinted as "The Rebirth of the Jewish Nation" in de Haas, *Louis D. Brandeis*, pp. 163, 168. Jews from Russia: "A Call to the Educated Jew," address

to Intercollegiate Menorah Association, published in *Menorah Journal*, January 1915, reprinted in Goldman, *Brandeis on Zionism*, as "A Call to the Educated Jew," pp. 59–69.

17. LDB, "A Call to the Educated Jew," p. 68.

18. Kallen, *Faith of Louis D. Brandeis*, p. 19.

19. Faneuil Hall speech reprinted as "True Americanism" in Goldman, *Brandeis on Zionism*, pp. 3–11.

20. Ibid.

21. Ibid.

22. Ibid.

23. LDB, "Zionism through Americanism," in Goldman, *Brandeis on Zionism*, p. 49. LDB's coworkers understood that his Zionism was an extension of his Progressivism. See, e.g., Felix Frankfurter's "Foreword" in Goldman, *Brandeis on Zionism*, pp. v–vi; Kallen, *Zionism and World Politics*, chap. 11; Malke Pronin, "Portrait of a Jew as an American," *Jewish Frontier*, November 1936, p. 25; Solomon Goldman, "A Practical Idealist," *New Palestine*, November 14, 1941, p. 4. Eliot and *Menorah Journal*: A. L. Todd, *Justice on Trial* (New York: McGraw-Hill, 1964), p. 183. The speech was printed as "True Americanism" in *Harper's Weekly*, 61 (July 10, 1915), p. 31. Cf. Julian Hawthorne, "Brandeis Explains Zionist Plan," *Boston American*, and Edward A. Filene, "Brandeis the Man and Zionist Leader," *Boston Sunday Post*, both July 4, 1915, BP, Scrapbook II.

24. LDB, "A Call to the Educated Jew."

25. LDB to Norman Hapgood, October 1, 1914, BP, NMF 62-1.

26. On becoming Zionists: address before the Knights of Zion convention, Chicago, January 2, 1916, reprinted as "Not by Charity Alone" in Goldman, *Brandeis on Zionism*, pp. 85, 87–88; address before the Federation of American Zionists convention, Philadelphia, July 7, 1916, reprinted as "Democracy Means Responsibility" in Goldman, *Brandeis on Zionism*, pp. 91–92. Subscriptions: receipts, BP, Addendum, Box 15. Reading: LDB to Stephen Wise, July 21, 1916, BP, Z 6-2; LDB to de Haas, September 13, 1917, *Letters*, IV, 307. Kallen, *Zionism and World Politics*, p. 23.

27. LDB, "Jewish Problem" and "The Fruits of Zionism" in Goldman, *Brandeis on Zionism*, pp. 31, 56–58.

28. LDB, "Jewish Problem," pp. 24–26.

29. Chaim Weizmann, *Trial and Error* (New York: Greenwood, 1949), pp. 309, 456.

14. Zionism Reconsidered

1. Urofsky, *American Zionism*, p. 145: see, e.g., LDB to de Haas, April 24, 1917, *Letters*, IV, 283; to same, May 4, 8, 10, August 7, and November 22, 1917, *Letters*, IV, 288–290, 302, 322; to Rothenberg, February 18, 1917, in Solomon Goldman, ed., *The Words of Justice Brandeis* (New York: Schumann, 1953), p. 112. LDB to well-wishers: see letters in BP, NMF 78-1. Jerusalem: LDB to de Haas, January 19, 1918, *Letters*, IV, 336.

2. Urofsky, *American Zionism*, chap. 3; Shapiro, *Leadership*, chaps. 1, 2.

3. Urofsky, *American Zionism*, pp. 75–76; Shapiro, *Leadership*, pp. 38, 59.

4. Urofsky, *American Zionism*, pp. 164–171; Shapiro, *Leadership*, pp. 78–81.

5. Congress movement: Urofsky, *American Zionism*, pp. 179–180; Shapiro, *Leadership*, pp. 80–98.

6. Carnegie Hall address, January 24, 1916, reprinted as "The Common Cause of the Jewish People" in Goldman, *Brandeis on Zionism*, p. 105; see "Jewish Rights and the Congress" in de Haas, *Brandeis*, pp. 218–231. LDB to Lipsky, March 29, 1916, BP, Z 1-4; to Actions Committee, May 15, 1916, *Letters*, IV, 184–185; to Henry Friedenwald, June 14, 1916, BP, Z 11-2; to Eustace Sutherland Campbell Percy, June 26, 1916, *Letters*, IV, 236; to Lipsky, about Henry Moskowitz, May 31, 1916, BP, Z 1-4. LDB on Congress and democracy: Horace M. Kallen, *The Faith of Louis D. Brandeis, Zionist* (New York: Hadassah, n.d.), p. 30.

7. Urofsky, *American Zionism*, chap. 5; Shapiro, *Leadership*, pp. 94–96.

8. LDB to I. A. Abrahams, February 17, 1915, BP, Z 7-1 (the Palestinian members of the Committee were Arthur Ruppin, Ephraim Cohen, and Aaron Aaronsohn); to Morgenthau, February 8, 1915, BP, Z 12-3; to Wise, February 13, 1915, BP, Z 6-2; to Ruppin, March 8, 1914, *Letters*, III, 473; to Morgenthau, December 22, 1915, BP, Z 14-3; to Wise, April 3, 1916, BP, Z 6-2; to Otto Warburg, April 9, 1916, *Letters*, IV, 160.

9. LDB to Morgenthau, June 25, 1915, *Letters*, III, 542; to Ruppin, March 8, 1915, *Letters*, III, 473.

10. LDB to Otto Warburg, April 9, 1916, *Letters*, IV, 160; cf. IV, 164 n.1; LDB to Sokolow, April 2, 1917, BP, Z 22-2; Urofsky, *American Zionism*, p. 154; Morgenthau, *World's Work*, 43 (December 1921), pp. 138–145.

11. LDB to Ruppin, March 8, 1915, *Letters*, III, 474; Urofsky, *American Zionism*, p. 154. Bryan and Lansing: LDB to Charles A. Cowen, March 26, 1919, *Letters*, IV, 388; LDB to Daniels and Bryan, March 5, 1915, *Letters*, III, 465 and 465, n. 1; LDB to Wise, October 15, 1915, BP, Z 6-2; Lief, *Brandeis*, p. 324; Bryan to LDB, March 27, 1919, quoted in Mason, *Brandeis*, p. 456; Urofsky, *American Zionism*, p. 205.

12. State Department: Urofsky, *American Zionism*, p. 206; PC report reprinted as "American Aid" in Goldman, *Brandeis on Zionism*, p. 73 (no date is given but internal evidence suggests the report was written in 1915).

13. *Letters*, IV, 281, n. 1; Urofsky, *American Zionism*, p. 208.

14. LDB to de Haas, April 24, May 8, and May 10, 1917, *Letters*, IV, 283, 288–289, 290; see cable to James Armand de Rothschild, May 15, 1917, BP, Z 22-2. LDB to Alice Brandeis, June 25, 1919, BP, M 4-3; to Alfred, June 30, 1919, M 4-1; to Alice, August 8, 1919, BP, M 4-3; to Balfour, October 28, 1920, *Letters*, IV, 495 and 495 n. 2.

15. Blanche E. C. Dugdale, *Arthur James Balfour* (London: Hutchinson, 1936), II, 231. Weizmann, *Trial and Error*, pp. 193, 194; see pp. 176–194, 200–208 for Weizmann's version of the history of the declaration. For other views

of LDB's impact on the declaration see Mason, *Brandeis*, pp.453–455; Lief, *Brandeis*, p. 406; Shapiro, *Leadership*, p.129; Richard Ned Lebow, "Woodrow Wilson and the Balfour Declaration," *Journal of Modern History*, 40 (December 1968), 501–523.

16. LDB to Bernard A. Rosenblatt, November 10, 1920, *Letters*, IV, 499; to Mack et al., February 6, 1921, *Letters*, IV, 530.

17. LDB on Aaronsohn: Address to Young Men's Hebrew Association of Chelsea, Massachusetts, May 18, 1913, reprinted as "To Be a Jew" in Goldman, *Brandeis on Zionism*, pp. 39–40; LDB, "The Jewish Problem" in Goldman, *Brandeis on Zionism*, p. 27.

18. LDB to David Lubin, September 29, 1918, *Letters*, IV, 346; to Weizmann, January 13, 1918, *Letters*, IV, 335; statement to American delegation of the London Conference, July 14, 1920, reprinted as "Efficiency in Public Service" in Goldman, *Brandeis on Zionism*, p. 124; LDB to Weizmann, April 12, 1918, *Letters*, IV, 342.

19. Pittsburgh Platform: in de Haas, *Louis D. Brandeis*, pp. 96–97; LDB ᵗo Weizmann, January 13, 1918, *Letters*, IV, 335.

20. Zeeland Program: in LDB, *Bigness*, p. 251; LDB, address before the 2nd Annual Conference of Palestine Land Development Council, May 27, 1923, reprinted as "The Pilgrims Had Faith" in Goldman, *Brandeis on Zionism*, pp. 126, 132; "Call to the Educated Jew" in Goldman, *Brandeis on Zionism*, pp. 63–66.

21. LDB, "The Pilgrims Had Faith" in Goldman, *Brandeis on Zionism*, p. 130. Message to conference of Jewish organization,February 17, 1924, reprinted as "The Only Promising Road" in Goldman, *Brandeis on Zionism*, p. 143. LDB's conversation with Solomon Goldman, September 1941, in Goldman, *Brandeis on Zionism*, p. 51.

22. Weizmann, *Trial and Error*, pp. 217–223, 232–236, 245–247; FF-LC Boxes 161, 162; LDB to Robert Szold, August 19, 1930, *Letters*, V, 449.

23. Goldman, *Words of Justice Brandeis*, pp. 50–51. Playgrounds: Louis E. Levinthal, *Louis Dembitz Brandeis* (Washington, D.C.: Zionist Organization of America, n.d.), p. 12.

24. LDB to Julian Mack, October 20, 1929, BP, Z 36-2; to Robert Szold, August 19, 1930, *Letters*, V, 449; to Bernard Flexner, April 8, 1940, *Letters*, V, 637.

25. Need for land: LDB to Julian Mack, July 20, 1930, BP, Z 42-1; to Robert Szold, August 19, 1930, *Letters*, V, 449; to Szold, March 3, 1931, BP, Z 49-2; to Szold, July 11, 1932, *Letters*, V, 506; to Wise, August 9, 1934, *Letters*, V, 545; to Szold, *Letters*, V, 593–594. Negotiations with Hussein: LDB to Neumann, January 27, 1933, *Letters*, V, 513–514; *Letters*, V, 507, n. 1; Emmanuel Neumann, "The Nation-Builder," *The New Palestine*, November 14, 1941, p. 8.

26. Goldman, *Brandeis on Zionism*, pp. 146–147.

27. LDB to Alice, August 1, 1919, BP, M 4-3; "Palestine Has Developed Jewish Character" in Goldman, *Brandeis on Zionism*, pp. 145–146; LDB address before Palestine Development League, Boston, June 24, 1923, printed as "Re-

alization Will Not Come as a Gift" in Goldman, *Brandeis on Zionism*, pp. 137, 142.

28. LDB to Alice, August 5, 1919, *Letters*, IV, 422; also see *Letters*, IV, 421, n. 1. Malaria: "Palestine Has Developed Jewish Character" in Goldman, *Brandeis on Zionism*, p. 146; "Realization Will Not Come as a Gift" in Goldman, *Brandeis on Zionism*, p. 138; LDB to Jack Mosseri, September 24, 1919, *Letters*, IV, 426–427 and 427, n. 1; to Rothschild, October 28, 1919, *Letters*, IV, 436; de Haas, *Louis D. Brandeis*, pp. 116–117.

29. Urofsky, *American Zionism*, pp. 265–270, 273–275; Shapiro, *Leadership*, pp. 138–155.

30. Phillips, *Frankfurter Reminisces*, pp. 178–188; Lief, *Brandeis*, pp. 463–464.

31. Urofsky, *American Zionism*, pp. 275–278; Shapiro, *Leadership*, pp. 145–150, 161–162; Weizmann, *Trial and Error*, pp. 260–262; Kallen, *Zionism and World Politics*, pp. 281–284, n. 1.

32. LDB to Wise, November 13, 1920, *Letters*, IV, 501–502.

33. ZOA convention: Urofsky, *American Zionism*, pp. 281–294; Shapiro, *Leadership*, pp. 175–179.

34. LDB to FF, April 10 and 26, 1921, *Letters*, IV, 549, 553; to Mack, April 27, 1921, *Letters*, IV, 556. Also see to Wise et al., February 18, 1921, *Letters*, IV, 534.

35. The memorial volume is in BP.

36. LDB to Mack, November 17, 1920, *Letters*, IV, 506; to Alfred, June 12, 1921, *Letters*, IV, 566, n. 1.

37. Urofsky, *American Zionism*, pp. 336–340; Shapiro, *Leadership*, pp. 184–186, 194–195; de Haas, *Louis D. Brandeis*, pp. 146–147; Bernard Flexner, "Brandeis and the Palestine Economic Corporation," *The New Palestine*, November 14, 1941, pp. 15–17. Contributions: Mason, *Brandeis*, p. 692. Stipends: LDB to de Haas, August 10, 1924, BP, Addendum, Box 19; to Henrietta Szold, April 3, 1922, BP, Addendum, Box 19. Will: BP, Addendum, Box 5.

38. Rose G. Jacobs, "Justice Brandeis and Hadassah," pp. 18–19.

39. LDB to World Zionist Organization, June 19, 1921, *Letters*, IV, 567; to de Haas about Lipsky, quoted in Mason, *Brandeis*, p. 413.

40. Goldman, "A Practical Idealist," p. 6; Neumann, "The Nation-Builder," p. 7; de Haas, *Louis D. Brandeis*, p. 149; Jacobs, "Justice Brandeis and Hadassah," p. 17.

41. Urofsky, *American Zionism*, p. 362; Shapiro, *Leadership*, pp. 244–245; *New York Times*, November 12, 1929; LDB to Zionist Organization of America, June 28, 1930, *Letters*, V, 429–430; LDB to ZOA, November 1931, printed as "A Zionist's Vow" in Goldman, *Brandeis on Zionism*, p. 154.

42. Samuel Ben-Zvi, "Justice Brandeis and Ein Hashofet," *The New Palestine*, November 14, 1941, p. 10. Also *Letters*, V, 618, n. 2.

43. "The Chief": Kallen, *Faith of Louis D. Brandeis*, p. 26. LDB, "The Pilgrims Had Faith" in Goldman, *Brandeis on Zionism*, p. 130.

44. Pittsburgh Platform quoted in de Haas, *Louis D. Brandeis*, p. 96.

15. Mr. Brandeis Goes to Washington

1. Todd, *Justice on Trial*, pp. 21–34; Mason, *Brandeis*, p. 465.

2. Lief, *Brandeis*, p. 346; Hapgood, *Changing Years*, p. 192. Although Hapgood, as cited, claims that the idea of appointing Brandeis was Wilson's, in a 1932 letter he recalled that the first person to suggest Brandeis to Wilson was the president's physician, Admiral Cary Grayson. Both Gregory and McAdoo credited themselves with the idea: cf. *Letters*, IV, 25, n. 2. As Mason comments about the after-the-fact disagreement, Wilson knew Brandeis well enough and admired him sufficiently to need no prompting. Mason, *Brandeis*, p. 467 n., quoting Hapgood to Ray Stannard Baker, May 10, 1932. La Follette: Todd, *Justice on Trial*, p. 37; La Follette and La Follette, *La Follette*, p. 568. Gompers: Todd, *Justice on Trial*, pp. 120, 259. Anderson: Lief, *Brandeis*, p. 347.

3. Alice to Alfred, January 31, 1916, quoted in Mason, *Brandeis*, p. 466; LDB to Alfred, January 28, 1916, BP, NMF 77-1; LDB to Alfred, February 12, 1916, quoted in Mason, *Brandeis*, p. 469. Concern over health: Lief, *Brandeis*, p. 347. Edward F. McClennen, "Better that a Man's Own Works . . . ," *The New Palestine*, November 14, 1941, p. 21.

4. G. J. Karger to Taft, January 29, 1916, quoted in Arthur Link, *Confusions and Crises* (Princeton, N.J.: Princeton University Press, 1964), p. 325.

5. McAdoo's: Mason, *Brandeis*, p. 466; Lief, *Brandeis*, p. 348: Todd, *Justice on Trial*, p. 70. Press: *Washington Post*, January 29, 1916. La Follette: to LDB, March 22, 1916, quoted in Mason, *Brandeis*, p. 491.

6. Brandeis's "brief": stenographic transcript of Brandeis-McClennen conference, March 22, 1916, pp. 1–6, BP, NMF 85-2.

7. Wickersham: Todd, *Justice on Trial*, pp. 81–82, 131–132, 161, 179–181, 237–239. Taft: Mason, *Brandeis*, p. 538; Todd, *Justice on Trial*, p. 257. AJC: ibid., pp. 217–218.

8. LDB to Alfred, March 2, 1916, BP, SC 2-1; LDB to McClennen, February 19, 1916, BP, NMF 76-2. Walsh: Melvin I. Urofsky, *Louis D. Brandeis and the Progressive Tradition* (Boston: Little, Brown, 1981), p. 106; Todd, *Justice on Trial*, pp. 95, 174, 176.

9. Todd, *Justice on Trial*, pp. 71, 77, 106, 107, 149–162, 257; Mason, *Brandeis*, pp. 472–473; Lief, *Brandeis*, p. 377. Copies of all letters sent to the subcommittee are in BP, NMF 75-1 and 75-2, and in U.S., Congress, Senate, Committee on the Judiciary, *Hearings before the Subcommittee on the Nomination of Louis D. Brandeis to be an Associate Justice of the Supreme Court of the United States*, 64th Cong., 1st sess., 1916, 2 vols. Copies of many are also in FF-LC Box 127. Higginson: Todd, *Justice on Trial*, p. 257.

10. Eliot to Charles A. Culberson, May 17, 1916, quoted in Todd, *Justice on Trial*, pp. 228–229; McClennen to Nutter, May 24, 1916, quoted in Mason, *Brandeis*, p. 501. Students' petition: Todd, *Justice on Trial*, p. 141. Dinner: ibid., pp. 209–215. Support: ibid., pp. 134, 152–153; Mason, *Brandeis*, p. 482.

11. Berle to Sen. William E. Chilton, February 18, 1916, BP, NMF 75-1. Letters: Todd, *Justice on Trial*, pp. 136, 250; Ellerton James: ibid., p. 93.

12. LDB to Hapgood, February 1, 1916, BP, NMF 77-1, 77-2. Gregory to LDB, quoted in Mason, *Brandeis*, pp. 467–468. LDB to Alfred, BP, NMF 77-1.

13. LDB to Louise Malloch, February 13, 1916, BP, NMF 77-1. LDB to McClennen, February 12, 1916, BP, NMF 76-2. Most of these letters are in BP, NMF 76-2. A sampling can be found in *Letters*, IV. See, e.g., February 17, 19, 23, 26, 28, and March 9, 1916. Malloch: See, e.g., LDB to Anderson, March 6, BP, NMF 77-1; to FF, March 18 and April 3, 1916, BP, NMF 77-1.

14. LDB to Emerson, March 17, 1916, BP, NMF 77-1. Letter-writing: Todd, *Justice on Trial*, pp. 210–211.

15. Editorials: See, e.g., Todd, *Justice on Trial*, p. 177. LDB to Croly, February 11, 1916, BP, NMF 78-1. Lippmann: *New Republic*, March 11, 1916, p. 139. LDB to Lippmann, February 21, 1916, BP, NMF 77-1.

16. Taft: LDB to Hapgood, March 14, BP, NMF 77-2, including reference to talk with FF; Lippmann in *New Republic*, March 18, 1916. Articles: *Harper's Weekly*, April 1, 1916; *Survey*, March 16, 1916; *Letters*, IV, 119, n. 5. "Brief": LDB to McClennen, April 3, BP, NMF 76-2, *New York World*, April 25, 1916; cf. Mason, *Brandeis*, pp. 495–496. *Independent*: LDB to Holt, June 14, 1916, BP, NMF 79-1.

17. "Morgenthau": Reported in Morgenthau's diary for April 1, 1916. Lief, *Brandeis*, pp. 391–392; Todd, *Justice on Trial*, p. 211.

18. Subcommittee vote and report: *Hearings . . . on the Nominatio. of Louis D. Brandeis*, vol. II. Zionist meeting: Mason, *Brandeis*, p. 498; Todd, *Justice on Trial*, p. 212. Wilson's letter: May 5, 1916. *Hearings . . . on the Nominatin of Louis D. Brandeis*, vol. II, pp. 5–7. Hapgood's apartment: Todd, *Justice on Trial*, pp. 221–226.

19. Todd, *Justice on Trial*, p. 245.

20. LDB's activism in fight: cf. Mason, *Brandeis*, pp. 483–499; Urofsky, *Louis D. Brandeis and the Progressive Tradition*, pp. 108–109.

21. WW to Morgenthau, June 5, 1916, quoted in Todd, *Justice on Trial*, p. 247; WW quoted in Hapgood, *Changing Years*, p. 193.

22. Mason, *Brandeis*, p. 511; Todd, *Justice on Trial*, p. 248; Lief, *Brandeis*, pp. 394–395.

23. Congratulatory letters are collected in BP, NMF 78-81. Resignations: LDB to J. W. Beatson, June 16, 1916, BP, NMF 11-1 re Economic League; to Leon Sanders, June 26, 1916, BP, NMF 73-5, re Hebrew Immigrant Aid Society; to Massachusetts Civil Service Association, September 25, 1916, BP, NMF 73-4; and similar letters in BP, NMF 73-4. Zionists: LDB to Hugo Pam, July 21, BP, Z 16-3; to Felix Warburg, July 21, BP, NMF 71-6; to Wise, July 21, BP, Z 6-2.

24. LDB to Edward White, June 29, 1916, and White to LDB, July 17, 1916, both BP, M 17-1; Malloch, law firm resignation: Lief, *Brandeis*, p. 396.

25. Vacation: LDB to Morris L. Cooke, July 24, 1916, BP, NMF 70-1. Washington: Dean Acheson, *Morning and Noon* (Boston: Houghton Mifflin, 1965), pp. 41–42, 63; Holmes: Mason, *Brandeis*, p. 570; Lief, *Brandeis*, p. 424.

26. LDB's convictions: Paul Freund, *On Understanding the Supreme Court* (Boston: Little, Brown, 1949), p. 52.

27. *Arizona* v. *California*, 283 U.S. 423, 463-4 (1931). Cf. *Swift Co.* v. *Hocking Valley Ry.*, 243 U.S. 281 (1917); *Bilby* v. *Stewart*, 246 U.S. 255 (1918); *Sugarman* v. *U.S.*, 249 U.S. 182 (1919); *Babour* v. *Ga.*, 249 U.S. 454 (1919); *Collins* v. *Miller*, 252 U.S. 364 (1920); *Terrace* v. *Thompson*, 263 U.S. 197 (1923); *Oliver Co.* v. *Mexico*, 264 U.S. 440 (1924); *Willing* v. *Chicago*, 277 U.S. 274 (1928). Constitutional determination: *Chastleton Corp.* v. *Sinclair*, 264 U.S. 543, 549 (1924) (concurring in part). Local law: *Railroad Comm.* v. *Los Angeles*, 280 U.S. 145, 163 (1929) (dissenting).

28. *International News Service* v. *Associated Press*, 248 U.S. 215, 248, 263, 262, 267 (1918) (dissenting).

29. LDB's pro-press prejudice: Mason says this and quotes Learned Hand in agreement. Mason, *Brandeis*, p. 579 n. Money trust: *Eisner* v. *Macomber*, 252 U.S. 189, 220–1 (1920). Sutherland: quoted in Samuel Konefsky, *The Legacy of Holmes and Brandeis* (New York: Macmillan, 1956), p. 278 n. *New State Ice Co.* v. *Liebmann*, 285 U.S. 262, 279–280.

30. *New State Ice Co.* v. *Liebmann*, 285 U.S. 287–300; 287–290 n. 8–17.

31. Ibid., 306–310.

32. Ibid., 310–311.

33. Ibid., 288–290 n. 13, 14, 16–18.

34. *Yarborough* v. *Yarborough*, 290 U.S. 202 (1933); *Bradford Electric Light Co.* v. *Clapper*, 284 U.S. 221 (1931); *John Hancock* v. *Yates*, 299 U.S. 178 (1936); Freund, *On Understanding the Supreme Court*, pp. 66–67.

35. *Carter* v. *Carter*, 298 U.S. 238 (1936); *Adkins* v. *Children's Hospital*, 261 U.S. 525 (1923).

36. *Hammer* v. *Dagenhart*, 247 U.S. 251, 277–281 (1922). *Atherton Mills* v. *Johnston*, 259 U.S. 11, 12–15 (1922).

37. "Memorandum": BP-HLS, reprinted in Alexander Bickel, ed., *The Unpublished Opinions of Mr. Justice Brandeis* (Cambridge: Harvard University Press, 1957), pp. 5–14. Case moot: 259 U.S. 15–16. *Bailey* v. *Drexel*, 259 U.S. 20 (1922).

38. Quoted in Bickel, *Unpublished Opinions*, pp. 16–17. Brandeis did not dissent when the 1922 decision was handed down. Although his dissent would not have affected the Court's 8-1 ruling, the sentence from the draft of *Atherton* and Brandeis's concurrence with Holmes in *Hammer* make it clear he considered the act constitutional. Bickel argues convincingly that intra-Court politics and an eye towards his own continued effectiveness on the Court led Brandeis to maintain silence here. Ibid., pp. 18–19.

39. Kelley and Gompers: LDB to FF, June 16, 1922, *Letters*, V, 53, n. 4; September 19, 1922, *Letters*, V, 63. Bailey: LDB to FF, June 16, 1922, *Letters*, V, 52. Remedy: LDB to FF, September 19, 1922, *Letters*, V, 64.

40. *Whitney* v. *Calif.*, 274 U.S. 357, 372, 379–380 (1927) (concurring).

41. *Ashwander* v. *TVA*, 297 U.S. 288, 341–348 (1936).

42. Walton Hamilton, "The Jurist's Art." *Columbia Law Review* 31(1931),

1073, reprinted in Felix Frankfurter, ed., *Mr. Justice Brandeis* (New Haven: Yale University Press, 1932), pp. 171, 176. Frankfurter, "The Constitution," in *Mr. Justice Brandeis*, p. 52. LDB's impact: see particularly *Galveston Electric Co. v. City of Galveston*, 258 U.S. 388 (1922); *South Western Bell v. Public Service Commission*, 262 U.S. 276, 289 (1923) (concurring); *McCardle v. Indianapolis Water Co.*, 272 U.S. 400, 421 (1926) (dissenting); *St. Louis and O'Fallon Ry. v. U.S.* 279 U.S. 461, 488 (1929) (dissenting); *Railroad Commission v. Los Angeles Ry.* 280 U.S. 145, 158 (1929) (dissenting); *United Ry. v. West*, 280 U.S. 234, 255 (1930) (dissenting). Cf. Hamilton, "Jurist's Art," pp. 171–192; Henry Wolf Biklé, "Mr. Justice Brandeis and the Regulation of Railroads" in Frankfurter, *Mr. Justice Brandeis*, pp. 143–168; Mason, *Brandeis*, pp. 547–553; Mason, *Brandeis, Lawyer and Judge in the Modern State* (Princeton, N.J.: Princeton University Press, 1933), pp. 182–202; Louis L. Jaffe, "The Contributions of Justice Brandeis to Administrative Law," *Iowa Law Review*, 18 (1932–1933), 213; Harry Shulman, "The Demise of Swift v. Tyson," *Yale Law Journal*, 47 (1937–1938), 1336, all of which cite relevant cases.

16. Law and Civil Liberties

1. Taft to Henry Stimson, May 18, 1928, quoted in Bickel, *Unpublished Opinions*, p. 220. Holmes quotation: Mark DeWolfe Howe, *The Holmes-Pollock Letters* (Cambridge: Harvard University Press, 1941), II, 215. The case in which LDB dissented was *Casey v. U.S.*, 276 U.S. 413 (1928).

2. Holmes and Brandeis: cf. Mason, *Brandeis*, chap. 36; Bickel, *Unpublished Opinions*, chap. 10; Konefsky, *Legacy of Holmes and Brandeis*. LDB on Holmes: Felix Frankfurter, "Memorandum," FF-LC Box 128, p. 14; BP-HLS, Untitled Notebook, Box 114-7, pp. marked August 4, 1924, 3–5. The memorandum is a typescript, reportedly put together by Alexander Bickel, of handwritten notes made by Frankfurter after talks with LDB, 1922–1926. The originals, in BP-HLS 114-7 and 114-8, are difficult to read, but differ in small ways from the typescript, apparently because of the problems presented by FF's handwriting. Where the two versions differ, the BP-HLS archives have been used for this volume. Holmes's version: Holmes to Pollock, Howe, *Holmes-Pollock Letters*, II, 13–14.

3. Instances: Frankfurter, "Memorandum," p. 16. Durant: LDB to FF, January 7, 1927, *Letters*, V, 260. Sainte-Beuve: Holmes to FF, July 12, 1923, Holmes papers, HLS, quoted in Bickel, *Unpublished Opinions*, p. 230.

4. Futility of experience: Oliver Wendell Holmes, *Collected Legal Papers* (New York: Peter Smith, 1952), p. 306. Malthus: Holmes to LDB, April 20, 1919, BP, SC 4-2. Holmes to FF, December 3, 1925, Holmes Papers, HLS, quoted in Bickel, *Unpublished Opinions*, p. 230.

5. David Riesman, "Notes for an Essay on Justice Brandeis," sent to FF, May 22, 1936, FF-LC Box 127, pp. 1–2.

6. *Truax v. Corrigan*, 257 U.S. 312, 355–357 (1921) (dissenting).

7. *Jay Burns Baking Co. v. Bryan*, 264 U.S. 504, 517, 519–534 (1924) (dissenting).

8. *American Column and Lumber Co. v. U.S.*, 257 U.S. 377, 414–418

(1921) (dissenting); *Boston Store* v. *American Gramophone Co.*, 246 U.S. 8, 27–28 (1918) (concurring); *Frost* v. *Corp. Commission of Oklahoma*, 278 U.S. 515, 528, 536, 538–546 (1929); *New State Ice Co.* v. *Liebmann*, 285 U.S. 262, 280 (1932) (dissenting).

9. *Pennsylvania Coal Co.* v. *Mahon*, 260 U.S. 393, 415, 416 (1922). LDB dissent: 260 U.S. 416, 422.

10. LDB told FF about Holmes's opinion, " 'Due Process'—the thing that prevailed with him in the Mahon case." FF, "Memorandum," FF-LC Box 224, p. 24. For Brandeis and Holmes's earlier disputes over property rights and due process, cf. Bickel's discussion of *Bullock* v. *Florida*, 254 U.S. 513 (1921), in Bickel, *Unpublished Opinions*, chap. 10. LDB on Holmes: to FF, January 13, 1923, *Letters*, V, 83; FF, "Memorandum," FF-LC Box 224, pp. 21, 27; original BP-HLS Notebook marked "Chatham," 114-8, pp. 21–22; Untitled Notebook, p. 2. "Benjamin" refers to Holmes.

11. *Truax* v. *Corrigan*, 257 U.S. 312, 344, 354, 357–70 (1921).

12. Early Holmes: Konefsky, *The Legacy of Holmes and Brandeis*, pp. 185–186, 188–189; immaterial: Holmes to Pollock, *Holmes-Pollock Letters*, I, 163.

13. David Riesman, "Notes for an Essay on Justice Brandeis," unpublished letter to Felix Frankfurter, May 22, 1936, FF-LC, p. 2. *Myers* v. *U.S.*, 52, 240, 293 (1926).

14. *Frohwerk* v. *United States*, 249 U.S. 204 (1919); *Gitlow* v. *New York*, 268 U.S. 652 (1925); *Schenck* v. *U.S.*, 249 U.S. 47 (1919).

15. Clear and present danger: *Schenck* v. *U.S.* at 52.

16. Ibid., at 52.

17. LDB on *Schenck* and Holmes: FF, "Memorandum," p. 23. *Frohwerk* v. *United States*.

18. *Abrams* v. *United States*, 250 U.S. 616, 630 (1919).

19. *Schaefer* v. *U.S.*, 251 U.S. 266 (1920).

20. LDB in *Schaefer*: 251 U.S. 466, 482, 483, 484–485, 487–492, 494.

21. Ibid. at 495.

22. *Pierce* v. *United States*: 252 U.S. 239, 256–263, 264, 272–273 (1920); LDB on Pitney: FF, "Memorandum," p. 4.

23. LDB on *Schaefer* and *Pierce*: FF, "Memorandum," pp. 22–23. LDB on *Debs* v. *U.S.*, 249 U.S. 211 (1919): FF memorandum, p. 23.

24. *Gilbert* v. *Minnesota*, 254 U.S. 325 (1920).

25. *Gilbert* quotation, ibid. at 327; Holmes's concurrence: ibid. at 334.

26. LDB in *Gilbert*: 254 U.S. 325, 334, 335–336, 342, 343.

27. Mining: *Pennsylvania Coal* v. *Mahon*, 260 U.S. 393 (1922); tenants: *Block* v. *Hirsh*, 256 U.S. 135 (1921). LDB on *Block*: to FF, *Letters*, IV, 550.

28. *United States ex rel. Milwaukee Social Democratic Publishing Company* v. *Burleson*, 255 U.S. 407, 417, 432, 436 (1921).

29. LDB on Fourteenth: FF, "Memorandum," pp. 19, 20–21. *Meyer* v. *Nebraska*, 262 U.S. 390 (1923). Common tongue: *Bartels* v. *Iowa*, 262 U.S. 404, 412 (1923). Fourteenth: FF, "Memorandum," p. 20. The section of Frankfurter's notes referred to here is mistranscribed in the Library of Congress typescript. The original (notebook titled "Chatham," BP-HLS 114-8, p. 19) reads as follows:

Long talk on topic of due process as to freedom of speech and foreign language cases. Agreed
1) d.p. (due process) should be restricted to procedural regularity or
2) in favor of repeal but
3) while it is, must be applied to substantive laws and so as to things that are fundamental.
Right to Speech
Right to Education
Right to choice of profession
Right to locomotion
are such "fundamental" rights not to be impaired or withdrawn except by "clear and present danger" test.

The major mistake in the FF-LC typescript is that the first right mentioned has been transcribed as "Right to appeal." (Other mistakes include "application" instead of "topic" in the first sentence, as well as lesser mistakes that do not alter the meaning). The handwritten version, closely studied, clearly says "Speech." This interpretation is bolstered by a continuation of the paragraph on the next page, which says "Whereas right to your education and to utter speech is fundamental *except* clear and present danger" (p. 20).

30. *Olmstead* v. *United States*, 277 U.S. 438, 471 (1928) (dissenting); *Whitney* v. *California*, 274 U.S. 357, 372 (1927) (concurring).

31. *Casey* v. *U.S.*, 276 U.S. 413 (1928).

32. Ibid. at 421–425.

33. *Olmstead* v. *United States* at 474, 475–476.

34. Ibid. at 473–477.

35. Ibid. at 472, quoting Marshall in *McCulloch* v. *Maryland*, 17 U.S. (4 Wheat.) 316, 409 (1819). Search and seizure: *Boyd* v. *U.S.*, 255 U.S. 298 (1921); *Ex parte Jackson*, 96 U.S. 727 (1878), all cited at 277 U.S. 473–477; Fourth Amendment: 277 U.S. at 478; men of zeal: 277 U.S. at 479.

36. *Olmstead* v. *United States* at 485.

37. Memorandum: March 21, 1938, BP-HLS 48-7. Cf. other folders in Box 48 for various memoranda, working notes, and drafts. Holmes's dissent: 277 U.S. 469; cf. Howe, *Holmes-Pollock Letters*, II:222. Standards: Fannie Brandeis's notes of 1931 conversation, BP, Addendum, Box I. LDB to FF, June 15, 1928, *Letters*, V, 345.

38. LDB and Warren, "The Right to Privacy," Thomas M. Cooley, *Cooley on Torts* (Chicago: Callaghan, 2nd ed., p. 29, 1875); reference is in the article, p. 193. Home: 277 U.S. at 474. Television: BP-HLS 48-7.

39. Government spying: LDB to FF, June 22, 1926, *Letters*, V, 224; June 23, 1926, *Letters*, V, 224–225; June 25, 1926, *Letters*, V, 225–226; July 2, 1926, *Letters*, V, 227–228; July 16, 1926, *Letters*, V, 229. Cf. LDB to FF, May 25, 1924, and February 4, 1927, FF-LC Box 27. In 1920 Attorney General Mitchell Palmer rounded up over 4,000 suspected radicals, deporting 556. Sedition: LDB was referring to reparations for Alien-Sedition Act.

40. "Un-American": LDB to FF, November 26, 1920, *Letters*, IV, 510.

ACLU: LDB to FF, May 21, 1927, *Letters*, V, 285–286; May 25, 1927, *Letters*, V, 287. The editor was Lowell Mellett; the author, Ruth Furness. Appropriations cuts: LDB to FF, June 23, 1926, *Letters*, V, 225. Transcripts of the wiretap on Frankfurter's telephone were obtained in 1977 by historian Lincoln A. Robbins. *New York Times*, September 15, 1977, p. B 21, c. 1–4.

41. *Whitney* v. *California*, 274 U.S. 357 (1927).

42. Ibid. at 372, 373.

43. Court in 1928: see cases cited, ibid., at 373; Holmes for unanimous court: *Schenck* v. *U.S.*, 249 U.S. 47 (1919). Majority in *Whitney*: 274 U.S. at 371–372.

44. *Whitney* v. *California*, 274 U.S. at 374.

45. Ibid. at 375.

46. Ibid. at 376, 377–378.

47. Ibid. at 379.

48. Ibid. at 375. Johnson: quoted in Bickel, *Unpublished Opinions*, p. 163; Acheson, *Morning and Noon*, p. 102.

49. Mason, *Brandeis*, p. 566. *"The Anti-Bar Law"*: Argument of L. D. Brandeis before the Joint Ctte on Liquor Law of the Massachusetts Legislature. February 27, 1891, BP, Scrapbooks, Clippings I.

50. Selling liquor: *Albrecht* v. *U.S.*, 273 U.S. 1 (1927); flask: *U.S.* v. *One Ford Coupe*, 272 U.S. 321 (1926); losses: *Ruppert* v. *Caffey*, 251 U.S. 264 (1920).

51. Louisville statute: *Buchanan* v. *Worley*, 245 U.S. 60 (1917); restrictive covenant: *Corrigan* v. *Buckley*, 271 U.S. 323 (1926). *South Covington* v. *Kentucky*, 252 U.S. 399 (1920). *Gong Lum* v. *Rice*. 275 U.S. 278 (1927).

52. *Wan* v. *United States*, 266 U.S. 1 (1924). Holmes: *Moore* v. *Dempsey*, 261 U.S. 86 (1923). Scottsboro: *Powell* v. *Alabama*, 287 U.S. 45 (1932); Scottsboro II: *Norris* v. *Alabama*, 294 U.S. 587 (1935). *Hollins* v. *Oklahoma*, 295 U.S. 394 (1935); *Hale* v. *Kentucky*, 303 U.S. 613 (1938).

53. Primaries: *Nixon* v. *Condon*, 286 U.S. 73 (1932); party convention: *Grovey* v. *Townsend*, 295 U.S. 45 (1936).

54. *New Negro Alliance* v. *Grocery Co.*, 303 U.S. 552, 561 (1938). McReynolds's dissent: ibid., 563–564.

55. *Missouri ex rel. Gaines* v. *Canada*, 305 U.S. 337 (1938).

56. Frankfurter and NAACP: H. N. Hirsch, *The Enigma of Felix Frankfurter* (New York: Basic Books, 1981), p. 71; Richard Kluger, *Simple Justice* (New York: Knopf, 1976), p. 115. Howard University: Kluger, *Simple Justice*, p. 125; Houston: Ibid., pp. 115–116, 125, 156, 201. *Shelley* v. *Kraemer*, 334 U.S. 1 (1928); Houston brief: Kluger, *Simple Justice*, pp. 253–254.

57. Margold: LDB to FF, February 11, 1928, *Letters*, V, 322; February 29, 1928, *Letters*, V, 325–326; March 29, 1928, *Letters*, V, 333–334; April 21, 1928, *Letters*, V, 336–337. Margold Report: unpublished report, "Preliminary Report to the Joint Committee Supervising the Expenditure of the 1930 Appropriation by the American Fund for Public Service to the N.A.A.C.P.," Margold Papers, Library of Congress, NAACP Papers, Container 200; also in New York City 42nd St. Library.

58. Sharecroppers: *Webb* v. *O'Brien*, 263 U.S. 313, 326 (1923). *Frick* v. *Webb*, 263 U.S. 326, 334 (1923). LDB to FF, November 20, 1923, *Letters*, V, 104–105.

59. Naturalized Chinese: 275 U.S. 475; 275 U.S. 78 (1927). LDB to FF, September 26, 1927, *Letters*, V, 303. Brandeis unclear: *Letters*, V, 303, n. 1. Other cases handled by the Court included *Ng Fung* v. *White*, 259 U.S. 273 (1921), *Ozawa* v. *U.S.*, 260 U.S. 178 (1922), *Toyota* v. *U.S.*, 268 U.S. 402 (1924), *Terrace* v. *Thompson*, 263 U.S. 197 (1923), and *Porterfield* v. *Webb*, 263 U.S. 313 (1923).

60. Harlan in *Plessy* v. *Ferguson*, 163 U.S. 537 (1896).

61. *Near* v. *Minnesota*, 283 U.S. 697 (1931). Oral argument: *New York Times*, January 31, 1931.

62. Law schools: Paul L. Murphy, *The Constitution in Crisis Times, 1918–1969* (New York: Harper and Row, 1972), pp. 74–75. Among the social scientists hired by the three law schools were Walton Hamilton, Harold Lasswell, Robert L. Hale, and Sheldon Glueck. Civil Rights Act: *Heart of Atlanta* v. *United States*, 379 U.S. 241 (1964); *Katzenbach* v. *McClung*, 379 U.S. 294 (1964).

63. Remedial use of racial classifications; see, e.g., *U.S.* v. *Montgomery*, 395 U.S. 225 (1969); *Swann* v. *Charlotte-Mecklenburg*, 402 U.S. 1 (1970); *Davis* v. *Board*, 402 U.S. 33 (1970).

64. See, e.g., Justice Brennan in *Frontiero* v. *Richardson*, 411 U.S. 677 (1973) (women); abortions: *Roe* v. *Wade*, 410 U.S. 113 (1973); poor women: Justice Marshall in *Maher* v. *Roe*, 432 U.S. 438, 454 (1977) (dissenting); medical students: *Regents* v. *Bakke*, 438 U.S. 265, (1978); black children: *Brown* v. *Board*, 347 U.S. 483 (1954); prisoners: *Rhodes* v. *Chapman*, 452 U.S. 337 (1981); death penalty: *Furman* v. *Georgia*, 408 U.S. 238 (1972).

17. The Curse of Bigness

1. *Liggett* v. *Lee*, 288 U.S. 517, 533, 536 (1933). LDB's dissent: ibid. at 533, 542–543, 547.

2. Ibid. at 548–549, 557, 564–567.

3. Ibid. at 568–569.

4. Ibid. at 564–569, n. 50–61; 580.

5. *Quaker City Cab Co.* v. *Pennsylvania*, 277 U.S. 389, 403, 410–411 (1928) (dissenting).

6. Felix Frankfurter, "Mr. Justice Brandeis and the Constitution" in Felix Frankfurter, ed., *Mr. Justice Brandeis* (New Haven: Yale University Press, 1933), p. 123; LDB quoted by Paul Freund in introduction to Bickel, *Unpublished Opinions*, p. xv.

7. *Hitchman Coal and Coke Co.* v. *Mitchell*, 245 U.S. 229, 263, 271 (1917) (dissenting).

8. *Duplex Printing Co.* v. *Deering*, 254 U.S. 443, 479, 483–488 (1921) (dissenting).

9. Alexis de Tocqueville, *Democracy in America* (New York: Adlard, 1835; reprinted New York: Knopf, 1945), I, 280.

10. LDB in *Duplex* v. *Deering*, 254 U.S. at 479–482.

11. Ibid. at 488.

12. *Truax* v. *Corrigan*, 257 U.S. 312, 354, 357–370.

13. *Bedford Cut Stone* v. *Journeymen Cutter's Association*, 274 U.S. 37 (1927); LDB at 274 U.S. 64–67.

14. See, e.g., Bickel, *Unpublished Opinions*, chaps. 4 and 5, the latter dealing with *United Mine Workers* v. *Coronado*, 259 U.S. 344 (1922).

15. Holmes to Laski, December 11, 1930, quoted in Bickel, *Unpublished Opinions*, p. 222. Laski to Holmes, January 13, 1918: Mark de Wolfe Howe, ed., *Holmes-Laski Letters* (Cambridge: Harvard University Press, 1953), I, 127. Stone to LDB, March 1, 1933, BP, HLS 82-12. Frankfurter on LDB: Frankfurter, "Mr. Justice Brandeis and the Constitution," pp. 51, 52.

16. Paul Freund, "Driven by Passion," in *Sunday Herald*, November 11, 1956, p. 3, FF-LC Box 128. Hurst: letter to author, November 18, 1977. Acheson: *Morning and Noon*, pp. 93–94, 103; Magruder speech, Temple Israel, Boston, October 31, 1941, HLS Magruder Papers 33-9, pp. 11–13; Acheson, *Morning and Noon*, p. 94.

17. *Myers* v. *U.S.*, 272 U.S. 52, 250, 293 (1927) (dissenting).

18. NRA and AAA: LDB to Elizabeth Brandeis Raushenbush, *Letters*, V, 537. LDB to Hapgood: October 27, 1934.

19. LDB in oil case: quoted in Mason, *Brandeis*, p. 618. The cases were *Panama Refining Co.* v. *Ryan* and *Amazon Petroleum Corp.* v. *Ryan*, 293 U.S. 388 (1935).

20. LDB's vote as surprise: Mason, *Brandeis*, p. 619; Arthur Schlesinger, Jr., *The Politics of Upheaval* (Boston: Houghton Mifflin, 1960), pp. 283–284. FDR on Isaiah: quoted in Melvin I. Urofsky, *Louis D. Brandeis and The Progressive Tradition* (Boston: Little, Brown, 1981), p. 162. LDB to FF, June 17, 1923, *Letters*, V, 98. Webb-Kenyon Act was upheld in *Clark Distilling* v. *Western Maryland*, 242 U.S. 311 (1917). Cardozo: *Schechter* v. *U.S.*, 295 U.S. 495, 551 (1935) (concurring).

21. *Humphrey's Executor* v. *United States*, 295 U.S. 602 (1935); *Louisville* v. *Radford*, 295 U.S. 555, 581–586, 589–590, 602.

22. LDB to FF: FF, "Memorandum," FF-LC Box 128, p. 24. *Erie Railroad* v. *Tompkins*, 304 U.S. 64, 78 (1938), overruling *Swift* v. *Tyson*, 16 Pet. 1 (1842). *Louisville* v. *Radford*, 295 U.S. at 590–595, 599, 600–601. I am grateful to Professor Willard Hurst for pointing out that Brandeis rarely used facts to strike down legislation. Interview with Hurst, September 24, 1980.

23. LDB to Corcoran: quoted in Schlesinger, *The Politics of Upheaval*, p. 280. "Black Monday" is Schlesinger's phrase.

24. *U.S.* v. *Butler*, 297 U.S. 1, 62–63 (1936).

25. Ibid. at 87.

26. LDB to FF, June 5, 1927, *Letters*, V, 292–293. Felix Frankfurter and James M. Landis, *The Business of the Supreme Court* (New York: Macmillan, 1928), pp. vii–viii.

27. LDB-FF conversations: FF, "Memorandum," FF-LC Box 128; original in BP-HLS 114-7, 114-8.

18. Style and Politics on the Court

1. A list of LDB's clerks, by year, is in Mason, *Brandeis*, p. 690.

2. Acheson, *Morning and Noon*, pp. 57, 82.

3. LDB to Alfred, September 11, 1926, BP, M 4-4; interview with Willard Hurst, September 24, 1980: Lief, *Brandeis*, p. 423; interview with H. Thomas Austern, October 22, 1978: interview with Paul Freund, October 28, 1977. *Liggett* v. *Lee*, 288 U.S. 517, 541 (1933). The factual material is in BP-HLS 81-1, 81-2; bibliographies are in BP-HLS 81-3, 81-4.

4. Patent case: interview with Austern. Footnotes: Acheson, *Morning and Noon*, p. 80. Austern told the same story in interview. Accuracy: see Riesman, "Notes for an Essay," p. 3.

5. Acheson, *Morning and Noon*, pp. 96–97; interview with Willard Hurst. Patent case: interview with Austern.

6. Draft with sixty changes: interview with Austern. Delivering opinions from memory: "Justice Brandeis," *St. Louis Post-Dispatch* (no byline), reprinted in Louisville newspaper (name unclear), November 13, 1931, in Louisville Free Public Library, Kentucky Authors Scrapbook, Part I.

7. Acheson, *Morning and Noon*, pp. 82–83. Magruder to FF: FF-HLS Box 20. Date appears to be 1916. Landis in *Whitney*: BP-HLF 44-7; see particularly Landis to LDB, August 16, 1926. Riesman in *Carter*: "Doubts and Hesitations," BP-HLS 97-8.

8. *Shafer* v. *Farmers Grain Co.*, 268 U.S. 189 (1925); LDB to McCurdy, June 26, July 19, and August 18, 1923, BP-HLS. *McGrain*: BP-HLS 38-7. See letters to and from LDB and Landis, BP-HLS 38-7; drafts, etc., BP-HLS 38-6.

9. *Myers*: Landis notes, BP-HLS 39-10; Ege's memorandum BP-HLS 38-9. Mysterious hand: interviews with Freund, Austern, Riesman. LDB's schedule: Lief, *Brandeis*, p. 472; Nathaniel Nathanson, "Mr. Justice Brandeis," *American Jewish Archives*, 15 (1963), 8.

10. Description of LDB: interview with Austern. Journalists' accounts: R. L. Duffus, "Brandeis, at 75, Still the Fighter," *New York Times*, November 8, 1931; Carson C. Hathaway, "Justice Brandeis Reaches 70 Years" (no name of newspaper or date); S. T. Williamson, "Our Leading Dissenter," *New York Times*, January 27, 1932; R. L. Duffus (no title), *New York Times*, magazine section, November 8, 1936; Mildred Adams, "Three Venerable Justices Who Refuse to Grow Old," *New York Times*, December 8, 1929; all in Louisville Free Public Library, Kentucky Authors Scrapbook, Box 8.

11. Acheson, *Morning and Noon*, pp. 181, 227. Magruder to LDB, Magruder Papers, HLS, 33-9. LDB to Magruder, July 3, 1932; August 18, 1932; Alice to Magruder, January 5, 1943; all Magruder Papers, HLS 33-7. Presentation of bronze head: Minutes of January 10, 1945 (date unclear in original) meeting of Visiting Committee to accept gift, FF-LC Box 127.

12. "Two-person team" and clerks' hours: interview with Hurst.

13. LDB to FF, January 28, 1928, *Letters*, V, 320. On Shulman: to same, October 13, 1929, *Letters*, V, 404; also on Page and Friendly. Problems with

Goldsmith: LDB to FF, October 7, 1928, *Letters*, V, 358–359; October 12, *Letters*, V, 359–360; October 15, *Letters*, V, 361.

14. Liva Baker, *Felix Frankfurter* (New York: Coward-McCann, 1969), pp. 41–42; Philipps, *Frankfurter Reminisces*, pp. 77–80; Nelson Lloyd Dawson, *Louis D. Brandeis, Felix Frankfurter, and the New Deal* (Hamden, Conn.: Archon Books, 1980), pp. 1–2; Hirsch, *Enigma of Felix Frankfurter*, pp. 31–32.

15. FF's "extracurricular" activities: Dawson, *Louis D. Brandeis, Felix Frankfurter*, pp. 4–5; Hirsch, *Enigma of Felix Frankfurter*, pp. 45, 69–73, 78, 90–94. Also see Chapter 19. FF's fiancée: LDB to Marion Denman, November 3, 1919, quoted in Hirsch, *Enigma of Felix Frankfurter*, p. 85.

16. Lief, *Brandeis*, p. 423; Acheson, *Morning and Noon*, pp. 81–82, 99; interviews with Hurst, Austern, and Riesman. *Senn* v. *Tile Layers Protective Union*, 301 U.S. 468 (1937): letter from Hurst to author, October 3, 1980. LDB's comments to Hurst and Nathanson: interview with Hurst; Nathanson to FF, March 4, 1935, FF-LC, Box 127. The comment to Nathanson was made in connection with LDB's opinion in *Nashville, Chattanooga & St. Louis Railway* v. *Walters*, 294 U.S. 405 (1935), which the Court had handed down that day. Riesman memorandum, FF-LC, Box 127, p. 3.

17. Interview with Freund; interview with Austern.

18. Remark about *Muller*: Acheson, *Morning and Noon*, p. 53. Bullitt: interview with Riesman. Denmark: interview with Freund.

19. Acheson, *Morning and Noon*, pp. 87, 123. Clerks' recollections: author's interviews with Freund and Austern; Landis to LDB, August 16, 1926, BP-HLS 44-7; Riesman to LDB, BP-HLS 97-8. Contact with Frankfurter: Acheson, *Morning and Noon*, pp. 51–53; Nathanson, "Mr. Justice Brandeis," p. 12; LDB to FF, December 1, 1916, *Letters*, IV, 268; November 25, 1920, *Letters*, IV, 510; October 23, 1922, *Letters*, V, 74; November 9, 1926, *Letters*, V, 255; September 29, 1929, *Letters*, V, 397. Also see LDB to William Rice, Jr., May 25, 1937, *Letters*, V, 589.

20. Author's interview with Riesman, Austern, and Hurst: Acheson, *Morning and Noon*, pp. 49–50.

21. Mack: author's interview with Austern. Marion Frankfurter quoted in Joseph P. Lash, "A Brahmin of the Law: A Biographical Essay" in *The Diaries of Felix Frankfurter*, ed. Joseph P. Lash (New York: W. W. Norton, 1975), p. 51. Modest home: author's interview with Austern; records: author's interview with Riesman. Asceticism: Riesman memorandum, FF-LC, Box 127, p. 3. Cryptanalyst: Acheson, *Morning and Noon*, p. 58. Typesetter: BP, SC-13. Printer: BP-HLS 37-14. The case involved was *Lambert* v. *Yellowley*, 272 U.S. 581 (1926).

22. *Harvard Law Review*: LDB to FF, January 24, 1926, *Letters*, V, 204; to same, June 25, 1926, *Letters*, V, 225. Other reviews: LDB to FF, May 11, 1924, *Letters*, V, 129; June 16, 1927, *Letters*, V, 294. Also see LDB to FF, May 14, 1923, *Letters*, V, 94.

23. *Adams* v. *Tanner*, 244 U.S. 590, 597, 603 n. 3, 613 nn. 1–3, 615 n. 1 (1917) (dissenting). *Erie Railroad* v. *Tompkins*, 304 U.S. 72 nn. 3, 4; 73 nn. 5, 6; 74 n. 7; 75 nn. 9, 10; 77 nn. 20–22. Topics for *Review*: see, e.g., LDB to FF,

March 8, 1925, cited in David W. Levy and Bruce Allen Murphy, "Preserving the Progressive Spirit in a Conservative Time," *Michigan Law Review*, 78 (August 1980), 1252, 1290 n. 190; May 2, 1926, *Letters*, V, 221; June 25, 1926, *Letters*, V, 226–227; August 15, 1926, cited in Levy and Murphy, "Preserving the Progressive Spirit," p. 1289; October 15, 1926, *Letters*, V, 235; November 30, 1926, *Letters*, V, 247–248; June 2, 1927, *Letters*, V, 290; July 27, 1927, cited in Levy and Murphy, "Preserving the Progressive Spirit," p. 1289; October 29, 1927, *Letters*, V, 306; December 6, 1927, *Letters*, V, 315; March 16, 1928, V, 329–330; and letters cited in Levy and Murphy, "Preserving the Progressive Spirit," pp. 1286–91. LDB, FF, and common law article: ibid., p. 1291. Birthday reviews: *Columbia Law Review*, v. 31; *Yale Law Journal*, v. 41; *Harvard Law Review*, v. 45; all November 1931.

24. McReynolds: Mason, *Brandeis*, p. 628, citing memorandum from Hurst to Mason. Twenty-four opinions: Chester A. Newland: *Innovation in Judicial Technique: The Brandeis Opinion* (Pocatello, Idaho: Idaho State University Press, 1960), pp. 1, 5–6.

25. The best work on the subject of intracourt politics is Walter Murphy, *Elements of Judicial Strategy* (Chicago: University of Chicago Press, 1964).

26. "play politics": FF, "Memorandum," BP-HLS 114-8, p. 3; second copy in FF-LC Box 224, p. 16. Number of LDB's opinions was calculated by Mason in *Brandeis*, pp. 627–628.

27. LDB on dissents: FF, "Memorandum," FF-LC Box 224, pp. 6, 8–9, 18. *United Zinc & Chemical Co. v. Britt*, 258 U.S. 268 (1922); LDB's comments, FF, "Memorandum," p. 26. Holmes's need to " 'shoot them off' ": ibid., p. 17.

28. FF, "Memorandum," pp. 5, 8, 9. Pitney: ibid., p. 25. The case was probably *Citizens National Bank of Cincinnati v. Durr*, 257 U.S. 99 (1921).

29. LDB to Alice, December 4, 1918, *Letters*, IV, 370. There is no indication of which case was involved. Case in which technique worked: FF, "Memorandum," p. 26. *Hamilton v. Kentucky Distilleries & Wine Company*, 251 U.S. 146 (1919), discussed in ibid., p. 23.

30. *McCarthy v. Arndstein*, 262 U.S. 355 (1923): LDB's memorandum is in BP-HLS 16-15, 16-16, 17-1. *St. Louis, Brownsville and Mexico Railroad Company v. United States* (1925): the note is in BP-HLS 29-11. "Next drafts": e.g., *Truax v. Corrigan*, 257 U.S. 312 (1921), BP-HLS 7-7, 7-8, 7-10; *Galveston Electric Co. v. Galveston*, 258 U.S. 388 (1922), BP-HLS 10-2, 10-3, 10-4; *Great Northern Ry. Co. v. Merchants Elevator Co.*, 259 U.S. 285 (1922), BP-HLS 10-6. See Stone to LDB, March 1, 1933, BP-HLS 82-12, re *Liggett v. Lee*.

31. Memoranda turned into dissents: *Pierce*, BP-HLS 4-1, 4-2; *Duplex*, BP-HLS 5-9, 5-10; *Gilbert*, BP-HLS 5-13; *New State Ice*, BP-HLS 76-1, 76-3; *Liggett*, BP-HLS 81-7, 81-11, 82-7; also see *Portsmouth Harbor Land and Hotel Co. v. U.S.*, 260 U.S. 327 (1922), BP-HLS 19-2. Tactical reasons: There are numerous examples in the HLS papers as well as in Bickel, *Unpublished Opinions*. Memorandum in *Truax*: FF, "Memorandum," p. 1. *United Mine Workers v. Coronado*, 259 U.S. 344 (1922); Bickel, *Unpublished Opinions*, chap. 5. LDB's comments: FF, "Memorandum," FF-LC Box 224, pp. 2, 3; BP-HLS 114-8, "Chatham: #1," p. 9.

32. *McCarthy* v. *Arndstein*, 262 U.S. 355 (1923); Taft's note is in BP-HLS 17-1. *Atlantic Coast Line Railroad* v. *Watts*, 262 U.S. 413 (1923); note in BP-HLS 13-8. Taft to LDB, December 23, 1922, BP-HLS 20-1, referring to *Southern Railway Company* v. *Watts*, 260 U.S. 519 (1923).

33. Drafts with colleagues' comments are in BP-HLS. Sutherland's comment refers to *U.S.* v. *Wycoff Pipe*, 271 U.S. 262 (1926); Sanford's to *Atlantic Coast Line Railroad* v. *Watts*; Holmes's to the same; Pitney's to *Ruppert* v. *Caffey*, 251 U.S. 264 (1920). LDB to Stone: April 25, 1923, BP-HLS 28-46, referring to *Marr* v. *U.S.*, 268 U.S. 536 (1925). LDB to Van Devanter, May 19, 1926, *Letters*, V, 221 (it is not clear what case this letter was about).

34. Not discussing other justices with outsiders: Elizabeth Glendower Evans, "People I Have Known: Louis D. Brandeis, Tribune of the People," *La Follette's Magazine* (no date), pp. 188, 189, BP, Scrapbook 2; Willard Hurst, quoted in Mason, *Brandeis*, p. 538; Acheson, *Morning and Noon*, pp. 66–71; interviews with Hurst and Riesman. LDB-FF conversations in Chatham: FF's notes in FF-LC Box 224, in a typescript version probably made by Alexander Bickel. The originals, which are difficult to decipher, are in BP-HLS 114-7, 114-8. See FF to Marion Denman Frankfurter, July 2, 1924, FF-LC Box 120; July 7, 1924, FF-LC Box 121. On Van Devanter and Clarke: FF, "Memorandum," FF-LC Box 224, pp. 2, 6, 7, 8. The case in which Van Devanter persuaded Sutherland and Sanford not to dissent was *Jay Burns Baking Co.* v. *Bryan*, 264 U.S. 504 (1924). On Day: FF, "Memorandum," p. 2; also see p. 22. LDB on "lobbying": FF, "Memorandum," p. 8; also see pp. 16–17, 22.

35. McReynolds's majority opinion: FF, "Memorandum," p. 9. The case was *Sonneborn Brothers* v. *Cureton*, 262 U.S. 506 (1923). On Van Devanter's role: FF, "Memorandum," pp. 9, 10.

36. LDB on Taft: conference room, FF, "Memorandum," p. 22; *certiorari*, ibid., p. 21; mind, ibid., pp. 14–15; legislative matters, ibid., p. 28. For LDB's relationship with Taft, see Mason, *Brandeis*, pp. 538–539; for Taft's involvement with the Harding administration, see Henry Pringle, *The Life and Times of William Howard Taft* (New York: Farrar & Rinehart, 1939), I, 267 and II, 626–637, 827–833; Walter F. Murphy, "In His Own Image," in *1961 Supreme Court Review* (Chicago: University of Chicago Press, 1961), p. 159; Walter F. Murphy, "Chief Justice Taft and the Lower Court Bureaucracy," *Journal of Politics*, 24 (1962), 453; Walter F. Murphy, *Elements of Judicial Strategy* (Chicago: University of Chicago Press, 1964), passim. *Sonneborn Brothers* v. *Cureton*, 262 U.S. 506 (1923); comment, FF, "Memorandum," p. 7. Taft taking suggestions from LDB: FF, "Memorandum," p. 22, referring to *Railroad Commission of Wisconsin* v. *Chicago, Burlington & Quincy Railroad Co.*, 257 U.S. 563 (1922). Talking with Taft: FF, "Memorandum," pp. 3, 26, 27; Taft vapid: ibid., p. 12.

37. LDB on Holmes: FF, "Memorandum," pp. 1, 3, 14, 15, 18, 27.

38. On Sutherland: FF, "Memorandum," p. 6; Sanford, ibid., p. 8, also see pp. 26, 28; McReynolds, ibid., pp. 9, 12; Pitney, ibid., pp. 17, 22; Butler, ibid., p. 26; McKenna, ibid., p. 25. Other comments on justices (LDB did discuss the justices with his clerks) are in Acheson, *Morning and Noon*, pp. 66–71.

39. LDB's chats with White: Acheson, *Morning and Noon*, p. 60. Dinner with Clarke: LDB to Alfred, October 23, 1921, BP, M 4-4. Van Devanter: Phillips, *Frankfurter Reminisces*, p. 60. Treating justices with respect: Acheson, *Morning and Noon*, p. 94. Courtesy and self-restraint: Acheson, ibid., p. 94; also see Murphy, *Elements of Judicial Strategy*, p. 201 n.

19. Isaiah's Extrajudicial Activities

1. LDB to John B. Winslow, February 23, 1917, BP, SC 3-1; Acheson, *Morning and Noon*, p. 59; Mason, *Brandeis*, pp. 585, 613–614, 628. On Hughes: William O. Douglas, *The Court Years* (New York: Random House, 1980), p. 213.

2. LDB to FF, November 19, 1916, *Letters*, IV, 266; to same, November 25, 1916, *Letters*, V, 266–267. FF's bank account: LDB to FF, June 2, 1927, *Letters*, V, 290; Nelson Lloyd Dawson, *Louis D. Brandeis, Felix Frankfurter, and the New Deal* (Hamden, Conn.: Archon Books, 1980), pp. 4–5.

3. LDB to FF, January 6, 1923, FF-LC Box 26. LDB to FF, September 24, 1925, FF-LC Box 27; to FF, June 2, 1927, FF-LC Box 27; to Julian Mack, March 11, 1934, BP, Z 58-1.

4. LDB to Laski, November 29, 1928, BP, M 18-3; to same, August 3, 1925, BP, M 18-3. FF and Supreme Judicial Court: FF quoted in Phillips, *Frankfurter Reminisces*, p. 232. FF as solicitor general: Hirsch, *Enigma of Felix Frankfurter*, p. 103; Dawson, *Louis D. Brandeis, Felix Frankfurter*, pp. 47–48; Max Freedman, ed., *Roosevelt and Frankfurter: Their Correspondence, 1928–1945* (Boston: Little, Brown, 1967), pp. 110–114. FF, "Memorandum," FF-LC Box 128, mentions consulting only LDB and Solicitor General Thacher. Freedman, *Roosevelt and Frankfurter*, p. 114.

5. Judge Friendly: quoted in Leonard Baker, "The Franklin D. Roosevelt Presidency, Louis D. Brandeis, and Felix Frankfurter," paper delivered at Hofstra University, March 6, 1982, p. 3. I am grateful to Mr. Baker for giving me access to this material. LDB to FF, September 24, 1925, FF-LC Box 127. Hapgood, *Changing Years*, p. 42.

6. Relatives: see, e.g., letters to Alfred discussing payments to "Aunt Minna" (referred to by Otto Wehle in a letter of acknowledgment as the "March instalment"), "Virgie and Louise" (quarterly payments), and "Rudolph's family" (quarterly payments); LDB to Alfred, February 27, 1909, BP, NMF 11-10; Otto Wehle to LDB, March 3, 1909, BP, NMF 11-10; LDB to Wehle, March 31, 1909, enclosing "April payment," BP, NMF 11-10. De Haas: LDB to de Haas, August 10, 1924, BP, NMF 19-18. LDB sent money, probably amounting to $650 a month, through June, 1929. See various letters from LDB to de Haas in BP, NMF 19-18; LDB to Julian Mack and Stephen Wise, November 3, 1921, *Letters*, V, 27–28; to Mack, January 3, 1932, BP, P 52-1; to Mack, December 1934, *Letters*, V, 549. Szold: LDB signed an agreement with a few other wealthy Zionists to establish a $1,000 quarterly stipend for Henrietta Szold, at least through 1939. LDB to Mack, March 11, 1916, BP, Z 11-1; LDB to Mack, November 6, 1925, *Letters*, V, 191–192; to Robert Szold, June 28, 1939, *Letters*,

V, 620. *Harper's Weekly*: LDB to Hapgood, December 22, 1913, BP, NMF 64-1; to Alfred, May 28, 1913, BP, NMF 42-1. Also see LDB to Alfred, January 11, 1914, BP, M 4-1; to H. W. Ashley, January 31, 1914, BP, NMF 69-1; to Hapgood, May 28, 1913, BP, NMF 52-1.

7. Letter from Lewis H. Weinstein to Prof. Robert M. Cover, May 20, 1982; from Weinstein to author, June 2, 1982; from Weinstein to Editor of the *Harvard Law Record*, April 16, 1982, p. 11. I am grateful to Prof. Cover for putting me in touch with Mr. Weinstein, senior partner of Foley, Hoag & Eliot, in Boston. John P. Frank, review article, *Journal of Legal Education*, 32 (1982), 435. Frank also notes that LDB gave money to Wilbur Katz and James Landis for specific projects. ibid., p. 436.

8. LDB to Mack, January 12, 1922, FF-LC Box 26; to same, March 11, 1934, BP, Z 58-1; LDB to de Haas, April 7, 1920, *Letters*, IV, 248; LDB to McClennen, October 30, 1932, BP, NMF 20-2. Nelson Dawson has noted that LDB also gave FF money to help in the publication of a casebook and to cover expenses resulting from Marion Frankfurter's illness. Dawson, *Louis D. Brandeis, Felix Frankfurter*, pp. 4–5.

9. Suggestions from LDB to FF: December 30, 1920, January 4, 1921, March 9 and 27, 1921, *Letters*, IV, 520, 521, 542, 547–548; September 24, 25, 30, 1922, June 3, 1924, September 29, 1924, October 5, 1925, January 24, 1926, February 2, 1928, March 29, 1928, September 2 and 13, 1928, July 21, 1929, August 27, 1929, September 23, 1929, 64-65, 65, *Letters*, V, 64–71, 131, 141, 188–189, 203, 324, 333–334, 352, 353, 381, 382, 390.

10. Capitalism: LDB to FF, September 30, 1922, *Letters*, V, 65–71. Croly: LDB to Alice, December 2, 1918, *Letters*, IV, 367; to FF, December 10, 1920, *Letters*, IV, 517–518; to FF, April 10, 1921, *Letters*, IV, 549. LDB as *NR* editor: Levy and Murphy, "Preserving the Progressive Spirit," p. 1282, italics in original.

11. Mason, *Brandeis*, p. 588. LDB to Kellogg, April 25, 1920, BP, SC 5-2; April 30, 1920, *Letters*, IV, 462; cf. *The Survey*, 45 (November 13, 1920), pp. 183–228; to Kellogg, November 7, 1920, BP, SC 5-2.

12. LDB to Kellogg, June 9, 1924, *Letters*, V, 133; March 11, 1928, *Letters*, V, 329; March 13, 1928, SUNY-Albany; April 2, 1928, BP, M 5-1. Kellogg to LDB, March 15, 1928, SUNY-Albany; March 28, 1928, SUNY-Albany. LDB to Beulah Amidon, January 11, 1928, SUNY-Albany. LDB to Kellogg, May 24, 1936, *Letters*, V, 569, n. 1; to Leila E. Colburn, August 2, 1936, *Letters*, V, 575; cf. *Survey Graphic*, 25, November 1936, pp. 598–602. LDB to Charles Amidon, February 11, 1916, BP, NMF 78-1; May 2, 1916, BP, NMF 77-2. LDB's will: BP, WB 50338.

13. Zionist meeting: Urofsky, *American Zionism*, p. 362; Shapiro, *Leadership*, p. 240; *New York Times*, November 25, 1929; LDB to FF, November 29, 1929, *Letters*, V, 413.

14. Administration friends: LDB to Alfred, March 23, 1917, BP, M 4-1; to Hapgood, May 15, 1917, *Letters*, IV, 293; to Alice, October 16, 1917, *Letters*, IV, 314; to Alfred, December 1, 1917, BP, M 4-1; Alice, December 3, 1918, *Letters*, IV, 369; to Alfred, March 25, 1919, BP, M 4-1; to FF, January 18, 1920, *Letters*, IV, 444; to Alfred, December 11, 1920, BP, M 4-4. Hapgood, *Changing*

Years, p. 233. Josephus Daniels, "Prophetic Leadership," *Opinion*, 12 (November 1941), 8. Daniels as intermediary: Hapgood, *Changing Years*, p. 233; Daniels to FDR, September 26, 1934, cited in Walter F. Murphy, *Elements of Judicial Strategy* (Chicago: University of Chicago Press, 1964), pp. 148, 233 n. 96.

15. Prohibition message: Hapgood, *Changing Years*, p. 194. Appointing Hoover: Hapgood, *Changing Years*, pp. 195–196; Melvin I. Urofsky, *Louis D. Brandeis and the Progressive Tradition* (Boston: Little, Brown, 1981), p. 130; LDB to Hapgood, July 21, 1917, quoted in Mason, *Brandeis*, p. 520; LDB to Alfred, September 17 and October 7, 1917, BP, M 4-1; LDB to Alfred, November 27, 1920, BP, M 4-4. Members of war government: Urofsky, *Progressive Tradition*, p. 130.

16. LDB and Masaryk: Lief, *Brandeis*, pp. 406–407; LDB to Alfred, October 14, 1917, BP, M 4-1; to Alice, October 14, 1917, *Letters*, IV, 316. LDB and Straus: Straus to Hoover, November 18, 1918. LDB initialled one copy and noted that it was based on a conversation in "early November." FF-HLS Box 20; cf. Murphy, *Judicial Strategy*, p. 148.

17. Harding's cabinet: LDB to Alfred, January 16, 1921; February 6, 1921; March 1 and 23, 1921; September 16, 1921; October 15, 1921; all BP, M 4-4. Walsh: Lief, *Brandeis*, p. 440. *Black & White Taxi Co.* v. *Brown & Yellow Taxi Co.*, 276 U.S. 518 (1928); LDB to FF, April 21, 1928, and February 21, 1929, *Letters*, V, 336–337, 369. LDB and Moore: LDB to FF, March 4, 1928, and April 21, 1928, *Letters* V, 326, 337. Mexico and Nicaragua: LDB to FF, March 29, 1927, *Letters*, V, 277. Other visitors during 1920s: LDB to Alfred, November 27, 1920; March 9 and 23, 1921; May 6, 1921; October 27 and 31, 1921; November 4, 1921; October 3, 1924; October 31, 1927; all BP, M 4-4; LDB to Susan Brandeis Gilbert, November 14, 1922, *Letters*, V, 76; to FF, September 16, 1923, *Letters*, V, 100; to FF, May 18, 1924, *Letters*, V, 130; to FF, November 7, 1924, *Letters*, V, 151; to FF, May 21, 1927, *Letters*, V, 151; to FF, January 1, 1925, *Letters*, V, 155–156; to FF, May 25, 1927, *Letters*, V, 287; to FF, February 11, 1928, *Letters*, V, 322; to FF, March 4, 1928, *Letters*, V, 326–327; to FF, September 23, 1928, *Letters*, V, 354; to FF, October 1, 1928, *Letters*, V, 355; to FF, December 2, 1929, *Letters*, V, 414; Acheson, *Morning and Noon*, p. 110.

18. Shipstead Bill: LDB to FF, February 11, 1928, *Letters*, V, 322, 323 n. 2.

19. LDB to Hapgood, July 21, 1917, quoted in Mason, *Brandeis*, p. 520; Mason interview with LDB, July 22, 1940, cited in Mason, *Brandeis*, p. 518. LDB to FF, April 5, 1920, *Letters*, IV, 456; to Alfred, June 20, 1920, BP, M 4-4; to Alfred, September 6, 1921, BP, Unmarked Folder; to FF May 20, 1923, *Letters*, V, 95; to FF, January 11, 1924, *Letters*, V, 111; to FF, April 6, 1924, *Letters*, V, 124; to FF, January 6, 1926, *Letters*, V, 199; to FF, July 25, 1926, *Letters*, V, 230; to FF, October 28, 1926, *Letters*, V, 237. LDB for Al Smith: to FF, September 2, 1928, *Letters*, V, 352; October 15, 1928, *Letters*, V, 361: November 6, 1928, *Letters*, V, 362; November 8, 1928, *Letters*, V, 362; also LDB to Harold Laski, November 29, 1928, *Letters*, V, 364.

20. Stevens: LDB to FF, November 29, 1925, *Letters*, V, 195. Commission

on Law: LDB to FF, March 17, 1929, *Letters*, V, 374; to FF, April 3, 1929, *Letters*, V, 375. Eastman: LDB to FF, December 2, 1929, *Letters*, V, 414, 415 n. 4. Conversation with Hoover: quoted in conversation with Mason, June 26, 1940, reported in Mason, *Brandeis*, p. 601.

21. FF and LDB: Freedman, *Roosevelt and Frankfurter*, pp. 10–13; Hirsch, *Enigma of Felix Frankfurter*, p. 100; FF to Lippmann, 1930, quoted in Hirsch, ibid., pp. 100–101. FF and "Frank": Freedman, *Roosevelt and Frankfurter*, pp. 11, 281, 293. LDB's "requests": LDB to FF, November 4, 1928, *Letters*, V, 364 n. 2; to FF, November 14, 1928, *Letters*, V, 363. McAdoo: LDB to Fannie Brandeis, July 11, 1932, *Letters*, V, 505.

22. FDR-LDB conversation: Phillips, *Frankfurter Reminisces*, pp. 239–240; LDB to FF, November 24, 1932, FF-LC Box 98; Dawson, *Louis D. Brandeis, Felix Frankfurter,* p. 44.

23. LDB on Cabinet: to FF, February 23, 1933, FF-LC Box 28. LDB talking to Perkins: Perkins to FF, April 5, 1933, quoted in Dawson, *Louis D. Brandeis, Felix Frankfurter,* p. 52. Perkins and Black: LDB to FF, May 14, 1933, quoted in Dawson, ibid, p. 53; cf. p. 202 n. 49. Sprague: Dawson, ibid., p. 53.

24. Harold L. Ickes, *The Secret Diary of Harold L. Ickes* (New York: Simon & Schuster, 1953), quoted in Dawson, *Louis D. Brandeis, Felix Frankfurter,* p. 49. Margold: LDB to FF, March 13, 1933, FF-LC Box 28; also see Dawson, ibid., p. 50. Dawson's information about LDB and the New Deal relies heavily on the Frankfurter papers in the Library of Congress, which are cited. Some of the papers, unfortunately, were stolen after Dawson completed his research.

25. Johnson: LDB to FF, August 14, 1933, FF-LC Box 28, quoted in Dawson, *Louis D. Brandeis, Felix Frankfurter*, p. 65. Raushenbush plan: author's interview with Elizabeth Brandeis Raushenbush; LDB to Laski, February 28, 1932, *Letters*, V, 497–498; Elizabeth Brandeis, "Wisconsin Tackles Job Security," *The Survey*, 67 (December 15, 1931), 295–296; Elizabeth Brandeis, "Employment Reserves vs. Insurance," *The New Republic*, 76 (September 27, 1933), 177–179. LDB on Johnson: to Elizabeth Brandeis Raushenbush, November 17, 1933, *Letters*, V, 526–527.

26. Johnson, who was being treated for alcoholism, caused a tempest in a teapot by defending himself in a radio speech and maintaining that he had been "in constant touch" with Brandeis about the matter. As LDB's letter to Elizabeth (November 17, 1933) and another to Frankfurter indicate, LDB's only involvement had been to warn against the size of the NIRA and to urge a more federalized system. LDB to FF, September 22, 1935, FF-LC, Box 28. Some newspapers, apparently assuming that the "constant touch" implied LDB's approval of the NIRA, demanded that he recuse himself from any case involving it. LDB chose to ignore them and the incident died down after LDB voted with the Court to overturn the NIRA. LDB to FF, September 25, 1935, FF-LC, Box 28; Bernard Bellush, *The Failure of the NRA* (New York: Norton, 1975), pp. 122, 132–133; Arthur M. Schlesinger, Jr., *The Coming of the New Deal* (Boston: Houghton Mifflin, 1958), p. 105. Donald Richberg, "The Industrial Liberalism of Justice Brandeis," *Columbia Law Review*, vol. 31, reprinted in Felix Frankfurter, *Mr. Justice Brandeis* (New Haven: Yale University Press, 1932), pp. 127–140. Rich-

berg and FDR: Richberg to LDB, January 1, 1934, BP, G 9-2. LDB to Richberg, August 13, 1933, *Letters*, V, 518. LDB, Lilienthal, and Morgan: Lilienthal to LDB, August 21, 1933, BP, G 6-1; Dawson, *Louis D. Brandeis, Felix Frankfurter*, p. 82. Interview with Elizabeth Brandeis Raushenbush; Schlesinger, *Coming of the New Deal*, p. 328; LDB to Ickes, June 14, 1933, BP, G 6-1.

27. Rosenman: LDB to FF, September 20, 1933, cited in Dawson, *Louis D. Brandeis, Felix Frankfurter*, p. 91; to FF, September 23, 1933, quoted in Dawson, ibid., p. 91. Thompson to FDR, November 25, 1932, SUNY-Albany. LDB and Moley: Schlesinger, *Coming of the New Deal*, p. 236; LDB to FF, September 20, 1933, cited in Dawson, *Louis D. Brandeis, Felix Frankfurter*, p. 91; LDB to FF, September 23, 1933, cited in Dawson, ibid., p. 91. Moley to FF, October 31, 1935, FF-HLS Box 20. Moley was then editor of *Today*.

28. Corcoran and Cohen: Arthur M. Schlesinger, Jr., *The Politics of Upheaval* (Boston: Houghton Mifflin, 1960), p. 227; Corcoran to FF, October 10, 1933, quoted in Dawson, ibid., pp. 95–96; Corcoran to FF, December 30, 1933, LDB to FF, December 30, 1933, LDB to FF, January 10, 1934, all cited in Dawson, ibid., p. 96; Corcoran to FF, November 16, 1933 and December 30, 1933, FF-LC Box 116; LDB to FF, December 17, 1933, FF-LC Box 115. Court-packing plan: Dawson, ibid., p. 141, quoting Robert Sherwood, *Roosevelt and Hopkins* (New York: Harper & Bros., 1948). Drafting statutes: Schlesinger, *Coming of the New Deal*, pp. 442, 456–457, 466. Rexford Tugwell, *The Art of Politics as Practiced by Three Great Americans* (New York: Doubleday, 1958), pp. 247–248. Channels of communication: Schlesinger, *Coming of the New Deal*, p. 223; Dawson, *Louis D. Brandeis, Felix Frankfurter*, pp. 94–98; Joseph P. Lash, *From the Diaries of Felix Frankfurter* (New York: Norton, 1975), p. 52.

29. Wehle: Murphy, *Judicial Strategy*, p. 151. FDR to Hapgood, July 22, 1935, quoted in Dawson, *Louis D. Brandeis, Felix Frankfurter*, p. 134. Hapgood to FDR, June 1935, and FDR to Hapgood, May 25, 1937 and January 25, 1937, SUNY-Albany. FDR to Wise: quoted in Mason, *Brandeis*, p. 597; also see Schlesinger, *Politics of Upheaval*, p. 222; FDR to LDB, June 18, 1940, quoted in Mason, *Brandeis*, p. 636.

30. LDB to Wise, May 18, 1933, *Letters*, V, 516. FF to FDR, May 27,1933, *Letters*, V, 516 n. 1; Wise to FDR, January 1937 and LDB to Wise, January 19, 1936, *Letters*, V, 564; Wise to FDR in summer 1936 and LDB to Wise, September 4, 1936, *Letters*, V, 576; FF to FDR, April 22, 19, and 27, 1938, in Freedman, *Roosevelt and Frankfurter*, pp. 452–453, 455, 456; Benjamin Cohen to Missy LeHand, October 13, 1938, about FF talk with FDR on October 16, 1938, in Freedman, ibid, p. 465; FF to FDR, November 25, 1938, in ibid., p. 466; cf. ibid., pp. 495–496. FDR's reluctance: Frank Freidel, *Franklin D. Roosevelt: Launching the New Deal* (Boston: Little, Brown, 1973), pp. 393–395. Perkins: Freidel, ibid., pp. 394–395. LDB to Wise, September 4, 1936, *Letters*, V, 576; cf. 577 n. 1. LDB to Robert Szold, September 5, 1936, *Letters*, V, 577–581. Wise and Szold to London: LDB to Szold, July 12, 1937, *Letters*, V, 590–591; January 2, 1938, *Letters*, V, 593; January 16, 1938, *Letters*, V, 593–594.

31. Zionists urging Christians: LDB to Szold, October 12, 1938, BP, M 18-

2; November 11, 1938, *Letters*, V, 603–604. LDB and FDR: LDB to FF, October 16, 1938, *Letters*, V, 603; cf. n. 1.

32. White Paper: LDB to FDR, March 16, 1939, *Letters*, V, 613–614; April 17, 1939, *Letters*, V, 616; May 4, 1939, *Letters*, V, 617; FDR to LDB, March 23, 1939, *Letters*, V, 614 n. 3. LDB and FDR meeting: LDB to Wise, October 24, 1939, *Letters*, V, 629. Wallace: LDB to FDR, December 4, 1939, *Letters*, V, 631; FDR to LDB, December 16, 1939, *Letters*, V, 631 n. 2 and 635 n. 1; cf. LDB to FDR, December 20, 1939, *Letters*, V, 635. No meeting: LDB to FDR, June 14, 1940, *Letters*, V, 642; FDR to LDB, June 18, 1940, *Letters*, V, 642 n. 1.

33. LDB to FDR, April 26, 1941, *Letters*, V, 651; FDR to LDB, May 5, 1941, *Letters*, V, 652 n. 3.

34. LDB to Elizabeth Brandeis Raushenbush, September 16, 1933, *Letters*, V, 520. Meetings: Schlesinger, *Coming of the New Deal*, pp. 302–303; *Letters*, V, 531 n. 2. LDB on Perkins: LDB to Elizabeth Brandeis Raushenbush, April 20, 1934, *Letters*, V, 536; April 22, 1934, *Letters*, V, 537.

35. Perkins and Committee: Schlesinger, *Coming of the New Deal*, pp. 301–303. LDB and FDR meeting: LDB to Elizabeth Brandeis Raushenbush, June 8, 1934, *Letters*, V, 539–540; cf. Corcoran to FF, June 18, 1934, FF-LC Box 149. Committee recommendation: Schlesinger, *Coming of the New Deal*, pp. 304–306. LDB on "social worker error": to Elizabeth Brandeis Raushenbush, June 7, 1935, *Letters*, V, 555; Goethe quotation, to same, September 19, 1935, *Letters*, V, 560.

36. Interview with Harold Putnam of the *Boston Globe*, Summer, 1940, quoted in Mason, *Brandeis*, p. 621. FF to FDR, October 14, 1941, quoted in Dawson, *Louis D. Brandeis, Felix Frankfurter*, p. 167. There is no doubt about Brandeis's admiration for Jefferson and Roosevelt. He did not usually list Lincoln among the great presidents, however, and Frankfurter, always anxious to ingratiate himself with Roosevelt, may have altered Brandeis's comment in a way he thought would please the president. On the other hand, the quotation may be accurate.

37. Margaret Truman, *Harry S. Truman* (New York: Pocket Books, 1974), p. 116. Guests: untitled, *Opinion*, 12 (November 1941), p. 11, in FF-LC Box 128; Schlesinger, *Politics of Upheaval*, pp. 222–223. Mrs. R. M. Boeckel to A. T. Mason, March 9, 1944, quoted in Mason, *Brandeis*, p. 604. Teas: Marquis Childs, *I Write From Washington* (New York: Harper, 1942), p. 43. "Emissaries": Mason, *Brandeis*, p. 606.

38. Mason, *Brandeis*, p. 626. Wheeler bill: Lief, *Brandeis*, p. 471. LDB on Court-packing plan: cited in statement of Corcoran to Harry Hopkins, quoted in Dawson, *Louis D. Brandeis, Felix Frankfurter*, p. 140. Letter to committee: Mason, *Brandeis*, p. 626, citing interview with Wheeler. Dawson's version is that three senators, including Wheeler, went to Hughes on March 18, 1937, to ask him to appear. He said at least one other justice should go and asked LDB, who said no justice should go. Hughes then suggested a letter; LDB agreed. Dawson, *Louis D. Brandeis, Felix Frankfurter*, pp. 144–145, citing Hughes Papers, Library of Congress.

39. Cabell Phillips, *The Truman Presidency* (New York: Penguin, 1969), pp. 27, 31. Truman on LDB: Merle Miller, *Plain Speaking: An Oral Biography of Harry S. Truman* (New York: Berkley Publishing, 1974), pp. 150–151, 440. Acheson quoted in ibid., p. 406; cf. Schlesinger, *Politics of Upheaval*, pp. 222–223. Truman and transportation: Truman, *Truman*, p. 112; Miller, *Plain Speaking*, pp. 153–155. Brandeis, Truman, and size: Truman, *Truman*, p. 116. Truman on investigation: Miller, *Plain Speaking*, pp. 155–156. Truman on railroads: ibid., pp. 359–360. Truman on rights: quoted in Miller, ibid., pp. 441, 443.

40. Truman on Palestine: Miller, *Plain Speaking*, p. 232. Truman and Wise: ibid., pp. 230, 232–233. Barkley: Alben W. Barkley, *That Reminds Me* (Garden City, N.Y.: Doubleday, 1954), p. 96. LDB and McDonald: LDB to Mack, October 17, 1933, *Letters*, V, 525. McDonald and refugees: FF to FDR, November 23, 1933, enclosing letter from McDonald about German Jews, in Freedman, *Roosevelt and Frankfurter*, pp. 167–168, 173–174; LDB to Robert Szold, November 24, 1938, *Letters*, V, 606.

41. Suggestions: LDB to Elizabeth Brandeis Raushenbush, October 14, 1939, *Letters*, V, 625–626.

42. Shulman memorandum, FF-HLS 188-8. I am grateful to Professor H. N. Hirsch for bringing this memorandum to my attention.

43. LDB on public works: Lash, *Diaries of Frankfurter*, pp. 134, 135; Schlesinger, *Politics of Upheaval*, p. 236; FF to LDB, August 31, 1934, BP, G 9-2; Dawson, *Louis D. Brandeis, Felix Frankfurter*, pp. 30–31, 72, 91. Need for other points in memorandum: ibid., pp. 17, 91, 94, 114; Schlesinger, *Politics of Upheaval*, p. 328; LDB to FF, September 30, 1922, *Letters*, V, 66; Hirsch, *Enigma of Frankfurter*, pp. 106, 113. LDB to Elizabeth Brandeis Raushenbush, November 19, 1933, *Letters*, V, 527–528.

44. Public works and spending: LDB to FF, January 31, 1933, quoted in Dawson, *Louis D. Brandeis, Felix Frankfurter*, p. 31; *Journal of David Lilienthal*, cited in ibid., pp. 30–31. Lowering prices: LDB to Hapgood, May 25, 1936, and June 12, 1936, quoted in Mason, *Brandeis*, p. 622. "Many men are all wool": letter from David Riesman to author, October 31, 1977; Mason, *Brandeis*, p. 620.

45. Mason, *Brandeis*, pp. 620–621. The journalists are not identified.

46. Schlesinger, *Politics of Upheaval*, p. 387. Hapgood to FDR, February 20, 1936, SUNY-Albany (original in FDR Library, Hyde Park); FDR to Hapgood, February 24, 1936, SUNY-Albany.

47. Those in the "other camp": Schlesinger, *Politics of Upheaval*, pp. 233–234. LDB to Robert Bruère, February 25, 1922, BP, NMF M 12-3.

48. C. Herman Pritchett, *The Roosevelt Court* (New York: Macmillan, 1948), p. 265. James MacGregor Burns, *Roosevelt: The Lion and the Fox* (New York: Harcourt, Brace, 1956), p. 334. Schlesinger, *Politics of Upheaval*, p. 561.

49. LDB to FF, January 16, 1921, *Letters*, IV, 528–529. The results of the Cleveland survey were summarized by J. W. Love in "Justice in the Stocks," *The Survey*, 47 (October 29, 1921), pp. 135–145.

50. LDB on provinces: quoted in Schlesinger, *Politics of Upheaval*, p. 222.

He gave the same kind of advice to his law clerks. Nathanson, "Mr. Justice Brandeis," p. 13.

51. Lief, *Brandeis*, p. 441. LDB to Grady: September 22, 1927, November 18, 1927, January 22, 1928, March 9, 16, 25, 1928, May 9, 13, 16, 27, 1928, June 24, 1928, *Letters*, V, 302, 311, 319, 329, 331, 331–332, 338, 340–341, 341, 342–343, 346. LDB on Grady: to Alfred, November 2, 1927, BP, M 4-4. Urging friends to help: LDB to FF, February 9, 1928, *Letters*, V, 321; June 15, 1928, *Letters* , V, 344–345; July 14, 1928, *Letters*, v, 348; October 10, 1929, *Letters*, V, 402; November 15, 1929, *Letters*, V, 410–411; also see LDB to David K. Niles, April 25, 1933, *Letters*, V, 515. LDB to Grady, January 22, 1928, *Letters*, V, 319; March 9, 1928, *Letters*, V, 328; March 16, 1928, *Letters*, V, 331; August 6 and September 2, 1932, BP, I 1-4. *Other People's Money*: LDB to Louis B. Wehle, January 19, 1932, *Letters*, V, 493–494; to same, February 10, 1932, *Letters*, V, 496; to Hapgood, March 13, 1932, *Letters*, V, 499; to Grady, September 2, 1932, BP, I 1-4.

52. Committee of Visitors: James Landis, "Mr. Justice Brandeis and the Harvard Law School," *Harvard Law Review*, 55 (1941), 184. Interest in school: LDB to FF, April 2, 1922, April 6, 1923, October 5, 1928, and September 26, 1929, *Letters*, V, 48, 90, 356, 374. Special donations: LDB to Roscoe Pound, July 20, 1914, *Letters*, III, 287–288; to same, December 10, 1914, *Letters*, III, 383; to same, March 27, 1916, *Letters*, IV, 134; to FF, April 22, 1922, *Letters*, V, 50; to FF, December 14, 1922, *Letters*, V, 78; to FF, December 19, 1922, *Letters*, V, 80. General fund-raising: to FF, June 16, 1922, January 6, 1924, March 29, 1927, May 25, 1927, *Letters*, V, 52–53, 109–110, 276, 288. For additional information about LDB and the Law School, cf. LDB to Christopher Langdell, December 30, 1889, BP, Scrapbook I; to Langdell, April 10, 1893, *Letters*, I, 113; to Charles W. Eliot, April 25 and 28, 1893, *Letters*, I, 113–116; to Eliot, March 30, 1894, *Letters*, I, 117; to Roscoe Pound, November 7, 1912, *Letters*, II, 712; Joseph H. Beale to LDB, January 22, 1913, BP, NMF 56-3; LDB to Beale, January 23, 1913, BP, NMF 56-3; LDB to FF, January 24, 1913, BP, NMF 56-3; FF to LDB, January 27, 1913, BP, NMF 56-3.

53. Funding professorship: LDB to Winfred Denison, July 12, 1913, BP, NMF 1-N-1; to Roscoe Pound, July 12, 1913, *Letters*, III, 135-136. FF "radical": LDB to FF, May 2, 1920, *Letters*, IV, 463, and April 6, 1927, *Letters*, V, 278; LDB to Pound, quoted in Phillips, *Frankfurter Reminisces*, p. 170. LDB to Chafee, May 19, 1921, *Letters*, IV, 558; to FF, May 20, 1921, *Letters*, IV, 559; to FF, June 2, 1921, *Letters*, IV, 561; to Chafee, June 5, 1921, *Letters*, IV, 564. Pound: LDB to Pound, May 28, 1919, *Letters*, IV, 395; to Alice, June 14, 1919, *Letters*, IV, 400; to FF, September 6, 1921, *Letters*, V, 11; to FF, December 14, 1925, *Letters*, V, 196–197. LDB to Laski, April 3, 1916, BP, NMF 77-1, and February 1, 1917, *Letters*, IV, 270–271. Clerks and faculty members: to FF, June 17, 1923, *Letters*, V, 98; January 10, 1926, *Letters*, V, 201; June 22, 1926, *Letters*, V, 224; February 26, 1927, *Letters*, V, 273; February 11, 1923, *Letters*, V, 322; October 1, 1928, *Letters*, V, 355; November 15, 1929, *Letters*, V, 411; also see to Alice, April 20, 1920, *Letters*, IV, 458–459.

54. Awards: Todd, *Justice on Trial*, p. 117. Fellowship: LDB to Mack, November 14, 1926, *Letters*, V, 244; to FF, November 15, 1926, *Letters*, V, 245.

55. LDB to FF, October 9, 1924, *Letters*, V, 143; October 25, 1924, *Letters*, V, 146–147; January 1, 1925, *Letters*, V, 155–156. LDB to Mack, quoted in LDB to FF, January 1, 1925, *Letters*, V, 156.

56. Collections to College: LDB to Adele Brandeis, September 24, 1924, BP, M 15-1; servant's mistake: LDB to same, September 29, 1924, BP, M 4-4. LDB to Alfred, February 18, 1925, BP, M 4-4; to same, January 23, 1927, BP, M 4-4. Burden in Louisville: LDB to Frederick Wehle, November 19, 1925, quoted in Flexner, *Mr. Justice Brandeis*, p. 5.

57. Departmental libraries: LDB to Charles Tachau, August 25, 1928, quoted in Flexner, *Mr. Justice Brandeis*, p. 46. Letter to nephew: LDB to Wehle, October 28, 1924, quoted in ibid., pp. 23–24. University to be cosmopolitan: LDB to Charles Tachau, April 22, 1926, quoted in ibid., pp. 32–33; cf. p. 4. Zionist library: LDB to Tachau, April 29, 1926, quoted in ibid., pp. 40–41; to Stella and Emily Dembitz, May 17, 1926, BP, M 4-4; to Dean Warwick Anderson, June 4, 1926, quoted in Flexner, ibid., pp. 37–40.

58. Kentuckiana, etc.: LDB to Alfred, June 22, 1926, cited in Flexner, *Mr. Justice Brandeis*, pp. 43–44; Alfred to President of University, quoted in ibid., pp. 42–43; LDB to Alfred, January 16, 1927, BP, M 4-4; to Fannie Brandeis, October 21, 1926, BP, M 15-1; to same, October 20, 1924, BP, M 4-4. Official reports: LDB to Alfred, June 4, 1925, BP, M 4-4. Involving others: Flexner, *Mr. Justice Brandeis*, pp. 27–30; LDB to Alfred, January 16, 1927, BP, M 4-4; to Robert N. Miller, June 8, 1925, BP, Notebook; to FF, June 22, 1926, *Letters*, V, 224. Soliciting aid: Flexner, *Mr. Justice Brandeis*, pp. 34–35, 54, 77; LDB to Joseph Rauch, September 23, 1929, BP, M 4-6; to Rauch, October 13, 1929, BP, M 16-1.

59. LDB to Alfred, January 16, 1927, BP, M 4-4. Ashes: Marlin Vole to FF, April 18, 1959, FF-LC Box 127.

60. Lief, *Brandeis*, p. 480.

61. LDB quoted in *Boston Globe*, November 16, 1904, BP, Clippings Box I, referring to meeting on November 15, 1904.

62. On Jefferson: LDB to FF, March 14, 1926, *Letters*, V, 209; June 22, 1926, *Letters*, V, 224; also see to Alfred, May 19, 1926, BP, M 4-4. From Bowers: LDB to FF, July 3, 1927, SUNY-Albany. The book referred to is actually Claude Bowers, *Jefferson and Hamilton* (Boston: Houghton Mifflin, 1924). Monticello and return: LDB to Alice Grady, September 22, 1927, *Letters*, V, 302; to Alfred, September 22, 1927, BP, M 4-4. Cf. to Alfred, September 20 and 26, 1927, BP, M 4-4. Nock: LDB to FF, December 6, 1927, *Letters*, V, 315. LDB to Pauline Goldmark, November 15, 1929, *Letters*, V, 411.

63. Boycott: LDB to Wise, September 18, 1933. The book was Genevieve Helen Lisitzky's *Thomas Jefferson*, published earlier that year. On Nock: LDB to Bernard Flexner, November 16, 1940, *Letters*, V, 647–648; Flexner to LDB, November 19, 1940, SUNY-Albany.

64. *Ashwander* v. *T.V.A.*, 297 U.S. 288 (1935).

65. For an extensive account of justices giving advice to presidents, see Murphy, *Judicial Strategy*, pp. 73–77, 147–155. Civil Rights Act: *Heart of Atlanta* v. *U.S.*, 379 U.S. 241 (1964); *Katzenbach* v. *McClung*, 379 U.S. 294 (1964). *United States* v. *Nixon*, 418 U.S. 683 (1974).

66. Douglas, *The Court Years*, p. 253. Letter to the editor of the *Nation* from Charles Yale Harrison, one of the defense attorneys, quoting from a letter by Bartolomeo Vanzetti, October 7, 1926; letter to the editor of the *Nation* from Norman Hapgood, October 6, 1926.

67. *Adkins* v. *Children's Hospital*, 261 U.S. 525 (1923); *Continental Illinois* v. *Chicago*, 294 U.S. 648 (1935). Principles: *New State Ice Co.* v. *Liebmann*, 285 U.S. 262, 280 (1932) (dissenting); *Whitney* v. *California*, 274 U.S. 357, 374 (1927) (concurring); *United States* v. *Butler*, 297 U.S. 1 (1936).

68. Mason and Lief both apparently believed that LDB was not at all involved in New Deal policymaking. When I first raised the possibility with Paul Freund, who, in addition to serving as one of LDB's clerks and becoming his friend, has written extensively about him, Freund's initial reaction was incredulity. Interview with Freund, October 28, 1977. Court-packing plan: note 38. Secretary Hull: interview with Freund.

69. *Myers* v. *U.S.*, 272 U.S. 52, 240, 293–295 (1926) (dissenting).

20. Possibilities and Limitations

1. LDB, *Bigness*, p. 45.

2. LDB conversation with FF: quoted in FF's entry in his diary for October 17, 1946, in Joseph P. Lash, ed., *From the Diaries of Felix Frankfurter* (New York: Norton, 1975), p. 271. LDB said essentially the same thing to Dean Acheson twenty years earlier. Acheson, *Morning and Noon*, p. 78. Congress: LDB to FF, November 9, 1933, FF-LC Box 115. Paul A. Freund, "Mr. Justice Brandeis," *Harvard Law Review*, 55 (1941), p. 195.

3. Alvin Johnson to LDB, quoted in Bickel, *Unpublished Opinions*, p. 163. Conversation with Acheson: quoted in Acheson, *Morning and Noon*, p. 100. Conversation with niece: memorandum of conversation with Fannie Brandeis, 1931, BP, Misc.

4. Dante and Kant: quoted in Solomon Goldman, ed., *The Words of Justice Brandeis* (New York: Schumann, 1953), p. 152. Canoeing: LDB to Huston Thompson, June 23, 1934, *Letters*, V, 541.

5. James MacGregor Burns, *Roosevelt: The Lion and The Fox* (New York: Harcourt, Brace, 1956), p. 223; also see Arthur M. Schlesinger, Jr., *The Politics of Upheaval* (Boston: Houghton Mifflin, 1960), p. 337.

6. Berle working in LDB's office: Adolf A. Berle, Jr., *Power Without Property* (New York: Harcourt, Brace, 1959), p. 13. Remarks on LDB's birthday: "The Way of An American," *Survey Graphic*, 25 (November 1936), 297. Later remarks: Berle, *Power Without Property*, p. 14. The remainder of the book is predicated on the inevitability of corporate and government bigness.

7. LDB to Frank A. Fetter, November 26, 1940, *Letters*, V, 648.

8. *Economist* quoted in William Leuchtenburg, *Franklin D. Roosevelt and*

the New Deal, 1932–1940 (New York: Harper & Row, 1963), p. 326. Burns, *Roosevelt*, p. 238.

9. "Grand Coalition": ibid., pp. 264–288.

10. First and Second New Deals: see, e.g., Burns, *Roosevelt*; Arthur M. Schlesinger, Jr., *The Coming of New Deal* (Boston: Houghton Mifflin, 1958) and *Politics of Upheaval*. NRA in 1938: Leuchtenburg, *Franklin D. Roosevelt*, p. 163.

11. Max Lerner, *New York Herald Tribune*, March 3, 1935, quoted in Nelson Lloyd Dawson, *Louis D. Brandeis, Felix Frankfurter, and the New Deal* (Hamden, Conn.: Archon Books, 1980), p. 33.

12. New Deal Court: see C. Herman Pritchett, *The Roosevelt Court* (New York: Macmillan, 1948). Paul L. Murphy, *The Constitution in Crisis Time* (New York: Harper & Row, 1971), p. 172.

13. Jury trial and police behavior: *Norris* v. *Alabama*, 294 U.S. 587 (1935); *Pierre* v. *Louisiana*, 306 U.S. 354 (1939); *Smith* v. *Texas*, 311 U.S. 128 (1940); *Hill* v. *Texas*, 316 U.S. 400 (1942); *Akins* v. *Texas*, 325 U.S. 398 (1945). Voting rights: *Grovey* v. *Townsend*, 295 U.S. 45 (1935); *U.S.* v. *Classic*, 313 U.S. 299 (1941). Right to travel: *Edwards* v. *California*, 314 U.S. 160 (1941). For the Court in the 1950s, 1960s, and early 1970s, see, e.g., Leonard W. Levy, ed., *The Supreme Court Under Earl Warren* (New York: New York Times-Quadrangle Books, 1972); Alexander M. Bickel, *Politics and the Warren Court* (New York: Harper & Row, 1965); Alexander M. Bickel, *The Supreme Court and the Idea of Progress* (New York: Harper & Row, 1970); Archibald Cox, *The Warren Court* (Cambridge: Harvard University Press, 1968); Philip B. Kurland, *Politics, the Constitution, and the Warren Court* (Chicago: University of Chicago Press, 1970); Anthony Lewis, ed., *The Warren Court* (New York: Chelsea House, 1970).

14. Questions about judicial action: Fred P. Graham, *The Self-Inflicted Wound* (New York: Macmillan, 1970); William F. Swindler, *Court and Constitution in the Twentieth Century* (Indianapolis: Bobbs-Merrill, 1970); Donald L. Horowitz, *The Courts and Social Policy* (Washington, D.C.: The Brookings Institution, 1977); Richard Y. Funston, *Constitutional Counter-Revolution?* (Cambridge: Schenkman, 1977); Alexander M. Bickel, *The Least Dangerous Branch* (Indianapolis: Bobbs-Merrill, 1962); Leonard Levy, ed., *Judicial Review and the Supreme Court* (New York: Harper & Row, 1967); David F. Forte, ed., *The Supreme Court in American Politics* (Lexington, Mass.: D.C. Heath, 1972). There are many more books on the issue and their number continues to grow. The best way to see the growth of doubt about the extent of judicial policymaking is to note the difference in tone in the essays published each year in Philip M. Kurland, ed., *The Supreme Court Review* (Chicago: University of Chicago Press, 1969–1982). Women's movement and the Court: the best work, even though somewhat dated, remains Jo Freeman: *The Politics of Women's Liberation* (New York: McKay, 1975).

15. LDB's repeated comments to FF about the ACLU and the NAACP can be found throughout *Letters*, IV and V. LDB to Hapgood, July 21, 1917, quoted in Mason, *Brandeis*, p. 520.

16. LDB to Jenny Brandeis, Feburary 13, 1939, quoted in Mason, *Brandeis*, p. 634.

17. "Remarks of Mr. Justice Frankfurter at the funeral service of Mr. Justice Brandeis," FF-LC Box 128.

18. Acheson, *Morning and Noon*, p. 103. Nathanson, "Mr. Justice Brandeis," p. 15. Quote in BP, NMF 17-5; cf. Horace M. Kallen, *The Faith of Louis D. Brandeis, Zionist* (New York: Hadassah, n.d.), p. 15.

19. LDB to Alfred, May 26, 1927, BP, M 4-4.

Bibliography

There are numerous secondary sources, all listed in the notes. Only primary sources and those secondary sources that were relied on heavily are cited below.

Archives

Brandeis, Louis Dembitz. Papers. Harvard Law School. Cambridge, Massachusetts.
Brandeis, Louis Dembitz. Papers. State University of New York. Albany, New York.
Brandeis, Louis Dembitz. Papers. University of Louisville. Louisville, Kentucky.
Frankfurter, Felix. Papers. Harvard Law School. Cambridge, Massachusetts.
Frankfurter, Felix. Papers. Library of Congress. Washington, D.C.

Interviews (all with the author)

Austern, Thomas H. October 22, 1978. Washington, D.C.
Baldwin, Roger. May 19, 1981. Telephone interview.
Freund, Paul A. October 28, 1977. Cambridge, Massachusetts.
Hurst, Willard H. September 24, 1980. Madison, Wisconsin.
Raushenbush, Elizabeth Brandeis. September 23 and 24, 1980. Madison, Wisconsin.
Riesman, David. December 4, 1977. Cambridge, Massachusetts.
Tachau, Mary Kay. June 12, 1980. Louisville, Kentucky.

Works by Louis Dembitz Brandeis

"Liability of Trust-Estates on Contracts Made for Their Benefit." *American Law Review*, 15 (1881), 275–288.

With Samuel D. Warren, Jr. "The Watuppa Pond Cases." *Harvard Law Review*, 2 (1888–1889), 195–211.

"The Harvard Law School." *The Green Bag*, 1 (January 1889), 10–25.

With Samuel D. Warren, Jr. "The Law of Ponds." *Harvard Law Review*, 3 (1889–1890), 1–22.

With Samuel D. Warren, Jr. "The Right to Privacy." *Harvard Law Review*, 4 (1890–1891), 193–220.

Notes on Business Law. 2 vols. Privately printed, 1884–1896.

"An Economic Exhortation to Organized Labor." *National Civic Federation Monthly Review*, March 1905, pp. 20–24.

"Wage Earner's Life Insurance." *Collier's Weekly*, 37 (September 15, 1906), 16–17, 28, 30.

"Financial Condition of the New York, New Haven & Hartford Railroad Company, and of the Boston & Maine Railroad." Privately printed, 1907.

"Massachusetts' Substitute for Old Age Pensions." *The Independent*, 65 (July 16, 1908), 125–128.

"Massachusetts' Old Age Annuities." *American Federationist*, 15 (August 1908), 595–597.

"Massachusetts Savings Insurance and Annuity Banks." *The Banker's Magazine*, 78 (August 1908), 186–188.

"The Proposed Railroad Merger." *New England Magazine*, May 1908, pp. 267–269.

"Boston and Maine Pensions." *Survey Weekly*, June 19, 1909, p. 22.

"The New Conception of Industrial Efficiency." *Journal of Accountancy*, 12 (May 1911), 35–42.

"Organized Labor and Efficiency." *The Survey*, 26 (April 22, 1911), 148–156.

"Our New Peonage: Discretionary Pensions." *The Independent*, 72 (July 25, 1912), 187–191.

"The Preferential Shop." *Human Engineering*, 2 (August 1912), 179–181.

"Shall We Abandon the Policy of Competition?" *Case and Comment*, 18 (February 1912), 494–496.

"Trusts, Efficiency and the New Party." *Collier's Weekly*, 49 (September 14, 1912), 14–15.

"Competition." *American Legal News*, 44 (January 1913), 5–14.

"How Far Have We Come on the Road to Industrial Democracy?" *La Follette's Weekly*, May 13, 1913, p. 5.

"Price Maintenance, Competition That Kills." *Harper's Weekly*, 57 (November 15, 1913), pp. 10–12.

"The Solution of the Trust Problem." *Harper's Weekly*, 58 (November 8, 1913), 18–19.

With Josephine Goldmark. *Women in Industry*. New York: National Consumers' League (n.d.).

Business—A Profession. Boston: Small, Maynard, 1914.

"Efficiency and Social Ideals." *The Independent*, November 30, 1914, p. 80.

Other People's Money and How the Bankers Use It. New York: Stokes, 1914.

"Efficiency by Consent." *Harper's Weekly*, December 11, 1915, p. 61.

"The Constitution and the Minimum Wage." *The Survey*, 33 (February 7, 1915), 490–494, 521–524.
"The Living Law." *Illinois Law Review*, 10 (February 1916), 461–471.
The Curse of Bigness, ed. Osmond K. Fraenkel. New York: Viking Press, 1934.

Other Major Sources

Abrams, Richard M. *Conservatism in a Progressive Era*. Cambridge: Harvard University Press, 1964.
Acheson, Dean. *Morning and Noon*. Boston: Houghton Mifflin, 1965.
Baldwin, Roger. "Affirmation of Democracy." *Jewish Frontier*, 3 (November 1936), 10.
Ben-Zvi, Samuel. "Justice Brandeis and Ein Hashofet." *The New Palestine*, 32 (November 14, 1941), 10–12.
Bernard, Burton C. "Brandeis in St. Louis." *St. Louis Bar Journal*, 11 (1964), 54–60.
Bickel, Alexander M., ed. *The Unpublished Opinions of Mr. Justice Brandeis*. Cambridge: Harvard University Press, 1957.
Brandeis, Elizabeth. "Employment Reserves vs. Insurance." *The New Republic*, September 27, 1933, pp. 177–179.
———. "Wisconsin Tackles Job Security." *The Survey*, 15 (December 15, 1931), 295–296.
de Haas, Jacob. *Louis D. Brandeis: A Biographical Sketch*. New York: Bloch, 1929.
Evans, Elizabeth Glendower. "Memoirs." Evans Mss., Schlesinger Library, Radcliffe College, Cambridge, Massachusetts.
Filene, Edward A. "Brandeis the Man and Zionist Leader." *Boston Sunday Post*, July 4, 1915.
———. "Louis D. Brandeis As We Know Him." *Boston Post*, July 14, 1915.
Flexner, Bernard. "Brandeis and the Palestine Economic Corporation." *The New Palestine*, 32 (November 14, 1941), 15–16.
———. *Mr. Justice Brandeis and the University of Louisville*. Louisville, Ky.: University of Louisville Press, 1938.
Frankfurter, Felix, assisted by Josephine Goldmark. *The Case for the Shorter Work Day*. New York: National Consumers' League, 1915.
——— and James M. Landis. *The Business of the Supreme Court*. New York: Macmillan, 1928.
Freund, Paul. "Driven by Passion." *Boston Sunday Herald*, November 11, 1956.
———. "Mr. Justice Brandeis." *Harvard Law Review*, 55 (1941), 195–196.
———. "Mr. Justice Brandeis: A Centennial Memoir." *Harvard Law Review*, 70 (1957), 769–792.
———. *On Understanding the Supreme Court*. Boston: Little, Brown, 1949.
Gal, Allon. *Brandeis of Boston*. Cambridge: Harvard University Press, 1980.
Goldman, Solomon, ed. *Brandeis on Zionism*. Washington, D.C.: Zionist Organization of America, 1942.
Goldman, Solomon, ed., *The Words of Justice Brandeis*. New York: Schumann, 1953.

Goldmark, Alice, and Josephine Goldmark. *Democracy in Denmark*. Washington, D.C.: National Home Library Foundation, 1936.

Goldmark, Josephine. *Fatigue and Efficiency*. New York: Russell Sage Foundation, 1912.

———. *Impatient Crusader: Florence Kelley's Life Story*. Urbana: University of Illinois Press, 1953.

———. *Pilgrims of '48*. New Haven: Yale University Press, 1930.

Hamilton, Walton N. "The Jurist's Art." *Columbia Law Review*, 33 (1931), 1073–93.

Hapgood, Norman. *The Changing Years*. New York: Farrar & Rinehart, 1930.

Hirsch, H. N. *The Enigma of Felix Frankfurter*. New York: Basic Books, 1981.

Jacobs, Rose G. "Justice Brandeis and Hadassah." *The New Progressive*, 32 (November 14, 1941), 17–19.

Jaffe, Louis L. "The Contributions of Justice Brandeis to Administrative Law." *Iowa Law Review*, 18 (1932–1933), 213–227.

Kaplan, Jacob J. "Mr. Justice Brandeis, Prophet." *The New Palestine*, 32 (November 14, 1941), 27–28.

Katz, Irving. "Henry Lee Higginson vs. Louis Dembitz Brandeis." *New England Quarterly*, 41 (1968), 67–80.

Konefsky, Samuel J. *The Legacy of Holmes and Brandeis*. New York: Macmillan, 1956.

Kraines, Oscar. "Brandeis' Philosophy of Scientific Management." *Western Political Quarterly*, 13 (March 1960), 191–201.

La Dame, Mary. *The Filene Store: A Study of Employees' Relation to Management in a Retail Store*. New York: Russell Sage Foundation, 1930.

La Follette, Belle, and Fola La Follette. *Robert M. La Follette*. New York: Macmillan, 1953.

Landis, James. "The Legislative History of the Securities Act of 1933." *George Washington Law Review*, 28 (1959), 29–49.

———. "Mr. Justice Brandeis and the Harvard Law School." *Harvard Law Review*, 55 (1941), 184–190.

Levy, David W., and Bruce Allen Murphy. "Preserving the Progressive Spirit in a Conservative Time." *Michigan Law Review*, 78 (1980), 1248–1298.

Lief, Alfred, ed. *The Brandeis Guide to the Modern World*. Boston: Little, Brown and Co., 1941.

———. *Brandeis: The Personal History of an American Ideal*. New York: Stackpole, 1936.

———. ed. *The Social and Economic Views of Mr. Justice Brandeis*. New York: Vanguard Press, 1930.

McClennen, Edward F. "Better That a Man's Own Works . . ." *The New Palestine*, 32 (November 14, 1941), 20–22.

———. "Louis D. Brandeis as a Lawyer." *Massachusetts Law Quarterly*, 33 (1948), 1–28.

McPherson, John Bruce. "The New York Cloakmaker's Strike." *Journal of Political Economy*, 19 (March 1911), 153–187.

Magruder, Calvert C. "Mr. Justice Brandeis." *Harvard Law Review*, 55 (1941), 193–194.

Mann, Arthur. *Yankee Reformers in the Urban Age*. Cambridge: Harvard University Press, 1954.

Mason, Alpheus T. *Brandeis: A Free Man's Life*. New York: Viking Press, 1946.

——. *Brandeis, Lawyer and Judge in the Modern State*. Princeton, N.J.: Princeton University Press, 1933.

——. *The Brandeis Way: A Case Study in the Workings of Democracy*. Princeton, N.J.: Princeton University Press, 1938.

Mersky, Roy. *Louis Dembitz Brandeis, 1856–1941: A Bibliography*. New Haven, Conn.: Yale Law School, 1958.

Morgenthau, Henry. "All in a Lifetime: The Campaign of 1916." *World's Work*, 43 (December 1921), 138–145.

Nathanson, Nathaniel L. "Mr. Justice Brandeis: A Law Clerk's Recollections of the October Term, 1934." *American Jewish Archives*, 15 (1963), 6–13.

Neumann, Emmanuel. "The Nation-Builder." *The New Palestine*, 32 (November 14, 1941) 7–9.

Phillips, Harlan B., ed. *Felix Frankfurter Reminisces*. New York: Reynal, 1960.

Poole, Ernest. "Brandeis: A Remarkable Record of Unselfish Work Done in the Public Interest." *American Magazine*, February 1911, 481–493.

Riesman, David. "Notes for an Essay on Justice Brandeis." Unpublished letter to Felix Frankfurter, May 22, 1936. FF-LC.

Shapiro, Yonathan. *Leadership of the American Zionist Organization, 1897–1903*. Urbana: University of Illinois Press, 1971.

Shulman, Harry. "The Demise of *Swift* v. *Tyson*." *Yale Law Journal* 47 (1937–1938), 1336–1353.

Solomon, Barbara M. *Ancestors and Immigrants*. Cambridge: Harvard University Press, 1959.

Staples, Henry Lee, and Alpheus T. Mason. *The Fall of a Railroad Empire*. Syracuse, N.Y.: Syracuse University Press, 1947.

Todd, Alden L. *Justice on Trial: The Case of Louis D. Brandeis*. New York: McGraw-Hill, 1964.

Tugwell, Rexford. *The Art of Politics as Practiced by Three Great Americans*. New York: Doubleday, 1958.

Urofsky, Melvin I. *A Mind of One Piece: Brandeis and American Reform*. New York: Scribner, 1971.

——. *American Zionism from Herzl to the Holocaust*. Garden City, N.Y.: Doubleday, 1975.

—— and David Levy. *Letters of Louis D. Brandeis*. 5 vols. Albany: State University of New York Press, 1972–1978.

U.S. Congress. House. Committee on Interstate and Foreign Commerce. *Hearings on H.R. 13305*. 63rd Cong., 2nd sess., 1915.

——. Committee on Investigation of United States Steel Corporation. *Hearings before the Committee on Investigation of the United States Steel Corporation*. 62nd Cong., 3rd sess., 1912, 8 vols.

————. Committee on the Judiciary. *Hearings on Trust Legislation.* 63rd Cong., 2nd sess., 1914.

U.S. Congress. Senate. Committee on Interstate Commerce. *Hearings on Control of Corporations, Persons, and Firms Engaged in Interstate Commerce.* 62nd Cong., 2nd sess., 1911.

————. *Hearings on Bills Relating to Trust Legislation.* 63rd Cong., 2nd sess., 1914.

————. Committee on the Judiciary. *Hearings before the Subcommittee on the Nomination of Louis D. Brandeis to be an Associate Justice of the Supreme Court of the United States.* 64th Cong., 1st sess., 1916, 2 vols.

Weizmann, Chaim. *Trial and Error.* Philadelphia: Jewish Publication Society of America, 1949.

Wise, Stephen. "Battling with Wilson for Justice to the Jew." *The Jewish Tribune,* March 14, 1924, p. 22.

Wyatt, Edith F. "The New York Cloakmaker's Strike." *McClure's,* 34 (April 1911), 708–711.

Zimmern, Alfred. *The Greek Commonwealth.* Oxford: Clarendon Press, 1912, 1915, 1921, 1924, 1931.

Index

ABOUT THE AUTHOR

Philippa Strum is professor of political science, Brooklyn College, City University of New York, and a director of the American Civil Liberties Union. Among her publications are *The Supreme Court and Political Questions* and *Presidential Power and American Democracy*.